second canadian edition

Strategic **Management**

Competitiveness and Globalization

CONCEPTS

second canadian edition

Strategic **Management**
Competitiveness and Globalization

CONCEPTS

Michael A. **Hitt**
Arizona State University

R. Duane **Ireland**
University of Richmond

Robert E. **Hoskisson**
The University of Oklahoma

W. Glenn **Rowe**
The University of Western Ontario

Jerry P. **Sheppard**
Simon Fraser University

THOMSON
NELSON

Australia   Canada   Mexico   Singapore   Spain   United Kingdom   United States

THOMSON

NELSON

Strategic Management: Competitiveness and Globalization—Concepts
Second Canadian Edition
Michael A. Hitt, R. Duane Ireland, Robert E. Hoskisson,
W. Glenn Rowe, and Jerry P. Sheppard

Associate Vice-President,
Editorial Director:
Evelyn Veitch

Senior Acquisitions Editor:
Anthony Rezek

Senior Executive Marketing
Manager:
Don Thompson

Senior Developmental Editor:
Karina Hope

Photo Researcher and
Permissions Coordinator:
Terri Rothman

Production Editor:
Tammy Scherer

Copy Editor:
Mariko Obokata

Proofreader:
Rodney Rawlings

Indexer:
Elizabeth Bell

Senior Production Coordinator:
Kathrine Pummell

Creative Director:
Angela Cluer

Interior Design:
Tammy Gay

Cover Design:
Peter Papayanakis

Cover Image:
Chad Baker/Photodisc Red/
Getty Images

Compositor:
Rachel Sloat

Printer:
Transcontinental

Library and Archives Canada
Cataloguing in Publication

Strategic management :
competitiveness and globalization :
concepts / Michael A. Hitt ...
[et al.].—2nd Canadian ed.

Includes indexes.
ISBN 0-17-641601-3

1. Strategic planning—
Textbooks. 2. Strategic planning—
Canada—Case studies. I. Hitt,
Michael A.

HD30.28.S728 2005   658.4'012
C2004-906846-6

To my grandson, Mason, and my granddaughter, Michelle. Pa Pa loves you.

—Michael A. Hitt

To Mary Ann and to Rebecca and Scott, our children. I love each of you deeply. Always remember that "When you need me, call my name; because without you, my life just wouldn't be the same."

—R. Duane Ireland

To my loving and supportive wife, Kathy Hall Hoskisson, with whom life is much more special, and to my wonderful children, who are uniquely wonderful examples to me.

—Robert E. Hoskisson

To Fay and Gillian. Fay, you make me complete. I love you both so much and I am so very proud of all that you have done.

—W. Glenn Rowe

To a new arrival—Bailey—and to two departures— Rocky and Barb. To my family, I love you. To my bright light in this cloudy place, Marnie. To Jesse, Benjamin, and Bailey, yes we can do that now. To my parents, Rocky and Rose. To Harvey and Barb.

—Jerry P. Sheppard

Brief Contents

Contents

Chapter 4 The Internal Environment: Resources, Capabilities,
and Core Competencies   98

Part 2 *Strategic Actions: Strategy Formulation 134*

Chapter 5 Business-Level Strategy   136

Chapter 12 Organizational Structure and Controls   356

Chapter 13 Strategic Leadership 394

About This Book

As with the earlier Canadian edition, to develop this second Canadian edition of *Strategic Management: Competitiveness and Globalization—Concepts*, we have carefully integrated cutting-edge research with practical applications that examine companies competing in global markets. We continue to use this approach because we strongly believe that melding research findings with managerial practices provides you, our readers, with a comprehensive, timely, and accurate explanation of how companies use the strategic management process to successfully compete in the 21st century's dynamic and challenging competitive landscape. Our goals in preparing this edition remain as they were for the first edition: (1) to introduce the strategic management process in a way that illustrates both traditional approaches and the dynamics of strategic change; (2) to describe the full set of strategic management tools, techniques, and concepts available, as well as how firms use them to develop competitive advantages; and (3) to present contemporary strategic thinking and issues affecting 21st century firms and the strategic decisions made in those companies. Thus, our major goal in preparing this edition has been to present you, our readers, with a concise, complete, accurate, up-to-date, and interesting explanation of the strategic management process as it is used by firms competing in the global economy.

Using an engaging, action-oriented writing style, we have taken great care to sharpen our presentation of strategic management tools and concepts. We have carefully rewritten the chapters to make them clear and concise. Although we fully describe all relevant parts of the strategic, and interesting, management process, the chapters in this edition are more succinct. However, the noticeable reduction in chapter length has not come at the expense of informative, practical examples. In fact, while reading the chapters, you'll find descriptions of many different types of firms as we explore the strategic management process. These examples are current and show how firms are competing in today's constantly changing global environment.

New Features and Updates

Many new features and updates to this edition enhance the book's value.

- All new chapter *opening cases* (14 in total).
- All new *Strategic Focus boxes* (one to three per chapter for a total of 38).
- New *company-specific examples* illustrating each chapter's central themes.
- *Full coverage of strategic issues that are prominent in the 21st century competitive landscape.* Chapter 14, for example, has been rewritten to focus on strategic entrepreneurship. Important in established firms as well as in start-up ventures, strategic entrepreneurship is concerned with combining opportunity-seeking behaviour with advantage-seeking behaviour. As we describe in the all-new Chapter 14, firms that learn how to use a strategic perspective to identify and exploit entrepreneurial opportunities increase their ability to outperform their rivals. In Chapter 6, we've sharpened the discussion of patterns of competition that occur between firms as they try to outperform each other.

- *Discussion of new topics.* In this edition, we discuss the use of the balanced scorecard as a means of measurement and control and the concept of corporate social responsibility as a performance measure (Chapter 2). These new tools are gaining importance as parts of an effective strategic management process.
- A continued emphasis on *global coverage*, with more emphasis on the international context and issues, both in the chapters and the cases.
- Updated *review questions* at the end of each chapter.
- *Experiential exercises* at the end of each chapter. New to this edition, these exercises present real-life strategic management issues and are followed by questions. The exercises can be individual or group-based, and are sophisticated, yet simple to use.
- Enhanced readability and pedagogical treatment.

These new features and updates provide a unique competitive advantage for this book. With 14 new opening cases and 38 new Strategic Focus boxes, we offer 52 major case examples in the chapters. In addition, virtually all of the shorter examples used throughout each chapter are completely new.

This new edition also emphasizes a global advantage with comprehensive coverage of international concepts and issues. In addition to comprehensive coverage of international strategies in Chapter 9, references to and discussions of the international context and issues are included in every chapter. The opening cases, Strategic Focus boxes, and individual examples in each chapter cover numerous global issues.

Importantly, this new edition solidifies a research advantage for our book. For example, each chapter averages more than 100 references. On average, 60 percent of these references are new to this edition. Drawn from business literature and academic research, the materials in these references are vital to our explanations of how firms use the strategic management process.

The Book's Focus

The strategic management process is our book's focus. Organizations use the strategic management process to understand competitive forces and to develop competitive advantages. The magnitude of this challenge is greater today than it has been in the past. A new competitive landscape exists in the 21st century as a result of the technological revolution (especially in e-commerce) and increasing globalization. The technological revolution has placed greater importance on innovation and the ability to rapidly introduce new goods and services to the marketplace. The global economy, one in which goods and services flow relatively freely among nations, continuously pressures firms to become more competitive. By offering either valued goods or services to customers, competitive firms increase the probability of earning above-average returns. Thus, the strategic management process helps organizations identify what they want to achieve as well as how they will do it.

The Strategic Management Process

Our discussion of the strategic management process is both traditional and contemporary. In maintaining tradition, we examine important materials that have historically been a part of understanding strategic management. For example, we thoroughly examine the concept of performance (see Chapter 2), how to analyze a firm's external environment (see Chapter 3), and how to analyze a firm's internal environment (see Chapter 4).

Contemporary Treatment

To explain the aforementioned important activities, we keep our treatments contemporary. In Chapter 4, for example, we emphasize the importance of identifying and determining the value-creating potential of a firm's resources, capabilities, and core competencies. The strategic actions taken as a result have a direct link with the company's ability to establish a competitive advantage, achieve strategic competitiveness, and earn above-average returns.

Our contemporary treatment is also shown in the chapters on the dynamics of strategic change in the complex global economy. In Chapter 6, for example, we discuss the competitive rivalry between firms and the outcomes of their competitive actions and responses. Chapter 6's discussion suggests a firm's strategic actions are influenced by its competitors' actions and reactions. Thus, competition in the global economy is fluid, dynamic, and fast-paced. Similarly, in Chapter 8, we explain the dynamics of strategic change at the corporate level, specifically addressing the motivation and consequences of mergers, acquisitions, and restructuring (e.g., divestitures) in the global economy.

We also emphasize that the set of strategic actions, known as strategy formulation and strategy implementation (see Figure 1.1 on page 8), must be carefully integrated for the firm to be successful.

Contemporary Concepts

Contemporary topics and concepts are the foundation for our in-depth analysis of the strategic actions that firms take to implement strategies. In Chapter 11, for example, we describe how different corporate governance mechanisms (e.g., boards of directors, institutional owners, and executive compensation) affect strategy implementation. Chapter 12 explains how firms gain a competitive advantage by effectively using organizational structures that are properly matched to different strategies. The vital contributions of strategic leaders are examined in Chapter 13. In the all-new Chapter 14, we describe the important relationship between the ability to find and exploit entrepreneurial opportunities through competitive advantages.

Key Features

Several features are included in this book to increase its value for you.

Knowledge Objectives

Each chapter begins with clearly stated knowledge objectives. Their purpose is to emphasize key strategic management issues you will learn while studying each chapter. To both facilitate and verify learning, you can revisit the knowledge objectives while preparing answers to the review questions that are presented at the end of each chapter.

Opening Cases

An opening case follows the knowledge objectives in each chapter. The opening cases describe current strategic issues in modern companies such as Magna Corporation, Southwest Airlines, WestJet, the Hudson's Bay Company, and Alcan Inc., among many others. The purpose of the opening cases is to demonstrate how specific firms apply an individual chapter's strategic management concepts. Thus, the opening cases serve as a direct and often distinctive link between the theory and application of strategic management in different organizations and industries. In the opening case in Chapter 3, we discuss the impact of such events as 9/11, SARS, "mad cow" disease, and the power outage of August 2003.

Key Terms

Key terms that are critical to understanding the strategic management process are bold-faced throughout the chapters. Definitions of the key terms appear in chapter margins as well as in the text. Other terms and concepts throughout the text are italicized, signifying their importance.

Strategic Focus Segments

Each chapter presents between one and three all-new Strategic Focus boxes. As with the opening cases, the Strategic Focus boxes highlight a variety of high-profile organizations, situations, and concepts and describe issues that can be addressed by applying a chapter's strategy-related concepts.

End-of-Chapter Summaries

Closing each chapter is a summary that revisits the concepts outlined in the knowledge objectives. The summaries are presented in a bulleted format to highlight a chapter's concepts, tools, and techniques.

Review Questions

Review questions are directly tied to each chapter's knowledge objectives, prompting readers to reexamine the most important concepts in each chapter.

Experiential Exercises

Each experiential exercise provides an action-oriented opportunity for readers to enhance their understanding of strategic management. Materials come to life as readers use a chapter's materials to answer questions concerned with strategic management issues. We appreciate the work of Luis Flores, Northern Illinois University, who developed several of these experiential exercises.

Examples

In addition to the opening cases and Strategic Focus boxes, each chapter is filled with real-world examples of companies in action. These examples illustrate key strategic management concepts and provide realistic applications of strategic management.

Indexes

Besides the traditional end-of-book subject and name indexes, we offer a company index as well. The company index includes the names of the hundreds of organizations discussed in the text. The three indexes help to locate where subjects are discussed, a person's name is used, and a company's actions are described.

Support Material For the Instructor

Instructor's Resource CD-ROM

Key ancillaries (Instructor's Resource Manual, Test Bank, ExamView® Testing Software, and PowerPoint® Slides) are provided on CD-ROM (ISBN 0-17-640761-8), giving instructors the ultimate tool for customizing lectures and presentations. See the descriptions on the following page.

Instructor's Resource Manual

The manual provides instructors with a wealth of additional material and presentations that effectively complement the text. Using each chapter's knowledge objectives as an organizing principle, the manual has been completely revised to integrate the best knowledge on teaching strategic management to maximize student learning. The manual includes ideas about how to approach each chapter and how to emphasize essential principles with additional examples that can be used to explain points and to stimulate active discussions in your classrooms. Lecture outlines, detailed answers to the review questions at the end of each chapter, additional assignments, and transparency masters are also included, along with instructions for using each chapter's experiential exercise. Flexible in nature, these exercises can be used in class or in other ways, such as homework or as an out-of-classroom assignment.

Test Bank

The test bank has been thoroughly revised and enhanced for this edition and includes new questions for each opening case and Strategic Focus box, as well as a set of scenario-based questions for each chapter to add an innovative problem-solving dimension to exams. All objective questions are linked to chapter knowledge objectives and are ranked by difficulty level, among other measures.

ExamView® Testing Software

All of the test questions are available in ExamView®, a computerized format available in Windows and Macintosh versions. ExamView® is easy-to-use test-creation software that makes it possible for instructors to easily and efficiently create, edit, store, and print exams.

PowerPoint® Slides

An all-new set of PowerPoint® slides designed to be used with this text can be down-loaded from the website at www.hitt2e.nelson.com. The easily followed presentations include clear figures based on the text and innovative adaptations to illustrate the text concepts.

Videos

Management and Strategy (ISBN 0-324-17170-6) is a 45-minute video of short clips providing news and information about firms and current strategic management issues that are of particular relevance to students of strategic management, using the resources of Turner Learning/CNN, the world's first 24-hour all-news network. A separate multi-media integration guide, developed by Ross Stapleton-Gray (PhD, CISSP, chief university spokesperson on IT security issues for the University of California), accompanies the videotape and provides video descriptions, topical guides, and discussion questions for each clip.

Entrepreneurship and Strategy (ISBN 0-324-26131-4) is a 45-minute video based on the remarkable resources of "Small Business School," the series on PBS stations, Worldnet, and the Web. It looks at seven firms that capitalized on their beginnings and used strategic management to grow market share and create competitive advantage. A resource guide within the Instructor's Resource Manual describes each segment and provides discussion questions.

Corporate Strategy (ISBN 0-324-11488-5) is a 45-minute video featuring corporate strategy situations for classroom viewing. A resource guide within the Instructor's Resource Manual describes each segment and provides discussion questions.

Simulations

Strategic Management in the Marketplace (ISBN 0-324-16867-5) is a unique and adaptable Web-based simulation that has been tailored to use with our text for the strategic management course. We worked closely with Ernest Cadotte of the University of Tennessee and his colleagues at Innovative Learning Solutions, Inc. to develop this product. Designed around important strategic management tools, techniques, and concepts, the simulation is easy to administer.

The Global Business Game (ISBN 0-324-16183-2) simulation challenges students to deal with a host of strategic issues in a global context and make decisions that will lead to the firm's success. We worked with author Joseph Wolfe to prepare the second edition of this simulation, which includes clear operational instructions that closely match topics in the text.

For the Student

Infotrac® College Edition

Infotrac® College Edition gives students access—anytime, anywhere—to an online database of full-text articles from hundreds of scholarly and popular periodicals, including *Newsweek* and *Fortune*. Fast and easy search tools help you find just what you're looking for from among tens of thousands of articles, updated daily, all at a single site. For more information or to log on, please visit http://www.infotrac-college.com. Just enter your passcode as provided on the subscription card packaged free with new copies of *Strategic Management*.

For the Student and Instructor

Website—www.hitt2e.nelson.com

This edition's website offers students and instructors access to several useful resources, including quizzes for self-testing, Web links, and a wealth of other material.

Acknowledgments

We want to thank those who helped us prepare the second Canadian edition. The professionalism, guidance, and support provided by the editorial and production teams of Evelyn Veitch, Anthony Rezek, Karina Hope, Tammy Scherer, Mariko Obokata, and Rodney Rawlings are gratefully acknowledged. We appreciate the excellent work of our research assistants: Kerry Hendricks and Marnie Young. In addition, we owe a debt of gratitude to our colleagues at Texas A&M University, Arizona State University, the University of Richmond, the University of Oklahoma, the University of Western Ontario, and Simon Fraser University. Finally, we are sincerely grateful to those who took time to read and provide feedback on drafts of either this second Canadian edition or the previous edition of our book. Their insights and evaluations have enhanced this text, and we list them below with our thanks.

Kamal Argheyd, Concordia University

Don Ausman, University of Alberta

David Barrows, York University

Robert Blunden, Dalhousie University

Barry Boothman, University of New Brunswick

Michele Bowring, University of Manitoba

Alan Chapelle, Malaspina University-College

Shamsud Chowdhury, Athabasca University

Christopher Gadsby, British Columbia Institute of Technology

Robert Gephart, University of Alberta

Ann Gregory, Memorial University of Newfoundland

Ike Hall, British Columbia Institute of Technology

Jack Ito, University of Regina

Knud Jensen, Ryerson University

Ian Lee, Carleton University

Lee Maguire, Ryerson University

Alfie Morgan, University of Windsor

Jean-Marie Nkongolo-Bakenda, University of Regina

Brad Olson, University of Lethbridge

Laurie Turner, Humber College

Tom Wesson, York University

Final Comments

Organizations face exciting and dynamic competitive challenges in the 21st century. These challenges, and effective responses to them, are explored in this second Canadian edition of *Strategic Management: Competitiveness and Globalization*. The strategic management process conceptualized and described in this text offers valuable insights and knowledge to those committed to successfully meeting the challenge of dynamic competition. Thinking strategically, as this book challenges you to do, increases the likelihood that you will help your company achieve strategic success. In addition, continuous practice with strategic thinking and the use of the strategic management process gives you skills and knowledge that will contribute to career advancement and success. Finally, we want to wish you all the best and nothing other than complete success in all of your endeavours.

Michael A. Hitt

R. Duane Ireland

Robert E. Hoskisson

W. Glenn Rowe

Jerry P. Sheppard

Part One

Strategic Management Inputs

Chapter One

Strategic Management and Strategic Competitiveness

Knowledge Objectives

Studying this chapter should provide you with the strategic management knowledge needed to:

1. Define strategic competitiveness, competitive advantage, and above-average returns.

2. Describe the 21st-century competitive landscape and explain how globalization and technological changes shape it.

3. Use the industrial organization (I/O) model to explain how firms can earn above-average returns.

4. Use the resource-based model to explain how firms can earn above-average returns.

5. Describe strategic intent and strategic mission and discuss their value.

6. Define stakeholders and describe their ability to influence organizations.

7. Describe strategists' work.

8. Explain the strategic management process.

Sittin' on Top of the World

Canada is sitting on top of the world! At least as a geographic truth, Canada does sit on top of the world. Yet, it seems that geographic placement does not fully describe the full extent to which Canadians are not just a tiny population safely tucked away in a frozen corner of North America.

To the surprise of many, Canada has in recent years been given a rather trendy designation. "Indeed, a cautious case can now be made that Canada is now rather cool," noted Britain's *Economist* magazine in late 2003. At about the same time, a less directly stated measure of Canada's coolness could be found in the *Washington Post*. Remembering the 1960s' centre of left-leaning liberalism in the U.S., the *Post* noted that "Just when you had all but forgotten that carbon-based life exists north of the 49th parallel, those sly Canadians have redefined their entire nation as Berkeley North."

While neither the *Economist* nor the *Washington Post* is the last word in defining "cool," there are signs that these publications were on to something. A half-century ahead of the U.S. in government support for socialized medicine (including regulated drug prices), serious consideration of decriminalizing small amounts of marijuana, and legalizing gay marriages make Canada's neighbours to the south seem positively Victorian. All of these initiatives have contributed to the growth, or potential for growth, in some Canadian industries. An increasing flock of online prescription drug providers has cropped up in Canada to supply over-charged Americans. Cannabis cultivation has become one of British Columbia's largest industries! Finally, the impact gay marriages will have on Canada's tourism industry is anyone's guess.

The biggest surprise is that, like Canadians themselves, Canadian businesses are not just a tiny population safely tucked away in a frozen corner of North America. If making assumptions about the two countries based on their population size, we may tend to view Canada as something less, relative to the industrial might of the U.S. Yet there are a number of industries where Canada is home not only to world-class commercial competitors, but to dominant companies in their industries.

The world's largest aluminum company in terms of sales is Montreal-based Alcan Inc. While one might be tempted to account for Alcan's rise based on its access to Canada's abundant natural resources, the real story is somewhat different. Alcan's rise to the top is a story of good beginnings, consistent expansion, the occasional odd government ruling, and some interesting merger strategies.

Alcan's good beginnings were in Shawinigan, Quebec—the site of its first production facility. From 1901 to 1928, the company operated as a subsidiary of the Aluminum Company of America (Alcoa). This relationship with the Americans proved to be a blessing. Alcoa's antitrust problems forced it to divest, not only its interests in

Montreal-based Alcan Inc. is the world's largest aluminum company in terms of sales.

(continued)

Alcan, but most of its interests outside the United States. Ownership of these interests was ceded to Alcan, and the Canadian company instantly became an international player. At a time when most companies operated in just their home market, Alcan was spun off from Alcoa with operations in Canada, seven European countries, Japan, and South America.

Alcan remained a major player and, in the decades that followed, added operations throughout Europe, Asia, Australia, and the Americas—including its parent's turf, the U.S. In a move designed to make it the industry leader, Alcan proposed a three-way merger between itself and two European rivals, Switzerland's Alusuisse and France's Pechiney. On this occasion, government watchdogs were not kind to Alcan. The divestments needed to gain regulatory approval were too great, and Pechiney withdrew from the deal, leaving Alusuisse to become part of Alcan. Then, in 2003, Alcan bought Pechiney outright and immediately surpassed the size of former parent, market leader Alcoa.

Alcan is not the only Canadian industry leader. Like Alcan, EnCana is a Canadian resource company that employed mergers to rise to become one of the world's largest companies in its field. After CP Rail spun off PanCanadian Energy in 2001, Gwyn Morgan, CEO of Alberta Energy, seized the opportunity to create one of the world's largest independent oil and gas producers by merging the two companies into one, in early 2002.

EnCana is not the only industry leader in Canada that is immersed in oil. McCain Foods Limited can make such a claim more arguably than any company. McCain is the leading maker of french fries, producing almost one-third of the world's french fries.

While no one would think a group of street performers would create an organization that is a half-billion dollar business and dominates the world of live entertainment, particularly in one of its centres—Las Vegas. However, this is exactly what Cirque du Soleil has done. Within 20 years, Cirque has performed in more than 130 cities and played to more than 130 million people. In a recent year, Cirque was simultaneously performing seven different shows on four continents. Cirque has IMAX movies, CDs, and boutiques. It now has permanent facilities in Las Vegas and Walt Disney World. The whole operation is still run from where it began—Montreal. Cirque has moved off the street, however, and now is run from a 600-employee, $40 million headquarters.

The world has opened its doors to Cirque, and chances are they are Canadian doors. The world's largest door maker is Toronto's Masonite International. Philip Orsino started with the company in 1982. To get the company to the top, he merged it with Premdor in 1989 and Masonite Corp. in 2001. However, Orsino grew the $2.5 billion company with more than just smart mergers. The company has a well-thought-out strategy—it focuses only on doors and on intelligent decisions for locating their production—the company has 70 locations in 12 countries. Doors are heavy to transport and locating close to customers turns out to be a critical consideration.

SOURCES: G. Marr, 2003, Doormaker to the world, *National Post* (*Financial Post*), November 4, FP7; Q. Hardy, 2003, Inside dope, *Forbes*, November 10, 28; B. Bregman, 2003, The holistic oil baron, *Maclean's* (Toronto ed.), January 13, 30–34; S. Burgess, 2003, They really like us, eh? *Maclean's* (Toronto ed.), October 13, 53–55; Canada's new spirit, 2003, *Economist*, September 27, 15; The entertainers: Cirque du Soleil, 2000, *Maclean's* (Toronto ed.), September 4, 45–46; McCain Foods Limited, 2003, *McCain website*, http://www.mccain.com/ McCainWorldWide/Leadership/, accessed October 20, 2003; MilkPEP, 2003, *MilkPEP's Why Milk website*, http://www.whymilk.com/ bios/cirque_du_soleil.html, accessed October 20, 2003; Metal center news online, 2000, *Metal Center News website*, http://www.metalcenter news.com/2000/May00/0500min_1.htm, May; J. Baglole, 2003, Personal health (a special report): health costs / prevention—getting the gray out…, *Wall Street Journal* (Eastern ed.), February 11, R6.

The actions undertaken by companies such as Alcan, EnCana, McCain, Cirque du Soleil, and Masonite are designed to help the firms achieve strategic competitiveness and earn above-average returns. **Strategic competitiveness** is achieved when a firm successfully formulates and implements a value-creating strategy. When a firm implements such a strategy and other companies are unable to duplicate it or find it too costly to imitate,[1] this firm has a **sustained (or sustainable) competitive advantage** (hereafter called competitive advantage). An organization is assured of a competitive advantage only after others' efforts to duplicate its strategy have ceased or failed. In addition, when a firm achieves a competitive advantage, it normally can sustain the advantage for only a certain period.[2] The speed with which competitors are able to acquire the skills needed to duplicate the benefits of a firm's value-creating strategy determines how long the competitive advantage will last.[3]

Understanding how to exploit a competitive advantage is important for firms to earn above-average returns.[4] **Above-average returns** are returns in excess of what an investor expects to earn from other investments with a similar amount of risk. **Risk** is an investor's uncertainty about the economic gains or losses that will result from a particular investment.[5] Returns are often measured in terms of accounting figures, e.g., return on assets or return on equity. Alternatively, returns can be measured on the basis of stock market returns, such as monthly returns (end-of-period stock price less beginning-of-period stock price, divided by the beginning price, as a percentage return).

Firms without a competitive advantage or firms that are not competing in an attractive industry earn, at best, average returns. **Average returns** are returns equal to those an investor expects to earn from other investments with a similar amount of risk. In the long run, an inability to earn at least average returns results in failure. Failure occurs because investors withdraw their investments from those firms earning less than average returns.

Dynamic in nature, the **strategic management process** (see Figure 1.1 on page 8) is the full set of commitments, decisions, and actions required for a firm to achieve strategic competitiveness and earn above-average returns.[6] Relevant strategic inputs derived from analyses of the internal and external environments are necessary for effective strategy formulation and implementation. In turn, effective strategic actions are a prerequisite to achieving the desired outcomes of strategic competitiveness and above-average returns. Thus, the strategic management process is used to match the conditions of an ever-changing market and competitive structure with a firm's continuously evolving resources, capabilities, and competencies (the sources of strategic inputs). When effective strategic actions take place in the context of carefully integrated strategy formulation and implementation, the result is desired strategic outcomes.[7]

In the remaining chapters of this book, we use the strategic management process to explain what firms should do to achieve strategic competitiveness and earn above-average returns. These explanations demonstrate why some firms consistently achieve competitive success while others fail to do so.[8] As you will see, the reality of global competition is a critical part of the strategic management process.[9]

Several topics are discussed in this chapter. First, we define the concept of strategy from different perspectives. As part of this discussion, we examine two models that suggest the strategic inputs needed to select the strategic actions that will achieve strategic competitiveness. The first model (industrial organization) suggests that the external environment is the primary determinant of a firm's strategic actions. The key to this model is identifying and competing successfully in an attractive (i.e., profitable) industry.[10] The second model (resource-based) suggests that a firm's unique resources and capabilities are the critical link to strategic competitiveness.[11] Comprehensive explanations in this chapter and the next three chapters show that, through the combined use of these models, firms obtain the strategic inputs needed to formulate and implement strategies successfully.

Strategic competitiveness is achieved when a firm successfully formulates and implements a value-creating strategy.

A **sustained** or **sustainable competitive advantage** occurs when a firm implements a value-creating strategy and other companies are unable to duplicate it or find it too costly to imitate.

Above-average returns are returns in excess of what an investor expects to earn from other investments with a similar amount of risk.

Risk is an investor's uncertainty about the economic gains or losses that will result from a particular investment.

Average returns are returns equal to those an investor expects to earn from other investments with a similar amount of risk.

The **strategic management process** is the full set of commitments, decisions, and actions required for a firm to achieve strategic competitiveness and earn above-average returns.

Figure 1.1   The Strategic Management Process

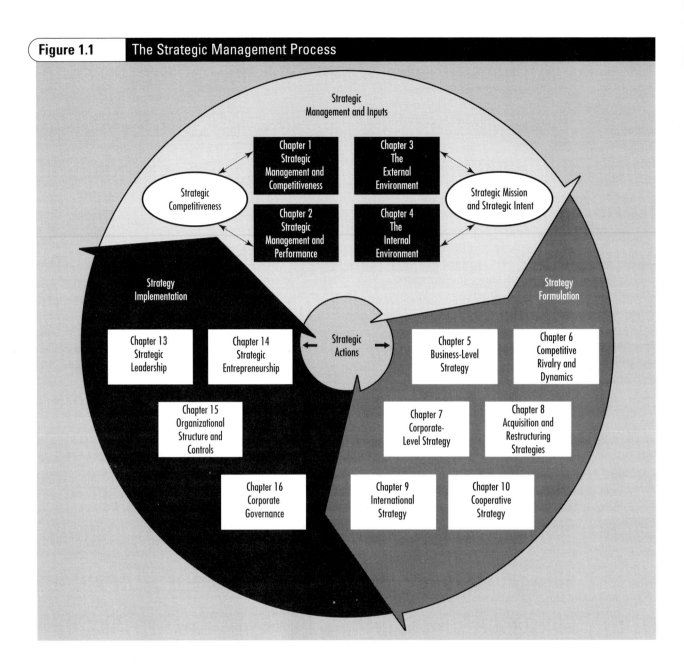

Next, we examine the challenge of strategic management. This brief discussion highlights the fact that strategic actions taken to achieve and then maintain strategic competitiveness demand the best efforts of managers, employees, and their organizations on a continuous basis.[12] Third, we describe the 21st-century competitive landscape, created primarily by the emergence of a global economy and rapid technological changes. This landscape provides the context of opportunities and threats within which firms strive to meet the competitive challenge.

To manoeuvre the organization through the competitive landscape, the firm must have a reasonable destination and a map for getting there—in other words, a strategic mission and strategic intent. Analysis of the firm's external and internal environments helps provide it with the information required to develop its strategic intent and strategic mission (defined later in this chapter, on page 21). As shown in Figure 1.1, strategic intent and strategic mission influence strategy formulation and implementation actions.

The chapter's discussion then turns from the notion of strategic intent and mission to the stakeholders that organizations serve. The degree to which stakeholders' needs can be met increases directly with enhancements in a firm's strategic competitiveness and its ability to earn above-average returns. Closing the chapter are introductions to organizational strategists and the elements of the strategic management process.

What Is Strategy?

For simplicity, we can define **strategy** as an integrated and coordinated set of commitments and actions designed to exploit core competencies and gain a competitive advantage. Yet, in reality, defining strategy is a bit more complicated. There may be no single agreed-to definition of strategy. Some of the diversity in the definitions of strategy is presented in Table 1.1.[13]

> **Strategy** is an integrated and coordinated set of commitments and actions designed to exploit core competencies and gain a competitive advantage.

McGill University's Henry Mintzberg gives five definitions of strategy: a plan, a ploy, a pattern, a position, and a perspective. Mintzberg's notion of plan refers to an organization's undertaking of a conscious and intended course of action to deal with a situation. Strategy as a ploy refers to a firm's attempts to implement some kind of specific manoeuvre intended to outwit a competitor or opponent. The third view of strategy is that it is a pattern of fairly consistent actions rather than a set of intended courses of actions. Strategy as a position reflects placing the organization in a particular environment (i.e., a market niche) that puts the organization at a competitive advantage and allows it to produce a higher than normal rate of return. Lastly, strategy may reflect a perspective—the organization's "ingrained way of perceiving the world" (i.e., there's the right way, the wrong way, and the way we do it here).[14]

Mintzberg makes another important contribution to our understanding of strategy when he differentiates among intended, emergent, and realized strategies (see Figure 1.2 on page 10).[15] Intended strategies are those plans or conscious courses of actions required to deal with a specific situation that lead to deliberate strategies. Intended strategies are usually top-down from senior management and reflect a hierarchical view of strategy. This hierarchical perspective suggests that corporate senior managers are responsible for the corporate mission and objectives, business unit senior managers are responsible for business unit strategies flowing from corporate missions and objectives,

Table 1.1	Alternative Definitions of Strategy

"The formulation of basic organizational missions, purposes, and objectives; policies and program strategies to achieve them; and the methods needed to assure that strategies are implemented to achieve organizational ends" (Steiner & Miner, 1977:7).

"A unified, comprehensive, and integrated plan designed to ensure that the basic objectives of the enterprise are achieved" (Glueck, 1980:9).

"The pattern or plan that integrates an organization's major goals, policies, and action sequences into a cohesive whole. A well formulated strategy helps to marshal and allocate an organization's resources into a unique and viable posture based on its relative internal competencies and shortcomings, anticipated changes in the environment, and contingent moves by intelligent opponents" (Quinn, 1980).

"The way to achieve organizational goals" (Hatten & Hatten, 1988:1).

"Strategy is a pattern of resource allocation that enables firms to maintain or improve their performance. A good strategy is a strategy that neutralizes threats and exploits opportunities while capitalizing on strengths and avoiding or fixing weaknesses" (Barney, 1997:17).

Figure 1.2 | Intended, Emergent, and Realized Strategies

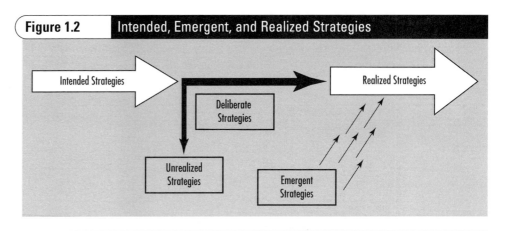

and functional area managers within the division are responsible for tactics and policies that flow from the business unit strategies.

Emergent strategies are patterns of actions that come about over time in an unintended manner. They are actions and decisions that a firm's senior managers may not have intended to pursue but nevertheless have ended up pursuing. They may be a byproduct of other intended strategies or may be strategies that emerge from bottom up, as opposed to top down. Emergent strategies are thus those strategies that result from the pattern of everyday actions and behaviours engaged in by managers and employees almost without conscious thought or planning. What is important about this view of strategy is the awareness that realized strategies are the result of how people in an organization (senior managers, middle managers, and employees) conduct themselves as they go about their daily activities. This means that senior managers must appreciate the need for all members of their organizations to be aware of, understand, embrace, and, on a day-to-day basis, act in accordance with the proposed strategy of the firm and its subordinate business units. In an organization where senior managers do not have a clear mission or clear objectives—and therefore, no clear strategy—the actions that emerge may destroy shareholder wealth. Thus, the need to develop a clear strategy is critical to the success of the organization. To this end, we now turn to two models used in strategic analysis to generate the strategic inputs needed to successfully formulate and implement strategies.

The I/O and Resource-Based Models of Above-Average Returns

The industrial organization, or I/O model (examined in Chapter 3), specifies that the industry a firm chooses to compete in has a stronger influence on the firm's performance than the decisions that managers make inside the firm.[16] According to this view, a firm's performance is determined mainly by a range of industry properties, including economies of scale, barriers to market entry, diversification, product differentiation, and the degree of concentration of firms in the industry.[17]

The I/O model has four underlying assumptions. One, the external environment imposes constraints that determine the strategies that result in above-average returns. Two, firms competing in an industry control similar resources and pursue similar strategies. Three, resources to implement strategies are mobile across firms, and resource differences between firms will be short-lived. Four, organizational decision makers are rational and committed to acting to maximize the firm's profits.[18] The I/O model challenges firms to locate the most attractive industry and learn how to use their resources to implement the strategy required by the industry's characteristics.

The five forces model of competition is an analytical tool used to help firms with this task. The model suggests that an industry's profitability is a function of interactions among suppliers, buyers, competitive rivalry, product substitutes, and potential entrants to the industry.[19] Firms can earn above-average returns by producing standardized products at lower cost (a cost-leadership strategy) or by making differentiated products that can command a premium price (a differentiation strategy).

As shown in Figure 1.3, the I/O model suggests that above-average returns are earned when firms implement the strategy dictated by the characteristics of the general environment, the industry environment, and the competitor environment. Companies that develop or acquire skills needed to implement these strategies are likely to succeed; those that do not are likely to fail. This model suggests that external characteristics, rather than the firm's unique internal resources and capabilities, primarily determine its returns.

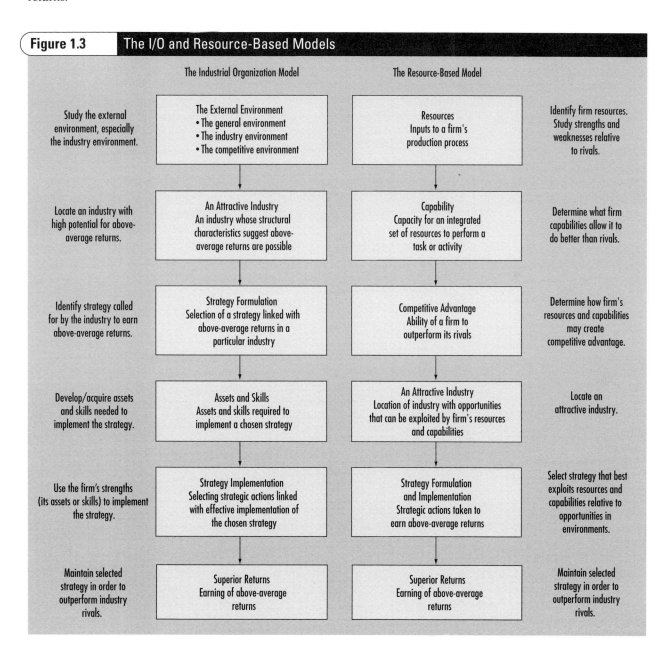

Figure 1.3   The I/O and Resource-Based Models

The Industrial Organization Model

The Resource-Based Model

Study the external environment, especially the industry environment.

The External Environment
• The general environment
• The industry environment
• The competitive environment

Resources
Inputs to a firm's production process

Identify firm resources. Study strengths and weaknesses relative to rivals.

Locate an industry with high potential for above-average returns.

An Attractive Industry
An industry whose structural characteristics suggest above-average returns are possible

Capability
Capacity for an integrated set of resources to perform a task or activity

Determine what firm capabilities allow it to do better than rivals.

Identify strategy called for by the industry to earn above-average returns.

Strategy Formulation
Selection of a strategy linked with above-average returns in a particular industry

Competitive Advantage
Ability of a firm to outperform its rivals

Determine how firm's resources and capabilities may create competitive advantage.

Develop/acquire assets and skills needed to implement the strategy.

Assets and Skills
Assets and skills required to implement a chosen strategy

An Attractive Industry
Location of industry with opportunities that can be exploited by firm's resources and capabilities

Locate an attractive industry.

Use the firm's strengths (its assets or skills) to implement the strategy.

Strategy Implementation
Selecting strategic actions linked with effective implementation of the chosen strategy

Strategy Formulation and Implementation
Strategic actions taken to earn above-average returns

Select strategy that best exploits resources and capabilities relative to opportunities in environments.

Maintain selected strategy in order to outperform industry rivals.

Superior Returns
Earning of above-average returns

Superior Returns
Earning of above-average returns

Maintain selected strategy in order to outperform industry rivals.

Alternatively, the resource-based model assumes each organization's unique collection of resources and capabilities are the primary basis for the firm's strategy and returns rather than industry characteristics. **Resources** are inputs into a firm's production process, such as capital equipment, the skills of individual employees, patents, finances, and talented managers. A **capability** is the capacity for a set of resources to perform a task or an activity in an integrative manner. This model suggests that capabilities evolve and must be managed dynamically.[20] Furthermore, firms acquire different resources and develop unique capabilities, and since resources may not be highly mobile across firms, the differences in resources may be the real basis for competitive advantage.

In the resource-based model, the strategy chosen should allow a firm to best exploit its core competencies relative to opportunities in the external environment. Not all firm resources and capabilities have the potential to be the basis for a core competency. This potential is realized when resources and capabilities are (1) valuable—allowing a firm to take advantage of opportunities or neutralize external threats; (2) rare—possessed by few current or potential competitors; (3) costly to imitate—when other firms either cannot obtain them or are at a cost disadvantage in obtaining them; and (4) organized to be exploited—firms have the correct structure, control and reward systems to support each advantage.[21] When these four criteria are met, resources and capabilities become core competencies. **Core competencies** are resources and capabilities that serve as sources of competitive advantage for a firm. Often related to functional skills, core competencies, when developed and applied throughout a firm, may result in strategic competitiveness.

Research findings suggest both environment and firm characteristics play roles in determining a firm's profitability. These findings show that about 20 percent of the variance in a firm's profitability is determined by the industries in which the firm operates, and 36 percent of the variance in profitability could be attributed to the firm's characteristics and actions.[22] Thus, there is likely a reciprocal relationship between the environment and the firm's strategy, thereby affecting the firm's performance.[23] As a result, executives must integrate the two models to develop the most effective strategy.

The Challenge of Strategic Management

The goals of achieving strategic competitiveness and earning above-average returns are challenging, not only for large firms such as IBM, but also for those as small as a local computer retail outlet or a dry cleaner. As suggested in the opening case, on page 5, the performances of some companies, such as Alcan, EnCana, McCain, Cirque, and Masonite, have more than met strategic management's challenge to date.

For other firms, the challenges are substantial in the dynamic competitive landscape. Evidence the rapid changes experienced by Nortel Networks. During the 1990s, Nortel's overall performance was among the best—it was one of the top wealth producers throughout the decades.[24] However, in 2001, the firm experienced significant reductions in its stock price. These setbacks were so severe that shareholders launched numerous lawsuits against the company.[25] Some investors have placed the blame for Nortel's downfall squarely on the shoulders of former CEO John Roth. However, others are quick to point out that all companies in the sector have been decimated.[26] As well, Nortel's top management argued that their new strategic actions would, over time, regain the high performance once enjoyed by the firm.[27]

The most significant challenge can simply be staying in business. From the year 2000, onward, 10,000 Canadian businesses per year filed have for bankruptcy.[28] Because data about business start-ups and failures are usually incomplete, the actual number of companies closing their doors typically exceeds the official count.[29] These statistics suggest that competitive success is transient.[30] Thomas J. Watson Jr., formerly IBM's chairman,

---

Resources are inputs into a firm's production process, such as capital equipment, the skills of individual employees, patents, finances, and talented managers.

A **capability** is the capacity for a set of resources to perform a task or an activity in an integrative manner.

Core competencies are resources and capabilities that serve as sources of competitive advantage for a firm over its rivals.

once cautioned people to remember that "corporations are expendable and that success—at best—is an impermanent achievement which can always slip out of hand."[31]

Successful performance may be transient and impermanent, as Fruit of the Loom (FTL) found. It was once a highly successful company, with a strong global brand and good financial performance. In the middle of a relatively robust economy in the late 1990s, FTL suffered losses and needed to close several factories. In December 1999, the company filed for bankruptcy protection. The firm had made a number of strategic mistakes, but the most serious blunder was that it did not keep pace with reconfigurations being made by others to the global value chain. This is when Montreal-based competitor Gildan Activewear came in. Gildan used cheap offshore labour to keep costs down and handled its non-Canadian sales out of its Barbados office to drastically lower its tax bill. By the time Fruit of the Loom figured out Gildan's strategy, FTL was well on its way to bankruptcy court, and Gildan was becoming North America's number one T-shirt maker. This is not to say that Gildan's performance might not also be transient and impermanent. Gildan's sales have declined since 2000, and FTL has new backing since being bought by Warren Buffet's Berkshire Hathaway.[32]

It is interesting to note that a survey showed CEOs did not place "strong and consistent profits" as their top priority; in fact, it was ranked fifth. A "strong and well-thought-out strategy" was regarded as the most important factor to make a firm the most respected in the future. Ranking second, third, and fourth were "maximizing customer satisfaction and loyalty," "business leadership and quality products and services," and "concern for consistent profits,"[33] respectively. These rankings are consistent with the view that no matter how good a product or service is, the firm must select the right strategy and then implement it effectively.[34]

CEOs' concern for strategy is well founded, as shown by the case of Eaton's described in the following Strategic Focus box, "The Impermanence of Success," on page 14. Some firms create their own problems by formulating the wrong strategy or by poorly implementing an effective strategy. Although Eaton's clearly had the opportunity maintain its existence, it failed—in a very public and spectacular way—to do so. Furthermore, it squandered its historic market leadership in the course of its decline.

In recognition of strategic management's challenge, Andrew Grove, Intel's former CEO, noted that only paranoid companies survive and succeed. Firms must continuously evaluate their environments and decide on the appropriate strategy. By choosing a strategy, a firm decides to pursue one course of action over others. The firm's executives are thus setting priorities for the firm's competitive actions.

Firms can select effective or ineffective strategies. For example, the choice by Eaton's to stop stressing the importance of marketing its brand was likely an ineffective one. The purpose of this book is to explain how firms develop and implement effective strategies. Partly because of Grove's approach described above, Intel continuously strives to improve in order to remain competitive. For Intel and others that compete in the 21st century's competitive landscape, Grove believes that a key challenge is to try to do the impossible—namely, to anticipate the unexpected.[35]

The 21st-Century Competitive Landscape[36]

The fundamental nature of competition in many of the world's industries is changing.[37] The pace of this change is relentless and is increasing. Even determining the boundaries of an industry has become challenging. Consider, for example, how advances in interactive computer networks and telecommunications have blurred the definition of the television industry. Because of these advances, the near future will find firms such as ABC, CBC, CBS, NBC, CTV, and HBO competing not only among themselves but also with companies such as AT&T, Microsoft, Rogers, Sony, Bell, and Telus.

The Impermanence of Success

For Eaton's, the routes of their failure can be traced back as far as 1952, when U.S. retailing giant Sears formed a joint venture with Simpson's—a major competitor of Eaton's. Eaton's seemed to underestimate the power of the new venture. The view seemed to be that the new suburban Simpsons-Sears stores were too distant to matter much to the downtown merchants who ran Eaton's. Yet Sears had a long history of successfully operating suburban stores; it opened its first store in 1928, in Aurora, Illinois. Within a quarter-century, Simpsons-Sears equalled Eaton's $1.6 billion sales level. Eaton's sales froze at that level while Sears continued to grow. By the time Eaton's arrived in bankruptcy court, Sears' sales had tripled from mid-1970s levels. About $1 billion of these sales came from Sears catalogue sales—a market Eaton's had abandoned in 1976 (the Sears catalogue phone number is the most frequently called toll-free number in Canada).

One of Eaton's biggest mistakes lay in its on-and-off support for marketing the Eaton's brand. In the 1970s, Eaton's moved from being a traditional style department store to a modern retailer. The company began to sell the idea of "the store and the customer's relationship with the store." Eaton's greatest marketing strength was evident from 1970 to 1980. By the end of the 1980s, Eaton's began losing sight of the importance of keeping its brand exciting—including its withdrawal of support for the Santa Claus parade in 1982. When the recession hit in the early 1990s, Eaton's abandoned marketing its brand in favour of a more price-orientated approach. Eaton's tried to rebuild its brand in the mid-1990s, but the move came too late, and Eaton's fell into bankruptcy in early 1997.

After Eaton's initial reorganization, it cut product lines and moved into upscale clothing with its Diversity in-store boutiques. This move alienated older loyal customers and failed to attract the younger customers that Eaton's sought. Part of the failure to attract new customers stemmed from Eaton's advertising store changes before it had begun to implement them. Potential new customers, curious enough to look at the new Eaton's, came to find the same old store. As well, competitors, both specialty retailers and other department stores, occupied the niche Eaton's sought. Others were selling the same clothing lines in stores with a decor and ambiance that Eaton's attempted to achieve. Eaton's was perceived as staid, despite trying to be trendy, and in the end, Eaton's found it was accepted as neither.

In the 1990s, Eaton's traditional core customers were older than the average Canadian. These customers were also growing more price-sensitive due to a recession at the beginning of the 1990s. Customers were able to exercise their price-sensitive impulses because of the arrival in Canada of Wal-Mart in 1995. From 1994 to 1998, Eaton's share of the Canadian department store market fell from 14.3 percent to 7.2 percent—on average, a reduction of between $400 million and $500 million in sales, every year for three to four years!

Finally, Eaton's made two serious financial missteps in reorganization. First, Eaton's closed only 25 percent of its stores, while many argued the company should have closed better than half of its outlets. The remaining stores would have been the best performing ones in the chain. Secondly, Eaton's raised hundreds of millions of dollars by selling half the firm to the public. Critics noted that twice the amount of funds was really needed to turn around the company.

After failing to keep its traditional customers, failing to acquire new customers, and saddling itself with too many poorly performing stores and too little cash, Eaton's ended up back in bankruptcy. Bought out by Sears, there was some hope for rehabilitation of the Eaton's name. However, in five short years, the Eaton's name went from retailing icon to a name synonymous with failure. Even Sears, with all its resources, could not save the name, and by 2003, the last of the Eaton's stores became Sears' outlets.

SOURCES: J. Sheppard & S. Chowhury, 2004, Riding the wrong wave: organizational failure as a failed turnaround, *Simon Fraser University Faculty of Business Working Paper*; R. McQueen, 1999, *The Eatons: The rise & fall of Canada's royal family*, Toronto: Stoddart Publishing; P. Allossery, 1999, How a love affair went sour, *National Post*, August 17, C4; M. Janigan, 1998, Hard times at Eaton's, *Maclean's* (Toronto ed.), November 30, 62; J. Schofield, 1999, The retail revolution: shoppers are shaking up the market, and Wal-Mart is winning, *Maclean's* (Toronto ed.), March 1, 34.

Other characteristics of the 21st-century competitive landscape are noteworthy as well. Conventional sources of competitive advantage, such as economies of scale and huge advertising budgets, are not as effective as they once were. Moreover, the traditional managerial mind-set is unlikely to lead a firm to strategic competitiveness. Managers must adopt a new mind-set that values flexibility, speed, innovation, integration, and the challenges that evolve from constantly changing conditions. The conditions of the competitive landscape result in a perilous business world, one where the investments required to compete on a global scale are enormous, and the consequences of failure are severe.[38]

Hypercompetition is a term often used to capture the realities of the 21st-century competitive landscape. Hypercompetition results from the dynamics of strategic manoeuvring among global and innovative combatants. It is a condition of rapidly escalating competition, based on price-quality positioning, competition to create new know-how and establish first-mover advantage, and competition to protect or invade established product or geographic markets.[39] In a hypercompetitive market, firms often aggressively challenge their competitors in the hopes of improving their own competitive position and, ultimately, their own performance.[40] Several factors create hypercompetitive environments and the 21st-century competitive landscape. The two primary drivers are the emergence of a global economy and rapid technological change.

The Global Economy

A **global economy** is one in which goods, services, people, skills, and ideas move freely across geographic borders. Relatively unfettered by artificial constraints, such as tariffs, the global economy significantly expands and complicates a firm's competitive environment.[41] Unprecedented opportunities and challenges are associated with the emergence of the global economy. For example, by 2015, China's total gross domestic product (GDP) is projected to be greater than Japan's (although its per capita output will likely be lower).[42] Europe is now the world's largest single market, with 700 million potential customers. In addition, the European market also has a GDP of $8 trillion, which is comparable to that of the United States.[43] However, as the competitiveness rankings in Table 1.2 on page 16 indicate, individual European countries, vary greatly in their level of competitiveness.

Achieving improved competitiveness allows a country's citizens to have a higher standard of living. Some believe that entrepreneurial activity will continue to influence living standards during the 21st century. For example, a report describing European competitiveness concluded that, "it is only through the creation of more new businesses and more fast-growing businesses that Europe will create more new jobs and achieve higher levels of economic well-being for all of its citizens."[44] The role of entrepreneurship is discussed further in Chapter 14. A country's competitiveness is achieved through the accumulation of individual firms' strategic competitiveness in the global economy. To be competitive, a firm must view the world as its marketplace. For example, Procter & Gamble believes that it still has tremendous potential to grow internationally because the global market for household products is not as mature as it is in North America.

Although a commitment to viewing the world as a company's marketplace creates a sense of direction, it is not without risks. For example, the Canadian dollar's rise against the U.S. dollar in 2003 meant that many firms with substantial U.S. interests would see significant changes in their reported income. Vancouver's Sierra Systems, a $150 million information-technology services company, lost almost two-thirds of its income (from 40 cents a share before exchange losses to 14 cents after taking dollar changes into account) because of a higher dollar.[45]

A **global economy** is one in which goods, services, people, skills, and ideas move freely across geographic borders.

Table 1.2	World Competitiveness Rankings				
Country	2004 Rank	2003 Rank	2002 Rank	2001 Rank	2000 Rank
USA	1	1	1	1	1
Singapore	2	4	8	3	2
Canada	3	6	7	9	8
Australia	4	7	10	12	11
Iceland	5	8	11	10	10
Hong Kong	6	10	13	4	9
Denmark	7	5	6	15	12
Finland	8	3	3	5	6
Luxembourg	9	2	2	2	3
Ireland	10	11	9	7	5
Sweden	11	12	12	11	14
Taiwan	12	17	20	16	17
Austria	13	14	15	14	18
Switzerland	14	9	5	8	7
Netherlands	15	13	4	6	4
Malaysia	16	21	24	28	26
Norway	17	15	14	19	16
New Zealand	18	16	18	21	20
Germany*	19	20	17	13	13
U.K.*	20	19	16	17	15

*For purposes of comparability across five years, we eliminated places not ranked for all years (e.g., Zhejiang, which was ranked 19th in 2004 and 38th in 2003, and Bavaria, which was ranked 20th in 2004 and 31st in 2003; no other country or region added in the 2000–04 period was ranked in the top 20).

SOURCE: From *World Competitiveness Yearbook 2004*, IMD, Switzerland, http://www02.imd.ch/documents/wcy/content/pastranking.pdf, accessed July 18, 2004. Reprinted with permission of IMD.

The March of Globalization

Globalization is the increasing economic interdependence among countries as reflected in the flow of goods and services, financial capital, and knowledge across country borders.[46] In globalized markets and industries, financial capital might be obtained in one national market and used to buy raw materials in another one. Manufacturing equipment bought from a third national market can then be used to produce products that are sold in yet a fourth market. Thus, globalization increases the range of opportunities for companies competing in the 21st-century competitive landscape.

Wal-Mart, for instance, is trying to achieve boundary-less retailing with global pricing, sourcing, and logistics. Most of Wal-Mart's original international investments were in Canada and Mexico, in close proximity to the United States. However, the company has now moved into several other countries, including Argentina, Brazil, Indonesia, and China. By the end of 2000, Wal-Mart was the largest retailer in the world. Wal-Mart changes the structure of business in many countries it enters. For example, in Mexico, it has reduced the prominence of distributors and middlemen with its 600 stores. By 2003, the number of Wal-Mart outlets outside the U.S. was double number of stores in the U.S.[47]

The internationalization of markets and industries makes it increasingly difficult to think of some firms as domestic companies. For example, what could be more Canadian than Tim Hortons? Yet, Tim Hortons is owned by Wendy's International, based in Dublin, Ohio. The largest individual shareholder of Wendy's stock is Ron Joyce, past

CEO of Tim Hortons and a Canadian.[48] So does that make Tim Hortons a U.S. company and Wendy's a Canadian one? The lines are becoming increasingly blurred with the growth of international investments.

It is difficult to think automobile firms as European, Japanese, or American. Instead, they can be more accurately classified as global companies striving to achieve strategic competitiveness in the 21st-century competitive landscape. For example, Ford launched a car in Japan that it had built in Europe.[49]

Some believe that because of the enormous economic benefits it can generate, globalization will not be stopped. It has been predicted that genuine free trade in manufactured goods among North America, Europe, and Japan would add 5 to 10 percent to the three regions' annual economic output, and free trade in their service sectors would boost aggregate output by another 15 to 20 percent. Realizing these potential gains in economic output requires a commitment from the industrialized nations to cooperatively stimulate the higher levels of trade necessary for global growth. In 2001, global trade in goods and services accounted for approximately 25 percent of the world's GDP.[50]

Global competition has increased performance standards in many dimensions, including quality, cost, productivity, product introduction time, and operational efficiency. Moreover, these standards are not static; they are exacting, requiring continuous improvement from a firm and its employees. As they accept the challenges posed by these increasing standards, companies improve their capabilities, and individual workers sharpen their skills. Thus, in the 21st-century competitive landscape, only firms capable of meeting, if not exceeding, global standards typically earn strategic competitiveness.[51]

The development of emerging and transitional economies is also changing the global competitive landscape and significantly increasing competition in global markets.[52] The economic development of Asian countries (outside of Japan) is increasing the significance of Asian markets. Firms in the emerging economies of Asia, such as South Korea, however, are becoming major competitors in global industries. Companies such as Cemex are moving more boldly into international markets and are making important investments in Asia. Cemex, a cement producer headquartered in Mexico, also has significant investments in North America and Latin America. Thus, international investments come from many directions and are targeted for multiple regions of the world.

There are risks with these investments (a number of them are discussed in Chapter 9). Some people refer to these risks as the "liability of foreignness."[53] Research suggests that firms, in their early ventures, are challenged into international markets and can encounter difficulties by entering too many different or challenging international markets. First, performance may suffer in early efforts to globalize until a firm develops the skills required to manage international operations.[54] Additionally, the firm's performance may suffer with substantial investment in globalization. In this instance, firms may overdiversify internationally beyond their ability to manage these diversified operations.[55] The outcome can sometimes be quite painful to these firms.[56] Thus, entry into international markets, even for firms with substantial experience in such markets, first requires careful planning and selection of the appropriate markets to enter, followed by developing the most effective strategies to successfully operate in those markets.

Global markets are attractive strategic options for some companies, but they are not the only source of strategic competitiveness. In fact, for most companies, even for those capable of competing successfully in global markets, it is critical to remain committed to the domestic market.[57] In the 21st-century competitive landscape, firms are challenged to develop the optimal level of globalization that results in appropriate concentrations on a company's domestic and global operations.

In many instances, strategically competitive companies are those that have learned how to apply competitive insights gained locally (or domestically) on a global scale.[58] These companies do not impose homogeneous solutions in a pluralistic world. Instead, they nourish local insights so that they can modify and apply them appropriately in different regions of the world. Moreover, strategically competitive companies are sensitive to globalization's potential effects. Firms with strong commitments to global success evaluate these possible outcomes in making their strategic choices.

Technology and Technological Changes

There are three categories of trends and conditions through which technology is significantly altering the nature of competition.

Increasing Rate of Technological Change and Diffusion

Both the rate of change of technology and the speed at which new technologies become available and are used have increased substantially over the last 15 to 20 years. Consider the following rates of technology diffusion: It took the telephone 35 years to get into about 25 percent of all homes in the North America. It took TV 26 years. It took radio 22 years. It took PCs 16 years. It took the Internet 7 years.[59]

Perpetual innovation is a term used to describe the speed and consistency at which new, information-intensive technologies replace older technologies. The shorter product life cycles resulting from these rapid diffusions of new technologies place a competitive premium on being able to quickly introduce new goods and services into the marketplace. In fact, when products become somewhat indistinguishable because of the widespread and rapid diffusion of technologies, speed to market may be the primary source of competitive advantage (see Chapter 6).[60]

There are other indicators of rapid technology diffusion. Some evidence suggests that it takes only 12 to 18 months for firms to gather information about their competitors' research and development and product decisions.[61] In the global economy, competitors can sometimes imitate a firm's successful competitive actions within a few days. Consider, for example, approximately 75 percent of the product-life gross margins for a typical personal computer are earned within the first 90 days of sales.[62] Once a source of competitive advantage, the protection that firms possessed previously through their patents has been stifled by the current rate of technological diffusion. Today, patents are thought by many to be an effective way of protecting proprietary technology only for pharmaceutical and chemical industries. Indeed, many firms competing in the electronics industry often do not apply for the patents in order to prevent competitors from gaining access to technological knowledge included in the patent application.

The other factor in technological change is the development of disruptive technologies that destroy the value of existing technology and create new markets.[63] Some have referred to this concept as a Schumpeterian innovation, from the work by the economist Joseph A. Schumpeter, who suggested that such innovation emerged from a process of creative destruction, in which existing technologies are replaced by new ones. Others refer to this outcome as radical or breakthrough innovation.[64] The development and use of the Internet for commerce is an example of a disruptive technology.

The Information Age

Dramatic changes in information technology have occurred in recent years. Personal computers, cellular phones, artificial intelligence, virtual reality, and massive databases (e.g., LexisNexis) are a few examples of how information is used differently as a result of technological developments. An important outcome of these changes is that the ability to effectively and efficiently access and use information has become an important source of competitive advantage in virtually all industries.

Companies are building electronic networks that link them to customers, employees, vendors, and suppliers. These networks, designed to conduct business over the Internet, are referred to as e-business;[65] and e-business is big business. North American e-business sales total more than $300 billion. It is predicted that e-business will eventually represent 75 to 80 percent of the gross domestic product.[66] In one respect, Canadians have emerged as global Internet leaders. The majority of Canadian home and business Internet users connect using broadband connections. This places Canada second only to South Korea among the world's leaders in use of high-speed connections.[67]

Both the pace of change in information technology and its diffusion will continue to increase. For instance, the number of personal computers in use is expected to reach 278 million by 2010. The declining costs of information technologies and the increased accessibility to them are also evident in the 21st-century competitive landscape. The global proliferation of relatively inexpensive computing power and its linkage on a global scale via computer networks combine to increase the speed and diffusion of information technologies. Thus, the competitive potential of information technologies is now available to companies of all sizes throughout the world, not only to large firms in Europe, Japan, and North America.

The Internet provides an infrastructure that allows the delivery of information to computers in any location. Access to significant quantities of relatively inexpensive information yields strategic opportunities for a range of industries and companies. Retailers, for example, use the Internet to provide abundant shopping privileges to customers in multiple locations. The pervasive influence of electronic commerce, or e-business, is creating a new culture, referred to as e-culture, that affects the way managers lead, organize, think, and develop and implement strategies.[68]

Increasing Knowledge Intensity

Knowledge (information, intelligence, and expertise) is the basis of technology and its application. In the 21st-century competitive landscape, knowledge is a critical organizational resource and is increasingly a valuable source of competitive advantage.[69] As a result, many companies now strive to transmute the accumulated knowledge of individual employees into a corporate asset. Some argue that the value of intangible assets, including knowledge, is growing as a proportion of total shareholder value.[70] The probability of achieving strategic competitiveness in the 21st-century competitive landscape is enhanced for the firm that realizes its survival depends on the ability to capture intelligence, transform it into usable knowledge, and diffuse it rapidly throughout the company.[71] Firms accepting this challenge shift their focus from merely obtaining information to exploiting that information to gain a competitive advantage over rival firms.[72]

To earn above-average returns, firms must be able to adapt quickly to changes in their competitive landscape. Such adaptation requires that the firm develop strategic flexibility. **Strategic flexibility** is a set of capabilities used to respond to various demands and opportunities existing in a dynamic and uncertain competitive environment. Thus, it involves coping with uncertainty and the accompanying risks.[73]

Firms should develop strategic flexibility in all areas of their operations. To achieve strategic flexibility, many firms have to develop organizational slack—resources that allow the firm some flexibility to respond to environmental changes.[74] When larger changes are required, firms may have to undergo strategic reorientations. Such reorientations can drastically change a firm's competitive strategy.[75] Strategic reorientations often result from a firm's poor performance. For example, when a firm earns negative returns, its stakeholders (discussed later in this chapter) are likely to pressure top executives to make major changes.[76] To be strategically flexible on a continuing basis, a firm needs to develop the capacity to learn. Continuous learning provides the firm with new and up-to-date sets of skills, which allow the firm to adapt to its environment as the firm encounters changes.[77]

Following a well-thought-out strategy in the high-tech field is important. Yet, as illustrated in the Strategic Focus box on page 20, "The Clean New World," being flexible, learning, and

Strategic flexibility is a set of capabilities used to respond to various demands and opportunities existing in a dynamic and uncertain competitive environment.

The Clean New World

"The days of the internal-combustion gas engine were drawing to a close and we felt certain that hydrogen fuel-cell technology was the strongest contender to replace it." At least that's how Pierre Rivard explains the founding of Mississauga's Hydrogenics Corporation. Rivard, and partners Joe Cargnelli and Boyd Taylor, began the company in 1995. All three were engineers with a range of business experience. As researchers investigating hydrogen fuel cells at the University of Toronto, Rivard and Cargnelli saw the commercial potential of their work and started Hydrogenics to start a revolution. Cargnelli notes that "the potential for this technology to completely change the world is on par with the microcomputer." To keep the cause alive, Rivard notes, "We attract some of the best minds in the world. They want to work here because they honestly believe we're working toward a cause rather than working for a company,"

The three founders immediately struck upon the triple-market approach that still drives the company. The first product market was in-vehicle fuel cells to power ultra-quiet vehicles whose only exhaust is water vapour. However, numerous scientific breakthroughs and a great deal of capital are required before we will see a commercially viable hydrogen-powered vehicle. This is where Hydrogenics' two other product markets come in. The first of these markets are for generators—anything from small, portable units for the military to huge stationary units for office towers. They are technically easier to develop than in-vehicle fuel cells but mastering them will provide Hydrogenics with a base to build on for developing fuel cells for vehicles. In 2003, Hydrogenics sold its first commercial generators, six power modules to Vancouver-based General Hydrogen.

Hydrogenics final market stream is fuel-cell testing equipment. Every fuel-cell system is made up of a series of components called stacks. Every company entered in the race to develop fuel-cell technology is focused on creating new and better stacks. Hydrogenics' test units—"big metal boxes pocked with dials and gauges"—allow fuel-cell developers to monitor and control the effects of temperature, pressure, and other variables on a stack. Simply, the founders of Hydrogenics realized that they would need testing equipment to facilitate their own fuel-cell research, so why not build it and sell it to others as well. Each unit brings in a gross profit of between $15,000 and $75,000 and helps fund other Hydrogenics product research.

While this three-product market strategy has worked well for the company, Hydrogenics has also been careful to establish quality cooperative strategies. Ottawa cooperated with the company by chipping in with critical seed funding for the initial Hydrogenics research, then Hydrogenics established a relationship with GM that allowed it to take on a significant role in GM's stack development. Between 1997 and 1999, Hydrogenics's revenue jumped from less than $150,000 to more than $3.5 million.

With its association with GM to back it, Hydrogenics was able to secure $6 million in venture capital between late 1998 and early 2000. This allowed the company to develop and market its initial testing devices. With an order backlog and R&D costs growing, Hydrogenics raised $128 million with an initial public offering (IPO) in October 2000. Strategically, Hydrogenics made all the right moves: intelligent product market, growth, and partner choices. Luck was on the company's side as well. Right after the IPO, the market for tech stocks imploded, and Hydrogenics stock has yet to regain its IPO price. Yet, even with the growing cloud over tech stocks, the fundamental strategy of the company, along with the enormous importance of Hydrogen fuel cell development compelled GM to purchase 24 percent of Hydrogenics in October 2001. The two firms are now engaged in joint R&D efforts. GM has first rights to any innovations related to vehicular fuel cells, but Hydrogenics can use any new developments in noncompeting products.

Finally, Hydrogenics's strategy includes maintaining its lead in a consolidating industry. To that end, the company purchased two competing fuel-cell test system makers. The company's purchase of Greenlight Power Technologies in 2003 made Hydrogenics the largest producer of hydrogen fuel-cell testing equipment in the world.

SOURCE: Lee Oliver, 2003 PROFIT 100: The Top 5—Hydrogenics Corp.: Generation H. PROFITguide.com http://www.profitguide.com/profit100/2003/article.asp?ID=1254 (March 24, 2004) © 2003 Rogers Inc. © 2000–2004 PROFIT, Your Guide to Business Success. All Rights Reserved.

making the necessary changes with regard to products and partnerships—plus a little luck— allowed Mississauga's Hydrogenics Corporation reach the top of the Profit 100.

As the Hydrogenics story illustrates, the need for a vision to drive an organization is critical. Without such a vision, the organization is truly directionless. With this focus in mind, we need to turn our attention to the concepts of strategic intent and strategic mission.

Strategic Intent and Strategic Mission

To guide the organization through the competitive landscape, it must have a reasonable destination and a map for getting there—in other words, a strategic mission and strategic intent. Analysis of the firm's external and internal environments help provide it with the information required to develop both its strategic intent and its strategic mission.

Strategic Intent

Strategic intent is the leveraging of a firm's resources, capabilities, and core competencies to accomplish the firm's goals in the competitive environment.[78] Strategic intent exists when all employees and levels of a firm are committed to the pursuit of a specific (and significant) performance criterion. Some argue that strategic intent provides employees with the only goal worthy of personal effort and commitment: to unseat the best or remain the best, worldwide.[79] Strategic intent has been effectively formed when employees believe fervently in their company's product and when they are focused totally on their firm's ability to outperform its competitors.

For example, Unilever has stated its strategic intent to make Dove a megabrand—to make Dove to personal care products what Coke is to soft drinks. For 40 years, Dove signified a bar of soap. However, in recent years, Unilever has been developing other personal care products under the Dove brand, including deodorant, vitamins, body wash, and facial tissues. Dove helped propel Unilever to become the largest producer of bar soap with more than $1 billion in sales worldwide.[80]

It is not enough for a firm to know its own strategic intent. Performing well demands that the firm also identify its competitors' strategic intent. Only when these intentions are understood can a firm become aware of the resolve, stamina, and inventiveness (traits linked with effective strategic intents) of those competitors.[81] For example, Unilever must identify and understand Procter & Gamble's strategic intent with its Olay brand. A company's success may be also grounded in a keen and deep understanding of the strategic intent of customers, suppliers, partners, and competitors.[82]

Strategic Mission

As the preceding discussion shows, strategic intent is internally focused. It is concerned with identifying the resources, capabilities, and core competencies on which a firm can base its strategic actions. Strategic intent reflects what a firm is capable of doing with its core competencies and the unique ways the core competencies can be used to exploit a competitive advantage.

Strategic mission flows from strategic intent. Externally focused, **strategic mission** is a statement of a firm's unique purpose and the scope of its operations in product and market terms.[83] A strategic mission provides general descriptions of the products a firm intends to produce and the markets it will serve using its core competencies. An effective strategic mission establishes a firm's individuality and is inspiring and relevant to all stakeholders.[84] Together, strategic intent and strategic mission yield the insights required to formulate and implement strategies.

The strategic mission of Johnson & Johnson focuses on customers, stating that the organization's primary responsibility is "to the doctors, nurses, and patients, mothers and

Strategic intent is the leveraging of a firm's resources, capabilities, and core competencies to accomplish the firm's goals in the competitive environment.

Strategic mission is a statement of a firm's unique purpose and the scope of its operations in product and market terms.

fathers and all others who use our products and services."[85] An effective strategic mission is formed when the firm has a strong sense of both what it wants to do and the ethical standards that will guide behaviours in the pursuit of its goals.[86] Because Johnson & Johnson specifies the products it will offer in particular markets and presents a framework within which the firm operates, its strategic mission is an application of strategic intent.[87]

Research has shown that having an effective intent and mission and properly implementing them has a positive effect on performance as measured by growth in sales, profits, employment, and net worth.[88] When a firm is strategically competitive and earning above-average returns, it has the capacity to satisfy stakeholders' interests.

Stakeholders

Every organization involves a system of primary stakeholder groups with whom it establishes and manages relationships.[89] **Stakeholders** are the individuals and groups who can affect, and are affected by, the strategic outcomes achieved and who have enforceable claims on a firm's performance.[90] Claims on a firm's performance are enforced through the stakeholders' ability to withhold participation essential to the organization's survival, competitiveness, and profitability.[91] Stakeholders continue to support an organization when its performance meets or exceeds their expectations. Also, recent research suggests that firms that effectively managing stakeholder relationships outperform those that do not. Stakeholder relationships can therefore be managed to be a source of competitive advantage.[92]

Although organizations have dependency relationships with their stakeholders, they are not equally dependent on all stakeholders at all times; as a consequence, not every stakeholder has the same level of influence. The more critical and valued a stakeholder's participation is, the greater a firm's dependency on it. Greater dependence, in turn, gives the stakeholder more potential influence over a firm's commitments, decisions, and actions. As shown in the Strategic Focus box "Can Telus Satisfy All of Its Stakeholders?" on page 25, managers must find ways to either accommodate or insulate the organization from the demands of stakeholders controlling critical resources.[93]

Nortel regressed from being a star to most of its stakeholders to displeasing many of them. In particular, its substantial reduction in stock price concerned shareholders. The employee layoffs created concern and displeasure among Nortel's workforce, particularly because the need to cut costs was caused by poor strategic decisions that produced large inventories. At present, there seems to be hope, but much uncertainty, among Nortel's stakeholders.

Classification of Stakeholders

The parties involved with a firm's operations can be separated into at least three groups.[94] As shown in Figure 1.4, these groups are the capital market stakeholders (shareholders and the major suppliers of a firm's capital), the product market stakeholders (the firm's primary customers, suppliers, host communities, and unions representing the workforce), and the organizational stakeholders (all of a firm's employees, including both non management and management personnel).

Each stakeholder group expects that those making strategic decisions in a firm will provide the leadership through which the company's valued objectives will be accomplished.[95] The objectives of the various stakeholder groups often differ from one another, sometimes placing managers in situations where trade-offs have to be made. The most obvious stakeholders, at least in U.S. organizations, are shareholders—those who have invested capital in a firm in the expectation of earning a positive return on their investments. These stakeholders' rights are grounded in laws governing private property and private enterprise.

Stakeholders are the individuals and groups who can affect, and are affected by, the strategic outcomes achieved and who have enforceable claims on a firm's performance.

Figure 1.4   The Three Stakeholder Groups

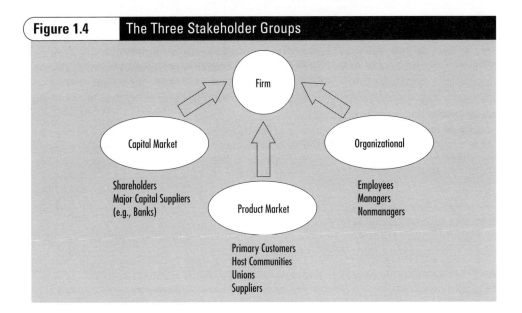

Shareholders want the return on their investment (and, hence, their wealth) to be maximized. Maximization of returns sometimes is accomplished at the expense of investing in a firm's future. Gains achieved by reducing investment in research and development, for example, could be returned to shareholders, thereby increasing the short-term return on their investments. However, this short-term enhancement of shareholders' wealth can negatively affect the firm's future competitive ability, and sophisticated shareholders with diversified portfolios may sell their interests if a firm fails to invest in its own future. Those making strategic decisions are responsible for a firm's survival in both the short and the long term. Accordingly, it is not in the interests of any stakeholders for investments in the company to be unduly minimized.

In contrast to shareholders, another group of stakeholders—the firm's customers—prefers that investors receive a minimum return on their investments. Customers could have their interests maximized when the quality and reliability of a firm's products are improved, but without a price increase. High returns to customers might come at the expense of lower returns negotiated with capital market shareholders. Because of potential conflicts, each firm is challenged to manage its stakeholders. First, a firm must carefully identify all important stakeholders. Second, it must prioritize them, in case it cannot satisfy all of them. Power is the most critical criterion in prioritizing stakeholders. Other criteria might include the urgency of satisfying each particular stakeholder group and the degree of importance of each shareholder to the firm.[96]

When the firm earns above-average returns, this challenge is lessened substantially. With the capability and flexibility provided by above-average returns, a firm can more easily satisfy multiple stakeholders simultaneously. When the firm is earning only average returns, however, the management of its stakeholders may be more difficult. With average returns, the firm is unable to maximize the interests of all stakeholders. The objective then becomes one of at least minimally satisfying each stakeholder. Trade-off decisions are made in light of how dependent the firm is on the support of its stakeholder groups. A firm earning below-average returns does not have the capacity to minimally satisfy all stakeholders. The managerial challenge in this case is to make trade-offs that minimize the amount of support lost from stakeholders.

Societal values also influence the general weightings allocated among the three stakeholder groups shown in Figure 1.4. Although all three groups are served by firms in the major industrialized nations, the priorities in their service vary because of cultural differences. It is important that those responsible for managing stakeholder relationships in a country outside their native land use a global mind-set. A **global mind-set** is the "capacity to appreciate the beliefs, values, behaviours, and business practices of individuals and organizations from a variety of regions and cultures."[97] Employing a global mind-set allows managers to better understand the realities and preferences existing in the world region and culture in which they are working. Thus, thinking globally means "taking the best [that] other cultures have to offer and blending that into a third culture."[98]

Capital Market Stakeholders

Shareholders and lenders both expect a firm to preserve and enhance the wealth they have entrusted to it. The returns they expect are commensurate with the degree of risk accepted with those investments (i.e., lower returns are expected with low-risk investments, and higher returns are expected with high-risk investments). Dissatisfied lenders may impose stricter covenants on subsequent borrowing of capital. Dissatisfied shareholders can reflect their dissatisfaction through several means, including selling their stock.

When a firm is aware of potential or actual dissatisfactions among capital market stakeholders, it may respond to their concerns. The firm's response to dissatisfied stakeholders is affected by the nature of its dependency relationship with them (which, as noted earlier, is also influenced by a society's values). The greater and more significant the dependency relationship is, the more direct and significant the firm's response becomes.

Product Market Stakeholders

Some might think that there is little commonality among the interests of customers, host communities, unions, and suppliers (product market stakeholders). However, all four groups can benefit as firms engage in competitive battles. For example, depending on product and industry characteristics, marketplace competition may result in lower product prices being charged to a firm's customers and higher prices paid to its suppliers (the firm might be willing to pay higher supplier prices to ensure delivery of the types of goods and services that are linked with its competitive success).

As is noted in Chapter 5, customers, as stakeholders, demand reliable products at the lowest possible prices. Host communities want companies willing to be long-term employers and providers of tax revenues without placing excessive demands on public support services. Union officials are interested in secure jobs, under highly desirable working conditions, for employees they represent. Suppliers seek loyal customers who are willing to pay the highest sustainable prices for the goods and services they receive. Thus, product market stakeholders are generally satisfied when a firm's profit margin yields the lowest acceptable return to capital market stakeholders (i.e., the lowest return lenders and shareholders will accept and still retain their interests in the firm).

Organizational Stakeholders

Employees—the firm's organizational stakeholders—expect the firm to provide a dynamic, stimulating, and rewarding work environment. Employees are usually satisfied working for a company that is growing and where they can actively developing their skills, especially those abilities that are needed to be effective team members and to meet or exceed global work standards. Workers who learn how to use new knowledge productively are critical to organizational success. In a collective sense, the education and skills of a firm's workforce are competitive weapons affecting strategy implementation and firm performance.[99]

Can Telus Satisfy All of Its Stakeholders?

Telus is Canada's second largest phone company and, with $7 billion in revenue, one of the largest companies in Western Canada. In 2001, Telus's net income was almost $500 million. It was one of the best companies in Canada to work for. Customers had dependable and reliable service. Product market, organizational, and capital market stakeholders were all being reasonably satisfied.

About this time, Telus management correctly realized that the industry was in for radical changes. Telecommunications would not be providing just good phone service. High-speed Internet, cell phone service, voice and video communication over Internet and wireless networks, and delivery of entertainment (television, video, and recordings) over telephone and cable lines were all technically possible and about to become commercially available. If Telus was not going to provide these services a whole host of new competitors was prepared to do so. These companies included Shaw, Rogers, and Sprint. Telus was already in the cell phone business and to secure its position had bought mobile phone competitor Clearnet.

In 2001, the market for tech stocks tanked and Telcom stocks went with them. From early 2001 to mid-2002 the company's stock lost three-quarters of its value. To bring the stock price back up, and to keep the company competitive in a tougher environment, without access to funding, the company executed some radical surgery: the 25,000 employee labour force would be cut by nearly 30 percent. About 7000 jobs would be lost. The charges for this downsizing, as well as restructuring charges for Telus's QuebecTel and Clearnet acquisitions, moved the company's $454 million profit in 2001 into a $229 million loss in 2002.

At this point the Telus story would take on all the makings of a great work of fiction: love, hate, violence, death, glory, greed … and the list could go on. Telus reduced unionized employees by about 5000 and managers by 2000. Customer call centres were reduced from 66 to 19. Because of the staff reductions, waiting times to get a customer representative on the phone rose from the CRTC's (Canadian Radio-television and Telecommunications Commission's) legally mandated 20 seconds to something closer to an hour; phone line repair and installation times went from days to weeks or, in some cases, months.

Horror stories piled up because of staff shortages. A disabled man lay helpless on the floor of his home for hours after his phone-linked Lifeline failed to work. When his pager went off, an on-call surgeon had to drive to where his cell phone would work because his home phone had been out for weeks, and he could not get cell phone coverage in his area. An 80-year-old woman was severely burned, and her family wondered if her subsequent death could have been prevented if their phone service had not been out for a week, delaying a critical call to 911.

Because of the poor service, harassment of customer service representatives increased. This harassment became so severe that the Telecommunications Workers Union (TWU) put out an alert to try to stop it. In a published piece, the TWU noted that Telus's problems were the company's fault and the public should not take out their frustration on the employees by berating TWU members.

Complaints to the CRTC mounted—about 4000 were received in 2003. In October 2003 alone, there were 1600 complaints against Telus. Bell Canada, a company twice the size of Telus, received 73 complaints that same month. In fact, complaints to the government were so numerous that the CRTC increased its quarterly review of Telus's quality of operations to a weekly review. Accompanying these disruptions were rumoured threats that the CRTC could and would lower Telus's phone rates if service levels did not improve. There were threats of lawsuits from customers due to the poor service.

At one point, shots were fired through the windows at the Telus headquarters building in Burnaby, B.C. Fortunately, there were no injuries. There was no known motive for the incident, and police insisted there was nothing to indicate that the gunshots had anything to do with the company or any specific complaints. However, a Telus vice-president did warn employees and customers to be watchful!

(continued)

Not that all the problems were Telus's fault. In the midst of all the other problems, a construction company drilled through a cable and left thousands of Telus customers in downtown Vancouver without phone service. Thousands of wire and fibre-optic lines had to be matched and re-connected. Even the forces of nature were aligned against the company as fires in B.C.'s interior caused disruption to the phone service of thousands.

Telus went from reasonably satisfying all its stakeholders to, apparently, hardly satisfying any. There were two bright spots among the stakeholders however: the shareholders and the competitors. In the same month that Telus had received a record number of complaints, CEO Darren Entwistle announced that the company had a $115 million profit. This 32-cent a share profit was 50 percent better than the average stock analyst's forecast. Perhaps realizing this happy stockholder news would not, in light of the service problems, go over well with the public, Entwistle apologized to the phone company's customers. He stated that management was to blame for the service problems and promised to improve the company's services by the end of the year. There were hopeful signs. The company had been hiring and training new service representatives, and wait times were declining. The wait times for Telus may well have compared favourably to competitors, such as Shaw and Sprint, however, Telus—being *the* phone company—may have been held to a higher standard. Hoping that customers would hold the company to high expectations, Sprint Canada put out advertisements promoting its local service to steal away disgruntled Telus customers.

Yet, Telus, for all its apparent problems, may not, on closer inspection, be as hard-nosed as the media has made it out to be. When forest fires caused service to go out on 5000 customers in the B.C. interior, the company got the lines back up and running in 72 hours. As part of fire relief efforts, Telus distributed 200 cell phones to firefighters to help them coordinate the fire containment efforts. The company set up phone lines for emergency centres, the Red Cross, and relief centres. Telus distributed 3000 "comfort kits" containing toiletries, comfort bears, T-shirts, toys, and videos to evacuation centres over the fire-ravaged area. Finally, the company established a toll-free assistance line for Telus employees who were hosting some of the 30,000 evacuees. As well, Telus still wins awards for its environmental efforts, quality of training and investor communications. Word of all these good works—and its improving customer service—may well put the company in a better light and win the back the hearts of a broad spectrum of Telus stakeholders. Time will tell.

SOURCES: Telus, 2003 *Telus website*, www.telus.com, accessed, November 7, 2003; S. Mertl, 2003, Telus battles image problem…, *Canadian Press*, November 5, http://money.canoe.ca/News/Sectors/Telecommunication/TELUS/2003/11/05/247892-cp.html; A. Ford, 2003, Telus eclipses analysts' forecasts, *Montreal Gazette*, November 1, B2; W. Boei, 2003, Telus CEO takes blame…, *Vancouver Sun*, November 1, H1; S. Hunter, 2003, RCMP probe Telus backlash theory after shots fired, *The Province*, October 31, A18; J. Jamieson , 2003, We love to hate Telus…, *The Province*, November 4, A34.

Setting and promoting the organization's mission in order to achieve the goals of the firm's strategy are essential components of the senior manager's job. Thus, the final section of this chapter deals with the role of the organizational strategist.

Organizational Strategists

Organizational strategists are the people responsible for the design and execution of strategic management processes. These individuals may be top-level managers, executives, the top management team, or general managers. Throughout this book, these names are used interchangeably. As will be discussed in Chapter 13, top-level managers can be a source of competitive advantage, as a result of the value created by their strategic decisions.

Small organizations may have a single strategist; in many cases, this person owns the firm and is deeply involved with its daily operations. At the other extreme, large, diversified firms have many top-level managers. In addition to the CEO and other top-level officials (e.g., the chief operating officer and chief financial officer), other managers within these companies are responsible for the performance of individual business units.

Top-level managers play critical roles in a firm's efforts to achieve its desired strategic outcomes. In fact, some analysts believe that every organizational failure is actually a failure of those who hold the final responsibility for the quality and effectiveness of a firm's decisions and actions. Failure can stem from changing strategic assumptions, which can cause the strategic mission to become a strategic blunder. Also, a firm's method of operating may entail routines that create strategic inertia, where established relationships create shackles that prevent change. Finally, a shared set of beliefs may become a dogma that prevents a change in corporate culture.[100] Strategic managers need to ask the right questions to overcome the inertia that success often creates.

Strategists make decisions on how resources will be developed or acquired, at what price they will be obtained, and how they will be used. Managerial decisions also influence the way information flows in a company, the strategies a firm chooses to implement, and the scope of its operations. In making these decisions, managers must assess the risk involved in taking the actions being considered and factor the risk into the decision.[101] Both the firm's strategic intent and the managers' strategic orientations affect the decisions. Additionally, how strategists complete their work and their patterns of interactions with others significantly influence the way a firm does business and affect its ability to develop a competitive advantage.

Critical to strategic leadership practices and the implementation of strategies, **organizational culture** refers to the complex set of ideologies, symbols, and core values that are shared throughout the firm and that influence how the firm conducts business. Thus, culture is the social energy that drives—or fails to drive—the organization. For example, Cirque du Soleil, one of the successful firms discussed in this chapter's opening case, on page 6, is known for having a unique and valuable culture. Its culture encourages employees to work hard but also to be creative and to have fun while doing so. These core values at Cirque provide a particular type of energy that drives the firm's efforts. Organizational culture thus becomes a potential source of competitive advantage.

Organizational culture refers to the complex set of ideologies, symbols, and core values that are shared throughout the firm and that influence how the firm conducts business.

After evaluating available information and alternatives, top-level managers must frequently choose among similarly attractive alternatives. The most effective strategists have the self-confidence necessary to select the best alternatives, allocate the required level of resources to them, and effectively explain to interested parties why certain alternatives were selected. [102] When choosing among alternatives, strategists are accountable for treating employees, suppliers, customers, and others with fairness and respect. Evidence suggests that trust can be a source of competitive advantage, thereby supporting an organizational commitment to treat stakeholders fairly and with respect.[103]

The Work of Effective Strategists

Perhaps not surprisingly, hard work, thorough analyses, a willingness to be brutally honest, a penchant for always wanting the firm and its people to accomplish more, and common sense are prerequisites to an individual's success as a strategist.[104] In addition to possessing these characteristics, effective strategists must be able to think clearly and ask many questions. But, in particular, top-level managers are challenged to "think seriously and deeply … about the purposes of the organizations they head or functions they perform, about the strategies, tactics, technologies, systems, and people necessary to attain these purposes and about the important questions that always need to be asked."[105]

Just as the Internet has changed the nature of competition, it is also changing strategic decision making. Speed has become a much more prominent competitive factor, and it makes strategic thinking even more critical. Most high-tech firms operate in hypercompetitive industry environments. As a result of the intense competition in these industries, some product life cycles have decreased from a period of one to two years to a period of six to nine months, leaving less time for a company's products to generate revenue. Speed and flexibility have become key sources of competitive advantage for companies competing in these industries. Thinking strategically, in concert with others, increases the probability of identifying bold, innovative ideas.[106] When these ideas lead to the development of core competencies, they become the foundation for taking advantage of environmental opportunities.

Our discussion highlights the nature of a strategist's work. The work is filled with ambiguous decision situations for which the most effective solutions are not always easily determined. However, the opportunities afforded by this type of work are appealing and offer exciting chances to dream and to act. The following words, given as advice to the late Time Warner chairman and co-CEO Steven J. Ross by his father, describe the opportunities in a strategist's work: There are three categories of people— the person who goes into the office, puts his feet up on his desk, and dreams for 12 hours; the person who arrives at 5 a.m. and works for 16 hours, never once stopping to dream; and the person who puts his feet up, dreams for one hour, then does something about those dreams.[107]

The organizational term used for a dream that challenges and energizes a company is strategic intent (discussed on page 21 in this chapter).[108] Strategists have opportunities to dream and to act, and the most effective ones provide a vision (the strategic intent) to effectively elicit the help of others in creating a firm's competitive advantage.

Predicting Outcomes of Strategic Decisions

Top-level managers attempt to predict the outcomes of their strategic decisions before they are implemented. In most cases, managers determine the outcomes only after the decisions have been implemented. For example, when Gabe Tsampalieros became CEO of Cara Foods in 1996, he moved the company from a holding company to a business focused on food. Just after the company had divested the Grand & Toy business supply concern and the Days Inn hotel locations, the Cara food businesses began to see big changes in the market. People were moving away from fast food to more upscale dining experiences. This upward shift negatively impacted Cara's Harvey's and Swiss Chalet chains. On top of this, Cara's catering business was subject to some of the pains that the airlines were feeling; one of Cara's major customers in the catering area was Air Canada. Cara would have to take a large write-off of its accounts receivable from Air Canada, when the later company went bankrupt.[109]

While it may have been difficult for Cara to predict the severe decline in the fortunes of Air Canada, it should have been much easier to predict the change in consumer tastes. In fact, Cara saw early on that the quick service segment was declining, and the company bought Montana's, Milestone's, and the licence to the Outback chain in Canada.[110] One means of helping managers understand the potential outcomes of their strategic decisions is to map their industry's profit pools, by following four steps: (1) define the pool's boundaries, (2) estimate the pool's overall size, (3) estimate the size of the value-chain activity in the pool, and (4) reconcile the calculations.[111] This approach appears to be what Cara followed in order to prompt its move into the higher priced segments.

A **profit pool** entails the total profits earned in an industry at all points along the value chain.

A **profit pool** entails the total profits earned in an industry at all points along the value chain.[112] Analyzing the profit pool in the industry may help a firm to understand the primary sources of profits in an industry, and thus, identify an opportunity that others are unable to recognize. After these sources have been identified, managers must link the profit potential identified to specific strategies. In a sense, managers map the profit potential of their departmental units by linking to the firm's overall profits. They can then better link the strategic actions considered to potential profits.[113]

Mapping profit pools and linking potential profits to strategic actions before they are implemented should be standard steps in the strategic management process. General Motors managers would have done well to take these actions when they decided to continue investing resources in the Oldsmobile brand instead of investing resources in the Saturn brand. The firm's investments in Oldsmobile in essence starved Saturn for resources, even though Oldsmobile was no longer a successful product in the market. Finally, after making a decision to stop marketing Oldsmobile, GM decided to invest $1.5 billion in developing a full line of Saturn products.[114]

The Strategic Management Process

As suggested by Figure 1.1, on page 8, the strategic management process is intended to be a rational approach to help a firm effectively respond to the challenges of the 21st-century competitive landscape. Figure 1.1 also outlines the topics examined in this book to study the strategic management process. Part 1 of this book shows how this process requires a firm to study its external environment (Chapter 3) and internal environment (Chapter 4) to identify marketplace opportunities and threats and to determine how to use its core competencies in the pursuit of desired strategic outcomes. With this knowledge, the firm forms its strategic intent to leverage its resources, capabilities, and core competencies and to win competitive battles. Flowing from its strategic intent, the firm's strategic mission specifies, in writing, the products the firm intends to produce and the markets it will serve when leveraging those resources, capabilities, and competencies.

The firm's strategic inputs provide the foundation for its strategic actions to formulate and implement strategies. Both formulating and implementing strategies are critical to achieving strategic competitiveness and earning above-average returns. As suggested in Figure 1.1 by the horizontal arrow linking the two types of strategic actions, implementation and formulation, must be simultaneously integrated. In formulating strategies, thought should be given to their implementation. Likewise, during implementation, effective strategists also seek feedback to improve the selected strategies. Only when these two sets of actions are carefully integrated can the firm achieve its desired strategic outcomes.

In Part 2 of this book, the formulation of strategies is explained. First, we examine the formulation of strategies at the business-unit level (Chapter 5). A diversified firm competing in multiple product markets and businesses has a business-level strategy for each distinct product market area. A company competing in a single product market has but one business-level strategy. In all instances, a business-level strategy describes a firm's actions that are designed to exploit its competitive advantage over rivals. On the other hand, business-level strategies are not formulated and implemented in isolation (Chapter 6). Competitors respond to and try to anticipate each other's actions. Thus, the dynamics of competition are an important input when selecting and implementing strategies.

For the diversified firm, corporate-level strategy (Chapter 7) is concerned with determining the businesses in which the company intends to compete and how resources are to be allocated among those businesses. Other topics vital to strategy formulation, particularly in the diversified firm, include the acquisition of other companies and, as appropriate, the restructuring of the firm's portfolio of businesses (Chapter 8) and the selection of an international strategy (Chapter 9). Increasingly important in a global economy, cooperative strategies are used by a firm to gain competitive advantage by forming advantageous relationships with other firms (Chapter 10).

To examine actions taken to implement strategies, we consider several topics in Part 3 of the book. First, the different mechanisms used to govern firms are explained (Chapter 11). With demands for improved corporate governance voiced by various stakeholders, organizations are challenged to satisfy stakeholders' interests and the attainment of desired strategic outcomes. Finally, the organizational structure and actions needed to control a firm's operations (Chapter 12), the patterns of strategic leadership appropriate for today's firms and competitive environments (Chapter 13), and renewal and innovation (Chapter 14) are addressed.

As noted earlier, competition requires firms to make choices to survive and succeed. Some of these choices are strategic in nature, including those of selecting a strategic intent and strategic mission, determining which strategies to implement, choosing an appropriate level of corporate scope, designing governance and organization structures to properly coordinate a firm's work, and, through strategic leadership, encouraging and nurturing organizational innovation.[115] The goal is to achieve and maintain a competitive advantage over rivals.

Primarily because they are related to how a firm interacts with its stakeholders, almost all strategic decisions have ethical dimensions.[116] Organizational ethics are revealed by an organization's culture; that is to say, a firm's strategic decisions are a product of the core values that are shared by most or all of a company's managers and employees. Especially in the turbulent and often ambiguous 21st-century competitive landscape, those making strategic decisions are challenged both to recognize that their decisions affect capital market, product market, and organizational stakeholders differently and to evaluate the ethical implications of their decisions.

As you will discover, the strategic management process examined in this book calls for disciplined approaches to the development of competitive advantage. These approaches provide the pathway through which firms will be able to achieve strategic competitiveness and earn above-average returns in the 21st century. Mastery of this strategic management process will effectively serve readers and the organizations for which they choose to work.

Summary

- Through their actions, firms seek strategic competitiveness and above-average returns. Strategic competitiveness is achieved when a firm has developed and learned how to implement a value-creating strategy. Above-average returns (in excess of what investors expect to earn from other investments with similar levels of risk) allow a firm to simultaneously satisfy all of its stakeholders.

- There are two major models of how a firm can formulate strategies to earn above-average returns. The I/O model suggests that the external environment is the primary determinant of the firm's strategies. Above-average returns are earned when the firm locates an attractive industry and successfully implements the strategy dictated by that industry's characteristics.

- The resource-based model assumes that each firm is a collection of unique resources and capabilities that determine its strategy. Above-average returns are earned when the firm is organized to exploit and uses its valuable, rare, and costly to imitate resources and capabilities (i.e., core competencies) as the source of its competitive advantage(s).

- In the 21st-century competitive landscape, the fundamental nature of competition has changed. As a result, managers making strategic decisions must adopt a new mind-set that is global in nature. Firms must learn how to compete in highly turbulent and chaotic environments that produce disorder and a great deal of uncertainty. The globalization of industries and their markets and rapid and significant technological changes are the two primary factors contributing to the 21st-century competitive landscape.

- Strategic intent and strategic mission are formed in light of the information and insights gained from studying a firm's internal and external environments. Strategic intent suggests how resources, capabilities, and core competencies will be leveraged to achieve desired outcomes. The strategic mission is an application of strategic intent. The mission is used to specify the product markets and the customers that a firm intends to serve through the leveraging of its resources, capabilities, and competencies.

- Stakeholders are those who can affect, and are affected by, a firm's strategic outcomes. Because a firm is dependent on the continuing support of stakeholders (shareholders, customers, suppliers, employees, host communities, etc.), they have enforceable claims on the company's performance. When earning above-average returns, a firm can adequately satisfy all stakeholders' interests. However, when earning only average returns, a firm's strategists must carefully manage all stakeholder groups in order to retain their support. A firm earning below-average returns must minimize the amount of support it loses from dissatisfied stakeholders.

- Organizational strategists are responsible for the design and execution of an effective strategic management process. Today, the most effective of these processes are grounded in ethical intentions and conduct. Strategists can be a source of competitive advantage. The strategist's work demands decision trade-offs, often among attractive alternatives. Successful top-level managers work hard, conduct thorough analyses of situations, behave brutally and with consistent honesty, and ask the right questions, of the right people, at the right time.

- Managers must predict the potential outcomes of their strategic decisions. To do so, they must first calculate the profit pools in their industry that are linked to the value chain activities. In so doing, they are less likely to formulate and implement an ineffective strategy.

Review Questions

1. What are strategic competitiveness, competitive advantage, and above-average returns?

2. What do the I/O model and resource-based model suggest a firm should do to earn above-average returns?

3. What are the characteristics of the 21st-century landscape? What two factors are the primary drivers of this landscape?

4. What are strategic intent and strategic mission? What is their value for the strategic management process?

5. What are stakeholders? How do the three primary stakeholder groups influence organizations?

6. How would you describe the work of organizational strategists?

7. What are the elements of the strategic management process? How are they interrelated?

Experiential Exercise

Strategic Mission Statements

Strategic intent and strategic mission influence strategy formulation and implementation actions. Below are brief mission statements of some of the firms mentioned in this chapter as they appear on the firms' websites (the firms are identified later). Refer to the mission statements to complete this exercise.

a. … an international organization founded in Quebec dedicated to the creation, production and performance of artistic works, whose mission is to invoke, provoke and evoke the imagination, the senses and the emotions of people around the world.

b. … governing objective of maximizing value…. Our corporate values guide our growth as a leading, respected and value-driven organization. These values … form the backbone of our corporate operating philosophy…. They guide us as we incorporate economic, environmental and social considerations into our long-term business strategy, daily activities and decisions.

c. Our mission: Energy for People. Our vision is to create a truly great company—one where quality work is the norm; where we stretch and strive to be the best we can be; and where great things are accomplished. Principles grace every decision and punctuate every interaction … stakeholders support our endeavours because we have earned their trust and respect.

d. … primary objective is to increase shareholder value by pursuing strategic growth through focusing on one product line … and expanding in all significant markets throughout the world … providing the highest quality engineered wood products at the best value. Increased sales … through innovative merchandising and marketing initiatives that emphasize quality, value and service.

e. Unleashing the power of Internet technologies to deliver the best solutions for Canadians at home, in the workplace and on the move.

Break into small groups of three to five students for this exercise.

1. A firm's strategic mission, as defined in this chapter, is a statement of the firm's unique purpose and the scope of its operations in product and market terms. Do the above statements serve as strategic mission statements? As a group, choose a statement you feel best achieves this purpose and one that does not. Be ready to defend your choices to the other groups.

2. As a group, identify an industry for which each statement seems to apply. Do any of the statements seem to apply to several industries? Discuss whether you feel the statements should be broader or narrower across industries to be effective strategic mission statements.

Statement	Industry
a.	
b.	
c.	
d.	
e.	

3. Refer to the list below to identify the firms. Based on the material in the text and your everyday knowledge of the firms and their products or services, which statement does your group feel most effectively reflects the firm's strategic intent and mission? Which statement is most closely tied to an individual firm and which to an individual industry?

a. … an international organization … (Cirque du Soleil);
b. … governing objective of maximizing value … (Alcan);
c. Our mission: Energy for People … (EnCana);
d. … primary objective is to increase shareholder value … (Masonite);
e. Unleashing the power of Internet technologies … (Telus)

Notes

1. C. A. Maritan, 2001, Capital investment as investing in organizational capabilities: An empirically grounded process model, *Academy of Management Journal*, 44: 513–31; C. E. Helfat, 2000, The evolution of firm capabilities, *Strategic Management Journal*, 21(special issue): 955–59; J. B. Barney, 1999, How firms' capabilities affect boundary decisions, *Sloan Management Review*, 40(3): 137–45.

2. W. Mitchell, 2000, Path-dependent and path-breaking change: Reconfiguring business resources following acquisitions in the U.S. medical sector, 1978–1995, *Strategic Management Journal*, 21(special issue): 1061–81; K. M. Eisenhardt & S. L. Brown, 1999, Patching: Restitching business portfolios in dynamic markets, *Harvard Business Review*, 77(3): 72–84.

3. E. Bonabeau & C. Meyer, 2001, Swarm intelligence, *Harvard Business Review*, 79(5): 107–14; D. Abell, 1999, Competing today while preparing for tomorrow, *Sloan Management Review*, 40(3): 73–81; D. J. Teece, G. Pisano, & A. Shuen, 1997, Dynamic capabilities and strategic management, *Strategic Management Journal*, 18: 509–33.

4. T. C. Powell, 2001, Competitive advantage: Logical and philosophical considerations, *Strategic Management Journal*, 22: 875–88; R. Coff, 1999, When competitive advantage doesn't lead to performance: The resource-based view and stakeholder bargaining power, *Organization Science*, 10: 119–33.

5. P. Shrivastava, 1995, Ecocentric management for a risk society, *Academy of Management Review*, 20: 118–38.

6. R. P. Rumelt, D. E. Schendel, & D. J. Teece (eds.), 1994, *Fundamental Issues in Strategy*, Boston: Harvard Business School Press, 527–30.

7. M. J. Epstein & R. A. Westbrook, 2001, Linking actions to profits in strategic decision making, *Sloan Management Review*, 42(3): 39–49.

8. Rumelt, Schendel, & Teece, *Fundamental Issues in Strategy*, 543–47.

9. M. A. Hitt, R. D. Ireland, S. M. Camp, & D. L. Sexton, 2001, Strategic entrepreneurship: Entrepreneurial strategies for wealth creation, *Strategic Management Journal*, 22(special issue): 479–91; S. A. Zahra, R. D. Ireland, & M. A. Hitt, 2000, International expansion by new venture firms: International diversity, mode of market entry technological learning and performance, *Academy of Management Journal*, 43: 925–50.

10. A. Nair & S. Kotha, 2001, Does group membership matter? Evidence from the Japanese steel industry, *Strategic Management Journal*, 22: 221–35; A. M. McGahan & M. E. Porter, 1997, How much does industry matter, really? *Strategic Management Journal*, 18(special summer issue): 15–30.

11. J. B. Barney, 2001, Is the resource-based "view" a useful perspective for strategic management research? Yes, *Academy of Management Review*, 26: 41–56.

12. M. A. Hitt, L. Bierman, K. Shimizu, & R. Kochhar, 2001, Direct and moderating effects of human capital on strategy and performance in professional service firms, *Academy of Management Journal*, 44: 13–28.

13. G. A. Steiner and J. B. Miner, 1977, *Management Policy and Strategy: Text, Readings and Cases*, New York: MacMillan, 7; W. F. Glueck, 1980, *Business Policy and Strategic Management*, New York: McGraw-Hill, 9; J. B. Quinn, 1980, *Strategies for Change: Logical Incrementalism*, Homewood, IL: Irwin; K. J. Hatten & M. L. Hatten, 1988, *Effective Strategic Management*, Englewood Cliffs, NJ: Prentice-Hall, 1; J. B. Barney, 1997, *Gaining and Sustaining Competitive Advantage*, Don Mills, ON: Addison-Wesley Publishing, 17.

14. H. Mintzberg, 1987, Five Ps for strategy, *California Management Review*, Fall, reprinted in H. Mintzberg & J. B. Quinn, 1996, *The Strategy Process: Concepts, Contexts and Cases*, Upper Saddle River, NJ: Prentice-Hall, 10–17.

15. Ibid., 12.

16. E. H. Bowman & C. E. Helfat, 2001, Does corporate strategy matter? *Strategic Management Journal*, 22: 1–23.

17. A. Seth & H. Thomas, 1994, Theories of the firm: Implications for strategy research, *Journal of Management Studies*, 31: 165–91.

18. Ibid., 169–73.

19. M. E. Porter, 1985, *Competitive Advantage*, New York: Free Press; M. E. Porter, 1980, *Competitive Strategy*, New York: Free Press.

20. C. Lee, K. Lee, & J. M. Pennings, 2001, Internal capabilities, external networks, and performance: A study on technology-based ventures, *Strategic Management Journal*, 22(special issue): 615–40; C. C. Markides, 1999, A dynamic view of strategy, *Sloan*

Management Review, 40(3): 55–72; Abell, Competing today while preparing for tomorrow.

21. J. B. Barney, 1991, Firm resources and sustained competitive advantage, *Journal of Management*, 17: 99–120; Barney, 1995, Looking inside for competitive advantage, *Academy of Management Executive*, 9(4): 56; Barney, 1997, *Gaining and Sustaining Competitive Advantage*; Barney, Is the resource-based "view" a useful perspective for strategic management research? Yes, 41–56.

22. A. M. McGahan, 1999, Competition, strategy and business performance, *California Management Review*, 413): 74–101; McGahan & Porter, How much does industry matter, really? 15–30.

23. R. Henderson & W. Mitchell, 1997, The interactions of organizational and competitive influences on strategy and performance, *Strategic Management Journal*, 18(special summer issue): 5–14; C. Oliver, 1997, Sustainable competitive advantage: Combining institutional and resource-based views, *Strategic Management Journal*, 18: 697–713; J. L. Stimpert & I. M. Duhaime, 1997, Seeing the big picture: The influence of industry, diversification, and business strategy on performance, *Academy of Management Journal*, 40: 560–83.

24. P. Bagnell, 1999, Nortel leads in creating value: Shareholder boost [Market Value Added], *Financial Post (National Post)*, July 3, C1, C4.

25. M. Lewis, 2001, Money managers consider legal moves: major shareholders, lawyers approached about class action. *Financial Post (National Post)*, February 27, C1, C10.

26. K. Macklem, 2002, Nortel's long struggle back, *Macleans*, November 11, 54–55.

27. Nortel Networks, 2002, Annual Report 2002 Nortel Networks Corporation, *Nortel Networks website*, www.nortelnetworks.com/corporate/investor/reports/collateral/nnc_eng_complete.pdf, accessed October 25, 2003.

28. Office of the Superintendent of Bankruptcy Canada, 2003, Bankruptcy Statistics, *Office of the Superintendent of Bankruptcy Canada website*, http://strategis.ic.gc.ca/epic/internet/inbsf-osb.nsf/en/h_br01011e.html, accessed October 25, 2003.

29. ABI World, 2001, Filing statistics, abiworld.org/stats/newstatsfront.

30. Rumelt, Schendel, & Teece, *Fundamental Issues in Strategy*, 530.

31. C. J. Loomis, 1993, Dinosaurs, *Fortune*, May 3, 36–46.

32. J. Kirby, 2001, The Chamandys built a $600m company … and what they've got is trouble with a capital T, *Canadian Business*, May 28: 58–61; S. Silcoff, 2001, Gildan cuts earnings forecast second time: T-shirt maker took hit from Fruit of the Loom buyout effort [Annual results], *Financial Post (National Post)*, December 8, FP3.

33. V. Marsh, 1998, Attributes: Strong strategy tops the list, *Financial Times*, http://www.ft.com, November 30.

34. J. Nocera, 1999, Five lessons from Iomega, *Fortune*, August 2, 251–54.

35. A. Reinhardt, 1997, Paranoia, aggression, and other strengths, *Business Week*, October 13, 14; A. S. Grove, 1995, A high-tech CEO updates his views on managing and careers, *Fortune*, September 18, 229–30.

36. This section is based largely on information featured in two sources: M. A. Hitt, B. W. Keats, & S. M. DeMarie, 1998, Navigating in the new competitive landscape: Building competitive advantage and strategic flexibility in the 21st century, *Academy of Management Executive*, 12(4): 22–42; R. A. Bettis & M. A. Hitt, 1995, The new competitive landscape, *Strategic Management Journal*, 16(special summer issue): 7–19.

37. D.Tapscott, 2001, Rethinking strategy in a networked world, *Strategy & Business*, 24(third quarter), 34–41.

38. R. D. Ireland & M. A. Hitt, 1999, Achieving and maintaining strategic competitiveness in the 21st century: The role of strategic leadership, *Academy of Management Executive*, 13(1): 43–57.

39. R. A. D'Aveni, 1995, Coping with hypercompetition: Utilizing the new 7S's framework, *Academy of Management Executive*, 9(3): 45–61.

40. W. J. Ferrier, 2001, Navigating the competitive landscape: The drivers and consequences of competitive aggressiveness, *Academy of Management Journal*, 44: 858–77.

41. D. G. McKendrick, 2001, Global strategy and population level learning: The case of hard disk drives, *Strategic Management Journal*, 22: 307–34; T. P. Murtha, S. A. Lenway, & R. Bagozzi, 1998, Global mind-sets and cognitive shifts in a complex multinational corporation, *Strategic Management Journal*, 19: 97–114.

42. T. A. Stewart, 1993, The new face of American power, *Fortune*, July 26, 70–86.

43. S. Koudsi & L. A. Costa, 1998, America vs. the new Europe: By the numbers, *Fortune*, December 21, 149–56.

44. E. Tucker, 1999, More entrepreneurship urged, *Financial Times*, June 22, 2.

45. CNEWS, 2003, Sierra Systems expects lower earnings, *CNEWS website*, October 27, http://www.canoe.ca/CNEWS/TechNews/2003/10/27/238580-cp.html.

46. V. Govindarajan & A. K. Gupta, 2001, *The Quest for Global Dominance*, San Francisco: Jossey-Bass.

47. D. Luhnow, 2001, Crossover success: How Nafta helped Wal-Mart reshape the Mexican market…, *Wall Street Journal*, August 31, A1; Govindarajan & Gupta, The Quest for Global Dominance; Wal-Mart, 2003, *2003 Annual Report*, Bentonville, Arkansas: Wal-Mart.

48. Wendy's International, 2003, *Wendy's International website*, http://www.wendys-invest.com/fin/owner, accessed October 30, 2003.

49. R. McNast, 1999, Tora, tora, taurus, *Business Week*, April 12, 6.

50. Govindarajan & Gupta, *The Quest for Global Dominance*; R. Ruggiero, 1997, The high stakes of world trade, *Wall Street Journal*, April 28, A18.

51. M. Subramaniam & N. Venkatraman, 2001, Determinants of transnational new product development capability: Testing the influence of transferring and deploying tacit overseas knowledge, *Strategic Management Journal*, 22: 359–78; S. A. Zahra, 1999, The changing rules of global competitiveness in the 21st century, *Academy of Management Executive*, 13(1): 36–42; R. M. Kanter, 1995, Thriving locally in the global economy, *Harvard Business Review*, 73(5): 151–60.

52. Zahra, Ireland, Gutierrez, & Hitt, 2000, Privatization and entrepreneurial transformation: Emerging issues and a future research agenda, *Academy of Management Review*, 25: 509–24.

53. S. Zaheer & E. Mosakowski, 1997, The dynamics of the liability of foreignness: A global study of survival in financial services, *Strategic Management Journal*, 18: 439–64.

54. D. Arnold, 2000, Seven rules of international distribution, *Harvard Business Review*, 78(6): 131–37; J. S. Black & H. B. Gregersen, 1999, The right way to manage expats, *Harvard Business Review*, 77(2): 52–63.

55. M. A. Hitt, R. E. Hoskisson, & H. Kim, 1997, International diversification: Effects on innovation and firm performance in product-diversified firms, *Academy of Management Journal*, 40: 767–98.

56. D'Aveni, Coping with hypercompetition: Utilizing the new 7S's framework, 46.

57. G. Hamel, 2001, Revolution vs. evolution: You need both, *Harvard Business Review*, 79(5): 150–56; T. Nakahara, 1997, Innovation in a borderless world economy, *Research-Technology Management*, May/June, 7–9.

58. J. Birkinshaw & N. Hood, 2001, Unleash innovation in foreign subsidiaries, *Harvard Business Review*, 79(3): 131–37; N. Dawar & T. Frost, 1999, Competing with giants: Survival strategies for local companies in emerging markets, *Harvard Business Review*, 77(2): 119–29.

59. K. H. Hammonds, 2001, What is the state of the new economy? *Fast Company*, September, 101–4.

60. K. H. Hammonds, 2001, How do fast companies work now? *Fast Company*, September, 134–42; K. M. Eisenhardt, 1999, Strategy as strategic decision making, *Sloan Management Review*, 40(3): 65–72.

61. C. W. L. Hill, 1997, Establishing a standard: Competitive strategy and technological standards in winner-take-all industries, *Academy of Management Executive*, 11(2): 7–25.

62. R. Karlgaard, 1999, Digital rules, *Forbes*, July 5, 43.

63. C. M. Christiansen, 1997, *The Innovator's Dilemma*, Boston: Harvard Business School Press.

64. G. Ahuja & C. M. Lampert, 2001, Entrepreneurship in the large corporation: A longitudinal study of how established firms create breakthrough inventions, *Strategic Management Journal*, 22(special summer issue): 521–43.

65. R. Amit & C. Zott, 2001, Value creation in e-business, *Strategic Management Journal*, 22(special summer issue): 493–520.

66. Ibid.

67. Statistics Canada, 2003, Broadband: High-speed access to the Internet, *The Daily*, September 23, Ottawa: Statistics Canada, http://www.statcan.ca/Daily/English/030923/d030923b.htm.

68. R. M. Kanter, 2001, *e-volve: Succeeding in the Digital Culture of Tomorrow*, Boston: Harvard Business School Press.

69. Hitt, Ireland, Camp, & Sexton, Strategic entrepreneurship, 479–91.

70. F. Warner, 2001, The drills for knowledge, *Fast Company*, September, 186–91; B. L. Simonin, 1999, Ambiguity and the process of knowledge transfer in strategic alliances, *Strategic Management Journal*, 20: 595–624.

71. L. Rosenkopf & A. Nerkar, 2001, Beyond local search: Boundary-spanning, exploration, and impact on the optical disk industry, *Strategic Management Journal*, 22: 287–306; T. H. Davenport & L. Prusak, 1998, *Working Knowledge: How Organizations Manage What They Know*, Boston: Harvard Business School Press.

72. D. F. Kuratko, R. D. Ireland, & J. S. Hornsby, 2001, Improving firm performance through entrepreneurial actions: Insights from Acordia Inc.'s corporate entrepreneurship

strategy, *Academy of Management Executive*, 15(4): 60–71; T. K. Kayworth & R. D. Ireland, 1998, The use of corporate IT standards as a means of implementing the cost leadership strategy, *Journal of Information Technology Management*, IX(4): 13–42.

73. K. R. Harrigan, 2001, Strategic flexibility in old and new economies, in M. A. Hitt, R. E. Freeman, & J. R. Harrison (eds.), *Handbook of Strategic Management*, Oxford, U.K.: Blackwell Publishers, 97–123.

74. J. L. C. Cheng & I. F. Kesner, 1997, Organizational slack and response to environmental shifts: The impact of resource allocation patterns, *Journal of Management*, 23: 1–18.

75. C. Markides, 1998, Strategic innovation in established companies, *Sloan Management Review*, 39(3): 31–42; V. L. Barker III & I. M. Duhaime, 1997, Strategic change in the turnaround process: Theory and empirical evidence, *Strategic Management Journal*, 18: 13–38.

76. M. A. Hitt, R. D. Ireland, & J. S. Harrison, 2001, Mergers and acquisitions: A value creating or value destroying strategy? In M. A. Hitt, R. E. Freeman, & J. S. Harrison (eds.), *Handbook of Strategic Management*, Oxford, U.K.: Blackwell Publishers, 384–408; W. Boeker, 1997, Strategic change: The influence of managerial characteristics and organizational growth, *Academy of Management Journal*, 40: 152–70.

77. R. T. Pascale, 1999, Surviving the edge of chaos, *Sloan Management Review*, 40(3): 83–94; E. D. Beinhocker, 1999, Robust adaptive strategies, *Sloan Management Review*, 40(3): 95–106; N. Rajagopalan & G. M. Spreitzer, 1997, Toward a theory of strategic change: A multi-lens perspective and integrative framework, *Academy of Management Review*, 22: 48–79.

78. G. Hamel & C. K. Prahalad, 1989, Strategic intent, *Harvard Business Review*, 67(3): 63–76.

79. Hamel & Prahalad, Strategic intent, 66.

80. J. E. Barnes, 2001, The making (or possible breaking) of a megabrand, *New York Times*, http://www.nytimes.com, July 22.

81. Hamel & Prahalad, Strategic intent, 64.

82. M. A. Hitt, D. Park, C. Hardee, & B. B. Tyler, 1995, Understanding strategic intent in the global marketplace, *Academy of Management Executive*, 9(2): 12–19.

83. R. D. Ireland & M. A. Hitt, 1992, Mission statements: Importance, challenge, and recommendations for development, *Business Horizons*, 35(3): 34–42.

84. W. J. Duncan, 1999, *Management: Ideas and Actions*, New York: Oxford University Press, 122–25.

85. R. M. Fulmer, 2001, Johnson & Johnson: Frameworks for leadership, *Organizational Dynamics*, 29 (3): 211–20.

86. P. Martin, 1999, Lessons in humility, *Financial Times*, June 22, 18.

87. I. M. Levin, 2000, Vision revisited, *Journal of Applied Behavioral Science*, 36: 91–107.

88. I. R. Baum, E. A. Locke, & S. A. Kirkpatrick, 1998, A longitudinal study of the relation of vision and vision communication to venture growth in entrepreneurial firms, *Journal of Applied Psychology*, 83: 43–54.

89. J. Frooman, 1999, Stakeholder influence strategies, *Academy of Management Review*, 24: 191–205.

90. T. M. Jones & A. C. Wicks, 1999, Convergent stakeholder theory, *Academy of Management Review*, 24: 206–21; R. E. Freeman, 1984, *Strategic Management: A Stakeholder Approach*, Boston: Pitman, 53–54.

91. G. Donaldson & J. W. Lorsch, 1983, *Decision Making at the Top: The Shaping of Strategic Direction*, New York: Basic Books, 37–40.

92. A. J. Hillman & G. D. Keim, 2001, Shareholder value, stakeholder management, and social issues: What's the bottom line? *Strategic Management Journal*, 22: 125–39.

93. R. E. Freeman & J. McVea, 2001, A stakeholder approach to strategic management, in M. A. Hitt, R. E. Freeman, & J. S. Harrison (eds.), *Handbook of Strategic Management*, Oxford, U.K.: Blackwell Publishers, 189–207.

94. Ibid.

95. A. McWilliams & D. Siegel, 2001, Corporate social responsibility: A theory of the firm perspective, *Academy of Management Review*, 26: 117–27; D. A. Gioia, 1999, Practicality, paradigms, and problems in stakeholder theorizing, *Academy of Management Review*, 24: 228–32.

96. Freeman & McVea, A stakeholder approach to strategic management; R. K. Mitchell, B. R. Agle, & D. J. Wood, 1997, Toward a theory of stakeholder identification and salience: Defining the principle of who and what really count, *Academy of Management Review*, 22: 853–86.

97. 1995, Don't be an ugly-American manager, *Fortune*, October 16, 225.

98. G. Dutton, 1999, Building a global brain, *Management Review*, May, 23–30.

99. Hitt, Bierman, Shimizu, & Kochhar, Direct and moderating effects of human capital.

100. D. N. Sull, 1999, Why good companies go bad, *Harvard Business Review*, 77(4): 42–52.

101. P. Bromiley, K. D. Miller, & D. Rau, 2001, Risk in strategic management research, in M. A. Hitt, R. E. Freeman, & J. S. Harrison (eds.), *Handbook of Strategic Management*, Oxford, U.K.: Blackwell Publishers, 259–88.

102. R. McGrath & I. MacMillan, 2000, *The Entrepreneurial Mindset*, Boston: Harvard Business School Press.

103. J.H. Davis, F.D. Schoorman, R.C. Mayer, & H.H. Tau, 2000, The trusted general manager and business unit performance: Empirical evidence of a competitive advantage, *Strategic Management Journal*, 21: 563–76.

104. W. C. Taylor, 1999, Whatever happened to globalization? *Fast Company*, September, 288–94.

105. T. Leavitt, 1991, *Thinking about Management*, New York: Free Press, 9.

106. K. Lovelace, D. L. Shapiro, & L. R. Weingart, 2001, Maximizing cross-functional new product teams' innovativeness and constraint adherence: A conflict communications perspective, *Academy of Management Journal*, 44: 779–93.

107. M. Loeb, 1993, Steven J. Ross, 1927–1992, *Fortune*, January 25, 4.

108. G. Hamel & C. K. Prahalad, 1994, *Competing for the Future*, Boston, MA: Harvard Business School Press, 129.

109. R. Thompson, 2003, Terrible timing in the airline food business: How Cara's CEO hit the rough with Air Canada meltdown, *Financial Post (National Post)*, July 11, FP1, FP6.

110. Ibid.

111. O. Gadiesh & J. L. Gilbert, 1998, How to map your industry's profit pool, *Harvard Business Review*, 76(3): 149–62.

112. O. Gadiesh & J. L. Gilbert, 1998, Profit pools: A fresh look at strategy, *Harvard Business Review*, 76(3): 139–47.

113. M. J. Epstein & R. A. Westbrook, 2001, Linking actions to profits in strategic decision making, *Sloan Management Review*, 42(3): 39–49.

114. 2001, Trading places, *Forbes*, http://www.forbes.com, June 14.

115. R. D. Ireland, M. A. Hitt, S. M. Camp, & D. L. Sexton, 2001, Integrating entrepreneurship and strategic management actions to create firm wealth, *Academy of Management Executive*, 15(1): 49–63; Rumelt, Schendel, & Teece, *Fundamental Issues in Strategy*, 9–10.

116. D. R. Gilbert, 2001, Corporate strategy and ethics as corporate strategy comes of age, in M.A. Hitt, R. E. Freeman, & J. S. Harrison (eds.), *Handbook of Strategic Management*, Oxford, U.K.: Blackwell Publishers, 564–82.

Chapter Two

Strategic Management and Firm Performance

Knowledge Objectives

Studying this chapter should provide you with the strategic management knowledge needed to:

1. Understand the ultimate goal of strategic management—to impact organizational performance.

2. Define performance, particularly the differences among above-average returns, average returns, and below-average returns.

3. Discuss the different ways in which organizational performance is measured.

4. Know the strengths and weaknesses of different measures of organizational performance.

5. Define corporate social responsibility, sustainability, and the triple bottom line.

The 2003 Best 50 Corporate Citizens

In recent years, a very different measure of firm performance is gaining prominence. This measure is corporate social responsibility. In 2002 and in 2003, Corporate Knights published its "Best 50 Corporate Citizens" list. These corporate citizens were rated on several categories, with weights assigned to each category. In its 2002 rankings, Corporate Knights used the December 31, 2001 TSX (Toronto Stock Exchange) 300 as its universe of firms to rate. In its 2003 rankings, it selected the largest 100 companies on the TSX 100 by market capitalization, as of December 31, 2002. The weightings were based on a stakeholder model that included shareholders, nature, employees, customers, and citizens. The weightings were as follows: community, 7.5 percent; employee relations/diversity, 15.0 percent; environment, 17.5 percent; product safety and business practices, 2 percent; international, 17.5 percent; corporate governance, 10.0 percent; and share performance (5 year), 12.5 percent. Corporate Knights obtained the corporate governance scores from the *Report on Business* corporate governance rankings and the share performances from Sustainable Investment Group Ltd. For the other five items, Corporate Knights asked three different research firms to use their own methodology to rate the top 100 TSX firms by market capitalization, using a scale of −100 to +100. An emphasis on durability was included: the firms were awarded scores based on demonstrating that their 2003 accomplishments were part of a sustained corporate social responsibility strategy going back several years. The three companies involved were EthicScan Canada Ltd., Sustainable Investment Group, and Innovest Strategic Value Advisors.

Founded in 1989, EthicScan's mission is to provide organizations, businesses, and individuals with the research and tools to bring an ethical dimension to their investing, purchasing, partnering, training, and managing decisions. Through independent research, EthicScan evaluates the environmental, labour, and social performance of approximately 1500 Canadian companies. Its researchers focus on 10 key criteria related to corporate social responsibility. The criteria and ratings reflect more than 50 expert opinions that are developed through a deliberately open, modified Delphi process. This panel of experts includes regulators, business persons, human rights advocates, and environmentalists. Its research emphasizes performance and results, as opposed to what companies wanted to do or said they would do through their guidelines and policies.

Sustainable Investment Group (SIG) was founded by Brian Schofield and Dr. Blair Feltmate in 1995. SIG focuses on the management of sustainable development-based pension and mutual funds. In addition to being a money manager, SIG also gives advice to firms on increasing their identified sustainable strengths and discovering and mitigating their sustainable weaknesses. SIG's goal is to analyze the relationships between two performance indicators: development that is sustainable and shareholder value creation SIG uses a proprietary management tool called the Sustainable Development Index (SDI) to assess companies' sustainable performance on 60 to 160 industry-specific measures related to social, economic, and environment issues. The financial industry is assessed using 60 measures, whereas the chemical industry is assessed using 115 measures. Companies receiving a SDI (r) score greater than 70 are rated as top-tier sustainable development practitioners, making them

Corporate Knights measures corporate social responsibility. Visit www.corporateknights.ca and see the most recent ranking of the top 50 Canadian corporations.

COURTESY OF CORPORATE KNIGHTS MAGAZINE

(continued)

eligible to be included in SIG's mutual and pension funds. In contrast to EthicScan's approach, SIG focuses on procedures and policies and includes in their deliberations how long these policies have been in place. The four key areas covered in SIG's assessment are societal, economic, environmental, and general issues.

Innovest Strategic Value Advisors is an investment advisory and research firm that analyzes drivers of risk and shareholder value that are considered non-traditional: strategic governance, labour relations, environment, and stakeholder capital. This investment advisor gives advice to institutional investors, decision makers in global Fortune 500 companies, governments, and non-governmental organizations (NGOs) internationally. Innovest collects data from firms, NGOs, trade publications, and governments. These data are used in a proprietary matrix with industry weightings developed from actual stock returns to assess performance within a company's industry or sector given the competitive dynamics within that industry or sector. After this step, the data are used as background material for direct interviews with each firm's senior executives. To highlight the relationship between sustainability and profitability, Innovest uses its analytical model in an explicit attempt to balance the environment and social investment risks against a firm's capacity to manage that risk.

eeBy using three different research methodologies and crunching them into one rating, Corporate Knights developed the list of the 50 best corporate citizens in Canada. The top 10 for 2003 were Alcan Inc., Royal Bank of Canada, Suncor Energy Inc., Nexen Inc., Canadian Imperial Bank of Commerce, Bank of Nova Scotia, Domtar Inc., Manitoba Telecom Services Inc., Nova Chemicals Corp., and BMO Financial Group. The Toronto-Dominion Bank came in at number 23. We will present the top 20 companies for 2003 and 2004 later in Chapter 2. Another measure of corporate social responsibility is the list of finalists for the GLOBE Awards. Each year The GLOBE Foundation and *The Globe and Mail* recognize outstanding achievement in the area of environmental stewardship by giving the "GLOBE Awards for Environmental Excellence." As they say on the GLOBE Awards website, it takes dedication, a competitive nature, and an ability to endure many challenges to work towards becoming a sustainable enterprise. The GLOBE Awards are presented at the EECO Environment and Energy Conference every May in Toronto. Later in this chapter we list the 2004 GLOBE Award winners and finalists and explain the categories and the criteria for each category. It seems that having average or above-average returns is no longer enough. These returns must be generated through ethical and environmentally and socially responsible actions.

SOURCES: The GLOBE Awards, *The GLOBE Awards website*, http://www.theglobeawards.ca/, accessed May 5, 2004; Corporate Knights, The 2003 best 50 corporate citizens, *Corporate Knights website*, http://www.corporateknights.ca, accessed May 5, 2004; Corporate Knights, Our methodology: How we find the best 50 corporate citizens in Canada, *Corporate Knights website*, http://www.corporateknights.ca, accessed May 5, 2004.

In Chapter 1, we stressed the importance of understanding how to exploit competitive advantages to ensure that a firm earns above-average returns. This is consistent with most definitions of strategy that have at least one attribute in common: they focus on the effect of a firm's strategy on performance in the short- and/or long-term. The definition of strategy as the allocation of resources to enable the maintenance or enhancement of performance illustrates this point very well.[1] In addition, this emphasis on performance is explicit in the description of the strategic management process in Chapter 1: *The strategic management process is the full set of commitments, decisions, and actions required for a firm to achieve strategic competitiveness and earn above-average returns.*[2]

An important question in the study of organizations is: What is performance? In some settings, the notion of performance is very clear. In athletics, the person who throws the javelin the furthest, the person who runs 100 metres the fastest, the person who jumps the highest in a pole vaulting competition—all of these people have outperformed their competition. In sports, the team that wins the Stanley Cup in the National Hockey League playoffs, the team that wins the World Series in baseball, the team that wins the National Basketball Association's league championship—these teams are considered to have outperformed the rest of the teams in their respective sports. However, in many organizations, the definition of performance is more complicated. In this chapter, we present one reasonable approach to defining performance. Then we examine several measures of organizational performance. Finally, we suggest that there is no single measure of performance that is flawless and that using multiple approaches is an appropriate perspective for conducting strategic analyses.[3]

Defining Performance Conceptually

To understand performance conceptually, it is necessary to define what is meant by an organization. An organization is an association of productive assets (including people) who have voluntarily come together to accomplish a set of goals—in the case of the business organization, the goal is to gain an economic advantage.[4] For the coming together to occur, there must be a point of equilibrium between contributions to the organization and inducements from the organization, such that people and other productive assets are willing to stay with the organization. In simple terms, it must be worth it for people and other productive assets to be involved with the organization.[5] In addition, owners of productive assets must be satisfied with the use of these assets by an organization and, therefore, be willing to permit the organization to retain the assets and continue to exist.[6] Further, the owners of assets will voluntarily make these assets available to an organization if, and only if, they are satisfied with the income they are receiving. They will only be satisfied if the income they are receiving—as adjusted for risk—is at least as high as the next best alternative.[7]

Building on the above insights, strategy researcher Jay Barney developed a conceptual definition of performance that compares the actual value created by an organization using its productive assets with the expected value that the assets' owners anticipated the organization would create.[8] The comparison of the actual value created with the value that owners expected leads to three levels of performance: below-normal, normal, and above-normal performance. Below-normal performance occurs when an organization's actual value created is less than the value owners expected. Normal performance occurs when the actual value created is equal to the expected value. Finally, above-normal performance occurs when the actual value created is greater than the expected value. The positive difference between actual value created and expected value is also known as economic rent. Barney argues that resources and capabilities that are sources of competitive disadvantage will lead to below-normal performance, while those that are sources of competitive parity will lead to normal performance, and those that are sources of either temporary or sustained competitive advantage will lead to above-normal performance. We will discuss these concepts in depth in Chapter 4.

Before proceeding further, we will define and briefly discuss the concept of value. One marketing researcher has defined value as what is received for what is given. In the context of creating customer value, he argues that customers give their money, time, energy, or effort, and incur psychological and sensory costs (negative aspects of the setting where the interaction takes place, such as noise, drafts, or uncomfortable seats). After a transaction, the customer will ask, "Did I receive more than I gave?"[9] If the answer is yes, value was created but if the answer is no, value was destroyed. For shareholders, value creation means receiving more from an investment than could have been received from another investment with similar risk. As a student, ask yourself whether you are receiving value for the money, time, and effort invested in buying and reading this textbook. Have shareholders who invested in Nortel over the years received more than they gave, considering the destruction of shareholder value by successive boards of directors, CEOs, and senior management teams?

The terms below-normal, normal, and above-normal performance were derived from microeconomic theory and refer to levels of firm performance achieved under conditions of perfect competition. If a firm uses its resources to create just enough value to fully compensate the owners of all resources (including a rate of return that is risk-adjusted for the suppliers of capital), it is achieving normal performance, and the owners of resources will keep those resources in that firm. These firms are surviving.[10] When firms are achieving below-normal performance, the owners of resources will move their resources to another firm where it is expected that they will be used to achieve at least normal performance. When this happens to all of a firm's resources, the firm no longer exists economically, and eventually may cease to exist legally. Certainly, firms such as Eaton's, Woodward's, and Canadian Airlines no longer exist economically because they have created less value than the owners of their resources expected them to create. Air Canada is fighting for its very existence in 2004 and may cease to exist. Firms achieving above-normal performance will retain its current productive resources and will attract even more productive resources. These firms can be said to be prospering.

Building on the above insights and using terminology from Chapter 1, we state that when a firm achieves strategic competitiveness and successfully exploits its competitive advantages, it is able to accomplish its primary objective—achieving above-average returns. **Above-average returns** are those returns in excess of what an investor expects to earn from other investments with a similar amount of risk. Firms that are competing without any competitive advantages will earn, at best, average returns.

Average returns are those returns equal to what an investor expects to earn given a similar amount of risk. If a firm does not achieve at least average returns, the result is failure. Failure occurs because the owners of productive assets will choose to withdraw their investments from these firms and invest in firms that are earning at least average returns. This last group of firms is said to be earning below-average returns. **Below-average returns** are those returns that are less than an investor expects given a similar level of risk. Table 2.1 presents the relationships among the expected value of a firm's resources, their actual value, and firm performance.

This conceptual approach to defining performance has several advantages.[11] It is consistent with the perspective from microeconomics, it is consistent with most definitions of performance developed in organization behaviour and organization theory, and it can be used to analyze the impact of a firm's resources, capabilities, and environment on its performance. Unfortunately, this definition of performance is hard to measure, and we present several measures of performance in the next section. It is suggested that those assessing performance use more than one measure of performance.

Above-average returns are those returns in excess of what an investor expects to earn from other investments with a similar amount of risk.

Average returns are those returns equal to what an investor expects to earn given a similar amount of risk.

Below-average returns are those returns that are less than an investor expects given a similar level of risk.

The Measure of Firm Performance

Firm performance can be measured through the use of a variety of techniques. All of these techniques have limitations, and they all have their critics and supporters. Because of the limitations associated with each technique, it is advisable that multiple measures of performance be used when conducting a strategic analysis of a firm. Eight approaches to measuring firm performance will be described in the following sections. We will review the strengths and weakness of several of these approaches when applicable.

Firm Survival and Performance

One measure of performance is the ability of a firm to survive over an extended period of time. Obviously, if a firm survives for an extended period of time, it is creating at least average returns as defined in Table 2.1. The logic behind this statement is that firms generating less than average returns will not survive in the long term unless they receive some kind of subsidy either from government (as was Air Canada's case for years) or some private benefactor.[12]

Strengths of Using Firm Survival

This measure of firm performance is relatively easy to use. It does not require detailed information about a firm's economic condition. The only information required is whether a firm is still continuing operations. If this is the case, then the firm must be generating average returns as, if it were not, the owners of the assets would have transferred them elsewhere.[13]

Weaknesses of Using Firm Survival

Unfortunately, the firm survival measure of performance has several important limitations. First, it is sometimes difficult to know when a firm no longer exists. Although determining when some firms no longer exist may be easy—as in the case of smaller firms, such as individually owned gas stations, restaurants, and small newspapers—for larger firms, it may not be so easy to assess whether a firm has ceased to exist. For example, in August 2001, Indigo merged with Chapters to become Indigo Books and

Table 2.1	The Relationships among Expected Value, Actual Value, and Firm Performance
Average Returns	A firm creates with its resources value **equal to** what owners of those resources expected the firm to create given similar levels of risk.
Below-Average Returns	A firm creates with its resources value **less than** what owners of these resources expected the firm to create given similar levels of risk.
Above-Average Returns	A firm creates with its resources value **greater than** what owners of these resources expected the firm to create given similar levels of risk.

SOURCE: Adapted with permission from Barney, Jay B., *Gaining and Sustaining Competitive Advantage* (2nd Edition), 27. © 2002. Reprinted by permission of Pearson Education, Inc., Upper Saddle River, NJ.

Music. Arguably, neither bookstore chain currently exists. But, the assets of both are relatively still intact, they each probably serve many of the same customers they served prior to being merged, and they compete in many of the same markets. In fact, the website is http://www.chapters.indigo.ca. Thus, have Indigo and Chapters ceased to exist? When Ontario's Small Fry Snack Foods purchased the trademarks, distribution system, and other key assets of the U.S. Humpty Dumpty corporation in order to continue the brand, did it keep Humpty Dumpty in existence?[14]

In addition, does a firm cease to exist when it declares bankruptcy? Air Canada filed for protection under the Companies' Creditors Arrangement Act on April 1, 2003, to facilitate its operational, commercial, financial, and corporate restructuring. As of May 2004, Air Canada was still operating, even though investors were withdrawing their offer of equity, as in the case of Trinity Time Investments Limited.[15] Similar to a legal acquisition, many bankrupt firms continue to use the same productive assets, service the same customers, and compete against the same firms. In fact, some firms appear to do better after declaring bankruptcy. There is some evidence that suggests the possibility that strategic bankruptcies—bankruptcies filed in order to deal with some specific problem[16]—may be a way to maintain or even improve performance. Some firms are declaring bankruptcies to enable restructuring with the intention of being a stronger, better performing firm in the future. Yet, research shows that any circumstance in which a strategic bankruptcy may be profitably employed is so limited as to be useless as a strategy.[17]

A second limitation is that the death of a firm can occur over an extended period of time. This is particularly true when a firm has generated above-average returns and therefore acquired many assets that are of value and whose liquidation can extend survival. During such times, it is not clear whether the firm is going out of business or facing temporary setbacks. This means that using survival as the only definition of performance may lead to results being ambiguous.[18]

Even firms that survive for an extended period of time may change themselves in such a way that analyzing them as one firm may be illogical. The Hudson's Bay Company is an example of a firm that has survived as a legal entity for more than three centuries. Obviously, the business activities of the Hudson's Bay Company in the 1700s (building and maintaining trading posts for the fur trade) are much different from the activities of the year 2005 (being the owner and operator of large department stores). Focusing solely on survival as one measure of performance would miss the transition that has taken place in the Hudson's Bay Company.[19]

A final limitation regarding the use of survival as a performance measure is that it does not provide any information concerning above-average returns. Survival only differentiates between below-average returns and average returns. Some of the firms generating at least average returns may be generating slightly above-average returns or well-above average returns. In strategic management, we are interested in conditions that enable firms to earn above-average returns. With a focus concentrated only on survival, these insights are not available.[20]

This is not to say that financial ratios and other indicators (such as the quality of the board of directors) that are related to survival are not important. Slack financial resources (e.g., high liquidity or low debt-to-equity ratio) and quality board members (e.g., boards that may have many personal connections with other corporate boards) will aid a firm's condition and chances for survival. In fact, in one piece of classic research, Edward Altman combined several financial measures that were indicative of a firm's likelihood of survival. His measure, known as Altman's Z (shown below) uses measures of profitability, liquidity, and solvency to evaluate a company's likelihood of bankruptcy or default on bondholders (major stakeholders).[21] Altman's Z Scores of less than 1.8 represent very high potential for failure, scores between 1.8 and 3.2 represent a grey zone, and scores greater than 3.2 indicate a the likelihood of survival.

Altman's Z = .012(WC/TA)+.014(RE/TA)+.033(EBIT/TA)+.006(MVE/BVE)+.100(SALE/TA)

where,   WC = Working Capital; TA = Total Assets

RE = Retained Earnings

EBIT = Earnings Before Interest & Taxes

MVE = Market Value of Equity; (Shares Outstanding $\times$ Average Market Value)

BVD = Book Value of Debt

SALE = Net Sales

However, we must note that the simple act of surviving (without looking at any indicators related to the likelihood of survival, such as the accounting measures discussed below or Altman's Z noted above) is insufficient to allow a complete picture of the performance of the organization.

Therefore, while survival is an important technique in assessing firm performance, it is only one measure. Other authors have suggested several reasons for the limited ability of survival as a performance measure. First, it is hard to apply to new organizations. Second, it gives no guidance to short-term decision making. Third, it is possible that a firm will survive because of the intervention of others, such as government support, therefore making the measure artificial. Finally, it is possible that focusing solely on survival may cause senior managers to ignore other important goals and objectives that are essential for the firm's long-term well-being.[22] We now turn our attention to accounting measures of performance.

Accounting Measures and Firm Performance

Accounting measures of firm performance are the most frequently used measures in strategic management.[23] Some would suggest that the reason for the popularity of accounting measures is that the data are easily available for publicly traded firms. Others contend that accounting numbers are important because managers use them when making strategic decisions and because accounting numbers actually provide insights into economic rates of return.[24] However, others have criticized accounting measures of performance because accounting numbers have a built-in short-term bias, are subject to manipulation by managers, and undervalue intangible assets.[25]

In defence of accounting data, it is necessary to understand that such criticisms were developed to defend large U.S. firms in anticompetition or antitrust suits against charges that these firms (e.g., IBM) were earning monopoly rents. Thus, it was important to argue that accounting rates of return did not reflect economic rates of return. In addition, some finance scholars note that stock exchanges (e.g., the Toronto Stock Exchange) put great emphasis on the quality of accounting data so that investors may better estimate a firm's future returns.[26] Finally, some researchers have defended the use of accounting measures of performance by arguing that if one assumes that stock market data are indicative of economic profits, then accounting information must also provide insights into economic performance to some degree, particularly if investors consider accounting numbers useful.[27] Thus, while accounting-based measures of performance may present certain problems, there is broad support for their use as a measure of financial performance.

The more common approach to using accounting data to assess firm financial performance is to use ratio analysis. Some of the more important ratios and what they mean with respect to firm performance are listed in Table 2.2. The categories most used are (1) profitability ratios (a measure of profitability is used as the numerator, and a measure of size is used as the denominator), (2) liquidity ratios (the ability of a firm to

Ratio	Calculation	What the Ratio Means
Profitability Ratios		
• Gross Profit Margin	$\dfrac{\text{(Sales} - \text{cost of goods sold)}}{\text{Sales}}$	Measures the revenue left to cover operating expenses after taking out the cost of procurement
• Operating Profit Margin	$\dfrac{\text{Profit before interest \& taxes}}{\text{Sales}}$	Assesses firm profitability without regard to interest charges as a result of the capital structure
• Net Profit Margin (Return on Sales)	$\dfrac{\text{Profit after taxes}}{\text{Sales}}$	After-tax profits per dollar of sales
• Return on Total Assets	$\dfrac{\text{Profit after taxes}}{\text{Total assets}}$	Measures the return on the total investment in the firm
	$\dfrac{\text{Profits after taxes} + \text{interest}}{\text{Total assets}}$	It is appropriate to add interest to the numerator to obtain a measure of returns to both debt and equity of investors
• Return on shareholders' equity	$\dfrac{\text{Profit after taxes (PAT)}}{\text{Total shareholders' equity}}$	Rate of return to shareholders given their investment in the firm
• Return on common equity	$\dfrac{\text{PAT} - \text{preferred stock dividends}}{\text{Total shareholders' equity}}$	Return on investment which common shareholders have made in the firm
• Earnings per share	$\dfrac{\text{PAT} - \text{preferred stock dividends}}{\text{\# of common shares outstanding}}$	Earnings available to common shareholders
Liquidity Ratios		
• Current ratio	$\dfrac{\text{Current assets}}{\text{Current liabilities}}$	Measure of ability to cover short-term debt by assets convertible to cash in approximately same period as short-term debt matures
• Quick ratio (Acid-Test Ratio)	$\dfrac{\text{Current assets} - \text{inventory}}{\text{Current liabilities}}$	Measure of ability to pay off short-term debt without relying on inventory (the most difficult current asset to convert to cash)
• Inventory to net working capital	$\dfrac{\text{Inventory}}{\text{Current assets} - \text{current liabilities}}$	Measure of the extent to which a firm's working capital is tied up in inventory
Leverage Ratios		
• Debt-to-assets ratio	$\dfrac{\text{Total debt}}{\text{Total assets}}$	Measures use of debt to finance operations
• Debt-to-equity ratio	$\dfrac{\text{Total debt}}{\text{Total shareholders' equity}}$	Measures use of debt relative to shareholders' investment in firm
• Long-term debt-to-equity ratio	$\dfrac{\text{Long-term debt}}{\text{Total shareholders' equity}}$	Measures the balance between debt and equity in the long-term capital structure of firm
• Times interest earned	$\dfrac{\text{Profits before interest and taxes}}{\text{Total interest charges}}$	Measures how much profits can decline before firm is unable to meet its interest obligations
• Fixed-charge coverage	$\dfrac{\text{Profits before taxes and interest} + \text{lease obligations}}{\text{Interest charges} + \text{lease obligations}}$	A more inclusive measure of ability of firm to handle all of its fixed-charge obligations

(continued)

Ratio	Calculation	What the Ratio Means
Activity Ratios		
• Accounts receivable turnover	$\dfrac{\text{Annual credit sales}}{\text{Accounts receivable}}$	Measures average time to collect on credit sales
• Average collection period	$\dfrac{\text{Accounts receivable}}{\text{Total sales}/365}$	Average time it takes to receive payment for a sale
• Inventory turnover	$\dfrac{\text{Cost of goods sold}}{\text{Average inventory}}$	Measures speed with which firm is turning over its inventory
• Fixed-assets turnover	$\dfrac{\text{Sales}}{\text{Fixed assets}}$	Measures sales productivity and plant & equipment utilization
• Total assets turnover	$\dfrac{\text{Sales}}{\text{Total assets}}$	Measures utilization of a firm's assets. If below industry average, a firm is not generating the volume expected given its investment in assets
Shareholders' Return and Other Ratios		
• Dividend yield on common stock	$\dfrac{\text{Annual dividends per share}}{\text{Current market price per share}}$	Measures return to common shareholders
• Price-earning ratio	$\dfrac{\text{Current market price per share}}{\text{After-tax earnings per share}}$	Indicates market perception of the firm. Usually, faster growing or less risky firms tend to have higher P/E ratios than more risky or slower growing firms
• Dividend payout ratio	$\dfrac{\text{Annual dividends per share}}{\text{After-tax earnings per share}}$	Indicates dividends paid out as a percentage of profits
• Cash flow per share	$\dfrac{\text{After-tax profits} + \text{depreciation}}{\text{\# of common shares outstanding}}$	Measures total cash per share available to firm
• Break-even analysis	$\dfrac{\text{Fixed costs}}{\text{Contribution margin}}$ Where Contribution Margin = (Selling price/unit) − (variable price/unit)	Measures the number of units of product or service that need to be sold to begin to make a profit on that product or service

pay its short-term debts), (3) leverage ratios (the amount of a firm's indebtedness), (4) activity ratios (the level of activity in a firm), and (5) miscellaneous ratios (ratios that do not fall into one of the previously mentioned categories).

The following sources are available to access Canadian and U.S. industry averages in order to judge a particular firm's ratios relative to its closest competitors in a particular industry:

- Statistics Canada, *Market Research Handbook*, available at http://www.statcan.ca/ english/ads/63-224-XPB.
- Dun & Bradstreet, *Industry Norms & Key Business Ratios*, available at http://www.dnb.ca/products/indnorm.html.
- L. Troy, 2004, *Almanac of Business and Industrial Financial Ratios*, Englewood Cliffs, NJ: Prentice-Hall.

Limitations Associated with Using Accounting Measures

There are three important limitations to using accounting measures to assess firm performance. These are managerial discretion, short-term bias, and valuing intangible resources and capabilities.[28]

Managerial Discretion

Managers have some discretion when they choose methods of accounting.[29] Managers decide when to account for revenues and/or costs, how to value inventory, and how to depreciate assets. Consequently, accounting measures of performance may reflect managerial preferences and interests.

Short-Term Bias

A second limitation is the built-in short-term bias in accounting measures.[30] This short-term bias occurs because longer term, multi-year investments are generally treated as costs in a year when they do not generate identifiable revenues. This means that investments in research and development, human resource management training and development, and market research may be expensed in the short term rather than viewed as an investment in the long term. If managers' bonuses are based on short-term financial results, they may reduce these types of strategic investments.

Valuable Intangible Resources and Capabilities

A third limitation is the valuation of intangible resources.[31] Intangible resources and capabilities are productive assets that have a significant effect on performance but are difficult to observe, describe, and value through the use of accounting measures. Resources such as brand awareness, a sense of affiliation and identity with the firm, trust and friendship among managers and employees, close relationships with suppliers and customers, and close relations with shareholders are hard to assess and measure but are critical components of firm success.[32]

These limitations do not mean that accounting measures are bad or should be ignored. They do suggest that judgment and care should be used when assessing firm performance using accounting measures. Next we will examine the multiple stakeholder view of performance.

Firm Performance and the Multiple Stakeholder Approach

The conceptual approach described earlier suggests a stakeholder approach to measuring performance.[33] This method views a firm's performance relative to the preferences of those stakeholders who are important to the firm and can impact firm performance. Stakeholders who may impact firm performance include customers, employees, suppliers, managers, top executives, equity holders, debt holders, communities where plants and offices are located, and governments (local, provincial, and federal). The problem is that different stakeholders may have differential interests in how the firm should be managed. These differential interests may be a result of how much of each resource is being supplied by each stakeholder and the effect that firm decisions will have on each stakeholder.

Different stakeholders use different criteria to judge firm performance. Consequently, it is difficult to formulate and implement strategies that will satisfy each stakeholder with an interest in the firm. Firms that sell their products at a lower than optimal price may satisfy their customers but may not have the financial resources to satisfy employees with better pay, managers with better furnishings, and governments with higher taxes.

While the multiple stakeholder approach to performance is intuitively appealing, it is very difficult to apply in performing strategic analyses that lead to formulating and implementing appropriate strategies. As one strategy researcher wrote, "Each stakeholding group, and perhaps each individual stakeholder, may define performance in an idiosyncratic way."[34] As a result, there may be several and varied dimensions firms may have to assess. This multiple approach could become very cumbersome and cause performance for the few very important stakeholders to deteriorate. Consequently, it may be necessary to adopt those measures that emphasize a few stakeholders over others. These stakeholders need not always be the owners, and in cases where others are more critical to the firm's interest in the short run, their interests may take precedent. For example, XWave Solutions of St. John's, Newfoundland, has decided to emphasize employee satisfaction as well as customer satisfaction. Senior managers at XWave consider that this will mean better service for customers and higher shareholder returns in the long term. This is similar to the philosophy followed by Starbucks. In the field of higher education, universities are becoming more student-oriented. This focus is a major shift from the 1980s when they were faculty-oriented. We would argue that universities must be faculty-, staff-, student-, and alumni-oriented if they are to satisfy some of their more important stakeholders. But this is difficult given the differing needs and perceptions of what value means even among this small group of stakeholders.

Present Value

One measure of performance, grounded in finance theory, is the present value of cash flows.[35] This approach seeks to avoid some of the limitations of other performance measures. It avoids short-term bias by measuring cash flows over time, and it values all resources made available to a firm by using the discount-rate concept. Firms that use the present-value approach estimate both their net cash flows and their expected discount rates for several years into the future. This approach allows them to assess firm performance and individual project performance on a forward-looking basis. Table 2.3 shows the relationship between a firm's net present value and firm performance.

Strengths and Weaknesses of Present-Value Measures

This method of measuring performance has several strengths. First, there is the close link between present value and the conceptual definition of performance proposed by Jay Barney.[36] In addition, research suggests that firms who apply present-value principles and invest in positive net present-value strategies are able to maximize the wealth of shareholders. These firms will probably also generate enough cash to satisfy other stakeholders, such as employees, managers, customers, suppliers, and governments.

However, there are also several weaknesses that have been highlighted in the literature. The first is the problem of accurately predicting cash flow patterns several years into the future. Misjudging these cash flows on projects worth several billion dollars

Table 2.3	The Relationships between Net Present Value and Firm Performance	
Net Present Value < 0	Below-average returns	
Net Present Value = 0	Average returns	
Net Present Value > 0	Above-average returns	

SOURCE: Adapted with permission from Barney, Jay B., *Gaining and Sustaining Competitive Advantage* (1st Edition), 145–61. © 1997. Reprinted by permission of Pearson Education, Inc., Upper Saddle River, NJ.

and lasting several decades may be problematic. Second, measuring the discount rate is problematic. When estimating the discount rate, the firm's systematic risk (beta) must be assessed. Unfortunately, the measurement of beta may be problematic and may change over time. Finally, many researchers question the adequacy of the economic model (the Capital Asset Pricing Model [CAPM]) on which the estimation of beta is based.[37]

Does this mean we should not use net present-value measures? Of course not! Just as we suggested with other measures, the use of net present value must be done with its limitations in mind. In fact, using this measure may allow for a deeper understanding of firm performance.

Market-Based Measures and Firm Performance

In recent years, strategy researchers have increasingly relied on market-based measures of firm performance, either alone or in conjunction with accounting-based measures, when assessing a firm's financial performance.[38] This increased use of market-based measures of firm performance may partially be a response to the criticisms of accounting-based measures outlined earlier. The theoretical basis for using market-based performance measures is that they are a more accurate reflection of a firm's economic performance than accounting-based measures. This argument is based on the semi-strong form of the efficient market hypothesis[39] that suggests that all publicly available information is immediately reflected in a firm's stock price. This assumption has led to the use of the Capital Asset Pricing Model (CAPM) to determine systematic (beta) and unsystematic risks, and risk-free firm returns (e.g., as measured by Jensen's Alpha, defined below).

Some researchers have argued that while accounting data may be used to measure the effects of a firm's strategies *post hoc*, they are not useful for assessing the economic value of a given strategy or for choosing between strategies that are being evaluated for possible implementation.[40] Another viewpoint suggests that market-based measures are intrinsically different from accounting-based measures because the former focus on the present value of future streams of income (e.g., on the expected value of future cash flows), whereas accounting-based measures focus on past performance.[41] Thus, we will examine several measures of firm performance based on stock market data. However, before we do, we will discuss the manner in which these measures are developed.

Stock Market Measures

Stock market measures are based on the assumption that capital markets are semi-strong form efficient. This means that all publicly available information is reflected in the price of a firm's equity and debt. Accepting this assumption allows us to develop measures of risk and performance for a publicly traded firm. To develop these measures we need prices for the firm's stock over a period of time and values for the market index on which the stock is traded. For example, let's take a hypothetical firm that is traded on the Toronto Stock Exchange. In our example, we will examine the change in our firm's closing stock price for a period of 250 trading days. We take these closing stock price changes and regress them (in a statistical procedure called linear regression) on the daily change in the closing values of the TSX 300. This is reflected below:

$$S - RFR = a + b(M - RFR) + e$$

where, S = the percentage change in daily closing stock prices over 250 trading days

RFR = a measure of the risk-free rate of return for each of the 250 trading days

a = Jensen's Alpha, the risk-free rate of return for the firm's stock b = beta, the systematic risk or risk associated with movements in the stock market

M = the percentage change in daily closing value of the stock market index (e.g., TSX 300) for each of the 250 trading days

e = the residual obtained when estimating alpha and beta

Once this regression is conducted, it is possible to obtain measures of risk. The standard deviation of "S" is used as the measure of total risk. Beta is used as the measure of systematic risk, and the standard deviation of "e" is used as the measure of unsystematic risk. Market performance can now be assessed using four different measures: (1) the Sharpe measure, (2) the Treynor measure, (3) Jensen's Alpha, and (4) the Appraisal Ratio.[42]

The Sharpe measure is used to assess return per unit of total risk. The formula is:

The Sharpe measure = (S − RFR) / Standard Deviation of "S"

The Treynor measure is used to assess return per unit of systematic risk. The formula is:

The Treynor measure = (S − RFR)/Beta

Jensen's Alpha is used to assess a risk-free return and is measured by "a"

Jensen's Alpha = a

The Appraisal Ratio is used to measure the risk free return per unit of unsystematic risk. The formula is:

Appraisal Ratio = Jensen's Alpha / Standard Deviation of "e"

In summary, the Sharpe measure compares a firm's stock market performance to the firm's total risk. The higher the value of the Sharpe measure, the better the firm is performing. The Treynor measure compares a firm's stock market performance to the firm's systematic risk. As with the Sharpe measure, a higher Treynor measures indicates better firm performance. Jensen's Alpha compares a firm's stock market performance to the firm's risk-adjusted expected performance. A Jensen's Alpha greater than zero (one standard deviation or more above the mean) suggests that the firm is outperforming the market and achieving above-average returns. A Jensen's Alpha equal to zero suggests that the firm is performing as well as the market and achieving average returns. A Jensen's Alpha less than zero (one standard deviation or more below the mean) suggests that the firm is underperforming the market and achieving below-average returns. Table 2.4 on page 50 summarizes the relationship between Jensen's Alpha and firm performance. The Appraisal Ratio is a measure of the abnormal return per unit of risk that the firm could diversify away by becoming more diversified in the scope of its product markets. The higher the Appraisal Ratio the better a firm is performing.

Limitations of Market Measures

The first limitation of these measures is that they were not originally designed for the measurement of firm performance, but for the assessment of investment portfolio performance. Recently, however, strategy researchers have used them as a measure of firm performance.[43] A related problem is that both the Sharpe and Treynor measures implicitly use the risk-free rate as the cost of capital. This application may not be as much of a problem as it once was for large, publicly traded firms in the United States. The cost of capital and the rate of return on capital are available for the largest 1000 U.S. firms from the Stern Stewart 1000 performance lists. Unfortunately, Stern Stewart has stopped publishing the Stern Stewart Canadian 300 performance list; the list was last available in 1999. This loss

Table 2.4	Relationship between Jensen's Alpha and Firm Performance
Jensen's Alpha < –1	Below-average returns
Jensen's Alpha = 0	Average returns
Jensen's Alpha > +1	Above-average returns

of this Canadian performance list has recently become a problem for Canadian firms. In addition, it is a problem when assessing smaller firms in both countries.

A second, related problem is that the Treynor measure uses the firm's systematic risk (beta), which assumes that any unsystematic risk is fully diversified away. This approach may be appropriate for investment portfolios but may not be appropriate for firms. For example, the beta of Fishery Products International (FPI) was found to be approximately 0.70 with only 10 percent of the variance explained by the change in the TSX 300 index. This measure suggests that most of the total risk in FPI is composed of unsystematic risk or risk inherent in the firm. This indicates that FPI has not diversified away all unsystematic risk—an assumption underlying the use of beta in the Treynor measure. Finally, some have questioned the use of market indexes. The TSX 300 is frequently criticized as being too heavily influenced by Nortel Networks. The TSX 300 weights each stock in the index by the number of shares each firm has outstanding. Critics argue that this gives Nortel's stock an inordinate amount of influence on the TSX 300. Some argue that weight should be capped at 10 percent, while others argue for the status quo, which reflects the reality of the TSX 300 index.[44] These arguments have become particularly relevant given the recent performance of Nortel's stock.

Although these four measures have limitations, they do provide insight into the ability of a firm to achieve above-average returns, average returns, or below-average returns. Empirically, the Sharpe measure, the Treynor measure, Jensen's Alpha, and the Appraisal Ratio are highly correlated. One study found that the correlations of the Sharpe measure, the Treynor measure, and Jensen's Alpha were in the 0.84 to 0.90 range.[45] Another study found that the Sharpe measure, the Treynor measure, and the Appraisal Ratio had correlations in the same range.[46] However, both studies found that the correlations between the accounting measures described earlier and the market measures were only in the 0.15 to 0.30 range. Although statistically significant, the results suggest that market measures tell us more about performance than the accounting measures do.

Market Value Added and Economic Value Added

Market Value Added (MVA) and Economic Value Added (EVA) are measures of performance that some firms may use to judge their performance. In this section, we describe these two concepts and, in the Strategic Focus box "Limitations of MVA and EVA" on page 53, discuss their limitations. These two concepts, developed by Stern Stewart, allow for the appraisal of performance and evaluation. They further suggest that using MVA and EVA will enhance benchmarking, assessing business and financial risk, setting goals, spotting investments, and screening acquisition targets, among others.[47]

Market Value Added

Market Value Added (MVA) is believed to be a definitive measure of firm performance, with performance being defined as shareholder wealth maximization through the most efficient management and allocation of resources. MVA is the difference between the cash that investors expect to receive (given the current market value of the firm) and the amount of cash that debt and equity holders have invested in the firm since its inception. For example,

Market Value Added (MVA) is the difference between the cash that investors expect to receive (given the current market value of the firm) and the amount of cash that debt and equity holders have invested in the firm since its inception.

for a firm that has received $20 billion from its debt holders and $15 billion from its equity holders, has retained $30 billion through its operations, and currently has a total market value of $75 million, the MVA equals $10 billion. This $10 billion represents the cumulative amount that the firm has increased its shareholder wealth. Of course, a negative MVA would represent the cumulative amount that the firm has reduced its shareholder wealth.[48]

Stern Stewart argues that not only is MVA a good measure of shareholder wealth creation or destruction but that it also captures the ability of a firm to manage scarce capital resources. The reasoning behind this argument is that MVA is considered an estimate of the net present value of all the firm's capital projects, both those currently being pursued and those that are being anticipated by investors. Just as a net present value analysis takes the up-front investment and subtracts it from the present value of the expected cash flows of a future project, MVA takes the capital investment in the firm to date and subtracts it from the firm's current gross market value (the expected present value of the firm's future cash flows). The difference is the firm's net present value. Positive MVAs suggest that firms are maximizing shareholder wealth and that these firms are efficiently allocating the resources flowing to them.[49]

Consequently, MVA shows how much shareholder wealth has been increased and how well the firm's senior leaders are managing the firm's capital. This measurement of firm performance is a better measure of success than rankings that focus on measures of size, such as sales, revenue, or market capitalization.

Changes in MVA over a period of time are significant and should be examined closely by a firm's stakeholders, as these changes may be a more effective measure than absolute MVA at a particular point in time. A positive increase in MVA means that the firm's market value grew more than the amount of any additional funds obtained through debt, equity, or retained earnings. This increase indicates that the firm's net present value increased and so did the wealth of its shareholders. A decrease in MVA means that the firm's net present value was reduced and that shareholder wealth was destroyed. Stern Stewart argue that a change in MVA could be the result of many factors, including a change in stock market values, changes in expectations for a specific industry, and/or the effectiveness of a firm's senior leaders and the strategic choices that they have made. In Table 2.5 on page 52, we include the top 20 and bottom 10 firms from the most recent listing of Stern Stewart's 1000 performance listing. As we mentioned earlier, the Canadian 300 is no longer available from Stern Stewart so we included firms from the U.S. list. Many of these firms are familiar and affect many aspects of our daily lives (e.g., Microsoft, Wal-Mart Stores, and General Motors).

Economic Value Added

Economic Value Added (EVA) is an internal measure of a firm's ability to generate MVA in the future. It is measured by taking the amount of operating capital at the beginning of each year and multiplying it by the difference between the rate of return on capital and the weighted average cost of the debt and equity capital employed. Measurements are made at the beginning of the year because new capital investments take at least a full year to reach maturity. As mentioned earlier, EVA is linked to MVA in that MVA is the present value of all projected EVAs.

Obviously, there are several ways to create shareholder value, but they all relate to doing one of the following three,[50] all of which will improve EVA:

- Improve return on capital already employed (i.e., generate more profits without employing more capital);
- Invest more capital in strategies that have a greater rate of return than the cost of the capital employed; and
- Withdraw capital from strategies or projects that have a cost of capital greater than their rate of return.

Economic Value Added (EVA) is an internal measure of a firm's ability to generate MVA in the future. It is measured by taking the amount of operating capital at the beginning of each year and multiplying it by the difference between the rate of return on capital and the weighted average cost of the debt and equity capital employed.

Table 2.5			The 2003 Stern Stewart Performance 1000 MVA Ranking				
MVA Rank 2002	MVA Rank 2001	MVA Rank 1997	Company Name	MVA 2002	EVA 2002	Return on Operating Capital 2002 (%)	Cost of Capital 2002 (%)
1	1	2	Microsoft Corp.	219 165	1 076	17.7	13.6
2	2	1	General Electric Co.	183 386	5 946	14.5	8.1
3	3	17	Wal-Mart Stores	182 769	2 935	13.0	8.8
4	7	14	Johnson & Johnson	116 396	2 839	15.0	9.0
5	11	5	Merck & Co.	103 664	3 872	19.1	8.7
6	13	4	Coca-Cola Co.	92 015	2 446	17.5	6.9
7	16	9	Procter & Gamble	89 722	1 925	13.0	8.0
8	10	6	Exxon Mobil Corp.	84 379	(2 174)	6.6	7.8
9	5	18	IBM	75 175	(8 032)	307.0	11.6
10	6	NR	Citigroup	68 078	2 964	13.1	10.3
11	22	40	Dell Computer Corp.	63 644	373	17.6	12.5
12	4	8	Intel Corp.	59 763	(3 736)	6.2	16.0
13	26	NR	United Parcel Service Inc.	57 672	875	13.1	8.6
14	17	15	Lilly (Eli) & Co.	57 066	1 096	15.5	8.8
15	24	NR	Fannie Mae	54 181	2 457	28.1	9.8
16	19	54	Oracle Corp.	54 132	1 412	122.7	13.1
17	9	10	Pfizer Inc.	52 579	(3 533)	6.6	9.1
18	21	26	Pepsico Inc.	49 655	1 083	10.6	7.0
19	23	13	Altria Group Inc.	49 478	5 985	14.3	6.1
20	18	27	Abbott Laboratories	48 176	1 562	15.9	8.6
991	995	1000	Kindred Healthcare Inc.	(12 052)	(772)	0.6	6.4
992	993	NR	Verisign Inc.	(12 165)	(4 517)	-15.0	15.1
993	947	56	Motorola	(14 314)	(5 849)	0.0	12.8
994	996	998	General Motors Corp.	(15 449)	(6 309)	1.8	7.0
995	495	NR	J P Morgan Chase & Co.	(25 499)	(3 646)	5.2	10.3
996	72	34	SBC Communications Inc.	(25 862)	(8 695)	4.8	10.4
997	999	487	JDS Uniphase Corp.	(36 006)	(10 902)	-12.8	14.1
998	1000	30	Lucent Technologies Inc.	(37 218)	(20 802)	-22.1	10.1
999	998	28	AT&T Corp.	(64 071)	(28 484)	-8.7	9.5
1000	997	99	AOL Time Warner Inc.	(83 005)	(32 747)	-8.0	9.4

SOURCE: The 2003 US EVA/MVA Annual 1000 Ranking Database. Reprinted with permission of Stern Stewart & Co.

The Balanced Scoreboard

The Balanced Scorecard is a relatively new way of measuring performance. The creators of this system, Robert S. Kaplan and David P. Norton, argue that the Balanced Scorecard is a synthesis of a firm's long-range competitive capabilities and its historical-cost financial accounting model. The goal is to integrate long-term and short-term perspectives into one performance management system. Financial measures tell about past events; however, they are inadequate for the evaluating and directing required for the creation of future value through investing in suppliers, employees, customers, processes, technology, and innovation. The Balanced Scorecard brings financial measures of previous performance together with measures of the drivers of future performance. Its measures and objectives are determined from an organization's vision and strategy.

Limitations of MVA and EVA

Several writers do not agree with the many benefits of MVA/EVA touted by Stern Stewart. The authors of an article in *CMA Management* listed seven weaknesses that they considered were associated with the use of MVA/EVA.[51] First, EVA does not assess economic value or profit. The authors argued that economic value is a firm's expected cash flows discounted at the firm's cost of capital. Economic profit is the difference in economic value at two different points in time. The authors suggested that EVA does not measure cash flow but measures accounting net income that has been accrued. In addition, they suggested that EVA does not measure future cash flows but past accounting income. Second, the authors argued that there is a lack of consistent definitions for EVA, capital, and net operating profit after taxes. Third, EVA is too complex in that it requires 160 accounting adjustments to the generally accepted accounting principles (GAAP). Fourth, EVA is an inadequate single measure for any decision in that it only measures short-term profitability, which is not appropriate. Fifth, given that EVA is a short-term measure, it may be inappropriate to reward managers based only on EVA. Sixth, EVA is not appropriate for capital budgeting.

Finally, EVA is easy for managers to manipulate. The authors suggest five ways that managers can manipulate EVA and reduce firm performance:

- EVA requires the capitalization of R&D. This could allow the capitalization of R&D expenditures as assets rather than as expenses when the expenditures have no future value.
- Managers could develop a short-term bias.
- Managers could decide to spend little or no time on quality improvement.
- EVA permits the capitalization of restructuring charges, which could lead to unnecessary restructuring.
- EVA permits the holding back of expenditures in asset accounts. Expenditures with no future value could be recorded as assets.

Brian Schofield, of the Canadian firm Sustainable Investment Group Ltd. (SIGL), argues for the use of EVA and argues against the suggested weaknesses described above.[52] He suggests that an educated approach to using some of the 160 adjustments is necessary. Because SIGL calculates quarterly EVAs for more than 125 firms, their calculations are based on explicit decisions regarding each of the 160 accounting adjustments and their applicability on an industry-specific basis. SIGL adds a few adjustments of its own and in total makes less than 20 adjustments—the 20 or so most meaningful to each firm and the industry in which it operates. Schofield's argument is that assessing the future direction of a firm's EVA and understanding its value-creating/destroying capabilities allows SIGL to derive likely scenarios for future stock prices. He concludes that EVA methodology, applied appropriately, is very valuable in unveiling hidden investment opportunities and over-valued projects and strategies.

The EVA and MVA methodologies are fairly new concepts, with many people for, and some against, their use. Although both have been used successfully by large firms such as General Electric (GE) and Coca-Cola, a major limitation is the proprietary nature of the methodology; to have EVA/MVA applied to your firm in accordance with the Stern Stewart philosophy means hiring consultants from Stern Stewart. Of course, as the methodology becomes better known, others will apply their own version of the Stern Stewart MVA/EVA techniques (as SIGL as done), and the current proprietary nature of the techniques will no longer be as much of a problem.

SOURCES: D. Keys, M. Azamhuzjaev, and J. MacKey, 1999, EVA: To boldly go? *CMA Management*, September, 30-33; B. Schofield, 2000, EVA, *CMA Management*, December/January, 8-9.

The framework used translates a firm's vision and strategy into operational terms by asking four interrelated questions, illustrated in Table 2.6. For each question, it is critical to identify the objectives, determine how each objective will be measured, and set appropriate targets and initiatives to achieve the targets. It is important to remember that each of these questions is interrelated with all of the others and that all the questions are driven by the organization's vision and strategy. Robert Kaplan and David Norton have written several articles and a book on the Balanced Scorecard, which the reader is encouraged to obtain and read for further information.[53]

Corporate Social Responsibility

As mentioned in the Strategic Focus box "Reputation as a Measure of Performance," one of the categories assessed in determining the most admired company in Canada is corporate social responsibility. When measuring corporate social responsibility, CEOs were asked to consider the following as part of a larger group of items: charitable donations, progressive environmental, product and workplace-safety practices, sensitivity to shareholders' rights issues, and trade association leadership. For the past three years, the top four companies, according to an Ipsos-Reid poll, were the RBC Financial Group, BCE Inc., Suncor Energy Inc., and Canadian Imperial Bank of Commerce. This list is very impressive, given the consistency of these companies in being recognized each year.

We mentioned in the opening case, on page 37, that many organizations, such as CorporateKnights.ca, are assessing Canadian firms on their corporate citizenry. Two other organizations that recognize outstanding corporate citizens are The GLOBE Foundation and *The Globe and Mail*. These two organizations sponsor the GLOBE Awards for Environmental Excellence. Awards are given in six categories, with the winner and up to three finalists being announced in each category. The categories are excellence in

Table 2.6		The Balanced Scoreboard				
	Area	Question	Objectives	Measures	Targets	Initiatives
Vision Strategy	Customer	To achieve our vision, how should we appear to our customers?				
	Financial	To succeed financially, how should we appear to our shareholders?				
	Internal Business Processes	To satisfy our shareholders and customers, what business processes must we excel at?				
	Learning & Growth	To achieve our vision, how will we sustain our ability to change and improve?				

SOURCE: Reprinted by permission of *Harvard Business Review*. Adapted from "Using the balanced scorecard as a Strategic Management System," by R. S. Kaplan and D. S. Norton (January–February), p. 76. Copyright © 1996 by the Harvard Business School Publishing Corporation, all rights reserved.

Reputation as a Measure of Performance

Another measure of performance is reputation. In Canada, there is an annual survey of Canada's most admired and respected corporations, sponsored by KPMG and conducted by Ipsos-Reid. The latest list available was published in January 2004, and, for the second year in a row, RBC Financial Group topped the list as the most respected and admired Canadian corporation as selected by Canadian chief executive officers (CEOs). The survey was conducted in the fall of 2003, and was based on interviews with 255 CEOs in Canada. Each company is assessed in nine categories: (1) best long-term investment value, (2) innovation and product/service development, (3) human resources management, (4) financial performance, (5) corporate social responsibility, (6) high quality service/product, (7) corporate governance, (8) customer service, and (9) top-of-mind most admired or respected. The innovation and product/service development category was topped by Research in Motion Ltd. WestJet Airlines Ltd. came first in two categories (high quality service/product and customer service), and it placed second overall, up from seventh in 2002, and 147th in 2001. The RBC Financial Group came first in the other six categories and retained its top place ranking from the previous year. We include a table with the top 25 firms for 2003 in this Strategic Focus. When the 2004 list is published, it will be interesting to review the results for Nortel, given the firing on April 28, 2004, of Frank Dunn, CEO; Doug Beatty, CFO; and Michael Gollogly, comptroller for "cause." Nortel had fallen to 41st place in 2002, down from 4th in 2001, but had climbed back to 21st in 2003. It is likely that if Nortel restated its earnings for 2003, as was being speculated on in 2004, its ranking in the 2004 poll will be lower than 21st.

The 2003 Honour Roll
The 25 Most Admired and Respected Canadian Corporations as Ranked by Canadian CEOs

Rank 2003	Score 2002	2001	Company Name	2003	2002	2001
1	1	2	RBC Financial Group	983	1106	589
2	7	147	WestJet Airlines Ltd.	357	217	6
3	3	3	BCE Inc.	344	320	413
4	5	7	Loblaw Companies Ltd.	251	266	136
5	2	1	Bombardier Inc.	227	463	841
6	8	6	Research in Motion Ltd.	196	199	149
7	12	24	Bank of Nova Scotia	179	170	49
8	19	—	EnCana Corporation	151	147	—
9	20	14	BMO Financial Group	150	148	77
10	4	8	Magna International Inc.	145	271	114
11	23	30	Canadian Tire Corporation Ltd.	141	114	43
12	17	18	Suncor Energy Inc.	140	149	60
13	16	10	CIBC	135	155	104
14	22	—	Four Seasons Hotels and Resorts	133	129	—
15	18	41	Manulife Financial Corporation	129	151	34
16	6	23	Dofasco Inc.	106	230	51
17	11	38	Wal-Mart Canada Corp.	104	173	38
18	9	5	TD Bank Financial Group / TD Canada Trust	103	183	209
19	24	21	GE Canada Inc.	99	113	54
20	15	25	Microsoft Canada Co.	92	157	48
20	13	29	Canadian National Railway Co.	92	44	52

(continued)

Rank 2003	Score 2002	2001	Company Name	2003	2002	2001
21	41	4	Nortel Networks Ltd.	90	43	373
22	10	13	IBM Canada Ltd.	88	176	81
23	33	245	Enbridge Inc.	82	60	1
24	35	51	TransCanada Pipelines Ltd.	81	57	15
25	30	24	Petro-Canada	75	75	49

Note: Microsoft Canada Co. and Canadian National Railway Co. tied for 20th place.
SOURCES: Ipsos-Reid, 2004, RBC Financial Group again selected by CEOs as Canada's most respected corporation for 2003, *Ipsos-Reid website*, http://www.ipsos-na.com/news/pressrelease.cfm?id=2019 (press release), January 19; M. Evans & W. Dabrowski, 2004, Nortel clears decks for admiral, *National Post*, Thursday, April 29, A1, A8.

brownfield redevelopment, corporate competitiveness, export performance, technology innovation and application, environmental performance, and sustainable investment and banking. Each of these categories has an environmental focus.[54]

The Brownfield Redevelopment award is given to a firm or local government that has demonstrated outstanding leadership in returning idle properties into thriving, revitalized communities or business areas. The corporate competitiveness award is presented for a proven record of environmental stewardship that has significantly contributed to economic competitiveness. The export performance award recognizes an environmental technology or service company that has succeeded in the global environmental marketplace. The technology innovation award is for technical ingenuity in the development and/or application of an innovative technology or process that has a significant environmental application. The environmental performance award is given to an association that has gone beyond regulatory compliance to develop a collective commitment to improving environmental performance. The sustainable investment and banking award is given to a company that operates in the financial markets and is integrating environmental factors into banking and investment decisions. The winners and finalists for each category are noted in Table 2.7.

As was mentioned earlier and in the opening case, the online magazine CorporateKnights.ca is assessing Canadian corporations on their corporate citizenry. CorporateKnights.ca assessed the largest 100 firms in terms of capitalization on the TSX 300 in 2003 and 2004 and listed the top 50 in each year. Table 2.8 on page 58 lists the top 20 firms from each of these two years.

Sustainability and the Triple Bottom Line

Many researchers are becoming concerned with the sustainability of the current growth-based market system that seems to be an outcome of a philosophy that gives little thought to the needs of society or the environment. There is a growing movement to include the triple bottom line when assessing performance. Sustainability is the recognition that the earth is a closed system with limits that we are approaching, not an open,

Table 2.7	The GLOBE Awards	
Category	**Winner**	**Finalists**
The Corporate Competitiveness Award	Toyota in Canada	Alcan Inc. Dupont Canada Suncor Energy
The Industry Association Award for Environmental Performance	Canadian Urban Transit Association	Canadian Steel Producers Association Canadian Plastics Industry Association
The Corporate Award for Technology Innovation and Application	Xantrex Technology Inc.	EcoTrans Technologies GPS Gas Protection System Inc.
The Industry Award for Export Performance	Carmanah Technologies Inc.	Fueling Technologies Inc. Lotek Wireless Inc. Trojan Technologies Inc.
The Capital Markets Award for Sustainable Investment & Banking	Innovest Strategic Value Advisors	Cleantech Venture Network The Ethical Funds Company
The Award for Excellence in Brownfield Redevelopment	Canada Lands Company's *Moncton Shops Project*	Low-Level Radioactive Waste Management Office's *Port Hope Waterworks Remediation Project* Nexen Inc. and Nexen Chemical's *Squamish Chemical Plant Site*

SOURCE: The GLOBE Awards, 2004, http://www.theglobeawards.ca, downloaded May 5, 2004. Reprinted with permission of the GLOBE Foundation.

boundless system. Sustainability is defined as the capability of present generations to meet their needs without compromising the capability of future generations to meet their needs. The triple bottom line is closely related to this definition of sustainability. It can be defined as a framework for measuring and reporting firm performance against economic, environmental, and social parameters. A few Canadian companies are starting to report their triple bottom line. BC Hydro is one such company, as indicated by the following quote from its website.[55]

"Our Triple Bottom Line Report documents the progress we have made towards our goal of balancing our business across three bottom lines: environmental, social and economic."

Corporate social responsibility has many aspects, and there is an increasing importance for senior leaders of companies to have an awareness they are being watched by shareholders, customers, employees, and other stakeholders who are interested in how the companies they invest in, work for, buy from, and interface with are interacting with society and the environment. In addition, there are many organizations that are assessing the ability of Canadian firms to interact in a responsible manner.

While assessing performance is difficult, it is expected that, as stakeholders require firms to be environmentally and socially responsible as well as financially responsible, measuring performance will become even more difficult. There is a growing sense that the firms that hope to achieve better financial performance are those that are also socially and environmentally responsible, as measured by their triple bottom line.

2004 Rank	Company Name	2003 Rank	Company Name
1	Zenon Environmental Inc.	1	Alcan Inc.
2	MDS Inc.	2	Royal Bank of Canada
3	Alcan Inc.	3	Suncor Energy Inc.
4	Dofasco Inc.	4	Nexen Inc.
5	Tembec Inc.	5	Cdn. Imperial Bank of Commerce
6	Bank of Montreal	6	Bank of Nova Scotia
7	Royal Bank of Canada	7	Domtar Inc.
8	TransAlta Corporation	8	Manitoba Telecom Services Inc.
9	Great-West Lifeco Inc.	9	Nova Chemicals Corp
10	Suncor Energy Inc.	10	BMO Financial Group
11	Enbridge Inc.	11	Enbridge, Inc.
12	TransCanada Pipelines Limited	12	Shell Canada Ltd.
13	Manitoba Telecom Services Inc.	13	Terasen Inc.
14	Husky Injection Molding Systems	14	Dofasco Inc.
15	Bank of Nova Scotia	15	EnCana Corporation
16	CGI Group Inc.	16	SNC-Lavalin Group Inc.
17	Husky Energy Inc.	17	Petro-Canada
18	Terasen Inc.	18	BCE Inc.
19	Falconbridge Limited	19	Fairmont Hotels & Resorts Inc.
20	Fairmont Hotels & Resorts Inc.	20	MDS Inc.

SOURCES: Corporate Knights, 2004, *Corporate Knights website*, http://www.corporateknights.ca/best50/2004best50.asp, accessed June 22, 2004; Corporate Knights, 2003, *Corporate Knights website*, http://www.corporateknights.ca/best50/2003best50.asp, accessed December 31, 2003.

Summary

- Performance is the comparison of the actual value created by an organization using its productive assets with the value that the assets' owners expected the organization to create. The comparison of actual value created with the value the owners of assets expected the organization to create leads to three levels of performance. These three levels are below-normal, normal, and above-normal performance. When an organization's actual value created is less than the value owners of assets expected, it is below-normal performance; when the actual value created is equal to the expected value, it is normal performance; and, when the actual value created is greater than the expected value, it is above-normal performance.

- Firm survival is one measurement of firm performance that is easily applied. If a firm survives over an extended period of time, it is creating at least average returns.

- One common approach to measuring firm performance is the use of accounting data. The type of data used are (1) profitability ratios (a measure of profitability is used as the numerator, and a measure of size is used as the denominator),

(2) liquidity ratios (the ability of a firm to pay its short-term debts), (3) leverage ratios (the amount of a firm's indebtedness), (4) activity ratios (the level of activity in a firm), and (5) miscellaneous ratios (ratios that do not fall into one of the previously mentioned categories).

- Another method of measuring firm performance is the stakeholder approach. This method views a firm's performance relative to the preferences of those stakeholders who are important to the firm and can impact firm performance. Some stakeholders who may impact firm performance are customers, employees, suppliers, managers, top executives, equity holders, debt holders, communities where plants and offices are located, and governments (local, provincial, and federal).

- Net present value begins with the measurement of future cash flows, discounts them using an appropriate discount rate, and then subtracts the up-front investment. This approach seeks to avoid some of the limitations of other performance measures. The net present value method avoids short-term bias by measuring cash flows over time, and it values all resources made available to a firm by using the discount rate concept. Firms that use the present-value approach estimate their net cash flows and expected discount rates for several years into the future. This approach allows them to assess firm performance and individual project performance on a forward-looking basis.

- Market-based measures have been used to measure firm performance in recent years. The measures used have been the Sharpe measure, the Treynor measure, Jensen's Alpha, and the Appraisal Ratio. These measures rely on the assumptions underlying the Capital Asset Pricing Model, especially the semi-strong market efficiency argument, and have been criticized for this reason.

- Market Value Added is the difference between the cash that investors expect to receive (given the current market value of the firm) and the amount of cash that debt and equity holders have invested in the firm since its inception.

- Economic Value Added is an internal measure of a firm's ability to generate MVA in the future. It is measured by taking the amount of operating capital at the beginning of each year and multiplying it by the difference between the rate of return on capital and the weighted average cost of the debt and equity capital employed.

- Corporate Social Responsibility, Sustainability, and Triple Bottom Line are terms coming into the language of business, more and more, in recent years. Sustainability is defined as the capability of present generations to meet their needs without compromising the capability of future generations to meet their needs. The Triple Bottom Line is closely related to this definition of sustainability. It can be defined as a framework for measuring and reporting firm performance against economic, environmental, and social parameters. Both of these definitions embrace the concept of Corporate Social Responsibility.

Review Questions

1. Discuss the conceptual meaning of performance. Is this a theoretically sound way to think about firm performance? Does this conceptual definition help us focus on the challenge of strategic management? Explain.

2. Briefly describe survival as a performance measure. What are its strengths and weaknesses?

3. Why are accounting measures of performance so popular? Is their continued use to measure performance justified? Why?

4. Is the stakeholder approach a useful performance measure? Describe how you would use this measure.

5. Net present value is a well-grounded financial performance measure. Discuss this measure conceptually, based on your finance textbooks. Do the authors of these textbooks agree or disagree with the limitations discussed in this chapter?

6. Market-based measures have been used recently to measure performance. Borrow an investment textbook from one of your finance friends, and use material from these textbooks to conceptually discuss whether market-based measures are appropriate for assessing firm performance.

7. Describe in detail what the measures Market Value Added and Economic Value Added mean. Are they valid measures of firm performance?

8. Briefly discuss the underlying principles of The Balanced Scorecard.

9. Discuss the concepts of Corporate Social Responsibility, Sustainability, and Triple Bottom Line. Are these valid ways of describing an organization's performance?

Experiential Exercise

Go to the website of a Canadian company that you would like to work for after graduation. Assess this company using accounting-based measures and market-based measures.

In addition, assess this company's level of corporate social responsibility. After conducting this assessment, determine whether you would still want to work there.

1. J. B. Barney, 1997, *Gaining and Sustaining Competitive Advantage*, Don Mills, Ontario: Addison-Wesley Publishing Company, 30–64.
2. R. P. Rumelt, D. E. Schendel, & D. J. Teece (eds.), 1994, *Fundamental Issues in Strategy*, Boston: Harvard Business School Press, 527–30; A. D. Meyer, 1991, What is strategy's distinctive competence? *Journal of Management*, 17: 821–33.
3. W. G. Rowe & J. L. Morrow Jr. 1999, A note on the dimensionality of the firm financial performance construct using accounting, market and subjective measures, *Canadian Journal of Administrative Sciences*, 16(1): 58–70.
4. A. Alchian & H. Demsetz, 1972, Production, information costs, and economic organization, *American Economic Review*, 62: 777–95; R. H. Coase, 1937, The nature of the firm, *Economica*, 4: 386–405; R. H. Hall, 1987, *Organizations: Structures, Processes, and Outcomes*, 4th ed., Engelwood Cliffs, N.J.: Prentice-Hall Inc.; M. C. Jensen & W. H. Meckling, 1976, Theory of the firm: Managerial behavior, agency costs, and ownership structure, *Journal of Financial Economics*, 3: 305–60; J. P. Sheppard, 1994, Strategy and bankruptcy: An exploration into organizational death, *Journal of Management*, 20: 795–833; H. A. Simon, 1976, *Administrative Behavior*, 3rd ed., New York: MacMillan.
5. Barney, *Gaining and Sustaining Competitive Advantage*; Simon, *Administrative Behavior*.
6. Barney, *Gaining and Sustaining Competitive Advantage*; Coase, The nature of the firm; Jensen and Meckling, Theory of the firm: Managerial behavior, agency costs, and ownership structure.
7. Alchian & Demsetz, Production, information costs, and economic organization; Barney, *Gaining and Sustaining Competitive Advantage*.
8. Barney, *Gaining and Sustaining Competitive Advantage*.
9. J. G. Barnes, 2001, *Secrets of Customer Relationship Marketing: It's All about How You Make Them Feel*, Montreal, QC; McGraw-Hill.
10. Sheppard, Strategy and bankruptcy: An exploration into organizational death.
11. Barney, *Gaining and Sustaining Competitive Advantage*.
12. Barney, *Gaining and Sustaining Competitive Advantage*; H. Demsetz, 1973, Industry structure, market rivalry, and public policy, *Journal of Law and Economics*, 16: 1–9.
13. Barney, *Gaining and Sustaining Competitive Advantage*.
14. Financial Post, 2000, Small Fry takes big steps into U.S. with Humpty Dumpty assets, *Financial Post (National Post)*, January 26, C8.
15. 2003, News release, Air Canada to restructure under CCAA, April 1, http://micro.newswire.ca/13213-2.html; 2004, News release, Air Canada to pursue alternatives to Trinity Investment: Business as usual for Air Canada's customers, April 2, http://micro.newswire.ca/13213-2.html.
16. K. J. Delaney, 1992, *Strategic Bankruptcy: How Corporations and Creditors Use Chapter 11 to Their Advantage*, Berkeley, CA: University of California Press; W. N. Moulton & H. Thomas, 1993, Bankruptcy as a deliberate strategy: Theoretical considerations and empirical evidence, *Strategic Management Journal*, 14(2): 125–35; J. P. Sheppard, 1992, When the going gets tough, the tough go bankrupt: The questionable use of Chapter 11 as a strategy, *Journal of Management Inquiry*, 1(3): 183–92.
17. J. P. Sheppard, 1993, Corporate diversification and survival, *Journal of Financial and Strategic Decisions*, 6(1): 113–32.
18. Barney, *Gaining and Sustaining Competitive Advantage*.
19. Ibid.
20. Barney, *Gaining and Sustaining Competitive Advantage*; M. E. Porter, 1980, *Competitive Strategy*, New York: Free Press; R. P. Rumelt, D. Schendel, & D. Teece, 1991, Strategic management and economics, *Strategic Management Journal*, 12(winter special issue), 5–29.
21. Altman, E. I., 1968, Financial ratios, discriminant analysis and the prediction of corporate bankruptcy, *The Journal of Finance*, 23(4): 589–609; Altman, E. I., 1982, *Corporate Financial Distress: A Complete Guide to Predicting, Avoiding, and Dealing with Bankruptcy*, New York: John Wiley and Sons.
22. Barney, *Gaining and Sustaining Competitive Advantage*; R. M. Kanter & D. Brinkerhoff, 1981, Organizational performance: Recent developments in measurement, *Annual Review of Sociology*, 7: 321–49.
23. Rowe & Morrow Jr., A note on the dimensionality of the firm financial performance construct using accounting, market and subjective measures; Barney, *Gaining and Sustaining Competitive Advantage*.
24. I. Horowitz, 1984, The misuse of accounting rates of return: Comment, *American Economic Review*, 74: 492–93; R. Jacobson, 1987, The validity of ROI as a measure of business performance, *American Economic Review*, 77: 470–78; W. F. Long & D. J. Ravenscraft, 1984, The misuse of accounting rates of return: Comment, *American Economic Review*, 74: 494–500.
25. G. Bentson, 1982, Accounting numbers and economic values, *Antitrust Bulletin*, Spring, 161–215; F. M. Fisher & J. J. McGowan, 1983, On the misuse of accounting rates of return to infer monopoly profits, *American Economic Review*, 73: 82–97; R. L. Watts & J. L. Zimmerman, 1978, Towards a positive theory of the determination of accounting standards, *Accounting Review*, 53: 112–33; R. L. Watts & J. L. Zimmerman, 1990, Positive accounting theory: A ten-year perspective, *Accounting Review*, 65: 131–56.
26. T. E. Copeland & J. F. Weston, 1983, *Financial Theory and Corporate Policy*, Reading, MA: Addison-Wesley.
27. Long & Ravenscraft, The misuse of accounting rates of return.
28. Rowe & Morrow Jr., A note on the dimensionality of the firm financial performance construct using accounting, market and subjective measures; Barney, *Gaining and Sustaining Competitive Advantage*.
29. Watts & Zimmerman, Towards a positive theory of the determination of accounting standards; Watts & Zimmerman, Positive accounting theory: A ten-year perspective.
30. Barney, *Gaining and Sustaining Competitive Advantage*.
31. H. Itami, 1987, *Mobilizing Invisible Assets*, Cambridge, MA: Harvard University Press; Barney, *Gaining and Sustaining Competitive Advantage*.
32. Barney, *Gaining and Sustaining Competitive Advantage*.
33. R. W. Sexty, 1995, *Canadian Business and Society*, Scarborough, ON: Prentice Hall Canada Inc.
34. Barney, *Gaining and Sustaining Competitive Advantage*, 46.
35. S. A. Ross, 1996, *Fundamentals of Corporate Finance*, 2nd Canadian ed., Toronto, ON: Irwin; Barney, *Gaining and Sustaining Competitive Advantage*.
36. Barney, *Gaining and Sustaining Competitive Advantage*.
37. W. F. Sharpe, G. J. Alexander, J. V. Bailey, & D. J. Fowler, 1997, *Investments*, 2nd Canadian ed., Scarborough, ON: Prentice Hall Canada Inc.; Z. Bodie, A. Kane, A. J. Marcus, S. Perrakis, & P. J. Ryan, 1997, *Investments*, 2nd Canadian ed., Toronto: McGraw-Hill Ryerson Ltd.
38. Rowe & Morrow Jr., A note on the dimensionality of the firm financial performance construct using accounting, market and subjective measures; R. E. Hoskisson, M. A. Hitt, R. A. Johnson, & D. D. Moesel, 1993, Construct validity of an objective (entropy) categorical measure of diversification strategy, *Strategic Management Journal*, 14: 215–35; R. E. Hoskisson, R. A. Johnson, & D. D. Moesel, 1994, Corporate divestiture intensity in restructuring firms: Effects of governance, strategy, and performance, *Academy of Management Journal*, 37(5): 1207–51.
39. Z. Bodie, A. Kane, & A. J. Marcus, 1993, *Investments*, 2nd ed., Boston, MA: Irwin.
40. M. Hergert & D. Morris, 1989, Accounting data for value chain analysis, *Strategic Management Journal*, 10: 175–88.
41. A. Seth, 1990, Value creation in acquisitions: A re-examination of performance issues, *Strategic Management Journal*, 11: 99–115.
42. Sharpe, Alexander, Bailey, & Fowler, *Investments*; Bodie, Kane, Marcus, Perrakis, & Ryan, *Investments*.
43. Rowe & Morrow Jr., A note on the dimensionality of the firm financial performance construct using accounting, market and subjective measures; R. E. Hoskisson, M. A. Hitt, R. A. Johnson, & D. D. Moesel, Construct validity of an objective (entropy) categorical measure of diversification strategy; Hoskisson, Johnson, & Moesel, Corporate divestiture intensity in restructuring firms: Effects of governance, strategy, and performance.
44. A. Bell, 1999, Nortel's might skews stock market, *Report on Business (Globe and Mail)*, October 13, B1.
45. Hoskisson, Hitt, Johnson, & Moesel, Construct validity of an objective (entropy) categorical measure of diversification strategy.
46. W. G. Rowe, 1996, *Persistence and Change in CEO Succession Processes*, College Station, TX: Texas A&M University, unpublished doctoral dissertation.
47. I. Ross, 1998, The 1997 Stern Stewart Performance 1000, *Journal of Applied Corporate Finance*, 10(4): 116–20; I. Ross, 1997, The 1996 Stern Stewart Performance 1000, *Journal of Applied Corporate Finance*, 8(4): 115–28; L. Walbert, 1995, The 1994 Stern Stewart Performance 1000, *Journal of Applied Corporate Finance*, 7(4): 104–18.
48. Stern Stewart Management Services, 1997, *The Stern Stewart Performance 1000*, New York: Stern Stewart Management Services.

49. Ibid.
50. Ibid.
51. D. Keys, M. Azamhuzjaev, & J. MacKey, 1999, EVA: To boldly go? *CMA Management*, September, 30–33.
52. B. Schofield, 2000, EVA, *CMA Management*, December/January, 8–9.
53. R. S. Kaplan & D. P. Norton, 1992, The balanced scorecard—measures that drive performance, *Harvard Business Review*, January–February, 71–79; R. S. Kaplan & D. P. Norton, 1996, Using the balanced scorecard as a strategic management system, *Harvard Business Review*, January–February, 71–79; R. S. Kaplan & David P. Norton, 1996, *The Balanced Scorecard: Translating Strategy into Action*, Boston: Harvard Business School Press.
54. The GLOBE Awards, *GLOBE Awards website*, http://www.theglobeawards.ca, accessed May 5, 2004.
55. L. Preston, 2001, Sustainability at Hewlett-Packard: From theory to practice, *California Management Review*, 43(3), Spring, 26–37; SustainAbility, 2003, The triple bottom line, *SustainAbility website*, http://www.sustainability.com/philosophy, accessed December 31, 2003; U. Balakrishnan, T. Duvall, & P. Priomeaux, 2003, Rewriting the bases of capitalism: Reflexive modernity and ecological sustainability as the foundations of a new normative framework, *Journal of Business Ethics*, 47: 299–314; B.C. Hydro, Reports and performance, *B.C. Hydro website*, http://www.bchydro.com/info/reports/reports846.html, accessed May 6, 2004.

3

Chapter Three

The External Environment: Opportunities, Threats, Industry Competition, and Competitor Analysis

Knowledge Objectives

Studying this chapter should provide you with the strategic management knowledge needed to:

1. Explain the importance of analyzing and understanding the firm's external environment.

2. Define and describe the general environment and the industry environment.

3. Discuss the four activities of the external environmental analysis process.

4. Name and describe the general environment's six segments.

5. Identify the five competitive forces and explain how they determine an industry's profit potential.

6. Define strategic groups and describe their influence on the firm.

7. Describe what firms need to know about their competitors and different methods used to collect intelligence about them.

Terrorism, SARS, the Iraq War, "Mad Cow Disease," and a Power Outage: A Firm's External Environment in the 21st Century

When terrorists flew airplanes into the twin towers of the World Trade Center and into the Pentagon, and crashed a third plane in Pennsylvania, on September 11, 2001, the world of business was changed forever. However, certain industries were affected more than others and in different ways. Firms in the insurance, air travel, financial services, and tourism industries took much of the initial brunt of the economic fall-out from the attacks. For example, air travel in Canada and the United States was halted for several days after the attacks, and demand was lower for some time following its resumption. Many scheduled conventions were either cancelled or conducted with fewer participants than planned. In the short term, however, demand for other means of travel, such as trains and buses, increased significantly.

In Canada, four events, with international relevance, occurred in 2003, and created economic upheaval for firms in numerous industries within the city of Toronto and across Canada. Toronto, the capital city of the province of Ontario, is well known as the home of the world's tallest building—the CN Tower and the world's longest street—Yonge Street. It is Canada's largest city and is home to a population of more than 2.5 million people. The city is well known as the cultural (with more than 100 ethnic groups represented), entertainment and financial capital of Canada. Canada depends on its trade—with more than 150 partners—to account for approximately 25 percent of the country's gross domestic product (GDP). The economy of Ontario mirrors that of the country, with a significant proportion of its trade (91 percent of exports and 76 percent of imports) being conducted with the United States, which borders the province to the south.

The first event, an outbreak of Severe Acute Respiratory Syndrome (SARS), appeared in Toronto, in March 2003, when a woman who had just returned from China, where SARS originated, died from the disease. Analysts estimated that the Canadian economy would suffer losses of between $1.5 billion and $2.1 billion, with much of the loss taking place in the Toronto area. Compounded by what analysts suggest was unnecessarily heavy media coverage, tourism and hospitality sectors went into a tailspin. In addition, hospitals and health care establishments experienced upheavals, as officials struggled to contain the spread of the disease in the face of critical scrutiny by the local population and the world's press.

During the outbreak, the Conference Board of Canada revised growth projections for Toronto downward, estimating that the impact of SARS on tourism, excluding airport traffic, would be at about $350 million, a 9 percent decrease from the previous year. Additionally, non–tourism-related retail sales would also go down by about

SARS was one of several external events that all Canadian organizations had to deal with in 2003.

© ANDREW WALLACE/REUTERS/LANDOV

(continued)

$380 million. The SARS outbreak was heavily reported worldwide along with WHO (World Health Organization) advisories that were issued against non-essential travel to Toronto.

Although the number of deaths attributed to SARS in Canada was a small fraction (approximately 4 percent) of the total number of SARS-related deaths worldwide, industry reports repeatedly cited massive cancellations in programs, meetings, conventions, and performances across the Greater Toronto Area. The first Canadian SARS outbreak was traced to Scarborough Grace Hospital, and retail businesses in the heavily populated Scarborough neighbourhood were severely affected. A number of businesses folded as there was a significant reduction in the number of shoppers venturing into the predominantly Chinese district. The city sought emergency financial relief from the provincial and federal governments to support those hardest hit, especially people in mandatory quarantine, health care workers, and employees in tourism, transportation, and retail sectors. It was not until late November 2003, when SARS was not visible anywhere worldwide, that the strict screening measures, instituted when SARS was first reported in Toronto, were scaled back, as officials agreed that a SARS epidemic was no longer an immediate threat.

Other events that affected Canada in 2003 included the U.S.-led war on Iraq, the reappearance of BSE (Bovine Spongiform Encephalopathy, better known as "Mad Cow Disease") in Canada, and a power outage in August that plunged most of Ontario and the northeastern United States into darkness. Canada's role in the Iraqi war sparks a point of debate among analysts and has been cited as negatively impacting the relationship between Canada and the United States, its closest neighbour and largest trading partner, with whom daily trade is valued at approximately $1.4 billion. On one side, the Canadian government is recognized for maintaining a position of not engaging in the war against Iraq without prior commitment from the United Nations; on the other hand, the government is charged with conning the majority of Canadians into believing it was not involved with the war, while internationally, it stands as the third strongest contributor behind Britain and Australia. Of issue, is the extent to which the Canadian position on the war against Iraq's arms policies and terrorism has impacted its international trade relationships and thereby the country's economy and trade.

Prior to May 2003, there had only been one detected case of BSE, in an animal that had been imported from Britain to a farm near Alberta. In that incident, in 1993, the Canadian government opted to destroy the animal and its herd mates. In the ensuing public debate amid bans on exports of Canadian cattle and beef products to several trade partners, eventually more than 350 animals were destroyed, and their owners were compensated. Canada's beef exports are approximately $2.2 billion annually, having risen sharply in recent years. Of this amount, approximately 39 percent is derived from the cattle industry in Alberta. Canada's large beef market is the United States, with Mexico, Japan, and South Korea also providing significant markets. During the 2003 case, the U.S. suspended all shipments of cattle, beef, and animal feed. The U.S. restriction was followed shortly by Japan and South Korea, with South Korea extending the ban to include Canadian dairy products. Industry analysts estimate that Canadian beef producers were losing $27 million per day as a result of the restrictions.

On a hot summer's day in mid-August 2003, the lights went out—the result of a massive power failure in Ohio that wiped out most of the power to Ontario and the northeastern United States. The Canadian economy once again faced the economic effects of activities in its wider operating environment. Statistics showed a reduction of about 3.8 percent in worldwide exports and an even larger reduction of 5.9 percent in imports. Reports from Statistics Canada suggest that the automotive industry accounted for most of the declines, as its output was reduced.

In more gripping reports, analysts suggest that "the energy crisis had the power to jolt the Canadian economy dangerously close to recession." During the blackout, hundreds of thousands of workers in Ontario at the federal, provincial, and municipal level, as well as employees in the not-for-profit and private sectors were off work for days as the province struggled to return the flickering energy supply to normal. As a cap to the declining situation, estimates from the retail sector also suggested big losses, with an estimated drop in sales of about 40 percent, compared to purchases in the previous week.

Overall, 2003 provided significant events that individually were sufficient to severely affect Canada's national economy because of their combined impact on businesses in several industries. Undoubtedly, an understanding of the broader context—the dynamics of relationships between Canada and the United States at the highest national level, in which the events took place—might have influenced the strategies employed by businesses both before and during the year. Of significance is the continued uncertainty in Canada–U.S. relations, although it is expected that our relations will be better under the leadership of Paul Martin (Canada's Prime Minister as of December 2003) than they were under Jean Chrétien, Martin's predecessor.

Few, if any, businesses were prepared for either the terrorist attacks on the United States on September 11, 2001, or the events that took place in Canada in 2003. However, these events provided a dramatic illustration of the dynamic environment within which firms operate and to which they must be able to respond. The many significant effects of the external environment (illustrated by the very few discussed in this opening case) suggest the substantial importance of the strategies that firms employ and of the ability required to adapt or change strategies in order to survive or prosper, in a rapidly changing landscape.

SOURCES: T. Hunt, 2003, Blackout highlights U.S., Canada feuds, *Canadian Press*, August 15; D. Meisner, 2003, Energy woes may jolt economy to brink of recession, *Canadian Press*, August 20; J. Thorpe, 2003, Blackout dims Ontario financial outlook: Adds to likelihood province will fall into deficit, analysts say, *Financial Post*, August 20; J. Makarenko, 2001, Canada's perspective and role, the war on global terrorism: Canada's role, *Canadian Centre for Cyber Citizenship website*, 2003, www.mapleleafweb.com, October 23; A. Segal & E. Missio, 2002, Canada's stance on an Iraq attack, *CBC News Online*, updated January 2003; R. Sanders, 2003, Canada—More "willing" than we seem, *Peace and Environment News*, www.canadawebpages.com/pc-editorial, April; H. Valentine, 2003, The post-Iraq economic slowdown, *Le Québécois Libre*, no. 123, April; J. Makarenko, 2003, Mad Cow: The science and the story, *CBC News Online*, May; J. Makarenko, 2003, Mad Cow Disease in Canada, *Canadian Centre for Cyber Citizenship website*, www.mapleleafweb.com/education/spotlight, June 17; T. Godfrey, 2003, SARS cutting Toronto economic growth, cnews.canoe.ca, May 2; J. Poirier, 2003, SARS has impacted economy: Fewer Americans crossing the border, *Sarnia Observer*, http://www.theobserver.ca, April 25; S. Feldman & D. Drache, 2003, Questioning media involvement in Toronto SARS outbreak, *York University website*, www.yorku.ca/yfile/archive, October 31; K. Leslie, 2003, Eves steps up delivery of SARS funds, *CNEWS*, http://www.cnews.canoe.ca, May 1; CTV.ca news staff, 2003, Ottawa adds $10 million to Toronto SARS recovery plan, *CTV News website*, http://www.ctv.ca, May 11; CBC News, 2003, Cumulative SARS cases as of June 17, 2003, *CBC News website*, http://www.cbc.ca/news/indepth/background/sars_cases.html, June 18; CBC News, 2003, SARS will cost Toronto $1 billion: Conference Board, *CBC News website*, http://toronto.cbc.ca/regional/servlet/View?filename=to_cost20030502, May 2; A. Michaels, 2001, Hope for an early deal on WTC insurance, *Financial Times*, http://www.ft.com, December 14; J. Fuerbringer, 2001, As the economic ground zero shudders, ripples spread, *New York Times*, http://www.nytimes.com, September 24; A. Brady & T. Locke, 2001, Cancellation of meetings and conferences deal a heavy blow to convention cities, *Wall Street Journal*, September 21, A8.

Companies' experiences and research suggest that the external environment affects firm growth and profitability.[1] Major political events such as the terrorist attacks on September 11, 2001, the strength of different nations' economies at different times, and the emergence of new technologies are a few examples of conditions in the external environment that affect firms in the United States and throughout the world. External environmental conditions such as these confront firms with both threats and opportunities, which, in turn, have major effects on those firms' strategic actions.[2]

Airlines changed their strategies in response to the threats in their external environment, taking a number of actions to reduce their costs while simultaneously enticing customers to return to air travel. All airlines but Southwest reduced their number of flights and personnel, and some eliminated routes as well. Southwest Airlines had substantial cash on hand, based on a conscious strategy to have funds available to operate during an emergency or crisis situation. Southwest Airlines' financial resources and human capital afforded it strategic flexibility.[3]

This chapter focuses on what firms can do to analyze and understand the external environment. As the discussion in the opening case vividly shows, the external environment influences the firm's strategic options, as well as the decisions made in light of them. The firm's understanding of the external environment is matched with knowledge about its internal environment (discussed in the next chapter) to form its strategic intent, to develop its strategic mission, and to take strategic actions that result in strategic competitiveness and above-average returns (see Figure 1.1, on page 8).

As noted in Chapter 1, the environmental conditions in the current global economy differ from those previously faced by firms. Technological changes and the continuing growth of information gathering and processing capabilities demand more timely and effective competitive actions and responses.[4] The rapid sociological changes occurring in many countries affect labour practices and the nature of products demanded by increasingly diverse consumers. Governmental policies and laws also affect where and how firms may choose to compete.[5] Deregulation and local government changes, such as those in the global electric utilities industry, affect not only the general competitive environment, but also the strategic decisions made by companies competing globally. To achieve strategic competitiveness, firms must be aware of and understand the different dimensions of the external environment.

Firms understand the external environment by acquiring information about competitors, customers, and other stakeholders to build their own base of knowledge and capabilities.[6] Firms may use this base to imitate the capabilities of their able competitors (or to imitate successful firms in other industries) and to build new knowledge and capabilities to achieve a competitive advantage. On the basis of the new information, knowledge, and capabilities, firms may take actions to buffer themselves against environmental effects or to build relationships with stakeholders in their environment.[7] To build their knowledge and capabilities and to take actions that buffer or build bridges to external stakeholders, organizations must effectively analyze the external environment.

The General, Industry, and Competitor Environments

An integrated understanding of the external and internal environments is essential for firms, in order to understand the present and predict the future.[8] As shown in Figure 3.1, a firm's external environment is divided into three major areas: the general, industry, and competitor environments.

The **general environment** is composed of dimensions in the broader society that influence an industry and the firms within it.
The **general environment** is composed of dimensions in the broader society that influence an industry and the firms within it.[9] We group these dimensions into six environmental segments: demographic, economic, sociocultural, global, technological, and political/legal. Examples of elements analyzed in each of these segments are shown in Table 3.1 on page 68.

Figure 3.1 | The External Environment

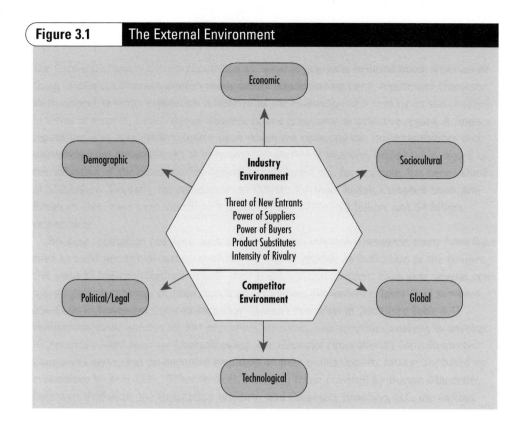

Firms cannot directly control the general environment's segments and elements. Accordingly, successful companies gather the information required to understand each segment and its implications for the selection and implementation of appropriate strategies. For example, the terrorist attacks in the United States on September 11, 2001, surprised most businesses throughout the world. As explained in the opening case, on page 63, this single set of events had substantial effects on the Canadian and U.S. economies.

The **industry environment** is the set of factors that directly influences a firm and its competitive actions and competitive responses: the threat of new entrants, the power of suppliers, the power of buyers, the threat of product substitutes, and the intensity of rivalry among competitors. In total, the interactions among these five factors determine an industry's profit potential. The challenge is to locate a position within an industry where a firm can favourably influence those factors or where it can successfully defend against their influence. The greater a firm's capacity to favourably influence its industry environment, the greater is the likelihood that the firm will earn above-average returns.

The way in which companies gather and interpret information about their competitors is called *competitor analysis*. Understanding the firm's competitor environment complements the insights provided by studying the general and industry environments.

Analysis of the general environment is focused on the future, analysis of the industry environment is focused on the factors and conditions influencing a firm's profitability within its industry, and analysis of competitors is focused on predicting the dynamics of competitors' actions, responses, and intentions. In combination, the results of the three analyses that the firm uses to understand its external environment influence the firm's strategic intent, strategic mission, and strategic actions. Although we discuss each analysis separately, performance improves when the firm integrates the insights provided by analyses of the general environment, the industry environment, and the competitor

The **industry environment** is the set of factors that directly influences a firm and its competitive actions and competitive responses: the threat of new entrants, the power of suppliers, the power of buyers, the threat of product substitutes, and the intensity of rivalry among competitors.

Table 3.1	The General Environment: Segments and Elements

Demographic Segment

Population size	Geographic distribution
Income distribution	Age structure
Ethnic mix	Immigration

Economic Segment

Inflation rates	Personal savings rates
Interest rates	Business savings rates
Trade deficits	Budget surpluses/deficits
Trade surpluses	Gross domestic product

Sociocultural Segment

Women in the workforce	Concerns about the environment
Workforce diversity	Shifts in work/career preferences
Attitudes about quality of work life	Shifts in preferences regarding product/services characteristics

Global Segment

Important political events	Newly industrialized countries
Critical global moments	Different cultural and institutional attributes

Technological Segment

Product innovations	New communication technologies
Process innovations	Focus of private and government-supported
Knowledge applications	R&D expenditures

Political/Legal Segment

Antitrust laws	Educational philosophies and policies
Taxation laws	Regulation/deregulation policies
Labour training laws	Philosophies regarding government economic
Deregulation philosophies	involvement/ownership

environment, and is illustrated by our discussion of the I/O model of above-average returns, which we discuss in the next section.

The I/O Model of Above-Average Returns

From the 1960s through the 1980s, the external environment was the primary determinant of strategies that firms pursued in order to be successful.[10] The industrial organization (I/O) model of above-average returns explains the dominant influence of the external environment on a firm's strategic actions. This model specifies that the industry in which a firm chooses to compete has a stronger influence on the firm's performance than the choices that managers make inside their organizations.[11] The firm's performance is believed to be determined primarily by a range of industry properties, including economies of scale, barriers to market entry, diversification, product differentiation, and the degree of concentration of firms in the industry.[12] These industry characteristics are examined in later in this chapter.

Grounded in economics, the I/O model has four underlying assumptions. First, the external environment is assumed to impose pressures and constraints that determine the strategies that can result in above-average returns. Second, most firms competing within a particular industry, or within a certain segment of an industry, are assumed to control similar strategically relevant resources and to pursue similar strategies in light of those resources. The I/O model's third assumption is that resources used to implement strategies are highly mobile across firms. Because of resource mobility, any resource differences that might develop between firms will be short lived. Fourth, organizational decision makers are assumed to be rational and committed to acting in the firm's best interests, as shown by their profit-maximizing behaviours.[13] The I/O model challenges firms to locate the most attractive industry in which to compete. Because most firms are assumed to have similar strategically relevant resources that are mobile across companies, competitiveness generally can be increased only when firms find the industry with the highest profit potential and learn how to use their resources to implement the strategy required by the industry's structural characteristics.

The five forces model of competition is an analytical tool used to help firms with this task. The model (see Figure 3.3, on page 82) encompasses many variables and tries to capture the complexity of competition. The five forces model suggests that an industry's profitability (i.e., its rate of return on invested capital relative to its cost of capital) is a function of interactions among five forces: suppliers, buyers, competitive rivalry among firms currently in the industry, product substitutes, and potential entrants to the industry.[14] Using this tool, a firm is challenged to understand an industry's profit potential and the strategy necessary to establish a defensible competitive position, given the industry's structure. Typically, the model suggests that firms can earn above-average returns by either manufacturing standardized products or producing standardized services at costs below those of competitors (a cost-leadership strategy, discussed in detail in Chapter 5), or by manufacturing differentiated products for which customers are willing to pay a price premium (a differentiation strategy, described in depth in Chapter 5).

As shown in Figure 3.2 on page 70, the I/O model suggests that above-average returns are earned when firms implement the strategy dictated by the characteristics of the general, industry, and competitor environments. Companies that develop or acquire the internal skills needed to implement strategies required by the external environment are likely to succeed, while those that do not are likely to fail. Hence, this model suggests that external characteristics rather than the firm's unique internal resources and capabilities primarily determine returns.

Research findings support the I/O model. They show that approximately 20 percent of a firm's profitability can be explained by the industry. In other words, 20 percent of a firm's profitability is determined by the industry or industries in which it chooses to operate. This research also showed, however, that 36 percent of the variance in profitability could be attributed to the firm's characteristics and actions.[15] The results of the research suggest that both the environment and the firm's characteristics play a role in determining the firm's specific level of profitability. Thus, there is likely a reciprocal relationship between the environment and the firm's strategy, thereby affecting the firm's performance.[16] As the research suggests, successful competition mandates that a firm build a unique set of resources and capabilities. This development should be achieved within the dynamics of the environment in which a firm operates.

A firm is viewed as a bundle of market activities and a bundle of resources. Market activities are understood through the application of the I/O model. The development and effective use of a firm's resources, capabilities, and competencies are understood through the application of the resource-based model (discussed in Chapter 4). As a result, executives must integrate the two models to develop the most effective strategy.

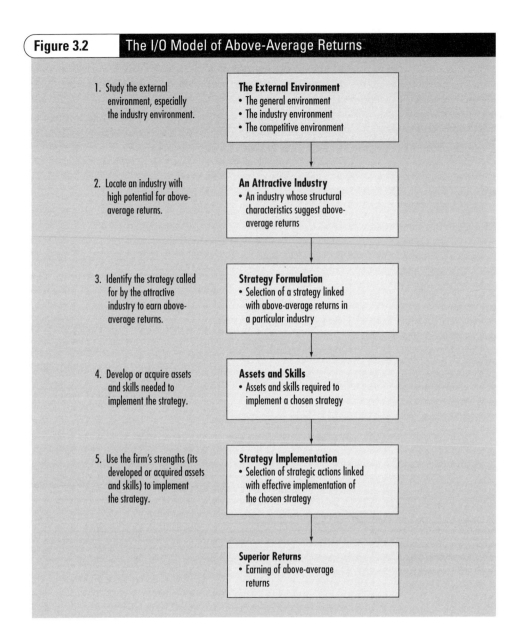

Figure 3.2 | The I/O Model of Above-Average Returns

1. Study the external environment, especially the industry environment.

The External Environment
- The general environment
- The industry environment
- The competitive environment

2. Locate an industry with high potential for above-average returns.

An Attractive Industry
- An industry whose structural characteristics suggest above-average returns

3. Identify the strategy called for by the attractive industry to earn above-average returns.

Strategy Formulation
- Selection of a strategy linked with above-average returns in a particular industry

4. Develop or acquire assets and skills needed to implement the strategy.

Assets and Skills
- Assets and skills required to implement a chosen strategy

5. Use the firm's strengths (its developed or acquired assets and skills) to implement the strategy.

Strategy Implementation
- Selection of strategic actions linked with effective implementation of the chosen strategy

Superior Returns
- Earning of above-average returns

External Environmental Analysis

Most firms face external environments that are highly turbulent, complex, and global—conditions that make interpreting them increasingly difficult.[17] To cope with what are often ambiguous and incomplete environmental data and to increase their understanding of the general environment, firms engage in a process called external environmental analysis. The continuous process includes four activities: scanning, monitoring, forecasting, and assessing (see Table 3.2). Those analyzing the external environment should understand that completing this analysis is a difficult, yet significant, activity.[18]

An important objective of studying the general environment is to identify opportunities and threats. An **opportunity** is a condition in the general environment that, if exploited, helps a company to achieve strategic competitiveness. The fact that 1 billion of the world's total population of 6 billion have cheap access to a telephone is a huge

An **opportunity** is a condition in the general environment that, if exploited, helps a company to achieve strategic competitiveness.

opportunity for global telecommunications companies.[19] And General Electric believes that "e-business represents a revolution that may be the greatest opportunity for growth that [the] Company has ever seen."[20]

A **threat** is a condition in the general environment that may hinder a company's efforts to achieve strategic competitiveness.[21] The once-revered firm Polaroid can attest to the seriousness of external threats. Polaroid was a leader in its industry and considered one of the top 50 firms in the United States, but filed for bankruptcy in 2001. When its competitors developed photographic equipment using digital technology, Polaroid was unprepared and never responded effectively. Mired in substantial debt, Polaroid was unable to reduce its costs to acceptable levels (and unable to repay its debt) and eventually had to declare bankruptcy.

Likewise, executives of Enron openly displayed contempt for regulators and consumer groups in its quest for fully deregulated energy markets. Jeffrey Skilling, former CEO of Enron stated, "We are on the side of angels. People want to have open, competitive markets." Unfortunately, Enron's shareholders and employees have been big losers in the meltdown when Enron filed for bankruptcy in 2001, the victim of the economy and reportedly questionable financing practices. Enron executives seemed to overlook the reporting of significant losses in the firm's energy trading business and were subject to U.S. Securities and Exchange Commission (SEC) and Congressional investigations in the United States.[22] As these examples indicate, opportunities suggest competitive possibilities, while threats are potential constraints.

Several sources can be used to analyze the general environment, including a wide variety of printed materials (such as trade publications, newspapers, business publications, and the results of academic research and public polls), trade shows, and suppliers, customers, and employees of public-sector organizations.[23] External network contacts can be particularly rich sources of information on the environment.[24] Much information can be obtained by people in the firm's boundary-spanning positions. Salespersons, purchasing managers, public relations directors, and customer service representatives, each of whom interacts with external constituents, are examples of individuals in boundary-spanning positions.[25]

> A **threat** is a condition in the general environment that may hinder a company's efforts to achieve strategic competitiveness.

Scanning

Scanning entails the study of all segments in the general environment. Through scanning, firms identify early signals of potential changes in the general environment and detect changes that are already under way.[26] When scanning, the firm often deals with ambiguous, incomplete, or unconnected data and information. Environmental scanning is critically important for firms competing in highly volatile environments.[27] In addition, scanning activities must be aligned with the organizational context; a scanning system designed for a volatile environment is inappropriate for a firm in a stable environment.[28]

Table 3.2	Components of the External Environmental Analysis
Scanning	Identifying early signals of environmental changes and trends
Monitoring	Detecting new developments through ongoing observations of environmental changes and trends
Forecasting	Developing projections of anticipated outcomes based on monitored changes and trends
Assessing	Determining the timing and importance of environmental changes and trends for firms' strategies and their management

Some analysts expect the pressure brought to bear by the early retirement trend on countries, such as the United States, France, Germany, and Japan, to be quite significant and challenging. Governments in these countries appear to be offering state-funded pensions to their future elderly populations, but the costs of those pensions cannot be met with the present taxes and social security contribution rates.[29] Firms selling financial planning services and options should analyze this trend to determine if it represents an opportunity for them to help governments find ways to meet their responsibilities. Interestingly, in Canada, the Prime Minister, the Right Honourable Paul Martin, said in a recent interview that he wanted to work as Prime Minister for 10 years. That would make him 75 when he steps down. He also suggested that we need to reconsider mandatory retirement at age 65.[30] Six of Canada's provinces (British Columbia, New Brunswick, Newfoundland and Labrador, Nova Scotia, Ontario, and Saskatchewan) have mandatory retirement at age 65. In the other four provinces (Alberta, Manitoba, Prince Edward Island, and Quebec) and Canada's three territories (Northwest Territories, Nunavut, and Yukon), mandatory retirement is considered discriminatory.[31]

As illustrated in the previous paragraph, the Internet provides multiple opportunities for scanning. Another example is Amazon.com, which records significant information about individuals visiting its website, particularly if a purchase is made. Amazon then welcomes them by name when they visit the website again. The firm even sends messages about specials and new products similar to those purchased in previous visits. Additionally, many websites and advertisers on the Internet obtain information from those who visit their sites using files called cookies. These files are saved to the visitors' hard drives, allowing customers to connect more quickly to the website, but also allowing the firm to solicit a variety of information. Because cookies are often placed without customers' knowledge, their use can be a questionable practice. A new privacy standard, Platform for Privacy Preferences, has been developed that provides more control over these digital messengers and allows users to block the cookies from their hard drives if desired.[32]

Monitoring

When *monitoring*, analysts observe environmental changes to determine whether an important trend is emerging from among those identified by scanning.[33] Critical to successful monitoring is the firm's ability to detect meaning in different environmental events and trends. For example, the size of the middle class of African-Americans continues to grow in the United States. With increasing wealth, this group of citizens is beginning to more aggressively pursue investment options. In Canada, immigration is expected to have a major impact, especially as Canada gives special consideration to the immigration of skilled workers and businesspersons. In the last decade, the United Nations Human Development Index ranked Canada, five times, as the best country in the world to live.[34] Companies in the financial planning sector could monitor these changes in the economic segment to determine the degree to which a competitively important trend and a business opportunity are emerging. By monitoring trends, firms can be prepared to introduce new goods and services at the appropriate time to take advantage of the opportunities these trends provide.

Effective monitoring requires the firm to identify significant stakeholders. Because the importance of different stakeholders can vary over a firm's life cycle, careful attention must be given to the firm's needs and its stakeholder groups over time. Scanning and monitoring are particularly important when a firm competes in an industry with high technological uncertainty. Scanning and monitoring not only provide the firm with information, they also serve as a means of importing new knowledge about markets and how to successfully commercialize new technologies that the firm has developed.[35]

Forecasting

Scanning and monitoring are concerned with events and trends in the general environment at a point in time. When *forecasting*, analysts develop feasible projections of what might happen, and how quickly, as a result of the changes and trends detected through scanning and monitoring.[36] For example, analysts might forecast the time that will be required for a new technology to reach the marketplace, the length of time before different corporate training procedures are required to deal with anticipated changes in the composition of the workforce, or how much time will elapse before changes in governmental taxation policies affect consumers' purchasing patterns.

Assessing

The objective of assessing is to determine the timing and significance of the effects of environmental changes and trends on the strategic management of the firm.[37] Through scanning, monitoring, and forecasting, analysts are able to understand the general environment. Going a step further, the intent of assessment is to specify the implications of that understanding for the organization. Without assessment, the firm is left with data that may be interesting but are of unknown competitive relevance.

For example, Ford, General Motors, and DaimlerChrysler sold an increased number of vehicles in the U.S. automobile market in 2001. However, in past years, all three firms lost market share in vehicles to competitors such as Honda, Toyota, Volkswagen, Audi, and BMW. The primary reason for the U.S. firms' increase in sales levels, in 2001, was their offers to sell the vehicles at 0 percent interest on loans. Without these generous loans, high-volume sales are unlikely to persist. Thus, firms must assess the reasons for sales, relative to their competitors, to be able to accurately forecast future sales.

Segments of the General Environment

The general environment is composed of segments (and their individual elements) that are external to the firm (see Table 3.1, on page 68). Although the degree of impact varies, these environmental segments affect each industry and its firms. The challenge to the firm is to scan, monitor, forecast, and assess those elements in each segment that are of the greatest importance. Resulting from these efforts should be a recognition of environmental changes, trends, opportunities, and threats. Opportunities are then matched with a firm's core competencies (the matching process is discussed further in Chapter 4).

The Demographic Segment

The **demographic segment** is concerned with a population's size, age structure, geographic distribution, ethnic mix, and income distribution.[38] Demographic segments are analyzed on a global basis because of their potential effects across countries' borders and because many firms compete in global markets.

> The **demographic segment** is concerned with a population's size, age structure, geographic distribution, ethnic mix, and income distribution.

Population Size

Before the end of 1999, the world's population grew to 6 billion, from 5 billion in 1987. Combined, China and India accounted for one-third of the 6 billion. Experts speculate that the population might stabilize at 10 billion after 2200, if the deceleration in the rate of increase in the world's head count continues. By 2050, India (with a projected population of more than 1.5 billion) and China (with a projected population of almost 1.5 billion people) are expected to be the most populous countries. Canada, by comparison, has 31.1 million people, even though, at 9.98 million km^2, it is the world's second largest country, in land mass. Canada's population grew from 28.8 million in

1996 to 31 million in 2001 with net immigration accounting for approximately 780,000 new members of Canada's population. Its population is expected to reach only 32.2 million by 2026.[39]

Observing demographic changes in populations highlights the importance of this environmental segment. For example, some advanced nations have a negative population growth, after discounting the effects of immigration. In some countries, including the United States and several European nations, couples are averaging fewer than two children. This birthrate will produce a loss of population over time (even with the population living longer on average). However, some forecasters believe that a baby boom will occur in the United States during the first 12 years of the 21st century and that by 2012, the annual number of births could exceed 4.3 million. Such a birthrate in the United States would equal the all-time high that was set in 1957. Canada's population only grew 609,000 (by number of births minus number of deaths) from 1996 to 2001 (less than the net increase of 780,000 from immigration versus emigration mentioned in the previous paragraph). This figure was down from 987,000 between 1986 and 1991, and down from 912,000 between 1991 and 1996. These projections suggest major 21st-century challenges and business opportunities for firms in Europe, the United States, and Canada.[40]

Age Structure

In some countries, the population's average age is increasing. In the United States, for example, the percentage of the population aged 65 and older increased less in the 1990s than the population younger than 65 years of age. However, in the period 2010 to 2020, the population aged 65 and older is projected to grow by 35.3 percent. In Canada, with a lower death rate (7.2 per 1000 versus 8.6 per 1000 for the U.S.), the proportion of the population aged 65 and older is expected to increase 97 percent, from 12.7 percent in 2001 to 21.4 percent in 2026.[41] Contributing to this growth are increasing life expectancies in both countries. This trend may suggest numerous opportunities for firms to develop goods and services that meet the needs of an increasingly older population. For example, GlaxoSmithKline has created a program for low-income elderly people without prescription drug coverage. The program provides drugs to these individuals at a 25 percent reduction in price. In so doing, the firm is able to increase its sales and provide an important service to a population who might not be able to afford the drugs otherwise.[42]

It has been projected that up to one-half of the females and one-third of the males born at the end of the 1990s in developed countries could live to be 100 years old, with some of them possibly living to be 200 or more. Also, the odds that a U.S. baby boomer (a person born between the years 1946 and 1964) will reach age 90 are now one in nine. If these life spans become a reality, a host of interesting business opportunities and societal issues will emerge. For example, the effect on individuals' pension plans will be significant and will create potential opportunities for financial institutions, as well as possible threats to government-sponsored retirement and health plans.[43]

Geographic Distribution

For decades, the U.S. population has been shifting from the north and east to the west and south. Similarly, the trend of relocating from metropolitan to non-metropolitan areas continues and may well accelerate after the terrorist attacks in New York City and Washington, D.C. These trends are changing local and state governments' tax bases. In turn, business firms' decisions regarding location are influenced by the degree of support that different taxing agencies offer. In Canada, we see a couple of different effects. In 2001, the percentage of the population living in rural areas and small towns was 20.3 percent, down from 21.5 percent in 1996. On the other hand, there was growth in Canada's extended Golden Horseshoe, the area consisting of the urban centres of Oshawa, Toronto,

Hamilton, the St. Catharines–Niagara region, Kitchener–Waterloo, Guelph, and Barrie. This area had an increase of 9.2 percent from 1996 to 2001, accounting for 22 percent of Canada's population and 59 percent of Ontario's population, in 2001.

Another outcome is the doughnut effect. In several census metropolitan areas in Canada, the areas around core municipalities are growing faster than the cores themselves. The larger the difference, the more pronounced the doughnut effect is considered to be. For example, the most prominent doughnut effect noted in the 2001 Canadian Census data, was around the core municipality of Saskatoon. The core municipality's population increased 1.6 percent, while the population of the municipalities around this core increased 14.6 percent. In the 27 census metropolitan areas in Canada, the growth in core municipalities was 4.3 percent from 1996 to 2001, while growth in the surrounding municipalities was around 8.5 percent.[44]

The geographic distribution of populations throughout the world is also affected by the capabilities resulting from advances in communications technology. Through computer technologies, for example, people can remain in their homes, communicating with others in remote locations to complete their work.

Ethnic Mix

The ethnic mix of countries' populations continues to change. Within Canada, the ethnicity of provinces and their cities varies significantly. For firms, the challenge is to be sensitive to these changes. Through careful study, companies can develop and market products that satisfy the unique needs of different ethnic groups. Changes in the ethnic mix also affect a workforce's composition.

Workforce diversity is a sociocultural issue. Effective management of a culturally diverse workforce can produce a competitive advantage. For example, heterogeneous work teams have been shown to produce more effective strategic analyses, more creativity and innovation, and higher quality decisions than homogeneous work teams. However, evidence also suggests that to achieve these outcomes, diverse work teams are difficult to manage.[45]

Income Distribution

Understanding how income is distributed within and across populations informs firms of different groups' purchasing power and their discretionary income. Studies of income distributions suggest that, although living standards have improved over time, variations exist within and between nations.[46] Of interest to firms are the average incomes of households and individuals. For instance, the increase in dual-career couples has had a notable effect on average incomes. Although real income has been declining in general, the income of dual-career couples has increased. These figures yield strategically relevant information for firms.

The Economic Segment

The health of a nation's economy affects individual firms and industries. Because of this correlation, companies study the economic environment to identify changes, trends, and their strategic implications.

The **economic environment** refers to the nature and direction of the economy in which a firm competes or may compete.[47] Because nations are interconnected as a result of the global economy, firms must scan, monitor, forecast, and assess the health of economies outside their host nation. For example, many nations throughout the world are affected by the U.S. economy, and this impact is especially evident in Canada. In 2002, 83.8 percent of Canada's exports were destined for the U.S., from where Canada received 71.5 percent of its imported goods.

The **economic environment** refers to the nature and direction of the economy in which a firm competes or may compete.

The U.S. economy declined into a recession in 2001, which extended into 2002, despite efforts to revive the economy by the U.S. government. The economy looked to be on the mend by mid-2002. For Canada, the impact was felt most on its exports. From 1999 to 2000, Canada's exports to the United States grew 16.2 percent. However, from 2000 to 2001, they fell 2 percent. They fell another 2 percent from 2001 to 2002.[48]

A proposal that could affect Canada is one supported by DaimlerChrysler's CEO Jürgen E. Schrempp. Schrempp, a strong proponent of completing a transatlantic integration between Europe and North America, supports largely unrestricted trade and believes that economic integration between Europe and North America is logical in that "Europe and the United States each account for close to 20 percent of the other's trade in goods while services account for more than 38 percent of bilateral trade." Principles developed by the Transatlantic Business Dialogue (a group of businesspersons and politicians) could support an integration effort. The principles include the removal of all trade barriers and differing regulatory controls and the acceptance of a product in all parts of the transatlantic marketplace once it has been approved.[49] Creating truly borderless commerce that permits free trade among nations is a significant challenge, however, because of differing regulations for trade between separate countries.

While bilateral trade can enrich the economies of the countries involved, it also makes each country more vulnerable to negative events. For example, the September 11, 2001 terrorist attacks in the United States have had more than a $100 billion negative effect on the U.S. economy. As a result, the European Union (E.U.) also suffered negative economic effects because of the reduction in bilateral trade between the U.S. and the E.U.[50]

As our discussion of the economic segment suggests, economic issues are intertwined closely with the realities of the external environment's political/legal segment. We will discuss the political/legal segment next.

The Political/Legal Segment

The **political/legal segment** is the arena in which organizations and interest groups compete for attention, resources, and a voice of overseeing the body of laws and regulations guiding the interactions among nations.

The **political/legal segment** is the arena in which organizations and interest groups compete for attention, resources, and a voice of overseeing the body of laws and regulations guiding the interactions among nations.[51] Essentially, this segment represents how organizations try to influence government and how governments influence them. Constantly changing, the segment influences the nature of competition (see Table 3.1, on page 68).

Firms must carefully analyze a new political administration's business-related policies and philosophies. Antitrust laws, taxation laws, industries chosen for deregulation, labour training laws, and the degree of commitment to educational institutions are areas in which an administration's policies can affect the operations and profitability of industries and individual firms. It is expected that Paul Martin's Liberal government will be very different from Jean Chrétien's Liberal government. Often, firms develop a political strategy to influence governmental policies and actions that might affect them. The effects of global governmental policies on a firm's competitive position increase the importance of forming an effective political strategy.[52]

Today, business firms across the globe confront an interesting array of political/legal questions and issues. For example, the debate continues over trade policies. Some believe that a nation should erect trade barriers to protect products manufactured by its companies. Others argue that free trade across nations serves the best interests of individual countries and their citizens. The International Monetary Fund (IMF) classifies trade barriers as restrictive when tariffs total at least 25 percent of a product's price. At the other extreme, the IMF stipulates that a nation has open trade when its tariffs are between 0 percent and 9 percent. To foster trade, New Zealand initially cut its tariffs from 16 percent to 8.5 percent and then to 3 percent in 2000. Colombia reduced its tariffs to less than 12 percent. The IMF classifies this percentage as "relatively open."[53] While controversial, a number of countries (including Canada, the United States, nations in the European Union, Japan, Australia, Chile, Singapore, and Mexico) are working together to reduce or eventually eliminate trade barriers.

How government agencies can affect business is discussed in the next Strategic Focus box, "Government Can Have a Large Effect on Businesses: Canada's Softwood Industry Dispute with the United States Government," which explains some of the effects that governments have on how business is conducted. The regulations related to softwood lumber show the power of government entities and suggest how important it is for firms to have a political strategy.

The Sociocultural Segment

The **sociocultural segment** is concerned with a society's attitudes and cultural values. Because attitudes and values form the cornerstone of a society, they often drive demographic, economic, political/legal, and technological conditions and changes. Thus, companies must understand the implications of a society's attitudes and its cultural values to offer products that meet consumers' needs.

> The **sociocultural segment** is concerned with a society's attitudes and cultural values.

A significant trend in many countries is wider workforce diversity. The growing gender, ethnic, and cultural diversities in the workforce create challenges and opportunities,[54] such as combining the best of both men's and women's traditional leadership styles for a firm's benefit and identifying ways to facilitate all employees' contributions to their firms. Some companies provide training to nurture women's and ethnic minorities' leadership potential. Changes in organizational structure and management practices often are required to eliminate subtle barriers that may exist. Learning to manage diversity in the domestic workforce can increase a firm's effectiveness in managing a globally diverse workforce, as the firm acquires a greater international presence.

Another manifestation of changing attitudes toward work is the continuing growth of contingency workers (part-time, temporary, and contract employees) throughout the global economy. This trend is significant in several parts of the world, including Canada, Japan, Latin America, Western Europe, and the United States. The fastest growing group of contingency workers is in the technical and professional area. Contributing to this growth are corporate restructurings and a breakdown of lifetime employment practices. Because of tight labour markets for technical and professional workers, the agencies providing these contingency workers are offering multiple inducements to those they hire.

Another major sociocultural trend is the continued growth of suburban communities in Canada and abroad. The increasing number of people living in the suburbs has a number of effects. For example, because of the resulting often-longer commute times to urban businesses, there is pressure for better transportation systems and superhighway systems (e.g., outer beltways to serve the suburban communities such as the Express Toll Route [ETR 407] from Hamilton, Ontario, to Ajax, Ontario, that also spans a 108 km section north of downtown Toronto). On the other hand, some businesses are locating in the suburbs closer to their employees. Suburban growth also has an effect on the number of electronic telecommuters, which is expected to increase rapidly in the 21st century. This work-style option is feasible because of changes in the technological segment, including the Internet's rapid growth and evolution.[55]

The Technological Segment

Pervasive and diversified in scope, technological changes affect many aspects of societies. These effects occur primarily through new products, processes, and materials. The **technological segment** includes the institutions and activities involved with creating new knowledge and translating that knowledge into new outputs, products, processes, and materials.

> The **technological segment** includes the institutions and activities involved with creating new knowledge and translating that knowledge into new outputs, products, processes, and materials.

Government Can Have a Large Effect on Businesses: Canada's Softwood Industry Dispute with the United States Government

Governmental entities can have major effects on businesses. Essentially, a government establishes the rules by which business is conducted within the country's boundaries or the geographic region being governed. Federal government regulations generally have the most profound effects on business.

The nature of government impact on business activity varies, depending on the level of government and the purpose of involvement. Typically, government might be involved with regulating industry; additionally one level of government may become instrumental to local business by facilitating government interventions from another governmental level or by supporting avenues and opportunities for industry through the opening of the community to international or other external economies, such as hosting athletic, trade, and cultural expositions.

The size and impact of government intervention will also vary. At a lower level, but no less significant to the community served, is the impact of municipal interventions in creating infrastructure with long-term implications for local business growth. At a significant international level is the case of Canada and the United States as trading partners.

At trading levels generating almost $500 billion in two-way trade every year, the Canada–United States trade relationship is the largest worldwide. Both countries enjoy the position of being the other's single largest recipient of exports and, conversely, import transactions. Government action on either side that challenges or supports the relationship will have far-reaching effects on industries across both nations.

For example, the future of the softwood lumber product, which is one of Canada's largest exports to the United States, contributing $9.4 billion (US$6.1 billion) in export earnings in 2001 alone, is currently undergoing severe pressure. Both Canadian and U.S. citizens benefit from the softwood lumber trade. In Canada, approximately 80,000 Canadians and 300 communities depend on the forestry sector; while in the United States, lumber producers are unable to meet product demand, so its market is supported by imports from Canada (currently about one-third of U.S. total consumption of the product). Additionally, U.S. housing and wood-related industries employ in excess of 7 million American workers.

At the heart of the softwood lumber issue is the legality of a 27 percent tariff charged on Canadian lumber entering the U.S. The history of Canada's softwood disputes with the U.S. is a long one, dating back as far as the 1820s. In 2003, the most recent stage of a 20-year dispute was observed by the world as international organizations, such as the North American Free Trade Agreement and the World Trade Organization (NAFTA and WTO, respectively) were appealed to, in order to arbitrate differences on the issue. Several government institutions on both sides of the issue, such as the Canadian Department of Foreign Affairs and International Trade, Canadian provincial governments, the U.S. International Trade Commission, and the U.S. Department of Commerce, have become embroiled in the debate.

With much to be lost on both sides, individuals and organizations in Canada and the U.S. have created avenues for the dissemination of information to create awareness within the citizenry of both countries. The actions of both governments are under close scrutiny on an issue that will have a large effect on businesses on both sides of the border.

SOURCES: Department of Foreign Affairs and International Trade, 2003, Softwood lumber: Canada pleased with NAFTA ruling on threat of injury, *Department of Foreign Affairs and International Trade website*, http://webapps.dfait-maeci.gc.ca/minpub/Publication.asp?publication_id=380317&Language=E (news release), September 5; Department of Foreign Affairs and International Trade, 2004, Softwood lumber: Canada's legal challenges, *Department of Foreign Affairs and International Trade website*, http://www.dfait-maeci.gc.ca/eicb/softwood/legal_action-en.asp, accessed January 20, 2004; U.S./Canada Partnership for Growth, 2003, Survey shows Americans lack knowledge about importance of U.S. trading relationship with its next door neighbour, *U.S. / Canada Partnership for Growth website*, http://www.partnershipforgrowth.org/Pollfeb21.pdf (press release), February 21.

Given the rapid pace of technological change, it is vital for firms to thoroughly study the technological segment. The importance of these efforts is suggested by the finding that early adopters of new technology often achieve higher market shares and earn higher returns. Thus, executives must verify that their firm is continuously scanning the external environment to identify potential substitutes for technologies that are in current use, as well as to spot newly emerging technologies from which their firms could derive competitive advantage.[56]

Numerous surveys suggest that executives are aware of the potential of a major technological development—the Internet. A survey completed by Booz Allen Hamilton in partnership with the *Economist* revealed that (1) 92 percent of executives who participated in the survey believed that the Internet would continue to reshape their companies' markets, (2) 61 percent thought that effective use of the Internet would facilitate efforts to achieve their firms' strategic goals, and (3) 30 percent noted that their competitive strategies had already been altered because of the Internet's influence.[57]

The value of the Internet is shown in its use by Staples Inc., the office supply superstores. Staples invested $250 million to create Staples.com to continue its market share leadership in the industry. The firm's online sales reached approximately $1 billion by 2001, up from $99 million in 1999, accounting for 10 percent of the company's total annual sales. Thomas Steinberg, founder and CEO of Staples, forecasted that sales on the Internet would reach $50 billion annually and represent 25 percent of the office supply industry's total sales in the next few years.[58]

Among its other valuable uses, the Internet is an excellent source of data and information for a firm to use to understand its external environment. Access to experts on topics from chemical engineering to semiconductor manufacturing, to Statistics Canada, to the United States Library of Congress, and even to satellite photographs is available through the Internet. Other information available through this technology includes Security and Exchange Commission (SEC) filings, information on firms publicly traded on the Toronto Stock Exchange, information from the United States Bureau of the Census, new patent filings, and stock market updates.

Another use of Internet technology is conducting business transactions between companies, as well as between a company and its customers. According to Dell Computer Corporation's CEO Michael Dell, the Internet also has great potential as a business-organization system. Dell uses this technology to reduce its paperwork flow, to more efficiently schedule its payments, and to coordinate its inventories. Dell accomplishes these tasks by linking personal computers with network servers, which the firm's CEO believes have the potential to revolutionize business processes "in a way that blurs traditional boundaries between supplier and manufacturer, and manufacturer and customer. This will eliminate paper-based functions, flatten organization hierarchies, and shrink time and distance to a degree not possible before."[59] Thus, a competitive advantage may accrue to the company that derives full value from the Internet, in terms of both e-commerce activities and transactions taken to process the firm's workflow.

While the Internet was a significant technological advance providing substantial power to companies utilizing its potential, wireless communication technology is predicted to be the next critical technological opportunity. By 2003, handheld devices and other wireless communications equipment were being used to access a variety of network-based services. The use of handheld computers with wireless network connectivity, web-enabled mobile phone handsets, and other emerging platforms (i.e., consumer Internet access devices) is expected to increase substantially, soon becoming the dominant form of communication and commerce.[60]

Clearly, the Internet and wireless forms of communications are important technological developments for many reasons. One reason for their importance, however, is that they facilitate the diffusion of other technology and knowledge critical for achieving and maintaining a competitive advantage.[61] Technological knowledge is particularly important. Certainly, on a global scale, the technological opportunities and threats in the general environment have an effect on whether firms obtain new technology from external sources (such as licensing and acquisition) or develop it internally.

The Global Segment

The **global segment** includes relevant new global markets, existing markets that are changing, important international political events, and critical cultural and institutional characteristics of global markets.[62] Globalization of business markets creates both opportunities and challenges for firms. For example, firms can identify and enter valuable new global markets. Many global markets (such as those in some South American nations and in South Korea and Taiwan) are becoming borderless and integrated.[63] In addition to contemplating opportunities, firms should recognize potential threats in these markets as well. For instance, companies with home bases in Europe and North America may be subject to terrorist threats in certain parts of the world (such as Middle Eastern regions and parts of Asia).

China presents many opportunities and some threats for international firms, and its recent admission to the World Trade Organization (WTO) is expected to create even greater opportunities for firms in all countries. A Geneva-based organization, the WTO establishes rules for global trade. China's membership in this organization suggests the possibility of increasing and less restricted participation by this country in the global economy.[64] In return for gaining entry to the WTO, China agreed to reduce trade barriers in multiple industries, including telecommunications, banking, automobiles, movies, and professional services (for example, the services of lawyers, physicians, and accountants). These reduced barriers are likely part of the reason that Star TV's Rupert Murdoch realized a major goal of entering the Chinese market. In 2001, Star TV, News Corporation, and Chinese television authorities announced an agreement to launch a 24-hour entertainment channel for the wealthy Chinese cities of Guangzhou and Zhaoqing. The purpose of the channel is to establish a relationship and a track record, with the hope of expanding it to other cities and regions of China, a huge potential market.[65]

Moving into international markets extends a firm's reach and potential. Toyota receives almost 50 percent of its total sales revenue from outside Japan, its home country. More than 60 percent of McDonald's sales revenues and almost 98 percent of Nokia's sales revenues are from outside their home countries. Because the opportunity is coupled with uncertainty, some view entering new international markets to be entrepreneurial.[66] Firms can increase the opportunity to sell innovations by entering international markets. The larger total market increases the probability that the firm will earn a return on its innovations. Certainly, firms entering new markets can diffuse new knowledge they have created and learn from the new markets as well.[67]

Firms should recognize the different sociocultural and institutional attributes of global markets. Companies competing in South Korea, for example, must understand the societal values placed on hierarchical order, formality, and self-control, as well as on duty rather than rights. Furthermore, the Korean ideology emphasizes communitarianism, a characteristic of many Asian countries. Korea's approach differs from those of Japan and China, however, in that it focuses on Inhwa, or harmony. Inhwa is based on a respect of hierarchical relationships and obedience to authority. Alternatively, the approach in China stresses Guanxi-personal relationships or good connections, while in Japan, the focus is on Wa, or group harmony and social cohesion. The institutional context of Korea suggests a major emphasis on centralized planning by the government. Indeed, the emphasis by many South Korean firms on growth is the result of a government policy to promote economic development.[68]

The **global segment** includes relevant new global markets, existing markets that are changing, important international political events, and critical cultural and institutional characteristics of global markets.

Firms based in other countries that compete in these markets can learn from their host countries. For example, the cultural characteristics above suggest the value of relationships. In particular, Guanxi communicates social capital's importance when doing business in China, a factor that is important for success in most markets around the world.[69]

Global markets offer firms more opportunities to obtain the resources needed for success. For example, the Kuwait Investment Authority is the second largest shareholder of DaimlerChrysler. Additionally, Global Crossing sought financial assistance from potential investors in Europe and Asia, but it was to no avail, as Global Crossing, citing overcapacity in the telecommunications network market as the primary cause of its problems, filed for bankruptcy in 2001.[70] Alternatively, globalization can be threatening. In particular, companies in emerging market countries may be vulnerable to larger, more resource-rich, and more effective competitors from developed markets.

Additionally, there are risks in global markets. A few years ago, Argentina's market was full of promise, but in 2001, Argentina experienced a financial crisis that placed it on the brink of bankruptcy.[71] Thus, the global segment of the general environment is quite important for most firms. As a result, it is necessary to have a top management team with the experience, knowledge, and sensitivity that are necessary to effectively analyze this segment of the environment.[72]

A key objective of analyzing the general environment is identifying anticipated changes and trends among external elements. With a focus on the future, the analysis of the general environment allows firms to identify opportunities and threats. Also critical to a firm's future operations is an understanding of its industry environment and its competitors; these issues are considered next.

Industry Environment Analysis

An **industry** is a group of firms producing products that are strategically equivalent or close substitutes. In the course of competition, these firms influence one another. Typically, industries include a rich mix of competitive strategies that companies use in pursuing strategic competitiveness and above-average returns. In part, these strategies are chosen because of the influence of an industry's characteristics.[73] Some believed that technology-based industries, in which e-commerce is a dominant means of competing, differ from their more traditional predecessors and that free exchange of information improved the competitiveness of the industries. However, while there were features of the e-commerce and information technology industries that differed from more traditional industries, the economic recession of 2001 and early 2002 showed the vulnerability of these industries.

Compared to the general environment, the industry environment has a more direct effect on the firm's strategic competitiveness and above-average returns, as exemplified in the Strategic Focus box, "Firms with Different Experiences in Economic Recession," on page 83. The intensity of industry competition and an industry's profit potential (as measured by the long-run return on invested capital) are a function of five forces of competition: the threats posed by new entrants, the power of suppliers, the power of buyers, product substitutes, and the intensity of rivalry among competitors (see Figure 3.3 on page 82).

The five forces model of competition expands the arena for competitive analysis. Historically, when studying the competitive environment, firms concentrated on companies with which they competed directly. However, firms must search more broadly to identify current and potential competitors by identifying potential customers as well as the firms serving them. Competing for the same customers and thus being influenced by how customers value location and firm capabilities in their decisions is referred to as the

An **industry** is a group of firms producing products that are strategically equivalent or close substitutes.

Figure 3.3 | The Five Forces of Competition Model

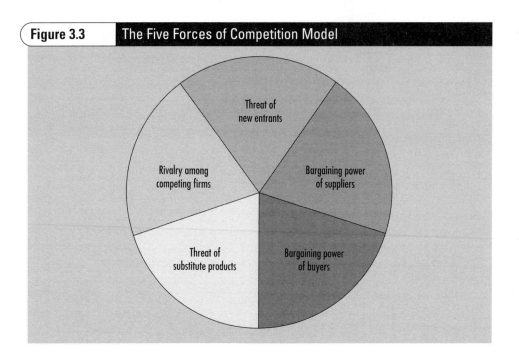

market microstructure. Understanding this area is particularly important, because in recent years, industry boundaries have become blurred. For example, in the electrical utilities industry, cogenerators (firms that also produce power) are competing with regional utility companies. Moreover, telecommunications companies now compete with broadcasters, software manufacturers provide personal financial services, airlines sell mutual funds, and automakers sell insurance and provide financing. In addition to focusing on customers rather than specific industry boundaries to define markets, geographic boundaries are also relevant. Research suggests that different geographic markets for the same product can have considerably different competitive conditions.[74]

The five forces model recognizes that suppliers can become a firm's competitors (by integrating forward), as can buyers (by integrating backward). Several firms have integrated forward in the pharmaceutical industry by acquiring distributors or wholesalers. In addition, firms choosing to enter a new market and those manufacturing products that are adequate substitutes for existing products can become competitors of a company.

Threat of New Entrants

Evidence suggests that companies often find it difficult to identify new competitors.[75] Knowledge about the new entrants in an industry is important because these new competitors can threaten the market share of existing competitors. One reason new entrants pose such a threat is that they bring additional production capacity. Unless the demand for a good or service is increasing, additional capacity holds consumers' costs down, resulting in less revenue and lower returns for competing firms. Often, new entrants have a keen interest in gaining a large market share. As a result, new competitors may force existing firms to be more effective and efficient and to learn how to compete on new dimensions (for example, using an Internet-based distribution channel).

The likelihood that firms will enter an industry is a function of two factors: barriers to entry and the retaliation expected from current industry participants. Entry barriers make it difficult for new firms to enter an industry and often place them at a competitive disadvantage, even when they are able to enter. As such, high entry barriers increase the returns for existing firms in the industry.[76]

Firms with Different Experiences in Economic Recession

In times of economic recession (typically defined as an overall slowing of economic activity; more specifically, a decline in GDP for two or more quarters in succession), firms generally experience heightened challenges to their successful business operations. The outlook on the Canadian economy after the 2001 terrorist attacks on the World Trade Centre was decidedly bleak. Analysts, because of the significant trade relationship between the two countries, projected an almost unitary response (i.e., a 1 percent decline in U.S. real GDP leading to an approximate 1 percent decline in export volumes) in Canada to the anticipated negative growth in the United States economy.

Understandably, the airline industry was severely affected by the attacks. Amidst reports on cancelled conventions, increased fear of flying, cancelled flights, and burgeoning insurance rates, the airline industry moved to layoff thousands of workers and to re-evaluate the viability of routes.

Despite ominous headlines and the realities being experienced by many in the air transport sector, a small airline company started back in 1996, with a well-researched business plan and the support of local businesses—WestJet—defied the odds. Using the Southwest Airlines low-cost model, WestJet began operations with 3 aircraft and 220 employees offering service to five destinations in Western Canada. After experiencing success with its initial public offering in July 1999, WestJet went on to expand operations by adding three destinations in Eastern Canada in the same year. It was recognized as the most successful low-cost carrier in Canadian history and produced performance figures that earned it recognition as the second most profitable airline in North America, second only to Southwest Airlines, whose example it modelled.

In 2001, just five years after its first revenue flight, WestJet ended the year with a fleet of 27 aircraft and collected $478 million in revenue, which produced a net income of $37 million. This positive showing is in stark contrast to other airlines, such as Canada 3000, which failed in November 2001, United Airlines and US Airways, which both shelved their low-fare operations, and Delta, which significantly scaled back its own low-fare subsidiary. Air Canada's response to the industry was to launch Tango, in October 2001, and then Zip in September 2002—both airline-within-an-airline operations designed to respond to the demand for no-frills/low-fare travel within the domestic market. It did not help, as by April of 2003, Air Canada had filed for protection under the Companies' Creditors Arrangement Act (CCAA).

Of note, in both 2001 and 2002, at a time when many airlines were grappling with significant reductions in capacity in order to deal with the projected decline in traffic, WestJet added two new destinations to its services, a trend that continued in 2003. WestJet's eighth year of operations was celebrated with first quarter 2004 results indicating 29 consecutive quarters of profitability.

The information technology (IT) industry in Canada and the United States has suffered with the economic recession. While many companies in the IT industry have ceased to operate and others have filed for bankruptcy with hopes of surviving, the IT industry is consolidating, and many consider it has a bright future. Oracle's CEO, Larry Ellison, argues that the industry is maturing, but others disagree. Former stars Cisco and Sun Microsystems have retreated but are preparing for improved markets. General Electric continued to spend heavily on its IT infrastructure when its competitors were severely reducing their IT spending. GE's intent was to be ahead of its competition as the economy improved. In particular, firms investing in wireless communications technology may be the future winners. For example, 80 percent of the cell phones sold in 2001 contained Texas Instruments' DSP or analogue chip.

SOURCES: Conference Board of Canada, 2001, *Implications of the Terrorist Attack for the Canadian Economy, Special Report*, September; WestJet, 2003, WestJet renewal annual information form 2002, *WestJet website*, www.westjet.com, accessed December 29, 2003; WestJet, 2004, *WestJet website*, http://www.westjet.com/pdffile/investorFactSheet.pdf (fact sheet), accessed June 26, 2004; R. Waters, 2001, Oracle chief dispels fantasy of young IT sector, *Financial Times*, http://www.ft.com, accessed December 14, 2003; S. Lohr, 2001, After the fall, a tech star stays scrappy, *New York Times*, http://www.nytimes.com, accessed September 30, 2003; E. Williams, 2001, Mixed signals, *Forbes*, May 28, 80–89; D. Lyons, 2001, Lion in winter, *Forbes*, April 30, 68–70.

Barriers to Entry

Existing competitors try to develop barriers to entry. In contrast, potential entrants seek markets in which the entry barriers are relatively insignificant. The absence of entry barriers increases the probability that a new entrant can operate profitably. There are several kinds of potentially significant entry barriers.

Economies of Scale. Economies of scale are "the marginal improvements in efficiency that a firm experiences as it incrementally increases its size."[77] Therefore, as the quantity of goods produced during a given period increases, the cost of manufacturing each unit declines. Economies of scale can be developed in most business functions, such as marketing, manufacturing, research and development, and purchasing. Increasing economies of scale enhance a firm's flexibility. For example, a firm may choose to reduce its price and capture a greater share of the market. Alternatively, it may keep its price constant to increase profits. In so doing, it likely will increase its cash flow, a strategy that is helpful in times of recession, as RadioShack was able to do in 2001.[78]

New entrants face a dilemma when confronting current competitors' scale economies. Small-scale entry places them at a cost disadvantage. Alternatively, large-scale entry, in which the new entrant manufactures large volumes of a product to gain economies of scale, risks strong competitive retaliation.

Also important for the firm to understand are instances of current competitive realities that reduce the ability of economies of scale to create an entry barrier. Many companies now customize their products for large numbers of small customer groups. Customized products are not manufactured in the volumes necessary to achieve economies of scale. Customization is made possible by new flexible manufacturing systems (this point is discussed further in Chapter 5). In fact, the new manufacturing technology facilitated by advanced computerization has allowed the development of mass customization in some industries. Mass customized products can be individualized to the customer in a very short time, often within a day. Mass customization is becoming increasingly common in manufacturing products.[79] Companies manufacturing customized products learn how to respond quickly to customers' desires rather than developing scale economies.

Product Differentiation. Over time, customers may come to believe that a firm's product is unique. This belief can result from the firm's service to the customer, effective advertising campaigns, or being the first to market a good or service. Companies such as Coca-Cola, PepsiCo Inc., and the world's automobile manufacturers spend a great deal of money on advertising to convince potential customers of their products' distinctiveness. Customers valuing a product's uniqueness tend to become loyal to both the product and the company producing it. Typically, new entrants must allocate many resources over time to overcome existing customer loyalties. To combat the perception of uniqueness, new entrants frequently offer products at lower prices. This decision, however, may result in lower profits or even losses.

Capital Requirements. Competing in a new industry requires the firm to have resources to invest. In addition to physical facilities, capital is needed for inventories, marketing activities, and other critical business functions. Even when competition in a new industry is attractive, the capital required for successful market entry may not be available, in order to pursue an apparent market opportunity. For example, entering the steel and defence industries would be very difficult because of the substantial resource investments required to be competitive. One way a firm could enter the steel industry, however, is with a highly efficient mini-mill. Alternatively, a firm might enter the defence industry through the acquisition of an existing firm, because the knowledge requirements would be minimal.

Switching Costs. Switching costs are the one-time costs customers incur when they buy from a different supplier. The costs of buying new ancillary equipment and of retraining employees, and even the psychic costs of ending a relationship, may be incurred in switching to a new supplier. In some cases, switching costs are low, such as when the consumer switches to a different soft drink. Switching costs can vary as a function of time. For example, in terms of hours toward graduation, the cost to a student to transfer from one university to another as a freshman is much lower than it is when the student is entering the senior year. Occasionally, a decision made by manufacturers to produce a new, innovative product creates high switching costs for the final consumer. Customer loyalty programs, such as airlines awarding frequent flier miles, are intended to increase the customer's switching costs.

If switching costs are high, a new entrant must offer either a substantially lower price or a much better product to attract buyers. Usually, the more established the relationship between parties, the greater is the cost incurred to switch to an alternative offering.

Access to Distribution Channels.   Over time, industry participants typically develop effective means of distributing products. Once a relationship with its distributors has been developed, a firm will nurture it to create switching costs for the distributors.

Access to distribution channels can be a strong entry barrier for new entrants, particularly in consumer nondurable goods industries (e.g., in grocery stores where shelf space is limited) and in international markets. Thus, new entrants need to persuade distributors to carry their products, either in addition to or in place of those currently distributed. Price breaks and cooperative advertising allowances may be used for this purpose; however, those practices reduce the new entrant's profit potential.

Cost Disadvantages Independent of Scale.   Sometimes, established competitors have cost advantages that new entrants cannot duplicate. Proprietary product technology, favourable access to raw materials, desirable locations, and government subsidies are examples. Successful competition requires new entrants to reduce the strategic relevance of these factors. Delivering purchases directly to the buyer can counter the advantage of a desirable location; new food establishments in an undesirable location often follow this practice. Similarly, automobile dealerships located in unattractive areas (perhaps in a city's downtown area) can provide superior service (such as picking up the car to be serviced and then delivering it to the customer) to overcome a competitor's location advantage.

Government Policy.   Through licensing and permit requirements, governments can also control entry into an industry. Liquor retailing, banking, and trucking are examples of industries in which government decisions and actions affect entry possibilities. Also, governments often restrict entry into some utility industries because of the need to provide quality service and the capital requirements necessary to do so. The European Competition Commission's blocking of GE's acquisition of Honeywell is a prime example of government actions controlling entry to a market.[80] Also, the agreement among governments to restrict the output of steel places substantial restrictions on new entrants to that industry.

Expected Retaliation

Firms seeking to enter an industry also anticipate the reactions of firms in the industry. An expectation of swift and vigorous competitive responses reduces the likelihood of entry. Vigorous retaliation can be expected when the existing firm has a major stake in the industry (e.g., it has fixed assets with few, if any, alternative uses), when it has substantial resources, and when industry growth is slow or constrained. For example, any firms that attempt to enter the steel or IT industries at the current time can expect significant retaliation from existing competitors.

Locating market niches not being served by incumbents allows the new entrant to avoid entry barriers. Small entrepreneurial firms are generally best suited for identifying and serving neglected market segments. When Honda first entered the U.S. market, it concentrated on small-engine motorcycles, a market that firms such as Harley-Davidson ignored. By targeting this neglected niche, Honda avoided competition. After consolidating its position, Honda used its strength to attack rivals by introducing larger motorcycles and competing in the broader market. Competitive actions and competitive responses between firms, such as Honda and Harley-Davidson, are discussed fully in Chapter 6.

Bargaining Power of Suppliers

Increasing prices and reducing the quality of its products are potential means used by suppliers to exert power over firms competing within an industry. If a firm is unable to recover cost increases by its suppliers through its pricing structure, its profitability is reduced by its suppliers' actions. A supplier group is powerful when

- It is dominated by a few large companies and is more concentrated than the industry to which it sells.
- Satisfactory substitute products are not available to industry firms.
- Industry firms are not a significant customer for the supplier group.
- Suppliers' goods are critical to buyers' marketplace success.
- The effectiveness of suppliers' products has created high switching costs for industry firms.
- It poses a credible threat to integrate forward into the buyers' industry. Credibility is enhanced when suppliers have substantial resources and provide a highly differentiated product.

The automobile manufacturing industry is an example of an industry in which suppliers' bargaining power is relatively low, demonstrated by the actions taken by Nissan and Toyota. Recently these two firms placed significant pressure on their suppliers to provide parts at reduced prices. Toyota, for example, requested price reductions of up to 30 percent. As a result of the success of its requests, Nissan reduced its purchasing costs by $2.25 billion annually. Because auto parts suppliers sell their products to a small number of large firms and they aren't credible threats to integrate forward, they have little power relative to automobile manufacturers such as Toyota and Nissan.[81]

Bargaining Power of Buyers

Firms seek to maximize the return on their invested capital. Alternatively, buyers (customers of an industry or firm) want to buy products at the lowest possible price—the point at which the industry earns the lowest acceptable rate of return on its invested capital. To reduce their costs, buyers bargain for higher quality, greater levels of service, and lower prices. These outcomes are achieved by encouraging competitive battles among the industry's firms. Customers (buyer groups) are powerful when

- They purchase a large portion of an industry's total output.
- The sales of the product being purchased account for a significant portion of the seller's annual revenues.
- They could switch to another product at little, if any, cost.
- The industry's products are undifferentiated or standardized, and the buyers pose a credible threat if they were to integrate backward into the sellers' industry.

Armed with greater amounts of information about the manufacturer's costs and the power of the Internet as a shopping and distribution alternative, consumers appear to be increasing their bargaining power in the automobile industry. One reason for this shift is that individual buyers incur virtually zero switching costs when they decide to purchase from one manufacturer rather than another, or from one dealer as opposed to a second or third one. These realities are forcing companies in the automobile industry to become more focused on the needs and desires of the people actually buying cars, trucks, minivans, and sport utility vehicles. These conditions of the market, combined with the recession in 2001 and early 2002, helped to form the basis for Nissan and Toyota pressuring their suppliers to reduce costs. In so doing, they can better serve and satisfy their customers who have considerable power.

Threat of Substitute Products

Substitute products are goods or services from outside a given industry that perform similar or the same functions as a product that the industry produces. For example, as a sugar substitute, NutraSweet places an upper limit on sugar manufacturers' prices—NutraSweet and sugar perform the same function, but with different characteristics. Other product substitutes include fax machines instead of overnight deliveries, plastic containers rather than glass jars, and tea substituted for coffee. Recently, firms have introduced to the market several low-alcohol, fruit-flavoured drinks that many customers substitute for beer. For example, Smirnoff's Ice was introduced with advertising similar to the type often used for beer. Other firms have introduced lemonade with 5 percent alcohol (e.g., Doc Otis Hard Lemon) and tea and lemon combinations with alcohol (e.g., BoDean's Twisted Tea). These products are increasing in popularity, especially among younger people, and as product substitutes, they have the potential to reduce overall sales of beer.[82]

In general, product substitutes present a strong threat to a firm when customers face few, if any, switching costs and when the substitute product's price is lower or its quality and performance capabilities are equal to or greater than those of the competing product. Differentiating a product along dimensions that customers value (such as price, quality, after-service sale, and location) reduces a substitute's attractiveness.

Intensity of Rivalry among Competitors

Because an industry's firms are mutually dependent, actions taken by one company usually invite competitive responses. Thus, in many industries, firms actively compete against one another. Competitive rivalry intensifies when a firm is challenged by a competitor's actions or when an opportunity to improve its market position is recognized.

Firms within industries are rarely homogeneous; they differ in resources and capabilities and seek to differentiate themselves from competitors.[83] Typically, firms seek to differentiate their products from competitors' offerings in ways that customers value and ways that will provide a competitive advantage. Visible dimensions on which rivalry is based include price, quality, and innovation. The rivalry between competitors, such as Fuji and Kodak, Airbus and Boeing, and Sun Microsystems and Microsoft, is intense.

The firms described in the next Strategic Focus box, "The High Stakes of Competitive Rivalry," on page 88, are taking different competitive actions and competitive responses in their efforts to be successful. Airbus is using a first mover strategy (explained in Chapter 6), Fuji is buying equity in a local competitor and infusing it with resources, Sun must improve the effectiveness of its web service to achieve even competitive parity, and Samsung is taking advantage of a major shift in technology to differentiate its products from those of its rivals.

As suggested by this Strategic Focus box, various factors influence the intensity of rivalry between or among competitors. Next, we discuss the most prominent factors that affect the intensity of firms' rivalries.

Numerous or Equally Balanced Competitors

Intense rivalries are common in industries with many companies. With multiple competitors, it is common for a few firms to believe that they can act without eliciting a

The High Stakes of Competitive Rivalry

While most industries produce situations where multiple firms compete against each other, there are some industries in which two major competitors compete head-to-head in multiple markets. Among these competitors are Fuji and Kodak, Airbus and Boeing, and Sun Microsystems and Microsoft. Fuji and Kodak have had an almost storied rivalry over the last decade. For example, Kodak invested heavily in developing digital products. Fuji was aware that Kodak was ahead in serving the digital market, so it decided to capture market share in the traditional film market in hopes of changing Kodak's strategy. Fuji engaged in severe price competition in the U.S. market, capturing major gains in market share from Kodak. Eventually, Kodak shareholders became dissatisfied, and Kodak had to respond. It reduced its prices and investment in R&D, slowing its move into digital products. Recently, however, Kodak has made major strides in capturing the high potential Chinese film market with approximately 50 percent of the market. To combat Kodak, Fuji, with 30 percent of the Chinese market, is negotiating to acquire equity in Lucky Film, China's only film manufacturer, which has 20 percent of the market. If the acquisition is finalized, Fuji will contribute financial capital, technology, and management, while Lucky will provide the manufacturing and distribution.

For a number of years, Airbus and Boeing have competed directly to serve the large airline market. During most of that time, Boeing was the clear winner with a majority of the market with its 700 (including the 727, 737, 747, 757, and 767) series of aircraft. In recent years, Airbus has begun to capture a greater share of this market. Boeing didn't react quickly to these changes, but when Airbus announced that it would produce a new super jumbo jet aircraft, Boeing responded with an announcement that it would develop a larger version of its 747. However, Airbus was the clear winner here, taking all of the contracts in head-to-head competition. Boeing gave up and dropped its plans to develop the larger aircraft. Instead, it announced the development of a smaller and much faster aircraft, but it will need to invest much time and money to do so. Boeing was not prepared well for the future and seemed to be resting on its laurels. As a result, Airbus has captured leadership of the global large aircraft market.

Scott McNealy became a success at a relatively young age. As CEO of Sun Microsystems, he is wealthy, with approximately $668 million in Sun equity. Given the economic travails of 2001 and 2002, he considered retiring to a less stressful life, but he still has a major goal to achieve. He believes that he must stop Sun's rival Microsoft from dominating the Internet and has stated, "It is mankind against Microsoft." The rivalry between Microsoft and Sun seems to be almost personal between McNealy and Microsoft's Bill Gates. McNealy faces a tough challenge—Microsoft leads Sun in four of six markets in which they compete, and Microsoft executed its web strategy effectively. Additionally, Sun was not profitable in 2001, while Microsoft was. As a result, Sun's stock price faltered, while Microsoft's increased. For Sun to reverse its performance and to successfully challenge Microsoft, it must be effective in providing web services. While Sun is unlikely to beat Microsoft, it needs to curb Microsoft's advance to keep it from dominating the web.

These three competitions are unique, in that, in each instance, only two major rivals are involved. In contrast, Samsung faces many competitors in the consumer electronics market, including five with higher market shares (and three of those rivals have more than twice Samsung's annual sales in this market). Nevertheless, Samsung established a goal to become the leader in this market by 2005. Just as Sony became a major player in the consumer electronics market with analogue technology and the Trinitron colour TV, Samsung is attempting to take the market with digital technology. Samsung executives believe that the change from analogue to digital technology levelled the competitive playing field. The current battle is for mind share to be followed by the battle for market share.

SOURCES: P. Burrows, 2001, Face-off, *Business Week*, November 19, 104–10; H. Brown, 2001, Look out, Sony, *Forbes*, June 11, 96–101; D. Michaels, 2001, Airbus's "Honest Abe" attitude adds fuel to rivalry with Boeing, *Wall Street Journal Interactive*, http://interactive.wsj.com, April 3; J. Kynge, 2001, Fuji considers Chinese tie-up to rival Kodak, *Financial Times*, http://www.ft.com, February 27.

response. However, evidence suggests that other firms generally are aware of competitors' actions, often choosing to respond to them. At the other extreme, industries with only a few firms of equivalent size and comparable power also tend to have strong rivalries. The large and often similar-sized resource bases of these firms permit vigorous actions and responses. The Fuji/Kodak and Airbus/Boeing competitive battles exemplify intense rivalries between pairs of relatively equivalent competitors.

Slow Industry Growth

When a market is growing, firms try to effectively use resources to serve an expanding customer base. Growing markets reduce the pressure to take customers from competitors. However, rivalry in nongrowth or slow-growth markets becomes more intense as firms battle to increase their market shares by attracting competitors' customers.

Typically, battles to protect market shares are fierce. Certainly, this has been the case with Fuji and Kodak. The instability in the market that results from these competitive engagements reduces profitability for firms throughout the industry, as is demonstrated by the commercial aircraft industry. The market for large aircraft is expected to decline or grow only slightly over the next few years. To expand market share, Boeing and Airbus will compete aggressively in terms of the introduction of new products, and product and service differentiation. Both firms are likely to win some and lose other battles. In early 2002, Airbus seemed to have an edge over Boeing in this market segment.

High Fixed Costs or High Storage Costs

When fixed costs account for a large part of total costs, companies try to maximize the use of their productive capacity. Doing so allows the firm to spread costs across a larger volume of output. However, when many firms attempt to maximize their productive capacity, excess capacity is created on an industry-wide basis. To then reduce inventories, individual companies typically cut the price of their product and offer rebates and other special discounts to customers. These practices, however, often intensify competition. The pattern of excess capacity at the industry level followed by intense rivalry at the firm level is observed frequently in industries with high storage costs. Perishable products, for example, lose their value rapidly with the passage of time. As their inventories grow, producers of perishable goods often use pricing strategies to sell products quickly.

Lack of Differentiation or Low Switching Costs

When buyers find a differentiated product that satisfies their needs, they frequently purchase the product loyally over time. Industries with many companies that have successfully differentiated their products have less rivalry, resulting in lower competition for individual firms.[84] However, when buyers view products as commodities (those products with few differentiated features or capabilities), rivalry intensifies. In these instances, buyers' purchasing decisions are based primarily on price and, to a lesser degree, service. Film for cameras is an example of a commodity. Thus, the competition between Fuji and Kodak is expected to be strong.

The effect of switching costs is identical to that described for differentiated products. The lower the buyers' switching costs, the easier it is for competitors to attract buyers through pricing and service offerings. High switching costs, however, at least partially insulate the firm from rivals' efforts to attract customers. Interestingly, the switching costs—such as pilot and mechanic training—are high in aircraft purchases, yet, the rivalry between Boeing and Airbus remains intense because the stakes for both are extremely high.

High Strategic Stakes

Competitive rivalry is likely to be high when it is important for several of the competitors to perform well in the market. For example, although Samsung is diversified and is a market leader in other businesses, it has targeted market leadership in the consumer electronics market. This market is quite important to Sony and its major competitors, such as Hitachi, Matsushita, NEC, and Mitsubishi. Thus, we can expect substantial rivalry in this market over the next few years.

High strategic stakes can also exist in terms of geographic locations. For example, Japanese automobile manufacturers are committed to a significant presence in the Canadian and U.S. marketplaces, due to North America's ranking as the world's single largest market for auto manufacturers' products. Because of the stakes involved in these two countries for Japanese and U.S. manufacturers, rivalry among firms in the global automobile industry is highly intense. It should be noted that while close proximity tends to promote greater rivalry, physically proximate competition has potentially positive benefits as well. For example, when competitors are located near each other, it is easier for suppliers to serve them, and the competitors can develop economies of scale that lead to lower production costs. Additionally, communications with key industry stakeholders, such as suppliers, are facilitated and more efficient when they are close to the firm.[85]

High Exit Barriers

Sometimes, companies continue competing in an industry even though the returns on their invested capital are low or negative. Firms making this choice likely face high exit barriers, which include economic, strategic, and emotional factors causing companies to remain in an industry when the profitability of doing so is questionable. Common exit barriers are

- Specialized assets (assets with values linked to a particular business or location).
- Fixed costs of exit (such as labour agreements).
- Strategic interrelationships (relationships of mutual dependence, such as those between one business and other parts of a company's operations, including shared facilities and access to financial markets).
- Emotional barriers (aversion to economically justified business decisions because of fear for one's own career, loyalty to employees, and so forth).
- Government and social restrictions (more common outside the United States, these restrictions often are based on government concerns for job losses and regional economic effects). For example, Fishery Products International, headquartered in St. John's, Newfoundland and Labrador, is required by an act of the provincial legislature to remain in the fishing industry and to remain headquartered in St. John's.

Interpreting Industry Analyses

Effective industry analyses are products of careful study and interpretation of data and information from multiple sources. A wealth of industry-specific data is available to be analyzed. Because of globalization, international markets and rivalries must be included in the firm's analyses. In fact, research shows that in some industries, international variables are more important as determinants of strategic competitiveness than domestic variables. Furthermore, because of the development of global markets, a country's borders no longer restrict industry structures. In fact, movement into international markets enhances the chances of success for new ventures, as well as more established firms.[86]

Following study of the five forces of competition, the firm can develop the insights required to determine an industry's attractiveness in terms of its potential to earn adequate or superior returns on its invested capital. In general, the stronger competitive forces are, the lower the profit potential for an industry's firms. An unattractive industry has low entry barriers, suppliers and buyers with strong bargaining positions, strong competitive threats from product substitutes, and intense rivalry among competitors. These industry characteristics make it very difficult for firms to achieve strategic competitiveness and earn above-average returns. Alternatively, an attractive industry has high entry barriers, suppliers and buyers with little bargaining power, few competitive threats from product substitutes, and relatively moderate rivalry.[87]

Strategic Groups

A set of firms emphasizing similar strategic dimensions to use a similar strategy is called a **strategic group**.[88] The competition between firms within a strategic group is greater than the competition between a member of a strategic group and companies outside that strategic group. In other words, intra-strategic group competition is more intense than is inter-strategic group competition.

A **strategic group** is a set of firms emphasizing similar strategic dimensions to use a similar strategy.

Firms in a strategic group treat a number of strategic dimensions similarly, including their extent of technological leadership, product quality, pricing policies, distribution channels, and customer service. In describing patterns of competition within strategic groups, there is evidence suggesting that "organizations in a strategic group occupy similar positions in the market, offer similar goods to similar customers, and may also make similar choices about production technology and other organizational features." Thus, membership in a particular strategic group defines the essential characteristics of the firm's strategy.[89]

The notion of strategic groups can be useful for analyzing an industry's competitive structure. Such analyses can be helpful in diagnosing competition, positioning, and the profitability of firms within an industry. Research has found that strategic groups differ in performance, suggesting their significance in conducting industry analysis. Interestingly, research also suggests that strategic group membership remains relatively stable over time, making analysis easier and more useful.[90]

Using strategic groups to understand an industry's competitive structure requires the firm to plot companies' competitive actions and competitive responses along strategic dimensions, such as pricing decisions, product quality, and distribution channels. This process shows the firm how certain companies are competing similarly, in terms of how they use similar strategic dimensions. For example, there are unique radio markets because consumers prefer different music formats and programming (news radio, talk radio, and so forth). Typically, a radio format is created through choices made regarding music or nonmusic style, scheduling, and announcer style.[91] It is estimated that approximately 30 different radio formats exist, suggesting that there are 30 strategic groups in this industry. The strategies within each of the 30 groups are similar, while the strategies across the total set of strategic groups are dissimilar. Thus, firms could increase their understanding of competition in the commercial radio industry by plotting companies' actions and responses in terms of important strategic dimensions, such as those we have mentioned.

Strategic groups have several implications. First, because firms within a group offer similar products to the same customers, the competitive rivalry among them can be intense. The more intense the rivalry, the greater is the threat to each firm's profitability. Second, the strengths of the five industry forces (the threats posed by new entrants, the power of suppliers, the power of buyers, product substitutes, and the intensity of rivalry among competitors) differ across strategic groups. Third, the closer the strategic groups are in terms of their strategies, the greater is the likelihood of rivalry among the groups.

Chapter 3 / The External Environment

Competitor Analysis

The competitor environment is the final part of the external environment requiring study. Competitor analysis focuses on each company against whom a firm directly competes. For example, Fuji and Kodak, Airbus and Boeing, and Air Canada and WestJet should be keenly interested in understanding each other's objectives, strategies, assumptions, and capabilities. Furthermore, intense rivalry creates a strong need to understand competitors. In a competitor analysis, the firm seeks to understand

- What drives the competitor, as shown by its *future objectives*.
- What the competitor is doing and can do, as revealed by its *current strategy*.
- What the competitor believes about the industry, as shown by its *assumptions*.
- What the competitor's possibilities are, as shown by its capabilities (its *strengths and weaknesses*).[92]

Information about these four dimensions helps the firm prepare an anticipated response profile for each competitor (see Figure 3.4). Thus, the results of an effective competitor analysis help a firm understand, interpret, and predict its competitors' actions and responses.

Critical to an effective competitor analysis is gathering data and information that can help the firm understand its competitors' intentions and the strategic implications resulting from them. Useful data and information combine to form **competitor intelligence**, the set of data and information the firm gathers to better understand and better anticipate competitors' objectives, strategies, assumptions, and capabilities. In competitor analysis, the firm should gather intelligence not only about its competitors, but

Competitor intelligence is the set of data and information the firm gathers to better understand and better anticipate competitors' objectives, strategies, assumptions, and capabilities.

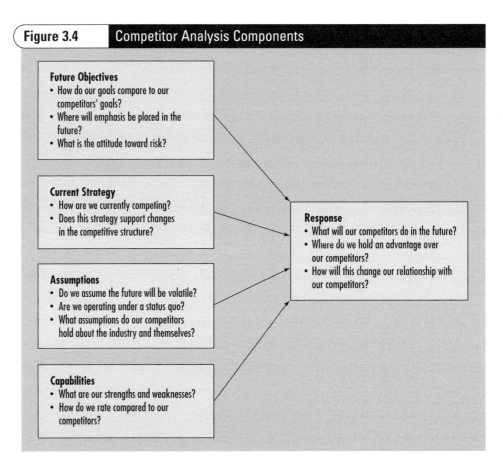

Figure 3.4   Competitor Analysis Components

Future Objectives
- How do our goals compare to our competitors' goals?
- Where will emphasis be placed in the future?
- What is the attitude toward risk?

Current Strategy
- How are we currently competing?
- Does this strategy support changes in the competitive structure?

Assumptions
- Do we assume the future will be volatile?
- Are we operating under a status quo?
- What assumptions do our competitors hold about the industry and themselves?

Capabilities
- What are our strengths and weaknesses?
- How do we rate compared to our competitors?

Response
- What will our competitors do in the future?
- Where do we hold an advantage over our competitors?
- How will this change our relationship with our competitors?

also regarding public policies in countries across the world. Intelligence about public policies "provides an early warning of threats and opportunities emerging from the global public policy environment, and analyzes how they will affect the achievement of the company's strategy."[93]

Through effective competitive and public policy intelligence, the firm gains the insights needed to create a competitive advantage and to increase the quality of the strategic decisions it makes when deciding how to compete against its rivals. Claire Hart, CEO of Factiva, a news and information service, believes that competitor intelligence helped her firm to move from the number three to the number two position in her industry. Additionally, she states that competitor intelligence will play an important role in her firm's efforts to reach its objective of becoming the top firm in the industry.[94]

Firms should follow generally accepted ethical practices in gathering competitor intelligence. Industry associations often develop lists of these practices that firms can adopt. Practices considered both legal and ethical include (1) obtaining publicly available information (such as court records, competitors' help wanted advertisements, annual reports, and financial reports of publicly held corporations), and (2) attending trade fairs and shows to obtain competitors' brochures, view their exhibits, and listen to discussions about their products.

In contrast, certain practices (including blackmail, trespassing, eavesdropping, and stealing drawings, samples, or documents) are widely viewed as unethical and often are illegal. To protect themselves from digital fraud or theft that occurs through competitors breaking into their employees' personal computers (PCs), some companies buy insurance to protect against PC hacking. Chubb's new ForeFront plan, for example, offers up to $10 million coverage against digital fraud, theft, and extortion. Cigna's information asset protection division sells anti-hacker policies that cover up to 10 percent of a firm's revenues. The number of clients making claims seems to suggest the value of these policies.[95]

Some competitor intelligence practices may be legal, but a firm must decide whether such practices are ethical, given the image the firm desires as a corporate citizen. Especially with electronic transmissions, the line between legal and ethical practices can be difficult to determine. For example, a firm may develop website addresses that are very similar to those of its competitors and thus occasionally receive e-mail transmissions that were intended for its competitors. According to legal experts, the legality of this e-mail snagging remains unclear.[96] Nonetheless, the practice is an example of the challenges companies face when deciding how to gather intelligence about competitors while simultaneously determining what to do to prevent competitors from learning too much about them.

In 2001, Procter & Gamble (P&G) notified Unilever that its own rules regarding gathering intelligence on competitors were violated when obtaining information on Unilever practices. Thus, P&G returned more than 80 documents that were taken from Unilever's trash bins. The two firms then negotiated a potential settlement. Unilever wanted P&G to delay several of its planned new product launches, but P&G resisted. Moreover, both firms had to take special care in the negotiations not to violate antitrust laws, thereby spurring regulators to take actions. Therefore, for several reasons, competitive intelligence must be handled with sensitivity.[97]

Open discussions of intelligence-gathering techniques can help a firm to ensure that people understand its convictions to follow ethical practices for gathering competitor intelligence. An appropriate guideline for competitor intelligence practices is to respect the principles of common morality and the right of competitors not to reveal certain information about their products, operations, and strategic intentions.[98]

Despite the importance of studying competitors, evidence suggests that only a relatively small percentage of firms use formal processes to collect and disseminate competitive intelligence. Beyond this, some firms forget to analyze competitors' future objectives as they try to understand their competitors' current strategies, assumptions, and capabilities, which will yield incomplete insights about those competitors.[99]

Summary

- The firm's external environment is challenging and complex. Because of the external environment's effect on performance, the firm must develop the skills required to identify opportunities and threats existing in that environment.

- The external environment has three major parts: (1) the general environment (elements in the broader society that affect industries and their firms), (2) the industry environment (factors that influence a firm, its competitive actions and responses, and the industry's profit potential), and (3) the competitor environment (in which the firm analyzes each major competitor's future objectives, current strategies, assumptions, and capabilities).

- The external environmental analysis process has four steps: scanning, monitoring, forecasting, and assessing. Through environmental analysis, the firm identifies opportunities and threats.

- The general environment has six segments: demographic, economic, sociocultural, global, technological, and political/legal. For each segment, the firm wants to determine the strategic relevance of environmental changes and trends.

- Compared to the general environment, the industry environment has a more direct effect on the firm's strategic actions.

The five forces model of competition includes the threat of entry, the power of suppliers, the power of buyers, product substitutes, and the intensity of rivalry among competitors. By studying these forces, the firm finds a position in an industry where it can influence the forces in its favour or where it can buffer itself from the power of the forces, in order to increase its ability to earn above-average returns.

- Industries are populated with different strategic groups. A strategic group is a collection of firms that follow similar strategies along similar dimensions. Competitive rivalry is greater within a strategic group than it is among strategic groups.

- Competitor analysis informs the firm about the future objectives, current strategies, assumptions, and capabilities of the companies with whom it competes directly.

- Different techniques are used to create competitor intelligence—the set of data, information, and knowledge that allows the firm to better understand its competitors and thereby predict their likely strategic and tactical actions. Firms should use only legal and ethical practices to gather intelligence. The Internet enhances firms' capabilities to gather insights about competitors and their strategic intentions.

Review Questions

1. Why is it important for a firm to study and understand the external environment?

2. What are the differences between the general environment and the industry environment? Why are these differences important?

3. What is the external environmental analysis process? What does the firm want to learn as it scans, monitors, forecasts, and assesses its external environment?

4. What are the six segments of the general environment? Explain the differences among them.

5. How do the five forces of competition in an industry affect its profit potential? Explain.

6. What is a strategic group? Of what value is knowledge of the firm's strategic group in formulating that firm's strategy?

7. What is the importance of collecting and interpreting data and information about competitors? What practices should a firm use to gather competitor intelligence and why?

Environmental Analysis

The results of an environmental analysis provide crucial knowledge for the firm's strategic decisions. The following activities can be worked in small groups or individually and then discussed in class.

General environment activity. As the manager of environmental analysis for an up-and-coming competitor to Wal-Mart, you've been asked to identify two trends for each of the segments of the general environment and to evaluate the potential impact of those trends on the firm's future strategy. Provide your findings in the table below.

Segment	Trend	Impact on Strategy
Demographic	1.	
	2.	
Economic	1.	
	2.	
Political/legal	1.	
	2.	
Sociocultural	1.	
	2.	
Technological	1.	
	2.	
Global	1.	
	2.	

Industry environment activity. You've also been asked to provide a brief analysis of the industrial environment and the five forces model of competition. Indicate in the following table the strength (high, medium, low) of each force on your industry and its impact on your firm's strategy.

Five Forces Model	Strength	Impact on Strategy
Bargaining power of suppliers		
Bargaining power of buyers		
Threats of substitute products		
Rivalry of competing firms		
Threat of new entrants		

Notes

1. J. Song, 2002, Firm capabilities and technology ladders: Sequential foreign direct investments of Japanese electronics firms in East Asia, *Strategic Management Journal*, 23: 191–210; D. J. Ketchen Jr. & T. B. Palmer, 1999, Strategic responses to poor organizational performance: A test of competing perspectives, *Journal of Management*, 25: 683–706; V. P. Rindova & C. J. Fombrun, 1999, Constructing competitive advantage: The role of firm-constituent interactions, *Strategic Management Journal*, 20: 691–710.
2. P. Chattopadhyay, W. H. Glick, & G. P. Huber, 2001, Organizational actions in response to threats and opportunities, *Academy of Management Journal*, 44: 937–55.
3. H. Lee & M. A. Hitt, 2002, Top management team composition and characteristics as predictors of strategic flexibility, working paper, University of Connecticut; A. Edgecliffe-Johnson, 2001, Southwest braced to weather trouble, *Financial Times*, http://www.ft.com, October 2; L. Zuckerman, 2001, With seats empty, airlines cut fares to bargain levels, *New York Times*, http://www.nytimes.com, December 18.
4. R. J. Herbold, 2002, Inside Microsoft: Balancing creativity and discipline, *Harvard Business Review*, 80(1): 73–79; C. M. Grimm & K. G. Smith, 1997, *Strategy as Action: Industry Rivalry and Coordination*, Cincinnati: South-Western; C. J. Fombrun, 1992, *Turning Point: Creating Strategic Change in Organizations*, New York: McGraw-Hill, 13.
5. J. M. Mezias, 2002, Identifying liabilities of foreignness and strategies to minimize their effects: The case of labor lawsuit judgments in the United States, *Strategic Management Journal*, 23: 229–44.
6. R. M. Kanter, 2002, Strategy as improvisational theater, *MIT Sloan Management Review*, 43(2): 76–81; S. A. Zahra, A. P. Nielsen, & W. C. Bogner, 1999, Corporate entrepreneurship, knowledge, and competence development, *Entrepreneurship: Theory and Practice*, 23(3): 169–89.
7. M. A. Hitt, J. E. Ricart, I Costa, & R. D. Nixon, 1998, The new frontier, in M. A. Hitt, J. E. Ricart I Costa, & R. D. Nixon (eds.), *Managing Strategically in an Interconnected World*, Chichester: John Wiley & Sons, 1–12.

8. S. A. Zahra & G. George, 2002, International entrepreneurship: The current status of the field and future research agenda, in M. A. Hitt, R. D. Ireland, S. M. Camp, & D. L. Sexton (eds.), *Strategic Entrepreneurship: Creating a New Mindset*, Oxford, U.K.: Blackwell Publishers, 255–88; W. C. Bogner & P. Bansal, 1998, Controlling unique knowledge development as the basis of sustained high performance, in M. A. Hitt, J. E. Ricart I Costa, & R. D. Nixon (eds.), *Managing Strategically in an Interconnected World*, Chichester: John Wiley & Sons, 167–84.

9. L. Fahey, 1999, *Competitors*, New York: John Wiley & Sons; B. A. Walters & R. L. Priem, 1999, Business strategy and CEO intelligence acquisition, *Competitive Intelligence Review*, 10(2): 15–22.

10. R. E. Hoskisson, M. A. Hitt, W. P. Wan, & D. Yiu, 1999, Swings of a pendulum: Theory and research in strategic management, *Journal of Management*, 25: 417–56.

11. E. H. Bowman & C. E. Helfat, 2001, Does corporate strategy matter? *Strategic Management Journal*, 22: 1–23.

12. A. Seth & H. Thomas, 1994, Theories of the firm: Implications for strategy research, *Journal of Management Studies*, 31: 165–91.

13. Ibid., 169–73.

14. M. E. Porter, 1985, *Competitive Advantage*, New York: Free Press; M. E. Porter, 1980, *Competitive Strategy*, New York: Free Press.

15. A. M. McGahan, 1999, Competition, strategy and business performance, *California Management Review*, 41(3): 74–101; A. M. McGahan & M. E. Porter, 1997, How much does industry matter, really? *Strategic Management Journal*, 18(special summer issue): 15–30.

16. R. Henderson & W. Mitchell, 1997, The interactions of organizational and competitive influences on strategy and performance, *Strategic Management Journal*, 18(special summer issue), 5–14; C. Oliver, 1997, Sustainable competitive advantage: Combining institutional and resource-based views, *Strategic Management Journal*, 18: 697–713; J. L. Stimpert & I. M. Duhaime, 1997, Seeing the big picture: The influence of industry, diversification, and business strategy on performance, *Academy of Management Journal*, 40: 560–83.

17. R. D. Ireland & M. A. Hitt, 1999, Achieving and maintaining strategic competitiveness in the 21st century: The role of strategic leadership, *Academy of Management Executive*, 13(1): 43–57; M. A. Hitt, B. W. Keats, & S. M. DeMarie, 1998, Navigating in the new competitive landscape: Building strategic flexibility and competitive advantage in the 21st century, *Academy of Management Executive*, 12(4): 22–42.

18. J. K. Sebenius, 2002, The hidden challenge of cross-border negotiations, *Harvard Business Review*, 80(3): 76–85; J. Kay, 1999, Strategy and the delusion of grand designs, Mastering strategy (Part One), *Financial Times*, September 27, 2.

19. R. Karlgaard, 1999, Digital rules: Technology and the new economy, *Forbes*, May 17, 43.

20. General Electric, 2000, GE overview, *General Electric website*, http://www.ge.com, January 12.

21. V. Prior, 1999, The language of competitive intelligence: Part four, *Competitive Intelligence Review*, 10(1): 84–87.

22. A. Berenson & R. A. Oppel Jr., 2001, Once mighty Enron strains under scrutiny, *New York Times*, http://www.nytimes.com, October 28; C. H. Deutsch, 2001, Polaroid, deep in debt since 1988, files for bankruptcy, *New York Times*, http://www.nytimes.com, October 13.

23. G. Young, 1999, "Strategic value analysis" for competitive advantage, *Competitive Intelligence Review*, 10(2): 52–64.

24. M. A. Hitt, R. D. Ireland, S. M. Camp, & D. L. Sexton, 2001, Strategic entrepreneurship: Entrepreneurial strategies for wealth creation, *Strategic Management Journal*, 22(special summer issue): 479–91.

25. L. Rosenkopf & A. Nerkar, 2001, Beyond local search: Boundary-spanning exploration, and impact in the optical disk industry, *Strategic Management Journal*, 22: 287–306.

26. D. F. Kuratko, R. D. Ireland, & J. S. Hornsby, 2001, Improving firm performance through entrepreneurial actions: Acordia's corporate entrepreneurship strategy, *Academy of Management Executive*, 15(4): 60–71; D. S. Elenkov, 1997, Strategic uncertainty and environmental scanning: The case for institutional influences on scanning behavior, *Strategic Management Journal*, 18: 287–302.

27. K. M. Eisenhardt, 2002, Has strategy changed? *MIT Sloan Management Review*, 43(2): 88–91; I. Goll & A. M. A. Rasheed, 1997, Rational decision-making and firm performance: The moderating role of environment, *Strategic Management Journal*, 18: 583–91.

28. R. Aggarwal, 1999, Technology and globalization as mutual reinforcers in business: Reorienting strategic thinking for the new millennium, *Management International Review*, 39(2): 83–104; M. Yasai-Ardakani & P. C. Nystrom, 1996, Designs for environmental scanning systems: Tests of contingency theory, *Management Science*, 42: 187–204.

29. R. Donkin, 1999, Too young to retire, *Financial Times*, July 2, 9.

30. S. Chase, 2003, Martin opposes mandatory retirement, *Globe and Mail*, December 20, A1.

31. Human Resources and Development Canada, 2003, Legislative framework: mandatory retirement, *Human Resources and Development Canada website*, http://www110.hrdc-drhc.gc.ca/worklife/aw-retirement-legislative-02-en.cfm, accessed July 20, 2004.

32. B. Richards, 2001, Following the crumbs, *Wall Street Journal*, http://interactive.wsj.com, October 29.

33. Fahey, *Competitors*, 71–73.

34. Canada Law, Make the Canadian advantage your own, *Canada Law website*, http://www.canada-law.com/canadian_advantage.html, accessed December 29, 2003; G. Yip, 1999, The road to wealth, *Dallas Morning News*, August 2, D1, D3; Y. Luo & S. H. Park, 2001, Strategic alignment and performance of market-seeking MNCs in China, *Strategic Management Journal*, 22: 141–55.

35. I. M. Jawahar & G. L. McLaughlin, 2001, Toward a prescriptive stakeholder theory: An organizational life cycle approach, *Academy of Management Review*, 26: 397–414; M. Song & M. M. Montoya-Weiss, 2001, The effect of perceived technological uncertainty on Japanese new product development, *Academy of Management Journal*, 44: 61–80; H. Yli-Renko, E. Autio, & H. J. Sapienza, 2001, Social capital, knowledge acquisition, and knowledge exploitation in young technologically-based firms, *Strategic Management Journal*, 22(special summer issue): 587–613.

36. Fahey, *Competitors*. 71–77.

37. Fahey, *Competitors*, 75–77.

38. L. Fahey & V. K. Narayanan, 1986, *Macroenvironmental Analysis for Strategic Management*, St. Paul, MN: West Publishing Company, 58.

39. Aneki, Largest countries in the world, *Aneki website*, http://www.aneki.com/largest.html, accessed December 29, 2003; Statistics Canada, 1996 Census of Canada–Population and Dwelling Counts, *Statistics Canada website*, http://www.statcan.ca/Daily/English/970415/d970415.htm, accessed July 11, 2004; Statistics Canada, Population, provinces and territories, *Statistics Canada website*, http://www.statcan.ca/english/Pgdb/demo02.htm, accessed July 11, 2004; D. Fishburn, 1999, *The World in 1999*, The Economist Publications, 9; 1999, Six billion … and counting, *Time*, October 4, 16.

40. J. F. Coates, J. B. Mahaffie, & A. Hines, 1997, *2025: Scenarios of US and Global Society Reshaped by Science and Technology*, Greensboro, NC: Oakhill Press; R. Poe & C. L. Courter, 1999, The next baby boom, *Across the Board*, May, 1; 1999, World Future Society, Trends and forecasts for the next 25 years, *World Future Society*, 3; Statistics Canada, *Statistics Canada website*, http://www.statcan.ca/english/Pgdb/, accessed December 29, 2003.

41. 2001, Fewer seniors in the 1990s, *Business Week*, May 28, 30; Statistics Canada, *Statistics Canada website*, http://www.statcan.ca/english/Pgdb/, accessed December 29, 2003.

42. M. Peterson & M. Freudenheim, 2001, Drug giant to introduce discount drug plan for the elderly, *New York Times*, http://www.nytimes.com, October 3.

43. D. Stipp, 1999, Hell no, we won't go! *Fortune*, July 19, 102–8; G. Colvin, 1997, How to beat the boomer rush, *Fortune*, August 18, 59–63; J. MacIntyre, 1999, Figuratively speaking, *Across the Board*, November/December, 15; Colvin, How to beat the boomer rush, 60.

44. Statistics Canada, Shift and growth within large metropolitan areas: The donut effect, http://geodepot.statcan.ca/Diss/Highlights/Page10/Page10_e.cfm, accessed July 11, 2004, 9–11.

45. G. Dessler, 1999, How to earn your employees' commitment, *Academy of Management Executive*, 13(2): 58–67; S. Finkelstein & D. C. Hambrick, 1996, *Strategic Leadership: Top Executives and Their Effect on Organizations*, Minneapolis: West; L. H. Pelled, K. M. Eisenhardt, & K. R. Xin, 1999, Exploring the black box: An analysis of work group diversity, conflict, and performance, *Administrative Science Quarterly*, 44: 1–28.

46. E. S. Rubenstein, 1999, Inequality, *Forbes*, November 1, 158–60.

47. Fahey & Narayanan, *Macroenvironmental Analysis for Strategic Management*, 105.

48. Statistic Canada, *Statistics Canada website*, http://www.statcan.gc.ca/english/Pgdb/gblec02a.htm, accessed on December 29, 2003.

49. J. E. Schrempp, 1999, The world in 1999, Neighbours across the pond, *Economist*, 28.

50. J. L. Hilsenrath, 2001, Shock waves keep spreading, changing the outlook for cars, hotels-even for cola, *Wall Street Journal*, http://interactive.wsj.com, October 9.

51. G. Keim, 2001, Business and public policy: Competing in the political marketplace, in M. A. Hitt, R. E. Freeman, J. S. Harrison (eds.), *Handbook of Strategic Management*, Oxford, U.K.: Blackwell Publishers, 583–601.

52. A. J. Hillman & M. A. Hitt, 1999, Corporate political strategy formulation: A model of approach, participation, and strategy decisions, *Academy of Management Review*, 24: 825–42.

53. M. Carson, 1998, *Global Competitiveness Quarterly*, March 9, 1.

54. C. A. Bartlett & S. Ghoshal, 2002, Building competitive advantage through people, *MIT Sloan Management Review*, 43(2): 33–41.

55. R. Fishman, 2000, The American metropolis at century's end: Past and future influences, *Housing Policy Debate*, 11(1): 199–213.

56. A. Afuah, 2002, Mapping technological capabilities into product markets and competitive advantage: The case of cholesterol drugs, *Strategic Management Journal*, 23: 171–79; X. M. Song, C. A. Di Benedetto, & Y. L. Zhao, 1999, Pioneering advantages in manufacturing and service industries, *Strategic Management Journal*, 20: 811–36.

57. 1999, Business ready for Internet revolution, *Financial Times*, May 21, 17.

58. G. Rifkin, 2001, New economy: Re-evaluating online strategies, *New York Times*, http://www.nytimes.com, June 25.

59. M. Dell, 1999, The world in 1999, The virtual firm, *Economist*, 99.

60. 2001, *Technology Forecast: 2001–2003*, PricewaterhouseCoopers, Menlo Park, CA.

61. M. A. Hitt, R. D. Ireland, & H. Lee, 2000, Technological learning, knowledge management, firm growth and performance, *Journal of Technology and Engineering Management*, 17: 231–46.

62. S. Zahra, R. D. Ireland, I. Gutierrez, & M. A. Hitt, 2000, Privatization and entrepreneurial transformation: Emerging issues and a future research agenda, *Academy of Management Review*, 25: 509–24.

63. A. K. Gupta, V. Govindarajan, & A. Malhotra, 1999, Feedback-seeking behavior within multinational corporations, *Strategic Management Journal*, 20: 205–22.

64. Wall Street Journal, 1999, China and the U.S. sign trade deal, clearing hurdle for WTO entry, *Wall Street Journal*, www.interactive.wsj.com, November 15.

65. J. Kynge, 2001, Murdoch achieves Chinese goal with Star TV deal, *Financial Times*, http://www.ft.com, December 19.

66. R. D. Ireland, M. A. Hitt, S. M. Camp, & D. L. Sexton, 2001, Integrating entrepreneurship and strategic management actions to create firm wealth, *Academy of Management Executive*, 15(1): 49–63; J. W. Lu & P. W. Beamish, 2001, The internationalization and performance of SMEs, *Strategic Management Journal*, 22(special summer issue): 565–86.

67. M. Subramaniam & N. Venkatraman, 2001, Determinants of transnational new product development capability: Testing the influence of transferring and deploying tacit overseas knowledge, *Strategic Management Journal*, 22: 359–78; P. J. Lane, J. E. Salk, & M. A. Lyles, 2001, Absorptive capacity, learning and performance in international joint ventures, *Strategic Management Journal*, 22: 1139–61.

68. S. H. Park & Y. Luo, 2001, Guanxi and organizational dynamics: Organizational networking in Chinese firms, *Strategic Management Journal*, 22: 455–77; M. A. Hitt, M. T. Dacin, B. B. Tyler, & D. Park, 1997, Understanding the differences in Korean and U.S. executives' strategic orientations, *Strategic Management Journal*, 18: 159–67; T. Khanna & K. Palepu, 1999, The right way to restructure conglomerates in emerging markets, *Harvard Business Review*, 77(4): 125–34; Hitt, Dacin, Tyler, & Park, Understanding the differences in Korean and U.S. executives' strategic orientations.

69. Park & Luo, Guanxi and organizational dynamics: Organizational networking in Chinese firms; M. A. Hitt, H. Lee, & E. Yucel, 2002, The importance of social capital to the management of multinational enterprises: Relational capital among Asian and Western firms, *Asia Pacific Journal of Management*, 19(2/3): 353–72.

70. 2002, Global Crossing denies resemblance to Enron, *Richmond Times Dispatch*, March 22, B15; S. Romero, 2001, Global crossing looks overseas for financing, *New York Times*, http://www.nytimes.com, December 20; T. Burt, 2001, DaimlerChrysler in talks with Kuwaiti investors, *Financial Times*, http://www.ft.com, February 11.

71. J. Fuerbringer & R. W. Stevenson, 2001, No bailout is planned for Argentina, *New York Times*, http://www.nytimes.com, July 14; K. L. Newman, 2000, Organizational transformation during institutional upheaval, *Academy of Management Review*, 25: 602–19.

72. M. A. Carpenter & J. W. Fredrickson, 2001, Top management teams, global strategic posture and the moderating role of uncertainty, *Academy of Management Journal*, 44: 533–45.

73. Y. E. Spanos & S. Lioukas, 2001, An examination into the causal logic of rent generation: Contrasting Porter's competitive strategy framework and the resource-based perspective, *Strategic Management Journal*, 22: 907–34.

74. S. Zaheer & A. Zaheer, 2001, Market Microstructure in a global B2B network, *Strategic Management Journal*, 22: 859–73; Hitt, Ricart, Costa, & Nixon, The new frontier; Y. Pan & P. S. K. Chi, 1999, Financial performance and survival of multinational corporations in China, *Strategic Management Journal*, 20: 359–74; G. R. Brooks, 1995, Defining market boundaries, *Strategic Management Journal*, 16: 535–49.

75. P. A. Geroski, 1999, Early warning of new rivals, *Sloan Management Review*, 40(3): 107–16.

76. K. C. Robinson & P. P. McDougall, 2001, Entry barriers and new venture performance: A comparison of universal and contingency approaches, *Strategic Management Journal*, 22(special summer issue): 659–85.

77. R. Makadok, 1999, Interfirm differences in scale economies and the evolution of market shares, *Strategic Management Journal*, 20: 935–52.

78. T. McGinnis, 2001, Improving free cash flow, *Forbes*, http://www.forbes.com, December 21.

79. R. Wise & P. Baumgartner, 1999, Go downstream: The new profit imperative in manufacturing, *Harvard Business Review*, 77(5): 133–41; J. H. Gilmore & B. J. Pine, II, 1997, The four faces of mass customization, *Harvard Business Review*, 75(1): 91–101.

80. P. Spiegel, 2001, Senator attacks 'protectionist' EU over GE deal, *Financial Times*, http://www.ft.com, June 21.

81. C. Dawson, 2001, Machete time: In a cost-cutting war with Nissan, Toyota leans on suppliers, *Business Week*, April 9, 42–43.

82. G. Khermouch, 2001, Grown-up drinks for tender taste buds, *Business Week*, March 5, 96.

83. T. Noda & D. J. Collies, 2001, The evolution of intraindustry firm heterogeneity: Insights from a process study, *Academy of Management Journal*, 44: 897–925.

84. D. L. Deephouse, 1999, To be different, or to be the same? It's a question (and theory) of strategic balance, *Strategic Management Journal*, 20: 147–66.

85. W. Chung & A. Kalnins, 2001, Agglomeration effects and performance: Test of the Texas lodging industry, *Strategic Management Journal*, 22: 969–88.

86. W. Kuemmerle, 2001, Home base and knowledge management in international ventures, *Journal of Business Venturing*, 17: 99–122; G. Lorenzoni & A. Lipparini, 1999, The leveraging of interfirm relationships as a distinctive organizational capability: A longitudinal study, *Strategic Management Journal*, 20: 317–38.

87. M. E. Porter, 1980, *Competitive Strategy*, New York: Free Press.

88. M. S. Hunt, 1972, Competition in the major home appliance industry, 1960–1970, doctoral dissertation, Harvard University; Porter, *Competitive Strategy*, 129.

89. H. R. Greve, 1999, Managerial cognition and the mimetic adoption of market positions: What you see is what you do, *Strategic Management Journal*, 19: 967–88; R. K. Reger & A. S. Huff, 1993, Strategic groups: A cognitive perspective, *Strategic Management Journal*, 14: 103–23.

90. M. Peteraf & M. Shanely, 1997, Getting to know you: A theory of strategic group identity, *Strategic Management Journal*, 18(special issue): 165–86; A. Nair & S. Kotha, 2001, Does group membership matter? Evidence from the Japanese steel industry, *Strategic Management Journal*, 22: 221–35; J. D. Osborne, C. I. Stubbart, & A. Ramaprasad, 2001, Strategic groups and competitive enactment: A study of dynamic relationships between mental models and performance, *Strategic Management Journal*, 22: 435–54.

91. Greve, Managerial cognition, 972–73.

92. Porter, *Competitive Strategy*, 49.

93. P. M. Norman, R. D. Ireland, K. W. Artz, & M. A. Hitt, 2000, Acquiring and using competitive intelligence in entrepreneurial teams, paper presented at the Academy of Management, Toronto, Canada; C. S. Fleisher, 1999, Public policy competitive intelligence, *Competitive Intelligence Review*, 10(2): 24.

94. Fuld & Co., 2001, CEO interview: Claire Hart, President and CEO, *Factiva*, http://www.dowjones.com, April 4.

95. V. Drucker, 1999, Is your computer a sitting duck during a deal? *Mergers & Acquisitions*, July/August, 25–28; J. Hodges, 1999, Insuring your PC against hackers, *Fortune*, May 24, 280.

96. M. Moss, 1999, Inside the game of e-mail hijacking, *Wall Street Journal*, November 9, B1, B4.

97. A. Jones, 2001, P&G to seek new resolution of spy dispute, *Financial Times*, http://www.ft.com, September 4.

98. J. H. Hallaq & K. Steinhorst, 1994, Business intelligence methods: How ethical? *Journal of Business Ethics*, 13: 787–94.

99. L. Fahey, 1999, Competitor scenarios: Projecting a rival's marketplace strategy, *Competitive Intelligence Review*, 10(2): 65–85.

4

Chapter Four

The Internal Environment: Resources, Capabilities, and Core Competencies

Knowledge Objectives

Studying this chapter should provide you with the strategic management knowledge needed to:

1. Explain the need for firms to study and understand their internal environment.

2. Define value and discuss its importance.

3. Describe the differences between tangible and intangible resources.

4. Define capabilities and discuss how they are developed.

5. Describe four criteria used to determine whether resources and capabilities are core competencies.

6. Explain how value chain analysis is used to identify and evaluate resources and capabilities.

7. Define outsourcing and discuss the reasons for its use.

8. Discuss the importance of preventing core competencies from becoming core rigidities.

Reputation as a Source of Competitive Advantage

The Oxford Dictionary defines reputation as "what is generally believed about a person or thing," while the thesaurus offers many substitutes including fame, repute and character. With respect to firms, reputation is defined as the evaluation of a firm by its stakeholders, in terms of respect, knowledge or awareness, and emotional or affective regard. A firm's reputation is an intangible resource upon which the company can build capabilities and, ultimately, core competencies. A company's reputation is also very important in regard to the valuation of the company. The reputation of Coca-Cola, for example, has been valued at $52 billion. Similarly, the reputations of Gillette, Eastman Kodak, Campbell Soup, and Wrigley's Gum have been valued at $12 billion, $11 billion, $9 billion, and $4 billion, respectively.

Because reputation has been such a distinguishing intangible resource, many firms have tried to build perceptual measures of this asset that provide an indication of the competitive value of their reputations to both their rivals and stakeholders. Each year, several periodicals publish rankings of firms, based on reputation. For instance, Ipsos-Reid surveyed 255 CEOs in November 2003 to ascertain Canada's top firms in 2003 (see Table 4.1). *Fortune* magazine surveys 10,000 executives, directors, and securities analysts to develop its America's Most Admired Companies list. The *Financial Times* World's Most Respected Companies survey has an exclusive emphasis on peer evaluation—its ratings are based on evaluations by peer CEOs. Other services, including those provided by Burson-Marsteller, Delahaye Medialink, the Reputation Institute, and Corporate Branding, LLC, use various approaches to rank their clients' reputations. Each ranking service maintains that its ranking provides a unique and valuable perspective.

Research suggests that in the current global environment, there is a growing suspicion of the corporate world, making it even more important for firms to maintain a good reputation. Still present in the public's mind are recent scandals, such as those that occurred at Enron and WorldCom, the collapse of Nortel, and Martha Stewart's battle over charges of insider trading. Consequently, the notion of reputation, as intangible as it may first seem, has much to add to a firm's ongoing search for sustainable competitive advantage.

During his two decades as GE's CEO, Jack Welch (left) guided the firm to consistent growth, earning a legendary reputation for his leadership style. Jeff Immelt (right) took over from Welch on September 10, 2001, and faced the toughest economy in 20 years, skepticism about financial reporting, and uncertainty. He quickly responded by tightening costs, providing full disclosure in reporting, and reaching out to the customer. "This is not just a job," Immelt says. "This is a passion. This is my life."

Charles Fombrun and colleagues have argued that many ranking services are in the business of public relations rather than academic measurement. In their research, Fombrun and his colleagues use 20 attributes to develop a reputational quotient. These attributes are divided into six reputation categories: emotional appeal, social responsibility, financial performance, vision and leadership, workplace environment, and products and services.

A firm can develop intangible distinctions between itself and its rivals within each reputation category. These value-creating distinctions help the firm develop the type of reputation that can become a core competence.

Jeff Immelt succeeded Jack Welch as GE's CEO in September of 2001. It is expected that he will enhance GE's reputation as Welch did after he took over from Reg Jones in 1981.

© DOUG KANTER/AFP

(continued)

Southwest Airlines (further discussed in Chapter 5) has an *emotional appeal* based on its reputation for being a maverick in the rather commodity-like airline industry. Since cofounder and now retired CEO Herb Kelleher took over in 1978, the company has not lost money in any year. Despite fare wars, recessions, oil crises, the events of September 11, 2001, and other disasters plaguing the industry at large and creating massive losses for larger airlines, such as Delta, United, and American, Southwest's reputation has helped to sustain its competitive advantage during difficult industry cycles. Following a business model very similar to Southwest Airlines, WestJet has developed a reputation as a low-fare air carrier now operating across Canada from Victoria, British Columbia, to St. John's, Newfoundland and Labrador. In 2002, WestJet ranked seventh in the 8th Annual Survey of Canada's Most Respected Corporations, conducted by Ipsos-Reid between August 6 and November 30, 2002. In 2003, it received the Most Respected Corporation title for Innovative Practices in the third annual survey of Alberta's Most Respected Corporations, presented by the *Alberta Venture* magazine. Finally, in 2003, WestJet ranked second overall in the 9th Annual Survey of Canada's Most Respected Corporations, conducted by Ipsos-Reid.

Many firms have built their reputations by emphasizing *social responsibility*. The Body Shop, 3M, and DuPont are all firms whose environmental expenditures created an environmentally based competitive advantage. On the other hand, a firm's reputation and image can both suffer when it is involved in a disaster. For example, Exxon lost its reputation in the area of social responsibility following the Valdez oil tanker disaster, and it faced a long road to regain the public's respect. Firestone tire failures on Ford's Explorers hurt the reputations of both Ford and Firestone. Nine out of ten Canadian shareholders say that analysts and fund managers need to take a firm's social and environmental performance into account when determining a firm's value.

Under former CEO Jack Welch, General Electric (GE) enjoyed consistently high *financial performance* over a number of years, and, in the process, built a reputation for steady value creation for its shareholders. It will be interesting to see if GE retains its reputation as a competitive advantage under the leadership of its new CEO, Jeffrey Immelt.

Welch also helped GE's reputation for its financial performance with his *vision* and *leadership*. Many of the corporations mentioned above also attribute their success to leaders who produced and communicated a strategic mission (see Chapter 1) to their employees, fostering the implementation of the firm's strategic intent. Apple has risen, fallen, and risen again through various leaders, but Steven Jobs, in particular, has had a significant influence on Apple's fortunes over the years, as cofounder and CEO.

If a company can hire better skilled people because of its reputation for building human capital, it will likely increase its intellectual capital (the sum of everything that everybody in the company knows) relative to other firms and enhance the reputation of its *workplace environment*.[1] Intellectual capital can provide a competitive advantage for the firm as it competes against its rivals. But, without a strong reputation for treating employees fairly and professionally, it is unlikely that a firm will attract and retain the people required for it to be a leader in intellectual capital.

The most recognized reputational attribute is a firm's brand or trademark. Two Canadian companies, Aliant and TD Canada Trust, had to build their brands after they were formed from the merger of four and two companies, respectively. In the case of Aliant Inc. (TSX:Alt), a multifaceted communications company operating from offices in Nova Scotia, New Brunswick, Newfoundland and Labrador, and Prince Edward Island, with a market focus of Atlantic Canada, the process of branding took more than four years. Originally a merger of four provincial telephone companies (NBTel, MTT, IslandTel, and NewTel) in

March 1999, the resulting giant Aliant (currently Atlantic Canada's largest publicly traded company) found the process of building a brand to be a considerable undertaking. Aliant's particular challenge required delicate handling of existing (internal and external) images and perceptions of going concerns that had to be altered even while introducing a new brand. To further complicate the process each of the acquired telephone companies had been established in its own community for more than 100 years, which meant that the company also had to establish itself as part of those communities.

In contrast to Aliant's careful and long-term transition process, is the approach of TD Canada Trust. TD Bank Financial Group acquired Canada Trust in 2000. Both financial institutions were high market-value firms with strong images. Rather than comparing the brands in search of common traits, the TD Canada Trust strategy focused on creating a new brand, based on detailed customer research. TD Canada Trust's senior vice president of advertising and marketing services said the biggest challenge was "to ensure that everyone not only understood what our positioning is, but also how they could reinforce it in the job they do. ... The internal education process is really critical."

SOURCES: M. Johne, 2003, Forging a new identity after a merger or acquisition is critical to maintaining a strong client base, *CMA Management*, April; I. Jack, 2003, Shareholders support social values, poll finds, *Financial Post*, March 14, F5; http://c0dsp.westjet.com/internet/sky/about/index.jsp, accessed July 20, 2004; M. Boyle, 2002, The shiniest reputations in tarnished times, *Fortune*, March 4, 70–72; G. Khermouch, 2002, What makes a boffo brand, *Business Week* (special issue), spring, 20; A. Diba & L. Munoz, 2001, How long can they stay? *Fortune*, February 19, http://www.fortune.com; T. A. Stewart, 2001, Intellectual capital, *Fortune*, May 28, http://www.fortune.com; C. J. Fombrun, N. A. Gardberg, & M. J. Barnett, 2000, Opportunity platforms and safety nets: Corporate citizenship and reputational risk, *Business and Society Review*, 105(1): 85–106; D.L. Deephouse, 2000, Media reputation as a strategic resource: An integration of mass communication and resource-based theories, *Journal of Management*, 26: 1091–1112; C. Eidson & M. Master, 2000, Top ten ... most admired ... most respected: Who makes the call? *Across the Board*, 37(3): 16–22; P. M. Morgan & J. G. Covin, 2000, Environmental marketing: A source of reputational, competitive and financial advantage, *Journal of Business Ethics*, 23(3): 299–311; J. A. Petrick, R. F. Scherer, J. D. Brodzinski, J. F. Quinn, & M. F. Ainina, 1999, Global leadership skills and reputational capital: Intangible resources of sustainable competitive advantage, *Academy of Management Executive*, 13(1): 58–69.

The firms mentioned in the opening case have used their resources and capabilities to create reputation as a source of competitive advantage. Organizations that rely on reputation as a competitive advantage want that advantage to be *sustainable*. Table 4.1 lists several Canadian firms that have sustained their reputations (e.g., RBC Financial Group and Bombardier), increased their reputation (e.g., WestJet, from 147th in 2001 to 2nd in 2003), and some whose reputation have declined (e.g., Nortel). The data in Table 4.1 is from a survey sponsored by KPMG and conducted by Ipsos-Reid. As discussed in Chapter 1 and Chapter 3, several factors in the global economy, including the rapid development of the Internet's capabilities, have made it increasingly difficult for firms to develop a competitive advantage that can be sustained for any period of time.[2] Under these circumstances, firms try to create advantages that can be sustained over a long period of time. Regardless of its sustainability, however, a competitive advantage is developed when firms use the strategic management process to implement strategies that uniquely use a firm's resources, capabilities, and core competencies. In addition, it can be seen in Table 4.1 that some firms destroyed their reputation and dropped precipitously in the annual survey. Two firms that were in the top 10 in 2000 had dropped out of the top 20 by 2003, while one firm had rebounded to 19th in 2003, from 24th in 2002. These were Nortel (1st in 2000, 4th in 2001, 41st in 2002, and 21st in 2003), Imperial Oil (7th in 2000, 15th in 2001, and not in the top 20 in 2002 or 2003), and General Electric of Canada (9th in 2000, 21st in 2001, 24th in 2002, and 19th in 2003). Nortel was expected to be out of the top 25 again in 2004, given the firing of CEO Frank Dunn and several of his senior officers because of accounting irregularities.

The importance of competitive advantage is highlighted by the statement that "competitive advantage continues to provide the central agenda in strategy research."[3] Competitive advantage research is critical because "resources are the foundation for strategy and [the] unique bundles of resources [that] generate competitive advantages leading to wealth creation."[4] To identify and successfully use their competitive advantages over time, firms think constantly about their strategic management process and how to increase the value it creates.[5] As this chapter's discussion indicates, firms achieve strategic competitiveness and earn above-average returns when their unique core competencies are effectively leveraged to take advantage of opportunities in the external environment.

Increasingly, people are a key source of competitive advantage as organizations compete in the global economy.[6] At Walt Disney Company, for example, the importance of intellectual capital has become increasingly apparent. Walt Disney Studios, which in recent years has led the movie industry in market share, is experiencing competitive difficulties. The company's top strategic leaders, Chairman Michael D. Eisner and President Peter Schneider, are focusing on greater financial discipline in the studio, at a time when Disney is producing fewer movies and generating less impact on the market. This focus on cost cutting has lead to corporate downsizing and, many believe, the loss of some of the creative fire in Disney's animation division. The firm "has become ... famous in recent years for the people who have left [the studio]." One of the firm's recent animated productions, *Atlantis: The Lost Empire*, did not generate as much excitement in the marketplace as past Disney releases, which suggests that Disney's cost cutting and loss of significant employees have seriously decreased the quality, quantity, and especially the creative aspect of that all-important resource—intellectual capital.[7]

The RBC Financial Group ranked first in six of the nine categories assessed by Ipsos-Reid. RBC Financial Group ranked first in best long-term investment value, human resources management, financial performance, corporate social responsibility, corporate governance, and top-of-mind most admired or respected. WestJet Airlines ranked first in two categories—high quality service/product and customer service. Research in Motion ranked first in one category—innovation and product/service development.

| Table 4.1 | Canada's Most Admired Companies in 2003, 2002, and 2001 | |

2003 The Top Ten	2002 The Top Ten	2001 The Top Ten
1. RBC Financial Group	1. RBC Financial Group	1. Bombardier
2. WestJet	2. Bombardier	2. RBC Financial Group
3. BCE Inc.	3. BCE Inc.	3. BCE Inc.
4. Loblaw Companies Ltd.	4. Magna International Inc.	4. Nortel
5. Bombardier Inc.	5. Loblaw Companies Ltd.	5. Toronto Dominion Bank
6. Research in Motion	6. Dofasco	6. Research in Motion
7. Bank of Nova Scotia	7. WestJet	7. Loblaw Companies Ltd.
8. EnCana Corporation	8. Research in Motion	8. Magna International
9. BMO Financial Group	9. TD Canada Trust	9. Power Corporation
10. Magna International	10. IBM Canada	10. Canadian Imperial Bank

SOURCE: 2004. Ipsos-Reid Corporation, *Canada's Most Respected Corporations: The Ninth Annual Survey.* © Ipsos-Reid http://www.ipsos-na.com/news/pdf/media/mr040119-1.pdf (March 24, 2004).

Over time, the benefits of any firm's value-creating strategy can be duplicated by its competitors. In other words, all competitive advantages have a limited life.[8] The question of duplication is not *if* it will happen, but *when*. In general, the sustainability of a competitive advantage is a function of three factors: (1) the rate of core competence obsolescence because of environmental changes, (2) the availability of substitutes for the core competence, and (3) the imitability of the core competence.[9]

The challenge in all firms is to effectively manage current core competencies while simultaneously developing new ones.[10] In the words of Michael Dell, CEO of Dell Computer Corporation, "No [competitive] advantage and no success is ever permanent. The winners are those who keep moving. The only constant in our business is that everything is changing. We have to be ahead of the game."[11] Only when firms develop a continuous stream of competitive advantages do they achieve strategic competitiveness, earn above-average returns, and remain ahead of competitors (see Chapter 6).

In Chapter 3, we examined general, industry, and competitor environments. Armed with this knowledge about the realities and conditions of their environments, firms have a better understanding of marketplace opportunities and the goods or services through which they can be pursued. In this chapter, we focus on the firm itself. Through an analysis of its internal environment, a firm determines what it *can do*—that is, the actions permitted by its unique resources, capabilities, and core competencies. As discussed later in this chapter, core competencies are a firm's source of competitive advantage. The magnitude of that competitive advantage is a function primarily of the uniqueness of the firm's core competencies compared to those of its competitors.[12] Matching what a firm *can do* with what it *might do* (a function of opportunities and threats in the external environment) allows the firm to develop strategic intent, pursue its strategic mission, and select and implement its strategies. Outcomes resulting from internal and external environmental analyses are shown in Figure 4.1 on page 104.

We examine several topics in this chapter, beginning with a review of the resource-based model of above-average returns. We then discuss the importance and challenge of studying the firm's internal environment. Next, we examine the roles of resources, capabilities, and core competencies in developing sustainable competitive advantage. Included in this discussion are the techniques firms can use to identify and evaluate resources and capabilities

Chapter 4 / The Internal Environment

| Figure 4.1 | Outcomes from External and Internal Environmental Analyses |

By studying the external environment firms identify	By studying the internal environment firms determine
• What they *might* choose to do	• What they *can* do

and the criteria for selecting core competencies from among them. Resources, capabilities, and core competencies are not inherently valuable, but if they create value when the firm uses them to perform certain activities they may result in a source of competitive parity, temporary competitive advantage, or sustained competitive advantage. Accordingly, we also discuss in this chapter the value chain concept and examine four criteria to evaluate core competences that establish competitive advantage.[13]

The Resource-Based Model of Above-Average Returns

The resource-based model assumes that each organization is a collection of resources and capabilities, a few of which are unique and provide the basis for a firm's strategy and its primary source of above-average returns. This model suggests that capabilities evolve and must be managed dynamically in pursuit of above-average returns.[14] According to the model, differences in firms' performances across time are due primarily to their unique resources and capabilities rather than the structural characteristics of the industry in which they operate. This model also assumes that firms acquire different resources and develop unique capabilities. Therefore, not all firms competing within a particular industry possess the same resources and capabilities. Additionally, the model assumes that resources may not be highly mobile across firms and that the differences in resources are the basis of competitive advantage.

Resources are inputs into a firm's production process, such as capital equipment, the skills of individual employees, patents, finances, and talented managers. In general, a firm's resources can be classified into three categories: physical, human, and organizational capital. Described later in this chapter, resources are either tangible or intangible in nature.

Individual resources alone may not yield a competitive advantage.[15] In general, competitive advantages are formed through the combination and integration of sets of resources. A **capability** is the capacity for a set of resources to perform a task or an activity in an integrative manner. Through the firm's continued use, capabilities become stronger and more difficult for competitors to understand and imitate. As a source of competitive advantage, a capability "should be neither so simple that it is highly imitable, nor so complex that it defies internal steering and control."[16]

The resource-based model of superior returns is shown in Figure 4.2. Instead of focusing on the accumulation of resources necessary to implement the strategy dictated by conditions and constraints in the external environment (see Chapter 3, "The I/O Model of Above-Average Returns," on page 68), the resource-based view suggests that a firm's unique resources and capabilities provide the basis for a strategy. The strategy chosen should allow the firm to best exploit its core competencies relative to opportunities in the external environment.

Not all of a firm's resources and capabilities have the potential to be the basis for competitive advantage. This potential is realized when resources and capabilities are valuable, rare, costly to imitate, and organized to be exploited.[17] Resources are *valuable*

Resources are inputs into a firm's production process, such as capital equipment, the skills of individual employees, patents, finances, and talented managers.

A **capability** is the capacity for a set of resources to perform a task or an activity in an integrative manner.

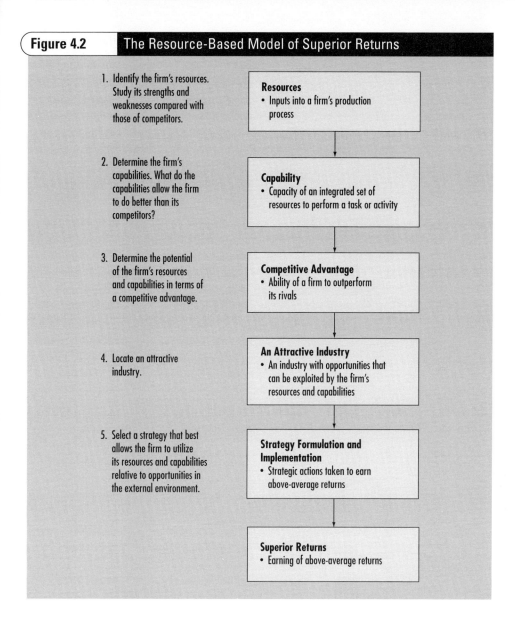

Figure 4.2 The Resource-Based Model of Superior Returns

1. Identify the firm's resources. Study its strengths and weaknesses compared with those of competitors.

Resources
• Inputs into a firm's production process

2. Determine the firm's capabilities. What do the capabilities allow the firm to do better than its competitors?

Capability
• Capacity of an integrated set of resources to perform a task or activity

3. Determine the potential of the firm's resources and capabilities in terms of a competitive advantage.

Competitive Advantage
• Ability of a firm to outperform its rivals

4. Locate an attractive industry.

An Attractive Industry
• An industry with opportunities that can be exploited by the firm's resources and capabilities

5. Select a strategy that best allows the firm to utilize its resources and capabilities relative to opportunities in the external environment.

Strategy Formulation and Implementation
• Strategic actions taken to earn above-average returns

Superior Returns
• Earning of above-average returns

when they allow a firm to take advantage of opportunities or neutralize threats in its external environment. They are *rare* when possessed by few, if any, current and potential competitors. Resources are *costly to imitate* when other firms either cannot obtain them or are at a cost disadvantage in obtaining them, compared with the firm that already possesses them. Finally, resources are *organized to be exploited* when they have the appropriate structure, control systems and reward systems that nurture resources and capabilities.

When these four criteria are met, resources and capabilities become core competencies. **Core competencies** are resources and capabilities that serve as a source of sustained competitive advantage for a firm over its rivals. Often related to a firm's functional skills, core competencies, when developed, nurtured, and applied throughout a firm, may result in strategic competitiveness.

Managerial competencies are important in most firms. For example, they have been shown to be critically important to successful entry into foreign markets.[18] Such competencies may include the capability to effectively organize and govern complex and

Core competencies are resources and capabilities that serve as a source of sustained competitive advantage for a firm over its rivals.

diverse operations and the capability to create and communicate a strategic vision.[19] Managerial capabilities are critical to a firm's ability to take advantage of its resources.

Another set of important competencies is product related. Included among these competencies is the capability to develop innovative new products and to re-engineer existing products to satisfy changing consumer tastes.[20] Firms must also continuously develop their competencies to keep them up-to-date. This development requires a systematic program for updating old skills and introducing new ones.

Dynamic core competencies are especially important in rapidly changing environments, such as those that exist in high-technology industries. Thus, the resource-based model suggests that core competencies are the basis for a firm's competitive advantage, its strategic competitiveness, and its ability to earn above-average returns.

The Importance of Internal Analysis

In the global economy, traditional factors—such as labour costs, access to financial resources and raw materials, and protected or regulated markets—continue to be sources of competitive advantage, but to a lesser degree than before.[21] One important reason for this decline is that the advantages created by these sources can be overcome through an international strategy (discussed in Chapter 9) and by the relatively free flow of resources throughout the global economy.

Few firms can consistently make effective strategic decisions unless they can change rapidly. A key challenge to developing the ability to change rapidly is the fostering of an organizational setting in which experimentation and learning are expected and promoted.[22] The demands of 21st-century competition require top-level managers to rethink earlier concepts of the firm and competition.

In addition to the firm's ability to change rapidly, a different managerial mind-set is required for firms to be successful in the global economy. Most top-level managers recognize the need to change their mind-sets, but many hesitate to do so. In the words of the European CEO of a major U.S. company, "It is more reassuring for all of us to stay as we are, even though we know the result will be certain failure … than to jump into a new way of working when we cannot be sure it will succeed."[23] Jacques Nasser, Ford Motor Company's former CEO, was quite outspoken in his belief that all employees—especially senior-level executives—have to change their mind-set from concentrating on their own area of operation to encompassing a view of the company in its entirety.

Also critical is that managers view the firm as a *bundle* of heterogeneous resources, capabilities, and core competencies that can be used to create an exclusive market position.[24] This perspective suggests that individual firms possess at least some resources and capabilities that other companies do not—at least not in the same combination. Resources are the source of capabilities, some of which lead to the development of a firm's core competencies.[25] Figure 4.3 illustrates the relationships among resources, capabilities, and core competencies and shows how firms use them to create strategic competitiveness. Essentially, the mind-set needed in the global economy requires decision makers to define their firm's strategy in terms of a *unique competitive position*, rather than strictly in terms of operational effectiveness. For instance, Michael Porter argues that quests for productivity, quality, and speed based on a number of management techniques—total quality management (TQM), benchmarking, time-based competition, and re-engineering—have resulted in operational efficiency, but have not resulted in strong sustainable strategies.[26] As we discussed in Chapter 1, strategic competitiveness results when the firm satisfies the operational efficiency demands of its external environment while simultaneously using its own unique capabilities to establish a viable strategic position. Because of its importance to business-level strategies, strategic positioning is discussed in greater detail in Chapter 5.

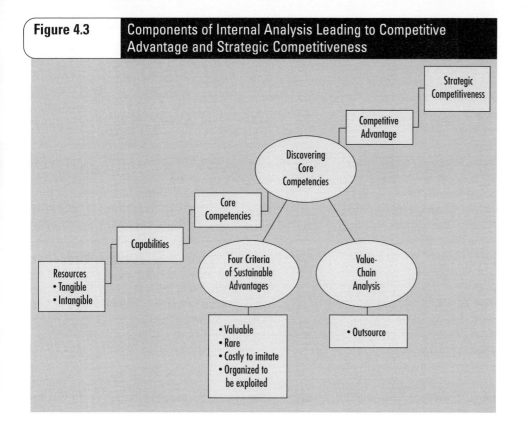

Creating Value

By exploiting core competencies and meeting the demanding standards of global competition, firms create value for customers.[27] **Value** is measured by a product's performance characteristics and by its attributes for which customers are willing to pay.[28]

Ultimately, creating customer value is the source of a firm's potential to earn above-average returns. A firm's intentions regarding value creation affects its choice of business-level strategy (see Chapter 5) and its organizational structure (see Chapter 12).[29] In Chapter 5's discussion of business-level strategies, we note that value is created by a product's low cost, by its highly differentiated features, or by a combination of low cost and high differentiation, compared to competitors' offerings. A business-level strategy is effective only when its use is grounded in exploiting the firm's current core competencies while actions are being taken to develop the core competencies that will be needed to effectively use tomorrow's business-level strategy. Thus, successful firms continuously examine the effectiveness of current and future core competencies.[30]

During the last several decades, the strategic management process was concerned largely with understanding the characteristics of the industry in which a firm competed and, in light of those characteristics, determining how a firm should position itself relative to its competitors. This emphasis on industry characteristics and competitive strategy may have understated the role of the firm's resources and capabilities in developing competitive advantage. In the current competitive landscape, core competencies, in combination with product-market positions, are the firm's most important sources of competitive advantage.[31] The core competencies of a firm, in addition to its analysis of its general, industry, and competitor environments, should drive its selection of strategies. By emphasizing core competencies when formulating strategies, companies learn to

Value is measured by a product's performance characteristics and by its attributes for which customers are willing to pay.

compete primarily on the basis of firm-specific differences, but they must be very aware of how things are changing as well.

The Challenge of Internal Analysis

The decisions that managers make in terms of the firm's resources, capabilities, and core competencies have a significant influence on the firm's ability to earn above-average returns.[32] Making these decisions—identifying, developing, deploying, and protecting resources, capabilities, and core competencies—may appear to be relatively easy. In fact, these tasks are as challenging and difficult as any other that managers face; moreover, such decisions are increasingly internationalized and linked with the firm's success.[33] Managers also face great pressure to pursue only those decisions that help the firm to meet the quarterly earning numbers expected by market analysts.[34] Recognizing the firm's core competencies is essential before the firm can make important strategic decisions, including those related to entering or exiting markets, investing in new technologies, building new or additional manufacturing capacity, or forming strategic partnerships.[35] Patterns of interactions between individuals and groups that occur as strategic decisions affect decision quality, as well as how effectively and quickly these decisions are implemented.[36]

The challenge and difficulty of making effective decisions are implied by preliminary evidence suggesting that one-half of organizational decisions fail.[37] Sometimes, mistakes are made as the firm analyzes its internal environment. Managers might, for example, select resources and capabilities as the firm's core competencies that do not create a competitive advantage. When a mistake occurs, decision makers must have the confidence to admit the error and take corrective actions.[38] A firm can still grow through well-intended errors—the learning generated by making and correcting mistakes can be important to the creation of new competitive advantages.[39] Moreover, firms can learn from the failure resulting from a mistake; that is, what not to do when seeking competitive advantage.[40]

To facilitate the development and use of core competencies, managers must have courage, self-confidence, integrity, the capacity to deal with uncertainty and complexity, and a willingness to both hold people accountable for their work and be held account-

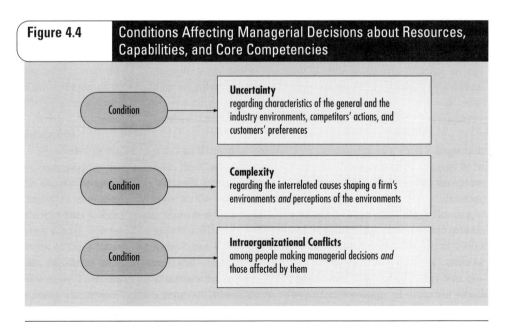

Figure 4.4 Conditions Affecting Managerial Decisions about Resources, Capabilities, and Core Competencies

SOURCE: Adapted from R. Amit and P. J. H. Schoemaker, 1993, Strategic and organizational rent, *Strategic Management Journal* 14: 33.

able themselves. Thus, difficult managerial decisions concerning resources, capabilities, and core competencies are characterized by three conditions: uncertainty, complexity, and intraorganizational conflicts (see Figure 4.4).[41]

Managers face *uncertainty* in terms of new proprietary technologies, rapidly changing economic and political trends, transformations in societal values, and shifts in customer demands.[42] Environmental uncertainty increases the *complexity* and range of issues to examine when studying the internal environment. Biases about how to cope with uncertainty affect decisions about the resources and capabilities that will become the foundation of the firm's competitive advantage. Finally, *intraorganizational conflict* surfaces when decisions are made about the core competencies to nurture and how they should be nurtured.

In making decisions affected by these three conditions, judgment should be used. *Judgment* is the capability of making successful decisions when no obviously correct model or rule is available, or when relevant data are unreliable or incomplete. In such situations, decision makers must be aware of possible cognitive biases. Overconfidence, for example, can often lower value when a correct decision is not obvious, such as making a judgment as to whether an internal resource is a strength or a weakness.[43]

When exercising judgment, decision makers demonstrate a willingness to take intelligent risks in a timely manner. In the current competitive landscape, executive judgment can be a particularly important source of competitive advantage, as over time, effective judgment allows a firm to build a strong reputation and retain the loyalty of stakeholders, whose support is linked to above-average returns.[44]

Significant changes in the value-creating potential of a firm's resources and capabilities can occur in a rapidly changing global economy.[45] Because these changes affect a company's power and social structure, inertia or resistance to change may surface. Even though these reactions may arise, decision makers should not deny the changes needed to assure the firm's strategic competitiveness. *Denial* is an unconscious coping mechanism used to block out and resist painful changes.[46] For example, Opel was once Germany's number one car. Of late, however, the GM-owned European automaker has suffered operating losses ($429 million in 2000 alone) and poor brand image. Concentrating on making changes in how the firm performs its primary and support activities, Carl-Peter Forster, head of Opel, candidly faced the problem and developed a restructuring plan that should reduce purchasing costs, streamline and modernize the firm's ineffective sales unit, and define new areas of potential growth beyond car sales. These actions, some of which could be painful, may improve the image of the firm's brand and, subsequently, its competitive ability.[47]

Because some people have a strong tendency to resist the changes needed to cope with intensely competitive environments, it is important to involve a range of individuals and groups when making changes in a firm's value-creating abilities.[48]

Resources, Capabilities, and Core Competencies

Resources, capabilities, and core competencies are the characteristics that form the foundation of competitive advantage. As mentioned earlier in this chapter, resources are the source of a firm's capabilities. Capabilities, in turn, are the source of a firm's core competencies, which form the basis of competitive advantages.[49] As shown in Figure 4.3, on page 107, combinations of resources and capabilities are managed to create core competencies. In this section, we define and provide examples of these building blocks of competitive advantage.

Resources

Broad in scope, resources cover a spectrum of individual, social, and organizational phenomena.[50] Typically, resources alone do not yield a competitive advantage.[51] In fact, a competitive advantage is created through the *unique bundling of several resources*.[52] For example, Amazon.com has combined service and distribution resources to develop its competitive advantages. The firm started as an online bookseller, directly shipping orders to customers. It quickly grew large and established a distribution network through which it could ship "millions of different items to millions of different customers." Compared to Amazon's use of combined resources, traditional bricks-and-mortar companies, such as Toys "Я" Us and Borders, found it hard to establish an effective online presence. These difficulties led them to develop partnerships with Amazon. Through these arrangements, Amazon now handles online presence and the shipping of goods for several firms, including Toys "Я" Us and Borders, which now can focus on sales in their stores. Arrangements such as these are useful to the bricks-and-mortar companies that are not accustomed to shipping such quantities of diverse merchandise directly to individuals.[53]

Tangible resources are assets that can be seen and quantified.

Intangible resources include assets that typically are rooted deeply in the firm's history and have accumulated over time.

Some of a firm's resources are tangible, while others are intangible. **Tangible resources** are assets that can be seen and quantified. Production equipment, manufacturing plants, and formal reporting structures are examples of tangible resources. **Intangible resources** include assets that typically are rooted deeply in the firm's history and have accumulated over time. Because they are embedded in unique patterns of routines, intangible resources are relatively difficult for competitors to analyze and imitate. Knowledge, trust between managers and employees, ideas, the capacity for innovation, managerial capabilities, organizational routines (the unique ways in which people work together), scientific capabilities, the firm's reputation for its goods or services, and the nature of its interactions with people (such as employees, customers, and suppliers) are all examples of intangible resources.[54]

The four types of tangible resources are financial, organizational, physical, and technological (see Table 4.2). The three types of intangible resources are human, innovation, and reputational (see Table 4.3).

Tangible Resources

As tangible resources, a firm's borrowing capacity and the status of its plant and equipment are visible. The value of many tangible resources can be established through financial statements, but because financial statements disregard some intangible resources, they do not account for the value of all of a firm's assets.[55] As such, each of the firm's sources of competitive advantage typically are not reflected fully on corporate financial statements. The value of tangible resources is also constrained because they are difficult to leverage—it is hard to derive additional business or value from a tangible resource. For example, an airplane is a tangible resource or asset, but, "You can't use the same airplane on five different routes at the same time. You can't put the same crew on five different routes at the same time. And the same goes for the financial investment you've made in the airplane."[56]

Although manufacturing assets are tangible, many of the processes to use these assets are intangible. Thus, the learning and potential proprietary processes associated with a tangible resource, such as manufacturing equipment, can have unique intangible attributes, such as quality, just-in-time management practices, and unique manufacturing processes that develop over time and create competitive advantage.[57]

Intangible Resources

As suggested above, compared to tangible resources, intangible resources are a superior and more potent source of core competencies.[58] In fact, in the global economy, "the success of a corporation lies more in its intellectual and systems capabilities than in its physical assets. [Moreover], the capacity to manage human intellect—and to convert it into useful products and services—is fast becoming the critical executive skill of the age."[59]

Table 4.2	Tangible Resources
Financial Resources	• The firm's borrowing capacity • The firm's ability to generate internal funds
Organizational Resources	• The firm's formal reporting structure and its formal planning, controlling, and coordinating systems
Physical Resources	• Sophistication and location of a firm's plant and equipment • Access to raw materials
Technological Resources	• Stock of technology, such as patents, trademarks, copyrights, and trade secrets

SOURCES: Adapted from J. B. Barney, 1991, Firm resources and sustained competitive advantage, *Journal of Management*, 17: 101; R. M. Grant, 1991, *Contemporary Strategy Analysis*, Cambridge, U.K.: Blackwell Business, 100–2.

Table 4.3	Intangible Resources
Human Resources	• Knowledge • Trust • Managerial capabilities • Organizational routines
Innovation Resources	• Ideas • Scientific capabilities • Capacity to innovate
Reputational Resources	• Reputation with customers • Brand name • Perceptions of product quality, durability, and reliability • Reputation with suppliers • For efficient, effective, supportive, and mutually beneficial interactions and relationships

SOURCES: Adapted from R. Hall, 1992, The strategic analysis of intangible resources, *Strategic Management Journal*, 13: 136–39; R. M. Grant, 1991, *Contemporary Strategy Analysis*, Cambridge, U.K.: Blackwell Business, 101–4.

There is some evidence that the value of intangible assets is growing, relative to that of tangible assets. John Kendrick, a well-known economist studying the main drivers of economic growth, identified a general increase in the contribution of intangible assets to U.S. economic growth since the early 1900s: "In 1929, the ratio of intangible business capital to tangible business capital was 30 percent to 70 percent. In 1990, that ratio was 63 percent to 37 percent."[60]

Because intangible resources are less visible and more difficult for competitors to understand, purchase, imitate, or substitute for, firms prefer to rely on intangible rather than tangible resources as the foundation for their capabilities and core competencies. In fact, the more unobservable (i.e., intangible) a resource is, the more sustainable the competitive advantage on which it is based. Another benefit of intangible resources is that, unlike most tangible resources, their use can be leveraged. With intangible resources, the larger the network of users, the greater the benefit to each party.[61] For instance, sharing knowledge among employees does not diminish its value for any one person. To the contrary, two people sharing their individualized knowledge sets often can be leveraged to create additional knowledge that, although new to each of them, contributes to performance improvements for the firm.[62]

As illustrated in the opening case, on page 99, the intangible resource of reputation is an important source of competitive advantage for companies such as WestJet, TD Canada Trust, Aliant, Coca-Cola, General Electric, and Southwest Airlines. Earned through the firm's actions, as well as its words, a value-creating reputation is a product of years of superior marketplace competence as perceived by stakeholders.[63] A well-known and highly valued brand name is an application of reputation as a source of competitive advantage. The Harley-Davidson brand name, for example, has such cachet that it adorns a limited-edition Barbie doll, a popular restaurant in New York City, and a line of L'Oreal cologne. Moreover, Harley-Davidson Motor Clothes annually generates more than $100 million in revenue and offers a broad range of clothing items, from black leather jackets to fashions for tots.[64]

Decision makers are challenged to understand fully the strategic value of their firm's tangible and intangible resources. The *strategic value of resources* is indicated by the degree to which they can contribute to the development of capabilities, core competencies, and, ultimately, competitive advantage. For example, as a tangible resource, a distribution facility is assigned a monetary value on the firm's balance sheet. The real value of the facility, however, is grounded in a variety of factors, such as its proximity to raw materials and customers, but also in intangible factors, such as the manner in which workers integrate their actions internally and with other stakeholders, such as suppliers and customers.[65]

Capabilities

As a source of capabilities, tangible and intangible resources are critical stepping stones in the pathway to the development of competitive advantage (as shown in Figure 4.3, on page 107). Capabilities are the firm's capacity to deploy resources that have been purposefully integrated to achieve a desired end state.[66] As the glue binding an organization together, capabilities emerge over time through complex interactions among tangible and intangible resources. The Strategic Focus box "Edward Jones (Canada)" demonstrates these complex interactions. Critical to the forming of competitive advantages, capabilities are often based on developing, carrying, and exchanging information and knowledge through the firm's human capital.[67] Because a knowledge base is grounded in organizational actions that may not be explicitly understood by all employees, repetition and practice increase the value of a firm's capabilities.

The foundation of many capabilities lies in the skills and knowledge of a firm's employees and, often, in their functional expertise. Hence, the value of human capital in developing and using capabilities and, ultimately, core competencies cannot be overstated. Firms committed to continuously developing their employees' capabilities seem to accept the adage that "the person who knows how will always have a job. The person who knows why will always be his boss."[68]

Global business leaders increasingly support the view that the knowledge possessed by human capital is among the most significant of an organization's capabilities and may ultimately be at the root of all competitive advantages. But firms must also be able to utilize the knowledge that they have and transfer it among their operating businesses.[69] For example, researchers have suggested that "in the information age, things are ancillary, knowledge is central. A company's value derives not from things, but from knowledge, know-how, intellectual assets, competencies—all of it embedded in people."[70] Given this reality, the firm's challenge is to create an environment that allows

Edward Jones (Canada): Building the Human Resource Capability; and AIC's Competitive Advantage

The number one spot on *Fortune* magazine's list of 100 best companies to work for in the U.S. has gone to Edward Jones (EJ) two years running. Additionally, in December 2002, the company earned the distinction of the number four spot in *The Globe and Mail Report on Business* magazine's annual listing of the 50 best companies to work for in Canada. In *Fortune's* annual survey, employees interviewed remain anonymous and participants are randomly selected. Responses to the employee survey comprise two-thirds of a company's score on the *Fortune* list. In the case of EJ, employee responses were consistent, and of the 79 percent of EJ employees polled, 95 percent agreed with the statement "I am proud to tell others I work here," while 83 percent said that they planned to work at the firm until retirement. Michael Holmes, chief human resources officer, is given much of the credit for the firm's recognition.

Holmes joined Edward Jones in 1996 and, very early in his tenure, identified employee turnover as the greatest problem facing the firm. He set about designing and implementing a series of initiatives focused on the firm's human resources. Initiatives included aligning firm compensation within the industry as well as recognizing location cost-of-living differences. Additionally, he brought screening and recruitment processes in-house, as a result of developing more effective tools internally, a move that resulted in annual savings of $2 million. Further, under his guidance, the human resources (HR) department conducted a series of in-house, in-depth surveys, using results to pinpoint traits consistent with successful leaders in the organization.

Beyond focus on its current situation, the department discussed and made an assessment on what it would take to be successful in the changing global operating environment. From this data, Holmes instituted an employee-assistance program and a company-wide diversity or inclusion program.

In the Canadian firm, principal Gary Reamey, indicates pride in the ranking "... because, in large part, it is the result of how associates view Edward Jones. ... We are many people working together, succeeding together, having fun together, and getting the job done." The firm has consistently been recognized as an employer of choice in national and international publications, including *Investment Executive's* annual survey of brokers, and the *Registered Representatives* magazine's annual survey of the nation's eight largest financial services firms in the U.S.

The recognition of the value of human resources as key to the success of the firm has not been lost on newcomer AIC. The company's mantra—Buy, Hold, and Prosper—has delivered returns and performance that belie the organization's relative youth. Behaving consistently, AIC's stated goal is to create long-term wealth for its clients, achieved through strict adherence to investment discipline and philosophy. Following principles that help investment decisions, AIC investors are expected to prosper over the long run through the preservation of capital, growth of capital, and the minimization of taxes.

Since being purchased, in 1987, AIC has racked up an enviable number of awards, including Best Global Balanced Fund for 2001 and several achievements by both Chairman and Chief Executive Officer Michael Lee-Chin and Chief Investment Officer Jonathan Wellum.

AIC, today ranks as Canada's largest, privately held mutual fund organization and manages more than $14 billion dollars in assets, with a growing portfolio of 35 mutual funds, 12 segregated funds, and 17 corporate class funds. AIC recruitment policy reflects its Buy, Hold, Prosper philosophy: the company actively enlists the best candidates and strives to retain them through attractive compensation packages and a challenging work environment that enables them to prosper and thrive.

The company's respected portfolio management team shares a common vision and follows the firm's Buy, Hold, Prosper philosophy to evaluate and select the excellent businesses in which the company invests.

SOURCES: A. Meisler, 2003. Holmes Improvement, *Workforce Management*, August; http://www.edwardjones.com/cgi/getHTML.cgi?page=/entry/index.html, accessed July 20, 2004; *AIC website*, http://www.aic.com/, accessed November 29, 2003.

people to fit their individual pieces of knowledge together so that, collectively, employees possess as much organizational knowledge as possible.[71]

To help their firms develop an environment in which knowledge is widely spread across all employees, some organizations have created the new upper-level managerial position of chief learning officer (CLO). Establishing a CLO position highlights a firm's belief that "future success will depend on competencies that traditionally have not been actively managed or measured—including creativity and the speed with which new ideas are learned and shared."[72] In general, the firm should manage knowledge in ways that will support its efforts to create value for customers.[73]

As illustrated in Table 4.4, capabilities are often developed in specific functional areas (such as manufacturing, R&D, and marketing) or in a part of a functional area (for example, advertising). Research suggests a relationship between capabilities developed in particular functional areas and the firm's financial performance at both the corporate and business-unit levels,[74] suggesting the need to develop capabilities at both levels. Table 4.4 shows a grouping of organizational functions and the capabilities that some companies are thought to possess, in terms of all or a selection of those functions.

Core Competencies

Core competencies are resources and capabilities that serve as sources of a firm's sustained competitive advantage over its rivals, distinguishing a company competitively and reflect its personality. Core competencies emerge over time through an organizational process of accumulating and learning how to deploy different resources and capabilities. As measures of the capacity to take action, core competencies are the crown jewels of a com-

Table 4.4	Examples of Firms' Capabilities	
Functional Areas	**Capabilities**	**Examples of Firms**
Supply Chain	Effective use of procurement techniques	Starbucks
Distribution	Effective use of logistics management techniques	Wal-Mart
Human Resources	Motivating, empowering, and retaining employees	Royal Bank of Canada
Management Information Systems	Effective and efficient control of inventories through point-of-purchase data collection methods	Wal-Mart
Marketing	Effective promotion of brand-name products	Gillette McKinsey & Co.
	Effective Customer Service	Nordstrom
Management	Ability to envision the future of clothing	Gap, Inc.
	Effective organizational structure	PepsiCo
	Effective culture	WestJet
Manufacturing	Design and production skills yielding reliable products	Komatsu
	Product and design quality	Gap, Inc.
	Production of technologically sophisticated automobile engines	Mazda
	Miniaturization of components and products	Sony
Research & Development	Exceptional technological capability	Corning
	Development of sophisticated elevator control solutions	Motion Control
	Rapid transformation of technology into new products and processes	Chaparral Steel
	Deep knowledge of silver-halide materials	Kodak

pany, the activities the company performs especially well compared to its competitors and through which the firm adds unique value to its goods or services over a long period of time.[75]

Not all of a firm's resources and capabilities are *strategic assets*—that is, assets that have the potential to serve as a source of competitive advantage.[76] Some resources and capabilities may result in incompetence, because they represent competitive areas in which the firm is weak compared to its competitors. Thus, some resources or capabilities may stifle or prevent the development of a core competence. Firms with the tangible resource of financial capital, such as Microsoft, may be able to purchase facilities or hire the skilled workers required to manufacture products that yield customer value. However, firms without financial capital would have a weakness in their ability to buy or build new capabilities. To be successful, firms must locate external environmental opportunities that can be exploited through their capabilities, while avoiding competition in areas of weakness.[77]

An important question is "How many core competencies are required for the firm to have a sustained competitive advantage?" Responses to this question vary. McKinsey & Company recommends that its clients identify three or four competencies around which their strategic actions can be organized.[78] This approach suggests that organizing to exploit (support and nurture) more than four core competencies may prevent a firm from developing the focus it needs to fully exploit its competencies in the marketplace.

Firms should take actions that are based on their core competencies. Recent actions by Starbucks demonstrate this point. Growing rapidly, Starbucks decided that it could use the Internet as a distribution channel to bring about additional growth. The firm quickly realized that it lacks the capabilities required to successfully distribute its products through this channel and that its unique coffee, not the delivery of that product, is its competitive advantage. In part, this recognition caused Starbucks to renew its emphasis on existing capabilities to create more value through its supply chain. As a result, Starbucks has trimmed the number of its milk suppliers from 65 to fewer than 25 and negotiated long-term contracts with coffee-bean growers. The firm also decided to place automated espresso machines in its busy units. These machines reduce Starbucks' cost while providing improved service to its customers, who can now move through the line much faster. Using its supply chain and service capabilities in these manners allows Starbucks to strengthen its competitive advantages of coffee and the unique venue in which on-site customers experience it.[79]

Of course, not all resources and capabilities are core competencies. The next section discusses two approaches for identifying core competencies.

Building Core Competencies

Two tools help the firm identify and build its core competencies.[80] The first consists of four specific criteria of sustainable competitive advantage that firms can use to determine those resources and capabilities that are core competencies. Because the capabilities shown in Table 4.4 have satisfied these four criteria, they are core competencies. The second tool is the value chain analysis. Firms use this tool to select the value-creating competencies that should be maintained, upgraded, or developed and those that should be outsourced.

Four Criteria of Sustainable Competitive Advantage

As shown in Table 4.5 on page 116, capabilities that are valuable, rare, costly to imitate, and organized to be exploited are strategic capabilities. Also called core competencies, strategic capabilities are a source of competitive advantage for the firm over its rivals. Capabilities failing to satisfy the four criteria of sustainable competitive advantage are

Table 4.5	Four Criteria for Determining Core Competencies (Strategic Capabilities)
Valuable Capabilities	Help a firm to generate revenues by exploiting opportunities and/or to reduce costs by neutralizing threats.
Rare Capabilities	Those capabilities possessed by a few firms in a group of competitors.
Costly-to-Imitate Capabilities (Nonduplicable and Nonsubstitutable Capabilities)	Those capabilities that an organization's closest competitors have tried to duplicate or substitute for, but the cost exceeds the benefits. Three reasons a capability may be costly to imitate are: <ul><li>Historical: a unique capability, such as a brand name or organizational culture that has developed along a defined historical path</li><li>Ambiguous cause: the cause of a capability is not clear</li><li>Social complexity: interpersonal relationships, such as trust and friendship among managers, employees, suppliers, customers</li></ul>
Organized to Be Exploited	Appropriate structure to support capability Appropriate control systems to support capability Appropriate reward systems to support capability

SOURCE: Adapted with permission from Barney, Jay B., *Gaining and Sustaining Competitive Advantage* (1st Edition), 145–61. © 1997. Reprinted by permission of Pearson Education, Inc., Upper Saddle River, NJ.

not core competencies. Thus, as shown in Figure 4.5, every core competence is a capability, but not every capability is a core competence. Operationally, for a capability to be a core competence, it must be "valuable and nonsubstitutable, from a customer's point of view, unique and inimitable, from a competitor's point of view"[81] and organized to be exploited from the firm's point of view.

A sustained competitive advantage is achieved only when competitors have failed in their efforts to duplicate the benefits of a firm's strategy or when they lack the confidence to attempt imitation. For some period of time, the firm may earn a competitive advantage by using capabilities that are, for example, valuable and rare, but that are imitable.[82] In this instance, the length of time a firm can expect to retain its competitive advantage is a function of how quickly competitors can successfully imitate a good, service, or process. Sustainable competitive advantage results only when all four criteria are satisfied.

Valuable

Valuable capabilities allow the firm to exploit opportunities to generate revenues or neutralize threats to reduce costs. By effectively using capabilities to exploit opportunities, a firm is able to create value for customers.

Sometimes, firms' capabilities become valuable only through modifications that improve firms' ability to satisfy customers' needs. As individuals browse the Internet for information, for example, many feel that an insufficient amount of value is available online to make a purchase. About 3 percent of website visitors actually make a purchase,

Valuable capabilities allow the firm to exploit opportunities to generate revenues or neutralize threats to reduce costs.

Figure 4.5 Core Competence as a Strategic Capability

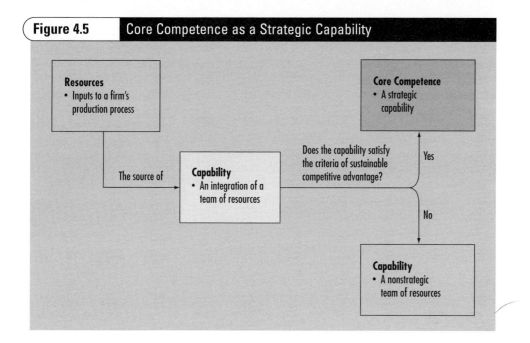

while 97 percent only browse. However, firms are learning to modify their websites to create more value for visitors, thereby converting them into buyers. The results from a recent study suggested that the order-conversion rate increased from 1.8 percent to 3.2 percent in 1999.[83] In this case, a valuable capability converts visitors into buyers. Over time, computer models that analyze website visits of consumers will play an important role in helping firms turn visitors into buyers. Interestingly, the models' real value may be that they make the website more like a human salesperson. "Think of the old-time shoe-store salesman who knew his customers, knew what they had bought for years, and knew who had to try on 11 pairs before one pair would feel right."[84]

In regard to value creation, e-commerce has a long way to go before a meaningful portion of it behaves like a human salesperson. However, this capability is what most e-businesses, such as Amazon.com, seek to achieve. In fact, Amazon has amazingly high satisfaction levels among its website visitors as well as its buyers. "Customers love Amazon not because it offers the lowest prices—it doesn't—but because the experience has been crafted so carefully that most of us actually enjoy it."[85] Similarly, Wal-Mart, relying initially on its distribution capabilities to pursue an opportunity, started its business by offering startlingly low prices on a vast selection of brand-name goods. Analysts believe that Wal-Mart changed the way consumers thought about value, letting them know that they did not have to pay the prices charged by most retailers.[86]

Rare

Rare capabilities are possessed by few, if any, current or potential competitors. A key question managers answer when evaluating this criterion is, "How many rival firms possess these valuable capabilities?" From an economics perspective, a capability is considered rare when the number of firms possessing the capability is fewer than the number required for perfect competition. Capabilities possessed by many rivals are unlikely to be a source of competitive advantage for any one of them. Instead, valuable but common (i.e., not rare) resources and capabilities are sources of competitive parity.[87] Valuable and rare resources and capabilities are sources of temporary competitive advantage. These

Rare capabilities are possessed by a few, if any, current or potential competitors.

temporary competitive advantages result when firms develop and exploit capabilities that differ from those shared with their competitors but are capable of being imitated or substituted for by those same competitors.

For example, when Palm Computing was established, it had an operating system that was different from its competitors in the PC sector. Palm's software was designed to run on a small handheld device. The first product using the software, Apple's Newton, did not create enough value for consumers and failed. However, funding from U.S. Robotics allowed the founders to create better software and design the hardware, incorporating both into the PalmPilot, and the product was successful. The PalmPilot sold 350,000 units in 1994, 750,000 in 1995, and 1 million in 1996. In 1998, 3Com purchased Palm Computing and spun it into a separate corporation in 2000. However, its software is still a rare product and is licensed by 3Com's competitors, such as Handspring. Although Microsoft has a competing operating system, to this point, it has not been as successful as the Palm operating system and application software.[88] Thus, Palm's operating system and associated software are still rare.

Costly to Imitate

Costly to imitate capabilities are capabilities that other firms cannot easily imitate or substitute for.

Costly to imitate capabilities are capabilities that other firms cannot easily imitate or substitute for. Capabilities that are costly to imitate are created because of one, or a combination, of three reasons (see Table 4.5, on page 116). First, a firm sometimes is able to develop capabilities because of *unique historical conditions*. "As firms evolve, they pick up skills, abilities and resources that are unique to them, reflecting their particular path through history."[89] In other words, firms sometimes are able to develop capabilities because they were in the right place at the right time.[90]

A firm with a unique and valuable *organizational culture* (such as Canada's WestJet) that emerged in the early stages of the company's history "may have an imperfectly imitable advantage over firms founded in another historical period"[91]—a period when less valuable or less competitively useful values and beliefs strongly influenced the development of the firm's culture. This may be the case for the consulting firm McKinsey & Company. "It is that culture, unique to McKinsey and eccentric, which sets the firm apart from virtually any other business organization and which often mystifies even those who engage [its] services."[92] Briefly discussed in Chapter 1, organizational culture is "something that people connect with, feel inspired by, think of as a normal way of operating. It's in their hearts and minds, and its core is voluntary behavior."[93] An organizational culture is a source of advantage when employees are held together tightly by their belief in it.[94]

UPS has been the prototype in many areas of the parcel delivery business because of its excellence in products, systems, marketing, and other operational business capabilities. "Its fundamental competitive strength, however, derives from the organization's unique culture, which has spanned almost a century, growing deeper all along. This culture provides solid, consistent roots for everything the company does, from skills training to technological innovation."[95]

A second condition of being costly to imitate occurs when the link between the firm's capabilities and its competitive advantage is *causally ambiguous*.[96] In these instances, competitors can't clearly understand how a firm uses its capabilities as the foundation for competitive advantage. As a result, other firms are uncertain about the capabilities they should develop to duplicate the benefits of a competitor's value-creating strategy. Gordon Forward, CEO of Chaparral Steel, allows competitors to tour his firm's facilities. In Forward's words, competitors can be shown almost "everything and we will be giving away nothing because they can't take it home with them."[97] Contributing to Chaparral Steel's causally ambiguous operations is the fact that workers use the concept of *mentefacturing*, by which manufacturing steel is done by using their minds instead of their hands. "In mentefacturing, workers use computers to monitor operations and don't need to be on the shop floor during production."[98]

Social complexity is the third reason that capabilities can be costly to imitate. Social complexity means that at least some, and frequently many, of the firm's capabilities are the products of complex social phenomena. Interpersonal relationships, trust, friendships among managers and between managers and employees, and a firm's reputation with suppliers and customers are examples of socially complex capabilities. Nucor Steel has been able to create "a hunger for new knowledge through a high-powered incentive system for every employee." This socially complex process has allowed Nucor "to push the boundaries of manufacturing process know-how."[99]

Nonsubstitutable capabilities are capabilities that do not have strategic equivalents. This criterion for a capability to be a source of competitive advantage is "that there must be no strategically equivalent valuable resources that are themselves either not rare or imitable. Two valuable firm resources (or two bundles of firm resources) are strategically equivalent when they each can be separately exploited to implement the same strategies."[100] In general, the strategic value of capabilities increases as they become more difficult to substitute.[101] The more invisible capabilities are, the more difficult it is for firms to find substitutes and the greater the challenge is to competitors trying to imitate a firm's value-creating strategy. Firm-specific knowledge and trust-based working relationships between managers and nonmanagerial personnel are examples of capabilities that are difficult to identify and for which finding a substitute is challenging. However, causal ambiguity may make it difficult for the firm to learn and may stifle progress because the firm does not know how to improve processes that are not easily codified and thus ambiguous.[102]

For example, competitors are deeply familiar with Dell Computer's successful direct sales model. However, to date, no competitor has been able to imitate Dell's capabilities, as "there's no better way to make, sell, and deliver PCs than the way Dell does it, and nobody executes that model better than Dell."[103] Moreover, no competitor has been able to develop and use substitute capabilities that can duplicate the value Dell creates by using its capabilities. Thus, experience suggests that Dell's direct sales model capabilities are nonsubstitutable.

Organized to Be Exploited

The fourth criterion in our search for core competencies is the ability to be organized to be exploited. Being **organized to be exploited** means that firms have the correct structure, control systems, and reward systems to support each source of competitive parity, temporary competitive advantage, and sustained competitive advantage. For example if a firm is pursuing a product differentiation strategy (discussed in Chapter 5) that is difficult for competitors to imitate, it is important that the structure, controls, and rewards be characterized as follows. Appropriate structural characteristics for product differentiation are cross-functional/cross-divisional linkages, there is a willingness to utilize new structures to take advantage of new opportunities, and there is a willingness to have isolated areas of intense creative efforts. Control systems need to be flexible in the way they control activities, make allowances for creative people, and allow learning from innovative failures. Reward systems should not punish for failure but reward for risk-taking and creative flair, and be qualitative and subjective in measuring performance.[104]

If, on the other hand, a firm wants to pursue a cost leadership strategy (discussed in Chapter 5) that competitors would have trouble imitating, the structure, control systems, and reward systems must be characterized by other attributes. Structurally, the firm should have few layers in its reporting system, reporting relationships should be simple, and there should be a disciplined focus on a narrow range of business functions. The control system should be one where there is tight cost control; quantitative cost objectives;

Being **organized to be exploited** means that firms have the correct structure, control systems, and reward systems to support each source of competitive parity, temporary competitive advantage, and sustained competitive advantage.

Table 4.6	Outcomes from Combinations of the Four Criteria for Sustained Competitive Advantage: The VRIO Framework

Is the resource or capability ...

Variable?	Rare?	Costly to Imitate?	Organized to Be Exploited?	Competitive Consequences	Performance Implications
No	–	–	No	Competitive Disadvantage	Below-Average Returns
Yes	No	–	Yes	Competitive Parity	Average Returns
Yes	Yes	No	Yes	Temporary Competitive Advantage	Above-Average Returns
Yes	Yes	Yes	Yes	Sustained Competitive Advantage	Above-Average Returns

SOURCE: Adapted with permission from Barney, Jay B., *Gaining and Sustaining Competitive Advantage* (1st Edition), 167. © 1997. Reprinted by permission of Pearson Education, Inc., Upper Saddle River, NJ.

closely supervised labour, raw material, inventory, and other costs; and a philosophy of cost leadership. Compensation policies should reward for reducing costs, and there should be incentives for all members to be involved in cost reduction.[105]

In summary, sustainable competitive advantage is created only by using valuable, rare, costly to imitate, and organized-to-be-exploited capabilities. Table 4.6 shows the competitive consequences and performance implications resulting from combinations of the four criteria of sustainability. The analysis suggested by the table helps managers determine the strategic value of a firm's capabilities. Resources and capabilities falling into the first row in the table (i.e., resources and capabilities that are not valuable) should not be emphasized by the firm when formulating and implementing strategies. Capabilities yielding competitive parity and either temporary or sustainable competitive advantage, however, should be organized to be exploited. Large competitors, such as Coca-Cola and PepsiCo, may have capabilities that can yield only competitive parity. In such cases, the firms will nurture these capabilities while simultaneously trying to develop capabilities that can yield either a temporary or sustainable competitive advantage.

Value Chain Analysis

Value chain analysis allows the firm to understand the parts of its operations that create value and those that do not. Understanding these issues is important because the firm earns above-average returns only when the value it creates is greater than the costs incurred to create that value.[106] (When value created is greater than the costs incurred, the positive difference is similar to the concept of rent in economics.)

The value chain is a template that firms use to understand their cost position and to identify the multiple means that might be used to facilitate implementation of a chosen business-level strategy.[107] As shown in Figure 4.6, a firm's value chain is segmented into primary and support activities. **Primary activities** are involved with a product's physical creation, its sale and distribution to buyers, and its service after the sale. **Support activities** provide the support necessary for the primary activities to take place.

Primary activities are involved with a product's physical creation, its sale and distribution to buyers, and its service after the sale.

Support activities provide the support necessary for the primary activities to take place.

Figure 4.6 | The Basic Value Chain

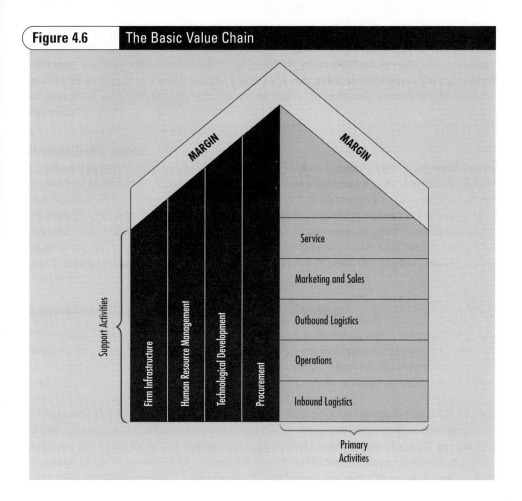

The value chain shows how a product moves from the raw-material stage to the final customer. For individual firms, the essential idea of the value chain is "to add as much value as possible as cheaply as possible, and, most important, to capture that value." In a globally competitive economy, the most valuable links on the chain tend to belong to people who have knowledge about customers.[108] This locus of value-creating possibilities applies just as strongly to retail and service firms as to manufacturers. Moreover, for organizations in all sectors, the effects of e-commerce make it increasingly necessary for companies to develop value-adding knowledge processes to compensate for the value and margin that the Internet strips from physical processes.[109]

Table 4.7 lists the items to be studied to assess the value-creating potential of primary activities. In Table 4.8, the items to consider when studying support activities are shown. Often, a source of confusion is the difference between inbound logistics (see Table 4.7, on page 122) and procurement (see Table 4.8, on page 124). Procurement is everything done to obtain raw materials up to—but not including—the point where the firm takes ownership of the raw material. Inbound logistics is everything done from the point where the firm takes ownership of raw materials until they are used to create a product or service. As with the analysis of primary activities, the intent in examining these items is to determine areas where the firm has the potential to create and capture value. All items in both tables should be evaluated relative to competitors' capabilities. To be a source of competitive advantage, a resource or capability must allow the firm (1) to perform an activity in a manner that is superior to the way competitors perform it, or

Table 4.7	Examining the Value-Creating Potential of Primary Activities along the Value Chain
Inbound Logistics	Activities, such as materials handling, warehousing, and inventory control, used to receive, store, and disseminate inputs to a product.
Operations	Activities necessary to convert the inputs provided by inbound logistics into final product form. Machining, packaging, assembly, and equipment maintenance are examples of operations activities.
Outbound Logistics	Activities involved with collecting, storing, and physically distributing the final product to customers. Examples of these activities include finished-goods warehousing, materials handling, and order processing.
Marketing and Sales	Activities that induce customers to purchase products and that define the means by which the purchases are made. To effectively market and sell products, firms develop advertising and promotional campaigns, select appropriate distribution channels, and select, develop, and support their sales force.
Service	Activities designed to enhance or maintain a product's value. Firms engage in a range of service-related activities, including installation, repair, training, and adjustment.

Each activity should be examined relative to competitors' abilities. This evaluation is accomplished by using the VRIO Framework in Table 4.6, on page 120.

SOURCE: Adapted with permission of The Free Press, a Division of Simon & Schuster Adult Publishing Group, from *Competitive Advantage: Creating and Sustaining Superior Performance*, by Michael E. Porter, pp. 39–40, Copyright © 1985, 1988 by Michael E. Porter. All rights reserved.

(2) to perform a value-creating activity that competitors cannot complete. Only under these conditions does a firm create and capture value through its sources of temporary and sustained competitive advantage.

Sometimes, start-up firms create value by uniquely reconfiguring or recombining parts of the value chain. Federal Express (FedEx) changed the nature of the delivery business by reconfiguring outbound logistics (a primary activity) and human resource management (a support activity) to originate the overnight delivery business, creating value in the process. As shown in Figure 4.7, the Internet is changing many aspects of the value chain for a broad range of firms. As an example of many of these changes, see the Strategic Focus box, "Significant Changes in the Value Chains of Pharmaceutical Firms," on page 125, which describes the upheaval in the value chains of firms that has created many entry opportunities for new participants.

Rating a firm's capability to execute its primary and support activities is challenging. Earlier in the chapter, we noted that identifying and assessing the value of a firm's resources and capabilities requires judgment. Judgment is equally necessary when using value chain analysis, as there is no obviously correct model or rule available to help in the process.

As discussed in this Strategic Focus box, a significant change is occurring in the pharmaceutical industry's value chain. Millennium Pharmaceuticals has exploited an opportunity to reduce costs in the research and exploration upstream stage in the value chain

Figure 4.7 Prominent Applications of the Internet in the Value Chain

Firm Infrastructure
- Web-based, distributed financial, and ERP systems
- Online investor relations (e.g., information dissemination, broadcast conference calls)

Human Resource Management
- Self-service personnel and benefits administration
- Web-based training
- Internet-based sharing and dissemination of company information
- Electronic time and expense reporting

Technology Development
- Collaborative product design across locations and among multiple value-system participants
- Knowledge directories accessible from all parts of the organization
- Real-time access by R&D to online sales and service information

Procurement
- Internet-enabled demand planning; real-time available-to-promise/capable-to-promise and fulfillment
- Other linkage of purchase, inventory, and forecasting systems with suppliers
- Automated "requisition to pay"
- Direct and indirect procurement via marketplaces, exchanges, auctions, and buyer-seller matching

Inbound Logistics
- Real-time integrated scheduling, shipping, warehouse management, demand management and planning, and advanced planning and scheduling across the company and its suppliers
- Dissemination throughout the company of real-time inbound and in-progress inventory data

Operations
- Integrated information exchange, scheduling and decision making in in-house plants, contract assemblers, and components suppliers
- Real-time available-to-promise and capable-to-promise information available to the sales force and channels

Outbound Logistics
- Real-time transaction of orders whether initiated by an end consumer, a sales person, or a channel partner
- Automated customer-specific agreements and contract terms
- Customer and channel access to product development and delivery status
- Collaborative integration with customer-forecasting systems
- Integrated channel management including information exchange, warranty claims, and contract management (versioning, process control)

Marketing and Sales
- Online sales channels including websites and marketplaces
- Real-time inside and outside access to customer information, product catalogues, dynamic pricing, inventory availability, online submission of quotes, and order entry
- Online product configurators
- Customer-tailored marketing via customer profiling
- Push advertising
- Tailored online access
- Real-time customer feedback through web surveys, opt-in/opt-out marketing, and promotion response tracking

After-Sales Service
- Online support of customer service representatives through e-mail response management, billing integration, co-browse, chat, "call me now," voice-over-IP, and other uses of video streaming
- Customer self-service via websites and intelligent service request processing including updates to billing and shipping profiles
- Real-time field service access to customer account review, schematic review, parts availability and ordering, work-order update, and service parts management

← • Web-distributed supply chain management →

SOURCE: Reprinted by permission of *Harvard Business Review* from "Strategy and the Internet" by Michael E. Porter, March 2001, p. 75. Copyright © 2001 by the Harvard Business School Publishing Corporation, all rights reserved.

and has thereby created significant opportunity for itself. Furthermore, larger, more established pharmaceutical firms, recognizing Millennium's capabilities, have sought partnerships with Millennium. By using Millennium's platform for genetic exploration, these partners hope to accelerate the identification of genetic leads that will develop cures. Through partnering with firms such as Eli Lilly and Abbott Laboratories, Millennium has raised $1.8 billion, which, in turn, has helped the firm solidify its R&D platform even further.[110]

Table 4.8	Examining the Value-Creating Potential of Support Activities in the Value Chain
Procurement	Activities completed to purchase the inputs needed to produce a firm's products. Purchased inputs include items fully consumed during the manufacture of products (e.g., raw materials and supplies, as well as fixed assets—machinery, laboratory equipment, office equipment, and buildings).
Technological Development	Activities completed to improve a firm's product and the processes used to manufacture it. Technological development takes many forms, such as process equipment, basic research and product design, and servicing procedures.
Human Resource Management	Activities involved with recruiting, hiring, training, developing, and compensating all personnel.
Firm Infrastructure	Firm infrastructure includes activities such as general management, planning, finance, accounting, legal support, and governmental relations that are required to support the work of the entire value chain. Through its infrastructure, the firm strives to effectively and consistently identify external opportunities and threats, identify resources and capabilities, and support core competencies.

Each activity should be examined relative to competitors' abilities. This is accomplished by using the VRIO Framework in Table 4.6, on page 120.

What should a firm do about primary and support activities in which its resources and capabilities are not a source of competitive parity or competitive advantage? One solution could be outsourcing.

Outsourcing

Outsourcing is the purchase of a value-creating activity from an external supplier.

Concerned with how components, finished goods, or services will be obtained, **outsourcing** is the purchase of a value-creating activity from an external supplier.[111] In multiple global industries, the trend toward outsourcing continues at a rapid pace.[112]

In some industries, virtually all firms seek the value that can be captured through effective outsourcing. The automobile manufacturing and, more recently, the electronics industry are examples of such situations.[113] A number of examples of outsourcing are provided in the Strategic Focus box, "Significant Changes in the Value Chains of Pharmaceutical Firms."

Outsourcing is effective because few, if any, organizations possess the resources and capabilities required to achieve competitive superiority in all primary and support activities. With respect to technologies, for example, research suggests that few companies can afford to develop internally all the technologies that might lead to competitive advantage. By nurturing a smaller number of capabilities, a firm increases the probability of

Significant Changes in the Value Chains of Pharmaceutical Firms

Over the last few years, significant changes have taken place in the value chains of many pharmaceutical firms. The first medical remedies date back to the herbs and potions that people took to treat illnesses. In the pharmaceutical industry's early history, medical remedies began to be created through chemistry. Companies, especially in Germany, began to systematically isolate ingredients, test them for efficacy, and sell them as pills and serums. Firms such as Pfizer and Eli Lilly began during this phase and used a vertical integration strategy (defined in Chapter 7) along the value chain stages of research, testing, and delivery to the consumer.

In the 1960s, following Crick and Watson's discovery of DNA, biology and genetics became major sources of inputs to pharmaceutical firms. The genetic revolution brought two new *upstream*—or early stage—steps to the industry's value chain: research into the genes that cause disease and identification of the proteins that those genes produce. Highly specialized biotech firms, such as AmGen and Genentech, were started through these developments in the upstream research stage of the value chain. For the most part, small, rather than large, companies dominated this new segment of the value chain. With no small firm having market power, this segment was highly fragmented (i.e., the segment had a relatively large number of small firms competing against each other but with no one firm able to significantly influence the competition among them).

More recently, the mapping of the human genome has further expanded the industry. Firms such as Millennium Pharmaceuticals have been involved in human genome research and mapping. Many of these upstream biopharmaceutical companies are now seeking to move downstream (the later stages in the value chain) where larger, more established pharmaceutical companies are positioned with expertise in testing (preclinical trials and clinical trials) and delivery (manufacturing and marketing).

To expand downstream, many smaller biopharmaceutical firms have structured partnerships with the larger pharmaceutical firms, who invest in the smaller biotech firms. Biotech firms such as Celera, the major developer of the genome mapping project, and Millennium Pharmaceuticals have research platforms that are attractive to larger downstream pharmaceutical firms because they allow the smaller biotech firms to accelerate the process of identifying genetic leads to develop cures. For example, in the space of a week, rather than just studying one experiment, scientists can now study dozens of experiments. Leveraging information technology, in association with gene finding technologies, has improved productivity in the discovery stage, one of the early segments of the value chain. Once a lead looks promising, a move to the testing stage is possible.

Because the early testing stages take considerable time, many information and web-based strategies are employed. In the United States, 15 years and approximately $500 million are needed to develop a drug and complete its preclinical and clinical trials, before it can be brought to market. Any time that can be pared from the 15-year period will lead to reduced testing and staging costs. Small specialty online firms using a focus strategy (see Chapter 5) have sought to develop web-based approaches to help speed up the trial-testing phases of the value chain. For instance, Schering-Plough has contracted with Phase Forward Inc., whose system allows clinical investigators (doctors and researchers) to enter patient data directly to a website. This step eliminates error-checking of paper records and "can shave one to two years off getting a drug to market," says Phase Forward CEO Shiv Tasker. Datatrak, another trial contractor, offers online software that is estimated to cut the total trial time by 30 percent. Although these technologies are promising, they account for only a tiny fraction of all trials underway. One consultant suggests that "everyone is waiting for a Quicken for clinical trials."

Not only does the Internet offer reduced error-checking and time during the testing period, a web-based approach can cost $35 per patient, compared with $350 per person now spent on advertising for patients, phone calls, and other requirements of the trial period. The web-based

(continued)

approach also reduces error because the software automatically checks information as it is entered and catches most mistakes, however the web cannot speed up all pharmaceutical research. To determine how many cancer patients survived after two years of treatment, a two-year study is still required.

In regard to the value chain areas of manufacturing and marketing, although web-based technologies offer alternative methods of delivery of prescription medicines, 90 percent of customers placing orders on the Internet prefer to pick up their orders at a nearby store rather than have them shipped to their homes. For firms such as Walgreens, an extensive network of stores has a potent advantage, even as ordering has shifted to the Internet. Accordingly, although online operations, such as drugstore.com, were forecasted to make bricks-and-mortar pharmacies, such as Walgreens, obsolete by providing cheaper medicines to consumers through a more direct distribution from the producer, this has not turned out to be the case.

The value chain of pharmaceutical firms is changing drastically. In the upstream research stage, computer technologies speed the discovery of useful compounds, and the mapping of human genome project has fostered significant progress. Furthermore, testing time has the potential to be shortened through web-based strategies. Finally, significant changes have occurred in the downstream marketing and delivery of drugs. These changes in the value chain have created significant opportunities for new entrants as well as established producers.

SOURCES: D. Champion, 2001, Mastering the value chain: An interview with Mark Levin of Millennium Pharmaceuticals, *Harvard Business Review*, 79(6): 108–15; E. Licking, J. Carey, & J. Kerstetter, 2001, Bioinformatics, *Business Week*, spring (industrial/technology ed.), 166–70; B. O'Keefe, 2001, Post-genome, Celera now shoots for profits, *Fortune*, February 19, 226; M. E. Porter, 2001, Strategy and the Internet, *Harvard Business Review*, 79(3): 62–78; R. Burcham, 2000, New pharma business model: Can we survive it? *Pharmaceutical Executive*, November, 94–100; J. Carey & E. Licking, 2000, An Rx for drug trials, *Business Week*, December 11, EB66–EB68.

developing a competitive advantage because it will not become overextended. In addition, by outsourcing activities in which it lacks competence, the firm can fully concentrate on those areas in which it can create value.[114]

Other research suggests that outsourcing does not work effectively without extensive internal capabilities to effectively coordinate external sourcing as well as internal coordination of core competencies.[115] Dell Computer, for example, outsources most of its manufacturing and customer service activities, allowing the firm to concentrate on creating value through its service and online distribution capabilities.

However, as the Strategic Focus box "Outsourcing the Human Resources Function" indicates, a company should exercise caution when most firms in the industry are engaged in outsourcing. Although many firms in the athletic shoe industry (e.g., Nike and Reebok) outsource their manufacturing to countries with lower average wage, some companies, such as New Balance, have decided not to ship the bulk of their manufacturing overseas. Although there is some logic to the suggestion that low-skilled labour and codified technologies should be outsourced to countries with lower cost structures and comparative advantage, New Balance has successfully challenged this assumption. Instead of outsourcing all of its production, like most other shoe companies, 20 percent of New Balance's production is kept within the company by upgrading low-skill jobs to improve efficiency. While shoes are still cheaper to produce in China ($1.30 per shoe compared to $4.00 per shoe in the United States), New Balance's domestically produced shoes are made more efficiently (24 minutes per shoe compared with three hours per shoe in China). New Balance believes that the ability to produce domestically, with the added advantages of design and quality control, is worth the extra cost of only 4 percent of the typical $70 shoe. While not all low-skill jobs could be made more efficient, New Balance's practice raises questions regarding which capabilities to outsource, even when

Outsourcing the Human Resources Function

As globalization progresses and firms increasingly face new and greater numbers of competitors, good business sense dictates that firms re-evaluate how prepared they are to deliver in the changing market. This practice requires assessing their internal processes to determine where, and if, additional or new efficiencies may reside. Often this self-assessment involves asking questions and making hard decisions regarding resources, in particular, human resources.

When a business case presents itself in efficiencies gained both in time and cost, not to mention the added benefit of existing resources being released, to refocus in areas of core competencies, then decisions about outsourcing become patently clear and much easier to make. Recent surveys by the Outsourcing Institute of Jericho estimate that Canadian companies spent an estimated $66 billion on outsourcing in 2001, an increase of 20 percent over the preceding year. In another survey, 500 chief financial officers (CFOs) expressed positive attitudes about the value of outsourcing. A significant 89 percent suggested that outsourcing enhanced shareholder value, and as many as 43 percent of the CFOs had outsourcing strategies in place. At least some support and non-core functions were outsourced at 91 percent of the companies represented. A primary reason for outsourcing (cited by 70 percent of CFOs) lay in a firm decision to tap into sources of skills and talent that were not seen as being evident within the firm. Other reasons for outsourcing were to concentrate resources on the core business and to reduce headcount and concomitant expenses.

The Hewitt study suggests that the function most likely to be outsourced is information technology, followed by human resources in the number two spot, closely followed by facilities management, in third place. Some distance behind, finance and accounting takes the fourth place position.

A recent BMO deal in late April 2003, saw the BMO Financial Group sign a multi-year $750 million HR outsourcing deal with California-based Exult, Inc. Only the second large financial house to make such a move in as many years (CIBC signed a 7-year $227 million deal with EDS), BMO's deal is expected to realize an almost 50 percent reduction in its HR expenses.

Officially, Rose Patten, executive vice-president, Human Resources and head of the Office of Strategic Management at BMO stated "Our agreement with Exult will give us the freedom to focus on the strategic management of human resources while continuing to provide leading HR administrative services." Patten, who took over the HR portfolio in November 2001, had identified five important objectives for the organization:

- Improve talent management;
- Improve the performance management and compensation system;
- Increase employee engagement;
- Ensure the bank's institute for learning was meeting its goals; and
- Run the HR department more efficiently.

The fifth objective was crucial in the process leading to the decision to outsource. Evaluating several options, including upgrading technology, implementing portals for self-service, and seeking companies that perform these services for a living, led to cost-benefit and cultural-impact assessments of each route, and ultimately, the selection of the outsource route.

The process of outsourcing required a detailed due diligence process and much deliberation over what would be outsourced. Patten said it wasn't easy to determine: "Where do you draw the line between strategic and transactional?"

Although business process outsourcing (BPO) deals of the magnitude of BMO and CIBC are still rare, more questions are being asked. Outsourcing providers, such as Hewitt Associates (HA) (an HR outsourcing and consulting firm that bought out Cyborg Worldwide, an established payroll provider, to enable it to have a more complete HR BPO operation) are positioning themselves for what seems to be an emerging market.

In a recent study, the Outsourcing Institute of Jericho concluded that outsourcing is not only growing but is also evolving, and where previously outsourcing was typically limited to non–

(continued)

mission critical tasks or tasks that didn't actually touch the customer, today that practice is changing. The challenge becomes introducing a sophistication to manage the new portfolio of business relationships.

Still further industry discussions suggest that outsourcing is a complex business proposition, requiring expertise in developing and negotiating the right terms and conditions. Additionally, there is a process of preparation that a firm must go through before it is ideally ready to outsource, and once engaged in a BPO relationship, the firm faces a new challenge of effectively managing the relationship. Bottom line, experts seem to agree that outsourcing is more than about the money; it's a matter of best practices.

While outsourcing has produced significant savings across many industries, such as the automobile industry, the electronics industry, and apparel and back-office services, outsourcing can be carried too far. For instance, if a firm outsources its central areas of core competence, it can destroy sources of competitive advantage. Dell successfully uses outsourcing because the personal computer industry uses standardized modules, and this is not Dell's core competence. Cisco exploited the modular architecture of its routers to compete in the telecommunications switching business from the low end. The firm efficiently outsourced much of its manufacturing to suppliers and much of its new product development to the start-ups it had acquired.

SOURCES: Hewitt Associates, 2002, CFOs say outsourcing increases shareholder value, *Hewitt Associates website*, http://www.hewitt.com/hewitt/resource/newsroom/pressrel/2002/04-29-02.htm (new release), April 29; D. Brown, 2003, BMO signs major HR outsourcing deal, *Canadian HR Reporter*, June 2; W. G. Stopper, 2003, Point-Counterpoint: How does HR outsourcing impact the power and influence of the function? (current practices) (panel discussion), *Human Resources Planning*, March.

some appear to be logical candidates. Similarly, Canada's Roots produces most of its clothing in Canada to ensure quality, despite cost savings possible from making its clothes in the Far East. We further study Roots' strategy in Chapter 5.[116]

To verify that the appropriate primary and support activities are outsourced, four skills are essential for managers involved in outsourcing programs: strategic thinking, deal making, partnership governance, and managing change.[117] Managers should understand whether and how outsourcing creates competitive advantage within their company—they need to be able to think strategically.[118] To complete effective outsourcing transactions, these managers must also be deal makers, to be able to secure rights from external providers that can be fully used by internal managers. Managers must be able to oversee and govern appropriately the relationships that develop when the company decides to outsource services. Because outsourcing can significantly change how an organization operates, managers administering these programs must also be able to manage that change, including the resolution of employee resistance that accompanies any significant change effort.[119]

Core Competencies: Cautions and Reminders

Tools such as outsourcing can help the firm focus on its core competencies. However, evidence shows that the value-creating ability of core competencies should never be taken for granted. Moreover, the ability of a core competence to be a permanent competitive advantage can't be assumed, as all core competencies have the potential to become *core rigidities*. As Leslie Wexner, CEO of The Limited, Inc., says, "Success doesn't beget success. Success begets failure because the more that you know a thing works, the less likely you are to think that it won't work. When you've had a long string of victories, it's harder to foresee your own vulnerabilities."[120] Thus, each competence is a strength and a weakness—a strength because it is the source of competitive advantage and, hence, strategic competitiveness, and a weakness because, if emphasized when it is no longer competitively relevant, it can become a core rigidity and a source of organizational inertia.[121]

Events occurring in the firm's external environment create conditions through which core competencies can become core rigidities, generate inertia, and stifle innovation. "Often the flip side, the dark side, of core capabilities is revealed due to external events when new competitors figure out a better way to serve the firm's customers, when new technologies emerge, or when political or social events shift the ground underneath."[122] However, in the final analysis, changes in the external environment do not cause core capabilities or core competencies to become core rigidities; rather, strategic myopia and inflexibility, on the part of managers, are the cause.[123]

These shortcomings may be the case at Bavarian Motor Works (BMW). Historically, BMW's unique internal process for designing automobiles has been a competitive advantage that other firms have not been able to duplicate. The firm's design process has required extensive and complex cooperative interactions among a large group of engineers. Recently, to reduce costs, BMW created a system that enables its engineers to use computer simulations to crash-test the cars they have designed and thereby improve them. This technology codifies into a set of algorithms what formerly could be achieved only through complex social interaction among BMW engineers. As such, the firm has codified what had been a complex intangible resource (interactions among design engineers), jeopardizing what had been a competitive advantage. It is much easier for BMW's rivals to imitate a computer simulation than to understand the complex, often unobservable interactions among the firm's engineers. Thus, at least in part, this competitive advantage may not be as valuable as it once was. However, continuous learning by BMW design engineers may allow the firm to maintain its competitive advantage in the long run.[124]

Summary

- In the global landscape, traditional factors (e.g., labour costs and superior access to financial resources and raw materials) can still create a competitive advantage. However, competitive advantages derived in this manner, are seen in a declining number of instances. In the new landscape, the resources, capabilities, and core competencies in the firm's internal environment may have a relatively stronger influence on its performance than the conditions in the external environment. The most effective firms recognize that strategic competitiveness and above-average returns result only when core competencies (identified through the study of the firm's internal environment) are matched with opportunities (determined through the study of the firm's external environment).

- No competitive advantage lasts forever. Over time, rivals use their own unique resources, capabilities, and core competencies to form different value-creating propositions that duplicate the value-creating ability of the firm's competitive advantages. In general, the Internet's capabilities are reducing the sustainability of many competitive advantages. Thus, because competitive advantages are not sustainable on a permanent basis, firms must exploit their current advantages while simultaneously using their resources and capabilities to form new advantages that can lead to competitive success in the future.

- Effective management of core competencies requires careful analysis of the firm's resources (inputs to the production process) and capabilities (capacities for teams of resources to perform a task or activity in an integrative manner). To successfully manage core competencies, decision makers must be self-confident, courageous, and willing both to hold others accountable for their work and to be held accountable for the outcomes of their own efforts.

- Individual resources are usually not a source of competitive advantage. Capabilities, which are groupings of tangible and intangible resources, are a more likely source of competitive advantages, especially those that are relatively sustainable. A key reason is that the firm's nurturing and support of core competencies are based on capabilities that are less visible to rivals and, as such, are harder to understand and imitate.

- Increasingly, employees' knowledge is viewed as perhaps the most relevant source of competitive advantage. To gain maximum benefit from knowledge, efforts are taken to find ways for individuals' unique knowledge sets to be shared throughout the firm. The Internet's capabilities affect both the development and the sharing of knowledge.

- Only when a capability is valuable, rare, costly to imitate, and organized to be exploited is it a core competence and a source of competitive advantage. Over time, core competencies must be supported, but they cannot be allowed to become core rigidities. Core competencies are a source of competitive advantage only when they allow the firm to create value by exploiting opportunities in the external environment. When this is no longer the case, attention shifts to selecting or forming other capabilities that do satisfy the four criteria of sustainable competitive advantage.

- Value chain analysis is used to identify and evaluate the competitive potential of resources and capabilities. By studying their skills relative to those associated with primary and support activities, firms can understand their cost structure and identify the activities through which they can create value. Firms using the VRIO Framework (see Table 4.6, on page 120) to analyze activities in the value chain (see Table 4.7, on page 122, and Table 4.8, on page 124) do a much better job of assessing value-creating activities and their potential to be a source of competitive disadvantage, competitive parity, temporary competitive advantage, or sustained competitive advantage.

- When the firm cannot create value in either a primary or support activity (therefore, creating a source of competitive disadvantage), outsourcing should be considered. Used commonly in the global economy, outsourcing is the purchase of a value-creating activity from an external supplier. The firm must outsource only to companies possessing a competitive advantage in terms of the particular primary or support activity under consideration. In addition, the firm must continuously verify that it is not outsourcing activities that could create value. Finally, it is important to ensure that core competencies do not become core rigidities. Core rigidities are sources of organizational inertia and competitive disadvantage.

Review Questions

1. Why is it important for a firm to study and understand its internal environment?

2. What is value? Why is it critical for the firm to create value? How does it create value?

3. What are the differences between tangible and intangible resources? Why is it important for decision makers to understand these differences? Are tangible resources linked more closely to the creation of competitive advantages than intangible resources, or is the reverse true? Why?

4. What are capabilities? What must firms do to create capabilities?

5. What are the four criteria used to determine which of a firm's capabilities are core competencies? Why is it important for these criteria to be used?

6. What is value chain analysis? What does the firm gain when it successfully uses this tool?

7. What is outsourcing? Why do firms outsource? Will outsourcing's importance grow in the 21st century? If so, why?

8. What are core rigidities? Why is it vital that firms prevent core competencies from becoming core rigidities?

Experiential Exercise

Organizational Resources

The organizations listed in the table below have different capabilities, core competencies, and competitive advantages.

Part One. In small groups, consider each firm and use logic and consensus to complete the table. Alternatively, complete the table on an individual basis.

Organization	Capabilities	Core Competencies	Competitive Advantage
McDonald's			
CBC			
Canada Post			
Microsoft			

Part Two. Based on your responses to the table, compare each type of firm in terms of its resources and suggest some reasons for the differences.

	Is the resource or capability				Competitive Consequences: Competitive disadvantage Competitive parity Temporary competitive advantage Sustained competitive advantage	Performance Implications: Below-average returns Average returns Above-average returns
	Valuable?	Rare?	Costly to Imitate?	Organized to Exploit?		
McDonald's						
CBC						
Canada Post						
Microsoft						

Notes

1. C. A. Bartlett & S. Ghoshal, 2002, Building competitive advantage through people, *MIT Sloan Management Review*, 43(2): 34–41.
2. R. R. Wiggins & T. W. Ruefli, 2002, Sustained competitive advantage: Temporal dynamics and the incidence of persistence of superior economic performance, *Organization Science*, 13: 82–105.
3. M. J. Rouse & U. S. Daellenbach, 1999, Rethinking research methods for the resource-based perspective: Isolating sources of sustainable competitive advantage, *Strategic Management Journal*, 20: 487–94.
4. C. G. Brush, P. G. Greene, & M. M. Hart, 2001, From initial idea to unique advantage: The entrepreneurial challenge of constructing a resource base, *Academy of Management Executive*, 15(1): 64–78.
5. R. Makadok, 2001, Toward a synthesis of the resource-based and dynamic-capability views of rent creation, *Strategic Management Journal*, 22: 387–401; K. M. Eisenhardt & J. A. Martin, 2000, Dynamic capabilities: What are they? *Strategic Management Journal*, 21: 1105–21.
6. M. A. Hitt, L. Bierman, K. Shimizu, & R. Kochhar, 2001, Direct and moderating effects of human capital on strategy and performance in professional service firms: A resource-based perspective, *Academy of Management Journal*, 44: 13–28; J. Lee & D. Miller, 1999, People matter: Commitment to employees, strategy and performance in Korean firms, *Strategic Management Journal*, 20: 579–93.
7. R. Lyman & G. Fabrikant, 2001, Suddenly, high stakes for Disney's film and TV businesses, *New York Times Interactive*, http://www.nytimes.com, May 21.
8. E. Autio, H. J. Sapienza, & J. G. Almeida, 2000, Effects of age at entry, knowledge intensity, and imitability on international growth, *Academy of Management Journal*, 43: 909–24.
9. P. L. Yeoh & K. Roth, 1999, An empirical analysis of sustained advantage in the U.S. pharmaceutical industry: Impact of firm resources and capabilities, *Strategic Management Journal*, 20: 637–53.
10. D. F. Abell, 1999, Competing today while preparing for tomorrow, *Sloan Management Review*, 40(3): 73–81; D. Leonard-Barton, 1995, *Wellsprings of Knowledge: Building and Sustaining the Sources of Innovation*, Boston: Harvard Business School Press; R. A. McGrath, J. C. MacMillan, & S. Venkataraman, 1995, Defining and developing competence: A strategic process paradigm, *Strategic Management Journal*, 16: 251–75.
11. K. M. Eisenhardt, 1999, Strategy as strategic decision making, *Sloan Management Review*, 40(3): 65–72.
12. H. K. Steensma & K. G. Corley, 2000, On the performance of technology-sourcing partnerships: The interaction between partner interdependence and technology attributes, *Academy of Management Journal*, 43: 1045–67.
13. J. B. Barney, 2001, Is the resource-based "view" a useful perspective for strategic management research? Yes, *Academy of Management Review*, 26: 41–56.
14. C. Lee, K. Lee, & J. M. Pennings, 2001, Internal capabilities, external networks, and performance: A study on technology-based ventures, *Strategic Management Journal*, 22(special issue): 615–40; C. C. Markides, 1999, A dynamic view of strategy, *Sloan Management Review*, 40(3): 55–72; Abell, Competing today while preparing for tomorrow.
15. R. L. Priem & J. E. Butler, 2001, Is the resource-based "view" a useful perspective for strategic management research? *Academy of Management Review*, 26: 22–40.
16. P. J. H. Schoemaker & R. Amit, 1994, Investment in strategic assets: Industry and firm-level perspectives, in P. Shrivastava, A. Huff, & J. Dutton (eds.), *Advances in Strategic Management*, Greenwich, CT: JAI Press, 9.
17. Barney, Is the resource-based "view" a useful perspective for strategic management research? Yes; J. B. Barney, 1995, Looking inside for competitive advantage, *Academy of Management Executive*, 9(4): 49–61.
18. A. Madhok, 1997, Cost, value and foreign market entry mode: The transaction and the firm, *Strategic Management Journal*, 18: 39–61.
19. W. Kuemmerle, 2001, Go global—or not? *Harvard Business Review*, 79(6): 37–49.
20. G. Ahuja & C. M. Lambert, 2001, Entrepreneurship in the large corporation: A longitudinal study of how established firms create breakthrough inventions, *Strategic Management Journal*, 22(special issue): 521–43; A. Arora & A. Gambardella, 1997, Domestic markets and international competitiveness: Generic and product specific competencies in the engineering sector, *Strategic Management Journal*, 18(special summer issue): 53–74.
21. J. K. Sebenius, 2002, The hidden challenge of cross-border negotiations, *Harvard Business Review*, 80(3): 76–85; P. W. Liu & X. Yang, 2000, The theory of irrelevance of the size of the firm, *Journal of Economic Behavior & Organization*, 42: 145–65.
22. P. F. Drucker, 2002, They're not employees, they're people, *Harvard Business Review*, 80(2): 70–77; G. Verona, 1999, A resource-based view of product development, *Academy of Management Review*, 24: 132–42.
23. S. Ghoshal & C. A. Bartlett, 1995, Changing the role of top management: Beyond structure to processes, *Harvard Business Review*, 73(1): 96.
24. Barney, Is the resource-based "view" a useful perspective for strategic management research? Yes; V. P. Rindova & C. J. Fombrun, 1999, Constructing competitive advantage: The role of firm-constituent interactions, *Strategic Management Journal*, 20: 691–710; M. A. Peteraf, 1993, The cornerstones of competitive strategy: A resource-based view, *Strategic Management Journal*, 14: 179–91.
25. Barney, Is the resource-based "view" a useful perspective for strategic management research? Yes; T. H. Brush & K. W. Artz, 1999, Toward a contingent resource-based

theory: The impact of information asymmetry on the value of capabilities in veterinary medicine, *Strategic Management Journal*, 20: 223–50.

26. M. E. Porter, 1996, What is strategy? *Harvard Business Review*, 74(6): 61–78.

27. S. K. McEvily & B. Chakravarthy, 2002, The persistence of knowledge-based advantage: An empirical test for product performance and technological knowledge, *Strategic Management Journal*, 23: 285–305; P. J. Buckley & M. J. Carter, 2000, Knowledge management in global technology markets: Applying theory to practice, *Long Range Planning*, 33(1): 55–71.

28. Economist, 1998, *Pocket Strategy*, Value, London, UK: The Economist Books, 165.

29. J. Wolf & W. G. Egelhoff, 2002, A reexamination and extension of international strategy-structure theory, *Strategic Management Journal*, 23: 181–89; R. Ramirez, 1999, Value co-production: Intellectual origins and implications for practice and research, *Strategic Management Journal*, 20: 49–65.

30. S. W. Floyd & B. Wooldridge, 1999, Knowledge creation and social networks in corporate entrepreneurship: The renewal of organizational capability, *Entrepreneurship: Theory and Practice*, 23(3): 123–43; A. Campbell & M. Alexander, 1997, What's wrong with strategy? *Harvard Business Review*, 75(6): 42–51.

31. M. A. Hitt, R. D. Nixon, P. G. Clifford, & K. P. Coyne, 1999, The development and use of strategic resources, in M. A. Hitt, P. G. Clifford, R. D. Nixon, & K. P. Coyne (eds.), *Dynamic Strategic Resources*, Chichester: John Wiley & Sons, 1–14.

32. T. H. Davenport, 2001, Data to knowledge to results: Building an analytic capability, *California Management Review*, 43(2): 117–38; J. B. Barney, 1999, How a firm's capabilities affect boundary decisions, *Sloan Management Review*, 40(3): 137–45.

33. P. Westhead, M. Wright, & D. Ucbasaran, 2001, The internationalization of new and small firms: A resource-based view, *Journal of Business Venturing*, 16(4): 333–58; A. McWilliams, D. D. Van Fleet, & P. M. Wright, 2001, Strategic management of human resources for global competitive advantage, *Journal of Business Strategies*, 18(1): 1–24.

34. H. Collingwood, 2001, The earnings game: Everyone plays, nobody wins, *Harvard Business Review*, 79(6): 65–74.

35. Eisenhardt, Strategy as strategic decision making.

36. R. S. Dooley & G. E. Fryxell, 1999, Attaining decision quality and commitment from dissent: The moderating effects of loyalty and competence in strategic decision-making teams, *Academy of Management Journal*, 42: 389–402.

37. P. C. Nutt, 1999, Surprising but true: Half the decisions in organizations fail, *Academy of Management Executive*, 13(4): 75–90.

38. Ibid.

39. P. G. Audia, E. Locke, & K. G. Smith, 2000, The paradox of success: An archival and a laboratory study of strategic persistence following radical environmental change, *Academy of Management Journal*, 43: 837–53; D. A. Aaker & E. Joachimsthaler, 1999, The lure of global branding, *Harvard Business Review*, 77(6): 137–44.

40. G. P. West III & J. DeCastro, 2001, The Achilles heel of firm strategy: Resource weaknesses and distinctive inadequacies, *Journal of Management Studies*, 38: 417–42; G. Gavetti & D. Levinthal, 2000, Looking forward and looking backward: Cognitive and experimental search, *Administrative Science Quarterly*, 45: 113–37.

41. R. Amit & P. J. H. Schoemaker, 1993, Strategic assets and organizational rent, *Strategic Management Journal*, 14: 33–46.

42. R. E. Hoskisson & L. W. Busenitz, 2001, Market uncertainty and learning distance in corporate entrepreneurship entry mode choice. In M. A. Hitt, R. D. Ireland, S. M. Camp, & D. L. Sexton (eds.), *Strategic Entrepreneurship: Creating a New Integrated Mindset*, Oxford, U.K.: Blackwell Publishers, 151–72.

43. A. L. Zacharakis & D. L. Shepherd, 2001, The nature of information and overconfidence on venture capitalist's decision making, *Journal of Business Venturing*, 16: 311–32.

44. P. Burrows & A. Park, 2002, What price victory at Hewlett-Packard? *Business Week*, April 1, 36–37.

45. H. Thomas, T. Pollock, & P. Gorman, 1999, Global strategic analyses: Frameworks and approaches, *Academy of Management Executive*, 13(1): 70–82.

46. J. M. Mezias, P. Grinyer, & W. D. Guth, 2001, Changing collective cognition: A process model for strategic change, *Long Range Planning*, 34(1): 71–95.

47. U. Harnischfeger, 2001, Opel limits its ambitions in a grim market, *Financial Times*, http://www.ft.com, June 21.

48. N. Tichy, 1999, The teachable point of view, *Harvard Business Review*, 77(2): 82–83.

49. Brush, Greene, & Hart, From initial idea to unique advantage.

50. Eisenhardt & Martin, Dynamic capabilities: What are they?; M. D. Michalisin, D. M. Kline, & R. D. Smith, 2000, Intangible strategic assets and firm performance: A multi-industry study of the resource-based view, *Journal of Business Strategies*, 17(2): 91–117.

51. West III & DeCastro, The Achilles heel of firm strategy; D. L. Deeds, D. DeCarolis, & J. Coombs, 2000, Dynamic capabilities and new product development in high technology ventures: An empirical analysis of new biotechnology firms, *Journal of Business Venturing*, 15: 211–29.

52. S. Berman, J. Down, & C. Hill, 2002, Tacit knowledge as a source of competitive advantage in the National Basketball Association, *Academy of Management Journal*, 45: 13–31.

53. S. Shepard, 2001, Interview: The company is not in the stock, *Business Week*, April 30, 94–96.

54. M. S. Feldman, 2000, Organizational routines as a source of continuous change, *Organization Science*, 11: 611–29; A. M. Knott & B. McKelvey, 1999, Nirvana efficiency: A comparative test of residual claims and routines, *Journal of Economic Behavior & Organization*, 38: 365–83.

55. R. Lubit, 2001, Tacit knowledge and knowledge management: The keys to sustainable competitive advantage, *Organizational Dynamics*, 29(3): 164–78; S. A. Zahra, A. P. Nielsen, & W. C. Bogner, 1999, Corporate entrepreneurship, knowledge, and competence development, *Entrepreneurship: Theory and Practice*, 23(3): 169–89.

56. A. M. Webber, 2000, New math for a new economy, *Fast Company*, January/February, 214–24.

57. R. G. Schroeder, K. A. Bates, & M. A. Junttila, 2002, A resource-based view of manufacturing strategy and the relationship to manufacturing performance, *Strategic Management Journal*, 23: 105–17.

58. Brush & Artz, Toward a contingent resource-based theory.

59. J. B. Quinn, P. Anderson, & S. Finkelstein, 1996, Making the most of the best, *Harvard Business Review*, 74(2): 71–80.

60. Webber, New math for a new economy, 217.

61. Ibid., 218.

62. R. D. Ireland, M. A. Hitt, & D. Vaidyanath, 2002, Alliance management as a source of competitive advantage, *Journal of Management*. 28(3): 413–46.

63. D. L. Deephouse, 2000, Media reputation as a strategic resource: An integration of mass communication and resource-based theories, *Journal of Management*, 26: 1091–112.

64. M. Kleinman, 2001, Harley pushes brand prestige, *Marketing*, May 17, 16; G. Rifkin, 1998, How Harley-Davidson revs its brand, *Strategy & Business*, 9: 31–40.

65. G. Gavetti & D. Levinthal 2000, Looking forward and looking backward: Cognitive and experimental search, *Administrative Science Quarterly*, 45: 113–37; R. W. Coff, 1999, How buyers cope with uncertainty when acquiring firms in knowledge-intensive industries: Caveat emptor, *Organization Science*, 10: 144–61.

66. C. E. Helfat & R. S. Raubitschek, 2000, Product sequencing: Co-evolution of knowledge, capabilities and products, *Strategic Management Journal*, 21: 961–79.

67. Hitt, Bierman, Shimizu, & Kochhar, Direct and moderating effects of human capital on strategy and performance in professional service firms: A resource-based perspective; M. A. Hitt, R. D. Ireland, & H. Lee, 2000, Technological learning, knowledge management, firm growth and performance: An introductory essay, *Journal of Engineering and Technology Management*, 17: 231–46.

68. 1999, Thoughts on the business of life, *Forbes*, May 17, 352.

69. L. Argote & P. Ingram, 2000, Knowledge transfer: A basis for competitive advantage in firms, *Organizational Behavior and Human Decision Processes*, 82: 150–69.

70. G. G. Dess & J. C. Picken, 1999, *Beyond Productivity*, New York: AMACOM.

71. P. Coy, 2002, High turnover, high risk, *Business Week*, spring(special issue), 24.

72. T. T. Baldwin & C. C. Danielson, 2000, Building a learning strategy at the top: Interviews with ten of America's CLOs, *Business Horizons*, 43(6): 5–14.

73. D. F. Kuratko, R. D. Ireland, & J. S. Hornsby, 2001, Improving firm performance through entrepreneurial actions: Acordia's corporate entrepreneurship strategy, *Academy of Management Executive*, 15(4): 60–71; M. T. Hansen, N. Nhoria, & T. Tierney, 1999, What's your strategy for managing knowledge? *Harvard Business Review*, 77(2): 106–16.

74. M. A. Hitt & R. D. Ireland, 1986, Relationships among corporate level distinctive competencies, diversification strategy, corporate structure, and performance, *Journal of Management Studies*, 23: 401–16; M. A. Hitt & R. D. Ireland, 1985, Corporate distinctive competence, strategy, industry, and performance, *Strategic Management Journal*, 6: 273–93; M. A. Hitt, R. D. Ireland, & K. A. Palia, 1982, Industrial firms' grand strategy and functional importance, *Academy of Management Journal*, 25: 265–98.

75. K. Hafeez, Y. B. Zhang, & N. Malak, 2002, Core competence for sustainable competitive advantage: A structured methodology for identifying core competence, *IEEE Transactions on Engineering Management*, 49(1): 28–35; C. K. Prahalad & G. Hamel, 1990, The core competence of the corporation, *Harvard Business Review*, 68(3): 79–93.

76. C. Bowman & V. Ambrosini, 2000, Value creation versus value capture: Towards a coherent definition of value in strategy, *British Journal of Management*, 11: 1–15; T. Chi, 1994, Trading in strategic resources: Necessary conditions, transaction cost problems, and choice of exchange structure, *Strategic Management Journal*, 15: 271–90.

77. C. Bowman, 2001, "Value" in the resource-based view of the firm: A contribution to the debate, *Academy of Management Review*, 26: 501–2.

78. C. Ames, 1995, Sales soft? Profits flat? It's time to rethink your business, *Fortune*, June 25, 142–46.

79. N. D. Schwartz, 2001, Remedies for an economic hangover, *Fortune*, June 25, 130–38.

80. Barney, How a firm's capabilities; Barney, Looking inside for competitive advantage; J. B. Barney, 1991, Firm resources and sustained competitive advantage, *Journal of Management*, 17: 99–120.

81. C. H. St. John & J. S. Harrison, 1999, Manufacturing-based relatedness, synergy, and coordination, *Strategic Management Journal*, 20: 129–45.

82. Barney, Looking inside for competitive advantage.

83. M. Betts, 2001, Turning browsers into buyers, *Sloan Management Review*, 42(2): 8–9.

84. Ibid.

85. G. Colvin, 2001, Shaking hands on the Web, *Fortune*, May 14, 54.

86. R. Tomkins, 1999, Marketing value for money, *Financial Times*, May 14, 18.

87. Barney, Looking inside for competitive advantage, 52.

88. Brush, Greene, & Hart, From initial idea to unique advantage, 65–67.

89. Barney, Looking inside for competitive advantage, 53.

90. Barney, How a firm's capabilities, 141.

91. Barney, Firm resources, 108.

92. J. Huey, 1993, How McKinsey does it, *Fortune*, November 1, 56–81.

93. J. Kurtzman, 1997, An interview with Rosabeth Moss Kanter, *Strategy & Business*, 16: 85–94.

94. R. Burt, 1999, When is corporate culture a competitive asset? Mastering Strategy (Part Six), *Financial Times*, November 1, 14–15.

95. L. Soupata, 2001, Managing culture for competitive advantage at United Parcel Service, *Journal of Organizational Excellence*, 20(3): 19–26.

96. A. W. King & C. P. Zeithaml, 2001, Competencies and firm performance: Examining the causal ambiguity paradox, *Strategic Management Journal*, 22: 75–99; R. Reed & R. J. DeFillippi, 1990, Causal ambiguity, barriers to imitation, and sustainable competitive advantage, *Academy of Management Review*, 15: 88–102.

97. Leonard-Barton, *Wellsprings of Knowledge*, 7.

98. A. Ritt, 2000, Reaching for maximum flexibility, *Iron Age New Steel*, January, 20–26.

99. A. K. Gupta & V. Govindarajan, 2000, Knowledge management's social dimension: Lessons from Nucor Steel, *Sloan Management Review*, 42(1): 71–80.

100. Barney, Firm resources, 111.

101. Amit & Schoemaker, Strategic assets, 39.

102. S. K. McEvily, S. Das, & K. McCabe, 2000, Avoiding competence substitution through knowledge sharing, *Academy of Management Review*, 25: 294–311.

103. A. Serwer, 2002, Dell does domination, *Fortune*, January 21, 70–75.

104. J. B. Barney, 2002, *Gaining and Sustaining Competitive Advantage*. Upper Saddle River, NJ: Prentice-Hall.

105. Ibid.

106. M. E. Porter, 1985, *Competitive Advantage*, New York: Free Press, 33–61.

107. G. G. Dess, A. Gupta, J.-F. Hennart, & C. W. L. Hill, 1995, Conducting and integrating strategy research at the international corporate and business levels: Issues and directions, *Journal of Management*, 21: 376; Porter, What is strategy?

108. J. Webb & C. Gile, 2001, Reversing the value chain, *Journal of Business Strategy*, 22(2): 13–17; T. A. Stewart, 1999, Customer learning is a two-way street, *Fortune*, May 10, 158–60.

109. R. Amit & C. Zott, 2001, Value creation in e-business, *Strategic Management Journal*, 22(special issue): 493–520; M. E. Porter, 2001, Strategy and the Internet, *Harvard Business Review*, 79(3): 62–78.

110. D. Champion, 2001, Mastering the value chain: An interview with Mark Levin of Millennium Pharmaceuticals, *Harvard Business Review*, 79(6): 108–15.

111. J. Y. Murray & M. Kotabe, 1999, Sourcing strategies of U.S. service companies: A modified transaction-cost analysis, *Strategic Management Journal*, 20: 791–809.

112. S. Jones, 1999, Growth process in global market, *Financial Times*, June 22, 17.

113. A. Takeishi, 2001, Bridging inter- and intra-firm boundaries: Management of supplier involvement in automobile product development, *Strategic Management Journal*, 22: 403–33; H. Y. Park, C. S. Reddy, & S. Sarkar, 2000, Make or buy strategy of firms in the U.S., *Multinational Business Review*, 8(2): 89–97.

114. Hafeez, Zhang, & Malak, Core competence for sustainable competitive advantage; B. H. Jevnaker & M. Bruce, 1999, Design as a strategic alliance: Expanding the creative capability of the firm, in M. A. Hitt, P. G. Clifford, R. D. Nixon, & K. P. Coyne (eds.), *Dynamic Strategic Resources*, Chichester: John Wiley & Sons, 266–98.

115. Takeishi, Bridging inter- and intra-firm boundaries: Management of supplier involvement in automobile product development, 403–33.

116. 2004, *Roots website*, http://www.roots.com, March 8, 2004; A. Bernstein, 2001, Low-skilled jobs: do they have to move? *Business Week*, February 26, 94.

117. M. Useem & J. Harder, 2000, Leading laterally in company outsourcing, *Sloan Management Review*, 41(2): 25–36.

118. R. C. Insinga & M. J. Werle, 2000, Linking outsourcing to business strategy, *Academy of Management Executive*, 14(4): 58–70.

119. M. Katz, 2001, Planning ahead for manufacturing facility changes: A case study in outsourcing, *Pharmaceutical Technology*, March: 160–64.

120. G. G. Dess & J. C. Picken, 1999, Creating competitive (dis)advantage: Learning from Food Lion's freefall, *Academy of Management Executive*, 13(3): 97–111.

121. M. Hannan & J. Freeman, 1977, The population ecology of organizations, *American Journal of Sociology*, 82: 929–64.

122. Leonard-Barton, *Wellsprings of Knowledge*, 30–31.

123. West III & DeCastro, The Achilles heel of firm strategy; M. Keil, 2000, Cutting your losses: Extricating your losses when a big project goes awry, *Sloan Management Review*, 41(3): 55–68.

124. C. M. Christensen, 2001, The past and future of competitive advantage, *Sloan Management Review*, 42(2): 105–9.

Part Two

Strategic Actions:
Strategy Formulation

Chapter 5
Business-Level Strategy

Chapter 6
Competitive Rivalry and Competitive Dynamics

Chapter 7
Corporate-Level Strategy

Chapter 8
Acquisition and Restructuring Strategies

Chapter 9
International Strategy

Chapter 10
Cooperative Strategy

5

Chapter Five

Business-Level Strategy

Knowledge Objectives

Studying this chapter should provide you with the strategic management knowledge needed to:

1. Define business-level strategies.

2. Discuss the relationship between customers and business-level strategies in terms of *who*, *what*, and *how*.

3. Explain the differences among business-level strategies.

4. Use the five forces of competition model to explain how above-average returns can be earned through each business-level strategy.

5. Describe the risks of using each of the business-level strategies.

Developing and Using Carefully Designed Strategies: The Key to Corporate Success

Internet technology has a tremendous effect on how firms compete in the 21st century. In Chapter 3, we noted how the Internet affects both industry structures and the potential to operate profitably within them. Internet technology itself, however, is rarely a competitive advantage. This technology actually makes it more essential for a firm to develop well-designed, business-level strategies in order to detail how Internet technology can enable the success of the firm's other strategic actions. According to Michael Porter, many of the companies that succeed in the 21st century "... will be ones that use the Internet as a complement to traditional ways of competing, not those that set their Internet initiatives apart from their established operations."

Whatever business-level strategy the firm chooses, it should be carefully developed. Moreover, because of the importance of human capital to a company's competitive success, the ultimate effectiveness of a business-level strategy is strongly influenced by the quality of the people the organization employs. In light of environmental changes and the capabilities of Internet technology, companies across most industries are changing their business-level strategies. For example, an analysis of a number of property-casualty insurers shows that many of these companies have not effectively integrated the Internet into their business-level strategies. However, within this industry, the competitive pressures to have an effective online presence are influencing the actions many of these firms are taking to establish a competitive advantage while using their business-level strategy.

Networking firms, such as Nortel Networks, Cisco Systems, and Lucent Technologies, refocused their optical technology strategies in response to dramatically altered conditions in their environments. According to an analyst, Nortel's optical technology strategy is to "...compete in key segments of the industry, such as Internet data centres and broadband, and to dominate the optical market and grow related businesses off that." Nortel's concentration on serving only key segments of an industry demonstrates the use of the focused differentiation business-level strategy. With 75 percent of all North American Internet traffic riding across Nortel's optical network equipment, and more than 750 optical Internet customers worldwide, the firm is now working on making networks that are 20 times faster and capable of handling even more traffic.

Yet, Nortel is a research and development-oriented company that does not intend to lose out to other producers in hot market niches either. As wireless local area networks (LANs) grow in popularity, more laptop users will be able to connect to the Internet and corporate servers without plugging in an Ethernet cable. Typically, wireless access points are each hard-wired into a costly broadband connection. Nortel has come up with a way to extend such networks over a large area by wirelessly connecting sets of untethered access points. Each access point sends and receives signals from other access points in six directions to create a honeycomb-shaped mesh of wireless signals that are connected to a wired network at just a few points. Access points automatically route data

Wireless access points send and receive signals from other access points in six directions to create a honeycomb-shaped mesh.

CHAD BAKER/RYAN MCVAY/PHOTODISC/GETTY IMAGES

(continued)

by whatever nodes are fastest and route around off-line nodes. Thus, although Nortel is focusing in on certain segments, it has not lost sight of the other areas of its market that will demand attention in the future.

For its part, Cisco decided to place less emphasis on the enterprise market, in order to concentrate more on lucrative sales to service providers. Cisco also decided that part of its optical technology business-level strategy of focused differentiation would be to pursue opportunities for fibre-optic-related products in metropolitan area networks (MANs).

Lucent's strategy in the core optical technology market is to offer cheaper alternatives, while maintaining at least acceptable levels of differentiation, such as quality, with each alternative. These actions demonstrate Lucent's use of the cost leadership business-level strategy in this particular product line. Some of Lucent's recent customers are located in nations outside the United States. The firm's strategy appears to have been successful. Belgacom of Belgium and P&T Luxembourg recently chose Lucent to expand the capacity of the two parallel optical network connections between their networks in Belgium and Luxembourg. Lucent has also signed a contract with GNG Networks, one of the leading broadband Internet infrastructure providers in Korea, to provide a high-speed optical networking system for GNG's backbone network.

Smaller, nimbler companies, such as RedBack Networks, Sycamore Networks, and Ciena, are also creating new optical technology strategies. For the most part, these entrepreneurial ventures competing against Nortel, Cisco, and Lucent are using focused differentiation business-level strategies to serve the needs of particular market segments more effectively than companies with strategies aimed at serving all of a market. However, as will be discussed in the next chapter, one firm's strategies are met with responses from its competitors.

SOURCES: A. Wahl, 2004, Nortel's next big thing, *Canadian Business*, 77(3): 49–54; G. Anders, 2001, John Chambers after the deluge, *Fast Company*, July, 100–11; G. Biehn, 2001, Yes, you can profit from e-commerce, *Financial Executive*, May, 26–27; A. P. Burger, 2001, Getting your program back on track, *American Agent & Broker*, May, 69; S. Lee, 2001, Optical titans refocus, *InfoWorld*, April 2, 1, 29; M. E. Porter, 2001, Strategy and the Internet, *Harvard Business Review*, 79(3): 63–78; A. C. Trembly, 2001, Most PC insurers lack web strategy, *National Underwriter*, February 26, 1, 23; E. Zimmerman, 2001, What are employees worth? *Workforce*, February, 32–36; Lucent Technologies, *Lucent Technologies website*, http://www.lucent.com; *Nortel Networks website*, http://www.nortel.com, accessed February 28, 2004.

Strategy is concerned with making choices among two or more alternatives. When choosing a strategy, the firm decides to pursue one course of action instead of others. Indeed, the main point of strategy is to help decision makers choose among the competing priorities and alternatives facing their firm.[1] Business-level strategy is the choice a firm makes when deciding how to compete in individual product markets. The choices are important, as there is an established link between a firm's strategies and its long-term performance.[2] Thus, the choices Nortel, Cisco, and Lucent have made to develop their optical technology strategies will affect the degree to which the firms will be able to earn above-average returns while competing against companies such as RedBack Networks, Sycamore Networks, and Ciena.

Determining the businesses in which the firm will compete is a question of corporate-level strategy and is discussed in Chapter 7. Competition in individual product markets is a question of business-level strategy, which is this chapter's focus. For all types of strategies, companies must acquire the information and knowledge needed to make their choices by studying external environmental opportunities and threats, as well as by identifying and evaluating their internal resources, capabilities, and core competencies.

In Chapter 1, we defined a *strategy* as an integrated and coordinated set of commitments and actions designed to exploit core competencies and gain a competitive advantage. The different strategies that firms use to gain competitive advantages are shown in Figure 1.1, on page 8, in Chapter 1. As described in the individual chapters outlined in the figure, the firm tries to establish and exploit a competitive advantage when using each type of strategy. As explained in the opening case, on page 137, in the optical technology market, Lucent is using a cost leadership strategy, while Cisco and Nortel are using the focused differentiation business-level strategy. Each firm, by using the strategy it has chosen, hopes to develop a competitive advantage and exploit it for marketplace success.

Every firm needs a business-level strategy.[3] However, every firm may not use all the strategies—corporate-level, acquisition and restructuring, international, and cooperative—that are examined in Chapters 7 through 10. For example, the firm competing in a single-product market area in a single geographic location does not need either a corporate-level strategy to deal with product diversity or an international strategy to deal with geographic diversity. A local dry cleaner with only one location, offering a single service (the cleaning and pressing of clothes), in a single storefront does not require an explicit corporate-level strategy or an international strategy to be successful. In contrast, a diversified firm will use one of the several types of corporate-level strategies, as well as a separate business-level strategy for each product market area in which the company competes (the relationship between corporate-level and business-level strategies is further examined in Chapter 7). Thus, every firm—from the local dry cleaner to the multinational corporation—chooses at least one business-level strategy. Business-level strategy can be thought of as the firm's *core* strategy—the strategy that must be formed to describe how the firm will compete.[4]

Each strategy the firm uses specifies the desired outcomes and how they are to be achieved.[5] Integrating external and internal focuses, strategies reflect the firm's theory about how it intends to compete.[6] The fundamental objective of using each strategy is to create value for stakeholders. Strategies are purposeful, precede the actions to which they apply, and demonstrate a shared understanding of the firm's strategic intent and strategic mission.[7] An effectively formulated strategy marshals, integrates, and allocates the firm's resources, capabilities, and competencies so that the firm will be properly aligned with its external environment.[8] A properly developed strategy also rationalizes the firm's strategic intent and strategic mission along with the actions taken to achieve them.[9]

Information about a host of variables, including markets, customers, technology, worldwide finance, and the changing world economy must be collected and analyzed to properly form and use strategies.[10] As noted in the opening case, Internet technology affects how organizations gather and examine the information that must be carefully studied when choosing strategies.

A **business-level strategy** is an integrated and coordinated set of commitments and actions the firm uses to gain a competitive advantage by exploiting core competencies in specific product markets.

Business-level strategy, this chapter's focus, is an integrated and coordinated set of commitments and actions the firm uses to gain a competitive advantage by exploiting core competencies in specific product markets.[11] Only firms that continuously upgrade their competitive advantages over time are able to achieve long-term success with their business-level strategy.[12] Key issues the firm must address when choosing a business-level strategy are the good or service to offer customers, how to manufacture or create it, and how to distribute it to the marketplace.[13] Once formed, the business-level strategy reflects where and how the firm has an advantage over its rivals.[14] The essence of a firm's business-level strategy is "choosing to perform activities differently or to perform different activities than rivals."[15]

Customers are the foundation of successful business-level strategies. In fact, some believe that an effective business-level strategy demonstrates the firm's ability to "… build and maintain relationships to the best people for maximum value creation, both 'internally' (to firm members) and 'externally' (to customers)."[16] Thus, successful organizations think of their employees as internal customers who produce value-creating products for which customers are willing to pay.

Because of their strategic importance, this chapter opens with a discussion of customers. Three issues are considered in this analysis. In selecting a business-level strategy, the firm determines (1) *who* will be served, (2) *what* needs those target customers have that it will satisfy, and (3) *how* those needs will be satisfied. Descriptions of five business-level strategies follow the discussion of customers. These five strategies are sometimes called *generic* because they can be used in any business and in any industry.[17] Our analysis of these strategies describes how effective use of each strategy allows the firm to favourably position itself relative to the five competitive forces in the industry (see Chapter 3). In addition, we use the value chain (see Chapter 4) to show examples of the primary and support activities that are necessary to implement each business-level strategy. We also describe the different risks the firm may encounter when using one of these strategies. Organizational structures and controls that are linked with successful use of each business-level strategy are explained in Chapter 12.

Customers: Who, What, and How

Strategic competitiveness results only when the firm is able to satisfy a group of customers by using its competitive advantages to compete in individual product markets. The most successful companies constantly seek to chart new competitive space in order to serve new customers, as they simultaneously try to find ways to better serve existing customers.

Flexibility is important to the firm that emphasizes customers as a vital component of its strategies. For example, Air Canada's Aeroplan points program moved away from its strictly frequent flier rewards program to a more broadly based loyalty program. Aeroplan members still have to fly with Air Canada to acquire points, but redeeming their points involves more than just free flights. If you need to get the energy flowing in your home, a feng shui expert will come to give you remodelling tips: 20,000 points. Want to be a Viking for a day? Just 47,000 points will get you the experience at L'Anse aux Meadows in Newfoundland—complete with axe-throwing lessons and a costume. Test-drive Porsches on a test track for a day—114,000 points. The list goes on. For customers, the revised points program allows them to broaden the range of items for which they can redeem points. For Air Canada, the new program allows the company to convert its 100 billion unused points from a liability to an income item. It is expected that the move to expand the range of redemption options will broaden Air Canada's customer base to attract people interested in a more complete loyalty program.[18]

A key reason that the firm must satisfy customers with its business-level strategy is that returns earned from relationships with customers are the lifeblood of all organizations.[19] Executives at Washington D.C.-based Motley Fool capture this reality crisply by noting that, "the customer is the person who pays us."[20] The quality of these returns for Internet ventures is dictated by the conversion rate. The conversion rate measures returns by dividing the number of people who visit a site within a particular period by the number of visitors who take action (e.g., purchasing or registering) while visiting.[21]

The Importance of Effectively Managing Relationships with Customers

The firm's relationships with its customers are strengthened when it is committed to offering them superior value. In business-to-business transactions, superior value is often created when the firm's product helps its customers to develop a new competitive advantage or to enhance the value of its existing competitive advantages.[22] Receiving superior value enhances customers' loyalty to the firm that provides it. Evidence suggests that loyalty has a positive relationship with profitability. Ford Motor Company, for example, estimates that each percentage-point increase in customer loyalty—defined as how many Ford owners purchase a Ford product for their next vehicle—creates at least $100 million in additional profits annually.[23]

Selecting customers, deciding which of their needs the firm will try to satisfy, as well as how it fulfill those needs, are challenging tasks. One reason is that competition at the global level has created many attractive choices for customers. As discussed in Chapter 3, a having a large set of what appear to be equally attractive choices increases customers' power and influence, relative to companies offering products to them. Some even argue that increased choice and easily accessible information about the functionality of firms' products are creating increasingly sophisticated and knowledgeable customers, making it difficult to earn their loyalty.[24]

Several products are available to firms to help them better understand customers and manage relationships with them. For example, firms can use customer relationship management (CRM) software programs to develop web-based profiles of their customers and to fully integrate customer communications with back-office activities, such as billing and accounting.[25] California's Salesforce.com produces a popular CRM program that helps a firm's sales and marketing staffs communicate with customers: "A salesperson can, for instance, quickly check on the status of a customer account, while marketing people can collaborate to plan and execute promotional e-mail campaigns."[26] The unique attribute of Salesforce.com's program is that it is hosted and maintained entirely via the Internet. A successful CRM program can be a source of competitive advantage, as the firm uses knowledge gained from the program to improve strategy implementation processes.

A number of companies have become skilled at the art of *managing* all aspects of their relationship with their customers.[27] In the fast-paced, technologically sophisticated global economy, firms that participate in e-commerce (Internet-based ventures and firms that provide a strong Internet presence along with their storefront operations) can understand their customers and manage their relationships with them more effectively than those companies without an Internet presence. As noted in the opening case, the probability of successful competition increases even more when the firm carefully integrates Internet technology with its strategy, rather than using Internet technology on a "stand-alone basis."[28]

For example, Amazon.com is an Internet-based venture widely recognized for the quality of information it maintains about its customers and the services it renders. Cemex SA, a major global cement company based in Mexico, uses the Internet to link its customers, cement plants, and main control room, allowing the firm to automate orders and optimize truck deliveries in highly congested Mexico City. Analysts believe that

Cemex's integration of web technology with its cost leadership strategy is helping to differentiate it from its competitors.[29]

Bank of Montreal (BMO) launched a B2B (business-to-business) e-procurement system called FlexPort. The FlexPort system was designed to ease purchase order, invoicing and payment problems for customers and suppliers. Actually, FlexPort is more of a B2B2B system—the middle "B" being the bank. The data captured by FlexPort is translated by the bank and sent back to both buyers and sellers in formats they can each read and tie into their own accounting and office systems. This approach reduces problems of trying to adapt the systems of each company to make the B2B transaction work, and it saves BMO's clients time and money, as well as enhancing relationships between customers.[30]

Reach, Richness, and Affiliation

As the foundation on which e-commerce is linked with the firm's business-level strategy, Internet technology can help the firm establish a competitive advantage through its relationship with customers along the dimensions of reach, richness, and affiliation.

The *reach* dimension is about the firm's access and connection to customers. For instance, Canada's largest bookstore retailer by number of physical locations is Chapters.Indigo.ca. Chapters.Indigo.ca offers about 1 million titles to Canadians through the Internet and its more than 240 stores (under the Chapters, Indigo, W.H. Smith, and Coles names). By contrast, Amazon.com offers some 4.5 million titles and is located on millions of computer screens. Thus, Amazon.com's reach is significantly magnified relative to that associated with Chapters.Indigo.ca's physical bookstores or likely Internet users.[31]

Richness, the second dimension, is concerned with the depth and detail of the two-way flow of information between the firm and the customer. The potential of the richness dimension to help the firm establish a competitive advantage in its relationship with customers led financial services brokers, such as TD Waterhouse, to offer online services in order to better manage information exchanges with their customers. Broader and deeper information-based exchanges allow the firm to better understand its customers and their needs. Such exchanges also enable customers to become more knowledgeable of how the firm can satisfy them. Internet technology and e-commerce transactions have substantially reduced the costs of meaningful information exchanges with current and possible future customers.

Affiliation, the third dimension, is concerned with facilitating useful interactions with customers. For example, the Canadian government's National Research Council independently evaluates all types of innovative construction products, systems and services through its Institute for Research in Construction (IRC). Its evaluations are based on the latest technical research and expertise. Companies represent their own products, creating a situation in which its financial interests differ substantially from those of builders. Because the IRC's revenues come from sources other than the producer (e.g., through advertisements in its publications or on its website), builders using IRC-evaluated products or services feel they can trust the evaluations. Hence, the IRC provides a service that promotes a user's affiliation with the organization through its independence.[32]

As we discuss next, effective management of customer relationships, especially in an e-commerce era, helps the firm answer questions related to the issues of *who*, *what*, and *how* to serve.

Who: Determining the Customers to Serve

At any company, a crucial decision related to a business-level strategy is the decision about the target customers for the firm's goods or services (who).[33] To make this decision, companies divide customers into groups, based on differences in the customers' needs (needs are defined and further discussed in the next section). Called

market segmentation, this process clusters people with similar needs into individual and identifiable groups.[34] As part of its business-level strategy, the firm develops a marketing program to effectively sell products to its target customer groups.

Almost any identifiable human or organizational trait can be used to subdivide a market into segments that differ from one another on a given characteristic. Common characteristics on which customers' needs vary are illustrated in Table 5.1. Based on their core competencies and opportunities in the external environment, companies choose a business-level strategy to deliver value to target customers and satisfy their specific needs. For example, Rolls-Royce Motor Cars, Ltd. uses a focused differentiation strategy (defined and explained later in this chapter) to manufacture and sell Bentleys and Rolls-Royces. The firm considered both demographic characteristics (e.g., age and income) and socioeconomic characteristics (e.g., social class) (see Table 5.1) to identify its target customers. Customer feedback, as well as additional analyses, identified psychological factors (e.g., lifestyle choices) that allowed additional segmentation of the firm's core target customer group. Based on this information, the firm further segmented its target customer group into those *who want to drive* an ultra-luxury car themselves and those *who want to be driven* by a chauffeur in their ultra-luxury automobile. The Bentley targets the first individual, while the Rolls Royce satisfies the interests of the chauffeur-driven owner.[35]

Characteristics are often combined to segment a large market into specific groups that have unique needs. For example, burgers dominate the fast-food market. However, for college students interested in healthy eating, surveys suggest that subs are the dominant fast-food choice.[36] This more specific breakdown of the fast-food market for college students is a product of jointly studying demographic, psychological, and consumption-pattern characteristics (see Table 5.1). This knowledge suggests that on a relative basis, companies such as Toronto-based Mr. Sub should pursue a business-level strategy that targets college students with a desire for healthier foods more aggressively than should its Toronto-based rival Harvey's.

Demographic characteristics (see the discussion in Chapter 3 and Table 5.1) can also be used to segment markets into generations with unique interests and needs. Evidence

Table 5.1	Basis for Customer Segmentation

Consumer Markets
1. Demographic factors (age, income, sex, etc.)
2. Socioeconomic factors (social class, stage in the family life cycle)
3. Geographic factors (cultural, regional, and national differences)
4. Psychological factors (lifestyle, personality traits)
5. Consumption patterns (heavy, moderate, and light users)
6. Perceptual factors (benefit segmentation, perceptual mapping)

Industrial Markets
1. End-use segments (industry as identified in the North American Industry Classification System [NAICS])
2. Product segments (based on technological differences or production economics)
3. Geographic segments (defined by boundaries between countries or by regional differences)
4. Common buying factor segments (cut across product market and geographic segments)
5. Customer size segments

SOURCE: Adapted from S. C. Jain, 2000, *Marketing Planning and Strategy*, Cincinnati: South-Western College Publishing, 120.

suggests, for example, that direct mail is an effective communication medium for the World War II generation (those born before 1932). The values of the Swing generation (those born between 1933 and 1946) include taking cruises and purchasing second homes. Once financially conservative but now willing to spend money, members of this generation seek product information from knowledgeable sources. The Baby Boom generation (born between 1947 and 1964) are a generation we remember as organizing support for Pierre Trudeau's run at becoming Prime Minister. Members of this generation desire products that reduce the stress generated by juggling career demands, the needs of their older parents, and those of their own children. More conscious of hype, people in Generation X (born between 1965 and 1976) want products that deliver as promised. The Xers use the Internet as a primary shopping tool and expect visually compelling marketing. Members of this group are the fastest-growing segment of mutual fund shareholders, with their holdings overwhelmingly invested in stock funds.[37] Different marketing campaigns and distribution channels (e.g., Internet for Generation X customers, as compared to direct mail for the World War II generation) affect the implementation of strategies for those companies interested in serving the needs of different generations.

Increasing Segmentation of Markets

Companies frequently use sophisticated systems and programs to gather and interpret information about customers. Using these tools allows firms to gain the insights that are needed to further segment customers into specific groups that have unique needs. For example, many companies segment markets on a global basis. Indeed, because of increasing globalization of the world's economies, global market segmentation has become important to many firms' success. *Global market segmentation* is the process of identifying specific segments of potential customers—consumer groups across countries—with homogeneous attributes, who are likely to exhibit similar buying behaviour.[38]

Part of our discussion in the previous section suggests that companies are segmenting markets into increasingly specialized niches of customers with unique needs and interests. Generation Y (born between 1977 and 1984) is a market segment with specific characteristics that affect how firms use business-level strategies to serve these customers' needs. Analysis of purchasing patterns for this customer group shows that this segment prefers to buy in stores rather than online, but that they may use the Internet to study products prior to visiting a store to make a purchase. This preference suggests that companies targeting this segment might want to combine their storefront operations with a robust and active website.[39]

Another example of targeting specific market segments includes the effort by Travel Alberta to segment its domestic provincial vacationers. Travel Alberta found that such vacationers could be classifies into five groups: (1) the young urban-outdoor market, (2) the indoor-leisure traveller market, (3) the children-first market, (4) the fair-weather–friends market, and (5) the older cost-conscious traveller market. The young urban-outdoor market, (average age 38 years) is made up of budget-oriented males and females who are very active outdoors—camping, golfing, fishing, skiing, etc. The indoor-leisure travellers (average age 41 years) are mostly budget-oriented females, married, with children, living in the non-urban regions. Indoor museums, resorts, and shopping are key destinations for this group. The children-first market (average age 43 years) has the highest income of all groups. Activities that revolve around children and family are most important to this segment. The fair-weather–friends market (average age 44 years) is influenced by family or friends and weather conditions. Visiting family and friends is a key factor in making a travel decision. With moderate incomes and few budget concerns, they have the time and resources to travel. Banff, Lake Louise, and Edmonton are favourite locations. The older cost-conscious traveller (average age 45 years) is influenced by cost, value for money spent, and the sense of a safe and secure environment.

This group is more likely to take part in summer sports and leisure activities when travelling to places such as Banff, Lake Louise, and Jasper.

While all of the above groups depend on word of mouth to receive their information, there are differences in how to advertise to them. The Internet is more important for getting the word to the young urban-outdoor market, while television is more important for reaching the indoor-leisure travellers and children-first markets. Tourist information centres are important for targeting both the fair-weather–friends market and older cost-conscious travellers.[40]

Once their customer groups have been carefully segmented, companies are also improving their ability to provide individual goods and services with specific functionalities that can satisfy the unique needs of those groups. Sometimes, the needs of domestic and global customers are virtually identical. When customer needs and interests are homogeneous, or relatively so, across global markets, the firm has a single or only a few target customer groups rather than many.

What: Determining Which Customer Needs to Satisfy

Needs (*what*) are related to the benefits and features of a good or service.[41] A basic need of all customers is to buy products that create value for them. The generalized forms of value that products provide are either low cost with acceptable features or highly differentiated features with acceptable cost.

Successful firms constantly seek new customers as well as new ways to serve existing ones. As a firm decides *who* it will serve, it must simultaneously identify the targeted customer group's needs that the firm's goods or services can satisfy. Top-level managers play a critical role in recognizing and understanding these needs. The valuable insights they gain from listening to and studying customers influence product, technology, distribution, and service decisions. For example, Volkswagen AG planned to base several Volkswagen and Audi models on the same chassis and to use the same transmissions. Upper-level executives at the firm listened to concerns from customers about this decision, who asked why they should pay for the premiere Audi brand when they could obtain much of its technology at a lower cost by purchasing a Volkswagen product. As a result, Volkswagen AG planned to invest about $4 billion (CDN) during the next few years "to ensure that each of its brands retains a separate identity."[42]

Creating separate brand identities, such as Audi and Volkswagen, helps a firm's products convey benefits and features that customers want to purchase. In other words, brands can satisfy needs. Between 2000 and 2002, Air Canada executives launched no fewer than four different brands: Jazz, Jetz, Tango, and Zip, in late 2000. Jazz was simply Air Canada's reorganization and consolidation of its regional air carriers, Air BC, Air Nova, Air Ontario, and Canadian Regional. Jetz was Air Canada's sports and corporate charter brand. After the failure of the main professional sports team charter operator in Canada, Air Canada reconfigured three Boeing 737s and employed existing relationships with some of Canada's larger professional sports organizations to launch Jetz. Tango and Zip were Air Canada's discount carriers. Because both brands conveyed the same discount benefits and features Air Canada decided in 2003 to expand Zip and drop the Tango brand as a separate air carrier. As part of an operational consolidation, Zip was merged back into Air Canada in 2004.[43]

How: Determining Core Competencies Necessary to Satisfy Customer Needs

As explained in Chapters 1 and 4, *core competencies* are resources and capabilities that serve as a source of competitive advantage for the firm over its rivals. Firms use core competencies to implement value-creating strategies and thereby satisfy customers' needs (*how*). Only those firms with the capacity to continuously improve, innovate, and upgrade their competencies can expect to meet and hopefully exceed customers' expectations across time.[44]

Companies use different core competencies in their efforts to produce goods or services that can satisfy customers' needs. BCE Emergis, for example, emphasizes its core competence in e-commerce activities and technologies to develop new services. According to CEO Tony Gaffney, the company's objective is to "strengthen its position as the leading eBusiness provider in Canada and drive new business to profitability in the United States." BCE's eHealth unit will leverage the company's leadership in drug and dental claims processing in Canada to expand its services to include electronic reimbursement, dental settlements, and enhanced workers' compensation support on both sides of the border. In eFinance, the company will leverage its privileged relationships with major financial institutions in North America to develop in the mortgage industry. In the payments processing market, BCE Emergis tries to leverage banking relationships and its sales channels with new payment solutions, such as Visa use for bill payments.[45] And the previous items are just a short list.

All organizations, including BCE, must be able to use their core competencies (the *how*) to satisfy the needs (the *what*) of the target group of customers (the *who*) the firm has chosen to serve by using its business-level strategy. Next, we discuss the business-level strategies that firms use when pursuing strategic competitiveness and above-average returns.

Types of Business-Level Strategy

Business-level strategies are intended to create differences between the firm's position, relative to those of its rivals.[46] To position itself, the firm must decide whether it intends to *perform activities differently* or to *perform different activities*, as compared to its rivals.[47] Thus, the firm's business-level strategy is a deliberate choice about how it will perform the value chain's primary and support activities in ways that create unique value.

Successful use of a chosen strategy results only when the firm integrates its primary and support activities to provide the unique value it intends to deliver. Value is delivered to customers when the firm is able to use competitive advantages resulting from the integration of activities. Superior fit among primary and support activities forms an activity system. In turn, an effective activity system helps the firm establish and exploit its strategic position. In the next Strategic Focus box, "WestJet: Just a Southwest Clone?" on page 148, we use WestJet and Southwest Airlines to examine these issues in greater detail.

Favourably positioned firms, such as WestJet, have a competitive advantage over their industry rivals and are better able to cope with the five forces of competition (see Chapter 3). Favourable positioning is important, in that the universal objective of all companies is to develop and sustain competitive advantages.[48] Improperly positioned firms encounter competitive difficulties and likely will fail to sustain competitive advantages. For example, as noted in Chapter 1, ineffective responses to competitors, such as Wal-Mart, left Eaton's in a dead-end competitive position. These ineffective responses resulted from the inability of Eaton's to properly implement strategies that were appropriate in light of its external opportunities and threats and its internal competencies. Firms choose from among five business-level strategies to establish and defend their desired strategic position against rivals: *cost leadership, differentiation, focused cost leadership, focused differentiation,* and *integrated cost leadership/differentiation* (see Figure 5.1). Each business-level strategy helps the firm to establish and exploit a competitive advantage within a particular competitive scope.

When selecting a business-level strategy, firms evaluate two types of potential competitive advantage: "lower cost than rivals, or the ability to differentiate and command a

Figure 5.1 Five Business-Level Strategies

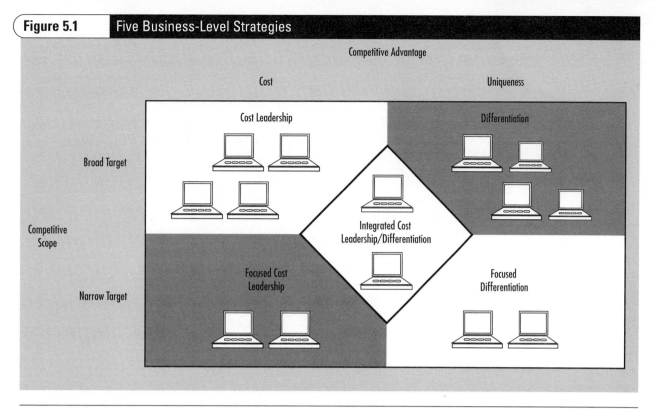

premium price that exceeds the extra cost of doing so."[49] Having lower cost derives from the firm's ability to perform activities differently from its rivals; being able to differentiate indicates the firm's capacity to perform different (and valuable) activities.[50] Competitive advantage is thus achieved within some scope.

Scope has several dimensions, including the group of product and customer segments served and the array of geographic markets in which the firm competes. Competitive advantage is sought by competing in many customer segments when implementing either the cost leadership or the differentiation strategy. In contrast, when using focus strategies, firms seek a cost competitive advantage or a differentiation competitive advantage in a *narrow competitive scope, segment,* or *niche*. With focus strategies, the firm "selects a segment or group of segments in the industry and tailors its strategy to serving them to the exclusion of others."[51]

None of the five business-level strategies is inherently or universally superior to the others.[52] The effectiveness of each strategy is contingent both on the opportunities and threats in a firm's external environment and on the possibilities provided by the firm's unique resources, capabilities, and core competencies. It is critical, therefore, for the firm to select an appropriate strategy in light of its opportunities, threats, and competencies.

Cost Leadership Strategy

The **cost leadership strategy** is an integrated set of actions designed to produce or deliver goods or services with features that are acceptable to customers at the lowest cost, relative to that of competitors.[53] Cost leaders' goods and services must have competitive levels of differentiation. Indeed, emphasizing cost reductions while ignoring competi-

The **cost leadership strategy** is an integrated set of actions designed to produce or deliver goods or services with features that are acceptable to customers at the lowest cost, relative to that of competitors.

WestJet: Just a Southwest Clone?

Launched in 1971, with service among three Texas cities, Southwest Airlines has followed its mission of "dedication to the highest quality of customer service delivered with a sense of warmth, friendliness, individual pride, and company spirit." Southwest has become the fifth largest U.S. carrier and eighth largest carrier in the world. Others have tried to copy the Southwest model in the U.S. with little to no success. Worldwide however, Southwest's model has been adopted, with adaptations, by a number of airlines: RyanAir and easyJet in Europe, and WestJet in Canada.

Relying on its mission to direct its activities, these companies offer short-haul, low-cost, point-to-point service between midsize cities and secondary airports in large cities. Like Dallas-based Southwest, Calgary's WestJet offers one class of seats and concentrates on flights shorter than 650 km. This focus permits a larger number of flights each day. Whenever possible, WestJet lands at small airports that charge low user fees. Both airlines use only one class of airplane (Boeing 737s) to reduce pilot training and maintenance costs. Neither airline serves in-flight meals. What they do offer customers are low prices, frequent departures, and an often-entertaining experience while in the air (a form of differentiation).

Since its inception in 1996, the company has grown to control 25 percent of the domestic market and has posted 29 consecutive quarters of profitability in an industry swimming in financial losses. Is this all from simply following the Southwest discount airline model? There may be a bit more to WestJet's success than that. If WestJet were to have a ten commandments, they may run, as Anthony A. Davis noted in *Profit* magazine, something like this:

1. *Find a successful model and copy it.* Copying a successful company is not plagiarism, it is benchmarking against the best. WestJet uses the Southwest notions of a happy corporate culture, profit sharing, and empowered employees. But the WestJet executives also looked at other companies, such as RyanAir, for ideas, and took the best they could find.
2. *Support your employees' efforts.* CEO Clive Beddoe believes that "If we have good relations with our employees, then the employees create good relationships with their customers." Beddoe makes sure he gets in the trenches if needed. The burly guy who checked your bags at WestJet on Christmas might have been Clive Beddoe. He has help change an airplane tire late at night in –30°C weather. He has helped replace an engine. "And when my wife and kids fly on WestJet, they help clean the planes, too," says Beddoe.
3. *Share the wealth.* While WestJet pays employees below industry average (in some cases 25 percent less), it boasts a renowned profit sharing and employee share purchase plan. Profit sharing has recently averaged 20 percent of an employee's base wage, and the more profitable the firm, the higher the profit percentage workers receive. Through the share purchase plan, WestJet matches the amount an employee invests in the firm. It is "lucrative enough to turn all our employees into partners," notes Beddoe. Seven of every eight employees own shares, and they invest an average of 13 percent of their salaries into the firm.
4. *Hire attitude; train skills.* Skills can be improved, but attitude is ingrained. WestJet has an extensive interview process. Potential frontline workers participate in group interviews, where the company tries to identify "fun and funky people." Applicants are required to tell stories and jokes, and play games. If the process fails, WestJet will quickly fire the person. The view is that one person with a poor attitude can infect others. The resulting employee turnover can incur costs to the firm when it needs to hire and train the replacements.
5. *Empower the frontline staff to give company money away.* In a recent year, WestJet gave away 2 percent of its annual revenues in guest credits to compensate customers for inconveniences such as late arrivals and overbookings. In discussing the frontline staff, chief operating officer (COO) Don Bell notes that, "From handing out flight credits to sending out for hamburgers to feed stranded passengers, they take care of things up front." Counter people have even bought a new wedding dress for a customer when hers was lost on a flight.

(continued)

6. *Embrace technology.* From installing fuel saving winglets on its 737s, to being an early propo-nent of online booking, WestJet tries to use new technology to drive down costs. Having clients book online can save 90 percent of the cost of conventional bookings. WestJet pro-motes online sales by offering air miles and discounts on web-purchased fares. About 70 per-cent of the firm's bookings are made online.

7. *Have a great business plan and get the money.* WestJet's founders raised their initial funding by creating a detailed business plan that clearly showed how Southwest had succeeded and how WestJet could do so as well. In one month, the founders raised enough capital to allow them to buy their first three 737s outright. Being well financed meant that WestJet could not be pushed out of the market quickly. Since then, WestJet has had a number of successful share offerings, and the company continues to be well financed.

8. *Maximize use of the assets.* A plane sitting on the ground does not earn money. To reduce wasted downtime, WestJet turns its planes around quickly and has signed deals to allow chartered use of its planes during the slow winter season. Also, WestJet rents out its three Calgary-based flight simulators, sublets hangar space in Calgary and Hamilton, and does some maintenance for other companies.

9. *Have a flexible workforce.* WestJet flight turnaround time is six minutes—the fastest in North America. They can do this by having everyone, from pilots to station agents, picking up garbage, vacuuming the carpets, and emptying the trash. Because WestJet has no union, no one says, "That's not my job." To address employee/management problems WestJet created a communications team (including one employee who sits on the board) to act as an employee association that meets regularly with management.

10. *Party*! WestJet celebrates its success. They do this sometimes randomly, and mostly boister-ously. Beddoe once rented a large sports bar in Calgary, just to throw a staff party. There was no reason, just for fun. More than 700 employees and the CEO showed up—Beddoe keeps returning to the trenches.

SOURCE: A. A. Davis, 2004, Sky high, *Profit*, 23(1): 20–23. © 2004 Rogers Inc.

The careful fit, or integration, among the airline's primary and support activities allows it to keep costs down, focus on customers, keep employees happy, and keep its work simple. This fit is instrumental to the development and use of the firm's two major competitive advantages—organi-zational culture and customer service. The importance of fit between primary and support activi-ties is a key to the sustainability of competitive advantage for all firms. As Michael Porter comments, "Strategic fit among many activities is fundamental not only to competitive advantage but also to the sustainability of that advantage. It is harder for a rival to match an array of inter-locked activities than it is merely to imitate a particular sales-force approach, match a process technology, or replicate a set of product features. Positions built on systems of activities are far more sustainable than those built on individual activities."

WestJet's tightly integrated primary and support activities make it difficult for competitors to imitate the firm's strategy. WestJet's culture influences these activities and their integration. WestJet's unique culture and supporting organizational rewards have become a competitive advantage that rivals have not been able to imitate. Careful integration of how WestJet employees perform the activities that support the firm's strategic themes reduces the probability that competitors will be able to successfully imitate its activity system.

SOURCES: C. Beddoe, 2003, How much is enough? *Maclean's*, 116(17): 40–41; T. Belden, 2001, Southwest Airlines' philosophy keeping it in front of pack now, *Richmond Times-Dispatch*, November 12, D29; M. Arndt, 2001, A simple and elegant flight pattern, *Business Week*, June 11, 118; 2001, The squeeze on Europe's air fares, *The Economist*, May 26, 57–58; P. Verberg, 2000, Prepare for takeoff, *Canadian Business*, 73(24): 94–98; J. Baglole, 2000, Fledgling is taking on Air Canada. ..., *Wall Street Journal* (eastern ed.), April 24, A26; M. E. Porter, 1996, What is strategy? *Harvard Business Review*, 74(6): 61–78; WestJet, 2004, *WestJet website*, http://www.westjet.com/pdffile/investorFactSheet.pdf (fact sheet), accessed June 26, 2004.

tive levels of differentiation is ineffective. At the extreme, concentrating only on reducing costs could find the firm very efficiently producing products that no customer wants to purchase. When the firm designs, produces, and markets a comparable product more efficiently than its rivals, there is evidence that it is successfully using the cost leadership strategy.[54] Firms using the cost leadership strategy sell no-frills, standardized goods or services (but with competitive levels of differentiation) to the industry's most typical customers. Cost leaders concentrate on finding ways to lower their costs, relative to those of their competitors, by constantly rethinking how to complete their primary and support activities (see Chapter 3) to further reduce costs while maintaining competitive levels of differentiation.[55]

As primary activities, inbound logistics (e.g., materials handling, warehousing, and inventory control) and outbound logistics (e.g., collecting, storing, and distributing products to customers) often account for significant portions of the total cost to produce goods and services. Research suggests that having a competitive advantage in terms of logistics creates more value when using the cost leadership strategy than when using the differentiation strategy.[56] Thus, cost leaders seeking competitively valuable ways to reduce costs may want to concentrate on the primary activities of inbound logistics and outbound logistics.

Cost leaders also carefully examine all support activities to find additional sources of potential cost reductions. Developing new systems for identifying the optimal combination of low cost and acceptable quality in the raw materials required to produce the firm's goods or services is an example of how the procurement support activity can facilitate successful use of the cost leadership strategy.

WestJet, mentioned in the previous Strategic Focus box, pursues a cost leadership strategy as a discount airline. Known for having personnel that are flexible in performing a wide range of jobs, WestJet also efficiently employs its people. WestJet averages 60 employees per aircraft, compared with the national industry average of 110. [57]

The company continues to look for chances to save money however. In one quarter of 2003 alone, the company reduced costs per available seat mile by almost 16 percent. This reduction was well after the company had already established itself as a frugal carrier. The cost savings does not mean the company hoards cash either. When the airline needs it, management will make investments in cost-saving advances. For example, WestJet installed vertical-blended winglets on the wingtips of its 737s at a cost to the company of $635,000 per plane. However, fuel cost is the biggest operating expense at the airline, and the fins reduced fuel consumption by 3 to 7 percent. At an average annual fuel bill of $4 million per plane, the winglets could pay for themselves in 30 to 60 months. Because the winglets last for 20 years, the improvement will pay for itself at least four times over.

However, WestJet does not lose sight of the need for differentiation. As mentioned in the Strategic Focus box, the company tries to make the flights fun and works at keeping customers satisfied. This, too, is part of its cost leadership formula. If customers are happy, they fly the airline. Their patronage means that planes fly closer to capacity, and costs are reduced because assets are better utilized.[58]

Another Calgary-based company that follows a cost leadership strategy is Liquidation World. While the company does provide buyers with low-cost items, it also allows companies with inventory problems to maximize the financial recovery from their situation. Liquidation World specializes "in purchasing and marketing merchandise from distress situations. Inventories are acquired through insurance and freight claims, bankruptcies, receiverships, buybacks, overproduction, cancelled orders … virtually any kind of problem situation." Because Liquidation World sells items through auctions or low-cost/low-rent facilities, the company is able to keep the cost of selling goods to a minimum. In the company's warehouses in provinces from Ontario westward, as well as in

Montana, Alaska, and the U.S. Pacific Northwest, buyers find an ever-changing array of low-cost products. Buyers receive more for their money, and sellers receive more for their goods.[59]

Having products available to customers at low cost demonstrates the firm's commitment to being the low-cost leader. By offering products in multiple locations rather than in only major metropolitan areas, Liquidation World also provides its target customers (budget-conscious consumers) with competitive levels of differentiation (e.g., location, convenience). Liquidation World captures the essence of the low-cost and competitive (but not the most) differentiation position by operating as a low-cost, value retailer.

As described in Chapter 4, firms use value chain analysis to determine the areas of the company's operations that create value and those that do not. Figure 5.2 illustrates the primary and support activities that allow a firm to create value through the cost leadership strategy. Companies unable to link the activities shown in this figure typically lack the resources, capabilities, and core competencies needed to successfully use the cost leadership strategy.

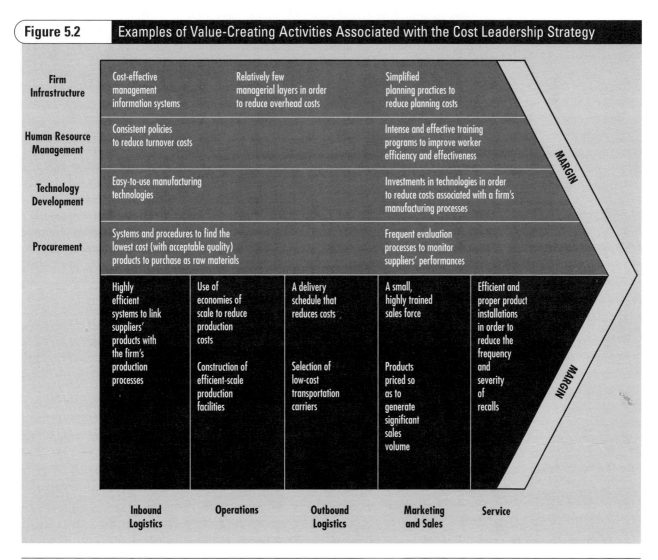

Figure 5.2 Examples of Value-Creating Activities Associated with the Cost Leadership Strategy

SOURCE: Adapted with permission of The Free Press, a Division of Simon & Schuster Adult Publishing Group, from *Competitive Advantage: Creating and Sustaining Superior Performance*, by Michael E. Porter, p. 47. Copyright © 1985, 1998 by Michael E. Porter. All rights reserved.

Effective use of the cost leadership strategy allows a firm to earn above-average returns, despite the presence of strong competitive forces (see Chapter 3). The next sections (one for each of the five forces) explain how firms are able to meet this challenge.

Rivalry with Existing Competitors

Having the low-cost position is a valuable defence against rivals. Because of the cost leader's advantageous position, rivals hesitate to compete on the basis of price. Nintendo is known for being able to produce systems for less cost. This ability makes it difficult for firms to compete against Nintendo on the basis of the price variable. Over the last few years, Nintendo has consistently priced its principal system $50 to $75 less than its rivals' entries. Game Cube went from the $300 range at introduction to less than half that price within a couple years.

At times, Microsoft, Sony, and Nintendo have all sold their systems at a loss to entice buyers. Retailing at about $50 to $75 each, the games are where the money is made. In fact, the game system market is so competitive that old-time video game maker Sega quit making its own system and now only makes games for other systems makers. Shying away from a price war, Microsoft has sought to lure customers to its late entry, higher priced Xbox with system Internet connectability. Sony tries to stay away from the price issue by using PlayStation 2's huge edge in its game lineup as its main selling point. With nearly 300 games for the North American market, the argument that the system is somewhat more versatile than rival Nintendo is one that therefore resonates positively with potential buyers.[60]

Bargaining Power of Buyers (Customers)

Powerful customers can force a cost leader to reduce its prices, but not below the level at which the cost leader's next-most-efficient industry competitor can earn average returns. Although powerful customers might be able to force the cost leader to reduce prices even below this level, they probably would not choose to do so. Prices that are low enough to prevent the next-most-efficient competitor from earning average returns would force that firm to exit the market, leaving the cost leader with less competition and in an even stronger position. Customers would thus lose their power and pay higher prices when they are forced to purchase from a single firm operating in an industry without competitive rivals.

Bargaining Power of Suppliers

The cost leader operates with margins greater than those of its competitors. Among other benefits, higher margins, relative to those of its competitors, make it possible for the cost leader to absorb its suppliers' price increases. When an industry faces substantial increases in the cost of its supplies, only the cost leader may be able to pay the higher prices and continue to earn either average or above-average returns. Alternatively, a powerful cost leader may be able to force its suppliers to hold down their prices, which would reduce the suppliers' margins in the process.

Potential Entrants

Through continuous efforts to reduce costs to levels that are lower than those of its competitors, a cost leader becomes highly efficient. Because ever-improving levels of efficiency enhance profit margins, they serve as significant entry barriers to potential competitors. New entrants must be willing and able to accept no-better-than-average returns until they gain the experience required to approach the cost leader's efficiency. To earn even average returns, new entrants must have the competencies required to match the cost levels of competitors other than the cost leader. The low profit margins (relative to margins earned by firms implementing the differentiation strategy) make it necessary for the cost leader to sell large volumes of its product to earn above-average returns. However, firms striving to be the cost leader must avoid pricing their products so low that their ability to operate profitability is reduced, even though volume increases.

Product Substitutes

Compared to its industry rivals, the cost leader also holds an attractive position in terms of product substitutes. A product substitute becomes an issue for the cost leader when its features and characteristics, in terms of cost and differentiated features, are potentially attractive to the firm's customers. When faced with possible substitutes, the cost leader has more flexibility than its competitors. To retain customers, it can reduce the price of its good or service. With still lower prices and competitive levels of differentiation, the cost leader increases the probability that customers will prefer its product rather than a substitute.

Competitive Risks of the Cost Leadership Strategy

The cost leadership strategy is not risk free. One risk is that the processes used by the cost leader to produce and distribute its good or service could become obsolete because of innovations by its competitors. These innovations may allow rivals to produce at costs lower than those of the original cost leader, or to provide additional differentiated features without increasing the product's price to customers.

A second risk is that too much focus by the cost leader on cost reductions may occur at the expense of trying to understand customers' perceptions of competitive levels of differentiation. However, the firm must simultaneously remain focused on understanding when a cost-reducing decision—one that eliminates those differentiated features that can create value in a low-cost environment—in order to reduce costs to still lower levels, would create an unattractive value proposition for customers. For example, even WestJet has contemplated selling chips and sandwiches on what had traditionally been meal-less flights, in order to give customers greater value.

A final risk of the cost leadership strategy concerns imitation. Using their own core competencies (see Chapter 4), competitors sometimes learn how to successfully imitate the cost leader's strategy. When this occurs, the cost leader must increase the value that its good or service provides to customers. Commonly, value is increased by selling the current product at an even lower price or by adding differentiated features that customers value while maintaining price.

Even cost leaders must be careful when reducing prices to a still lower level. If the firm prices its good or service at an unrealistically low level (a level at which it will be difficult to retain satisfactory margins), customers' expectations about a reasonable price become difficult to reverse.

Differentiation Strategy

The **differentiation strategy** is an integrated set of actions designed by a firm to produce or deliver goods or services (at an acceptable cost) that customers perceive as being different in ways that are important to them.[61] While cost leaders serve an industry's typical customer, differentiators target customers who perceive that value is added by the manner in which the firm's products are differentiated.

Firms must be able to produce differentiated products at competitive costs to reduce upward pressure on the price customers pay for them. When a product's differentiated features are produced through non-competitive costs, the price for the product can

The **differentiation strategy** is an integrated set of actions designed by a firm to produce or deliver goods or services (at an acceptable cost) that customers perceive as being different in ways that are important to them.

exceed what the firm's target customers are willing to pay. When the firm has a thorough understanding of what its target customers value, the relative importance they attach to the satisfaction of different needs, and the distinctive attributes for which they are willing to pay a premium, the differentiation strategy can be successfully used.[62]

Through the differentiation strategy, the firm produces non-standardized products for customers who value differentiated features more than they value low cost. For example, superior product reliability, product durability, and high-performance sound systems are among the differentiated features of Toyota Motor Corporation's Lexus products. The often-used Lexus promotional statement—The Relentless Pursuit of Perfection—suggests a strong commitment to overall product quality as a source of differentiation. However, Lexus offers its vehicles to customers at a competitive purchase price. As with Lexus products, a good or service's unique attributes, rather than its purchase price, provide the value for which customers are willing to pay.

Continuous success with the differentiation strategy results when the firm consistently upgrades differentiated features that customers value, without significant cost increases. Because a differentiated product satisfies customers' unique needs, firms following the differentiation strategy are able to charge premium prices. For customers to be willing to pay a premium price, a "firm must truly be unique at something or be perceived as unique."[63] The ability to sell a good or service at a price that substantially exceeds the cost of creating its differentiated features allows the firm to outperform rivals and earn above-average returns.

For example, because it pays meticulous attention to every detail of its business, the Eden restaurant at the Rimrock Resort Hotel in Banff has become one of only six restaurants in Canada with a five-diamond rating from the American Automobile Association. Long known for its superb food, great 24-hour service, a vast wine list, and spectacular views, in 2003, the Eden achieved this rating, the highest a hotel restaurant can achieve in North America. To arrive at this standard, the Eden managed to acquire Chef Yoshi Chubachi, in 2002. Because he has worked in top-notch restaurants in Japan, France, Switzerland, and across Canada, Chubachi developed a unique global cooking style that produces meals that taste and look like works of art. The restaurant specializes in five multi-course meals, each with a different theme, with wines chosen to match each dish. Many dishes use wild game (deer and bison) with interesting Asian flavours to provide that extra-special degree of uniqueness. Thus, the Eden's success rests on its ability to deliver unique meals in a special setting and sell a differentiated product and service at a price significantly higher than the costs of the food, staff, and rent.[64]

Rather than costs, a firm using the differentiation strategy always concentrates on investing in and developing features that differentiate a good or service in ways that customers value. Overall, a firm using the differentiation strategy seeks to be different from its competitors on as many dimensions as possible. The less similarity between a firm's goods or services and those of competitors, the more buffered it is from rivals' actions. Commonly recognized differentiated goods and services include Toyota's Lexus, Chanel handbags, and the Holt Renfrew shopping experience.

A product can be differentiated in many ways. Unusual features, responsive customer service, rapid product innovations and technological leadership, perceived prestige and status, different tastes, and engineering design and performance are examples of approaches to differentiation. There may be a limited number of ways to reduce costs (as demanded by successful use of the cost leadership strategy); however, virtually anything a firm can do to create real or perceived value is a basis for differentiation. The challenge is to identity features that create value for the customers that the firm has chosen to serve. As we see in the following Strategic Focus box, "Clothing Industry Competitiveness," firms can create a source of differentiation on the power of their brand, while others in the industry can quite successfully employ a cost leadership strategy.

Clothing Industry Competitiveness

Roots is Canada's leading independent manufacturer and retailer of high-quality clothing and accessories for men, women, and children. The Roots emphasis is on sportswear. Since its beginnings in Toronto, in 1973, Roots has branched out into many areas. In addition to apparel, the company has offered furniture, eyewear, watches, fragrances, and even a line of multivitamins. The company is firmly planted in Canada: 140 of the company's more than 200 stores are in Canada, with about 70 in Korea, 12 in Taiwan, and 7 in the U.S. It also sells some apparel lines through Sears Canada stores and Sears online, as well as through the Federated Department Stores throughout the United States. In addition there are about 55 Roots shops inside of Saks department stores in the U.S. By limiting its outlets and working closely with its retailers, Roots maintains tight control over the manner in which its products are presented to consumers.

To maintain and enhance the company's differentiation strategy, Roots spends significant time and effort to promote the differentiated quality and style of its clothing. The most well-known example of the Roots promotional acumen was the firm's outfitting of the 1998 Canadian Winter Olympic Team. The team's poorboy caps were such a fashion hit that for months Roots could not keep up with demand. This demand not only meant millions of dollars in sales but hundreds of millions of dollars in free advertising. In fact, other teams were so impressed with Roots styling that the company now outfits the Canadian, British, and U.S. Olympic teams, thus creating huge promotional value for its products, in markets whose combined population is about a dozen times larger than Canada's.

Differentiating its product as a quality product is not just a matter of image and style. The company adheres to "a motto of Quality and Integrity." The Roots production plants employ the latest equipment for the manufacture of clothing and accessories, use teamwork and task rotation to improve quality by reducing the tedium of an assembly line, and the vast majority of Roots apparel is made in Canada.

In contrast to the Roots differentiated strategy is the cost leadership strategy of Montreal's Gildan Activewear. As mentioned in Chapter 1, not only did Gildan use cheaper offshore labour to keep costs down and handle non-Canadian sales out of lower-tax countries, such as Barbados; but the company made careful choices that allowed it to build sales and production volumes for less cost. As well, Gildan invested heavily in cost-saving vertical integration. In addition, by selling its product as T-shirt blanks, which are, in due course, decorated with designs and logos for sale to consumers, Gildan was able to use the wholesale channel to grow rapidly as a manufacturer and marketer of high quality T-shirts in the Canadian, United States, and European imprinted-sportswear markets. Gildan's vertical integration involved moving into all aspects of producing its T-shirts: yarn spinning, knitting, dyeing, finishing, cutting, and sewing operations. These manufacturing processes are, as noted before, located in cost-efficient environments to constantly reinforce the company's position as a low-cost producer.

Gildan has also taken steps to ensure its costs stayed low in other areas of the value chain. Not only does Gildan constantly reinvest in state-of-the-art production equipment to keep costs low (and keep sales up by maintaining good quality), the company also employs cutting-edge technology in its marketing and distribution activities. To keep sales volumes high, Gildan ensures that customers receive what they need, by maintaining strong partnerships with distributors. Ensuring that the company can keep expanding when needed requires being able to access funds in the investment community. To insure investors are happy, the company won kudos for dropping its dual-class stock structure in 2004. Finally, to make certain sales do not flounder on accusations that the company runs sweatshops (to keep socially responsible buyers and, presumably, workers, happier) Gildan has become a participating member of the Fair Labor Association (F.L.A.). The F.L.A. is an independent U.S. verification agency that promotes adherence to international labour standards and the improvement of working conditions. It maintains an

(continued)

independent monitoring system to ensure participating companies comply with its code of conduct and undertakes recommendations for corrective measures when violations are found.

While these two Canadian companies look very different, they both emphasize consistent moves that will support their strategies. For Roots, this approach means stressing differentiation through continual emphasis on styling, quality, and promotion. For Gildan, the approach means stressing cost leadership through continual emphasis on cost reduction in every aspect of its own international value chain and that of its suppliers.

SOURCES: Roots, 2004, *Roots website*, http://www.roots.com, accessed March 8, 2004; Gildan Activewear, 2004, *Gildan Activewear website*, http://gildan.com, accessed March 8, 2004; S. Silcoff, 2004, Gildan in fashionable governance: T-shirt maker does away with dual-class structure, *National Post* (*Financial Post*) (national ed.), February 4, FP 1; D. MacDonald, 2003, Gildan joins fair-labour watchdog, *The Montreal Gazette* (final ed.), November 6, B4.

A firm's value chain can be analyzed to determine whether the firm is able to link the activities required to create value by using the differentiation strategy. Examples of primary and support activities that are commonly used to differentiate a good or service are shown in Figure 5.3. Companies without the core competencies needed to link these activities cannot expect to successfully use the differentiation strategy. Next, we explain how firms using the differentiation strategy can successfully position themselves in terms of the five forces of competition (see Chapter 3) to earn above-average returns.

Rivalry with Existing Competitors

Customers tend to be loyal purchasers of products that are differentiated in ways that are meaningful to them. As their loyalty to a brand increases, customers' sensitivity to an increase in prices is reduced. This is especially true of those purchasing high-end, big-ticket items (e.g., luxury automobiles).[65] The relationship between brand loyalty and price sensitivity insulates a firm from competitive rivalry. Thus, consulting giant McKinsey & Company is insulated from its competitors, even on the basis of price, as long as it continues to satisfy the differentiated needs of its customer group. Aurias Diamonds is similarly insulated from intense rivalry, as long as customers continue to perceive that its gems are a superior quality product.

Bargaining Power of Buyers (Customers)

The uniqueness of differentiated goods or services reduces customers' sensitivity to price increases. On the basis of a combination of unique materials and brand image, L'Oreal has developed a winning formula: a growing portfolio of international brands that has transformed the French company into the United Nations of beauty. Blink an eye, and L'Oreal has just sold 85 products around the world, from Maybelline eye makeup, Redken hair products, and Ralph Lauren perfumes to Helena Rubinstein cosmetics and Vichy skin care." L'Oreal is finding success in markets stretching from China to Mexico, while other consumer product companies falter. L'Oreal's differentiation strategy seeks to convey the allure of different cultures through its many products: "Whether it's selling Italian elegance, New York street smarts, or French beauty through its brands, L'Oreal is reaching out to more people across a bigger range of incomes and cultures than just about any other beauty products company in the world."[66]

L'Oreal seeks to satisfy customers' unique needs better than its competitors can. Some buyers are willing to pay a premium price for the firm's cosmetic items because, for these buyers, other products do not offer a comparable combination of features and cost. The lack of perceived acceptable alternatives increases the firm's power, relative to that of its customers.

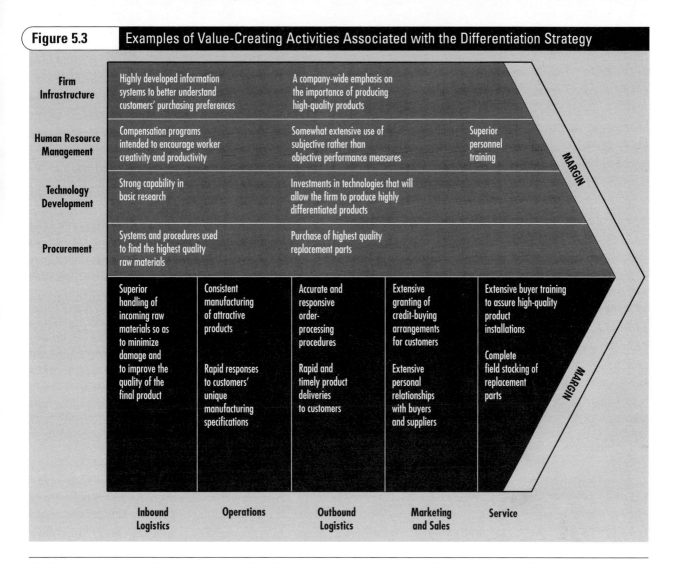

Figure 5.3	Examples of Value-Creating Activities Associated with the Differentiation Strategy

Firm Infrastructure
Highly developed information systems to better understand customers' purchasing preferences

A company-wide emphasis on the importance of producing high-quality products

Human Resource Management
Compensation programs intended to encourage worker creativity and productivity

Somewhat extensive use of subjective rather than objective performance measures

Superior personnel training

Technology Development
Strong capability in basic research

Investments in technologies that will allow the firm to produce highly differentiated products

Procurement
Systems and procedures used to find the highest quality raw materials

Purchase of highest quality replacement parts

MARGIN

Inbound Logistics	Operations	Outbound Logistics	Marketing and Sales	Service
Superior handling of incoming raw materials so as to minimize damage and to improve the quality of the final product	Consistent manufacturing of attractive products Rapid responses to customers' unique manufacturing specifications	Accurate and responsive order-processing procedures Rapid and timely product deliveries to customers	Extensive granting of credit-buying arrangements for customers Extensive personal relationships with buyers and suppliers	Extensive buyer training to assure high-quality product installations Complete field stocking of replacement parts

MARGIN

Bargaining Power of Suppliers

Because the firm using the differentiation strategy charges a premium price for its products, suppliers must provide high-quality components, driving up the firm's costs. However, the high margins the firm earns in these cases partially insulate it from the influence of suppliers, since higher supplier costs can be paid through these margins. Alternatively, because of buyers' relative insensitivity to price increases, the differentiated firm might choose to pass the additional cost of supplies on to the customer, by increasing the price of its unique product.

Potential Entrants

Customer loyalty and the need to overcome the uniqueness of a differentiated product present substantial entry barriers to potential entrants. Entering an industry under these conditions typically demands significant investments of resources and patience, while seeking customers' loyalty.

Chapter 5 / Business-Level Strategy

Product Substitutes

Firms selling brand-name goods and services to loyal customers are positioned effectively against product substitutes. In contrast, companies without brand loyalty face a higher probability of their customers switching either to products that offer differentiated features that serve the same function (particularly if the substitute has a lower price) or to products that offer more features and perform more attractive functions.

Competitive Risks of the Differentiation Strategy

As with the other business-level strategies, the differentiation strategy is not risk free. One risk is that customers might decide that the price differential between the differentiator's product and the cost leader's product is too large. In this instance, a firm may be offering differentiated features that exceed target customers' needs. The firm then becomes vulnerable to competitors that are able to offer customers a combination of features and a price that is more consistent with their needs.

Another risk of the differentiation strategy is that a firm's means of differentiation may cease to provide value for which customers are willing to pay. A differentiated product becomes less valuable if imitation by rivals causes customers to perceive that competitors offer essentially the same good or service, but at a lower price. For example, Walt Disney Company operates different theme parks, including The Magic Kingdom and Epcot Center. Each park offers entertainment and educational opportunities. However, Disney's competitors, such as Six Flags Corporation, also offer entertainment and educational experiences similar to those available at Disney's locations. To ensure that its facilities create value for which customers will be willing to pay, Disney continuously reinvests in its operations to more crisply differentiate them from those of its rivals.[67]

A third risk of the differentiation strategy is that experience can narrow customers' perceptions of the value of a product's differentiated features. For example, the value of the IBM name provided a differentiated feature for the firm's personal computers (PCs) for which some users were willing to pay a premium price in the early life cycle of the product. However, as customers familiarized themselves with the product's standard features, and as a host of other firms' PCs entered the market, IBM brand loyalty ceased to create the value for which some customers were willing to pay. The substitutes offered features similar to those found in the IBM product at a substantially lower price, reducing the attractiveness of IBM's product.

Responding to the effects of this reality, IBM now emphasizes service as a source of differentiation to drive product sales. Through IBM Global Services Inc., the firm is becoming product-service centred rather than remaining true to its origins, when it was product centred.[68] The firm's objective is to sell services to customers, especially when they purchase IBM hardware.[69] IBM's actions are an example of what a firm can do to offer new, value-creating differentiated features for its current customers, as well as to attract new customers.

Counterfeiting is the differentiation strategy's fourth risk. Makers of counterfeit goods—products that attempt to convey differentiated features to customers at significantly reduced prices—are a concern for many firms using the differentiation strategy. Fakes can damage the reputation of the company. For example, in 2002, children's clothing printed with counterfeit Molson beer logos was seized in Edmonton. A spokesperson for Molson said it was completely inappropriate to have its logos on children's clothing, and the company would never authorize such items. Poorly made fakes cannot only damage the reputation of the company, but they can also endanger the health and lives of consumers. In late 2003, the RCMP and Canada Customs seized almost 60,000 counterfeit Duracell batteries in Montreal. Cheaply made in China, these batteries held little power and did not contain protective standard features. The fakes not only contained mercury (a dangerous substance), but analysis showed they had the potential to explode.[70]

Focus Strategies

Firms choose a focus strategy when they want their core competencies to serve the needs of one particular industry segment or niche at the exclusion of others. Examples of specific market segments that can be targeted by a focus strategy include a (1) particular buyer group (e.g., youths or senior citizens), (2) different segment of a product line (e.g., products for professional painters or those for do-it-yourselfers), or (3) different geographic market (e.g., Eastern Canada or Western Canada).[71] Thus, the **focus strategy** is an integrated set of actions designed to produce or deliver goods or services that serve the needs of a particular competitive segment.

Although the breadth of a target is clearly a matter of degree, the essence of the focus strategy "is the exploitation of a narrow target's differences from the balance of the industry."[72] Firms using the focus strategy intend to serve a particular segment of an industry more effectively than industry-wide competitors. Firms succeed either when they effectively serve a segment whose unique needs are so specialized that broad-based competitors choose not to serve that segment or when they satisfy the needs of a segment being served poorly by industry-wide competitors.[73]

To satisfy the needs of financial customers in a particular geographic market, Vancouver City Savings Credit Union (VanCity) has positioned itself as an ethical financial services company serving the greater Vancouver region. Although it is Canada's largest credit union, 40 of its 41 branches are in the B.C. Lower Mainland or the neighbouring Fraser Valley (the 41st branch is in neighbouring Victoria).[74] Toronto's Home Capital Group is Canada's largest provider of nonstandard residential mortgages—even though Home Capital's $1.9 billion in assets represents only 2 percent of the mortgage market. Home Capital's clients include self-employed people, those with a short or limited credit history, and those with problem credit histories—potential clients that banks usually turn away. Although Home Capital charges between 1.5 and 2 percentage points higher than what banks charge, their clients are just as unlikely to default on their mortgage as other Canadians (only about 0.3 percent of Home Capital mortgages and 0.33 percent of national mortgages were in arrears at the end of 2003).[75] Through successful use of the focus strategy, firms such as Home Capital gain a competitive advantage in specific market niches or segments, even though they do not possess an industry-wide competitive advantage.[76]

Firms can create value for customers in specific and unique market segments by using the focused cost leadership strategy or the focused differentiation strategy.

The **focus strategy** is an integrated set of actions designed to produce or deliver goods or services that serve the needs of a particular competitive segment.

Focused Cost Leadership Strategy

Based in Sweden, Ikea, a global furniture retailer, follows the focused cost leadership strategy.[77] Young buyers desiring style at a low cost are Ikea's market segment. For these customers, the firm offers home furnishings that combine good design, function, and acceptable quality with low prices. According to the firm, "low cost is always in focus. This applies to every phase of our activities. The foundation is our range that shall offer good design and function at a low price."[78]

Ikea emphasizes several activities to keep its costs low. For example, instead of relying primarily on third-party manufacturers, the firm's engineers design low-cost, modular furniture ready for assembly by customers. Ikea also positions its products in room-like settings. Typically, competitors' furniture stores display multiple varieties of a single item in separate rooms, and their customers examine living room sofas in one room, tables in another room, chairs in yet another location, and accessories in still another area. In contrast, Ikea's customers can view different living combinations (complete with sofas, chairs, tables, and so forth) in a single setting, which eliminates the need for sales associates or decorators to help the customer imagine how a batch of furniture will look when placed in the customer's home. This approach requires fewer sales personnel, allowing Ikea to keep its costs low. A third practice that helps keep Ikea's costs low is expecting customers to transport their own purchases rather than providing delivery service.

Although a cost leader, Ikea also offers some differentiated features that appeal to its target customers, including in-store playrooms for children, wheelchairs for customer use, and extended hours. Stores outside those in the home country have Sweden Shops that sell Swedish specialties, such as herring, crisp bread, Swedish caviar, and gingerbread biscuits. Ikea believes that these services and products "are uniquely aligned with the needs of [its] customers, who are young, are not wealthy, are likely to have children, and, because they work for a living, have a need to shop at odd hours."[79] Thus, Ikea's focused cost leadership strategy finds the firm offering some differentiated features with its low cost products.

Focused Differentiation Strategy

Other firms implement the focused differentiation strategy in the pursuit of above-average returns. As noted earlier, firms can differentiate their products in many ways. Consider the following examples of firms using a focused differentiation strategy. Vancouver's Straight Line Designs is a custom furniture company that has a reputation for unique style and quality work. The company's whimsical and unusual designs focus on custom products aimed at children and the family. Straight Line's furniture is interactive and fun: metre-tall carrots with drawers, beds that look like castles, and cabinets that have virtually no straight lines. While some items are for personal use, many pieces are constructed for trade shows, movies and TV, malls, and retail stores—any place where Straight Line's eye-catching designs would draw people in. In the U.S., Get Well Network, Inc. provides products to augment the cable-connected television set found in most hospital rooms. With its charges posted to the hospital room bills, patients use the firm's interactive systems to watch pay-per-view movies and to connect to the Internet. StilicForce, a French firm, designed and sells the Trottibasket, a durable plastic basket that slides onto the vertical bar of a Razor scooter. Shaped like a cone, the Trottibasket is used to carry relatively small items the scooter rider needs to transport.[80]

In the next Strategic Focus box, "More Precious Than Diamonds," we discuss individual sources of differentiation that one Canadian industry has created to use the focused differentiation strategy. As described in the Strategic Focus box, the companies in the Canadian diamond industry use the focused differentiation strategy to target a narrow customer segment. While diamonds do appeal to the emotions of customers in a broad market, Canadian firms were able to target a customer group where the perceived value for its product could be enhanced in a narrow market segment. We also explain in the Strategic Focus box what capabilities and technologies were required to make the most of this opportunity.

Firms must be able to complete various primary and support activities in a competitively superior manner to achieve and sustain a competitive advantage and earn above-average returns with a focus strategy. The activities required to use the focused cost leadership strategy are virtually identical to the activities shown in Figure 5.2, on page 151, and the activities required to use the focused differentiation strategy are virtually identical to those shown in Figure 5.3, on page 157. Similarly, the manner in which each of these two focus strategies allows a firm to deal successfully with the five competitive forces parallel those described with respect to the cost leadership strategy and the differentiation strategy. The only difference is that the competitive scope changes from an industry-wide market to a narrow industry segment. Thus, a review of Figures 5.2 and 5.3 and the text regarding the five competitive forces yields a description of the relationship between each of the two focus strategies and competitive advantage.

More Precious Than Diamonds

What's more precious than diamonds? Canadian diamonds! At least that is the hope of the folks at Australia's BHP Billiton, Canada's Aber Diamond, and Britain's Rio Tinto. BHP owns the Ekati Diamond Mine in the Northwest Territories. Aber and Rio Tinto are joint owners of the Diavik Mine—also located about 300 km northeast of Yellowknife. Together these mines expect to be producing 10 percent of the world's diamond output for years to come. This makes Canada one of the world's six largest diamond producers. But with so much production what causes these Canadian stones to command at least a 20 percent premium on world markets? As we will see, Canadian diamonds can command a premium through a combination of the market's demand for certain types of diamonds, careful identification, certification, tracking, processing, and branding, The market demand for Canadian diamonds stems, in part, from the existence of products that have been labelled conflict diamonds, or blood diamonds.

As defined by the United Nations, "conflict diamonds are diamonds that originate from areas controlled by forces or factions opposed to legitimate and internationally recognized governments, and are used to fund military action in opposition to those governments, or in contravention of the decisions of the Security Council." Basically, conflict diamonds, which comprise 5 percent of the world's diamonds, are stones acquired by rebel forces and smuggled into legitimate markets so that their profits can be used to aid a rebellion. Buy these diamonds and you will have aided in the enslavement, maiming, or killing of innocent people in African nations such as Angola, the Democratic Republic of Congo, Liberia, and Sierra Leone. In addition, there are concerns that those smuggling the diamonds are using the money laundering that goes along with the activity to support terrorist groups such as Al-Queda.

Blood diamond is a term sometimes used to describe conflict diamonds, although authors such as Janine Roberts (2003, *Glitter and greed: The secret world of the diamond cartel*, New York: The Disinformation Company Ltd.) have used the term to describe any activity where poorly paid labour, working in poor conditions, mine, cut, or polish diamonds. Given that many diamonds might fall into this category, there have been calls to boycott diamonds altogether. As well, given what people spend on diamonds, spending a bit more to not buy them from sellers with blood on their hands, seems a small price to pay.

This is where the Canadian diamond industry comes in. Not only does the market present a demand for bloodless diamonds, but also the Canadian industry is uniquely placed to sell them. The industry has exceptional control over the gems since they are mined by only a few producers, in a remote, difficult to access location. As well, Canadian diamonds can claim to be mined in an environmentally and politically sensitive manner. Diamonds have their exact properties recorded via a process known as gemprinting (the gemological equivalent of human fingerprinting). Each diamond is audited from mine to shipment to the grading laboratory and is issued a numbered governmental certification of authenticity of origin that can be matched to the gemprinted diamond. Some of the gems are cut and polished by the handful of factories set up in Yellowknife by the Government of the Northwest Territories. Other diamonds are cut and polished by a handful of diamond cutters in Canada.

When the gems are cut, the stones are numbered and labelled on their girdle (the widest part around the diamond) using laser inscription. Since these identifiers are visible only under magnification, they do not impact the appearance of the diamond. For example, Canada's first branded diamond manufacturer, Sirius Diamonds, has received distinction around the world for the quality of products identified by their trademarked logos engraved on each diamond. Sirius introduced its Polar Bear logo as Canada's first branded diamond in 1999 and has since developed other images (fire and ice) and brands (Ideal Princess) to complement the original Polar Bear. The company also promotes the fact that, from the mine to the final polish, all work is done by Canadian crafters, in Canada.

(continued)

In addition, quality, and thus the premium that sellers can demand, can be raised beyond the simple bloodlessness of the diamonds. Additional quality selection will also produce a premium price. Ekati owner BHP has its own brand of diamonds called Aurias. Its high-end Aurias Select brand only sells diamonds that have no colour that is detectable to the unaided eye—a highly sought attribute. While high-quality diamonds usually have slight flaws, called inclusions, Aurias diamonds never have any inclusions visible to the unaided eye. Thus, even within the premium class of Canadian diamonds, super premiums can be created through careful selection.

SOURCES: Sirius Diamonds, 2004, *Sirius Diamonds website*, http://www.siriusdiamonds.com, accessed March 8, 2004; Aurias Diamonds, 2004, *Aurias Diamonds website*, http://www.aurias.com, accessed March 8, 2004; 2004, Diavik Mines, 2004, *Diavik Mines website*, http://www.diavik.ca, accessed March 7, 2004; United Nations, 2004, Conflict diamonds: Sanction and War: General Assembly adopts resolution on "conflict diamonds," *UN Conflict Diamonds website*, http://www.un.org/peace/africa/Diamond.html, accessed March 7, 2004; Amnesty International, 2004, Conflict diamonds: Did someone die for that diamond? *Amnesty International diamonds website*, http://www.amnestyusa.org/diamonds, accessed March 6, 2004; J. Roberts, 2003, The diamond empire, *Glitter and Greed website*, http://www.sparkle.plus.com, accessed March 6, 2004; S. Simpson, 2003, Mining giant puts city on world diamond map, *Vancouver Sun* (final ed.), June 24, D1; D. Finlayson, 2003, Canada's northern economy a diamond in the rough: Series: Northern tiger, *Vancouver Sun* (final ed.), June 10, D4; E. Lazarus, 2003, Ekati digs deep for brand identity, *Marketing Magazine*, 108(16): 2.

Competitive Risks of Focus Strategies

With either focus strategy, the firm faces the same general risks as does the company using either the cost leadership or the differentiation strategy on an industry-wide basis. However, focus strategies have three additional risks.

First, a competitor may be able to focus on a more narrowly defined competitive segment and outfocus the focuser. For example, Big Dog Motorcycles of Wichita, Kansas, is trying to outfocus Harley-Davidson, which is pursuing a broader focus differentiation strategy. While Harley focuses solely on producing heavyweight motorcycles, Big Dog builds motorcycles that target only the very high end of the heavyweight market—the high-end, premium cruiser market—with names such as Pitbull, Wolf, Mastiff, and Bulldog. Big Dog is careful to differentiate its products from those of Harley-Davidson, citing its larger motors, fat rear tires, unique state-of-the-art electronics, and 4-piston calibre brakes as examples of value-creating features. With additional value-creating differentiated features (e.g., performance capabilities made possible by larger engines), Big Dog may be able to better serve the unique needs of a narrow customer group.[81]

Second, a company competing on an industry-wide basis may decide that the market segment served by the focus strategy firm is attractive and worthy of competitive pursuit. For example, for years, sales at microbreweries grew at a phenomenal rate. This attracted the attention of big breweries, such as Molson, who introduced brands to appeal to this segment (e.g., Rickard's Red). Growth in the microbrewery segment peaked in the late 1990s. While neither the microbreweries' nor the big breweries' microbrew-targeted beers captured much market share, the products did encourage consumers to break out of their old brands and be more adventurous in their tastes. This change in consumer preference has allowed imported beers to move from less than 7 percent of the market in the late 1990s to more than 12 percent by 2003. The increase in consumption of imported beers has helped the big breweries. For example, Interbrew (who owns Labatt Breweries), was able to successfully introduce Canadians to its flagship Belgian brand, Stella Artois.[82] A risk associated with attracting big competitors is that another focuser may use the strategy to create a national firm, as Sleeman Brewing has done. Sleeman began as an Ontario microbrewery, then became a regional brewery. The firm then had the resources to buy other microbreweries in B.C. and Quebec, to create a national presence and become Canada's third largest brewery.[83]

The third risk involved with a focus strategy is that the needs of customers within a narrow competitive segment may become more similar to those of industry-wide customers as a whole. As a result, the advantages of a focus strategy are either reduced or eliminated. At some point, for example, the needs of Ikea's customers for stylish furniture may dissipate, although their desire to buy relatively inexpensive furnishings may not. If this change in needs were to happen, Ikea's customers might buy from large chain stores that sell comparatively standardized furniture at low costs.

Integrated Cost Leadership/Differentiation Strategy

Particularly in global markets, the firm's ability to integrate the means of competition necessary to implement the cost leadership and differentiation strategies may be critical to developing competitive advantages. Compared to firms implementing one dominant business-level strategy, the company that successfully uses an integrated cost leadership/differentiation strategy should be in a better position to (1) adapt quickly to environmental changes, (2) learn new skills and technologies more quickly, and (3) effectively leverage its core competencies while competing against its rivals.

In this chapter's first Strategic Focus box, "WestJet," on page 148, we saw how WestJet's activities demonstrate how a firm gains a competitive advantage by tightly integrating its primary and support activities. WestJet successfully uses the integrated cost leadership/differentiation strategy, allowing the firm to adapt quickly, learn rapidly, and meaningfully leverage its core competencies while competing against its rivals in the airline industry.

Vancouver's Nettwerk Productions began as a music publishing firm and has since expanded into a wide range of music-related ventures. The most visible of these ventures has been its management of an impressive list of Canadian recording stars, including the Barenaked Ladies, Gob, Our Lady Peace, Sum 41, Swollen Members, Treble Charger, and Chantal Kreviazuk. While music would seem the most differentiated of activities—particularly for a smaller player in the music business—Nettwerk's strategy also includes elements of cost leadership. Frequently, Nettwerk will contract with a relatively new artist as a less expensive entry into a relationship with that artist. By handling and developing new artists, the company can gain some loyalty at a very early and less-demanding stage of the musician's professional life. Nettwerk-managed musician Dayna Manning was still wearing braces on her first video for the song "My Addiction." Nettwerk recording artist Sarah McLachlan and Nettwerk-managed star Avril Lavigne were still in their teens when their relationships started with the company.[84]

Evidence suggests a relationship between successful use of the integrated strategy and above-average returns.[85] Thus, firms able to produce relatively differentiated products at relatively low costs can expect to perform well.[86] Indeed, a researcher found that the most successful firms competing in low-profit-potential industries were integrating the attributes of the cost leadership and differentiation strategies.[87] Other researchers have discovered that "businesses which combined multiple forms of competitive advantage outperformed businesses that only were identified with a single form."[88] The results of another study showed that the highest performing companies in the Korean electronics industry combined the value-creating aspects of the cost leadership and differentiation strategies.[89] This finding suggests the usefulness of integrated strategy in settings outside the United States. McDonald's is a global corporation with a strong global brand, offering products at a relatively low cost but with some differentiated features. Its global scale, relationships with franchisees, and rigorous standardization of processes allow McDonald's to lower its costs, while its brand recognition and product consistency are sources of differentiation allowing the restaurant chain to charge slightly higher prices.[90] Thus, the firm uses the integrated cost leadership/differentiation strategy.[91]

The future success of McDonald's has been questioned. The imitability of many of its newly designed sources of differentiation will affect the degree of success McDonald's can achieve with the integrated cost leadership/differentiation strategy. Major competitors, such as Burger King and Wendy's, may be able to imitate the value created through McDonald's new products and services, such as double drive-throughs and electronic menu boards. Additionally, both competitors have the resources to purchase technologies and equipment that reduce production costs. As a result, McDonald's must simultaneously seek new ways to differentiate its product offerings and storefront concepts and reduce its cost structure to successfully use the integrated strategy.[92]

A commitment to strategic flexibility (see Chapter 1) is necessary for firms such as McDonald's to effectively use the integrated cost leadership/differentiation strategy. Strategic flexibility results from developing systems, procedures, and methods that enable a firm to quickly and effectively respond to opportunities that reduce costs or increase differentiation. Flexible manufacturing systems, information networks, and total quality management systems are three sources of strategic flexibility that facilitate use of the integrated strategy. Valuable to the successful use of each business-level strategy, the strategic flexibility provided by these three tools is especially important to firms trying to balance the objectives of continuous cost reductions and continuous enhancements to sources of differentiation.

Flexible Manufacturing Systems

Modern information technologies have helped make flexible manufacturing systems (FMSs) possible. These systems increase the "flexibilities of human, physical, and information resources"[93] that the firm integrates to create differentiated products at low costs. A *flexible manufacturing system* is a computer-controlled process used to produce a variety of products in moderate, flexible quantities, with a minimum of manual intervention.[94] Particularly in situations where parts are too heavy for people to handle or when other methods are less effective in creating manufacturing and assembly flexibility, robots are integral to use of an FMS.[95] In spite of their promise, few companies are using the productive capabilities of an FMS (for example, only one in five Fortune 1000 companies is using an FMS).[96]

The goal of an FMS is to eliminate the "low-cost-versus-product-variety" trade-off that is inherent in traditional manufacturing technologies. Firms use an FMS to change quickly and easily from making one product to making another.[97] Used properly, an FMS allows the firm to respond more effectively to changes in its customers' needs, while retaining low-cost advantages and consistent product quality.[98] Because an FMS also enables the firm to reduce the lot size needed to manufacture a product efficiently, the firm increases its capacity to serve the unique needs of a narrow competitive scope. Thus, FMS technology is a significant technological advance that allows firms to produce a large variety of products at a relatively low cost. Levi Strauss, for example, uses an FMS to make jeans that fit women's exact measurements. Customers of Andersen Windows can design their own windows using proprietary software developed by the firm. Tire manufacturers Pirelli and Goodyear are turning to robots and other advanced technologies as part of their quest to transform the traditional time-consuming, complex, and costly method of making tires into a more flexible and responsive system.[99]

The effective use of an FMS is linked with a firm's abilities both to understand the constraints these systems may create (e.g., materials handling and the flow of supporting resources in scheduling) and to configure an effective mix of machines, computer systems, and people.[100] In service industries, the processes used must be flexible enough to both increase delivery speed and satisfy changing customer needs. McDonald's, for example, is testing three vision stores in three stages to learn how to reduce service times. In addition to installing more automated equipment, the company is experimenting with splitting counter service between two employees—one person taking the order and payment while the other assembles the order.[101] In industries of all types, effective mixes of the firm's tangible assets (e.g., machines) and intangible assets (e.g., people's skills) facilitate implementation of complex competitive strategies, especially the integrated cost leadership/differentiation strategy.[102]

Information Networks

By linking companies with their suppliers, distributors, and customers, information networks provide another source of strategic flexibility. Among other outcomes, these networks facilitate the firm's efforts to satisfy customer expectations, in terms of product quality and delivery speed.

As noted earlier, customer relationship management (CRM) is one form of an information-based network process that firms use to better understand customers and their needs. The effective CRM system provides a 360° view of the company's relationship with customers, encompassing all contact points, involving all business processes, and incorporating all communication media and sales channels.[103] The firm can then use this information to determine the trade-offs its customers are willing to make between differentiated features and low cost, knowledge that is vital for companies using the integrated cost leadership/differentiation strategy.

Information networks are also critical to the establishment and successful use of an enterprise resource planning (ERP) system. ERP is an information system used to identify and plan the resources required across the firm to receive, record, produce, and ship customer orders.[104] For example, W. C. Wood Co. has launched an ERP and supply chain management system for use in its three plants in Guelph, Ontario, and its Ottawa, Ohio plant. The system allows the company, a manufacture of large home appliances, to forecast inventory and plan production schedules. The company needed to be certain that when it says you can have the product on a certain day, that the product will be produced and in inventory by that time. This efficiency is particularly difficult to forecast in the home appliance market where a single store may sell only one freezer a week.[105] Full installations of an ERP system are expensive, running into the tens of millions of dollars for large-scale applications, but these systems can also save the same amounts in inventory carrying costs.

Improving efficiency on a company-wide basis is a primary objective of using an ERP system. Efficiency improvements result from the use of systems through which financial and operational data are moved rapidly from one department to another. Integrating data—across parties that are involved with detailing product specifications, manufacturing those products, and distributing them in ways that are consistent with customers' unique needs—enables the firm to respond with flexibility to customer preferences, relative to cost and differentiation.

Total Quality Management Systems

In the 1970s and 1980s, executives in Western nations recognized that their firms' success, and even their survival in some industries (e.g., automobile manufacturing), depended on developing an ability to dramatically improve the quality of their goods and services, while simultaneously reducing their cost structures. The relatively low costs of relatively high-quality products from a host of Japanese companies emphasized this message with resounding clarity.[106]

Focused on *doing things right* through efficiency increases, total quality management (TQM) systems are used in firms across multiple nations and economic regions to increase their competitiveness.[107] TQM systems incorporate customer definitions of quality, instead of those derived by the firm, and demand that the firm focus on the root causes of a problem rather than its symptoms.[108] Accepted widely as a viable means of improving the firm's competitiveness, TQM systems have been a worldwide movement since the early 1980s.[109]

A key assumption underlying the use of a TQM system is that "the costs of poor quality (such as inspection, rework, and lost customers, and so on) are far greater than the costs of developing processes that produce high-quality products and services."[110] This relationship may partially account for the financial difficulties Ford Motor Company experienced in mid-2001, when poor product quality and related production delays in the previous year were estimated to have cost Ford more than $1 billion in lost profits. A comparison of the estimated warranty costs for Ford and for two of its competitors also demonstrates the competitive disadvantage resulting from poor quality. Deutsche Bank estimated Ford's average warranty cost per vehicle at $650, GM's at $550, and Toyota's at $400.[111] Cost disadvantages such as these make it difficult to compete successfully against rivals (see Chapter 6) and to earn returns that satisfy investors' expectations.

Firms use TQM systems to achieve several specific objectives, including (1) at least meeting customers' expectations while striving to exceed them, especially in terms of quality, (2) focusing on work activities to drive out inefficiencies and waste in all business processes, and (3) incorporating improvements in all parts of the firm while continuously striving for additional improvement opportunities.[112] Achieving these objectives improves a firm's flexibility and facilitates use of all business-level strategies. However, the outcomes suggested by these objectives are particularly important to firms implementing the integrated cost leadership/differentiation strategy. The achievement of at least meeting (and perhaps exceeding) customers' expectations regarding quality is a differentiating feature, and eliminating process inefficiencies allows the firm to offer that quality at a relatively low cost. Thus, an effective TQM system helps the firm develop the flexibility needed to spot opportunities to simultaneously increase differentiation and/or reduce costs.

Competitive Risks of the Integrated Cost Leadership/Differentiation Strategy

The potential to earn above-average returns by successfully using the integrated cost leadership/differentiation strategy is appealing. However, experience shows that substantial risk accompanies this potential. Selecting a business-level strategy requires the firm to make choices about how it intends to compete.[113] Achieving the low-cost position in an industry, or in a segment of an industry, by using a focus strategy demands that the firm reduce its costs, consistently relative to the costs of its competitors. The use of the differentiation strategy, with either an industry-wide or a focused competitive scope (see Figure 5.1, on page 147), requires the firm to provide its customers with the differentiated goods or services they value and for which they are willing to pay a premium price.

The firm that uses the integrated strategy, yet fails to establish a leadership position, risks becoming stuck in the middle.[114] Being in this position prevents the firm from dealing successfully with the competitive forces in its industry and from having a distinguishable competitive advantage. Not only will the firm not be able to earn above-average returns, earning even average returns will be possible only when the structure of the industry in which it competes is highly favourable or if its competitors are also in the same position.[115] Without these conditions, the firm will earn below-average returns. Thus, companies implementing the integrated cost leadership/differentiation strategy, such as McDonald's, must be certain that their competitive actions allow them both to offer some differentiated features that their customers value and to provide them with products at a relatively low cost.

There is very little, if any, research evidence showing that the attributes of the cost leadership and differentiation strategies cannot be effectively integrated.[116] The integrated strategy, therefore, is an appropriate strategic choice for firms with the core competencies required to produce somewhat differentiated products at relatively low costs.

- A business-level strategy is an integrated and coordinated set of commitments and actions the firm uses to gain a competitive advantage by exploiting core competencies in specific product markets. Five business-level strategies (cost leadership, differentiation, focused cost leadership, focused differentiation, and integrated cost leadership/differentiation) are examined in the chapter. A firm's strategic competitiveness is enhanced when it is able to develop and exploit new core competencies faster than competitors can mimic the competitive advantages yielded by the firm's current competencies.

- Customers are the foundation of successful business-level strategies. When considering customers, a firm simultaneously examines three issues: who, what, and how. These issues respectively refer to the customer groups to be served, the needs those customers have that the firm seeks to satisfy, and the core competencies the firm will use to satisfy customers' needs. Increasing segmentation of markets throughout the global economy creates opportunities for firms to identify unique customer needs.

- Firms seeking competitive advantage through the cost leadership strategy produce no-frills, standardized products for an industry's typical customer. However, these low-cost products must be offered with competitive levels of differentiation. Above-average returns are earned when firms continuously drive their costs lower than those of their competitors, while providing customers with products that have low prices and acceptable levels of differentiated features.

- Competitive risks associated with the cost leadership strategy include (1) a loss of competitive advantage to newer technologies, (2) a failure to detect changes in customers' needs, and (3) the ability of competitors to imitate the cost leader's competitive advantage through their own unique strategic actions.

- The differentiation strategy enables firms to provide customers with products that have different (and valued) features. Differentiated products must be sold at a cost that customers believe is competitive, given the product's features, as compared to the cost/feature combination available through competitors' offerings. Because of their uniqueness, differentiated goods or services are sold at a premium price.

- Products can be differentiated along any dimension that a customer group values. Firms using this strategy seek to differentiate their products from competitors' goods or services along as many dimensions as possible. The less similarity with competitors' products, the more buffered a firm is from competition with its rivals.

- Risks associated with the differentiation strategy include (1) a customer group's decision that the differences between the differentiated product and the cost leader's good or service are no longer worth a premium price, (2) the inability of a differentiated product to create the type of value for which customers are willing to pay a premium price, (3) the ability of competitors to provide customers with products that have features similar to those associated with the differentiated product, but at a lower cost, and (4) the threat of counterfeiting, whereby competitors produce a cheap knock-off of a differentiated good or service.

- Through the cost leadership and the differentiated focus strategies, firms serve the needs of a narrow competitive segment (e.g., a buyer group, product segment, or geographic area). This strategy is successful when firms have the core competencies required to provide value to a narrow competitive segment that exceeds the value available from firms serving customers on an industry-wide basis.

- The competitive risks of focus strategies include (1) a competitor's ability to use its core competencies to outfocus the focuser by serving an even more narrowly defined competitive segment, (2) decisions by industry-wide competitors to serve a customer group's specialized needs that the focuser has been serving, and (3) a reduction in differences of the needs between customers in a narrow competitive segment and the industry-wide market.

- Firms using the integrated cost leadership/differentiation strategy strive to provide customers with relatively low-cost products that have some valued differentiated features. The primary risk of this strategy is that a firm might produce goods that do not offer sufficient value in terms of either low cost or differentiation. When this occurs, the company is stuck in the middle. Firms stuck in the middle compete at a disadvantage and are unable to earn more than average returns.

1. What is a business-level strategy?

2. What is the relationship between a firm's customers and its business-level strategy in terms of *who*, *what*, and *how*? Why is this relationship important?

3. What are the differences among the cost leadership, differentiation, focused cost leadership, focused differentiation, and integrated cost leadership/differentiation business-level strategies?

4. How can each one of the business-level strategies be used to position the firm, relative to the five forces of competition, in a way that permits the earning of above-average returns?

5. What are the specific risks associated with using each business-level strategy?

Experiential Exercise

Business-Level Strategy

Natural and organic foods are the fastest-growing segment of food retailing, and almost every supermarket in North America has begun offering at least a limited selection of these products. According to Pro Organics President Debra Boyle, "When we started, Canada had a $3-million-a-year industry." She now estimates national sales now approach $400 million annually.

Pro Organics started distributing organically grown produce in the late 1970s in Burnaby B.C. By 1996, the firm opened its second warehouse near Toronto. This move made the company Canada's first national organic food distributor. In 2000, Pro Organics set up a third distribution facility near Montreal.

Pro Organics purchases its products both locally and from all over the world, supporting organic farming on a global level, and prides itself on providing its customers with the highest-quality, least-processed, most flavourful, naturally preserved foods. While organic foods typically cost more than conventional foods, organic farming is not government subsidized, and organic products must meet stricter regulations governing growing, harvesting, transportation, and storage. All of these steps make the process more labour and management intensive.

Answer the following questions and be prepared to make a short presentation or to discuss your findings with the rest of the class.

1. What type of business-level strategy does Pro Organics appear to follow, based on the above information?

2. What are some of the risks Pro Organics faces with this strategy?

3. Use the following table and show how Pro Organics might apply each strategy to its business activities, based on the information given above (see Figure 5.2, on page 151 and Figure 5.3, on page 157).

Activities	Cost Leadership Strategy	Differentiation Strategy
Inbound Logistics		
Operations		
Outbound Logistics		
Marketing and Sales		
Service		

SOURCES: J. MacLellan, 2003, City woman tops in her field, *Burnaby Now* (final ed.), November 5, 16; Pro Organics, 2004, *Pro Organics website*, http://www.proorganics.com/home.html, accessed March 11, 2004.

1. J. Stopford, 2001, Should strategy makers become dream weavers? *Harvard Business Review*, 79(1): 165–69.

2. C. A. De Kluyver, 2000, *Strategic Thinking*, Upper Saddle River, NJ: Prentice-Hall, 3.

3. E. H. Bowman & C. E. Helfat, 2001, Does corporate strategy matter? *Strategic Management Journal*, 22: 1–23.

4. G. Hamel, 2000, *Leading the Revolution*, Boston: Harvard Business School Press, 71.

5. R. S. Kaplan & D. P. Norton, 2001, *The Strategy-Focused Organization*, Boston: Harvard Business School Press, 90.

6. J. B. Barney, 2002, *Gaining and Sustaining Competitive Advantage*, 2nd ed., Upper Saddle River, NJ: Prentice-Hall, 6; D. C. Hambrick & J. W. Fredrickson, 2001, Are you sure you have a strategy? *Academy of Management Executive*, 15(4): 48–59.

7. R. D. Ireland, M. A. Hitt, S. M. Camp, & D. L. Sexton, 2001, Integrating entrepreneurship and strategic management actions to create firm wealth, *Academy of Management Executive*, 15(1): 49–63.

8. M. A. Geletkanycz & S .S. Black, 2001, Bound by the past? Experience-based effects on commitment to the strategic status quo, *Journal of Management*, 27: 3–21; C. E. Helfat, 1997, Know-how and asset complementarity and dynamic capability accumulation: The case of R&D, *Strategic Management Journal*, 18: 339–60.

9. D. F. Kuratko, R. D. Ireland, & J. S. Hornsby, 2001, The power of entrepreneurial actions: Insights from Acordia, Inc., *Academy of Management Executive*, 15(4): 60–71; T. J. Dean, R. L. Brown, & C. E. Bamford, 1998, Differences in large and small firm responses to environmental context: Strategic implications from a comparative analysis of business formations, *Strategic Management Journal*, 19: 709–28.

10. L. Tihanyi, A. E. Ellstrand, C. M. Daily, & D. R. Dalton, 2000, Composition of top management team and firm international diversification, *Journal of Management*, 26: 1157–77; P. F. Drucker, 1999, *Management in the 21st Century*, New York: Harper Business.

11. P. Rindova & C. J. Fombrun, 1999, Constructing competitive advantage: The role of firm-constitute interactions, *Strategic Management Journal*, 20: 691–710; G. G. Dess, A. Gupta, J. F. Hennart, & C. W. L. Hill, 1995, Conducting and integrating strategy research at the international, corporate, and business levels: Issues and directions, *Journal of Management*, 21: 357–93.

12. Hamel, *Leading the Revolution*.

13. De Kluyver, *Strategic Thinking*, 7.

14. S. F. Slater & E. M. Olsen, 2000, Strategy type and performance: The influence of sales force management, *Strategic Management Journal*, 21: 813–29; M. E. Porter, 1998, *On Competition*, Boston: Harvard Business School Press.

15. M. E. Porter, 1996, What is strategy? *Harvard Business Review*, 74(6): 61–78.

16. B. Lowendahl & O. Revang, 1998, Challenges to existing strategy theory in a postindustrial society, *Strategic Management Journal*, 19: 755–73.

17. M. E. Porter, 1980, *Competitive Strategy*, New York: Free Press.

18. P. Vieira, 2004, Joyrides or feng shui? Spend your Aeroplan points on earth, *National Post (Financial Post)*, February, 26, FP1, FP6.

19. L. L. Berry, 2001, The old pillars of new retailing, *Harvard Business Review*, 79(4): 131–37; A. Afuah, 1999, Technology approaches for the information age, Mastering strategy (part one), *Financial Times*, September 27, 8.

20. N. Irwin, 2001, Motley Fool branches out, *Washington Post*, May 22, B5.

21. Knowledge@Wharton, 2001, Clicking with customers: New challenges in online conversion, *Knowledge@Wharton website*, http://knowledge.wharton.upenn.edu/index.cfm?fa=viewArticle&id=368, accessed July 23, 2004.

22. M. Schrage, 2001, Don't scorn your salespeople—you will soon be one, *Fortune*, May 14, 256; D. Peppers, M. Rogers, & B. Dorf, 1999, Is your company ready for one-to-one marketing? *Harvard Business Review*, 77(5): 59–72.

23. T. A. Stewart, 1999, *Intellectual Capital*, New York: Currency Doubleday, 144.

24. K. Ferguson, 2001, Closer than ever, *Business Week Small Biz*, May 21, 14–15; R. S. Winer, 2001, A framework for customer relationship management, *California Management Review*, 43(4): 89–105.

25. Ferguson, Closer than ever, 15.

26. M. Warner, 2001, Salesforce.com, *Fortune*, June 25, 164.

27. P. B. Seybold, 2001, Get inside the lives of your customers, *Harvard Business Review*, 79(5): 81–89.

28. M. E. Porter, 2001, Strategy and the Internet, *Harvard Business Review*, 79(3): 62–78.

29. L. Walker, 2001, Plugged in for maximum efficiency, *Washington Post*, June 20, G1, G4.

30. N. Sutton, 2002, FlexPort automates purchasing processes, *Computing Canada*, 28(11): 17.

31. Asontv, 2004, *Asontv website*, http://asontv.4t.com/chapters.html, accessed March 1, 2004; Indigo Books & Music, 2004, *Indigo Books & Music website*, http://www.chapters.indigo.ca, accessed March 1, 2004.

32. National Research Council Canada, 2004, *National Research Council Canada website*, http://irc.nrc-cnrc.gc.ca/ccmc/home_e.shtml, accessed March 1, 2004; P. Evans & T. S. Wurster, 1999, Getting real about virtual commerce, *Harvard Business Review*, 77(6): 84–94; S. F. Slater & J. C. Narver, 1999, Market-oriented is more than being customer-led, *Strategic Management Journal*, 20: 1165–68.

33. Knowledge@Wharton, 2001, How good, or bad, marketing decisions can make, or break, a company, *Knowledge@Wharton website*, http://www.knowledge.wharton.upenn.edu, accessed May 14, 2004.

34. W. D. Neal & J. Wurst, 2001, Advances in market segmentation, *Marketing Research*, 13(1): 14–18; S. C. Jain, 2000, *Marketing Planning and Strategy*, Cincinnati: South-Western College Publishing, 104–25.

35. Associated Press, 1999, Rolls Bentley targets U.S. drivers, *Dallas Morning News*, May 2, H5.

36. B. J. Knutson, 2000, College students and fast food-how students perceive restaurant brands, *Cornell Hotel and Restaurant Administration Quarterly*, 41(3): 68–74.

37. Wikipedia, 2004, Baby boomer, *Wikipedia website*, http://en.wikipedia.org/wiki/Baby_boomer; C. Burritt, 2001, Aging boomers reshape resort segment, *Lodging Hospitality*, 57(3): 31–32; J. D. Zbar, 2001, On a segmented dial, digital cuts wire finer, *Advertising Age*, 72(16): S12.

38. V. Kumar & A. Nagpal, 2001, Segmenting global markets: Look before you leap, *Marketing Research*, 13(1): 8–13.

39. Business Week, 2001, Is Gen Y shopping online? *Business Week*, June 11, 16.

40. S. Hudson & B. Ritchie, 2002, Understanding the domestic market using cluster analysis: A case study of the marketing efforts of Travel Alberta, *Journal of Vacation Marketing*, 8(3): 263–77.

41. D. A. Aaker, 1998, *Strategic Marketing Management*, 5th ed., New York: John Wiley & Sons, 20.

42. S. Miller, 1999, VW sows confusion with common platforms for models, *Wall Street Journal*, October 25, A25, A38.

43. Air Canada, 2004 Air Canada Jazz history, *Air Canada Jazz website*, http://www.aircanadaregional.ca/english/index.asp?id=25, accessed March 3; 2004, Air Canada expands Zip, *Prince George Citizen* (final ed.), February 5, 24; P. M. Rendon, 2003, Air Canada grounds Tango brand, *Marketing Magazine*, 108(34): 3; R. Milton, 2002, Speaking notes for Mr. Robert Milton, President & CEO, to 2002 Canadian Airline Investment Conference, Toronto, Ontario, June 14, *Air Canada website*, http://www.aircanada.ca/about-us/investor/can-airline_conf2002.html, accessed March 3, 2004; Air Canada, 2004, Air Canada Family, *Air Canada website*, http://www.aircanada.ca/acfamily/, accessed July 24, 2004.

44. A. W. King, S. W. Fowler, & C. P. Zeithaml, 2001, Managing organizational competencies for competitive advantage: The middle-management edge, *Academy of Management Executive*, 15(2): 95–106; Porter, Strategy and the Internet, 72.

45. Bell Canada Enterprises, 2003, BCE Emergis to focus on select business processes, http://www.bce.ca/en/news/releases/emergis/2003/12/17/70827.html (news release), accessed March 1, 2004.

46. M. E. Porter, 1988, *Competitive Advantage*, New York: Free Press, 26.

47. Porter, What is strategy?

48. Bowman & Helfat, Does corporate strategy matter? 1–4; B. McEvily & A. Zaheer, 1999, Bridging ties: A source of firm heterogeneity in competitive capabilities, *Strategic Management Journal*, 20: 133–56.

49. M. E. Porter, 1994, Toward a dynamic theory of strategy, in R. P. Rumelt, D. E. Schendel, & D. J. Teece (eds.), *Fundamental Issues in Strategy*, Boston: Harvard Business School Press, 423–61.

50. Porter, What is strategy? 62.

51. Porter, *Competitive Advantage*, 15.

52. G. G. Dess, G. T. Lumpkin, & J. E. McGee, 1999, Linking corporate entrepreneurship to strategy, structure, and process: Suggested research directions, *Entrepreneurship: Theory & Practice*, 23(3): 85–102; P. M. Wright, D. L. Smart, & G. C. McMahan, 1995, Matches between human resources and strategy among NCAA basketball teams, *Academy of Management Journal*, 38: 1052–74.

53. Porter, *Competitive Strategy*, 35–40.
54. J. A. Parnell, 2000, Reframing the combination strategy debate: Defining forms of combination, *Journal of Management Studies*, 9(1): 33–54.
55. C. Malburg, 2000, Competing on costs, *Industry Week*, October 16, 31.
56. D. F. Lynch, S. B. Keller, & J. Ozment, 2000, The effects of logistics capabilities and strategy on firm performance, *Journal of Business Logistics*, 21 (2): 47–68.
57. J. Baglole, 2000, Fledgling is taking on Air Canada, Southwest clone, plans make-or-break bet on nationwide service, *Wall Street Journal* (Eastern ed.), April 24, A26.
58. A. A. Davis, 2004, Sky high, *Profit*, 23(1), 20–23.
59. Liquidation World, 2004, *Liquidation World website*, http://www.liquidationworld.com, accessed March 2, 2004.
60. Inquirer newsdesk staff, 2003, Rumours of console price wars, E3 marks start of hostilities, *The Inquirer*, http://www.theinquirer.net/?article=9214, April 29, accessed March 3, 2004; R. Thompson & G. Marr, 2002, Video games: The new battle begins: Microsoft launches Internet strategy, Nintendo cuts prices, *National Post (Financial Post)* (national ed.), May 21, FP 1; 2001, New strategy is to make games, *Regina Leader Post* (final ed.) October 25, B 6.
61. Porter, *Competitive Strategy*, 35–40.
62. Ibid., 65.
63. Porter, *Competitive Advantage*, 14.
64. G. Semmens, 2003, Banff restaurant wins rare five-diamond award, *Calgary Herald* (final ed.), Nov 17, A1.
65. S. Freeman, 2002, U.S. car sales continued at strong clip in April: GM posts increase of 12.5% and Chrysler improves, but Ford shows 7.5% drop, *Wall Street Journal*, May 2, D3.
66. G. Edmonsdson, E. Neuborne, A. L. Kazmin, E. Thornton, & K. N. Anhalt, 1999, L'Oreal: The beauty of global branding, *Business Week e-biz*, June 28.
67. Barney, *Gaining and Sustaining Competitive Advantage*, 268.
68. L. B. Ward, 2001, Compaq changes direction, *Dallas Morning News,* June 26, D1, D12.
69. R. More, 2001, Creating profits from integrated product-service strategies, *Ivey Business Journal*, 65(5): 75–81.
70. A. Humphreys, 2003, Flood of fakes a lethal threat Series: Counterfeit Canada, *National Post* (national ed.), December 12, A.1.
71. Porter, *Competitive Strategy*, 98.
72. Porter, *Competitive Advantage*, 15.
73. Ibid., 15–16.
74. Vancouver City Savings Credit Union, 2004, *Vancouver City Savings Credit Union website*, http://www.vancity.com, accessed March 8, 2004.
75. M. Gutschi, 2003, Home Capital making risk pay: 2003 profit up 43%, *National Post* (national ed.), February 1, IN.1
76. Porter, *Competitive Advantage*, 15.
77. Porter, What is strategy? 67.
78. Ikea, 2004, *Ikea website*, http://www.ikea.com, accessed March 9, 2004.
79. Porter, What is strategy? 65.
80. Straight Line Designs, 2004, *Straight Line Designs website*, http://www.straightlinedesigns.com/mframe.htm, accessed March 9, 2004; E. McCarthy, 2001, Get Well Network enlivens patients' stay at hospital, *Washington Post*, May 7, E5; A. Overholt, 2001, Basket case, *Fast Company*, July, 60.
81. Big Dog Sportswear, *Big Dog Sportswear website*, http://www.bigdog.com, accessed July 24, 2004.
82. D. Alexander, 2003, Microbreweries on the decline, *National Post* (national ed.), February 1, D1.
83. Z. Olijnyk, 1998, Sleeman Breweries gets toehold in Quebec, *Financial Post Daily*, June 30, 3; A. Bryan, 1998, Sleeman Breweries sheds "micro" tag and eases its way into Quebec with purchase of Boucherville's Seigneuriale, *Montreal Gazette*, June 30, D1; E. Lazarus, 1999, New recipes: tough times are transforming BC's microbreweries, *Marketing Magazine*, March 1, 17–18.
84. Nettwek Management, 2004, *Nettwerk Management website*, http://www.nettwerkmanagement.com, accessed March 9, 2004; K. Gold, 2003, Music to his ears; Canadian manager Terry McBride, above, is a powerful player in recording industry, *Windsor Star* (final ed.), April 10, B 6.
85. Dess, Lumpkin, & McGee, Linking corporate entrepreneurship to strategy, 89.
86. P. Ghemawat, 2001, *Strategy and the Business Landscape*, Upper Saddle River, NJ: Prentice-Hall, 56.
87. W. K. Hall, 1980, Survival strategies in a hostile environment, *Harvard Business Review* 58(5): 75–87.
88. Dess, Gupta, Hennart, & Hill, Conducting and integrating strategy research, 377.
89. L. Kim & Y. Lim, 1988, Environment, generic strategies, and performance in a rapidly developing country: A taxonomic approach, *Academy of Management Journal*, 31: 802–27.
90. Ghemawat, *Strategy and the Business Landscape*, 56.
91. Ibid., 56.
92. A. K. Gupta & V. Govindarajan, 2001, Converting global presence into global competitive advantage, *Academy of Management Executive*, 15(2): 45–56.
93. R. Sanchez, 1995, Strategic flexibility in product competition, *Strategic Management Journal*, 16(summer special issue): 140.
94. Ibid., 105.
95. R. Olexa, 2001, Flexible parts feeding boosts productivity, *Manufacturing Engineering*, 126(4): 106–14.
96. I. Mount & B. Caulfield, 2001, The missing link, *Ecompany Now*, May, 82–88.
97. Ibid., 82.
98. Textile World, 2001, ABB: Integrated drives and process control, *Textile World*, April, 60–61.
99. M. Maynard, 2001, Tiremaking technology is on a roll, *Fortune*, May 28, 148B–48L; J. Martin, 1997, Give 'em exactly what they want, *Fortune*, November 10, 283–85.
100. R. S. Russell & B. W. Taylor III, 2000, *Operations Management*, 3rd ed., Upper Saddle River, NJ: Prentice-Hall, 262–64.
101. K. MacArthur, 2001, McDonald's sees 100% increase in U.S. sales, *AdAge website*, http://www.adage.com, accessed April 2, 2004.
102. J. B. Dilworth, 2000, *Operations Management: Providing Value in Goods and Services*, 3rd ed., Fort Worth, TX: The Dryden Press, 286–89; D. Lei, M. A. Hitt, & J. D. Goldhar, 1996, Advanced manufacturing technology, organization design and strategic flexibility, *Organization Studies*, 17: 501–23.
103. S. Isaac & R. N. Tooker, 2001, The many faces of CRM, *LIMRA's MarketFacts Quarterly*, Spring, 20(1): 84–89.
104. P. J. Rondeau & L. A. Litteral, 2001, The evolution of manufacturing planning and control systems: From reorder point to enterprise resource planning, *Production and Inventory Management*, 42(2): 1–7.
105. S. Schick, 2003, Appliance firm selects ERP for improved forecasting, *Computing Canada*, 29(5): 23.
106. D. Chatterji & J. M. Davidson, 2001, Examining TQM's legacies for R&D, *Research Technology Management*, 44(1): 10–12.
107. Kaplan & Norton, *The Strategy-Focused Organization*, 361; M. A. Mische, 2001, *Strategic Renewal: Becoming a High-Performance Organization*, Upper Saddle River, NJ: Prentice-Hall, 15.
108. J. Pfeffer, 1998, *The Human Equation: Building Profits by Putting People First*, Boston: Harvard Business School Press, 156.
109. W. M. Mak, 2000, The Tao of people-based management, *Total Quality Management*, July, 4–6.
110. J. R. Hackman & R. Wageman, 1995, Total quality management: Empirical, conceptual, and practical issues, *Administrative Science Quarterly*, 40: 310.
111. J. Muller, 2001, Ford: Why it's worse than you think, *Business Week*, June 25.
112. Chatterji & Davidson, Examining TQM's legacies for R&D, 11.
113. De Kluyver, *Strategic Thinking*, 3; C. H. St. John & J. S. Harrison, 1999, Manufacturing-based relatedness, synergy, and coordination, *Strategic Management Journal*, 20: 129–45.
114. Porter, *Competitive Advantage*, 16.
115. Ibid., 17.
116. Parnell, Reframing the combination strategy debate, 33.

6

Chapter Six

Competitive Rivalry and Competitive Dynamics

Knowledge Objectives

Studying this chapter should provide you with the strategic management knowledge needed to:

1. Define competitors, competitive rivalry, competitive behaviour, and competitive dynamics.

2. Describe market commonality and resource similarity as the building blocks of a competitor analysis.

3. Explain awareness, motivation, and ability as drivers of competitive behaviour.

4. Discuss factors affecting the likelihood a competitor will take competitive actions.

5. Discuss factors affecting the likelihood a competitor will respond to actions taken against it.

6. Explain competitive dynamics in slow-cycle, fast-cycle, and standard-cycle markets.

Classic Canadian Competitive Conflict

Great competitive rivalries have often been described as wars. Yet almost nothing compares to the commercial war fought across North America almost 200 years ago. Like the corporate battles of today, it involved companies with huge sums of money, lawyers, managers, hundreds of employees, mergers and takeovers, and the potential to dominate entire markets or, in failing to do so, to create financial ruin. However, it was truly a war, one with boats, guns, and cannons. Duels were fought, people were shot and killed; perpetrators were arrested. And, it was also almost totally Canadian.

Like many of the business battles that would succeed it, this one started because of the discovery and use of a new material. While it was not silicon for computer chips or steel for construction, its introduction was just as radical. It was beaver pelts for hat making. This fur had superior quality to any the Europeans had known and could be obtained from native trappers through simple barter. Anyone who could supply the material would have a competitive advantage over all other suppliers. There was one major problem—getting to the source. For the French, getting to the source of the pelts meant a journey of months or years, up inhospitable rivers and lakes and wintering in cold isolated places. The British found the journey easier because they were able to sail into Hudson's Bay.

Rather than get involved in an all-out competition to reach the source, British interests chartered a company to control the trade: the Hudson's Bay Company (HBC). The company received a monopoly on trade from the crown, in exchange for bearing the expense of colonizing the region. The company could seemingly monopolize the source of a product in high demand, they could transport the product more cheaply than potential competitors, and they had the capital—being a company—to set up the whole operation.

Where did this leave the French, and the later Scottish traders, operating out of Montreal? Certainly, with regard to access to a quick transportation route, they were at a competitive disadvantage. However, they did have one advantage over the HBC traders: they were, in modern terms, willing to give better service to their suppliers. The service was derived from going to the source. While HBC would have native trappers come to their trading posts, HBC's competitors would save trappers the trip by going to where the trappers were.

Through a series of complicated links, the Montreal traders eventually came together to form an association called the North West Company (NWC). NWC, and the enterprises that formed it, reconfigured the value chain by creating a requirement that one had to go to the source to get the pelts. This put HBC at a competitive disadvantage since it had neither the human resources nor capability to navigate upstream from its posts. HBC did, however, have the financial resources to hire those with navigational abilities, and the company was soon able to compete with the NWC in more directly sourcing furs. Since HBC was a company, it retained its earnings and had significant financial means; NWC, being an amalgamation of firms, distributed its earnings to members. Thus, HBC had the option to invest the full weight of its

The Battle of Seven Oaks exemplifies the competitive struggle between the Hudson's Bay Company and the North West Company.

HUDSON'S BAY COMPANY ARCHIVES, ARCHIVES OF MANITOBA/HBCA DOCUMENTARY ART, P-378 (N87-8)

(continued)

retained resources into new fields, should such a move be required. This move into new activities brought HBC and the North West Company into their most direct conflict.

As part of a scheme to move his fellow countrymen toward a better life, Thomas Douglas, the fifth Earl of Selkirk, became involved in the affairs of HBC. He bought sufficient stock in HBC to allow him to control the company, and then had HBC grant him about 30 million hectares around southern Manitoba, to establish a settlement. Talk about ambitious strategic intent. One problem was that the area included a number of important North West Company trading posts. While HBC was not directly settling these people, the company did provide transportation, provisions, and protection. The endeavour by Lord Selkirk was indistinguishable from the efforts of HBC, and was thus considered a threat to NWC. NWC began a campaign to dissuade colonists from making the trip. Letters to the editor appeared in newspapers where Lord Selkirk was recruiting, telling of the hardships settlers would face. Some of those who had signed on backed out, but enough were left to begin the project in 1811.

Despite the land grant crossing major NWC routes, there seemed little cause for concern. The first two waves of settlers were ill equipped. Yet, the behaviour of Selkirk's governor, Miles Macdonell, pitted the colonists against, not only the NWC, but the Métis who traded with them. First, HBC employees began surveying land on both sides of the Red River for the settlers' farms. While Lord Selkirk had legal advice that he was entitled to survey the land, this action ignored the reality that the Métis, who had lived there for three generations, felt they had legitimate right to the land. Second, when two more parties of settlers arrived in 1813 and 1814, Miles Macdonell, fearing he would not be able to feed them, seized tonnes of food supplies bound for NWC outposts. Later, he issued a proclamation that the NWC was to abandon its forts since they were on Lord Selkirk's land. In modern terms, Macdonell was trying to disrupt the NWC supply chain, and deny it resources by legal and other means.

The North West Company was no stranger to heavy-handed tactics. When needed, the NWC had used force when trading with the natives and the Métis. NWC partners ordered that employees resist all further seizures. They had Lord Selkirk's agents responsible for the food seizures—including the governor himself—arrested and shipped back east for trial. Finally, the NWC set out to destroy the Red River settlement. It offered free passage out of the area to any of the colonists who wished to go, and other settlers were hired away by NWC. NWC, with help from the Métis, threatened the settlers' crops and drove off their livestock. When less than a handful of colonists were left, Lord Selkirk's Fort Douglas and all other colony property were burned. By early 1815, Lord Selkirk's abilities to perform any activities in the area were essentially eliminated.

While NWC's use of force may have given it some temporary advantage, Lord Selkirk had tapped into an almost infinite supply of colonists. A fresh wave of settlers arrived in 1815, and settlers leaving the old colony were gathered up and rallied to return. Fort Douglas was rebuilt. Lord Selkirk's new governor, Robert Semple, had NWC managers arrested and sent east for trial. The NWC fort was then destroyed.

Like many modern businesses, both the NWC and HBC performed a variety of value chain activities—many of which were vulnerable to attack by competitors. NWC managers and their Métis associates, realizing this, proceeded to seize an HBC shipment, raid an HBC post, and then return their attention to the new Fort Douglas.

Domain selection can be critical in determining whether an organization survives. For the most part, this means selecting an industry or market niche that matches an organization's capabilities. In the case of Robert Semple, it meant not riding out from Fort Douglas to meet a passing party of NWC and Métis when he was badly out numbered and out-gunned. After each of the companies had raided each other's personnel and inventory, destroyed each other's facilities, and done battle in the courts, these two competitors set about the most direct competitive move imaginable—gunfire. After exchanging words with the NWC group, Robert Semple and more than 20 colonists were killed at Seven Oaks, in southern Manitoba. The NWC group then successfully threatened those at Fort Douglas with a similar fate, should they not surrender.

Continued competitive actions and responses occurred. Lord Selkirk hired Swiss merce-naries to capture the chief NWC post at Fort William. Seven Oaks provoked a new round of arrests—including an attempt to arrest Lord Selkirk. Both sides made dozens of charges in the courts. Cases dragged on for years. Cases were so badly handled that, at one point, the courts started the process all over again.

Lord Selkirk was so worn down by the whole proceeding that he was almost willing to sell out to representatives of Montreal's NWC. However, NWC partners in the West, weary of the battle, sent their own representatives to Lord Selkirk to discuss a merger. Like modern organizations, the death of the founders, or major builders of the corporation sig-nals major changes in organizations. In the end, the two people most likely to resist the merger—HBC's Lord Selkirk and NWC's Alexander Mackenzie—passed away in 1820. Later that year, the two companies merged, keeping the name of the older and more stable corporation—the future trade would all be routed through Hudson's Bay.

SOURCES: OnWar.com, 2000, Armed conflict events data: Seven Oaks massacre in Canada 1816, *OnWar website*, http://www.onwar.com/aced/data/charlie/canada1816.htm, accessed January 1, 2004; M. W. Campbell, 1983, *The North West Company*, Vancouver, BC: Douglas & McIntyre; D. Francis, 1982, *Battle for the West: Fur Traders and the Birth of Western Canada*, Edmonton, AB: Hurtig; G. C. Davidson, 1918, *The North West Company*, Berkeley, CA: University of California Press.

Firms operating in the same market, offering similar products and targeting similar customers are **competitors**.

Competitive rivalry is the ongoing set of competitive actions and competitive responses occurring between competitors as they compete against each other for an advantageous market position.

Competitive behaviour is the set of competitive actions and competitive responses the firm takes to build or defend its competitive advantages and to improve its market position.

All competitive behaviour—that is, the total set of actions and responses taken by all firms competing within a market—is called **competitive dynamics**.

Firms competing against each other in several product or geographic markets are engaged in **multimarket competition**.

Firms operating in the same market, offering similar products, and targeting similar customers are **competitors**.[1] Obviously, the Hudson's Bay Company (HBC) and the North West Company (NWC) were competitors. **Competitive rivalry** is the ongoing set of competitive actions and competitive responses occurring between competitors as they compete against each other for an advantageous market position. Competitive rivalry influences an individual firm's ability to gain and sustain competitive advantages.[2] In a sequence of firm-level moves, rivalry results from firms initiating their own competitive actions and then responding to actions taken by their competitors.[3] As is shown in the opening case, **competitive behaviour** is the set of competitive actions and competitive responses the firm takes to build or defend its competitive advantages and to improve its market position.[4] Through competitive behaviour, the firm tries to successfully position itself, relative to the five forces of competition (see Chapter 3), and to defend and use current competitive advantages, while building advantages for the future (see Chapter 4). Increasingly, as with the HBC and NWC, competitors engage in competitive actions and responses in multiple markets.[5]

All competitive behaviour—that is, the total set of actions and responses taken by all firms competing within a market—is called **competitive dynamics**. The relationships among these key concepts are shown in Figure 6.1.

This chapter focuses on competitive rivalry and competitive dynamics. The essence of these important topics is that a firm's strategies are dynamic in nature. Actions taken by one firm elicit responses from competitors that, in turn, typically result in responses from the firm that took the initial action.[6] This chain of events is illustrated in the opening case that describes HBC's and the North West Company's competitive rivalry as they competed against each other in several markets (e.g., package delivery and logistics services). Firms competing against each other in several product or geographic markets are engaged in **multimarket competition**.[7]

Another way of highlighting competitive rivalry's effect on the firm's strategies is by determining a strategy's success, not only by the firm's initial competitive actions, but also by how well it anticipates competitors' responses *and* by how well the firm responds to its competitors' initial actions (also called attacks).[8] Although competitive rivalry affects all types of strategies (e.g., corporate-level, acquisition, and international), its most dominant influence is on the firm's business-level strategy or strategies. Recall from

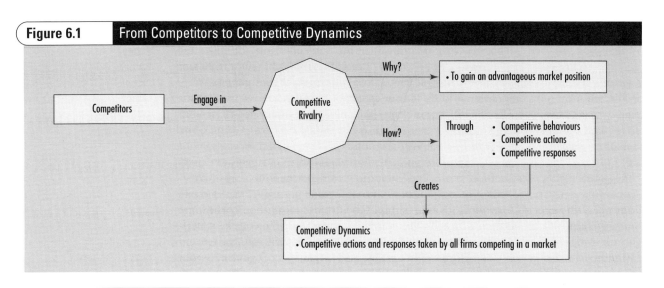

Figure 6.1   From Competitors to Competitive Dynamics

SOURCE: Adapted from M. J. Chen, 1996, Competitor analysis and interfirm rivalry: Toward a theoretical integration, *Academy of Management Review*, 21: 100–34.

Chapter 5 that business-level strategy is concerned with what the firm does to successfully use its competitive advantages in specific product markets.

In the global economy, competitive rivalry is intensifying,[9] meaning that the significance of its effect on firms' business-level strategies is increasing. In the automobile industry, for example, Ford Motor Company CEO William Ford Jr. believes that firms engage in cutthroat competition. Companies with strong brand names (e.g., Coca-Cola, GE, and Microsoft) increasingly rely on their brand names as ambassadors, when entering new markets or offering new products.[10] This reliance is especially noticeable for firms using a differentiation business-level strategy. Strong brands affect competitive rivalry. Companies without strong brands must find ways (e.g., price reductions) to reduce brand-name appeal to customers.[11] A competitor's decision to reduce prices likely will elicit a response from the firm with a strong brand, increasing competitive rivalry as a result.

An expanding geographic scope contributes to the increasing intensity in the competitive rivalry between firms. Some believe, for example, that an aptitude for cross-border management practices and a facility with cultural diversity find European Union firms emerging as formidable global competitors.[12] Similarly, former GE CEO Jack Welch believes that GE's most significant future competitive threats may be from companies not currently in prominent positions on the firm's radar screen, such as those in emerging countries.[13] Thus, the firm trying to predict competitive rivalry should anticipate that, in the future, it will encounter a larger number of increasingly diverse competitors. This trend also suggests that firms should expect competitive rivalry to have a stronger effect on their strategies' success than historically has been the case.[14]

We offer a model (see Figure 6.2) to show the activities involved with competitive rivalry at the firm level.[15] We study rivalry at the firm level because the competitive actions and responses the firm takes are the foundation for successfully building and using its competitive advantages to gain an advantageous market position.[16] Thus, we use the model in Figure 6.2 to help us explain competition between a particular firm and each of its competitors, as they compete for the most advantageous market position. Successful use of the model in Figure 6.2 allows companies to predict competitors' behaviour (actions and responses), which, in turn, has a positive effect on the firm's market position and its subsequent financial performance.[17] The sum of all the individual

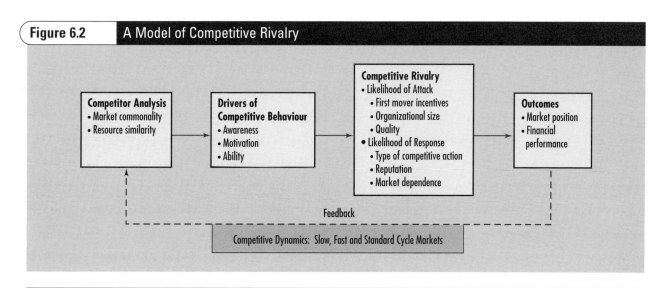

Figure 6.2   A Model of Competitive Rivalry

SOURCE: Adapted from M. J. Chen, 1996, Competitor analysis and interfirm rivalry: Toward a theoretical integration, *Academy of Management Review*, 21: 100–34.

rivalries modelled in Figure 6.2 that are occurring in a particular market reflects the competitive dynamics in that market.

The remainder of the chapter discusses the model shown in Figure 6.2. We first describe market commonality and resource similarity as the building blocks of a competitor analysis. Next, we discuss the effects of three organizational characteristics—awareness, motivation, and ability—on the firm's competitive behaviour. We then examine competitive rivalry in detail by describing both the factors that affect the likelihood a firm will take a competitive action and the factors that affect the likelihood a firm will respond to a competitor's action. In the chapter's final section, we turn our attention to competitive dynamics to describe how market characteristics affect competitive rivalry in slow-cycle, fast-cycle, and standard-cycle markets.

A Model of Competitive Rivalry

Over time, the firm takes many competitive actions and responses.[18] As noted earlier, competitive rivalry evolves from this pattern of actions and responses, as one firm's competitive actions have noticeable effects on competitors, eliciting their competitive responses.[19] This pattern shows that firms are mutually interdependent, that they feel each other's actions and responses, and that marketplace success is a function of both individual strategies and the consequences of their use.[20]

Increasingly too, executives recognize that competitive rivalry can have a major and direct effect on the firm's financial performance.[21] Research findings show that intensified rivalry results in decreased average profitability for all firms competing within an industry, supporting the importance of understanding these effects.[22] Rivalry in a number of markets demonstrates these points.

The first laser vision-correction clinics in North America were established in Canada, in the early 1990s. In 1997, the price of laser vision-correction surgery was $4800 for both eyes. The next year, the same procedure cost less than $3000. When the price was reduced to less than $1500 in 1998, laser surgery centres reported that business doubled. The price dropped to less than $1000 by the year 2000, and the industry started to consolidate.[23] Major Canadian competitor Icon Laser Eye Centres bought Lasik Eye Centres and, as their financial losses mounted, Icon started shutting down Lasik locations.[24] Dropping prices accompanied rising complaints that some doctors, seeking greater patient volumes in their clinics, were referring candidates who would likely be harmed by such surgery.[25] Competent after-surgery care—a costly item for the clinics—became hard to find at the low price. While larger chains were fighting each other on price, smaller, higher-priced clinics were managing to survive on the quality of their service and their after-surgery care.

The computer industry suffered pains when, in 2001, Dell Computer launched an intense price war in the PC business. This action caused prices for PCs and servers to drop by as much as 50 percent. Profit margins declined for all firms, including Dell.[26] CEO Michael Dell, however, believed that the direct sales model on which his firm's cost leadership strategy is based would enable it to better survive reduced profitability than Dell's competitors, and that, in the PC business, nimble execution direct sales strategy would be more important than economies of scale.[27] At the core of the intensified rivalry created by Dell's pricing action was the firm's intention of increasing its share of the PC market. Competitors responded to Dell's competitive action, intensifying rivalry in the process. The most dramatic response was Hewlett-Packard's merger with Compaq Computer.[28]

The intensity of rivalry within a particular market, such as what occurred in the PC market, is affected by many factors, including the total number of competitors, market characteristics, and the quality of individual firms' strategies. Firms that develop and use effective business-level strategies tend to outperform competitors in individual product markets, even when experiencing intense competitive rivalry.[29] According to some, Dell's use of an effective business-level strategy may contribute to its ability to frequently outperform its competitors. Indeed, it has been suggested that "Dell sets the standard for the industry, reflecting the strength of its direct sales model (strategy), and its superior cash flow management."[30]

We now turn directly to Figure 6.2 as our foundation for further discussion of competitive rivalry, such as that experienced in the laser eye surgery and PC markets.

Competitor Analysis

As noted above, a competitor analysis is the first step the firm takes to be able to predict the extent and nature of its rivalry with each competitor. Recall that a competitor is a firm operating in the same market, offering similar products, and targeting similar customers. The number of markets in which firms compete against each other (called market commonality, defined below) and the similarity in their resources (called resource similarity, also defined below) determine the extent to which the firms are competitors. Firms with high market commonality and highly similar resources are "... clearly direct and mutually acknowledged competitors."[31] However, being direct competitors does not necessarily mean that the rivalry between the firms will be intense. The drivers of competitive behaviour—as well as factors influencing the likelihood that a competitor will initiate competitive actions and will respond to its competitor's competitive actions—influence the intensity of rivalry, even for direct competitors.[32]

In Chapter 3, we discussed competitor analysis as a technique that firms use to understand their competitive environment. Along with the general and industry environments, the competitive environment comprises the firm's external environment. In the earlier chapter, we described how competitor analysis is used to help the firm *understand* its competitors. This understanding results from studying competitors' future objectives, current strategies, assumptions, and capabilities (see Figure 3.3, on page 82). In this chapter, the discussion of competitor analysis is extended to describe what firms study as the first step to being able to predict competitors' behaviour in the form of its competitive actions and responses. The discussions of competitor analysis in Chapter 3 and Chapter 6 are complementary, in that firms must first *understand* competitors (Chapter 3) before their competitive actions and competitive responses can be *predicted* (Chapter 6).

Market Commonality

Each industry is composed of various markets. The financial services industry has markets for insurance, brokerage services, banks, and so forth. Denoting an interest to concentrate on the needs of different, unique customer groups, markets can be further subdivided. The insurance market, for example, could be broken into market segments (e.g., commercial and consumer), product segments (e.g., health insurance and life insurance), and geographic markets (e.g., Western Europe and Southeast Asia).

In general, competitors agree about the different characteristics of individual markets that form an industry.[33] For example, in the transportation industry, there is an understanding that the commercial air travel market differs from the ground transportation market, which is served by firms such as MSM Transportation of Bolton, Ontario. Although differences exist, most industries' markets are related in terms of technologies used or core competencies needed to develop a competitive advantage.[34] For example, different types of transportation companies need to provide reliable and timely service. Commercial airline carriers, such as WestJet Airlines and Singapore Airlines, must therefore develop service competencies to satisfy their passengers, while MSM Transportation must develop such competencies to serve the needs of those using its fleet to ship their goods.

Firms competing in several or even many markets, some of which may be in different industries, are likely to come into contact with a particular competitor several times,[35] a situation bringing forth the issue of market commonality. **Market commonality** is concerned with the number of markets with which the firm and a competitor are jointly involved and the degree of importance of the individual markets to each.[36] Firms competing against one another in several or many markets engage in multimarket competition.[37] For example, sportswear retailers Roots Canada and Nike compete against each other in multiple geographic markets across the world,[38] while Manulife and Sun Life compete against each other in several market segments (e.g., institutional and retail) and product markets (e.g., life insurance and wealth management). Airlines, chemicals, pharmaceuticals, and consumer foods are other industries in which firms often simultaneously engage each other in multiple market competitions.

Firms competing in several markets have the potential to respond to a competitor's actions, not only within the market in which the actions are taken, but also in other markets where they compete with the rival. This potential complicates the rivalry between competitors. In fact, recent research suggests that "… a firm with greater multimarket contact is less likely to initiate an attack, but more likely to move (respond) aggressively when attacked."[39] Thus, in general, multimarket competition reduces competitive rivalry.[40]

Other research suggests that market commonality and multimarket competition sometimes occur almost by chance.[41] However, once it begins, the rivalry between originally unexpected competitors becomes intentional and oftentimes intense. This characteristic appears to be the case for telephone and cable companies. In the next Strategic Focus box, we describe the multimarket competition with which these firms are involved as well as some of the competitive actions and responses occurring between them.

For example, the competition between AOL and Microsoft is complex and intense, as each firm initiates competitive actions and responds to those of its competitor. The fact that they compete against each other in several markets has the potential to increase the scope and intensity of their rivalry. For example, actions taken by either AOL or Microsoft to improve its market position in instant messaging could result in a competitive response in the online music subscription service market. When predicting their competitor's actions and responses, AOL and Microsoft must consider the strong likelihood that some competitive responses will take place in a market other than the one in which a competitive action was taken.

Resource Similarity

Resource similarity is the extent to which the firm's tangible and intangible resources are comparable to a competitor's, in terms of both type and amount.[42] Firms with similar types and amounts of resources are likely to have similar strengths and weaknesses and use similar strategies.[43] The competition between competitors Shoppers Drug Mart and the Katz Group (which includes Rexall, PharmaPlus, Medicine Shoppe, IDA, Guardian) to be the largest drugstore chain in Canada demonstrates these expectations. These firms are using elements of an integrated cost leadership/differentiation strategy to offer relatively low-cost goods with some differentiated service features, such as services. Resource similarity, as shown by the firms' sales numbers ($5.4 billion for Shoppers; $6.0 billion for Katz), suggests that the firms might use similar strategies (in spite of the single Shoppers brand versus the multibranded Katz).

As our discussion shows, in a competitor analysis, the firm analyzes each of its competitors, in terms of market commonality and resource similarity. Determining market

Fighting for Air: Telcos after the Phone

You pick up the receiver, punch in a number, and—through the magic of electronics and through cables carrying innumerable strands of wire—someone you want to talk to answers at the other end. For almost 100 years, that's how the telephone worked. Then, the wires became cables of optical fibre, and the voice at the other end became voice mail, but the cable connection remained.

What is now driving the bottom-line at Canada's largest phone companies these days, however, is thin air: i.e., wireless services. Canada's largest telephone companies (telcos), Bell Canada, Telus, MTS, and Aliant, all rely on new services to generate profit growth. Among these services are, not only cell phones, but all kinds of wireless data transmission: text messaging, digital photo transmission, Internet access on cell phones, computers, personal data assistants, and whatever else comes along.

The telcos' traditional land-line services have come under increasing competition from several directions. First, there were technical changes. Not only were there cell phones, but also there was the potential for Voice over Internet Protocol (VoIP) to make inroads into traditional telephone service. VoIP, the use of the Internet to transmit voice communications, is relatively cheaper than traditional voice transmission. Thus, anyone providing Internet services could become a potential competitor. Second, there were the legal changes that allowed other telephone companies to compete in the industry. This trend started with providers such as MCI and Sprint supplying long-distance service over separate lines. Competition has been expanded to include local services, with the Canadian Radio-television and Telecommunications Commission (CRTC) sometimes forcing local phone companies to supply the connections to competitors' services. As a result, each local phone company that used to be a monopoly in its own geographic area can find itself competing both with other former phone company monopolies and new companies. Finally, both technology and the regulatory environment have conspired to bring other non–phone companies into the fray. Traditional cable companies, such as Rogers and Shaw, moved into providing Internet service years ago. With VoIP technology, both companies should be able to provide telephone services. As well, companies such as Rogers also compete with the big telcos because they all provide cell phone services.

In early 2004, upstart Primus Telecommunications unveiled a new low-cost, local residential phone service. Primus was a long-distance and Internet provider but its competitors and its 900,000 customers would henceforth have to view it as a phone company. This action would force Bell and Telus to accelerate their VoIP programs because of Primus' move into VoIP. At the same time, U.S. giant Verizon (a 21 percent owner of Telus) ordered $6 billion of equipment from Nortel Networks to move into greater use of VoIP. As well, Primus' move will force Shaw and Rogers to move into trying to provide local phone service one to two years earlier than planned.

Along with new competitors in traditional areas, telcos also face an increase in number of product features in their fight for profits and market share. All of the major cell phone competitors need to support text messaging, phones that transmit pictures, mobile computing, and technologies that are still on the drawing board. As well, they will have to come up with new products. Telus became the first Canadian telco to act as an online provider of music downloads with Puretracks. Other companies are sure to follow the lead.

SOURCES: M. Evans, 2004, Web play targets Bell, Telus,…, *Financial Post (National Post)*, January 9, FP1, FP4; D. Ebner, 2004, Internet rings in '04 as new phone…., *Globe and Mail*, January 7, B4; D. Ebner, 2004, 2004, Rogers sees healthy improvement in '04….,. *Globe and Mail*, January 6, B21; M. Evans, 2003, Wireless boosts BCE profit 28%…., *Financial Post (National Post)* October 30, FP01, FP08; 2003, Cablecaster, Telus teams with Puretracks for music downloads, *Cablecaster Magazine*, December 11, http://www.cablecastermagazine.com/article.asp?id=25325; T. Foran, 2000, Canada's cell phone companies in race to push out 3G wireless, *Network World Canada*, July 28, 24.

commonality isn't difficult. Shoppers and Katz, for example, are quite aware of the total number of markets in which they compete against each other, as well as the number of storefronts each operates. Recent statistics show that there are 600 Shoppers stores all across Canada and 1700 various drugstores owned by Katz all across Canada and in 11 Eastern and Midwestern states in the U.S. Thus, these firms compete against each other in many markets.[44]

In contrast to market commonality, assessing resource similarity can be difficult, particularly when critical resources are intangible (e.g., brand name, knowledge, trust, and the capacity to innovate) rather than tangible (e.g., access to raw materials and a competitor's ability to borrow capital). As discussed in Chapter 4, a competitor's intangible resources are difficult to identify and understand, making an assessment of their value challenging. Shoppers and Katz know the amount of each other's annual net income (a tangible resource). However, it is difficult for Shoppers and Katz to determine if any intangible resources its competitor possesses (e.g., knowledge and trust among employees) can lead to a competitive advantage.

The results of the firm's competitor analyses can be mapped for visual comparisons. In Figure 6.3, we show different hypothetical intersections between the firm and individual competitors, in terms of market commonality and resource similarity. These intersections indicate the extent to which the firm and those to which it has compared itself are competitors.[45] For example, the firm and its competitor displayed in quadrant I of Figure 6.3 have similar types and amounts of resources and use them to compete against each other in many markets that are important to each. These conditions lead to the conclusion that the firms modelled in quadrant I are direct and mutually acknowledged competitors. In contrast, the firm and its competitor shown in quadrant III share few markets and have little similarity in their resources, indicating that they aren't direct and mutually acknowledged competitors. The firm's mapping of its competitive relationship with rivals is fluid, as firms enter and exit markets and as companies' resources change in type and amount. Thus, the companies with whom the firm is a direct competitor change across time.

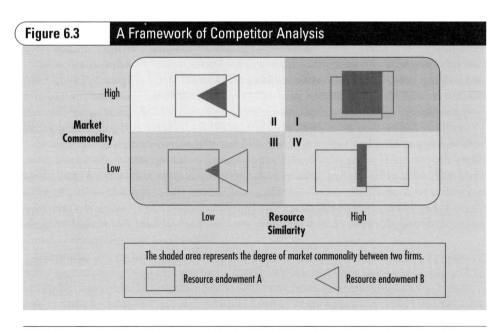

Figure 6.3   A Framework of Competitor Analysis

The shaded area represents the degree of market commonality between two firms.

☐ Resource endowment A   ◁ Resource endowment B

SOURCE: Adapted from M. J. Chen, 1996, Competitor analysis and interfirm rivalry: Toward a theoretical integration, *Academy of Management Review*, 21: 100–34.

Drivers of Competitive Actions and Responses

As shown in Figure 6.2, on page 177, market commonality and resource similarity influence the drivers (awareness, motivation, and ability) of competitive behaviour. In turn, the drivers influence the firm's competitive behaviour, as shown by the actions and responses it takes while engaged in competitive rivalry.[46]

Awareness, which is a prerequisite to any competitive action or response being taken by the firm or its competitor, refers to the extent to which competitors recognize the degree of their mutual interdependence that results from market commonality and resource similarity.[47] A lack of awareness can lead to excessive competition, resulting in a negative effect on all competitors' performance.[48] Awareness tends to be greatest when firms have highly similar resources (in terms of types and amounts) to use while competing against each other in multiple markets. Shoppers and Katz are fully aware of each other, as are Rona and Home Depot, and Wal-Mart and France's Carrefour. The last two firms' joint awareness has increased as they use similar resources to compete against each other for dominant positions in multiple European markets.[49] Awareness affects the extent to which the firm understands the consequences of its competitive actions and responses.

Motivation, which concerns the firm's incentive to take action or to respond to a competitor's attack, relates to perceived gains and losses. Thus, a firm may be aware of competitors, but may not be motivated to engage in rivalry if it perceives that, by responding, its position will neither improve nor be damaged.[50]

Market commonality affects the firm's perceptions and resulting motivation. For example, all else being equal, the firm is more likely to attack the rival with whom it has low market commonality than the one with whom it competes in multiple markets. The primary reason is that there are high stakes involved in trying to gain a more advantageous position over a rival with whom the firm shares many markets. As we mentioned earlier, multimarket competition can find a competitor responding to the firm's action in a market different from the one in which the initial action was taken. Actions and responses of this type can cause both firms to lose focus on core markets and to battle each other with resources that had been allocated for other purposes. Because of the high stakes of competition under the condition of market commonality, there is a high probability that the attacked firm will respond to its competitor's action in an effort to protect its position in one or more markets.[51]

In some instances, the firm may be aware of the large number of markets it shares with a competitor and may be motivated to respond to an attack by that competitor, but it lacks the ability to do so. *Ability* relates to each firm's resources and the flexibility those resources provide. Without available resources (e.g., financial capital and people), the firm lacks the ability to attack a competitor or respond to its actions. However, similar resources suggest similar abilities to attack and respond. When a firm faces a competitor with similar resources, careful study of a possible attack, before its initiation, is essential because the similarly resourced competitor is likely to respond to that action.

Resource dissimilarity also influences competitive actions and responses between firms, in that "the greater is the resource imbalance between the acting firm and competitors or potential responders, the greater will be the delay in response"[52] by the firm with a resource disadvantage. For example, Wal-Mart initially used its cost leadership strategy to compete only in small communities (those with a population of 25,000 or less). Using sophisticated logistics systems and extremely efficient purchasing practices as advantages, Wal-Mart created what was, at that time, a new type of value (primarily in the form of wide selections of products at the lowest competitive prices) for customers in small retail markets. Local stores, facing resource deficiencies, relative to Wal-Mart, lacked the ability to marshal resources at the pace required to respond quickly and effectively. However, even when facing competitors with greater resources (greater ability) or more attractive market positions, firms should eventually respond, no matter how daunting it may seem.[53] Choosing not to respond can ultimately result in failure, as happened with at least some local retailers who didn't respond to Wal-Mart's competitive actions.

Competitive Rivalry

As defined earlier in the chapter, *competitive rivalry* is the ongoing set of competitive actions and competitive responses occurring between competing firms for an advantageous market position. Because the ongoing competitive action/response sequence between a firm and a competitor affects the performance of both firms,[54] it is important for companies to carefully study competitive rivalry to successfully use their strategies. Understanding a competitor's awareness, motivation, and ability helps the firm to predict the likelihood of an attack by that competitor and how likely it is that a competitor will respond to the actions taken against it.

As we described above, the predictions drawn from study of competitors, in terms of awareness, motivation, and ability, are grounded in market commonality and resource similarity. These predictions are fairly general. The value of the final set of predictions the firm develops about each of its competitor's competitive actions and responses is enhanced by studying the "likelihood of attack" factors (e.g., first-mover incentives and organizational size) and the "likelihood of response" factors (e.g., the actor's reputation) that are shown in Figure 6.2, on page 177. Studying these factors allows the firm to develop a deeper understanding, in order to refine the predictions it makes about its competitors' actions and responses.

Strategic and Tactical Actions

A **competitive action** is a strategic or tactical action the firm takes to build or defend its competitive advantages or improve its market position.

A **competitive response** is a strategic or tactical action the firm takes to counter the effects of a competitor's competitive action.

A **strategic action** or a **strategic response** is a market-based move that involves a significant commitment of organizational resources and is difficult to implement and reverse.

A **tactical action** or a **tactical response** is a market-based move that is taken to fine-tune a strategy; it involves fewer resources and is relatively easy to implement and reverse.

Firms use both strategic and tactical actions when forming their competitive actions and competitive responses in the course of engaging in competitive rivalry.[55] A **competitive action** is a strategic or tactical action the firm takes to build or defend its competitive advantages or improve its market position. A **competitive response** is a strategic or tactical action the firm takes to counter the effects of a competitor's competitive action. A **strategic action** or a **strategic response** is a market-based move that involves a significant commitment of organizational resources and is difficult to implement and reverse. A **tactical action** or a **tactical response** is a market-based move that is taken to fine-tune a strategy; it involves fewer resources and is relatively easy to implement and reverse. Hyundai Motor Company's expenditures on research and development and plant expansion to support the firm's desire to be one of the world's largest carmakers by 2010[56] are strategic actions. The Strategic Focus box "Airplane Wars" describes strategic actions taken by competitors Airbus Industrie and Boeing.

A competitor's strategic action signals that significant amounts of resources are being committed to a project, and that, once underway, it will be difficult for the action to be reversed. As explained in the Strategic Focus box, Boeing and Airbus Industrie are initiating strategic actions that differ, based on the companies' interpretations of the future of air travel.

As the discussion in this Strategic Focus box indicates, Airbus and Boeing have committed significant amounts of organizational resources to develop the A380 and the 7E7, respectively. These actions will be difficult to reverse in that start-up development costs have been incurred, and expectations have been established for two customer groups—airline companies and travellers. Disappointing these groups could damage each firm's reputation for being an innovator as well as each company's objective to gain dominance over its major rival. On the other hand, even strategic actions should be reversed when dramatic external environmental changes (e.g., those caused by 9/11 and SARS) call their viability into serious question.

Airplane Wars: Airbus and Boeing Choose Different Strategic Actions

As competitors, Boeing and Airbus Industrie share multiple markets, have relatively similar resources (in terms of what is available for the commercial aircraft market), and have pursued similar strategies. However, based on their predictions of the air transport industry's future, they are taking different strategic actions regarding the manufacture of tomorrow's large commercial airliners.

The differences in the firm's strategic actions started to become visible in December 2000, when Airbus launched efforts to build the A380, the world's largest commercial aircraft. The 550–650-seat, double-decker super jumbo jet is designed to compete directly against the high end of Boeing's lucrative 747 series. The A380 is a primary challenger to the more than three-decade dominance of the 350-plus-seat commercial airliner market Boeing has enjoyed with its 747 series. Airbus has committed $12 billion to the A380's design and development, which is scheduled to make its commercial debut with Singapore Airlines in 2006. Airbus is touting the need for the A380, based on its belief that airline traffic will continue to grow, intensifying problems in already congested airport hubs.

In response to Airbus's A380, Boeing announced plans to build a 520-seat version of the 747 as a competing super jumbo aircraft. In March 2001, after failing to win orders for the 747X, Boeing changed direction and scrapped the project. As part of an evolving strategic action, Boeing made this decision before it committed significant levels of resources to design and build the 747X. Boeing's announcement effectively ceded the super jumbo jet market to Airbus.

Reflecting a radical change, Boeing also indicated that it believed that speed, not size, will be the most important consideration in the future of air travel. Rather than the continued dominance of the hub system, Boeing concluded, after further analyses, that passenger demand for increased point-to-point travel options will result in market fragmentation and a reduction in the importance of hub systems. In fragmented markets, Boeing believes that carriers will need speedy, long-range, mid-size planes to bypass major hubs for nonstop service from more remote destinations. In Boeing CEO Alan Mulally's words: "We decided point-to-point routes are the heart of the market. There was a lot of talk on large aircraft, but at the end of the day, after working with airlines, we decided to focus on longer range. ..." Based on these beliefs, Boeing started design development of its futuristic Sonic Cruiser, a 250-passenger jet designed to travel at 95 percent of the speed of sound and to fly above 40,000 feet. The Sonic Cruiser is expected to reduce air travel time by 20 percent, as a result of a radical new design, featuring a dramatically swept wing and two wing-mounted jet engines in the rear.

Industry experts estimate that because of fuel burn, the Sonic Cruiser's operating costs will be 12 percent to 15 percent higher than the 250-seat 767 that it will replace. To obtain revenues that exceed this higher operating cost will require the Sonic Cruiser to fly mostly business-class passengers, who are willing to pay a 20 percent premium over today's fares.

The reality of September 11, 2001 and fears of the spread of the SARS virus in 2003 challenged the viability of Airbus's and Boeing's evolving competitive actions regarding next-generation commercial jets. Previous predictions that airline traffic will continue to grow 5 percent annually over the next 20 years are being tested. Not only did airlines reduce flights and employees in response to lower passenger levels, they also decreased or cancelled orders for new aircraft. These actions affected both Boeing and Airbus. Boeing laid off 30,000 employees and cut production by 20 percent. Airbus received cancellation notices for 73 planes in a single month and halted plans for increasing capacity. This climate of severe uncertainty could potentially derail plans for development of the A380. Airbus requires 250 orders for the A380 project to be profitable. Even before September 11, the company had only 62 firm orders and 40 options to purchase.

There are signs that both companies may now be less willing to commit substantial resources

(continued)

Strategic Focus

to the design and potential development of an aircraft that differs radically from current commercial jets. For example, even though Boeing stated support of the Sonic Cruiser, it was forced to drop the very high speed that would have caused it to burn extra fuel. In the face of unclear demand and an unsettled Middle East with uncertain oil prices, a plane with poor fuel efficiency was not something Boeing was able to sell to prospective buyers. Boeing scaled back the plane's speed to 85 percent of the speed of sound and renamed it the 7E7. Even though Airbus has gone ahead with the A380, its now stated size is at the lowest end of the previously announced range. Thus, both firms are both continually thinking about and carefully rethinking the viability of their strategic actions, in light of a highly uncertain and unpredictable external environment.

SOURCES: M. Mecham, 2003, Tweaks to the concept…., *Aviation Week & Space Technology*, September 15, 31; Travel Biz, 2003, Qantas set to delay aircraft orders because of SARS, *Travel Biz website*, http://www.travelbiz.com.au/articles/fa/0c0160fa.asp April 24, accessed January 16, 2004, http://www.travelbiz.com.au/articles/fa/0c0160fa.asp; C. Matlack, 2002, Earth to Airbus: What's the flight plan? *Business Week*, January 21, 48; Economist, 2001, Place your bets, *Economist*, June 23, 60–61; H. Banks, 2001, Paper plane, *Forbes*, May 28, 52–53; G. Cramb & M. Odell, 2001, Companies and finance Europe: Airbus plans for expansion on hold, *Financial Times*, September 21, 33; S. Holmes, 2001, Boeing's sonic bruiser, *Business Week*, July 2, 64–68; S. Holmes, C. Dawson, & C. Matlack, 2001, Rumble over Tokyo, *Business Week*, April 2, 80–81; C. Matlack & S. Holmes, 2001, Why Airbus could go into a dive, *Business Week*, October 1, 83; S. McClenahen, 2001, Planely different, *Industry Week*, June 11, 68–72; A. Sequeo, 2001, Boeing plans to build smaller, faster jet, *Wall Street Journal*, March 20, A3; P. Sparaco, 2001, Airbus and Boeing snipe over speed versus size, *Aviation Week & Space Technology*, June 25, 26–27; P. Sparaco, 2001, Airbus thinks bigger, not faster, *Aviation Week & Space Technology*, June 18, 106–12; P. Sparaco, 2001, Airbus' production schedule riding out times, *Aviation Week & Space Technology*, September 24, 33.

Likelihood of Attack

In addition to market commonality, resource similarity, and the drivers of awareness, motivation, and ability, other factors also affect the likelihood a competitor will use strategic actions and tactical actions to attack its competitors. Three of these factors—first-mover incentives, organizational size, and quality—are discussed next.

First-Mover Incentives

A **first mover** is a firm that takes an initial competitive action in order to build or defend its competitive advantages or to improve its market position.

A **first mover** is a firm that takes an initial competitive action in order to build or defend its competitive advantages or to improve its market position. The first-mover concept has been influenced by the work of the famous economist Joseph Schumpeter, who argued that firms achieve competitive advantage by taking innovative actions[57] (innovation is defined and described in detail in Chapter 14). In general, first movers "allocate funds for product innovation and development, aggressive advertising, and advanced research and development."[58]

The benefits of being a successful first mover can be substantial. Especially in fast-cycle markets (discussed later in the chapter) where changes occur rapidly and where it is virtually impossible to sustain a competitive advantage for any period of time, "… a first mover may experience five to ten times the valuation and revenue of a second mover."[59] This evidence suggests that although first-mover benefits are never absolute, they are often critical to firm success in industries experiencing rapid technological developments and relatively short product life cycles.[60]

In addition to earning above-average returns until its competitors respond to its successful competitive action, the first mover can gain (1) the loyalty of customers who may become committed to the goods or services of the firm that first made them available and (2) market share that can be difficult for competitors to acquire during future competitive rivalry. For example, Yahoo! Japan moved first to establish an online auction market service in Japan. Rival eBay entered the market five months later. The delayed response by eBay, in an industry rife with rapid technological change, was a critical mistake, as shown by the fact that first mover Yahoo! Japan recently held 95 percent of the online auction market in Japan, while rival eBay's share was only 3 percent. A company official commented on Yahoo! Japan's first-mover incentive to establish an online auction market in Japan, "We knew catching up with a front-runner is hard, because in auctions, more buyers bring more sellers."[61]

The firm trying to predict its competitors' competitive actions might rightly conclude that the benefits we described above could serve as incentives to act as first movers. However, while a firm's competitors might be motivated to be first movers, they may lack the ability to do so. First movers tend to be aggressive and willing to experiment with innovation and take higher, yet reasonable levels of risk.[62] To be a first mover, the firm must have readily available the amount of resources that is required to significantly invest in R&D as well as to rapidly and successfully produce and market a stream of innovative products.

Organizational slack makes it possible for firms to have the ability (as measured by available resources) to be early movers into a market. *Slack* is the buffer or cushion provided by actual or obtainable resources that are not currently in use.[63] Thus, slack is composed of liquid resources that the firm can quickly allocate to support the actions, such as R&D investments and aggressive marketing campaigns, which lead to first mover benefits. This relationship between slack and the ability to be a first mover allows the firm to predict that a competitor who is a first mover likely has available slack and will probably take aggressive competitive actions to continuously introduce innovative products. Furthermore, the firm can predict that, as a first mover, a competitor will try to rapidly gain market share and customer loyalty in order to earn above-average returns until its competitors are able to effectively respond to its first move.

Firms studying competitors should realize that being a first mover carries risk. For example, it is difficult to accurately estimate the returns that will be earned from introducing product innovations to the marketplace.[64] Additionally, the first mover's cost to develop a product innovation can be substantial, reducing the slack available to it to support further innovation. Thus, the firm should carefully study the results a competitor achieves as a first mover. Continuous success by the competitor suggests additional product innovations, while lack of product acceptance over the course of the competitor's innovations may indicate less willingness in the future to accept the risks of being a first mover.

A **second mover** is a firm that responds to the first mover's competitive action, typically through imitation. More cautious than the first mover, the second mover studies customers' reactions to product innovations. In the course of doing so, the second mover also tries to identify any mistakes the first mover made so that it can avoid the resulting problems. Often, successful imitation of the first mover's innovations allows the second mover "... to avoid both the mistakes and the huge spending of the pioneers (first movers)."[65] Second movers also have the time to develop processes and technologies that are more efficient than those used by the first mover.[66] Greater efficiencies could result in lower costs for the second mover. Overall, the outcomes of the first mover's competitive actions may provide an effective blueprint for second and even late movers (as described below) as they determine the nature and timing of their competitive responses.[67]

Determining that a competitor thinks of itself as an effective second mover allows the firm to predict the competitor's tendency to respond quickly to first movers' successful, innovation-based market entries. If the firm itself is a first mover, then it can expect a successful second mover competitor to study its market entries and to respond quickly. As a second mover, the competitor will try to respond with a product that creates customer value exceeding the value provided by the first-mover's product. The most

A **second mover** is a firm that responds to the first mover's competitive action, typically through imitation.

successful second movers are able to rapidly and meaningfully interpret market feedback to respond quickly, yet successfully, to the first mover's successful innovations.[68]

A **late mover** is a firm that responds to a competitive action, but only after considerable time has elapsed after the first mover's action and the second mover's response. Typically, a late response is better than no response at all, although any success achieved from the late competitive response tends to be slow in coming and considerably less than that achieved by first and second movers. Thus, the firm competing against a late mover can predict that the late-mover competitor will likely enter a particular market only after both the first and second movers have entered the market and achieved success. Moreover, on a relative basis, the firm can predict that the late mover's competitive action will allow it to earn even average returns only when enough time has elapsed for the late mover to understand how to create value that is more attractive to customers than the value offered by the first and second movers' products. Although exceptions do exist, the firm can predict that as a competitor, the late mover's competitive actions will be relatively ineffective, certainly as compared to those initiated by first movers and second movers.

Organizational Size

An organization's size affects the likelihood that it will take competitive actions, the types of actions it will take, and their timing.[69] In general, compared to large companies, small firms are more likely to launch competitive actions and tend to be quicker in doing so. Smaller firms are thus perceived as nimble and flexible competitors who either defend their competitive advantages by relying on speed and surprise or, while engaged in competitive rivalry (especially with large companies), they develop new competitive advantages, to gain an advantageous market position.[70] Small firms' flexibility and nimbleness allow them to develop greater variety in their competitive actions, compared to large firms, which tend to limit the types of competitive actions used when competing with rivals.[71]

Compared to small firms, large firms are likely to initiate more competitive actions as well as strategic actions during a given time period.[72] Thus, when studying its competitors in terms of organizational size, the firm should use a measurement of size, such as total sales revenue or total number of employees, to compare itself with each competitor. The competitive actions the firm likely will encounter from competitors who are larger will be different from the competitive actions it will encounter from competitors who are smaller.

The organizational size factor has an additional layer of complexity associated with it. When engaging in competitive rivalry, the firm usually wants to take a large number of competitive actions against its competitors. As we have described, large organizations commonly have the slack resources required to launch a larger number of total competitive actions. On the other hand, smaller firms have the flexibility needed to launch a greater variety of competitive actions. Ideally, the firm would like to have the ability to launch a large number of unique competitive actions. A statement made by Herb Kelleher, former CEO of Southwest Airlines, addresses this matter: "Think and act big and we'll get smaller. Think and act small and we'll get bigger."[73]

In the context of competitive rivalry, Kelleher's statement can be interpreted to mean that relying on a limited number of types of competitive actions (which is the large firm's tendency) can lead to reduced competitive success across time, partly because competitors learn how to effectively respond to what is a limited set of competitive actions taken by a given firm. In contrast, remaining flexible and nimble (which is the small firm's tendency), in order to develop and use a wide variety of competitive actions, contributes to success against rivals.

Wal-Mart appears to be an example of a large firm that has the flexibility required to take many types of competitive actions. With $216 billion in sales and a $252 billion market capitalization, Wal-Mart is the world's largest company in terms of sales revenue. In only six years following its entry into the grocery market, Wal-Mart became one of the largest grocery retailers in the United States. This accomplishment demonstrates Wal-Mart's ability to successfully compete against its various rivals, even long-established grocers. In spite of its size, the firm remains highly flexible as it takes both strategic actions (e.g., rapid global expansion) and tactical actions.

Analysts believe that Wal-Mart's tactical actions are critical to its success and show a great deal of flexibility. For example, "every humble store worker has the power to lower the price on any Wal-Mart product if he spots it cheaper elsewhere."[74] Decision-making responsibility and authority have been delegated to the level of the individual worker to make certain that the firm's cost leadership strategy always results in the lowest prices for customers. Managers and employees both spend a good deal of time thinking about additional strategic and tactical actions, respectively, that might enhance the firm's performance. Thus, it is possible that Wal-Mart has met the expectation suggested by Kelleher's statement, in that it is a large firm that "...remains stuck to its small-town roots" in order to think and act like the small firm capable of using a wide variety of competitive actions.[75]

Oddly enough, one competitor that has, in part, used its small-town roots to survive the march of Wal-Mart is Canadian Tire. There is a sense that the local Canadian Tire is a local merchant. This is partly because they are usually locally owned franchises and partly because they are geographically convenient. Eighty-five percent of Canadians live within a 15-minute drive of their local Canadian Tire store. Although Canadian Tire has enlarged its stores to compete with Wal-Mart, the company has kept its product range simple by focusing on its three traditional areas: automotive, sports and leisure, and home products. The company has kept its customer coming back through its loyalty program—Canadian Tire money (cash-equivalent coupons that can only be used at Canadian Tire). It all seems to work. Even with Wal-Mart in the Canadian market, Canadian Tire claims that 9 out of 10 adult Canadians shop at Canadian Tire at least twice a year, and 40 percent of Canadians shop at Canadian Tire every week.

In the Strategic Focus box "Thinking and Acting Small" on page 190 we describe how a number of smaller Canadian competitors outperform their larger rivals. Although smaller than their primary competitors, their success has resulted in growth, partly at the expense of competitors. The competitive challenge for these companies will be to continue thinking and acting as a small firm as they become larger organizations.

In this Strategic Focus box the companies demonstrated flexibility in the variety of competitive actions they took. Some of these competitors used strategies that were exact opposites but equally profitable. All the strategies found a market niche and, particularly in the case of Dynatech Action, were flexible in their approach to obtaining valued customers.

Quality

Quality has many definitions, including well-established descriptions that relate to the production of goods or services with zero defects[76] and seeing the attainment of excellence as a never-ending cycle of continuous improvement.[77] From a strategic perspective, we consider quality to be an outcome of how the firm completes primary and support activities (see Chapter 3). Thus, **quality** exists when the firm's goods or services meet or exceed customers' expectations.

In addition to the more traditional manufacturing and service sectors, quality is also important in business-to-business (B2B) transactions.[78] Customers may be interested in measuring the quality of a firm's products against a broad range of dimensions. Sample quality dimensions for goods and services in which customers commonly express an interest are shown in Table 6.1 on page 191. Thus, in the eyes of customers, quality is about doing the right things, relative to performance measures that are important to them.[79]

Quality exists when the firm's goods or services meet or exceed customers' expectations.

Thinking and Acting Small

How did Brad Pedersen take Dynatech Action from a business in his basement apartment in Red Deer, Alberta, and, in 10 years, make it one of the twenty fastest growing private companies in Canada? He played with toys. Of course, they were the products his firm distributed—sporting goods and toys like Hula Hoops, compressed air rockets, and spy gear—and he found places to play with them that allowed for maximum exposure. Pedersen notes that, "The traditional media—TV, print and radio—weren't realistic for a start-up, so we got creative with low-budget ways of marketing."

The firm's first product, the X-zylo, was a gyroscopic cylinder that could be thrown the length of a football field, but retailers, preferring to work with large companies with a proven track record (e.g., Mattel and Hasbro), did not even return Pedersen's calls. That was when he started playing with the products. He travelled to events such as country fairs and the Calgary Stampede. He hired students to throw the X-zylo around, hang banners, set up contests, and hand out prizes. Not only did he sell thousands wherever went, but he managed to sign up numerous dealers in every town. The dealers would track Pedersen down to find out how they could get the product because customers were talking about it. Pedersen eventually got his product into Zellers and Canadian Tire by giving personal demonstrations to store managers in their parking lots.

Dynatech has stuck to the formula ever since. The company created a secret agent tour to promote its Wild Planet Spy Gear. A van decked out with Spy Gear logos visited 40 cities in 6 weeks. Dynatech even set up spy stations in the parking lots of retailers such as Toys "Я" Us, where children tried out listening devices and metal detectors. The effort helped boost Spy Gear sales by 200 percent.

Ever deal with a customer that you thought wasn't worth the trouble? How about telling them where to go? David Sutcliffe does it often. Sutcliffe is the chairman and CEO of Sierra Wireless, a wireless modem and phone manufacturer headquartered in Richmond, B.C. He sends potentially troublesome customers to the competition. When he refers customers to the competition, they "… think I'm joking, but I've done it more times than I can count over the last several years. … Our goal is not to earn 100 percent market share. It's to earn all of the profitable market share."

Sierra determines which clients are attractive by looking at how cost sensitive and demanding a client is likely to be. According to Sutcliffe, unprofitable customers "want the product 20 percent cheaper, but they also want you to spend a month customizing it for them, and they only plan to buy a low volume of product over two years." Sutcliffe steers these potential clients to other firms that could better meet their needs. "I give them a competitor's name, phone number, or e-mail address," he notes. "I know they're thinking I'm out of my mind. But if your competitors are so busy choking on those small orders, you can focus on and win the more profitable opportunities."

While Sierra Wireless sends small fussy customers down the road, Toronto-based C.J. Graphics welcomes them. The high-end printer specializes in the finesse jobs that big printers cannot do or do not want. Company president Jay Mandarino notes that "The work is too small for them, the attention to detail is too high, the stress is really high…. So they recommend us." C.J. Graphics has printed business cards for the British Royal Family, Hollywood celebrities, and the White House. While the company does sell everyday business cards for as low as 12¢ per card, they have also sold a set of business cards embossed with Italian calf leather for $4 per card.

SOURCES: C. Gulli, L. Pratt, & K. Shiffman, 2003, 10 amazing true stories of Canada's fastest growing companies, *Profit: The Magazine for Canadian Entrepreneurs*, June, 33–37; A. Wahl, 2003, Sierra's smart move, *Canadian Business*, October 14–26, 29; C. Burns & K. Shaw, 2002, The best issue: Best of the tests, *Network World*, November 11, 62–65; R. Seymour, 2002, Ideas that work: PROFIT 100 CEOs reveal their favourite management tips, *Profit: The Magazine for Canadian Entrepreneurs*, June, 66–70.

Quality is possible only when top-level managers support it and when its importance is institutionalized throughout the entire organization.[80] When quality is institutionalized and valued by all, employees and managers alike become vigilant about continuously finding ways to improve quality.[81]

Quality is a universal theme in the global economy and is a necessary but not sufficient condition for competitive success. In other words, "Quality used to be a competitive issue out there, but now it's just the basic denominator to being in the market."[82] Without quality, a firm's products lack credibility, and such products are not viewed by customers as viable options. Indeed, customers won't consider buying a product until they believe that it can satisfy at least their base-level expectations, in terms of quality dimensions that are important to them. For years, quality was an issue for Jaguar automobiles, as the carmaker endured frequent complaints from drivers about poor quality. As a result of recent actions addressing this issue, Jaguar quality has improved to the point where customers now view the cars as credible products.[83]

Poor quality also increases costs, which damages the firm's profitability. For example, as recently as 2002, Ford Motor Company ranked worst of the top seven global auto companies, in terms of quality. According to former Ford CEO Jacques Nasser, quality problems (which led to higher warranty expenses) and related production delays cost the firm more than $1 billion in lost profits, in 2000 alone.[84] The company failed to improve its quality rankings or turn a significant profit in the auto sector for 2001, 2002, and 2003.[85]

To improve quality or to maintain a focus on quality, firms often become involved with total quality management. **Total quality management (TQM)** is a "managerial innovation that emphasizes an organization's total commitment to the customer and to continuous improvement of every process through the use of data-driven, problem-solving approaches based on empowerment of employee groups and teams."[86] Through TQM, firms seek to (1) increase customer satisfaction, (2) cut costs, and (3) reduce the amount of time required to introduce innovative products to the marketplace.[87] Ford is

Total quality management (TQM) is a "managerial innovation that emphasizes an organization's total commitment to the customer and to continuous improvement of every process through the use of data-driven, problem-solving approaches based on empowerment of employee groups and teams."

Table 6.1	Quality Dimensions of Goods and Services

Product Quality Dimensions
1. *Performance*—Operating characteristics
2. *Features*—Important special characteristics
3. *Flexibility*—Meeting operating specifications over some period of time
4. *Durability*—Amount of use before performance deteriorates
5. *Conformance*—Match with pre-established standards
6. *Serviceability*—Ease and speed of repair
7. *Aesthetics*—How a product looks and feels
8. *Perceived quality*—Subjective assessment of characteristics (product image)

Service Quality Dimensions
1. *Timeliness*—Performed in the promised period of time
2. *Courtesy*—Performed cheerfully
3. *Consistency*—Delivering similar experiences to all customers each time
4. *Convenience*—Accessibility to customers
5. *Completeness*—Fully serviced, as required
6. *Accuracy*—Performed correctly each time

SOURCES: Adapted from J. W. Dean Jr. & J. R. Evans, 1994, *Total Quality: Management, Organization and Society*, St. Paul, MN: West Publishing Company; H. V. Roberts & B. F. Sergesketter, 1993, *Quality Is Personal*, New York: The Free Press; D. Garvin, 1988, *Managed Quality: The Strategic and Competitive Edge*, New York: The Free Press.

relying on TQM to help root out its quality flaws,[88] while competitor General Motors is "... scrambling to narrow the quality gap that its executives say is the main reason consumers shy away from GM."[89]

Quality affects competitive rivalry. The firm studying a competitor whose products suffer from poor quality can predict that the competitor's costs are high and that its sales revenue will likely decline until the quality issues are resolved. In addition, the firm can predict that the competitor likely won't be aggressive in terms of taking competitive actions, given that its quality problems must be corrected in order to gain credibility with customers. However, once corrected, that competitor is likely to take competitive actions emphasizing significant product quality improvements. Hyundai Motor Co.'s experiences illustrate these expectations.

Immediately upon becoming CEO of Hyundai Motor Co. in March 1999, Chung Mong Koo started touring the firm's manufacturing facilities. Appalled at what he saw, he told workers and managers alike that, "The only way we can survive is to raise our quality to Toyota's level."[90] To dramatically improve quality, a quality-control unit was established and significant resources (more than $1 billion annually) were allocated to research and development (R&D) in order to build cars that could compete on price and deliver on quality. Essentially, Chung Mong Koo introduced Hyundai to TQM through the decisions he made to improve the firm's performance.

Outcomes from Hyundai's focus on quality improvements are impressive. Survey results indicate that Hyundai's quality has improved dramatically in the last few years. One indicator of the dramatic quality improvement is the *Consumer Reports* rating of Hyundai that places it at a tie with Honda and behind only Toyota in the magazine's 2003 quality tests.[91]

While concentrating on quality improvements, Hyundai did not launch aggressive competitive actions, as competitors could predict would likely be the case. However, as could also be predicted by firms studying Hyundai as a competitor, improvements to the quality of Hyundai's products has helped the firm to become a more aggressive competitor. As a result of improved quality and the innovative outcomes from its R&D investments, Hyundai also introduced the Santa Fe in 2000. A well-conceived sport utility vehicle (SUV), the Santa Fe was designed and built to outperform Toyota's RAV4 and Honda's CR-V. The Santa Fe's introduction indicates that Hyundai is willing to aggressively attack its competitors in the SUV market with what has turned out to be an innovatively designed and quality-built product.[92]

Likelihood of Response

The success of a firm's competitive action is affected both by the likelihood that a competitor will respond to it, as well as by the type (strategic or tactical) of response and its effectiveness. As noted earlier, a competitive response is a strategic or tactical action the firm takes to counter the effects of a competitor's competitive action (see the opening case, on page 173). In general, a firm is likely to respond when the consequences of a competitor's action are better use of the competitor's competitive advantages or improvement in its market position, or when the action damages the firm's ability to use its advantages or when its market position becomes less defensible.[93]

In addition to market commonality, resource similarity and awareness, motivation, and ability, firms study three other factors—type of competitive action, reputation, and market dependence—to predict how a competitor is likely to respond to competitive actions.

Type of Competitive Action

Competitive responses to strategic actions differ from responses to tactical actions. These differences allow the firm to predict a competitor's likely response to a competitive action that has been launched against it. Of course, a general prediction is that strategic actions receive strategic responses while tactical responses are taken to counter the effects of tactical actions.

In general, strategic actions elicit fewer total competitive responses.[94] As with strategic actions, strategic responses, such as market-based moves, involve a significant commitment of resources and are difficult to implement and reverse. Moreover, the time needed for a strategic action to be implemented and its effectiveness to be assessed delays the competitor's response to that action.[95] Witness Eaton's critical delay in opening store locations in the suburbs after Sears began to successfully exploit the market. It was a strategic delay that cost market share and began Eaton's road to retailing oblivion (see the Strategic Focus box "The Impermanence of Success" in Chapter 1, on page 14). In contrast, a competitor likely will respond quickly to a tactical action, such as when an airline company almost immediately matches a competitor's tactical action of reducing prices in certain markets. Strategic actions or tactical actions that target a large number of a rival's customers are likely to be targeted with strong responses.[96]

Actor's Reputation

In the context of competitive rivalry, an actor is the firm taking an action or response while *reputation* is "... the positive or negative attribute ascribed by one rival to another based on past competitive behaviour."[97] Thus, to predict the likelihood of a competitor's response to a current or planned action, the firm studies the responses that the competitor has taken previously when attacked—past behaviour is assumed to be a reasonable predictor of future behaviour.

Competitors are more likely to respond to either strategic or tactical actions that are taken by a market leader.[98] For example, Home Depot is the world's largest home improvement retailer, the world's fourth largest retailer (behind the U.S.'s Wal-Mart, France's Carrefour, and Holland's Royal Ahold), and one of the world's 50 largest corporations. Known as an innovator in its core home improvement market, Home Depot also possesses the ability to develop successful new store formats. Home Depot can predict that its competitors carefully study its actions, especially the strategic actions, and competitors are likely to respond to such moves.

For all its resources and capabilities, however, Home Depot is not Canada's largest home-improvement chain. Home Hardware and Rona Home Centres are running neck and neck for first and second place. Both chains have their roots as associations of independent hardware retailers. The growth of Home Depot has forced both chains to re-evaluate their strategies.

Rather than compete directly with Home Depot, Home Hardware, based in St. Jacobs, Ontario, chose to segment the market. The company's Home Hardware stores have maintained their traditional lines of auto, paint, sporting goods, and housewares, along with plumbing, electrical, lawn, and farm supplies. Home Hardware also has larger Home Building Centre stores that look like Home Depot: lumber, paint, tools, and plumbing and electrical supplies, along with a wide range of other building materials. A third division, Home Hardware Building Centres, carries all the lines from the previous two divisions. Finally, Home Furniture sells large appliances, home electronics, and, of course, furniture.

Boucherville, Quebec-based Rona has instead chosen to move closer to the Home Depot by increasing the size of its stores. Rona has also increased the size of the chain by buying other big-box, Home Depot–sized home improvement stores. In the last several years, Rona has acquired competitors such as B.C.-based Revy Home Centres and Quebec-based Réno-Dépôt.[99]

Other evidence suggests that commonly successful actions, especially strategic actions, will be quickly imitated, almost regardless of the actor's reputation. For example, although a second mover, IBM committed significant resources to enter the PC market. When IBM was immediately successful in this endeavour, competitors such as Dell, Compaq, and Gateway responded with strategic actions to enter the market. IBM's reputation, as well as its successful strategic action, strongly influenced entry by these competitors. Thus, in terms of competitive rivalry, IBM could predict that responses would follow its entry to the PC market if that entry proved successful. In addition, IBM could predict that those competitors would try to create value in slightly different ways, such as Dell's legendary decision to sell directly to consumers rather than to use store-fronts as a distribution channel.

In contrast to a firm with a strong reputation, such as IBM, competitors are less likely to take responses against companies with reputations for competitive behaviour that is risky, complex, and unpredictable. The firm with a reputation as a price predator (an actor that frequently reduces prices to gain or maintain market share) generates few responses to its tactical pricing actions. The reason is that price predators, which typically increase prices once their market share objective is reached, lack credibility with their competitors.[100] The opposite of a price predator, in terms of reputation, Wal-Mart is widely recognized for its pricing integrity,[101] giving the firm a great deal of credibility when it launches a tactical action or response, based on the prices of its goods.

Dependence on the Market

Market dependence denotes the extent to which a firm's revenues or profits are derived from a particular market.[102] In general, firms can predict that competitors with high market dependence are likely to respond strongly to attacks threatening their market position.[103] Interestingly, the threatened firm in these instances tends not to respond quickly, suggesting the importance of an effective response to an attack on the firm's position in a critical market.

A firm such as Masonite International Corp. (see the opening case in Chapter 1, on page 5) would be expected to respond aggressively to an attack. Producing millions of interior and exterior doors each year, this Toronto-based door manufacturer is the world's market leader in producing doors for home use. Producing doors is all they do. Masonite's dominant market position provides the flexibility needed to respond aggressively, but carefully, to actions that might be taken by a competitor, such as Pella. Pella, a U.S. producer with more than $1 billion dollars in sales is best known as a manufacturer of high-end windows.[104] However, Pella also makes a full line of exterior doors. If Pella were to attack Masonite's markets, it should understand that Masonite's dependence on doors would induce it to respond aggressively to protect its position in that market.

Competitive Dynamics

Thus far in this chapter, we have discussed competitive rivalry. Competitive rivalry concerns the ongoing actions and responses between a firm and its competitors for an advantageous market position. On the other hand, competitive dynamics concern the ongoing actions and responses taking place among *all* firms competing within a market for advantageous positions. Such position should lead to improved performance (as discussed in the first two chapters).

To explain competitive rivalry, we described (1) factors that determine the degree to which firms are competitors (market commonality and resource similarity), (2) drivers of competitive behaviour for individual firms (awareness, motivation, and ability) and (3) factors affecting the likelihood a competitor will act or attack (first mover incentives, organizational size, and quality) and respond (type of competitive action, reputation, and market dependence). Building and sustaining competitive advantages are at the core of competitive rivalry, in that advantages are the link to a profitable market position.

To explain competitive dynamics, we discuss the effects of varying rates of competitive speed in different markets (called slow-cycle, fast-cycle, and standard-cycle markets, defined below) on the behaviour (actions and responses) of all competitors within a given market. Competitive behaviours as well as the reasons or logic for taking them are similar within each market type, but differ across market type.[105] Thus, competitive dynamics differ in slow-cycle, fast-cycle, and standard-cycle markets. The sustainability of the firm's competitive advantages is an important difference among the three market types.

As noted in Chapter 1, firms want to sustain their advantages for as long as possible, although no advantage is permanently sustainable. The degree of sustainability is affected by how quickly competitive advantages can be imitated and how costly it is to do so.

Slow-Cycle Markets

Slow-cycle markets are markets in which the firm's competitive advantages are shielded from imitation for what are commonly long periods of time and where imitation is costly.[106] Competitive advantages are sustainable in slow-cycle markets.

Building a one-of-a-kind competitive advantage that is proprietary leads to competitive success in a slow-cycle market. This type of advantage is difficult for competitors to understand. As discussed in Chapter 4, a difficult-to-understand and costly to imitate advantage results from unique historical conditions, causal ambiguity, and/or social complexity. Copyrights, geography, patents, and ownership of an information resource are examples of factors that can lead to one-of-a-kind advantages.[107] Once a proprietary advantage is developed, the firm's competitive behaviour in a slow-cycle market is oriented to protecting, maintaining, and extending that advantage. Thus, the competitive dynamics in slow-cycle markets involve all firms concentrating on competitive actions and responses that enable them to protect, maintain, and extend their proprietary competitive advantage.

Walt Disney Co. continues to extend its proprietary characters. Characters such as Mickey Mouse, Minnie Mouse, and Goofy have a unique historical development that was a result of Walt and Roy Disney's creativity and vision for entertaining people. Products based on the characters seen in Disney's animated films are sold through Disney's theme-park shops as well as through self-standing, retail outlets called Disney Stores. The list of character-based products is extensive, including everything from the characters themselves to clothing with the characters' images. Because patents shield it, the proprietary nature of Disney's advantage in terms of animated characters protects the firm from imitation by competitors.

Consistent with another attribute of competition in a slow-cycle market, Disney remains committed to protecting its exclusive rights to its characters and their use as shown by the fact that "… the company once sued a daycare centre, forcing it to remove the likeness of Mickey Mouse from a wall of the facility."[108] As with all firms competing in slow-cycle markets, Disney's competitive actions (e.g., building theme parks in France and Japan and other potential locations such as China) and responses (e.g., lawsuits to protect its right to fully control the use of its animated characters) maintain and extend its proprietary competitive advantage while protecting it. Disney has been able to establish, through actions and defend through responses, an advantageous market position as a result of its competitive behaviour.

Similarly, Toronto-based Nelvana is a global children's and family entertainment company that produces, markets, and distributes animation. With operations in Toronto, Los Angeles, London, Paris, Tokyo, and Shannon, Ireland, Nelvana's animation is aired on more than 360 broadcast outlets worldwide, spanning 50 different languages. The company has managed to build and maintain a stable of profitable animated series.

Slow-cycle markets are markets in which the firm's competitive advantages are shielded from imitation for what are commonly long periods of time and where imitation is costly.

Nelvana selects series with characters developed from a number of sources: Babar from the classic children's story, the Berenstain Bears and Corduroy from recent children's cartoons, Bob and Margaret from an animated short film, and Donkey Kong Country from game maker Nintendo.[109] Nelvana's competitive actions—global locations and a readily available outlets (Nelvana's parent, Corus Entertainment, owns YTV and a 40 percent interest in Teletoon)—have aided it in attracting program developers who want to turn their characters into an animated series. The competitive actions Nelvana has taken impact its competitive responses. Nelvana does not need to be as litigious as Disney because it has tapped external developers for the shows it produces. These developers would likely be the first to sue in the event of a copyright infringement.

The competitive dynamics generated by firms competing in slow-cycle markets are shown in Figure 6.4. In slow-cycle markets, firms launch a product (e.g., a new cartoon character or a new drug) that has been developed through a proprietary advantage (e.g., R&D) and then exploit it for as long as possible while the product is shielded from competition. Eventually, competitors respond to the action with a counterattack. In markets for drugs, for example, this counterattack commonly occurs as patents expire, creating the need for another product launch by the firm seeking a shielded market position.

Fast-Cycle Markets

Fast-cycle markets are markets in which the firm's competitive advantages aren't shielded from imitation and where imitation happens quickly and somewhat inexpensively.

Fast-cycle markets are markets in which the firm's competitive advantages aren't shielded from imitation and where imitation happens quickly and somewhat inexpensively. Competitive advantages aren't sustainable in fast-cycle markets.

Reverse engineering and the rate of technology diffusion in fast-cycle markets facilitate rapid imitation. A competitor uses reverse engineering to quickly gain the knowledge required to imitate or improve the firm's products, usually in only a few months. Technology is diffused rapidly in fast-cycle markets, making it available to competitors in a short period of time. The technology often used by fast-cycle competitors isn't proprietary, nor is it protected by patents, as is the technology used by firms competing in slow-cycle markets. For example, only a few hundred parts, which are readily available on the open market, are required to build a PC. Patents protect only a few of these parts, such as the microprocessor chips.[110]

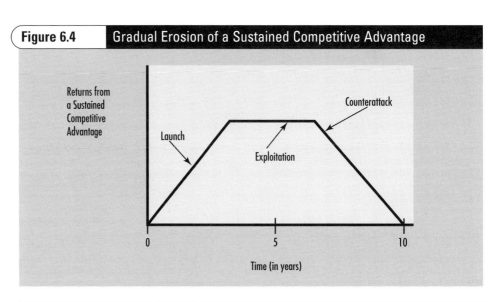

Figure 6.4 Gradual Erosion of a Sustained Competitive Advantage

SOURCE: Adapted from I. C. MacMillan, 1988, Controlling competitive dynamics by taking strategic initiative, *Academy of Management Executive*, II(2): 111–18.

Fast-cycle markets are more volatile than slow-cycle and standard-cycle markets. Indeed, the pace of competition in fast-cycle markets is almost frenzied, as companies rely on ideas and their resulting innovations as the engines of their growth. Because prices fall quickly in these markets, companies need to profit quickly from their product innovations. For example, rapid declines in the prices of microprocessor chips—produced by Markham, Ontario's ATI and those produced by NVIDIA and Intel (both of Santa Clara, California), among others—make it possible for personal computer manufacturers to continuously improve their graphics performance and reduce their prices to end users.[111]

Imitation of many fast-cycle products is relatively easy, as demonstrated by international and local PC vendors. All of these firms have partly or largely imitated IBM's initial PC design to create their products. Continuous declines in the costs of parts, as well as the fact that the information and knowledge required to assemble a PC is not especially complicated and is readily available, make it possible for additional competitors to enter this market without significant difficulty.[112]

The fast-cycle market characteristics described above make it virtually impossible for companies in this type of market to develop sustainable competitive advantages. Recognizing this vulnerability, firms avoid loyalty to any of their products, preferring to cannibalize their own products before competitors learn how to do so through successful imitation. This emphasis creates competitive dynamics that differ substantially from what is witnessed in slow-cycle markets. Instead of concentrating on protecting, maintaining, and extending competitive advantages, as is the case for firms in slow-cycle markets, companies competing in fast-cycle markets focus on learning how to rapidly and continuously develop new competitive advantages that are superior to those they replace. In fast-cycle markets, firms don't concentrate on trying to protect a given competitive advantage because they understand that the advantage won't exist long enough to extend it.

The competitive behaviour of firms competing in fast-cycle markets is shown in Figure 6.5. As suggested by the figure, competitive dynamics in fast-cycle markets are characterized by firms, in the course of competitive rivalry, taking actions and responses that are oriented to both rapid and continuous product introductions and the use of a

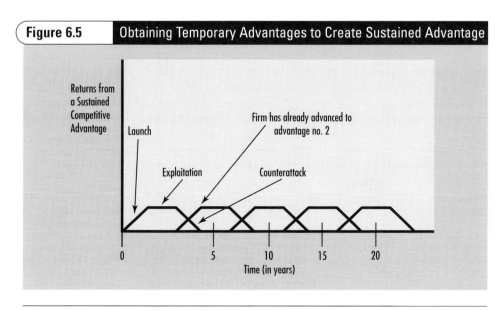

| Figure 6.5 | Obtaining Temporary Advantages to Create Sustained Advantage |

SOURCE: Adapted from I. C. MacMillan, 1988, Controlling competitive dynamics by taking strategic initiative, *Academy of Management Executive*, II(2): 111–18.

stream of ever-changing competitive advantages. The firm launches a product as a competitive action and then exploits the advantage associated with it, for as long as possible. However, the firm also tries to move to another temporary competitive before competitors can respond to the first one (see Figure 6.5). Thus, competitive dynamics in fast-cycle markets, in which all firms seek to achieve new competitive advantages before their competitors learn how to effectively respond to current competitive advantages, often result in rapid product upgrades as well as quick product innovations.[113]

As our discussion suggests, innovation has a dominant effect on competitive dynamics in fast-cycle markets. For individual firms, this means that innovation is a key source of competitive advantage. Through innovation, the firm can cannibalize its own products before competitors' can successfully imitate them.

In the fast-cycle computer graphics market, ATI, NVIDIA, and Intel all rely on innovation as a competitive advantage. There is evidence to suggest that the three companies are successful in this effort. ATI has been selected over NVIDIA to produce the next generation of graphics chips for Microsoft's Xbox and is involved with Korean giant Samsung to jointly develop its next-generation digital televisions.[114] NVIDIA, seeing the coming market need for quality handheld graphics in cell phones and PDAs, bought the R&D leader in the field, MediaQ. The purchase doubles NVIDIA's R&D staff and is likely to make NVIDIA a major player in the mobile graphics area.[115] While graphics capabilities on Intel's chips have met with mixed reviews, the chips do allow users run their systems faster and more efficiently.[116]

Standard-Cycle Markets

Standard-cycle markets are markets in which the firm's competitive advantages are moderately shielded from imitation and where imitation is moderately costly.

Standard-cycle markets are markets in which the firm's competitive advantages are moderately shielded from imitation and where imitation is moderately costly. Competitive advantages are partially sustainable in standard-cycle markets, but only when the firm is able to continuously upgrade the quality of its competitive advantages. The competitive actions and responses that form a standard-cycle market's competitive dynamics find firms seeking large market shares, trying to gain customer loyalty through brand names, and carefully controlling their operations to consistently provide the same usage experience for customers without surprises.[117]

Because of large volumes and the size of mass markets, the competition for market share is intense in standard-cycle markets. British/Dutch Unilever and the U.S.'s Procter & Gamble (P&G) compete in standard-cycle markets. A competitor analysis reveals that Unilever and P&G are direct competitors: they share multiple markets as they engage each other in competition in more 140 countries, and they have similar types and amounts of resources and follow similar strategies. One of the product lines in which these two firms aggressively compete against each other for market share is laundry detergents. The market for these products is large, with an annual sales volume of more than $7 billion in North America alone. The sheer size of this market highlights the importance of market share, as a mere percentage point gain in share translates into a $70 million increase in revenues. As analysts have noted, in a standard-cycle market, "It's a death struggle to incrementally gain share." For Unilever and P&G, this means that the firms must "… slog it out for every fraction of every share in every category in every market where they compete."[118]

Standard-cycle companies serve many customers in competitive markets. Because the capabilities on which their competitive advantages are based are less specialized, imitation is faster and less costly for standard-cycle firms than for those competing in slow-cycle markets. However, imitation is less quick and more expensive in these markets than in fast-cycle markets. Thus, competitive dynamics in standard-cycle markets rests midway between the characteristics of dynamics in slow-cycle and fast-cycle markets. The quickness of imitation is reduced and becomes more expensive for standard-cycle competitors when a firm is able to develop economies of scale by combining coordinated and integrated design and manufacturing processes with a large sales volume for its products.

Without scale economies, standard-cycle firms compete at a disadvantage. Recently, for example, some of Britain's well-known retailers, such as Marks & Spencer, reported continuing declines in sales volume. Entry to Britain by foreign competitors, including Sweden's Hennes & Mauritz, Spain's Zara, and Japan's Uniqlo, is contributing to this decline. According to analysts, these competitors rely on their global fashion sense and economies of scale to quickly imitate their British competitors. The global presence and resulting sales volumes of these global competitors increase the likelihood that these firms will develop and benefit from economies of scale. In contrast, Britain's home-grown retailers lack the presence and volume required to develop economies of scale and to make their competitive advantage costly to imitate.[119]

Innovation can also drive competitive actions and responses in standard-cycle markets, especially when rivalry is intense. Thus, innovation has a substantial influence on competitive dynamics, as it affects the actions and responses of all companies competing within a slow-cycle, fast-cycle, or standard-cycle market. We have emphasized the importance of innovation to the firm's strategic competitiveness in earlier chapters. Our discussion of innovation, in terms of competitive dynamics, extends the earlier discussions by showing the importance of innovation in all types of markets in which firms compete.

Innovation is vital to the competitive behaviour of consumer goods competitors in the food industry. Witness the development and expansion of the President's Choice product line. Launched as a limited line of quality, lower priced alternatives to branded supermarket food products, President's Choice has innovated and expanded to include pet foods, household products, lawn and garden products, and even financial products. President's Choice is a profitable line for its owner, the Loblaw Companies. Of course, the deck is stacked in Loblaw's favour. Being a supermarket chain itself, Loblaw will make money even if the consumer buys the competitor's brand.

Summary

- Competitors are firms competing in the same market, offering similar products, and targeting similar customers. Competitive rivalry is the ongoing set of competitive actions and competitive responses occurring between competitors as they compete against each other for an advantageous market position. The outcomes of competitive rivalry influence the firm's ability to sustain its competitive advantages, as well as the level (average, below-average, or above-average) of its financial returns.

- For the individual firm, the set of competitive actions and responses it takes while engaged in competitive rivalry is called competitive behaviour. Competitive dynamics is the set of actions taken by all firms that are competitors within a particular market.

- Firms study competitive rivalry in order to be able to predict the competitive actions and responses that each of its competitors likely will take. Competitive actions are either strategic or tactical in nature. The firm takes competitive actions to defend or build its competitive advantages or improve its market position. Competitive responses are taken to counter the effects of a competitor's competitive action. A strategic action or a strategic response requires a significant commitment of organizational resources, is difficult to successfully implement, and hard to reverse. In contrast, a tactical action or a tactical response requires fewer organizational resources and is easier to implement and reverse. For an airline company, for example, entering major new markets is an example of a strategic action or a strategic response, while changing its prices in a particular market is an example of a tactical action or a tactical response.

- A competitor analysis is the first step the firm takes to be able to predict its competitors' actions and responses. In Chapter 3, we discussed what firms do to *understand* competitors. This discussion is extended further in this chapter as we described what the firm does to *predict* competitors' market-based actions. Thus, understanding precedes prediction. Market commonality (the number of markets with which competitors are jointly involved and their importance to each competitor) and resource similarity (how comparable competitors' resources are, in terms of type and amount) are studied to complete a competitor analysis. In general, the greater the market commonality and resource similarity, the more firms acknowledge that they are direct competitors.

- Market commonality and resource similarity shape the firm's awareness (the degree to which it and its competitor understand their mutual interdependence), motivation (the firm's incentive to attack or respond), and ability (the quality of the resources available to the firm to attack and respond). Having knowledge of a competitor in terms of these characteristics increases the quality of the firm's predictions about a competitor's actions and responses.

- In addition to market commonality, resource similarity, resource awareness, motivation, and ability, three more specific factors affect the likelihood a competitor will take competitive actions. The first of these concerns first-mover incentives. First movers, those taking an initial competitive action, often earn above-average returns until competitors can successfully respond to the first mover's action and gain loyal customers. Not all firms can be first movers, as some firms may lack the awareness, motivation, or ability required to engage in this type of competitive behaviour. Moreover, some firms prefer to be a second mover (the firm responding to the first mover's action), because second movers, especially those acting quickly, can successfully compete against the first mover. By studying the first mover's product, customers' reactions to it, and the responses of other competitors to the first mover, the second mover can avoid the early entrant's mistakes and improve upon the customer value created by the first mover's good or service. Late movers, however (those that respond a long time after the original action was taken), commonly are lower performers and much less competitive.

   Organizational size, the second factor, tends to reduce the number of different types of competitive actions that large firms launch, while resulting in smaller competitors using a wide variety of actions. Ideally, the firm would like to initiate a large number of diverse actions when engaged in competitive rivalry.

The third factor, quality, dampens firms' abilities to take competitive actions, in that product quality is a base denominator to successful competition in the global economy.

- The type of action (strategic or tactical) initiated by the firm, the nature of a competitor's competitor behaviour, and the competitor's dependence on the market in which the action was taken are studied to predict a competitor's response to the firm's action. In general, the number of tactical responses taken exceeds the number of strategic responses. Competitors respond more frequently to the actions taken by the firm with a reputation for predictable and understandable competitive behaviour, especially if that firm is a market leader. In general, the firm can predict that when its competitor is highly dependent for its revenue and profitability in the market in which the firm took a competitive action, that competitor is likely to launch a strong response. However, firms that are more diversified across markets are less likely to respond to a particular action that affects only one of the markets in which they compete.

- Competitive dynamics concern the ongoing competitive behaviour occurring among all firms competing in a market for advantageous positions. Market characteristics, as well as the sustainability of firms' competitive advantages, affect the set of actions and responses that firms take while competing in a given market. In slow-cycle markets, where competitive advantages can be maintained, competitive dynamics find firms taking actions and responses that are intended to protect, maintain, and extend their proprietary advantages. In fast-cycle markets, competition is almost frenzied as firms concentrate on developing a series of temporary competitive advantages. This emphasis is necessary because firms' advantages in fast-cycle markets aren't proprietary and, as such, are subject to rapid and relatively inexpensive imitation. Standard-cycle markets are between slow-cycle and fast-cycle markets, as firms in standard-cycle markets are moderately shielded from competition as they use competitive advantages that are moderately sustainable. Competitors in standard-cycle markets serve mass markets and try to develop economies of scale to enhance their profitability. Innovation is vital to competitive success in each of the three types of markets. Firms should recognize that the set of competitive actions and responses taken by all firms differ according to the competitive dynamics of the market.

1. Who are competitors? How are competitive rivalry, competitive behaviour, and competitive dynamics defined in the chapter?

2. What is market commonality? What is resource similarity? How are these concepts the building blocks for a competitor analysis?

3. How do awareness, motivation, and ability affect the firm's competitive behaviour?

4. What factors affect the likelihood a firm will take a competitive action?

5. What factors affect the likelihood a firm will initiate a competitive response to the action taken by a competitor?

6. How is competitive dynamics in slow-cycle markets described in the chapter? In fast-cycle markets? In standard-cycle markets?

Experiential Exercise

Competitive Rivalry

Part One. Define a first mover and a second mover, and provide examples of firms for each category.

	First Mover	Second Mover
Examples		

Part Two. In the following table, list the advantages and disadvantages of being the first mover and of being the second mover.

	First Mover	Second Mover
Advantages		
Disadvantages		

Part Three. Based on the above information, what are the most important issues that you feel first and second movers must consider before initiating a competitive move?

Notes

1. M.-J. Chen, 1996, Competitor analysis and interfirm rivalry: Toward a theoretical integration, *Academy of Management Review*, 21: 100–34.

2. S. Jayachandran, J. Gimeno, & P. R. Varadarajan, 1999, Theory of multimarket competition: A synthesis and implications for marketing strategy, *Journal of Marketing*, 63(3): 49–66.

3. R. E. Caves, 1984, Economic analysis and the quest for competitive advantage, in *Papers and Proceedings of the 96th Annual Meeting of the American Economic Association*, 127–32.

4. G. Young, K. G. Smith, C. M. Grimm, & D. Simon, 2000, Multimarket contact and resource dissimilarity: A competitive dynamics perspective, *Journal of Management*, 26: 1217–36; C. M. Grimm & K. G. Smith, 1997, *Strategy as Action: Industry Rivalry and Coordination*, Cincinnati: South-Western College Publishing, 53–74.

5. H. A. Haveman & L. Nonnemaker, 2000, Competition in multiple geographic markets: The impact on growth and market entry, *Administrative Science Quarterly*, 45: 232–67.

6. G. Young, K. G. Smith, & C. M. Grimm, 1996, "Austrian" and industrial organization perspectives on firm-level competitive activity and performance, *Organization Science*, 73: 243–54.

7. K. G. Smith, W. J. Ferrier, & H. Ndofor, 2001, Competitive dynamics research: Critique and future directions, in M. A. Hitt, R. E. Freeman, & J. S. Harrison (eds.), *Handbook of Strategic Management*, Oxford, UK: Blackwell Publishers, 326.

8. G. S. Day & D. J. Reibstein, 1997, The dynamic challenges for theory and practice, in G. S. Day & D. J. Reibstein (eds.), *Wharton on Competitive Strategy*, New York: John Wiley & Sons, 2.

9. D. L. Deeds, D. DeCarolis, & J. Coombs, 2000, Dynamic capabilities and new product development in high technology adventures: An empirical analysis of new biotechnology firms, *Journal of Business Venturing*, 15: 211–99.

10. G. Khermouch, S. Holmes, & M. Ihlwan, 2001, The best global brands, *Business Week*, August 6, 50–57.

11. C. Lederer & S. Hill, 2001, See your brands through your customers' eyes, *Harvard Business Review*, 79(6): 125–33.

12. S. Crainer, 2001, And the new economy winner is … *Europe, Strategy & Business*, second quarter, 40–47.

13. J. E. Garten, 2001, The wrong time for companies to beat a global retreat, *Business Week*, December 17, 22.

14. Young, Smith, Grimm, & Simon, Multimarket contact and resource dissimilarity, 1230–33.

15. D. R. Gnyawali & R. Madhavan, 2001, Cooperative networks and competitive dynamics: A structural embeddedness perspective, *Academy of Management Review*, 26: 431–45.

16. Young, Smith, Grimm, & Simon, Multimarket contact and resource dissimilarity, 1217; M. E. Porter, 1991, Towards a dynamic theory of strategy, *Strategic Management Journal*, 12: 95–117.

17. S. Godin, 2002, Survival is not enough, *Fast Company*, January, 90–94.

18. S. J. Marsh, 1998, Creating barriers for foreign competitors: A study of the impact of anti-dumping actions on the performance of U.S. firms, *Strategic Management Journal*, 19: 25–37; K. G. Smith, C. M. Grimm, G. Young, & S. Wally, 1997, Strategic groups and rivalrous firm behavior: Toward a reconciliation, *Strategic Management Journal*, 18: 149–57.

19. W. J. Ferrier, 2001, Navigating the competitive landscape: The drivers and consequences of competitive aggressiveness, *Academy of Management Journal*, 44: 858–77; M. E. Porter, 1980, *Competitive Strategy*, New York: Free Press.

20. Smith, Ferrier, & Ndofor, Competitive dynamics research, 319.

21. K. Ramaswamy, 2001, Organizational ownership, competitive intensity, and firm performance: An empirical study of the Indian manufacturing sector, *Strategic Management Journal*, 22: 989–98.

22. K. Cool, L. H. Roller, & B. Leleux, 1999, The relative impact of actual and potential rivalry on firm profitability in the pharmaceutical industry, *Strategic Management Journal*, 20: 1–14.

23. H. Kent, 1999, Huge declines in price as competition heats up in Vancouver's booming laser-surgery market. *Canadian Medical Association Journal*, 161(7): 857–58.

24. V. Colliver, 2001, Left in the Lurch: Doctor walkouts, closures of Lasik Vision Medical Centers have patients scrambling, *San Francisco Chronicle*, April 4, D1.

25. LASIK Mainframe, 2003, Discount LASIK dangers: While searching for the best value, some have discovered first hand that cheaper sometimes isn't better …, *LASIK Mainframe web site*, http://www.lasikmainframe.com/discount_ lasik_dangers.htm, accessed January 14, 2004.

26. I. Sager, F. Keenan, C. Edwards, & A. Park, 2001, The mother of all price wars, *Business Week*, July 30, 32–35.

27. Economist, 2001, In the family's way, *Economist*, December 15, 56.

28. Sager, Keenan, Edwards, & Park, The mother of all price wars, 33.

29. W. P. Putsis Jr., 1999, Empirical analysis of competitive interaction in food product categories, *Agribusiness*, 15(3): 295–311.

30. Standard & Poor's, 2001, Dell Computer, Standard & Poor's stock report, http://www.standardandpoors.com, accessed December 8, 2001.

31. Chen, Competitor analysis, 108.

32. Ibid., 109.

33. E. Abrahamson & C. J. Fombrun, 1994, Macrocultures: Determinants and consequences, *Academy of Management Review*, 19: 728–55.

34. C. Salter, 2002, On the road again, *Fast Company*, January, 50–58.

35. Young, Smith, Grimm, & Simon, Multimarket contact, 1219.

36. Chen, Competitor analysis, 106.

37. J. Gimeno & C. Y. Woo, 1999, Multimarket contact, economies of scope, and firm performance, *Academy of Management Journal*, 42: 239–59.

38. H. Shaw, 2001, Roots to open 100 stores in China: "It has managed to create a global brand," *National Post* (national ed.), October 4, FP.1.

39. Young, Smith, Grimm, & Simon, Multimarket contact and resource dissimilarity, 1230.

40. J. Gimeno, 1999, Reciprocal threats in multimarket rivalry: Staking out "spheres of influence" in the U.S. airline industry, *Strategic Management Journal*, 20: 101–28; N. Fernandez & P. L. Marin, 1998, Market power and multimarket contact: Some evidence from the Spanish hotel industry, *Journal of Industrial Economics*, 46: 301–15.

41. H. J. Korn & J. A. C. Baum, 1999, Chance, imitative, and strategic antecedents to multimarket contact, *Academy of Management Journal*, 42: 171–93.

42. Jayachandran, Gimeno, & Varadarajan, Theory of multimarket competition, 59; Chen, Competitor analysis, 107.

43. J. Gimeno & C. Y. Woo, 1996, Hypercompetition in a multimarket environment: The role of strategic similarity and multimarket contact on competitive de-escalation, *Organization Science*, 7: 322–41.

44. M. Strauss, 2003, Katz shuts third of U.S. stores, Alta. drugstore firm suffers a setback, *Globe and Mail*, September 13, http://www.globeinvestor.com/servlet/ArticleNews/story/GAM/20030913/RKATZ, accessed January 15, 2004.

45. Chen, Competitor analysis, 107–8.

46. Ibid., 110.

47. Ibid., 110; W. Ocasio, 1997, Towards an attention-based view of the firm, *Strategic Management Journal*, 18(summer special issue): 187–206; Smith, Ferrier, & Ndofor, Competitive dynamics research, 320.

48. G. P. Hodgkinson & G. Johnson, 1994, Exploring the mental models of competitive strategists: The case for a processual approach, *Journal of Management Studies*, 31: 525–51; J. F. Porac & H. Thomas, 1994, Cognitive categorization and subjective rivalry among retailers in a small city, *Journal of Applied Psychology*, 79: 54–66.

49. Economist, 2001, Wal around the world, *Economist*, December 8, 55–56.

50. Smith, Ferrier, & Ndofor, Competitive dynamics research, 320.

51. Chen, Competitor analysis, 113.

52. Grimm & Smith, *Strategy as Action*, 125.

53. Economist, 2002, Blue light blues, *Economist*, January 29, 54; D. B. Yoffie & M. Kwak, 2001, Mastering strategic movement at Palm, *MIT Sloan Management Review*, 43(1): 55–63.

54. K. G. Smith, W. J. Ferrier, & C. M. Grimm, 2001, King of the hill: Dethroning the industry leader, *Academy of Management Executive*, 15(2): 59–70.

55. G. S. Day, 1997, Assessing competitive arenas: Who are your competitors? In G. S. Day & D. J. Reibstein (eds.), *Wharton on Competitive Strategy*, New York: John Wiley & Sons, 25–26.

56. M. Ihlwan, L. Armstrong, & K. Kerwin, 2001, Hyundai gets hot, *Business Week*, December 17, 84–86.

57. J. Schumpeter, 1934, *The Theory of Economic Development*, Cambridge, MA: Harvard University Press.

58. J. L. C. Cheng & I. F. Kesner, 1997, Organizational slack and response to environmental shifts: The impact of resource allocation patterns, *Journal of Management*, 23: 1–18.

59. F. Wang, 2000, Too appealing to overlook, *America's Network*, December, 10–12.

60. G. Hamel, 2000, *Leading the Revolution*, Boston: Harvard Business School Press, 103.

61. K. Belson, R. Hof, & B. Elgin, 2001, How Yahoo! Japan beat eBay at its own game, *Business Week*, June 4, 58.

62. Smith, Ferrier, & Ndofor, Competitive dynamics research, 331.

63. L. J. Bourgeois, 1981, On the measurement of organizational slack, *Academy of Management Review*, 6: 29–39.

64. M. B. Lieberman & D. B. Montgomery, 1988, First-mover advantages, *Strategic Management Journal*, 9: 41–58.

65. Economist, 2001, Older, wiser, webbier, *Economist*, June 30, 10.

66. M. Shank, 2002, Executive strategy report, IBM business strategy consulting, *IBM website*, http://www.ibm.com, March 14, 2002; W. Boulding & M. Christen, 2001, First-mover disadvantage, *Harvard Business Review*, 79(9): 20–21.

67. K. G. Smith, C. M. Grimm, & M. J. Gannon, 1992, *Dynamics of Competitive Strategy*, Newberry Park, CA: Sage Publications.

68. H. R. Greve, 1998, Managerial cognition and the mimetic adoption of market positions: What you see is what you do, *Strategic Management Journal*, 19: 967–88.

69. Smith, Ferrier, & Ndofor, Competitive dynamics research, 327.

70. M.-J. Chen & D. C. Hambrick, 1995, Speed, stealth and selective attack: How small firms differ from large firms in competitive behavior, *Academy of Management Journal*, 38: 453–82.

71. D. Miller & M.-J. Chen, 1996, The simplicity of competitive repertoires: An empirical analysis, *Strategic Management Journal*, 17: 419–40.

72. Young, Smith, & Grimm, "Austrian" and industrial organization perspectives.

73. B. A. Melcher, 1993, How Goliaths can act like Davids, *Business Week*, special issue, 193.

74. Economist, 2001, Wal around the world, 55.

75. Ibid., 55.

76. P. B. Crosby, 1980, *Quality Is Free*, New York: Penguin.

77. W. E. Deming, 1986, *Out of the Crisis*, Cambridge, MA: MIT Press.

78. T. Laseter, B. Long, & C. Capers, 2001, B2B benchmark: The state of electronic exchanges, *Strategy & Business*, fourth quarter, 32–42.

79. R. S. Kaplan & D. P. Norton, 2001, *The Strategy-Focused Organization*, Boston: Harvard Business School Press.

80. R. Cullen, S. Nicholls, & A. Halligan, 2001, Measurement to demonstrate success, *British Journal of Clinical Governance*, 6(4): 273–78.

81. K. E. Weick & K. M. Sutcliffe, 2001, *Managing the Unexpected*, San Francisco: Jossey-Bass, 81–82.

82. J. Aley, 1994, Manufacturers grade themselves, *Fortune*, March 21, 26.
83. J. Green & D. Welch, 2001, Jaguar may find it's a jungle out there, *Business Week*, March 26, 62.
84. J. Muller, 2001, Ford: Why it's worse than you think, *Business Week*, June 25, 80–89.
85. K. Lundegaard, 2003, The worst cars in America?—Hummer, Saab fare badly as key survey names poor performers for first time; a boost for Lexus, *Wall Street Journal* (eastern ed.), May 7, D1; J. Burt, 2003, Consumer Reports likes Hyundai, Chevy also on the "it" list, while Ford, Benz and VW make the other list, *TheCarConnection website*, March 17, http://www.thecarconnection .com/index.asp?article=5855, accessed January 17, 2004; Ford Motor Company, 2004, Ford Motor Company Annual and Quarterly reports, *Ford Motor Company website*, http://www.ford.com/en/company/investorInformation/ companyReports/financialResults/default.htm, accessed January, 17, 2004.
86. J. D. Westphal, R. Gulati, & S. M. Shortell, 1997, Customization or conformity: An institutional and network perspective on the content and consequences of TQM adoption, *Administrative Science Quarterly*, 42: 366–94.
87. S. Sanghera, 1999, Making continuous improvement better, *Financial Times*, April 21, 28.
88. Muller, Ford, 82.
89. J. White, G. L. White, & N. Shirouzu, 2001, Soon, the big three won't be, as foreigners make inroads, *Wall Street Journal*, August 13, A1, A12.
90. Ihlwan, Armstrong, & Kerwin, Hyundai gets hot, 84.
91. E. Eldridge, 2003, Hyundai's reliability rankings now tie Honda's …, *USA Today*, March 11, M1.
92. Ihlwan, Armstrong, & Kerwin, Hyundai gets hot, 85.
93. J. Schumpeter, 1950, *Capitalism, Socialism and Democracy*, New York: Harper; Smith, Ferrier, & Ndofor, Competitive dynamics research, 323.
94. M.-J. Chen & I. C. MacMillan, 1992, Nonresponse and delayed response to competitive moves, *Academy of Management Journal*, 35: 539–70; Smith, Ferrier, & Ndofor, Competitive dynamics research, 335.
95. M.-J. Chen, K. G. Smith, & C. M. Grimm, 1992, Action characteristics as predictors of competitive responses, *Management Science*, 38: 439–55.
96. M.-J. Chen & D. Miller, 1994, Competitive attack, retaliation and performance: An expectancy-valence framework, *Strategic Management Journal*, 15: 85–102.
97. Smith, Ferrier, & Ndofor, Competitive dynamics research, 333.
98. W. J. Ferrier, K. G. Smith, & C. M. Grimm, 1999, The role of competitive actions in market share erosion and industry dethronement: A study of industry leaders and challengers, *Academy of Management Journal*, 42: 372–88.
99. J. D'Arcy, 2000, The war for your home: The big-box renovation giants are locked in a death struggle to dominate Canada's suburbs, *Maclean's* (Toronto ed.), October 16, 54; Rona, 2004, *Rona website*, http://www.rona.ca, accessed January 17, 2004.
100. Smith, Grimm, & Gannon, *Dynamics of Competitive Strategy*.
101. Argus Research, 2001, Retail update 2001, *Argus Market Digest*, http://www. argusresearch.com, accessed December 28, 2001.
102. A. Karnani & B. Wernerfelt, 1985, Research note and communication: Multiple point competition, *Strategic Management Journal*, 6: 87–97.
103. Smith, Ferrier, & Ndofor, Competitive dynamics research, 330.
104. Pella Corporation, 2004, *Pella website*, http://www.pella.com, accessed January 18, 2004.
105. J. R. Williams, 1999, *Renewable Advantage: Crafting Strategy through Economic Time*, New York: Free Press.
106. R. Williams, 1992, How sustainable is your competitive advantage? *California Management Review*, 34(3): 29–51.
107. Ibid., 6.
108. Ibid., 57.
109. Nelvana, 2004, *Nelvana website*, http://www.nelvana.com, accessed January 19, 2004; Corus Entertainment, 2004, *Corus Entertainment website*, http://www.corusent.com, accessed January 19, 2004.
110. Williams, *Renewable Advantage*, 8.
111. P. N. Glaskowsky, 2003, Our 3-D future, Electronic Business, 29(12):12–13; A. MacLellan, 2003, ATI steals the show from NVIDIA for Xbox 2, EBN, August 18, 5; B. Gain, 2002, Intel's much anticipated 845G chipset bows to mixed reviews, EBN, May 27, 22; ATI Technologies Inc., 2002, ATI's FireGL professional workstation product line more affordable than ever, ATI website, http://www.ati.com/companyinfo/press/ 2002/4525.html (press release), accessed January 18, 2004; NVIDIA, 2004, NVIDIA website, http://www.nvidia.com/page/home, accessed January 18, 2004.
112. Williams, *Renewable Advantage*, 8.
113. R. Sanchez, 1995, Strategic flexibility in production competition, *Strategic Management Journal*, 16(summer special issue), 9–26.
114. 2003, ATI steals the show from NVIDIA for Xbox 2, EBN, August 18, 5; A. MacLellan, 2003, ATI to furnish chips for Samsung's digital TVs, EBN, November 10, 6.
115. NVIDIA, 2004, *NVIDIA website*, http://www.nvidia.com/page/home, accessed January 18, 2004.
116. B. Gain, 2002, Intel's much anticipated 845G chipset bows to mixed reviews, EBN, May 27, 22.
117. Williams, *Renewable Advantage*, 7.
118. K. Brooker, 2001, A game of inches, *Fortune*, February 5, 98–100.
119. Economist, 2001, High street woes, *Economist*, July 28, 56.

7

Chapter Seven

Corporate-Level Strategy

Knowledge Objectives

Studying this chapter should provide you with the strategic management knowledge needed to:

1. Define corporate-level strategy and discuss its importance to the diversified firm.

2. Describe the advantages and disadvantages of single-business strategies and dominant-business strategies.

3. Explain three primary reasons why firms move from single-business strategies and dominant-business strategies to more diversified strategies.

4. Describe how related-diversified firms create value by sharing or transferring core competencies.

5. Explain the two ways value can be created with an unrelated-diversification strategy.

6. Discuss the incentives and resources that encourage diversification.

7. Describe motives that can encourage managers to overdiversify a firm.

Magna International: A Diversified Automotive Conglomerate

Magna International Inc. is known as a leader in the automotive parts industry and is also one of the most diversified automotive parts suppliers worldwide. With approximately 72,000 employees in their manufacturing, product development, and engineering divisions located in North America, South America, Europe, Asia, and Mexico, Magna is an example of business growth through diversification strategies.

Focusing on automotive systems, Magna—through its 201 manufacturing divisions and 48 product development and engineering centres—designs, develops and manufactures automotive systems, assemblies, modules, and components, as well as engineering and assembling complete vehicles. Growing primarily through a related-linked corporate-level diversification strategy, Magna was started back in the 1950s as a one-person tool and die operation. The first auto part it manufactured was a sun-visor clip. Diversification began in earnest in the 1970s, when the automotive operations were expanded as part of a major product diversification strategy. A focus on growth in the 1980s confirmed Magna's plan to determine its growth and future through concentration on the automotive industry, consequently organizing its manufacturing divisions into automotive systems corporations and thereby becoming full-service suppliers for practically every system of the automobile.

Magna International was ranked 7th on the *Automotive News* list of the top 100 global original-equipment suppliers in 2002. Rankings were based on 2002 sales of $12.2 billion. Magna avers that it is the only supplier that can develop, engineer, test, and build a complete car.

Even while pursuing a related-linked diversification strategy, innovation at Magna was extremely creative, developing new systems to enhance existing work in the automotive business. In the 1990s, for example, Magna developed new hydroforming technology for use in its manufacturing processes. Expansion continued through acquisitions in its European division, and the spinoffs of a number of its operating arms into separate public companies: Decoma International Inc. (plastic exterior modules and systems group), Tesma International Inc. (global engines and transmission business), Magna Donnelly (automotive mirror and window systems and door handles), Intier Automotive (vehicle interior and closure components), Cosma (global metalforming supplier with products such as chassis stampings and bumper beams), and Magna Steyr (total vehicle engineering for original equipment manufacturer [OEM] clients with three distinct areas of work: vehicle technology, powertrain, and engineering).

Magna's operating principles are based on a decentralized operating structure, employee involvement, entrepreneurial managers, a widespread employee charter, and employee ownership. Its strategy of making a public offering of certain automotive systems groups has been cited as critical to Magna's success over the years. As a company, Magna felt it was necessary to preserve and renew the company's entrepreneurial culture by offering employees

Magna International founder Frank Stronach addresses shareholders at the 2004 annual general meeting.

© PETER JONES/REUTERS/LANDOV

(continued)

the opportunity for equity ownership in their place of work, to foster individual initiative and involvement and, thereby, a strong stake in the company's success.

Related-diversification strategies and the quest for ongoing innovation have also led the company, in 2000, to become a founding participant in Covisint, LLC, a business-to-business Internet exchange for the global automotive industry. More recently, Magna was poised to purchase a controlling stake in DaimlerChrysler's big transaxle plant in East Syracuse, New York. The purchase, to be handled through its spinoff Magna Steyr, would gain 68 percent controlling interests in the plant. The venture would make the company a major supplier of driveline components, and turn Magna Steyr into a global leader in four-wheel drive transfer cases. This move would almost also ensure new business from GM, Chrysler, BMW, and Ford.

Despite its success in the automotive industry, Magna has also ventured into areas of unrelated diversification, such as Magna Entertainment Corporation (MEC) and MI Developments Inc. (MID). MEC has earned recognition in the entertainment industry as the largest operator of thoroughbred racetracks in North America, and one of the world's leading simulcast providers of live thoroughbred racing. Key to the business is the ownership of approximately 12 thoroughbred racetracks and 2 standardbred tracks.

MEC has used the process of vertical integration to catapult its success by purchasing and holding, for strategic future development, significant real estate holdings (valued at $102.3 million, as at September 2003) beyond what is necessary for current operations. Additionally the corporation operates a growing off-track betting (OTB) network within the United States as well as a national account that enables customers to place bets by telephone and over the Internet, in effect making the product easily accessible to its customers. MEC went public in March 2000, with a distribution of approximately 15.7 million shares from Magna to its stockholders.

MID Inc., a thriving real estate business, was spun off to Magna shareholders in 2003. MID is listed as the fourth largest publicly held commercial real estate company in Canada (based on equity capitalization). Currently, MID has a controlling stake (96 percent of total voting power of its outstanding stock and 59 percent of total equity interests) in MEC. The investment in MEC is seen to be strategic, based on the expectation of co-development and joint venture opportunities, if and when MEC prepares to develop its excess lands.

MID property holdings include international, high-quality, income-producing properties (both industrial and commercial); properties being developed or being held for development; and properties being held for sale. Real estate assets include properties owned in Canada, the U.S., Mexico, and Europe.

SOURCES: Magna International, *Magna International Inc. website*, http://www.magna.com/magnaWeb.nsf/homepage?OpenFrameset, accessed May 11, 2004; P. Brieger, 2002, Magna plans to spin off Steyr unit (Nasdaq listing), *National Post*, June 15; Automotive News, 2002, Magna stays cautious despite record profit, *Automotive News*, November 11; G. Auer, 2003, Magna grows by offering complete cars, *Automotive News*, September 8; R. Sherefkin, 2003, Magna poised to run DCX plant: Proposed deal would allow automaker to unload an unwanted parts factory, *Automotive News*, September 22; Automotive News, 2003, What Magna would get, *Automotive News*, September 22; Magna Entertainment, *Magna Entertainment website*, http://www.magnaentertainment.com/MEC.Corporate/Home/, accessed May 11, 2004; MI Developments Inc., 2004, *MI Developments website*, http://www.midevelopments.com/index_2.html, accessed May 11, 2004.

Our discussions of business-level strategies (see Chapter 5) and the competitive rivalry and competitive dynamics associated with them (see Chapter 6) concentrate on firms competing in a single industry or product market.[1] When a firm chooses to diversify beyond a single industry and to operate businesses in several industries, it uses a corporate-level strategy of diversification. As explained in the opening case, Magna operates in multiple industries while using a related-linked corporate-level strategy. A corporate-level strategy of diversification allows the firm to use its core competencies to pursue opportunities in the external environment.[2]

Diversification strategies play a major role in the behaviour of large firms.[3] Strategic choices regarding diversification are, however, fraught with uncertainty.[4] A diversified company has two levels of strategy: business-unit (or competitive) strategies and corporate-level (or company-wide) strategies.[5] Each business unit in the diversified firm chooses a business-level strategy as its means of competing in individual product markets. The firm's corporate-level strategy is concerned with two key questions: what businesses should the firm be operating in, and how should the corporate office manage the group of businesses.[6] Defined formally, **corporate-level strategy** specifies actions taken by the firm to gain a competitive advantage by selecting and managing a group of different businesses competing in several industries and product markets. In the current global environment, when selecting new businesses and deciding how to manage them, top executives should view their firm's businesses as a portfolio of core competencies.[7] As with other strategic decisions, which may not be as complex, speed is critical when executives make changes to this portfolio.[8]

A corporate-level strategy is expected to help the firm earn above-average returns by creating value, just as with the diversified firm's business-level strategies.[9] Some suggest that few corporate-level strategies actually create value. A corporate-level strategy's value is ultimately determined by the degree to which "the businesses in the portfolio are worth more under the management of the company than they would be under any other ownership." Thus, effective corporate-level strategies create, across all business units, aggregate returns that exceed the level of returns without such strategies and contribute both to the firm's strategic competitiveness and its ability to earn above-average returns.[10]

Product diversification, a primary corporate-level strategy, concerns the scope of the industries and markets in which the firm competes, as well as "… how managers buy, create, and sell different businesses to match skills and strengths with opportunities presented to the firm." Successful diversification is expected to reduce variability in the firm's profitability since earnings are generated from several different business units. Because firms incur development and monitoring costs when diversifying, the ideal business portfolio measures diversification's costs and benefits, ensuring the benefits outweigh the costs. Increasingly, a number of traditional economy firms are diversifying into Internet and e-commerce businesses in attempts to develop a properly balanced portfolio.[11]

Diversification requires the crafting of a multibusiness or corporate-level strategy. Multibusiness strategies often involve the firm with many different industry environments and product markets and, as explained in Chapter 12, require unique organizational structures. In the opening case, on page 205, we describe Magna's use of a multibusiness strategy to compete in the real estate, hospitality, travel, and vehicle services markets. The prevailing logic of diversification suggests that the firm should diversify into additional markets when it has excess resources, capabilities, and core competencies with multiple value-creating uses.[12] The probability of success increases when top-level managers verify that the firm has an excess of value-creating resources, capabilities, and core competencies before choosing and implementing a corporate-level strategy.

Corporate-level strategy specifies actions taken by the firm to gain a competitive advantage by selecting and managing a group of different businesses competing in several industries and product markets.

We begin the chapter by examining different levels (from low to high) of diversification. Value-creating reasons for firms to use a corporate-level strategy are explored next. When diversification results in companies simultaneously competing against each other in multiple markets, they are engaging in multipoint competition. For example, the merger between Hewlett-Packard and Compaq Computer Corporation is expected to create a new firm that will be able to compete against IBM simultaneously in the attractive services market as well as in the PC and server markets.[13]

The chapter also describes using the vertical integration strategy as a means to gain power over competitors. Two types of diversification strategies denoting moderate to very high levels of diversification—related and unrelated—are then examined. The chapter also explores value-neutral incentives to diversify, as well as managerial motives for diversification, which can be value destructive.

Levels of Diversification

Diversified firms vary according to their level of diversification and the connections between and among their businesses. Figure 7.1 lists and defines five categories of businesses according to increasing levels of diversification. In addition to the single- and dominant-business categories, more fully diversified firms are classified into related and unrelated categories. A firm is related through its diversification when there are several links between its business units; for example, units may share products or services, technologies, or distribution channels. The more links among businesses, the more constrained is the relatedness of diversification. Unrelatedness refers to the absence of direct links between businesses.

Low Levels of Diversification

A firm pursing a *low level of diversification* uses either a single or a dominant corporate-level diversification strategy. A single-business diversification strategy is a corporate-level strategy wherein the firm generates 95 percent or more of its sales revenue from its core business area.[14] For example, focusing on the chewing-gum market, Wm. Wrigley Jr. Company uses a single-business strategy while operating in relatively few product markets. Wrigley's trademark chewing-gum brands include Spearmint, Doublemint, and Juicy Fruit. Sugarfree gums Hubba Bubba, Orbit, and Ice White were added in the 1990s. Its collaboration with Procter & Gamble to produce a dental chewing gum causes Wrigley to become slightly more diversified than it has been historically, although it is still using the single-business diversification strategy. The dental chewing gum will be marketed under P&G's Crest brand.[15]

WestJet Airlines is an example of a well-known Canadian firm that is pursuing a single-business diversification strategy in that all of its revenues come from the airline industry. It concentrates on flying passengers across Canada and does not appear to have any plans to diversify beyond the airline industry. Fishery Products International, of St. John's, Newfoundland and Labrador, is a very focused firm with 100 percent of its revenues coming from its products in the fishing industry.

With the dominant-business corporate-level diversification strategy, the firm generates between 70 percent and 95 percent of its total revenue within a single business area. Smithfield Foods, from Smithfield, Virginia, uses the dominant-business diversification strategy as shown by the fact that the majority of its sales are generated from raising and butchering hogs. Recently, however, Smithfield diversified into beef packing by acquiring Moyer Packing Co., a smaller beef processor. Smithfield also attempted to acquire IBP, the largest beef packer, but was outbid by Tyson Foods.[16] As we will discuss later in the chapter, Smithfield bought (in 1999) and sold (in 2004) Schneider Foods located in Kitchener, Ontario. Although it is still using the dominant-business diversification

Figure 7.1 — Levels and Types of Diversification

Low Levels of Diversification

Single business:
More than 95% of revenue comes from a single business.

Dominant business:
Between 70% and 95% of revenue comes from a single business.

Moderate to High Levels of Diversification

Related constrained:
Less than 70% of revenue comes from the dominant business, and all businesses share product, technological, and distribution linkages.

Related linked (mixed related and unrelated):
Less than 70% of revenue comes from the dominant business, and there are only limited links between businesses.

Very High Levels of Diversification

Unrelated:
Less than 70% of revenue comes from the dominant business, and there are no common links between businesses.

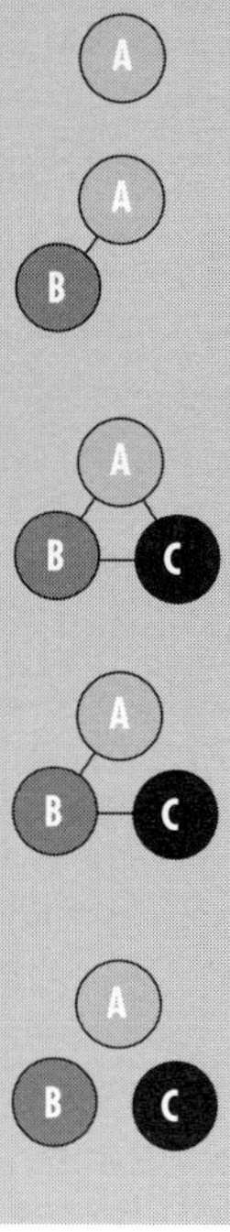

SOURCE: Adapted from R. P. Rumelt, 1974, *Strategy, Structure and Economic Performance*, Boston: Harvard Business School.

strategy, the firm's addition of beef packing operations suggests that its portfolio of businesses is becoming more diversified. If Smithfield were to become even more diversified, its corporate-level strategy could find the firm more accurately described as one that is moderately diversified.

Moderate and High Levels of Diversification

A firm generating more than 30 percent of its sales revenue outside a dominant business and whose businesses are related to each other in some manner uses a *related-diversification corporate-level strategy*. When the links between the diversified firm's businesses are rather direct, a *related-constrained diversification strategy* is being used. Canadian firms SNC-Lavalin and Nortel Networks and U.S. firms Campbell Soup, Procter & Gamble, Xerox, and Merck & Company all use a related-constrained strategy. A related-constrained firm shares a number of resources and activities between its businesses.

The diversified company with a portfolio of businesses with only a few links between them is called a mixed related and unrelated firm and is using the *related-linked diversification strategy* (see Figure 7.1). Canadian firms such as Bombardier and Rogers Communications and U.S. firms such as Johnson & Johnson, General Electric, and Schlumberger follow this corporate-level diversification strategy. Compared to related-constrained firms, related-linked firms share fewer resources and assets between their businesses, concentrating instead on transferring knowledge and competencies among the businesses.

A highly diversified firm, which has no relationships among its businesses, follows an unrelated-diversification strategy. Canadian firms Onex and Toromont Industries and

U.S. firms United Technologies, Textron, and Tenneco are examples of firms using this type of corporate-level strategy. Although many U.S. firms using the unrelated-diversification strategy have refocused to become less diversified, a number continue to have high levels of diversification. In Latin America and other emerging economies, such as China, Korea, and India, conglomerates (firms following the unrelated-diversification strategy) continue to dominate the private sector. For instance, in Taiwan, "the largest 100 groups produced one-third of the GNP [gross national product] in the past 20 years." Typically family-controlled, these corporations account for the greatest percentage of private firms in India. Similarly, the largest business groups in Brazil, Mexico, Argentina, and Colombia are family-owned, diversified enterprises. However, questions are being raised as to the viability of these large diversified business groups, especially in developed economies, such as Japan. In Canada, the percentage of unrelated-diversified firms is very low. One study found that only 2 percent of the largest 300 firms in Canada were using this corporate-level strategy.[17]

Reasons for Diversification

There are many reasons why firms use a corporate-level diversification strategy (see Table 7.1). Typically, a diversification strategy is used to increase the firm's value by improving its overall performance. Value is created either through related diversification or through unrelated diversification when the strategy allows a company's business units to increase revenues or reduce costs while implementing their business-level strategies. Another reason for diversification is to gain market power, relative to competitors. Often, this market power is achieved through vertical integration (see the discussion later in the chapter).

| Table 7.1 | Motives, Incentives, and Resources for Diversification |

Motives to Enhance Strategic Competitiveness
- Economies of scope (related diversification)
  Sharing activities
  Transferring core competencies
- Market power (related diversification)
  Blocking competitors through multipoint competition
  Vertical integration
- Financial economies (unrelated diversification)
  Efficient internal capital allocation
  Business restructuring

Incentives and Resources with Neutral Effects on Strategic Competitiveness
- Antitrust regulation
- Tax laws
- Low performance
- Uncertain future cash flows
- Risk reduction for firm
- Tangible resources
- Intangible resources

Managerial Motives (Value Reduction)
- Diversifying managerial employment risk
- Increasing managerial compensation

Other reasons for using a diversification strategy may not increase the firm's value; in fact, diversification could have neutral effects, increasing costs greater than the increase to revenues, or reducing both a firm's revenues and its value while increasing its costs. These reasons for diversification may be chosen to match and thereby neutralize a competitor's market power (e.g., to neutralize another firm's advantage by acquiring a distribution outlet similar to its rival) or to expand a firm's portfolio of businesses to reduce managerial employment risk (e.g., if one of the businesses in a diversified firm fails, the top executive of the firm remains employed). Because diversification can increase a firm's size and thus its managerial compensation, managers have motives to diversify a firm to a level that reduces its value. Diversification rationales that may have a neutral or negative effect on the firm's value are discussed in a later section.

To provide an overview of value-creating diversification strategies, Figure 7.2 illustrates operational relatedness and corporate relatedness. Study of these independent relatedness dimensions illustrates the importance of resources and key competencies. The figure's vertical dimension indicates sharing activities (operational relatedness), while the figure's horizontal dimension depicts corporate capabilities for transferring knowledge (corporate relatedness). The firm with a strong capability in managing operational synergy, especially in sharing assets between its businesses, falls in the upper-left quadrant, which also represents vertical sharing of assets through vertical integration. The lower-right quadrant represents a highly developed corporate capability for transferring a skill across businesses. This capability is located primarily in the corporate office. The use of either operational relatedness or corporate relatedness is based on a knowledge asset that the firm can either share or transfer.[18] Unrelated diversification is also illustrated in Figure 7.2 in the lower-left quadrant. As shown, the unrelated-diversification strategy creates value through financial economies rather than through either operational relatedness or corporate relatedness among business units.

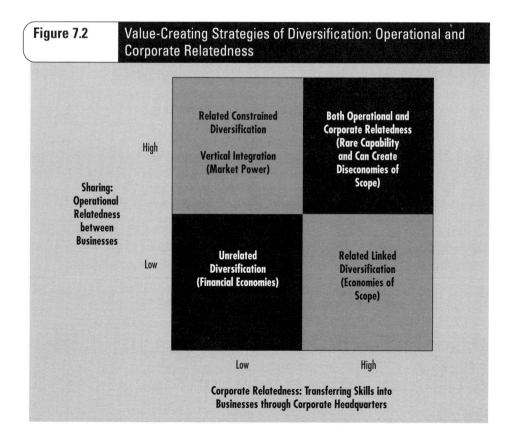

Figure 7.2   Value-Creating Strategies of Diversification: Operational and Corporate Relatedness

Related Diversification

Economies of scope are cost savings that the firm creates by successfully transferring some of its capabilities and competencies that were developed in one of its businesses to another of its businesses.

With the related-diversification corporate-level strategy, the firm builds upon or extends its resources, capabilities, and core competencies to create value. The company using the related-diversification strategy wants to develop and exploit economies of scope among its business units. Available to companies operating in multiple industries or product markets, **economies of scope** are cost savings that the firm creates by successfully transferring some of its capabilities and competencies that were developed in one of its businesses to another of its businesses.[19]

As illustrated in Figure 7.2, firms seek to create value from economies of scope through two basic kinds of operational economies: sharing activities (operational relatedness) and transferring skills or corporate core competencies (corporate relatedness). The difference between sharing activities and transferring competencies is based on how separate resources are jointly used to create economies of scope. Tangible resources, such as plant and equipment or other business-unit physical assets, often must be shared to create economies of scope. Less tangible resources, such as manufacturing know-how, also can be shared. However, when know-how is transferred between separate activities and there is no physical or tangible resource involved, a corporate core competence has been transferred as opposed to operational sharing of activities having taken place.

Operational Relatedness: Sharing Activities

Firms can create operational relatedness by sharing either a primary activity (e.g., raw material delivery systems from its suppliers, manufacturing operations, finished goods delivery systems to its customers, marketing and sales, and customer service) or a support activity (e.g., purchasing practices, human resource management practices, transfer of R&D, ability to take advantage of opportunities) (see Chapter 4's discussion of the value chain). Sharing activities is quite common, especially among related-constrained firms. Procter & Gamble's paper towel business and baby diaper business both use paper products as a primary input to the manufacturing process. The firm's joint paper production plant that produces inputs for the two divisions is an example of a shared activity. In addition, these two businesses are likely to share distribution channels and sales networks, because they both produce consumer products.

Firms expect activity sharing among units to result in increased strategic competitiveness and improved financial returns. For example, PepsiCo purchased Quaker Oats for $12 billion on August 10, 2001. Pepsi has done well in the recent past, but sales growth in carbonated beverages—a staple for PepsiCo—may have reached a point of market saturation and could even decline, because medical studies have linked soft drink consumption to childhood obesity. With the purchase of Quaker Oats, the maker of sports drink Gatorade, Pepsi hopes it has found a reliable growth driver. Gatorade is the market leader in sports drinks, with a 13 percent annual growth rate in sales revenue between 1998 and 2001. Pepsi is integrating Gatorade into its distribution channels, partly to increase Gatorade's market share outside the United States. Thus, Pepsi soft drinks (e.g., Pepsi Cola and Mountain Dew) and Gatorade are sharing the firm's outbound logistics activity. Similarly, the same distribution channels could be used to distribute Quaker Oats's healthy snacks and Frito Lay's salty snacks.[20]

Other issues affect the degree to which activity sharing creates positive outcomes. For example, activity sharing requires the distribution of strategic control over business units. One business unit manager may feel that another unit is receiving a disproportionate share of the gains. Such a perception could create conflicts between division managers.

Activity sharing also is risky because business-unit ties create links between outcomes. For instance, if demand for one business's product is reduced, there may not be sufficient revenues to cover the fixed costs required to operate the facilities being shared. Organizational difficulties such as these can prevent the success of activity sharing.[21]

Although activity sharing across business units isn't risk free, research shows that it can create value. For example, studies that examined acquisitions of firms in the same industry (called horizontal acquisitions), such as the banking industry, have found that sharing resources and activities, and thereby creating economies of scope, contributed to post-acquisition increases in performance and higher returns to shareholders. Additionally, firms that sold off related units, in which resource sharing was a possible source of economies of scope, have been found to produce lower returns than those that sold off businesses unrelated to the firm's core business. Still other research discovered that firms with more related units had lower risk. These results suggest that gaining economies of scope by sharing activities across a firm's businesses may be important in reducing risk and in creating value. Further, more attractive results are obtained through activity sharing when a strong corporate office facilitates it.[22]

Corporate Relatedness: Transferring of Core Competencies

Over tie, the firm's intangible resources, such as its know-how, become the foundation of core competencies. As suggested by Figure 7.2, corporate core competencies are complex sets of resources and capabilities that link different businesses, primarily through managerial and technological knowledge, experience, and expertise.[23]

Related-linked firms often transfer competencies across businesses, thereby creating value in at least two ways. First, the expense of developing a competence has been incurred in one unit. Transferring it to a second business unit eliminates the need for the second unit to allocate resources to develop the competence. Resource intangibility is a second source of value creation through corporate relatedness. Intangible resources are difficult for competitors to understand and imitate. Because of this difficulty, the unit receiving a transferred competence often gains an immediate competitive advantage over its rivals.

Currently, McDonald's is attempting to create value by transferring an intangible resource among businesses it has acquired. Chipotle Mexican Grill (a small Colorado chain of Mexican food restaurants), Donatos Pizza (a pizza restaurant chain), Boston Market (a nationally known U.S. chain specializing in home-style cooking), and Pret a Manger (a London, England chain offering eclectic food, such as smoked salmon sandwiches and sushi) are now owned by McDonald's. Efforts are underway from the corporate level to transfer McDonald's knowledge about all phases of the fast-food industry and restaurant operations to its newly acquired businesses. These actions demonstrate that McDonald's executives believe that the knowledge the company has gained from operating its core business can also create value in its other food venues—venues attracting customers who do not frequent McDonald's units. Interestingly, McDonald's stock price declined in early 2002, when questions surfaced about the firm's ability to maintain its historic growth and performance rates Although all of these acquired businesses are small, McDonald's believes that each can profitably grow by applying its knowledge in their unique settings. Estimates are that the new units could add 2 percent to McDonald's growth rate within a few years. However, McDonald's must be careful that efforts to increase sales in these smaller units do not divert attention away from its core business—selling fries, Big Macs, and milk shakes.[24]

A number of firms have successfully transferred some of their resources and capabilities across businesses. Virgin Industries transferred its marketing skills across travel, cosmetics, music, drinks, and a number of other businesses. Honda has developed and transferred its expertise in small and now larger engines for different types of vehicles, from motorcycles and lawn mowers to its range of automotive products.[25]

One way managers facilitate the transfer of competencies is to move key people into new management positions. However, a business-unit manager of an older division may be reluctant to transfer key people who have accumulated knowledge and experience critical to the business unit's success. Thus, managers with the ability to facilitate the transfer of a core competence may come at a premium, or the key people involved may not want to transfer. Additionally, the top-level managers from the transferring division may not want the competencies transferred to a new division to fulfill the firm's diversification objectives. Research suggests that transferring expertise in manufacturing-based businesses often does not result in improved performance.[26] Businesses in which performance does improve often demonstrate a corporate passion for pursuing skill transfer and appropriate coordination mechanisms for realizing economies of scope.

Market Power

Related diversification can also be used to gain market power. Market power exists when a firm is able to sell its products above the existing competitive level or to reduce the costs of its primary and support activities below the competitive level, or both.[27]

One approach to gaining market power through diversification is *multipoint competition*. Multipoint competition exists when two or more diversified firms simultaneously compete in the same product areas or geographic markets. As mentioned earlier, the actions taken by Hewlett-Packard (HP) in its merger with Compaq Computer Corporation demonstrate multipoint competition. This merger allows the combined firm to compete with other larger companies, such as IBM and Sun Microsystems. For example, HP and Compaq are now coordinating their efforts in PCs, servers, and services. The combined revenues of the two companies almost equal those of IBM. The merged firm will most likely compete directly with IBM in the server market and will continue to increase its services division as well.[28]

The preceding example illustrates the potential dynamics of multipoint competition. As a strategic action (see Chapter 6), HP and Compaq's decision to merge is partly a competitive response to IBM's success in servers and services.[29] Counterattacks are not common in multipoint competition because the threat of a counterattack may prevent strategic actions from being taken, or, more likely, firms may retract their strategic actions when faced with the threat of counterattack. Using a matching strategy, where the responding firm takes the same strategic action as the attacker, is a prominent form of response because it signals a commitment to defend the status quo without escalating rivalry.[30] This can be seen in the responses of media firms to the AOL Time Warner merger, as illustrated in the next Strategic Focus box, "Multipoint Competition among Media firms."

Some firms choose to create value by using vertical integration to gain market power (see Figure 7.2, on page 211). **Vertical integration** exists when a company produces its own inputs (backward integration) or owns its own source of distribution of outputs (forward integration). In some instances, firms partially integrate their operations, producing and selling their products by using both company units and outside sources.

Vertical integration is commonly used in the firm's core business to gain market power over rivals. Market power is gained as the firm develops the ability to save on its operations, avoid market costs, improve product quality, and, possibly, protect its technology from imitation by rivals. Market power also is created when firms have strong ties between their assets for which no market prices exist. Establishing a market price would result in high search and transaction costs, so firms seek to vertically integrate rather than remaining separate businesses.[31]

Smithfield Foods, located in Smithfield, Virginia, is a vertically integrated company with hog processing as its core business. Smithfield has vertically integrated backward by raising the hogs that it later processes in its plants. Most packaging plants operate profitably when the price of meat is low and suffer with high meat prices. In contrast, Smithfield can better control its costs because it owns the facilities that provide the raw materials required for its core processing operations. This control often results in Smithfield having market power over its competitors because it typically produces

Vertical integration exists when a company produces its own inputs (backward integration) or owns its own source of distribution of outputs (forward integration).

Multipoint Competition among Media Firms:
Content Is King at Disney

Following the announcement of the AOL Time Warner merger, other content-oriented media firms felt pressure to pursue distribution businesses. The merger provided a content company (AOL) with several distribution outlets (Time Warner). Time Warner already had distribution assets through its cable TV operations, and the merger with AOL added the largest Internet service provider (ISP). Vivendi Universal (discussed in the next Strategic Focus box), created through the merger of French utility conglomerate Vivendi with Seagram's, which owned Universal Studios and Universal Music, is seeking to match the content and distribution strategy developed by AOL Time Warner.

According to Walt Disney corporate website (http://disney.go.com/corporate), the firm's key objective is to be the world's premier family entertainment company through the ongoing development of its powerful brand and character franchises. Shown on the corporate website are performers Lebo M and Paulette Ivory from a production of the musical play, The Lion King, which builds on the company's movie characters by the same name. Walt Disney once remarked about his company, "I only hope we don't lose sight of one thing—that it was all started by a mouse."

Walt Disney Company, however, has resisted the pressure to imitate these competitive actions. The firm has been a strong force in the business of entertaining consumers for decades. True to its beginnings, Disney has grown to be one of the largest moviemakers in the industry— consistently producing hit movies. As the company grew and the media industry consolidated, it brought ABC and its affiliates under the Disney corporate umbrella, becoming a major competitor in the television network business. The diversified entertainment behemoth also built theme parks all over the world. According to Disney CEO Michael Eisner, all of the firm's business segments focus on one main product offering: content. In his view, Disney provides content—an actual, intellectual product made for consumption by the consumer.

The AOL Time Warner merger resulted in a battle in which AOL Time Warner cut Disney-owned ABC off from 3.5 million subscribers for 39 hours because of disputes between the two companies. There is much pressure, both from outside investors and inside executives, to expand Disney's distribution options. Some content producers have approached the company about bidding for AT&T Broadband, but Disney has resisted. Disney hopes that its content offerings will be so strong that consumers would complain if the Disney-owned channels were taken off the air, as was the case during the disagreement with AOL Time Warner.

To support "content is king" as the foundation for its competition position, Disney completed a transaction with News Corporation and Saban Entertainment Inc. to buy Fox Family Worldwide. This acquisition added more than 100 million subscribers to Disney's already vast cable operations, which include the Disney Channel, Toon Disney, SoapNet, and ESPN. Fox Family Worldwide also provides Disney with a rich library of content, including 6500 episodes of animated shows such as *Digimon*, *Spider-Man*, and *Mighty Morphin Power Rangers*. The company plans to integrate the Fox Family Channel with ABC's operations to air reruns of shows originally aired on the ABC Network or other Disney-owned channels. This "repurposing" will allow viewers to see their favourite shows outside of the normal viewing time. It will also allow Disney to make extra revenue from the shows, and the firm should be able to spread the cost across several outlets.

Disney sees itself as a creator of entertainment content rather than a distribution channel for entertainment content. Consistent with its vision, Disney continues to diversify in ways that add content to its substantial library, such as its acquisition of Fox Family Worldwide, and resists the temptation to add distribution capabilities, such as cable businesses like AT&T Broadband. Because of the multipoint competition for advertising, Disney may have to respond to the pressures for distribution assets. However, Disney encountered difficulties in its past attempts to do so, such as the go.com Internet portal. Thus, Disney feels pressure to move beyond its emphasis

(continued)

on content into new areas of competence to meet the competition, which is developing distribution channel capabilities.

SOURCES: B. Carter, 2001, Disney discusses strategy behind buying Fox Family, *New York Times*, http://www.nytimes.com, July 24; N. Deogun, S. Beatty, B. Orwall, & J. Lippman, 2001, Disney plans to acquire Fox Family for $3 billion and debt assumption, *Wall Street Journal Interactive*, http://www.interactive.wsj.com, July 23; G. Fabrikant & A. R. Sorkin, 2001, Disney is said to be close to acquiring Fox Family, *New York Times*, http://www.nytimes.com, July 23; J. Flint & B. Orwall, 2001, "ABC Family" cable channel will recycle network fare, *Wall Street Journal Interactive*, http://www.interactive.wsj.com, July 24; R. Grover, 2001, Fox Family enters the Mouse House, *Business Week Online*, http://www.businessweek.com, July 24; J. Guyon, 2001, Can Messier make cash flow like water? *Fortune*, September 3, 148–50; R. Linnett, 2001, Leap frog, *Advertising Age*, July 30, S12; S. Schiesel, 2001, For Disney's Eisner, the business is content, not conduits, *New York Times*, http://www.nytimes.com, July 2.

products at below the average industry production cost. Recent acquisitions of 10 U.S. and a few international meat-packaging companies are intended to support the firm's use of vertical integration to yield competitively attractive options to consumers. One of the international meat-packaging companies it purchased was Schneider Foods, from Kitchener, Ontario. Smithfield Foods had owned Schneider Foods for five years when it sold it to Maple Leaf Foods from Toronto, Ontario, with the deal closing on April 5, 2004. The acquisition gave Maple Leaf Foods incredible market power in the Canadian market. In addition, it was considered that Maple Leaf and Schneiders together would be a world-class, globally competitive food company. Interestingly, Maple Leaf had tried to buy Schneider's Foods five years previously, however, at that time, Smithfield Foods had been successful in its purchase bid.[32]

There are also limits to vertical integration. For example, an outside supplier may produce the product at a lower cost. As a result, internal transactions from vertical integration may be expensive and reduce profitability, relative to competitors. Also, bureaucratic costs may occur with vertical integration. Additionally, because vertical integration can require substantial investments in specific technologies, it may reduce the firm's flexibility, especially when technology changes quickly. Finally, changes in demand create problems in terms of capacity balance and coordination. If one division is building a part for another internal division, but the achievement of economies of scale requires the first division to manufacture quantities that are beyond the capacity of the internal buyer to absorb, it would be necessary to sell the parts outside the firm as well as to the internal division. Thus, although vertical integration can create value, especially through market power over competitors, it is not without risks and costs.

Many manufacturing firms no longer pursue vertical integration. In fact, deintegration is the focus of most manufacturing firms, such as Intel and Dell, and even among large automobile companies, such as Ford and General Motors, as they develop independent supplier networks. Such firms often manage their customers' entire product lines, and offer services ranging from inventory management to delivery and after-sales service. Performing business through e-commerce also allows vertical integration to be changed into virtual integration. Thus, closer relationships are possible with suppliers and customers through virtual integration (or electronic means of integration), allowing firms to reduce the costs of processing transactions while improving their supply-chain management skills and tightening the control of their inventories. "The longer the supply chain, the bigger the potential gains from B2B e-commerce, since it allows firms to eliminate the many layers of middlemen that hamper economic efficiency."[33]

Simultaneous Operational Relatedness and Corporate Relatedness

As Figure 7.2 suggests, some firms simultaneously seek operational and corporate forms of economies of scope. Because simultaneously managing two sources of knowledge is

Vivendi: From Water Treatment to Media Might

With a foundation in the water treatment business, the French firm Vivendi has diversified into various media businesses. This movement into media became more pronounced with Vivendi's announcement of its merger with Seagram's Universal Studios and Universal Music Group. At the time of this transaction, Vivendi CEO, Jean-Marie Messier described his vision of the future. The vision is one in which consumers can use either their cellular telephones or handheld computers to purchase music through an online music site and view movies through broadband subscription services. To realize this vision, Vivendi Universal acquired MP3.com, an online music-sharing website. Messier asserted that it was "a big step forward for Vivendi Universal's priority to develop an aggressive, legitimate, and attractive offering of our content to consumers." To overcome the powerful middlemen, such as Blockbuster video-rental chain and HBO cable network, and to reach his vision, Vivendi Universal has formed a joint venture with other studios (including Sony Pictures, AOL Time Warner's Warner Brothers, and Viacom's Metro-Goldwyn-Mayer) to create a digital video-on-demand platform. This service will allow direct broadband delivery of digital video to consumers.

When Vivendi Universal purchased Houghton Mifflin, a U.S. educational publisher, Messier asserted that it was "another step forward for Vivendi Universal to achieve world leadership in key content segments." He also said that leveraging the acquired content and technologies assets of Houghton Mifflin would allow Vivendi Universal "to capitalize on the growth of the education sector" and to match the publishing and content assets of AOL Time Warner.

In June 2001, Vivendi Universal further extended its reach by acquiring a larger stake in Elektrim Telekomunikacja, the telecommunication assets of Polish conglomerate Elektrim, which gave it control over that company, and, in effect, control over Polska Telefonia Cyfrowa (PTC), Eastern Europe's largest mobile-telephone operator. Vivendi already is one of the largest providers of mobile-phone service in Europe. Earlier, Vivendi joined forces with British telecommunications leader Vodafone to create Vizzavi, which was launched in France, in June 2000. "Vizzavi would be Messier's distribution arm in Europe, beaming content over the wireless web to Vivendi's 8 million and Vodafone's 48 million mobile-phone customers." This additional acquisition gave Vivendi Universal a strong foothold into the mobile-phone market in Eastern Europe, which fits nicely with its vision of the future.

The acquisition of MP3.com brought a number of assets to Vivendi Universal. First, even though Vivendi had fought with the online music distributors, MP3.com gave it a well-known online brand. More importantly for Vivendi, however, is the technology and know-how that the acquisition provides. Vivendi Universal and Sony Music have announced that they will also enter into the online music distribution business through a music service named Pressplay. The purchase of MP3.com brings into the company the demonstrated technology and experience that will be essential to Pressplay's success.

Vivendi Universal's acquisitions have extended the company's content and distribution network. The merger with Universal and the acquisition of Houghton Mifflin provided the company with well-known brands to produce content. By purchasing an online music distributor, Vivendi expanded its ability to put its content in front of the consumer for purchase. The procurement of a controlling stake in PTC gives the company a high performing cellular phone company and is a step into the future where people "see a trailer for a film on [their] ... mobile phone." By diversifying into different content and distribution areas, Vivendi Universal is building toward future in which it hopes to be a one-stop media outlet. In content businesses, Vivendi shares activities to produce movies, movie themes in its theme parks, and movie soundtracks. Additionally, it has the knowledge, through its phone acquisitions and alliances and the MP3.com acquisition, to transfer this expertise to improve distribution. However, because Vivendi's distribution is more dependent on mobile online technology than other large media firms, the success of Vivendi's approach remains an open question. Furthermore, it is hard to tell how the acquisitions are doing, relative to

(continued)

the basic water treatment assets, given that the income streams from these assets are hard to distinguish in the accounting reports. The increased emphasis on transparency regarding how a firm is generating its revenue and profits suggests that this could become an important issue.

SOURCES: C. Matlack, 2002, Memo to Jean-Marie Messier, *Business Week*, March 4, 56; Associated Press, 2001, MP3.com adds 1 millionth song; launches new subscriber service, *Detroit News Online*, http://www.detnews.com, June 14; D. Leonard, 2001, Mr. Messier is ready for his close-up, *Fortune*, September 3, 136–48; Dow Jones Newswire, 2001, France's Vivendi appears to win battle for mobile operator PTC in Poland, *Wall Street Journal Interactive*, http://www.wsj.com, June 28; B. Orwall, 2001, Five Hollywood studios enter venture to offer feature films of the Internet, *Wall Street Journal Interactive*, http://www.wsj.com, August 17; M. Richtel, 2001, Vivendi deal for MP3.com highlights trend, *New York Times*, http://www.nytimes.com, May 22; S. Schiesel, 2001, Vivendi will acquire Houghton Mifflin for $1.7 billion, *New York Times*, http://www.nytimes.com, June 2; A. R. Sorkin, 2001, Vivendi in deal to acquire MP3.com, *New York Times*, http://www.nytimes.com, May 21; A. Weintraub, R. Grover, & C. Matlack, 2001, Vivendi faces the music on the Web, *Business Week*, June 4, 43.

very difficult, such efforts often fail, creating diseconomies of scope.[34] Although this strategy is difficult to implement, if the firm is successful, it could create value that is hard for competitors to imitate.

Vivendi is trying to achieve both operational relatedness and corporate relatedness in the media business. The firm's strategy, as illustrated in the above Strategic Focus box, "Vivendi," may be difficult to achieve because its distribution of content is focused on mobile web technology.

As illustrated in the Strategic Focus box, a critical aspect of achieving both operational relatedness and corporate relatedness is how well a firm manages the sharing of activities *and* the transferring of knowledge. Disney, another media firm, has been successful in using both operational relatedness and corporate relatedness, although it has not developed distribution capabilities.

Disney's strategy is especially successful compared to Sony, when measured by revenues generated from successful movies. By using operational relatedness and corporate relatedness, Disney made $3 billion on the 150 products that were marketed with its movie, *The Lion King*. Sony's *Men in Black* was a super hit at the box office and earned $600 million, but box-office and video revenues were practically the entire success story. Disney was able to accomplish its great success by sharing activities regarding the *Lion King* theme within its movie and theme parks, music, and retail products divisions, while at the same time transferring knowledge into these same divisions, creating a music CD, *Rhythm of the Pride Lands*, and producing a video, *Simba's Pride*. In addition, there were *Lion King* themes at Disney resorts and Animal Kingdom parks. However, as is the case with Vivendi Universal, it is difficult for analysts from outside the firm to fully assess the value-creating potential of the firm pursuing both operational relatedness and corporate relatedness. As such, Disney's and Vivendi Universal's assets have been discounted somewhat because "the biggest lingering questions is whether multiple revenue streams will outpace multiple-platform overhead."[35]

Unrelated Diversification

Firms do not seek either operational relatedness or corporate relatedness when using the unrelated-diversification corporate-level strategy. An unrelated-diversification strategy (see Figure 7.2, on page 211) can create value through two types of financial economies. **Financial economies** are cost savings realized through improved allocations of financial resources based on investments inside or outside the firm.[36]

The first type of financial economy results from efficient internal capital allocations. This approach seeks to reduce risk among the firm's business units—for example, through the development of a portfolio of businesses with different risk profiles. The approach thereby reduces business risk for the total corporation. The second type of

Financial economies are cost savings realized through improved allocations of financial resources based on investments inside or outside the firm.

financial economy is concerned with purchasing other corporations and restructuring their assets. This approach finds the diversified firm buying other companies, restructuring their assets in ways that allows the purchased company to operate more profitably, and then selling the company for a profit in the external market. Toronto-based Onex is an example of a Canadian firm that achieves financial economies through risk reduction and the buying and selling of other firms to restructure their assets.

Efficient Internal Capital Market Allocation

In a market economy, capital markets are thought to efficiently allocate capital. Efficiency results from investors' purchasing of firm equity shares (ownership) that have high future cash-flow values. Capital is also allocated through debt as shareholders and debtholders try to improve the value of their investments by taking stakes in businesses with high-growth prospects.

In large diversified firms, the corporate office distributes capital to business divisions to create value for the overall company. Such an approach may provide gains from internal capital market allocation, relative to the external capital market.[37] While managing the firm's portfolio of businesses, the corporate office may gain access to detailed and accurate information regarding those businesses' actual and prospective performance.

The corporate office needs to convey its ability to create value in this manner to the market. One way firms have been conveying this ability is through tracking stocks, as General Motors has done for its Hughes Aerospace division.[38] GM created a new stock listing for the Hughes assets that conveyed better information to the market about this additional asset. This approach allows more scrutiny by the market and thus more transparency of increasingly complex and diversified internal operations.

Compared with corporate office personnel, investors have relatively limited access to internal information and can only estimate divisional performance and future business prospects. Although businesses seeking capital must provide information to potential suppliers (e.g., banks and/or insurance companies), firms with internal capital markets may have at least two informational advantages. First, the information provided to capital markets through annual reports and other sources might not include negative information, instead emphasizing positive prospects and outcomes. External sources of capital have limited ability to understand the dynamics inside large organizations. Even external shareholders, who have access to information, have no guarantee of full and complete disclosure.[39] Second, although a firm must disseminate information, that information also becomes simultaneously available to the firm's current and potential competitors. With insights gained by studying such information, competitors might attempt to duplicate a firm's competitive advantage. Thus, an ability to efficiently allocate capital through an internal market may help the firm protect its competitive advantages.

If intervention from outside the firm is required to make corrections to capital allocations, only significant changes are possible, such as forcing the firm into bankruptcy or changing the top management team. Alternatively, in an internal capital market, the corporate office can fine-tune its corrections, such as choosing to adjust managerial incentives or suggesting strategic changes in a division. Thus, capital can be allocated according to more specific criteria than is possible with external market allocations. Because it has less accurate information, the external capital market may fail to allocate resources adequately to high-potential investments, compared with corporate office investments. The corporate office of a diversified company can more effectively perform tasks such as the disciplining of underperforming management teams through resource allocations.[40]

Research suggests, however, that in efficient capital markets, the unrelated-diversification strategy may be discounted. "For years, stock markets have applied a conglomerate discount: they value diversified manufacturing conglomerates at 20 percent less, on average, than the value of the sum of their parts. The discount still applies, in good economic times and bad. Extraordinary manufacturers (e.g., GE) can defy it for a while, but more ordinary ones (e.g., Philips and Siemens) cannot."[41]

Some firms still use the unrelated-diversification strategy. These large diversified business groups are found in many European countries and throughout emerging economies. For example, research indicates that the conglomerate or unrelated-diversification strategy has not disappeared in Europe, where the number of firms using it has actually increased.[42] Although many conglomerates, such as ITT and Hansen Trust, have refocused, other unrelated-diversified firms have replaced them.

The Achilles heel of the unrelated-diversification strategy is that conglomerates in developed economies have a fairly short life cycle because financial economies are more easily duplicated than are the gains derived from operational relatedness and corporate relatedness. This is less of a problem in emerging economies, where the absence of a soft infrastructure (including effective financial intermediaries, sound regulations, and contract laws) supports and encourages use of the unrelated-diversification strategy. In fact, in emerging economies, such as those in India and Chile, diversification increases performance of firms affiliated with large diversified business groups.[43]

Restructuring

Financial economies can also be created when firms learn how to create value by buying and selling other companies' assets in the external market.[44] As in the real estate business, buying assets at low prices, restructuring them, and selling them at a price exceeding their cost generates a positive return on the firm's invested capital.

Selling underperforming divisions and placing the rest under rigorous financial controls increases a unit's value. Rigorous controls require that divisions follow strict budgets and account regularly for cash inflows and outflows to corporate headquarters. A firm creating financial economies, at least partly through rigorous controls, may have to use hostile takeovers or tender offers, because target firm managers often do not find this environment attractive and are less willing to be acquired. Hostile takeovers have the potential to increase the resistance of the target firm's top-level managers.[45] In these cases, corporate-level managers often are discharged, while division managers are retained, depending on how important each is to future operational success.

Creating financial economies by acquiring and restructuring other companies' assets requires an understanding of significant trade-offs. Success usually calls for a focus on mature, low-technology businesses because of the uncertainty of demand for high-technology products. Otherwise, resource allocation decisions become too complex, creating information-processing overload on the small corporate staffs of unrelated-diversified firms. Service businesses with a client orientation are also difficult to buy and sell in this way, because of their client-based sales orientation.[46]

Sales staffs of service businesses are more mobile than those of manufacturing-oriented businesses and may seek jobs with a competitor, taking clients with them. This is especially so in professional service businesses, such as accounting, law, advertising, consulting, and investment banking. Sears, Roebuck & Co. discovered this problem after its 1981 diversification into financial services by acquiring Coldwell Banker and Dean Witter Reynolds, Inc. The anticipated synergies in financial services did not materialize, and Sears' retail performance deteriorated. In 1992, Sears announced the divestiture of financial services and a refocusing on retail operations.[47]

Diversification: Incentives and Resources

The economic reasons given in the last section summarize conditions under which diversification strategies can increase a firm's value. Diversification, however, is also often undertaken with the expectation that it will prevent reductions in firm value. Thus, there are reasons to diversify that are value-neutral. In fact, some research suggests that all diversification leads to trade-offs and some suboptimization.[48] Nonetheless, as we explain next, several incentives may lead a firm to pursue further diversification.

Incentives to Diversify

Incentives to diversify come from both the external environment and a firm's internal environment. The term, incentive, implies that managers have choices. External incentives include antitrust regulations and tax laws. Internal incentives include low performance, uncertain future cash flows, and an overall reduction of risk for the firm. Several of the incentives are illustrated in the next Strategic Focus box, "Diversification Incentives Don't Always Lead to Success" on page 222, where we highlight actions being taken at Boeing, PepsiCo, Procter & Gamble (P&G), and Canadian firm Bombardier.

As the discussion in the Strategic Focus box indicates, there are incentives for the firm to use a diversification strategy. Diversification strategies taken in light of various incentives (e.g., PepsiCo's need to diversify its beverage line) sometimes increase the firm's ability to create value. Currently, it seems that Boeing and PepsiCo's diversification strategies are helping those firms create value. However, when a particular diversification strategy isn't creating the expected amount of value, which was determined to be the case by P&G upper-level decision makers and the new Bombardier CEO, Paul Tellier, firms must take corrective action to either reduce or increase the degree to which it is diversified.

Antitrust Regulation and Tax Laws

Government antitrust policies and tax laws sometimes provide incentives for firms to diversify. The tax effects of diversification stem not only from individual tax rates, but also from corporate tax changes. Some companies (especially mature ones) generate more cash from their operations than they can reinvest profitably. Some argue that *free cash flows* (liquid financial assets for which investments in current businesses are no longer economically viable) should be redistributed to shareholders as dividends.[49] However, when dividends are taxed more heavily than ordinary personal income, shareholders prefer that firms use free cash flows to buy and build companies in high-performance industries. If the firm's stock value appreciates over the long term, shareholders might receive a better return on those funds than if they had been redistributed as dividends, because, under capital-gains rules, they would be taxed more lightly when they sell their stock, than they would be if they had received dividends.

However, when the top individual, ordinary income-tax rate is reduced and the special capital-gains tax is also changed to treat capital gains as ordinary income, an incentive is created for shareholders to stop encouraging firms to retain funds for purposes of diversification. Tax law changes have also been known to influence an increase in divestitures of unrelated business units. This happened in the U.S. after 1984, when there were major changes to the U.S. tax laws. Thus, while individual tax rates for capital gains and dividends created a shareholder incentive to increase diversification before 1986, they encouraged less diversification after 1986, unless it was funded by tax-deductible debt. The elimination of personal interest deductions, as well as the lower attractiveness of retained earnings to shareholders, might prompt the use of more leverage by firms, for which interest expense is tax deductible.

Corporate tax laws also affect diversification. Acquisitions typically increase a firm's depreciable asset allowances. Increased depreciation (a non–cash-flow expense) produces lower taxable income, thereby providing an additional incentive for acquisitions.

A number of industries have experienced increased merger activity, due to industry-specific deregulation activity, including banking, telecommunications, oil and gas, and electric utilities, among others. For example, the electric utilities industry is deregulating throughout the developed world.[50] German utility companies, such as RWE, are finding

Diversification Incentives Don't Always Lead to Success

Boeing was in trouble in the late 1990s, after it acquired McDonnell Douglas. Besides performance problems associated with integrating the acquisition, Boeing's dominant segment—its civil-jet business—had slowed; the commercial jet market was only expanding by 5 percent per year. In response to these issues, Boeing decided to diversify.

In 2001, Boeing felt the effects of the airline industry's performance declines. Among other actions taken, the firm made the decision to lay off at least 30,000 employees before the end of 2002. However, because of the earlier performance problems and continuing uncertainty regarding the civilian airline industry, Boeing had already diversified over several years. Accordingly, the firm expects to benefit through its strong position as a space program supplier and particularly through its military and communications supply units. Because Boeing is a large producer of AWACS and C-17s for the U.S. Air Force, Boeing could benefit from the United States decision to enhance its air power after the September 11, 2001 terrorist attacks. Boeing expects that, in 2002, military sales could increase 10 percent and account for as much as 75 percent of sales increases across its various business units. The company announced that no defence-related workers would be affected by the planned layoffs.

Instead of focusing only on building jets and rockets, Boeing had also decided to move into services. In 2001, the firm won a $4 billion order from the U.S. Air Force to upgrade avionics on existing C-130 aircraft, which rival Lockheed Martin had built. Boeing recently entered the aircraft maintenance and services market and believes that it has significant growth potential in these two areas.

Boeing also released its plans for building air-traffic management systems, which it hopes to develop with the Federal Aviation Administration (FAA) when the agency overhauls the air-traffic control system. If the FAA partners with Boeing, the company believes that the market may be worth $70 billion annually. Boeing is also delving into the broadband communications market, hoping to provide airline passengers with live television and high-speed data links. In addition, the company recently opened an office in Europe to facilitate expansion of its financing company. Because of the terrorist crisis, many of the airlines have asked Boeing to refinance its current accounts, which will increase the returns from the firm's financing unit.

Some firms diversify, as did Boeing, because of unexpected poor performance. Others diversify because they expect future growth to slow. As mentioned earlier, PepsiCo, maker of Pepsi, acquired Quaker Oats in order to gain access to the increased growth associated with Gatorade in the sports drink segment. Thus, there are a number of incentives for firms to diversify beyond their successful business areas. However, not all of these efforts create value.

Procter & Gamble (P&G) has been divesting its non-core brands. In recent years, P&G diversified in an effort to boost sales, because many of its products, such as Pantene shampoo, compete in mature markets. Some of the products resulting from the diversification, such as its Olay line of cosmetics and artificial cooking fat Olestra, have failed. New CEO A.G. Lafley has decided to sell off the poorly performing brands and refocus on P&G's core, higher profit businesses by backing the company out of the food product business and other failed undertakings.

Bombardier made many acquisitions in the 1970s, 1980s, and 1990s. The acquisitions were intended to strengthen Bombardier's core business as well as to grow the company through diversification. However, in 2003, in spite of significant revenues of $21.3 billion, stock prices were declining, as many analysts reported the stock as "underperforming" or bearish. CEO Paul Tellier, recruited in December 2002, commenced several initiatives to restore Bombardier's margins and profitability. Bombardier changed its debt to capital ratio from 60 percent to 50 percent. Tellier then targeted excess capacity and implemented cost-cutting measures, including laying off thousands of employees and outsourcing equipment. A year later, in 2004, Tellier reflected, "Last April, in the first year, I announced an aggressive action plan that was designed to restructure the balance sheet, restore shareholder confidence, and get Bombardier back to profitability. We have

(continued)

made good on that plan and have met all of our commitments." Tellier moved next to restructure the business. Early in 2004, Bombardier announced a new management team and organizational structure to improve accountability and increase focus on project management at Bombardier Transportation. In addition, it disbanded its Industrial Division. In March 2004, Bombardier shares fell by approximately 12 percent as Tellier instituted additional measures under a three year $777 million restructuring program. The program includes closure of several production sites, global workforce reduction of approximately 6,600 positions, productivity improvement initiatives at five targeted sites, and procurement process improvements.

SOURCES: S. Holmes & S. Crock, 2002, The fortunes—and misfortunes—of war, *Business Week*, January 14, 90–91; Economist, 2001, Hard man Harry, *Economist*, June 9, 68; S. Jaffe, 2001, Do Pepsi and Gatorade mix? *Business Week Online*, http://www.businessweek.com, August 14; J. Lunsford & A. Pasztor, 2001, Boeing Co.'s course in terror's wake seen as a wider U.S. test, *Wall Street Journal*, September 20, A1, A8; E. Nelson, 2001, P&G expects to restore growth: Will pull the plug on failed projects, *Wall Street Journal Interactive*, http://www.wsj.com, June 18; Bombardier Inc., 2004, *Bombardier Inc. website*, www.bombardier.ca, accessed May 12, 2004; R. Bloom, 2004, Bombardier shares fall as investors digest revamp, *Globe and Mail*, Report on Business, March 19; S. Silcoff, 2004, Bombardier stock soars on 12 regional jet orders (Analysts say time to sell), *Financial Post*, February 11; D. DeCloet, 2004, Tellier may need to work miracles to boost margins, *Globe and Mail*, Report on Business, March 18.

deregulation challenging, in that it has produced lower electricity prices and limited profit growth. RWE, which easily raised $17 billion for acquisitions, hoped to diversify into utility markets in the United States and Europe to buffer deregulation's effects. CFO Klaus Sturany explained that the company was looking to purchase firms in the company's "core businesses: electricity, gas, water, and waste management ... [that] fit strategically."[51] Important to RWE is whether the acquisition is in a growth market, whether the quality of management is good, and whether existing profitability is high. RWE plans to find the most growth with water companies, but is also considering unregulated companies in the electricity generation sector. Such moves will require significant learning because most utilities have traditionally operated in slow-cycle markets.[52]

Deregulation moves in the financial services industry have also provided Canadian banks with opportunities. For example, Royal Bank has taken advantage of opportunities to improve its brokerage, trust, and insurance businesses. In addition to Dominion Securities (which Royal acquired control of in 1988), the Royal Financial Group expanded its brokerage business through its acquisition of investment dealer Richardson Greenshields in 1997. Royal purchased Royal Trust in 1993, and trust services were expanded in 1996 and 1997, by the acquisition of the institutional and pension custody businesses of TD Bank, Montreal Trust, and Scotiabank. Purchases of insurance businesses, such as Westbury Canadian Life (in 1996), the Canadian operations of Mutual of Omaha (in 1998), and Prudential's Canadian Life (in 2000), allowed a more solid foundation for RBC Insurance as well.[53]

Low Performance

Some research shows that low returns are related to greater levels of diversification. If "high performance eliminates the need for greater diversification," as in the case of Wm. Wrigley Jr. Co., then low performance may provide an incentive for diversification. Firms plagued by poor performance often take higher risks. Poor performance may lead to increased diversification as it did with Boeing (see the Strategic Focus box "Diversification Incentives Don't Always Lead to Success"), especially if resources exist to pursue a diversification strategy. Continued poor returns following additional diversification, however, may slow its pace and even lead to divestitures, as seems to be happening to Bombardier, as described in the Strategic Focus box. Thus, an overall

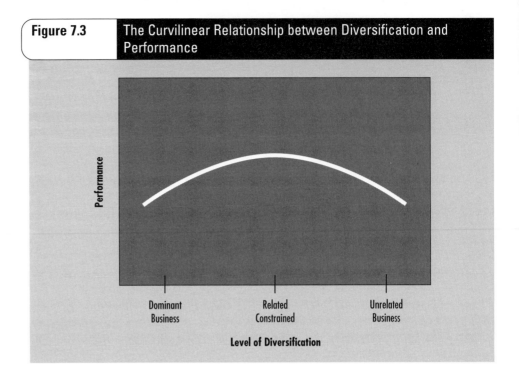

Figure 7.3 The Curvilinear Relationship between Diversification and Performance

Performance

Dominant Business

Related Constrained

Unrelated Business

Level of Diversification

curvilinear relationship, as illustrated in Figure 7.3, may exist between diversification and performance.[54]

As mentioned in the Strategic Focus box on page 222, Procter & Gamble may have diversified beyond its capabilities to manage the diversification. The company has had strong historical success in its consumer soaps, including Tide and Ivory, and in toothpaste (i.e., Crest). However, its Olay cosmetics and artificial cooking fat, Olestra, have not been successful, resulting in the firm's recent decision to refocus on its core brands. P&G's refocusing may suggest that its diversification level was producing poor returns (see diversification-performance curve in Figure 7.3).

Uncertain Future Cash Flows

As a firm's product line matures or is threatened, diversification may be taken as an important defensive strategy. Small firms and companies in mature or maturing industries sometimes find it necessary to diversify for long-term survival.[55] Certainly, this was one of the dominant reasons for diversification among railroad firms during the 1960s and 1970s. Railroads diversified primarily because the trucking industry was perceived to have significant negative effects for rail transportation and thus created demand uncertainty. Uncertainty, however, can be derived from supply, demand, and distribution sources. As explained earlier, PepsiCo acquired Quaker Oats to fortify its growth with Gatorade and healthy snacks. These products are projected to experience greater growth rates than Pepsi's soft drinks.

Firm Risk Reduction

Synergy exists when the value created by business units working together exceeds the value those same units create working independently.

Diversified firms pursuing economies of scope often have investments that are too inflexible to realize synergy among business units. As a result, a number of problems may arise. **Synergy** exists when the value created by business units working together exceeds the value those same units create working independently. However, as a firm increases its relatedness between business units, it also increases its risk of corporate failure, because synergy produces joint interdependence between business units, and the firm's flexibility to respond is constrained. This threat may force two basic decisions.

First, the firm may reduce its level of technological change by operating in more certain environments. This behaviour may make the firm risk averse and thus uninterested in pursuing new product lines that have potential, but are not proven. Alternatively, the firm may constrain its level of activity sharing and forego synergy's benefits. Either or both decisions may lead to further diversification. The former would lead to related diversification into industries in which more certainty exists. The latter may produce additional, but unrelated, diversification. Research suggests that a firm using a related-diversification strategy is more careful in bidding for new businesses, whereas a firm pursuing an unrelated-diversification strategy may be more likely to overprice its bid, because an unrelated bidder may not have full information about the acquired firm.[56]

Resources and Diversification

Although a firm may have incentives to diversify, it must also possess the resources required to create value through diversification. As mentioned earlier, tangible, intangible, and financial resources all facilitate diversification. Resources vary in their utility for value creation, however, because of differences in rarity and mobility—that is, some resources are easier for competitors to duplicate because they are not rare, valuable, costly to imitate, and nonsubstitutable (see Chapter 4). For instance, free cash flows are a financial resource that may be used to diversify the firm. Because financial resources are more flexible and common, they are less likely to create value, compared with other types of resources, and less likely to be a source of competitive advantage.[57]

However, as a financial resource, cash can be used to invest in other resources that can lead to more valuable and less imitable advantages. For example, Microsoft had $30 billion in cash reserves in 2001, and this reserve was growing by $1 billion every month. With this much cash in reserve (more, by far, than any other company), Microsoft was able to invest heavily in R&D, to gradually build a market presence with products such as Xbox, Microsoft's video game machine, and to make diversifying acquisitions of other companies and new business ventures. This level of cash creates significant flexibility, allowing Microsoft to invest in R&D so that it has the support required to possibly become a competitive advantage. As this example suggests, excess cash can be the conduit a firm needs to create more sustainable advantages.[58]

Tangible resources usually include the plant and equipment necessary to produce a product and tend to be less flexible assets. Any excess capacity often can be used only for closely related products, especially those requiring highly similar manufacturing technologies. Excess capacity of other tangible resources, such as a sales force, can be used to diversify more easily. Again, excess capacity in a sales force is more effective with related diversification, because it may be utilized to sell similar products. The sales force would be more knowledgeable about related-product characteristics, customers, and distribution channels. Tangible resources may create resource interrelationships in production, marketing, procurement, and technology, defined earlier as activity sharing. Intangible resources are more flexible than tangible physical assets in facilitating diversification. Although the sharing of tangible resources may induce diversification, intangible resources, such as tacit knowledge, could encourage even more diversification.[59]

Managerial Motives to Diversify

Managerial motives for diversification may exist independent of incentives and resources. Examples of managerial motives include managerial risk reduction and a desire for increased compensation. For instance, diversification may reduce top-level managers' employment risks (the risk of job loss or income reduction). That is, corporate executives may diversify a firm in order to diversify their own employment risk, as long as profitability does not suffer excessively.[60]

Diversification also provides an additional benefit to managers that shareholders do not enjoy. Diversification and firm size are highly correlated: as size increases, so does executive compensation. Large firms are more complex and difficult to manage; thus managers of larger firms usually receive more compensation.[61] Higher compensation may serve as a motive for managers to engage in greater diversification. Governance mechanisms, such as the board of directors, monitoring by owners, executive compensation, and the market for corporate control, may limit managerial tendencies to over-diversify. These mechanisms are discussed in more detail in Chapter 11.

On the other hand, governance mechanisms may not be strong, and in some instances managers may diversify the firm to the point that it fails to earn even average returns. The loss of adequate internal governance may result in poor relative performance, thereby triggering a threat of takeover. Although takeovers may improve efficiency by replacing ineffective managerial teams, managers may avoid takeovers through defensive tactics, such as "poison pills," or may reduce their own exposure to them with "golden parachute" agreements. Therefore, an external governance threat, although restraining managers, does not flawlessly control managerial motives for diversification.[62]

Most large publicly held firms are profitable because managers are positive stewards of firm resources and many of their strategic actions (e.g., diversification strategies) contribute to the firm's success. As mentioned, governance devices should be designed to deal with exceptions to the norms of achieving strategic competitiveness and increasing shareholder wealth. Thus, it is overly pessimistic to assume that managers usually act in their own self-interest as opposed to their firm's interest.[63]

Managers may also be held in check by concerns for their reputation. If positive reputation facilitates power, a poor reputation may reduce it. Likewise, a strong external market for managerial talent may deter managers from pursuing inappropriate diversification.[64] In addition, a diversified firm may police other diversified firms to acquire those poorly managed firms in order to restructure its own asset base. Knowing that their firms could be acquired if they are not managed successfully encourages managers to use value-creating strategies.

Even when governance mechanisms cause managers to correct a problem of poorly implemented diversification or overdiversification, these moves are not without trade-offs. For instance, firms that are spun off may not realize productivity gains, even though spinning them off is in the best interest of the divesting firm. Accordingly, the assumption that managers need disciplining may not be entirely correct, and sometimes governance may create consequences that are worse than those resulting from overdiversification. Governance that is excessive may cause a firm's managers to be overly cautious and risk averse.[65]

As shown in Figure 7.4, the level of diversification that can be expected to have the greatest positive effect on performance is based partly on how the interaction of resources, managerial motives, and incentives affects the adoption of particular diversification strategies. As indicated earlier, the greater the incentives and the more flexible the resources, the higher is the level of expected diversification. Financial resources (the most flexible) should have a stronger relationship to the extent of diversification than either tangible or intangible resources. Tangible resources (the most inflexible) are useful primarily for related diversification.

As discussed in this chapter, firms can create more value by effectively using diversification strategies. However, diversification must be kept in check by corporate governance (see Chapter 11). Appropriate strategy implementation tools, such as organizational

Figure 7.4

Figure 7.4 Summary Model of the Relationship between Firm Performance and Diversification

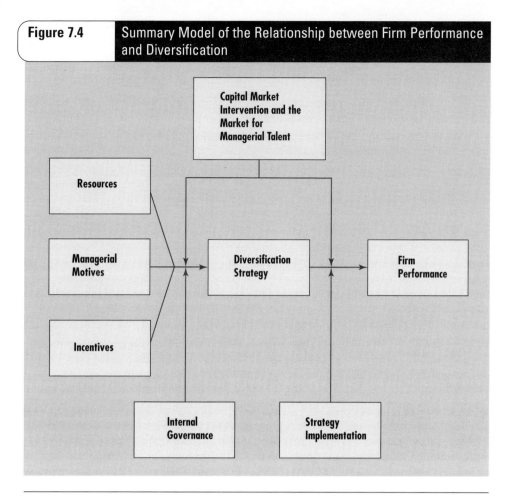

SOURCE: R. E. Hoskisson & M. A. Hitt, 1990, Antecedents and performance outcomes of diversification: A review and critique of theoretical perspectives, *Journal of Management*, 16: 498.

structures, are also important (see Chapter 12), as shown by the experiences of a number of Internet-based firms.

We have described corporate-level strategies in this chapter. In the next chapter, we discuss the use of mergers and acquisitions as a prominent means of firms to diversify. These trends toward more diversification through acquisitions, which have been partially reversed due to restructuring (see Chapter 8), indicate that learning has taken place regarding corporate-level diversification strategies. Firms performing well in their dominant business may not want to diversify. Moreover, firms that diversify should do so cautiously, choosing to focus on a relatively few, rather than many, businesses. In fact, research suggests that although unrelated diversification has decreased, related diversification has increased, possibly due to the restructuring that continued into the 1990s and early 21st century.[66]

In both emerging economies and industrialized countries, such as Germany, Italy and France, diversification has become the norm for the most successful firms. Subsequently, however, many of these diversified firms began to restructure. This sequence of diversification followed by restructuring mirrors the actions of firms in Canada, the United States, and the United Kingdom.[67]

In Europe, for example, many of the largest conglomerates are restructuring as a result of two elements' effects. First, deregulation across Europe is creating more competition, and the emergence of the European Union is causing firms to pursue pan-European strategies. Second, the realities of global competition are becoming prominent in Europe, resulting in corporate restructurings, and firms in several industries sectors are responding by restructuring to encourage long-term growth in both sales revenue and profitability.

As in Canada and the United States, these firms are finding that strategic competitiveness can be increased when they pursue a level of diversification that is appropriate for their resources (especially financial resources), core competencies, and the opportunities and threats in their external environment.[68]

Summary

- Using a single-business or dominant-business corporate-level strategy may be preferable to seeking a more diversified strategy, unless a corporation can develop economies of scope or financial economies between businesses, or unless it can obtain market power through additional levels of diversification. These economies and market power are the main sources of value creation when the firm diversifies.

- Related diversification creates value through the sharing of activities or the transfer of core competencies.

- Sharing activities usually involves sharing tangible resources between businesses. Transferring core competencies involves transferring core competencies developed in one business to another business. It also may involve transferring competencies between the corporate office and a business unit.

- Sharing activities is usually associated with the related-constrained diversification corporate-level strategy. Activity sharing is costly to implement and coordinate, may create unequal benefits for the divisions involved in the sharing, and may lead to fewer managerial risk-taking behaviours.

- Transferring core competencies is often associated with related-linked (or mixed related and unrelated) diversification, although firms pursuing both sharing activities and transferring core competencies can use it.

- Efficiently allocating resources or restructuring a target firm's assets and placing them under rigorous financial controls are two ways to accomplish successful unrelated diversification. These methods focus on obtaining financial economies.

- The primary reason a firm diversifies is to create more value. However, diversification is sometimes pursued because of incentives from tax and antitrust government policies, performance disappointments, uncertainties about future cash flow, or to reduce risk.

- Managerial motives to diversify (including to increase compensation) can lead to overdiversification and a reduction in the firm's value-creating ability. On the other hand, managers can also be good stewards of the firm's assets.

- Managers need to pay attention to both their firm's internal environment and its external environment when making decisions about the optimum level of diversification for their company. Of course, internal resources are important determinants of the direction that diversification should take. However, conditions in the firm's external environment may facilitate additional levels of diversification as might unexpected threats from competitors.

Review Questions

1. What is corporate-level strategy? Why is it important to the diversified firm?

2. What are the advantages and disadvantages of single-business and dominant-business strategies, compared with those of firms with higher levels of diversification?

3. What are three reasons that firms choose to become more diversified by moving away from either a single-business or a dominant-business corporate-level strategy?

4. How do firms share activities or transfer core competencies to obtain economies of scope when using a related-diversification strategy?

5. What are the two ways to obtain financial economies when using an unrelated-diversification strategy?

6. What incentives and resources encourage diversification?

7. What motives might encourage managers to diversify the firm beyond an appropriate level?

Diversification

As a member of the strategic management team for a very successful sporting goods firm that specializes in the manufacturing and marketing of soccer equipment, you have been asked to provide your thoughts as to whether the firm should diversify and to what extent.

Part One. List the advantages and disadvantages of diversification in the following table.

Part Two. Provide examples of related-diversification and unrelated-diversification areas that you feel might be appropriate for the firm, including some specific advantages and disadvantages that the firm might find for each.

Advantages	Disadvantages

Notes

1. M. E. Porter, 1980, *Competitive Strategy*, New York: The Free Press, xvi.
2. R. E. Hoskisson, R. A. Johnson, D. Yiu, & W. P. Wan, 2001, Restructuring strategies of diversified business groups: Differences associated with country institutional environments. In M. A. Hitt, R. E. Freeman, & J. S. Harrison (eds.), *Handbook of Strategic Management*, Oxford, UK: Blackwell Publishers, 433–63; Y. Luo, 2001, Determinants of entry in an emerging economy: A multilevel approach, *Journal of Management Studies*, 38: 443–72; T. B. Palmer & R. M. Wiseman, 1999, Decoupling risk taking from income stream uncertainty: A holistic model of risk, *Strategic Management Journal*, 20: 1037–62.
3. E. H. Bowman & C. E. Helfat, 2001, Does corporate strategy matter? *Strategic Management Journal*, 22: 1–23; M. A. Hitt, R. E. Hoskisson, & H. Kim, 1997, International diversification: Effects on innovation and firm performance in product-diversified firms, *Academy of Management Journal*, 40: 767–98.
4. R. L. Simerly & M. Li, 2000, Environmental dynamism, capital structure and performance: A theoretical integration and an empirical test, *Strategic Management Journal*, 21: 31–49; D. D. Bergh & M. W. Lawless, 1998, Portfolio restructuring and limits to hierarchical governance: The effects of environmental uncertainty and diversification strategy, *Organization Science*, 9: 87–102.
5. M. E. Porter, 1987, From competitive advantage to corporate strategy, *Harvard Business Review*, 65(3): 43–59.
6. Porter, From competitive advantage to corporate strategy; C. A. Montgomery, 1994, Corporate diversification, *Journal of Economic Perspectives*, 8: 163–78.
7. G. H. Stonehouse, J. D. Pemberton, & C. E. Barber, 2001, The role of knowledge facilitators and inhibitors: Lessons from airline reservations systems, *Long Range Planning*, 34(2): 115–38; B. Wysocki, Jr., 1999, Corporate America confronts the meaning of a "core" business, *Wall Street Journal*, November 9, A1, A4.
8. C. Meyer, 2001, The second generation of speed, *Harvard Business Review*, 79(4): 24–25.
9. H. Kwak, 2002, Maximizing value through diversification, *MIT Sloan Management Review*, 43(2): 10; R. A. Burgelman & Y. L. Doz, 2001, The power of strategic integration, *MIT Sloan Management Review*, 42(3): 28–38; C. C. Markides, 1997, To diversify or not to diversify, *Harvard Business Review*, 75(6): 93–99.
10. P. Wright, M. Kroll, A. Lado, & B. Van Ness, 2002, The structure of ownership and corporate acquisition strategies, *Strategic Management Journal*, 23: 41–53; C. C. Markides & P. J. Williamson, 1996, Corporate diversification and organizational structure: A resource-based view, *Academy of Management Journal*, 39: 340–67; A. Campbell, M. Goold, & M. Alexander, 1995, Corporate strategy: The question for parenting advantage, *Harvard Business Review*, 73(2): 120–32; T. H. Brush, P. Bromiley, & M. Hendrickx, 1999, The relative influence of industry and corporate on business segment performance: An alternative estimate, *Strategic Management Journal*, 20: 519–47; T. H. Brush & P. Bromiley, 1997, What does a small corporate effect mean? A variance components simulation of corporate and business effects, *Strategic Management Journal*, 18: 825–35; J. B. Barney, 2002, *Gaining and Sustaining Competitive Advantage*, 2nd ed., Upper Saddle River, NJ: Prentice-Hall.
11. D. D. Bergh, 2001, Diversification strategy research at a crossroads: Established, emerging and anticipated paths. In M. A. Hitt, R. E. Freeman, & J. S. Harrison (eds.), *Handbook of Strategic Management*, Oxford, UK: Blackwell Publishers, 363; C. Kim, S. Kim, & C. Pantzalis, 2001, Firm diversification and earnings volatility: An empirical analysis of U.S.-based MNCs, *American Business Review*, 19(1): 26–38; W. Lewellen, 1971, A pure financial rationale for the conglomerate merger, *Journal of Finance*, 26: 521–37; J. D. Fisher & Y. Liang, 2000, Is sector diversification more important than regional diversification? *Real Estate Finance*, 17(3): 35–40; H. von Kranenburg, M. Cloodt, & J. Hagedoorn, 2001, An exploratory story of recent trends in the diversification of Dutch publishing companies in the multimedia and information industries, *International Studies of Management & Organization*, 31(10): 64–86.
12. B. S. Silverman, 1999, Technological resources and the direction of corporate diversification: Toward an integration of the resource-based view and transaction cost economics, *Administrative Science Quarterly*, 45: 1109–24; D. Collis & C. A. Montgomery, 1995, Competing on resources: Strategy in the 1990s, *Harvard Business Review*, 73(4): 118–28; M. A. Peteraf, 1993, The cornerstones of competitive advantage: A resource-based view, *Strategic Management Journal*, 14: 179–91.
13. Bergh, Diversification strategy research at a crossroads, 369; N. Deogun, G. McWilliams, & M. Williams, 2001, Hewlett-Packard nears pact to buy Compaq for 26 billion in stock, *Wall Street Journal*, September 4, A1, A6.
14. R. P. Rumelt, 1974, *Strategy, Structure, and Economic Performance*, Boston: Harvard Business School; L. Wrigley, 1970, Divisional autonomy and diversification (Ph.D. dissertation), Boston, MA: Harvard Business School.
15. W. Heuslein, 2001, Wm. Wrigley Jr. Co.: Getting unstuck, *Forbes*, January 8, 138–39; T. Mason, 2001, Can gum and dental care mix? *Marketing*, August 23, 21.
16. S. Killman, 2001, Smithfield foods CEO welcomes backlash over its hog farms, *Wall Street Journal*, August 21, B4; J. Forster, 2001, Who's afraid of a little mud? *Business Week*, May 21, 112–13.
17. L. A. Keister, 2000, *Chinese Business Groups: The Structure and Impact of Inter-Firm Relations During Economic Development*, New York: Oxford University Press; T. Khanna & K. Palepu, 1997, Why focused strategies may be wrong for emerging markets, *Harvard Business Review*, 75(4): 41–50; C. Chung, 2001, Markets, culture and institutions: The emergence of large business groups in Taiwan, 1950s–1970s, *Journal of Management Studies*, 38: 719–45; S. Manikutty, 2000, Family business groups in India: A resource-based view of the emerging trends, *Family Business Review*, 13: 279–92; Economist, 1997, Inside story, *Economist*, December 6, 7–9;

K. Dewenter, W. Novaes, & R. H. Pettway, 2001, Visibility versus complexity in business groups: Evidence from Japanese keiretsus, *Journal of Business*, 74: 79–100; P. Kavanagh & W. G. Rowe, 2000, The mediating effect of risk on the diversification-firm value relationship: A Canadian perspective, working paper, St. John's, NL: Faculty of Business Administration, Memorial University of Newfoundland.

18. M. Farjoun, 1998, The independent and joint effects of the skill and physical bases of relatedness in diversification, *Strategic Management Journal*, 19: 611–30; R. E. Hoskisson & L.W. Busenitz, 2002, Market uncertainty and learning distance in corporate entrepreneurship entry mode choice. In M. A. Hitt, R. D. Ireland, S. M. Camp, & D. L. Sexton (eds.), *Strategic Entrepreneurship: Creating a New Mindset*, Oxford, UK: Blackwell Publishers, 150–72; R. Morck & B. Yeung, 1999, When synergy creates real value, Mastering Strategy (Part 7), *Financial Times*, November 8, 6–7.

19. B. Garette & P. Dussauge, 2000, Alliances versus acquisitions: Choosing the right option, *European Management Journal*, 18(1): 63–69; L. Capron, 1999, The long-term performance of horizontal acquisitions, *Strategic Management Journal*, 20: 987–1018; M. E. Porter, 1985, *Competitive Advantage*, New York: The Free Press, 328.

20. S. Jaffe, 2001, Do Pepsi and Gatorade mix? *Business Week Online*, http://www.businessweek.com, August 14.

21. M. L. Marks & P. H. Mirvis, 2000, Managing mergers, acquisitions, and alliances: Creating an effective transition structure, *Organizational Dynamics*, 28(3): 35–47.

22. G. Delong, 2001, Stockholder gains from focusing versus diversifying bank mergers, *Journal of Financial Economics*, 2: 221–52; T. H. Brush, 1996, Predicted change in operational synergy and post-acquisition performance of acquired businesses, *Strategic Management Journal*, 17: 1–24; H. Zhang, 1995, Wealth effects of U.S. bank takeovers, *Applied Financial Economics*, 5: 329–36; D. D. Bergh, 1995, Size and relatedness of units sold: An agency theory and resource-based perspective, *Strategic Management Journal*, 16: 221–39; M. Lubatkin & S. Chatterjee, 1994, Extending modern portfolio theory into the domain of corporate diversification: Does it apply? *Academy of Management Journal*, 37: 109–36; A. Van Oijen, 2001, Product diversification, corporate management instruments, resource sharing, and performance, *Academy of Management Best Paper Proceedings* (Business Policy and Strategy Division), CD-ROM; T. Kono, 1999, A strong head office makes a strong company, *Long Range Planning*, 32(2): 225.

23. M. Y. Brannen, J. K. Liker, & W. M. Fruin, 1999, Recontextualization and factory-to-factory knowledge transfer from Japan to the US: The case of NSK. In J. K. Liker, W. M. Fruin, & P. Adler (eds.), *Remade in America: Transplanting and Transforming Japanese Systems*, New York: Oxford University Press, 117–53; L. Capron, P. Dussauge, & W. Mitchell, 1998, Resource redeployment following horizontal acquisitions in Europe and the United States, 1988–1992, *Strategic Management Journal*, 19: 631–61; A. Mehra, 1996, Resource and market based determinants of performance in the U.S. banking industry, *Strategic Management Journal*, 17: 307–22; S. Chatterjee & B. Wernerfelt, 1991, The link between resources and type of diversification: Theory and evidence, *Strategic Management Journal*, 12: 33–48.

24. B. Horovitz, 2001, McDonald's tries a new recipe to revive sales, *USA Today*, July 10, 1–2; B. Johnson, 2004, presentation by Bill Johnson, CEO, McDonald's Canada, March 17, Richard Ivey School of Business, London, Ontario.

25. M. Maremont, 2000, For plastic hangers, you almost need to go to Tyco International, *Wall Street Journal*, February 15, A1, A10; R. Whittington, 1999, In praise of the evergreen conglomerate, Mastering Strategy (Part 6), *Financial Times*, November 1, 4–6; W. Ruigrok, A. Pettigrew, S. Peck, & R. Whittington, 1999, Corporate restructuring and new forms of organizing: Evidence from Europe, *Management International Review*, 39(special issue): 41–64.

26. C. St. John & J. S. Harrison, 1999, Manufacturing-based relatedness, synergy, and coordination, *Strategic Management Journal*, 20: 129–45; .

27. W. G. Shepherd, 1986, On the core concepts of industrial economics. In H. W. deJong & W. G. Shepherd (eds.), *Mainstreams in Industrial Organization*, Boston: Kluwer Publications.

28. D. Genesove & W. P. Mullin, 2001. Rules, communication, and collusion: Narrative evidence from the Sugar Institute Case, *American Economic Review*, 91: 379–98; J. Gimeno & C. Y. Woo, 1999, Multimarket contact, economies of scope, and firm performance, *Academy of Management Journal*, 42: 239–59; S. Lohr & S. Gaither, 2002, Hewlett Packard declares victory on the merger, *New York Times*, http://www.nytimes.com, March 20; N. Deogun, G. McWilliams, & M. Williams, 2001 Hewlett-Packard nears pact to buy Compaq for $26 billion in stock, *Wall Street Journal*, September 4, A1, A6.

29. A. Karnani & B. Wernerfelt, 1985, Multipoint competition, *Strategic Management Journal*, 6: 87–96.

30. Ibid.; H. A. Haveman & L. Nonnemaker, 2000, Competition in multiple geographic markets: The impact on growth and market entry, *Administrative Science Quarterly*, 45: 232–67; Genesove & Mullin, Rules, communication, and collusion.

31. O. E. Williamson, 1996, Economics and organization: A primer, *California Management Review*, 38(2): 131–46.

32. S. Killman, 2001, Smithfield foods CEO welcomes backlash over its hog farms, *Wall Street Journal*, August 21, B4; 2004, Maple Leaf Foods, Maple Leaf closes acquisition of Schneider Foods, *Maple Leaf Foods website*, http://www.mapleleaf.ca (press release) April 5, accessed May 11, 2004.

33. K. R. Harrigan, 2001, Strategic flexibility in the old and new economies. In M. A. Hitt, R. E. Freeman, & J. S. Harrison (eds.), *Handbook of Strategic Management*, Oxford, UK: Blackwell Publishers, 97–123; R. E. Kranton, & D. F. Minehart, 2001, Networks versus vertical integration, *The Rand Journal of Economics*, 3: 570–601; P. Kothandaraman & D. T. Wilson, 2001, The future of competition: Value-creating networks, *Industrial Marketing Management*, 30: 379–89; D. Stapleton, P. Gentles, J. Ross, & K. Shubert, 2001, The location-centric shift from marketplace to marketspace: Transaction cost-inspired propositions of virtual integration via an e-commerce model, *Advances in Competitiveness Research*, 9: 10–41.

34. K. M. Eisenhardt & D. C. Galunic, 2000, Coevolving: At last, a way to make synergies work, *Harvard Business Review*, 78(1): 91–111; R. Schoenberg, 2001, Knowledge transfer and resource sharing as value creation mechanisms in inbound continental European acquisitions, *Journal of Euro-Marketing*, 10: 99–114.

35. Eisenhardt & Galunic, Coevolving, 94; M. Freeman, 2002, Forging a model for profitability, *Electronic Media*, January 28, 1, 13.

36. D. D. Bergh, 1997, Predicting divestiture of unrelated acquisitions: An integrative model of ex ante conditions, *Strategic Management Journal*, 18(9): 715–32.; C. W. L. Hill, 1994, Diversification and economic performance: Bringing structure and corporate management back into the picture. In R. P. Rumelt, D. E. Schendel, & D. J. Teece (eds.), *Fundamental Issues in Strategy*, Boston: Harvard Business School Press, 297–321.

37. O. E. Williamson, 1975, *Markets and Hierarchies: Analysis and Antitrust Implications*, New York: Macmillan Free Press.

38. M. T. Billet & D. Mauer, 2001, Diversification and the value of internal capital markets: The case of tracking stock, *Journal of Banking & Finance*, 9: 1457–90.

39. R. Kochhar & M. A. Hitt, 1998, Linking corporate strategy to capital structure: Diversification strategy, type, and source of financing, *Strategic Management Journal*, 19: 601–10.

40. Ibid.; P. Taylor & J. Lowe, 1995, A note on corporate strategy and capital structure, *Strategic Management Journal*, 16: 411–14.

41. M. Kwak, 2001, Spinoffs lead to better financing decisions, *MIT Sloan Management Review*, 42(4): 10; O. A. Lamont & C. Polk, 2001, The diversification discount: Cash flows versus returns, *Journal of Finance*, 56: 1693–1721; R. Rajan, H. Servaes, & L. Zingales, 2001, The cost of diversity: The diversification discount and inefficient investment, *Journal of Finance*, 55: 35–79; Economist, 2001, Spoilt for choice, *Economist*, http://www.economist.com, July 5.

42. D. J. Denis, D. K. Denis, & A. Sarin, 1999, Agency theory and the reference of equity ownership structure on corporate diversification strategies, *Strategic Management Journal*, 20: 1071–76; R. Amit & J. Livnat, 1988, A concept of conglomerate diversification, *Journal of Management*, 14: 593–604; Whittington, In praise of the evergreen conglomerate, 4.

43. T. Khanna & J. W. Rivkin, 2001, Estimating the performance effects of business groups in emerging markets, *Strategic Management Journal*, 22: 45–74; T. Khanna & K. Palepu. 2000. Is group affiliation profitable in emerging markets? An analysis of diversified Indian business groups, *Journal of Finance*, 55: 867–92; T. Khanna & K. Palepu, 2000, The future of business groups in emerging markets: Long-run evidence from Chile, *Academy of Management Journal*, 43: 268–85.

44. R. E. Hoskisson, R. A. Johnson, D. Yiu, & W. P. Wan, 2001, Restructuring strategies and diversified business groups: Differences associated with country institutional environments. In M. A. Hitt, R. E. Freeman & J. S. Harrison (eds.), *Handbook of Strategic Management*, Oxford, UK: Blackwell Publishers, 433–63; S. J. Chang & H. Singh, 1999, The impact of entry and resource fit on modes of exit by multibusiness firms, *Strategic Management Journal*, 20: 1019–35.

45. J. S. Harrison, H. M. O'Neill, & R. E. Hoskisson, 2000, Acquisition strategy and target resistance: A theory of countervailing effects of pre-merger bidding and post-merger integration. In C. Cooper & A. Gregory (eds.), *Advances in Mergers and Acquisitions*, Vol. 1, Greenwich, CT: JAI/Elsevier, Inc, 157–82.

46. T. A. Doucet & R. M. Barefield, 1999, Client base valuation: The case of a professional service firm, *Journal of Business Research*, 44: 127–33.

47. S. Nambisan, 2001, Why service businesses are not product businesses, *MIT Sloan Management Review*, 42(4): 72–80; S. L. Gillan, J. W. Kensinger, & J. D. Martin, 2000, Value creation and corporate diversification: The case of Sears, Roebuck & Co., *Journal of Financial Economics*, 55: 103–37.

48. E. Stickel, 2001, Uncertainty reduction in a competitive environment, *Journal of Business Research*, 51: 169–77; S. Chatterjee & J. Singh, 1999, Are tradeoffs inherent in diversification moves? A simultaneous model for type of diversification and mode of expansion decisions, *Management Science*, 45: 25–41.

49. M. C. Jensen, 1986, Agency costs of free cash flow, corporate finance, and takeovers, *American Economic Review*, 76: 323–29.

50. R. F. Hirsh, 2000, *Power Loss: The Origins of Deregulation and Restructuring in the American Electric Power Industry*, Cambridge: MIT Press.

51. J. Ewing, 2001, Guten tag, America, *Business Week Online*, http://www.business week.com, July 27.

52. A. Lomi & E. Larsen, 2000, Strategic implications of deregulation and competition in the electricity industry, *European Management Journal*, 17(2): 151–63.

53. Royal Bank of Canada, 2000, *Royal Bank of Canada website*, http://www.rbc.com/history/quicktofuture/index.html, accessed July 20, 2004.

54. Y. Chang & H. Thomas, 1989, The impact of diversification strategy on risk-return performance, *Strategic Management Journal*, 10: 271–84; R. M. Grant, A. P. Jammine, & H. Thomas, 1988, Diversity, diversification, and profitability among British manufacturing companies, 1972–1984, *Academy of Management Journal*, 31: 771–801; Rumelt, *Strategy, Structure and Economic Performance*, 125; M. N. Nickel & M. C. Rodriguez, 2002, A review of research on the negative accounting relationship between risk and return: Bowman's paradox, *Omega*, 30(1): 1–18; R. M. Wiseman & L. R. Gomez-Mejia, 1998, A behavioral agency model of managerial risk taking, *Academy of Management Review*, 23: 133–53; E. H. Bowman, 1982, Risk seeking by troubled firms, *Sloan Management Review*, 23: 33–42; J. G. Matsusaka, 2001, Corporate diversification, value maximization, and organizational capabilities, *Journal of Business*, 74: 409–32; L. E. Palich, L. B. Cardinal, & C. C. Miller, 2000, Curvilinearity in the diversification-performance linkage: An examination of over three decades of research, *Strategic Management Journal*, 21: 155–74.

55. Simerly & Li, Environmental dynamism, capital structure and performance; J. C. Sandvig & L. Coakley, 1998, Best practices in small firm diversification, *Business Horizons*, 41(3): 33–40; C. G. Smith & A. C. Cooper, 1988, Established companies diversifying into young industries: A comparison of firms with different levels of performance, *Strategic Management Journal*, 9: 111–21.

56. N. M. Kay & A. Diamantopoulos, 1987, Uncertainty and synergy: Towards a formal model of corporate strategy, *Managerial and Decision Economics*, 8: 121–30; R. W. Coff, 1999, How buyers cope with uncertainty when acquiring firms in knowledge-intensive industries: Caveat emptor, *Organization Science*, 10: 144–61.

57. Chatterjee & Singh, Are tradeoffs inherent in diversification moves?; S. J. Chatterjee & B. Wernerfelt, 1991, The link between resources and type of diversification: Theory and evidence, *Strategic Management Journal*, 12: 33–48; Kochhar & Hitt, Linking corporate strategy to capital structure.

58. J. Greene, 2001, Microsoft: How it became stronger than ever, *Business Week*, June 4, 75–85; K. Haanes & O. Fjeldstad, 2000, Linking intangible resources and competition, *European Management Journal*, 18(1): 52–62.

59. L. Capron & J. Hulland, 1999, Redeployment of brands, sales forces, and general marketing management expertise following horizontal acquisitions: A resource-based view, *Journal of Marketing*, 63(2): 41–54; R. D. Smith, 2000, Intangible strategic assets and firm performance: A multi-industry study of the resource-based view, *Journal of Business Strategies*, 17(2): 91–117.

60. M. A. Geletkanycz, B. K. Boyd, & S. Finkelstein, 2001, The strategic value of CEO external directorate networks: Implications for CEO compensation, *Strategic Management Journal*, 9: 889–98; W. Grossman & R. E. Hoskisson, 1998, CEO pay at the crossroads of Wall Street and Main: Toward the strategic design of executive compensation, *Academy of Management Executive*, 12(1): 43–57; S. Finkelstein & D. C. Hambrick, 1996, *Strategic Leadership: Top Executives and Their Effects on Organizations*, St. Paul, MN: West Publishing Company; P. J. Lane, A. A. Cannella, Jr., & M. H. Lubatkin, 1998, Agency problems as antecedents to unrelated mergers and diversification: Amihud and Lev reconsidered, *Strategic Management Journal*, 19: 555–78; D. L. May, 1995, Do managerial motives influence firm risk reduction strategies? *Journal of Finance*, 50: 1291–1308; Y. Amihud and B. Lev, 1981, Risk reduction as a managerial motive for conglomerate mergers, *Bell Journal of Economics*, 12: 605–17.

61. S. R. Gray & A. A. Cannella, Jr., 1997, The role of risk in executive compensation, *Journal of Management*, 23: 517–40; H. Tosi & L. Gomez-Mejia, 1989, The decoupling of CEO pay and performance: An agency theory perspective, *Administrative Science Quarterly*, 34: 169–89; R. Bliss & R. Rosen, 2001, CEO compensation and bank mergers, *Journal of Financial Economics*, 1:107–38; S. Finkelstein & R. A. D'Aveni, 1994, CEO duality as a double-edged sword: How boards of directors balance entrenchment avoidance and unity of command, *Academy of Management Journal*, 37: 1070–108.

62. J. W. Lorsch, A. S. Zelleke, & K. Pick, 2001, Unbalanced boards, *Harvard Business Review*, 79(2): 28–30; R. E. Hoskisson & T. Turk, 1990, Corporate restructuring: Governance and control limits of the internal market, *Academy of Management Review*, 15: 459–77; R. C. Anderson, T. W. Bates, J. M. Bizjak, & M. L. Lemmon, 2000, Corporate governance and firm diversification, *Financial Management*, 29(1): 5–22; J. D. Westphal, 1998, Board games: How CEOs adapt to increases in structural board independence from management, *Administrative Science Quarterly*, 43: 511–37; J. K. Seward & J. P. Walsh, 1996, The governance and control of voluntary corporate spin offs, *Strategic Management Journal*, 17: 25–39; J. P. Walsh & J. K. Seward, 1990, On the efficiency of internal and external corporate control mechanisms, *Academy of Management Review*, 15: 421–58.

63. W. G. Rowe, 2001, Creating wealth in organizations: The role of strategic leadership, *Academy of Management Executive*, 15(1): 81–94; Finkelstein & D'Aveni, CEO duality as a double-edged sword.

64. E. F. Fama, 1980, Agency problems and the theory of the firm, *Journal of Political Economy*, 88: 288–307.

65. R. A. Johnson, 1996, Antecedents and outcomes of corporate refocusing, *Journal of Management*, 22: 439–83; C. Y. Woo, G. E. Willard, & U. S. Dallenbach, 1992, Spin-off performance: A case of overstated expectations, *Strategic Management Journal*, 13: 433–48; M. Wright, R. E. Hoskisson, & L. W. Busenitz, 2001, Firm rebirth: Buyouts as facilitators of strategic growth and entrepreneurship, *Academy of Management Executive*, 15(1): 111–25; H. Kim & R. E. Hoskisson, 1996, Japanese governance systems: A critical review. In S. B. Prasad (ed.), *Advances in International Comparative Management*, Greenwich, CT: JAI Press, 165–89.

66. L. Capron, W. Mitchell, & A. Swaminathan, 2001, Asset divestiture following horizontal acquisitions: A dynamic view, *Strategic Management Journal*, 22: 817–44; Bergh, Diversification strategy research at a crossroads, 370–71; W. M. Bulkeley, 1994, Conglomerates make a surprising come-back—with a '90s twist, *Wall Street Journal*, March 1, A1, A6; J. P. H. Fan & L. H. P. Lang, 2000, The measurement of relatedness: An application to corporate diversification, *Journal of Business*, 73: 629–60.

67. Khanna & Palepu, The future of business groups in emerging markets, 268–85; P. Ghemawat & T. Khanna, 1998, The nature of diversified business groups: A research design and two case studies, *Journal of Industrial Economics*, 46: 35–61.

68. W. P. Wan & R. E. Hoskisson, 2003, Home country environments, corporate diversification strategies, and firm performance, *Academy of Management Journal*, 46: 27–45.

Chapter Eight

Acquisition and Restructuring Strategies

Knowledge Objectives

Studying this chapter should provide you with the strategic management knowledge needed to:

1. Explain the popularity of acquisition strategies for firms competing in the global economy.

2. Discuss reasons firms use an acquisition strategy to achieve strategic competitiveness.

3. Describe seven problems that work against developing a competitive advantage using an acquisition strategy.

4. Name and describe attributes of effective acquisitions.

5. Define the restructuring strategy and distinguish among its common forms.

6. Explain the short-term and long-term outcomes of the different types of restructuring strategies.

MTS: Mega Telephone Synergy or Merger That Stinks?

In 2003, Winnipeg's Manitoba Telecom Services (MTS) was a relatively small, regional telephone competitor. The former provincial Crown-owned phone company was established in 1908, and had a dominant presence in Manitoba. Then, as today, it offered local, long-distance, wireless, data, and enhanced telecommunications services.

However, in early 2004, MTS announced a $1.7 billion friendly takeover bid for Toronto's Allstream. Allstream was a former AT&T Canada unit that emerged from a financial restructuring in 2003. Allstream had more than 10 percent of Canada's business telecom market and had become profitable after shedding billions of dollars of debt. As well, the company carried $3 billion of tax-loss carry-forwards that should eliminate the combined company's tax bill for the rest of the decade. MTS would also benefit from Allstream's reach outside Manitoba, accessing its extensive broadband fibre-optic network in Canada and through agreements with international service providers such as AT&T.

This acquisition would create a major new national challenger to Montreal's BCE and B.C.'s Telus. The takeover would create three well-financed national telecoms offering data, wireless, and voice services to corporate clients across most of the country. Mark Quigley, senior analyst with the Yankee Group in Canada, noted that the unexpected new player, "... really strengthens the marketplace as a whole.... At the end of the day, Telus and Bell are going to have to be that much better at what they do." The deal created a company with 7000 employees, annual revenue of more than $2 billion, a fibre optics–based national network, and more than $2.9 billion in assets.

So what could be wrong with creating a strong new competitor that possesses big technical and financial advantages? MTS management argued that this move would create Canada's "largest and most profitable alternative communication solutions provider." If you think that shareholders and regulators would support this move to create a viable new national competitor, you would be mostly, but not entirely, correct.

The Allstream takeover killed a plan backed by some shareholders to turn MTS into an income trust. Many MTS shareholders felt that they had been led to believe the company was leaning towards becoming a cash-producing income trust rather than moving toward a major acquisition. This caused investors to bid up MTS stock—analysts believed the company to be worth $55 to $60 per share as a trust. When the Allstream deal was announced, MTS shares fell 10 percent to $48 per share because it became less likely a trust conversion would happen. The short-run impact of the deal harmed shareholders.

Some MTS shareholders were so incensed by the Allstream takeover that they asked the Toronto Stock Exchange (TSX) to step in and—at a minimum—have the company put the purchase up to a shareholders' vote, or—in the extreme—stop the agreement altogether. What management claimed made good strategic sense for the company's long-run competitive survival was fairly unappealing to some of the investors in the short run. For a period of time, those in the business community had to wonder whether good strategic sense or financial expediency would win the day.

Manitoba Telecom Services hopes that acquiring Allstream's extensive broadband fibre-optic network will give it a competitive advantage in its marketplace.

© MATTHIAS KULKA/CORBIS/MAGMA

(continued)

The TSX, however, decided MTS management and directors were fulfilling their proper roles; instead of paying out cash as part of an income trust, the executives were using the company's resources to enhance its long-term future. As far as the feeling among some shareholders that they had been misled, MTS CEO Bill Fraser told investors, as far back as February 2003, that an income trust would be a long-term cash drain to the company and that, "We intend to be in business for another 100 years and we want to be sure that the framework that is established enables us to reinvest and grow the business."

There was also support for Fraser in the investment community. An analyst at CIBC World Markets warned that turning telecommunications companies, such as MTS, into income trusts would drain them of cash and leave them with inadequate resources to fight future competitive battles. Major capital investments in capacity are critical in the long run, and if a company like MTS lacks capacity in the future, it could be decimated by the competition. In the end, the smart strategic acquisition seems to have won the day.

SOURCES: Prince George Citizen, 2004, Manitoba Telecom shakes up phone biz, *Prince George Citizen*, March 19, 40; MTS, 2004, *MTS website*, http://www.mts.mb.ca, accessed April 10, 2004; M. Evans, 2004, Manitoba Tel won't rule out conversion, *National Post* (*Financial Post*), April 2, FP1; T. Corcoran, 2004, TSX saves MTS from corporate coup, *National Post* (*Financial Post*), April 2, FP11; T. Gignac, 2004, MTS, Allstream proposal praised: Analysts say merger creates new competition, *Calgary Herald*, March 20, E3.

In Chapter 7, we studied corporate-level strategies, focusing on types and levels of product diversification strategies that can build core competencies and create competitive advantage. As noted in that chapter, diversification allows a firm to create value by productively using excess resources.[1] In this chapter, we explore mergers and acquisitions, which are often combined with a diversification strategy, as a prominent strategy employed by firms throughout the world. The acquisition of Allstream by MTS is a horizontal acquisition, as Allstream competed with MTS in several markets. Still, each firm markets some different products in different geographic areas and has different strengths. As such, combining the two firms creates an opportunity for synergy to be developed beyond economies of scope.

In the latter half of the 20th century, acquisitions became a prominent strategy used by major corporations. Even smaller and more focused firms began employing acquisition strategies to grow and enter new markets. However, acquisition strategies are not without problems; a number of acquisitions fail to live up to expectations. Thus, we focus on how acquisitions can be used to produce value for the firm's stakeholders.[2] Before describing attributes associated with effective acquisitions, we examine the most prominent problems companies experience with an acquisition strategy. For example, when acquisitions contribute to poor performance, a firm may deem it necessary to restructure its operations. Closing the chapter are descriptions of three restructuring strategies, as well as the short-term and long-term outcomes resulting from their use. Setting the stage for these topics is an examination of the popularity of mergers and acquisitions and a discussion of the differences among mergers, acquisitions, and takeovers.

The Popularity of Merger and Acquisition Strategies

Acquisitions have been a popular strategy among North American firms for many years.[3] Increasingly, acquisition strategies are becoming more popular with firms worldwide. In fact, about 40 percent to 45 percent of the acquisitions in recent years have been made across country borders (i.e., a firm headquartered in one country acquiring a firm headquartered in another country).[4]

There were 55,000 acquisitions valued at $1.7 trillion in the 1980s, but acquisitions in the 1990s exceeded $14 trillion in value.[5] The number of mergers and acquisitions remains high—the annual value of acquisitions in the new millennium is still greater than the total for the entire decade of the 1980s. Based on a conversion of $1.30 CDN to $1 US, the annual value peaked in 2000, at $4.5 trillion, fell to about $2.3 trillion in 2001, fell further to about $1.8 trillion in 2002, and levelled off at about the same amount in 2003.[6] While such numbers may show optimism in being able to make an acquisition strategy pay off in good economic times, an acquisition strategy is sometimes used because of the uncertainty in the competitive landscape. A firm may also make an acquisition to increase its market power to counter a competitive threat, to enter a new market because of the opportunity available in that market, or to spread the risk due to the uncertain environment.[7] In addition, a firm may acquire other companies to provide options that allow the firm to shift its core business into different markets, as volatility brings undesirable changes to its primary markets.[8]

The strategic management process (see Figure 1.1, on page 8) calls for an acquisition strategy to increase a firm's strategic competitiveness as well as its returns to shareholders. Thus, an acquisition strategy should be used only when the acquiring firm will be able to increase its economic value through ownership and the use of an acquired firm's assets.[9]

Evidence suggests, however, that at least for acquiring firms, acquisition strategies may not result in these desirable outcomes. Studies by academic researchers have found that shareholders of acquired firms often earn above-average returns from an acquisition,

Chapter 8 / Acquisition and Restructuring Strategies

while shareholders of acquiring firms typically earn returns from the transaction that are close to zero.[10] In approximately two-thirds of all acquisitions, the acquiring firm's stock price falls immediately after the intended transaction is announced. We saw this happen in the opening case with the MTS–Allstream acquisition. This negative response is an indication of investors' skepticism about the likelihood that the acquirer will be able to achieve the synergies required to justify the premium paid to make the acquisition.[11]

Mergers, Acquisitions, and Takeovers: What Are the Differences?

A **merger** is a strategy through which two firms agree to integrate their operations on a relatively co-equal basis.

An **acquisition** is a strategy through which one firm buys a controlling, or 100 percent, interest in another firm with the intent of making the acquired firm a subsidiary business within its portfolio.

A **takeover** is a special type of an acquisition strategy wherein the target firm did not solicit the acquiring firm's bid.

A **merger** is a strategy through which two firms agree to integrate their operations on a relatively co-equal basis. There are not many true mergers, because one party is usually dominant. The classic case of the 1998 merger of Chrysler and Daimler-Benz was, in its time, touted as a merger of equals. Yet, not long after the companies merged, Daimler CEO Jürgen Schrempp replaced Chrysler's CEO with Daimler-Benz executive Dieter Zetsche. The merged organization was headquartered in Stuttgart, Germany, not Auburn Hill, Michigan. The company was incorporated as a German company and run under Germany's corporate governance rules. Given German labour laws, this meant that the board would be predominately German. In the end, the merger of equals was the Mercedes-Benz acquisition of Chrysler.[12]

An **acquisition** is a strategy through which one firm buys a controlling, or 100 percent, interest in another firm with the intent of making the acquired firm a subsidiary business within its portfolio. In this case, the management of the acquired firm reports to the management of the acquiring firm. While most mergers are friendly transactions, acquisitions include unfriendly takeovers. A **takeover** is a special type of an acquisition strategy wherein the target firm did not solicit the acquiring firm's bid. Oftentimes, takeover bids spawn bidding wars. For example, in January 2004, Atlanta's Cingular Wireless, the second largest wireless company in the U.S., made a $27 billion bid for AT&T Wireless, the third largest U.S. wireless operator. Five weeks later, Cingular won a bidding war against the U.K.'s Vodafone Group PLC. The final cost was $41 billion plus assumption of about $6 billion in debt—or about 75 percent more than the original offer made just a few weeks earlier.[13]

As well, other factors can impact the likelihood that unsolicited takeover bids will be launched. For example, the number of unsolicited takeover bids increased in the economic downturn in 2001–02. This activity is common in economic recessions, when poorly managed firms that are undervalued, relative to their assets, are more easily identified.[14]

Many takeover attempts are not desired by the target firm's managers and are referred to as hostile. These battles can get vicious. Witness Quebec's Axcan Pharma's attempt to take over Salix of North Carolina. After initially offering about $190 million for the company, the Salix board refused Axcan's offer. Axcan then offered $225 million, and the company and was still rebuffed. Axcan then put up its own slate of candidates for election to the Salix board. Shareholders sided with Salix's directors and voted more than 90 percent to reject the Axcan overtures. It was only then that Axcan declared the offer effectively dead.[15]

On a comparative basis, acquisitions are more common than mergers and takeovers. Accordingly, we will focus on acquisitions in this chapter.

Reasons for Acquisitions

In this section, we discuss reasons that support the use of an acquisition strategy. Although each reason can provide a legitimate rationale for an acquisition, the acquisition may not necessarily lead to a competitive advantage—a situation discussed in greater detail later in this chapter. Reasons for acquisitions are summarized in Figure 8.1.

Increased Market Power

A primary reason for an acquisition is to achieve greater market power.[16] Defined in Chapter 7, market power exists when a firm is able to sell its goods or services above competitive levels or when the costs of its primary or support activities are below those of its competitors. Market power usually is derived from the size of the firm and its resources and capabilities to compete in the marketplace.[17] Market power is also affected by the firm's share of the market. Therefore, most acquisitions designed to achieve greater market power entail buying a competitor, a supplier, a distributor, or a business in a highly related industry that will allow exercise of a core competence and permit the company to gain a competitive advantage in the acquiring firm's primary market. One goal in achieving market power is to become a market leader.[18] For example, the acquisition of Pechiney by Alcan, noted in the opening case of Chapter 1, on page 5, resulted in the firm becoming the world's number one aluminium producer.

Firms use horizontal, vertical, and related acquisitions to increase their market power.

Horizontal Acquisitions. The acquisition of a company competing in the same industry in which the acquiring firm competes is referred to as a *horizontal acquisition*. Horizontal acquisitions increase a firm's market power by exploiting cost-based and revenue-based synergies.[19] Research suggests that horizontal acquisitions of firms with similar characteristics result in higher performance than when firms with dissimilar characteristics combine their operations. Examples of important similar characteristics include strategy,

Figure 8.1	Reasons for Acquisitions

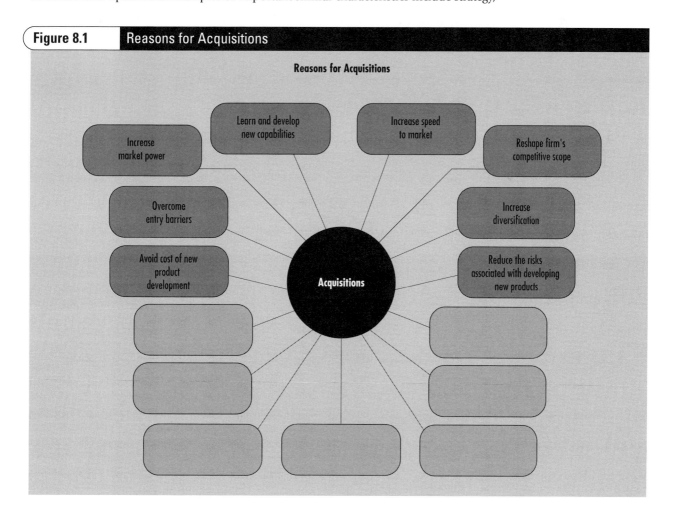

managerial styles, and resource allocation patterns. Similarities in these characteristics make the integration of the two firms proceed more smoothly.[20]

Horizontal acquisitions do not guarantee success. Some are successful, such as Alberta Energy's acquisition of PanCanadian Energy to create EnCana (discussed in the opening case of Chapter 1, on page 5). Others require a long time to achieve some semblance of order. For example, when Calgary's TransCanada Pipelines combined with Nova Corp.'s energy transmission businesses in 1998, their CEOs hailed the merger as a marriage "made in heaven." Nova, had a monopoly over gas collection and distribution in Alberta, and TransCanada operated the main pipeline to Central Canada and the U.S. Yet, it was also a marriage of necessity: Nova and TransCanada would have to face new competition from a $3.7 billion, 3000 km pipeline running from British Columbia to Chicago. The project had the backing of industry giants such as Duke Energy and Gulf Canada Resources. To survive, Nova and TransCanada had to join forces.[21] Yet, when the two organizations tried to work together, the resultant culture clash between the two organizations was dubbed "GI Joe meets Care Bear." For those managers who stayed at the new organization, the psychological wounds took years to heal.[22]

Vertical Acquisitions.   A *vertical acquisition* refers to a firm acquiring a supplier or distributor of one or more of its goods or services. A firm becomes vertically integrated through this type of acquisition, as it assumes control of additional parts of the value chain (see Chapter 4). An example of vertical integration is Aber Diamond Corp.'s $120 million acquisition of a majority interest in Harry Winston Inc. Toronto's Aber is a diamond marketer and mining concern (see Chapter 5's Strategic Focus box "More Precious Than Diamonds" on page 161). New York's Harry Winston, founded in 1912, is an old and respected jewellery retailer that has often been called the "jeweller to the stars." Aber's promotion of its Canadian diamonds would thus be aided by distribution through a high-end, high-profile retailer, such as Harry Winston.[23]

Related Acquisitions.   The acquisition of a firm in a highly related industry is referred to as a *related acquisition*. For example, in late 2003, Waterloo, Ontario-based Open Text bought Germany's IXOS. Although both provided software to run businesses' Enterprise Content Management (ECM) systems, they covered very different areas of the industry. Open Text specialized in knowledge management and document collaboration, and Ixos' specialized in groupware integration, transactions support, and Enterprise Resource Planning (ERP) applications. The combined company will be able to provide users with more complete solutions to their content management needs.[24]

Acquisitions intended to increase market power are subject to regulatory review, as well as to analysis by financial markets. For example, Canadian banks' attempts to merge with one another over the last decade or so have been thwarted by government concerns over the likely resulting loss of competition among the remaining players in industry. Thus, the banks have focused on international expansion rather than domestic merger. Thus, firms seeking growth and market power through acquisitions must understand the political/legal segment of the general environment (see Chapter 3) in order to successfully use an acquisition strategy.

As shown in the next Strategic Focus box, "Certainly Gaining Impetus with Acquisitions," horizontal, vertical, and related acquisitions can all play a role in creating an effective competitor. As well, horizontal acquisitions are often most effective when the acquiring firm integrates the acquired firm's assets with its assets, but only after evaluating and divesting excess capacity and assets that do not complement the newly combined firm's core competencies.[25]

Overcoming Entry Barriers

Barriers to entry (introduced in Chapter 3) are factors associated with the market or with the firms currently operating in the market that increase the expense and difficulty faced

Certainly Gaining *Impetus* with Acquisitions

Founded in 1976, CGI has become among the largest independent information technology (IT) and business process services firms in North America. With more than 20,000 employees, between $3 billion and $4 billion in sales, and an order backlog of more than $12 billion, this Montreal-based IT firm is a serious competitor. Even more impressive is that CGI clients include about 20 of the top 25 insurance carriers in the U.S. and about 15 of the top 25 insurance carriers in Canada. With all these things going for it, CGI can hardly be complacent. Its two largest rivals are U.S.-based giants EDS and IBM, firms that are, respectively, 5 and 25 times larger than CGI.

How does CGI manage to grow and thrive in its environment? Acquisitions and divestitures are a vital part of CGI's strategy. In 2003, after years of rivalry, CGI bought cross-town IT competitor Cognicase for $321 million. CGI followed this purchase with the sale of Cognicase's off-the-shelf Enterprise Resource Planning (ERP) products and related services to Nexxlink Technologies. In exchange, CGI received 35 percent equity interest in Nexxlink. CGI thus maintained its focus on the service aspects of the business that it does best, allowed Nexxlink to focus on products with which it is familiar, and gave itself a stake in a related product area.

CEO Serge Godin's most prized acquisition of 2003 was a somewhat smaller one, however. Godin's number one deal that year was the company's $53 million acquisition of The Underwriters Adjustment Bureau Ltd. The move marked CGI's efforts to extend its expertise in the insurance market and, according to Godin, "move up in the value chain and be an end-to-end IT services company." This purchase can be viewed as an essentially vertical acquisition to support CGI's strong commitment to its insurance industry customers.

In 2004, CGI bought U.S. IT consulting firm American Management Systems (AMS) for $1.1 billion. CGI then sold AMS's Defense and Intelligence Group to CACI International for $549 million. This sale cut the net cost to CGI by half. AMS added almost 5000 employees to CGI's workforce, increased its sales by $1 billion, and doubled the company's presence in the U.S. While CGI has an excellent record for absorbing new operations, the horizontal acquisition of AMS represented a new dimension in both size and CGI's approach to its new subsidiary. CGI employs the AMS name, along with its own, for the brand it uses in most of its U.S. operations. Michael Roach, CGI's chief operating officer explained that, "We think American Management Systems has a nice ring to it. ... That gives us a very good calling card, and helps us open more doors [in the U.S.]."

After completing more than 30 deals since 1998, CGI is still looking for acquisitions. However, as CGI's chief financial officer (CFO) Andre Imbeau notes, "Integration is the key to successful acquisition. ... If I had one goal today, it would be to show you [that] at CGI we handle acquisitions in a systematic, well-organized and structured manner."

SOURCES: CGI Group, 2004, *CGI website*, http://www.cgi.com, accessed April 12, 2004; A. Whal, 2004, Canadian invasion: CGI goes on the acquisition offensive, *Canadian Business*, March 15, 29; Wall Street Journal, 2004, CGI agrees to buy American Management, *Wall Street Journal*, March 11, 1; A. Whal, 2003 Resistance is futile: CGI has assimilated 29 companies since 1998: Here's how Cognicase became part of the collective, *Canadian Business Online*, June 15, accessed April 12, 2004; K. Marron, 2003, BPO boom, *Globe and Mail Report on Business*, September 26, 103; G. Hilson, 2002, CGI scores IT hat trick with three insurance firms…., *IT Business.ca*, February 5, accessed April 12, 2004.

by new ventures trying to enter that particular market. For example, well-established competitors may have substantial economies of scale in the manufacture of their products. In addition, enduring relationships with customers often create product loyalties that are difficult for new entrants to overcome. When facing differentiated products, new entrants typically must spend considerable resources to advertise their goods or services and may find it necessary to sell at a price below competitors' prices to entice customers.

Facing the entry barriers created by economies of scale and differentiated products, a new entrant may find the acquisition of an established company to be more effective than entering the market as a competitor offering a good or service that is unfamiliar to current buyers. In fact, the higher the barriers to market entry, the greater the probability that a firm will acquire an existing firm to overcome those barriers. Although an acquisition can be expensive, it does provide the new entrant with immediate market access.

Firms trying to enter international markets often face quite steep entry barriers.[26] In response, acquisitions are commonly used to overcome those barriers.[27] For example, in 2000, U.S.-based Best Buy decided to acquire B.C.'s Future Shop for $580 million, rather than try to enter the Canadian market on its own. The advantage for Best Buy is that it will have one less competitor when entering the Canadian market, and other U.S. companies will have to fight for market share with both the Future Shop and Best Buy names.[28]

For large multinational corporations, another indicator of the importance of entering and then competing successfully in international markets is the fact that five emerging markets (China, India, Brazil, Mexico, and Indonesia) are among the 12 largest economies in the world, with a combined purchasing power that is already one-half that of the Group of Seven industrial nations (Canada, United States, Japan, Britain, France, Germany, and Italy).[29] Being a play in these markets thus becomes critical for future growth, and entry barriers may make acquisition the most logical entry strategy.

Cross-Border Acquisitions.   Acquisitions made between companies with headquarters in different countries are called *cross-border acquisitions*. These acquisitions are often made to overcome entry barriers. In Chapter 10, we examine cross-border alliances and the reason for their use. Compared to a cross-border alliance, a firm has more control over its international operations through a cross-border acquisition.[30]

Historically, U.S. firms have been the most active acquirers of companies outside their domestic market. However, in the global economy, companies throughout the world are choosing this strategic option with increasing frequency. In recent years, cross-border acquisitions have represented as much as 45 percent of the total number of acquisitions made annually.[31] The CGI acquisition of AMS, discussed above, provides an example of this activity. Because of relaxed regulations, the amount of cross-border activity among nations within the European community also continues to increase. Accounting for this growth in a range of cross-border acquisitions, some analysts believe, is the fact that many large European corporations have approached the limits of growth within their domestic markets and thus seek growth in other markets. Additionally, they are trying to achieve market power to compete effectively throughout the European Union and thus have made acquisitions in other European countries.

Firms in all types of industries are completing cross-border acquisitions. In early 2004, Quebec drugstore market leader Jean Coutu bought more than 1500 Eckerd Drug Stores in the U.S. The purchase doubled Jean Coutu's revenues and tripled its number of stores and employees. Yet, limited growth opportunities in the Canadian market meant that Jean Coutu could not really afford to pass up the opportunity to buy up the Eckerd locations.[32] In the cosmetics industry, Japan's Shiseido created a new division to pursue mergers and acquisitions. With its growth long fuelled by acquisitions, the firm is now committed to emphasizing the cross-border variety, especially with European companies.

Cost of New-Product Development and Increased Speed to Market

Developing new products internally and introducing them successfully into the marketplace often requires significant investments of a firm's resources, including time, and thus makes it difficult to quickly earn a profitable return.[33] Also of concern to firms' managers is achieving adequate returns from the capital invested to develop and commercialize new products—an estimated 88 percent of innovations fail to achieve adequate returns. Perhaps contributing to these less than desirable rates of return is the successful imitation of approximately 60 percent of innovations within four years after the patents are obtained. Because of such outcomes, managers often perceive internal product development as a high-risk activity.[34]

Acquisitions are another means a firm can use to gain access both to new products and to current products that are new to the firm. Compared to internal product development processes, acquisitions provide more predictable returns as well as faster market entry. Returns are more predictable because the performance of the acquired firm's products can be assessed prior to completing the acquisition.[35] For these reasons, extensive bidding wars and acquisitions are more frequent in high-technology industries.[36]

Acquisition activity is also extensive throughout the pharmaceutical industry, where firms frequently use acquisitions to enter markets quickly, to overcome the high costs of developing products internally, and to increase the predictability of returns on their investments. The practice is not restricted to industry powerhouses, such as Pfizer of the U.S. or GlaxoSmithKline of the U.K. For example, in late 2002, Mississauga's Biovail— which, with about $1 billion in sales, is a relatively small player in the industry— acquired California-based Pharma Pass LLC and French-based Pharma Pass SA for $190 million to give its company new and novel drug delivery systems.[37]

As indicated previously, compared to internal product development, acquisitions result in more rapid market entries.[38] Acquisitions often represent the fastest means to enter international markets and help firms overcome the liabilities associated with such strategic moves.[39] Acquisitions provide rapid access both to new markets and to new capabilities. Using new capabilities to pioneer new products and to enter markets quickly can create advantageous market positions.[40] Pharmaceutical firms, for example, access new products through acquisitions of other drug manufacturers. They also acquire biotechnology firms both for new products and for new technological capabilities. Pharmaceutical firms often provide the manufacturing and marketing capabilities to take the new products developed by biotechnology firms to the market.[41]

Lower Risk Compared to Developing New Products

Because an acquisition's outcomes can be estimated more easily and accurately compared to the outcomes of an internal product development process, managers may view acquisitions as lowering risk.[42] The difference in risk between an internal product development process and an acquisition can be seen in the results of U.S. pharmaceutical giant Merck, given its strategy, relative to its competitors. Merck chose not to acquire new drugs but to develop them internally. This strategy made the company the world's largest and most successful pharmaceutical firm. However, since the start of the new millennium, Merck has experienced new-product development problems and now trails Pfizer and GlaxoSmithKline in the industry. Some analysts suggest that Merck may be unable to return to its former ranking unless it acquires another large and successful pharmaceutical firm.[43]

As with other strategic actions discussed in this book, the firm must exercise caution when using a strategy of acquiring new products rather than developing them internally. While research suggests that acquisitions have become a common means of avoiding risky internal ventures (and therefore risky R&D investments), acquisitions demand a premium and may also become a substitute for innovation.[44] Thus, acquisitions are not a risk-free alternative to entering new markets through internally developed products.

Increased Diversification

Acquisitions are also used to diversify firms. Based on experience and the insights resulting from it, firms typically find it easier to develop and introduce new products in markets currently served by the firm. In contrast, it is difficult for companies to develop products that differ from their current lines for markets in which they lack experience. Thus, it is uncommon for a firm to develop new products internally to diversify its product lines.[45] Using acquisitions to diversify a firm is the quickest and, typically, the easiest way to change its portfolio of businesses.[46]

Both related-diversification and unrelated-diversification strategies can be implemented through acquisitions. For example, one of Canada's most widely diversified conglomerates is Toronto's Onex Corporation. Sometimes referred to as a shopaholic, Onex's $17 billion in sales are derived from its interests in a diverse variety of industries—including electronic manufacturing, theatre exhibition, automotive products, and services for management, communications, and health care.[47] Yet, not all the company's purchases are completely unrelated. When moving into an industry, Onex typically follows up the initial purchase with additional investments in the same business line. For example, Onex went into the entertainment business after investing in a motion-picture production company in 1995. Onex then entered into a joint venture to build and operate theatres in 1999. In 2001, Onex, along with other partners, bought control of the Loews Cineplex theatre chain. They then bought Cinemex, Mexico's largest movie chain, in 2002. This was followed up with other related investments in theatres in Korea, the Canary Islands, and Europe.[48]

Research has shown the more related the acquired firm is to the acquiring firm, the greater is the probability that the acquisition will be successful.[49] Thus, horizontal acquisitions (through which a firm acquires a competitor) and related acquisitions tend to contribute more to the firm's strategic competitiveness than acquiring a company that operates in quite different product markets from those in which the firm competes.[50] For example, firms in the financial services industry have become more diversified over time, often through acquisitions into related industries, such as insurance. One study suggests that these firms are diversifying, not only to provide a more complete line of products for their customers, but also to create strategic flexibility. In other words, they diversify into some product lines to provide options for future services they may wish to emphasize. As noted earlier, such acquisitions are a means of dealing with an uncertain competitive environment.[51]

Reshaping the Firm's Competitive Scope

As discussed in Chapter 3, the intensity of competitive rivalry is an industry characteristic that affects the firm's profitability.[52] To reduce the negative effect of an intense rivalry on their financial performance, firms may use acquisitions to reduce their dependence on one or more products or markets. Reducing a company's dependence on specific markets alters the firm's competitive scope.

One of Canada's largest privately owned companies, The Jim Pattison Group, began in 1961, as a car dealership. Today, the group has interests in advertising, magazine distribution, and specialty packaging, among other industries. The company, by some analysts' estimates, is more of a grocery store chain than anything else, since the largest chunk of the company's revenues (about one-third) comes from its Overwaitea/Save-On-Foods food group and its Buy-Low Foods grocery stores. However, the fact that Jim Pattison is also North America's second largest magazine and newspaper distributor and owns the Ripley's Believe It or Not empire (more than 40 attractions in 8 countries) gives the organization a fairly wide scope of activities.[53]

Another example is that one of the arguments against Hewlett-Packard's acquisition of Compaq was that it would increase the firm's dependence on the highly competitive and volatile personal computer market. Thus, rather than using acquisitions to avoid competition, HP increased its emphasis in a market characterized by substantial competitive rivalry. Some major shareholders and analysts believe that HP should emphasize its printers and computer accessories businesses rather than its computers.

Learning and Developing New Capabilities

Some acquisitions are made to gain capabilities that the firm does not possess. For example, acquisitions may be used to acquire a special technological capability. Research has shown that firms can broaden their knowledge base and reduce inertia through acquisitions.[54] Therefore, acquiring other firms with skills and capabilities that differ from its own helps the acquiring firm to learn new knowledge and remain agile. Of course, firms are better able to learn these capabilities if they share some similar properties with the firm's current capabilities. Thus, firms should seek to acquire companies with different, but related and complementary, capabilities in order to build their own knowledge base.[55]

For example, in 2003, Angiotech, a small Vancouver-based pharmaceutical research lab, acquired two companies to aid in its development of innovative drug-loaded materials and devices. Angiotech's products are designed to lessen the complications resulting from surgery by using drugs as part of the materials and devices employed in surgical operations. One of the acquired companies added to Angiotech's knowledge of sprays and gels to reduce clotting after heart surgery. The other company gave Angiotech a knowledge base in a broad range of state-of-the-art biocompatible coatings for medical devices.[56]

Another example is California's Cisco Systems. One of its primary acquisition goals is to gain access to capabilities that the firm does not currently possess. Cisco executives emphasize the importance of learning throughout the organization.[57] They have developed an intricate process to quickly integrate the acquired firms and their capabilities (knowledge) after an acquisition. Although Cisco did suffer in the 2001–02 tech-stock collapse, the firm is expected to bounce back as the economy recovers.

Problems in Achieving Acquisition Success

Acquisition strategies based on the legitimate reasons described in this chapter can increase strategic competitiveness and help firms to earn above-average returns. However, acquisition strategies are not risk free. Potential problems with acquisition strategies and the previously discussed reasons for their use are shown in Figure 8.2.

Research suggests that 20 percent of all mergers and acquisitions are successful, approximately 60 percent produce disappointing results, and the last 20 percent are clear failures.[58] A study by market analyst Thomson Financial / First Call showed that the shares of the 20 most aggressive U.S. acquirers of the late 1990s dropped almost twice as much as the Dow Jones industrial average during the same period.[59] Successful acquisitions generally involve a well-conceived strategy in selecting the target, avoiding paying too high a premium, and an effective integration process.[60] As shown in Figure 8.2, several problems may prevent successful acquisitions.

Integration Difficulties
Integrating two companies following an acquisition can be quite difficult. Integration challenges include melding two disparate corporate cultures, linking different financial and control systems, building effective working relationships (particularly when management styles differ), and resolving problems regarding the status of the newly acquired firm's executives.[61]

The importance of a successful integration should not be underestimated. Without it, an acquisition is unlikely to produce positive returns. Thus, as suggested by a researcher studying the process, "managerial practice and academic writings show that the post-acquisition integration phase is probably the single most important determinant of shareholder value creation (and equally of value destruction) in mergers and acquisitions."[62]

Integration is complex and involves a large number of activities. When TD Bank took over Canada Trust, the deal was different from past bank acquisitions. First, the acquisition was under the intense scrutiny of regulators and required integrating 1500 branches, 44,000 employees, 10 million customers, $265 billion in assets, and an ATM

Figure 8.2 — Problems with and Reasons for Acquisitions

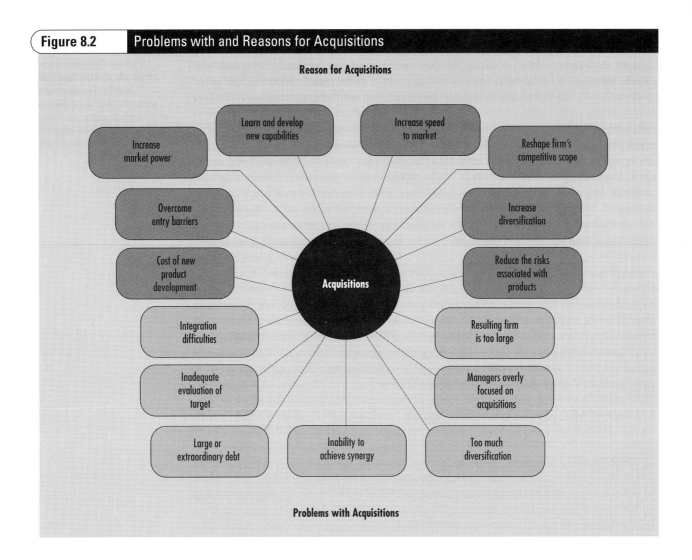

Reason for Acquisitions

Increase market power

Learn and develop new capabilities

Increase speed to market

Reshape firm's competitive scope

Overcome entry barriers

Increase diversification

Cost of new product development

Reduce the risks associated with products

Integration difficulties

Acquisitions

Resulting firm is too large

Inadequate evaluation of target

Managers overly focused on acquisitions

Large or extraordinary debt

Inability to achieve synergy

Too much diversification

Problems with Acquisitions

network that, at peak times, handled 700 transactions per second. Integrating the two companies' ATM networks was so complex, in fact, that it was accomplished in four waves—beginning with the East Coast. There were some early problems but these were fixed before large numbers of customers were impacted. Through the entire process, a special integration team kept things on schedule.[63]

It is important to maintain the human capital of the target firm after the acquisition. Much of an organization's knowledge is contained in its human capital.[64] Turnover of key personnel from the acquired firm can have a negative effect on the performance of the merged firm.[65] In the TD-Canada Trust merger, executives quickly let employees know how their jobs would be affected to ensure that key personal would not leave the company before a decision was made regarding their retention.[66] The loss of key personnel, such as critical managers, weakens the acquired firm's capabilities and reduces its value.

If implemented effectively, the integration process can have a positive effect on target firm managers and reduce the probability that they will leave.[67] In the two years after EnCana was created out of Alberta Energy and PanCanadian, its stock rose 14 percent and the company met its goal of reducing annual operating expenses by $250 million. To attain these successes, executives ensured the merged company came together quickly. Within six months after announcing the deal, shareholders and courts had given their approval, EnCana stock was trading in Toronto and New York, all layoffs of redundant employees had been substantially completed, and employees knew who their supervisors were and what their compensation would be.[68]

Inadequate Evaluation of Target

Due diligence is a process through which a potential acquirer evaluates a target firm for acquisition. In an effective due-diligence process, hundreds of items are examined in areas as diverse as the financing for the intended transaction, differences in cultures between the acquiring and target firm, tax consequences of the transaction, and actions that would be necessary to successfully meld the two workforces. Due diligence is commonly performed by investment bankers, accountants, lawyers, and management consultants specializing in that activity, although firms actively pursuing acquisitions may form their own internal due-diligence team.

The failure to complete an effective due-diligence process may easily result in the acquiring firm paying an excessive premium for the target company. In fact, research shows that without due diligence, "the purchase price is driven by the pricing of other 'comparable' acquisitions rather than by a rigorous assessment of where, when, and how management can drive real performance gains. [In these cases], the price paid may have little to do with achievable value."[69]

One nearly catastrophic example is Dynegy's November 2001 agreement to acquire its former rival, Enron, the once highly successful, then highly infamous, energy trading company. Months before the announcement, Enron's market value was about $90 billion. When the firm announced it had overstated earnings for several years, its value dropped and Dynegy agreed to buy Enron for only $12 billion. Within weeks, further serious financial problems were revealed and Enron's market value fell to about $360 million—3 percent of the price to which Dynegy had agreed. Dynegy withdrew its offer, and Enron filed a $13 billion lawsuit against Dynegy for backing out. Dynegy countersued to acquire Enron's largest pipeline for $2 billion, an amount agreed upon earlier in a separate deal. While Dynegy was eventually victorious in the lawsuit and countersuit, an effective due-diligence process on Dynegy's part may have revealed the true value of Enron, prior to any announced agreements.

In fact, Dynegy could have lost considerable value if it had completed the acquisition of Enron. It was saved because investors and lenders expressed concerns. While Dynegy obtained valuable pipeline assets for $2 billion, effective due diligence would have identified Enron's problems, and Dynegy would not have entered into a messy public commitment to acquire the firm.[70]

Large or Extraordinary Debt

To finance a number of acquisitions completed during the 1980s and 1990s, some companies significantly increased their levels of debt. A financial innovation called junk bonds helped make this increase possible. *Junk bonds* are a financing option through which risky acquisitions are financed with money (debt) that provides a large potential return to lenders (bondholders). Because junk bonds are unsecured obligations that are not tied to specific assets for collateral, during the 1980s, interest rates for these high-risk debt instruments sometimes reached between 18 percent and 20 percent.[71] Some prominent financial economists view debt as a means to discipline managers, causing them to act in shareholders' best interests.[72]

Junk bonds are now used less frequently to finance acquisitions, and the conviction that debt disciplines managers is less strong. Nonetheless, some firms still take on significant debt to acquire companies. For example, in 2001, Quebecor paid $5.4 billion for Groupe Vidéotron ltée—an acquisition that burdened the company with a huge

$8 billion total debt load. It also became a dubious investment because its cash flow never met its promise, due to increased competition from Bell ExpressVu's satellite TV.[73]

While there is less of a conviction that debt disciplines managers to run their companies better, the disciplining effects still exist. For example, in the 1990s, George Watson, an acquisitively aggressive CEO, headed TransCanada Pipelines Limted. Watson took the company into all kinds of unrelated and overseas businesses—and assumed huge debt to do so. When TransCanada bought up Nova Corp in 1998 (as discussed earlier in this chapter), the $15.6 billion in debt was more than the company's bankers could tolerate. Watson was disciplined—actually, he was fired. The firm's non–energy-distributing businesses were divested. The debt not only disciplined the CEO, but the company as well. The debt effectively took priority over the CEO's wishes and, in fact, over the CEO himself.[74]

High debt can have several negative effects on the firm. For example, because high debt increases the likelihood of bankruptcy, it can lead to a downgrade in the firm's credit rating by agencies such as Moody's and Standard & Poor's.[75] In addition, high debt may preclude needed investment in activities that contribute to the firm's long-term success, such as R&D, human resource training, and marketing.[76] Still, use of leverage can be a positive force in a firm's development, allowing it to take advantage of attractive expansion opportunities. However, too much leverage (e.g., extraordinary debt) can lead to negative outcomes, including postponing or eliminating investments (e.g., R&D expenditures) that are necessary to maintain strategic competitiveness over the long term.

Inability to Achieve Synergy

Derived from *synergos*, a Greek word that means "working together," synergy exists when the value created by units working together exceeds the value those units could create working independently (see Chapter 7). That is, synergy exists when assets are worth more when used in conjunction with each other than when they are used separately.[77] For shareholders, synergy generates gains in their wealth that they could not duplicate or exceed through their own portfolio diversification decisions.[78] Synergy is created by the efficiencies derived from economies of scale and economies of scope and by sharing resources (e.g., human capital and knowledge) across the businesses in the merged firm.[79]

A firm develops a competitive advantage through an acquisition strategy only when a transaction generates private synergy. *Private synergy* is created when the combination and integration of the acquiring and acquired firms' assets yield capabilities and core competencies that could not be developed by combining and integrating either firm's assets with another company. Private synergy is possible when firms' assets are complementary in unique ways; that is, the unique type of asset complement is not possible by combining either company's assets with another firm's assets.[80] Because of its uniqueness, private synergy is difficult for competitors to understand and imitate. However, private synergy is difficult to create. See the Strategic Focus box "Synergy Failures" for a few examples.

A firm's ability to account for costs that are necessary to create anticipated revenue-based and cost-based synergies affects the acquisition's success. Firms experience several expenses when trying to create private synergy through acquisitions. Called transaction costs, these expenses are incurred when firms use acquisition strategies to create synergy.[81] Transaction costs may be direct or indirect. Direct costs include legal fees and charges from investment bankers who complete due diligence for the acquiring firm. Indirect costs include managerial time to evaluate target firms and then to complete negotiations, as well as the loss of key managers and employees following an acquisition.[82] Firms tend to underestimate the sum of indirect costs when calculating the value of the synergy that may be created by combining and integrating the acquired firm's assets with the acquiring firm's assets.

Synergy Failures: When $1 + 1$ Equals $1\frac{1}{2}$

Almost by definition, synergy means that one plus one must equal more than two. In other words, for the merger of two companies to be financially justifiable, the combined company must be able to do better than the sum of its separate parts. Indeed, mergers and acquisitions make little sense if there is not some synergy involved. Yet, while most acquisitions begin with great optimism about the possible synergies to be achieved by the merged company, many fail to deliver on their promise.

In 2001, two huge U.S. companies spent billions to put together the deal to combine and form AOL Time Warner. The merged company hoped for synergies between AOL's technological/ Internet acumen and Time Warner's movie, video, and print content. In less than three years, the AOL name was quietly dropped from "AOL Time Warner." Not only were synergies nowhere near what were expected but the collapse of the tech-stock market made AOL a very junior partner in the valuation of the company.

Unfortunately, the Americans had no monopoly on this fuzzy notion of merging technology and content. Jean-Marie Messier, CEO of France's Vivendi, paid more than $30 billion to buy Canada's Seagram Co. Ltd. and its entertainment assets, Universal Studios and PolyGram Music. To create greater synergies, Messier later bought USA Networks and Houghton Mifflin Co., the U.S. text-book publisher. The expected synergies between Vivendi's telecommunications assets and Universal's content never materialized however, and Messier was, after only 19 months, demateri-alized from his position of CEO at the merged Vivendi Universal Entertainment.

Not to be left out, Jean Monty, CEO of Montreal's BCE, spent about $12 billion to buy long-distance carrier Teleglobe, the CTV television network, and control of *The Globe and Mail*. Combine all these with BCE's Sympatico website, and you can create the kind of synergy we have been talking about: none. Between the time Monty became CEO in 1998 and 2002, there was a steady decline in BCE's stock-market value and profits (which fell 90 percent during his tenure). Such synergy failures occurred, not only at BCE, but also at aggressive acquirers, such as Canada's Nortel Networks and JDS Uniphase.

In all of these cases, and many more, the sum of the parts was not even equal to what the companies were worth as stand-alone entities. As well, the whole problem is not restricted to tech stocks. Even mundane, or, in this case, morbid, businesses have failed to create synergies promised by acquisitions. In the early 1990s, B.C.'s Ray Loewen built the second largest funeral home chain in North America. Loewen was forced to step down as CEO after expected synergies from putting the company together failed to occur, and the Loewen Group missed earnings tar-gets too many times. About $4 billion in market capitalization disappeared between 1996 and 1999, when the company entered bankruptcy. After 30 months in bankruptcy, the company—renamed the Alderwoods Group—shed 200 of its 1100 funeral homes, 125 of its 400 cemeteries, and $2 bil-lion in debt. When measures as extreme as bankruptcy are employed to make a set of acquisi-tions work, it speaks volumes about the need to carefully evaluate the deal before getting involved.

SOURCES: Time Warner 2004, *Time Warner website*, http://www.timewarner.com/investors/faq/faq_z_04_merger.adp, accessed April 25, 2004; A. Grikscheit & M. Giansanti Cag, 2002, Extracting value from solid alliances, *Mergers and Acquisitions*, 37(6): 28; D. Olive, 2002, Merger: A strategy of growth by acquisition sent many high-flying companies tumbling into financial turmoil…., *Toronto Star*, August 27, C1; J. Bates & T. Mulligan, 2002, Convergence follies: The rise and demise of Vivendi's Messier, *Toronto Star*, July 7, C3; G. Norris, 2001, U.S. court OKs Loewen reorganization: Reborn Alderwoods if Canada also approves plan, *National Post (Financial Post)*, December 7, FP7; P. Kuitenbrouwer, 1999, Too big for their britches: From Burnaby to Hamilton, big consolidators are suffering…., *National Post (Financial Post)*, February 22, C12.

Too Much Diversification

As explained in Chapter 7, diversification strategies can lead to strategic competitiveness and above-average returns. In general, firms using related diversification strategies outperform those employing unrelated diversification strategies. However, conglomerates, formed by using an unrelated diversification strategy, also can be successful. For example, Virgin Group, the U.K. firm with interests ranging from cosmetics to trains, is successful.

At some point, firms can become overdiversified. The level at which overdiversification occurs varies across companies because each firm has different capabilities to manage diversification. Recall from Chapter 7 that related diversification requires more information processing than does unrelated diversification. The need for related diversified firms to process more information of greater diversity is such that they become overdiversified with a smaller number of business units, compared to firms using an unrelated diversification strategy.[83] Regardless of the type of diversification strategy implemented, however, declines in performance result from overdiversification, after which business units are often divested.[84] The pattern of excessive diversification followed by divestments of underperforming business units acquired earlier was frequently observed among North American companies[85] during the 1960s through the 1980s.[86]

Even when a firm is not overdiversified, a high level of diversification can have a negative effect on the firm's long-term performance. For example, the scope created by additional amounts of diversification often causes managers to rely on financial, rather than strategic, controls to evaluate business units' performances (financial and strategic controls are defined and explained in Chapters 12 and 13). Top-level executives often rely on financial controls to assess the performance of business units when they do not have a rich understanding of business units' objectives and strategies. Use of financial controls, such as return on investment (ROI), causes individual business-unit managers to focus on short-term outcomes at the expense of long-term investments. When long-term investments are reduced to increase short-term profits, a firm's overall strategic competitiveness may be harmed.[87]

Another problem resulting from too much diversification is the tendency for acquisitions to become substitutes for innovation. Typically, managers do not intend acquisitions to be used in that way. However, a reinforcing cycle evolves. Costs associated with acquisitions may result in fewer allocations to activities, such as R&D, that are linked to innovation. Without adequate support, a firm's innovation skills begin to atrophy. Without internal innovation skills, the only option available to a firm is to complete still additional acquisitions to gain access to innovation. Evidence suggests that a firm using acquisitions as a substitute for internal innovations eventually encounters performance problems.[88]

Managers Overly Focused on Acquisitions

Typically, a fairly substantial amount of managerial time and energy is required for acquisition strategies to contribute to the firm's strategic competitiveness. Activities with which managers become involved include (1) searching for viable acquisition candidates, (2) completing effective due-diligence processes, (3) preparing for negotiations, and (4) managing the integration process after the acquisition is completed.

Top-level managers do not personally gather all data and information required to make acquisitions. However, these executives do make critical decisions on the firms to be targeted, the nature of the negotiations, and so forth. Company experiences show that participating in and overseeing the activities required for making acquisitions can divert managerial attention from other matters that are necessary for long-term competitive success, such as identifying and taking advantage of other opportunities and interacting with important external stakeholders.[89]

For example, in 1996, Calgary entrepreneur Cameron Chell founded FutureLink, a professional services firm that aimed to be a leader in the emerging application service provider (ASP) industry. ASPs supply software to a company's computers on a subscription basis, so that companies do not need to buy expensive software up-front.[90] FutureLink established a server farm, a call centre, and a help desk in Calgary. To become the ASP leader, FutureLink then spent more than $1.1 billion to acquire a number of companies. In 1999, FutureLink purchased California's MicroVisions and Computer Networks, Detroit's Async Technologies, Maryland's VSI Technology Solutions, New York's Madison Group, and Toronto's Charon Systems. Although it became one of the top firms in the ASP business, FutureLink had concentrated more on making the acquisitions than integrating the purchased companies. Within a year, the firm's losses were double its revenues; within two years, the company was in bankruptcy; and today, it is no more.[91]

Acquisitions can consume significant amounts of managerial time and energy at both the acquiring and the target firms. In particular, managers in target firms may operate in a state of virtual suspended animation during an acquisition.[92] Although the target firm's day-to-day operations continue, most of the company's executives are hesitant to make decisions with long-term consequences until negotiations have been completed. Evidence suggests that the acquisition process can create a short-term perspective and a greater aversion to risk among top-level executives in a target firm.[93]

Too Large

Most acquisitions create a larger firm that should help increase its economies of scale. These economies can then lead to more efficient operations. For example, two sales organizations can be integrated using fewer sales reps because a sales rep can sell the products of both firms (particularly if the products of the acquiring and target firms are highly related).

Many firms seek increases in size because of the potential economies of scale and enhanced market power (discussed earlier). For example, Gruner+Jahr, a subsidiary of Germany's media giant, Bertelsmann AG, made $800 million in acquisitions in a six-month period during 2000, including the $450 million acquisition of *Fast Company*. Essentially, the goal was for Gruner+Jahr to become number one or two in the markets served and, simultaneously, gain economies of scale and market power.[94]

At some level, the additional costs required to manage the larger firm will exceed the benefits of the economies of scale and additional market power. In addition, the complexities generated by larger firm size often lead managers to implement more bureaucratic controls to manage the combined firm's operations. Bureaucratic controls are formalized supervisory and behavioural rules and policies designed to ensure consistency of decisions and actions across different units of a firm. However, through time, formalized controls often lead to relatively rigid and standardized managerial behaviour. Certainly, in the long run, the diminished flexibility that accompanies rigid and standardized managerial behaviour may produce less innovation. Because of innovation's importance to competitive success, the bureaucratic controls resulting from a large organization (i.e., built by acquisitions) can have a detrimental effect on performance.[95]

Effective Acquisitions

Earlier in the chapter, we noted that acquisition strategies do not consistently produce above-average returns for the acquiring firm's shareholders. Nonetheless, some companies are able to create value when using an acquisition strategy.[96] Results from a research study shed light on the differences between unsuccessful and successful acquisition strategies and suggest that there is a pattern of actions that can improve the probability of acquisition success.[97]

The study shows that when the target firm's assets are complementary to the acquired firm's assets, an acquisition is more successful, and there is a higher probability of creating synergy. In fact, integrating two firms with complementary assets frequently produces unique capabilities and core competencies.[98] With complementary assets, the acquiring firm can maintain its focus on core businesses and leverage the complementary assets and capabilities from the acquired firm. Oftentimes, targets were selected and groomed by establishing a working relationship sometime prior to the acquisition. As discussed in Chapter 10, strategic alliances are sometimes used to test the feasibility of a future merger or acquisition between the involved firms.[99]

The study's results also show that friendly acquisitions facilitate integration of the firms involved in an acquisition. Through friendly acquisitions, firms work together to find ways to integrate their operations to create synergy. In hostile takeovers, animosity often results between the two top-management teams, a condition that in turn affects working relationships in the newly created firm. As a result, more key personnel in the acquired firm may be lost, and those who remain may resist the changes necessary to integrate the two firms.[100] With effort, cultural clashes can be overcome, and fewer key managers and employees will become discouraged and leave.[101]

Additionally, effective due-diligence processes involving the deliberate and careful selection of target firms and an evaluation of the relative health of those firms (financial health, cultural fit, and the value of human resources) contribute to successful acquisitions. Financial slack, in the form of debt equity or cash, in both the acquiring and acquired firms, also has frequently contributed to success in acquisitions. While financial slack provides access to financing for the acquisition, it is still important to maintain a low or moderate level of debt after the acquisition, to keep debt costs low. When substantial debt was used to finance the acquisition, companies with successful acquisitions reduced the debt quickly, partly by selling off assets from the acquired firm, especially noncomplementary or poorly performing assets. For these firms, debt costs do not prevent long-term investments, such as R&D, and managerial discretion in the use of cash flow is relatively flexible.

Another attribute of successful acquisition strategies is an emphasis on innovation, as demonstrated by continuing investments in R&D activities. Significant R&D investments show a strong managerial commitment to innovation, a characteristic that is increasingly important to overall competitiveness, as well as acquisition success.

Flexibility and adaptability are the final two attributes of successful acquisitions. When executives of both the acquiring and the target firms have experience in managing change and learning from acquisitions, they will be more skilled at adapting their capabilities to new environments.[102] As a result, they will be more adept at integrating the two organizations, which is particularly important when firms have different organizational cultures.

Efficient and effective integration may quickly produce the desired synergy in the newly created firm. Effective integration allows the acquiring firm to keep valuable human resources in the acquired firm from leaving.[103]

The attributes and results of successful acquisitions are summarized in Table 8.1. Managers seeking acquisition success should emphasize the seven attributes that are listed.

For example, the attempted acquisition of Honeywell by GE had some but not all of the attributes of successful acquisitions summarized in Table 8.1. In 2001, Honeywell International agreed to be acquired by General Electric (GE). There seemed to be potential synergies between GE and Honeywell, especially in the aerospace businesses. GE's jet engines and Honeywell's avionic equipment businesses should fit well together. Yet, concern over potential dominance of this market is what later led European regulators to disapprove the acquisition. As well, it is unclear how much due diligence GE conducted prior to making its offer, since the deal was completed so quickly that there was no time to consult European lawyers on regulatory concerns. Finally, the deal had the

Table 8.1	Attributes of Successful Acquisitions

Attributes	Results
1. Acquired firm has assets or resources that are complementary to the acquiring firm's core business	1. High probability of synergy and competitive advantage by maintaining strengths
2. Acquisition is friendly	2. Faster and more effective integration and possibly lower premiums
3. Acquiring firm conducts effective due diligence to select target firms and evaluate the target firm's health (financial, cultural, and human resources)	3. Firms with strongest complementarities are acquired, and overpayment is avoided
4. Acquiring firm has financial slack (cash or a favourable debt position)	4. Financing (debt or equity) is easier and less costly to obtain
5. Merged firm maintains low to moderate debt position	5. Lower financing cost, lower risk (e.g., of bankruptcy), and avoidance of trade-offs that are associated with high debt
6. Sustained and consistent emphasis on R&D and innovation	6. Maintain long-term competitive advantage in markets
7. Has experience with change and is flexible and adaptable	7. Faster and more effective integration facilitates achievement of synergy

trappings of managerial hubris. GE CEO Jack Welch was planning to retire, and some analysts touted this acquisition as his last great strategic move.[104]

As we have learned, some acquisitions enhance strategic competitiveness. However, the majority of acquisitions that took place from the 1970s through the 1990s did not enhance firms' strategic competitiveness. In fact, "history shows that anywhere between one-third [and] more than half of all acquisitions are ultimately divested or spun off."[105] Thus, firms often use restructuring strategies to correct for the failure of a merger or an acquisition.

Restructuring

Defined formally, **restructuring** is a strategy through which a firm changes its set of businesses or financial structure.[106] From the 1970s, into the 2000s, divesting businesses from company portfolios and downsizing accounted for a large percentage of firms' restructuring strategies. Restructuring is a global phenomenon.[107]

The failure of an acquisition strategy often precedes a restructuring strategy. Among the famous restructurings taken to correct for an acquisition failure are (1) Trans-Canada Pipeline's $3 billion divestment of its international energy assets after its $14 billion merger with Nova, (2) AT&T's $7.4 billion purchase of NCR and subsequent spinoff of the company to shareholders in a deal valued at $3.4 billion, (3) Novell's purchase of WordPerfect for stock valued at $1.4 billion and its sale of the company to Corel for $124 million in stock and cash, and (4) Quaker Oats's acquisition of Snapple Beverage Company for $1.7 billion, only to sell it three years later for $300 million.[108]

In other instances, however, firms use a restructuring strategy because of changes in their external and internal environments. For example, opportunities sometimes surface

Restructuring is a strategy through which a firm changes its set of businesses or financial structure.

in the external environments that are particularly attractive to the diversified firm in light of its core competencies. In such cases, restructuring may be appropriate to position the firm to create more value for stakeholders, given the environmental changes.

As discussed next, there are three restructuring strategies that firms use: downsizing, downscoping, and leveraged buyouts.

Downsizing

Once thought to be an indicator of organizational decline, downsizing is now recognized as a legitimate restructuring strategy. *Downsizing* is a reduction in the number of a firm's employees and, sometimes, in the number of its operating units, but it may or may not change the composition of businesses in the company's portfolio. Thus, downsizing is an intentional proactive management strategy, whereas "decline is an environmental or organizational phenomenon that occurs involuntarily and results in erosion of an organization's resource base."[109]

In the late 1980s, early 1990s, and early 2000s, thousands of jobs were lost in private and public organizations in North America. One study estimates that 85 percent of *Fortune* 1000 firms have used downsizing as a restructuring strategy.[110] Moreover, in 2001, *Fortune* 500 firms laid off more than 1 million employees, or 4 percent of their collective workforce.[111]

Firms use downsizing as a restructuring strategy for different reasons. The most frequently cited reason is that the firm expects that cost reductions will lead to improved profitability and more efficient operations. For example, after being spun off from Hewlett-Packard (HP) in 1999, California's Agilent Technologies employed more than 40,000. Agilent sold thousands of different types of test equipment to engineers and scientists—cutting-edge items with technical sounding names, such as Ethernet-over-SONET mapper chips and cDNA microarrays. Essentially, Agilent was HP's historic testing-products business. Within five years, the company was hit with recession, the technology sector going bust, and market fears after 9/11. During this time, the company bled $3 billion in losses. To help it get through the hard times, the company laid off nearly one-third of its workforce. Agilent went from employing more than 45,000 employees in 2001, to fewer than 30,000 in 2004. The story of how the company managed this and was able to survive is discussed in the Strategic Focus box "Downsizing." In early 2004, the company was finally able to report a quarterly profit.[112]

Downscoping

Compared to downsizing, downscoping has a more positive effect on firm performance.[113] *Downscoping* refers to divestiture, spinoff, or some other means of eliminating businesses that are unrelated to a firm's core businesses. Commonly, downscoping is described as a set of actions that causes a firm to strategically refocus on its core businesses.

A firm that downscopes often also downsizes simultaneously. However, it does not eliminate key employees from its primary businesses in the process, because such action could lead to a loss of one or more core competencies. Instead, a firm that is simultaneously downscoping and downsizing becomes smaller by reducing the diversity of businesses in its portfolio.

By refocusing on its core businesses, the firm can be managed more effectively by the top management team. Managerial effectiveness increases because the firm has become less diversified, allowing the top management team to better understand and manage the remaining businesses.[114]

In general, North American firms use downscoping as a restructuring strategy more frequently than do European companies. Typically, the trend in Europe, Latin America, and Asia has been to build conglomerates. In Latin America, these conglomerates are

Downsizing: The Good, the Bad, and the Ugly

If there is such a thing as a good downsizing—and this is debatable—Agilent may have pulled it off. When the company first ran into trouble, CEO Ned Barnholt froze hiring, laid off 5000 temporary employees, and asked employees to aid in cost cutting. Within months, Agilent cut its travel expenses by 50 percent and its printer and PC purchases by 70 percent. Employees were not kept in the dark. They knew the company was having problems, and management was trying everything possible to save the company and jobs. As revenues fell, cost cutting was insufficient to prevent further losses. Instead of staff cuts, Barnholt announced a temporary 10 percent across-the-board salary cut. Employees were encouraged by management's move to save jobs.

Still, the firm was losing money, and 4000 full-time jobs needed to be cut. Employees were to be told they were being let go only by their direct managers, and there were to be no across-the-board position cuts. Everything was handled quickly on a division-by-division basis, looking at each program and each employee. More than 3000 managers went through a series of daylong training sessions at an outplacement firm to learn the right and wrong ways to let people go.

When 9/11 hit, the company's fortunes again went downhill. Another 4000 jobs needed to be cut. Employees were still generally upbeat about how management had treated them: the communication, empathy, and family bonding from the company were all positives. Yet the further Barnholt had to clean house, the less likely it was that those who remained were going to view him as the benevolent head of their corporate family. At some point, employee staff cuts can go too deep or, in the wrong hands, be handled so badly that they are the wrong cuts.

This brings us to bad downsizing. Management experts argue such downsizing is the norm, and it is bad for business. One study of downsizing data found that while large layoffs can boost stock prices for a couple of years, they do not lead to greater profits. Expenses drop, but revenues tend to drop as well. Remaining workers cope with what some have called survivor syndrome: anger, fear, anxiety, frustration, and decreased risk taking. As well, the remaining employees may feel overworked in an environment some have described as organizational anorexia—where the remaining staff are too thinly spread over the required tasks to perform the jobs necessary to keep the organization alive.

When Telus announced labour-force cuts in 2002, the company was having financial difficulties. Arguing for the cuts was the fact that the company's share price had dropped by more than 70 percent in the first half of 2002, and Moody's Investors Service downgraded half of Telus's $9 billion in debt to junk status. This downgrade would make credit—and investors—harder and more expensive to come by.

On the other hand, the company was battling for high-speed Internet market share, was about to face new competitors in the local telephone market, and was trying to enter the market for delivery of home entertainment. The company did not need service disruptions. Yet the loss of 6000 union employees could result in just such disruptions, given the company's powerful labour union. In fact, the layoffs did exacerbate an already strained union–management relationship. Telus and its union had not been able to come to an agreement regarding a labour contract, and workers had already been working without a contract for some time when news of the layoffs came. Whether it was the lack of staff from the layoffs or the survivors' attitudes toward customer service, disruptions were the end result of this process, as customers had to wait for extended periods to get service from the company (see the Strategic Focus box "Can Telus Satisfy All of Its Stakeholders?" on page 25, in Chapter 1).

As well, the layoffs caused some observers to question the company's priorities—in particular, whether Telus should keep up with CEO Darren Entwistle's expansion plans, or concentrate on paying down debt and improving operating profit. The argument was that, rather than cutting jobs, Entwistle should have been cutting his expansion plans and getting the company to function like an effective telecommunications competitor.

(continued)

Then there are those ugly downsizings. Nortel, like Agilent, was also hit with the technology sector going bust and market fears after 9/11. However, Nortel bled more than 10 times the red ink that Agilent spilled. Nortel totalled more than $30 billion in losses between 2000 and 2003. To stop the company from swimming further in red ink, two of every three employees—tens of thousand of workers—were let go. Divestments were made and plants were closed. As well, Nortel had to investigate how much of the missing red ink was from cost cutting and how much was from creative accounting. The need for such an investigation explains why some of the company's top finance people are among those who no longer work there.

The only bright spot in Nortel's ugly downsizing is the notion that the company has refocused on its research and development (R&D) mission. Aware that the company is, at its core, an R&D-driven enterprise (Nortel spent and still spends an exceptional one of every five dollars on R&D), top management has stressed that R&D will be internally developed. Management has stated a commitment that the company will not buy outside technology or start-ups, except under the unusual circumstances. So, at least for now, gone are Nortel's days of big-ticket acquisitions, and, if all goes well, gone are the huge financial losses.

SOURCES: M. Morrison, 2004, Stocks down sharply: TSX down 200 points after Nortel fires execs, *Whitehorse Star*, April 28, 16; J. Bagnall, 2004, Nortel CEO "finished" with downsizing, *Ottawa Citizen*, January 14, A1; B. Hill, 2003, Nortel workers brace for layoffs, *Ottawa Citizen*, October 16, C1; D. Roth, 2002, How to cut pay, lay off 8,000 people, and still have workers who love you, *Fortune*, 145(3) 62–66; H. Kirwan-Taylor, 2002, Are you suffering from … corporate anorexia, *Management Today*, December, 24; M. Anderson, 2002, Subject: Telus Corp, *National Post*, September 1, 31.

called grupos. Many Asian and Latin American conglomerates have begun to adopt Western corporate strategies in recent years and have been refocusing on their core businesses. This downscoping has occurred simultaneously with increasing globalization and with more open markets that have greatly enhanced the competition. By downscoping, these firms have been able to focus on their core businesses and improve their competitiveness.[115]

Among North American–based firms using downscoping as a restructuring strategy, Canadian Pacific has to be one of the champions. Between the early 1960s and early 1990s, Canadian Pacific had become a conglomerate that, at one time or another, had interests in steel and paper production, oil and gas development, coal and metals mining, heavy equipment manufacture, real-estate development, shipping, hotels, and communications—along with, air, sea, rail, and road transportation. By the mid- to late 1990s many of these interests were divested, and the company bolstered some of the segments it deemed were solid businesses—such as its hotels and its oil and gas business—while keeping its coal and rail and ship transportation. By 2001, however, company executives deemed that the company was still too diverse and that it would be in the best interest of investors if the company were split it into five different companies: CP Ships, CP Rail, Hotels, Mining (Fording Coal), and PanCanadian (later to become EnCana).[116]

Leveraged Buyouts

Leveraged buyouts are commonly used as a restructuring strategy to correct for managerial mistakes or because the firm's managers are making decisions that primarily serve their own interests rather than those of shareholders.[117] A *leveraged buyout* (LBO) is a restructuring strategy whereby a party buys all of a firm's assets in order to take the firm private. Once the transaction is completed, the company's stock is no longer traded publicly.

Usually, significant amounts of debt are incurred to finance the buyout; hence the term "leveraged" buyout. To support debt payments and to downscope the company to concentrate on the firm's core businesses, the new owners may immediately sell a number of assets.[118] It is not uncommon for those buying a firm through an LBO to restructure the firm to the point that it can be sold at a profit within a five-year to eight-year period.

Management buyouts (MBOs), employee buyouts (EBOs), and whole-firm buyouts are the three types of LBOs. EBOs are often called ESOPs, employee stock ownership plans. In whole-firm buyouts, an entire company is purchased instead of a part of it. Partly because of managerial incentives, MBOs (more so than EBOs and whole-firm buyouts) have been found to lead to downscoping, an increased strategic focus, and improved performance.[119] Research has shown that management buyouts can also lead to greater entrepreneurial activity and growth.

While there may be different reasons for a buyout, one motive is to protect against a capricious financial market, allowing the owners to focus on developing innovations and bringing them to the market.[120] As such, buyouts can represent a form of firm rebirth to facilitate entrepreneurial efforts and stimulate strategic growth.[121]

Restructuring Outcomes

The short-term and long-term outcomes resulting from the three restructuring strategies are shown in Figure 8.3. As indicated, downsizing does not commonly lead to a higher firm performance. Still, in free-market–based societies at large, downsizing has generated a host of entrepreneurial new ventures, as individuals who are laid off start their own businesses.

Research has shown that downsizing has contributed to lower returns for both North American and Japanese firms. Stock markets where downsizing firms' shares are traded have evaluated downsizing negatively. Investors concluded that downsizing would have a negative effect on companies' ability to achieve strategic competitiveness in the long term. Investors also seem to assume that downsizing occurs as a consequence of other problems in a company.[122] Ford's announcement in 2002 that it was downsizing by eliminating 35,000 jobs exemplifies this situation. Ford did experience significant performance problems due to its lack of competitiveness in the markets in which it competed.[123]

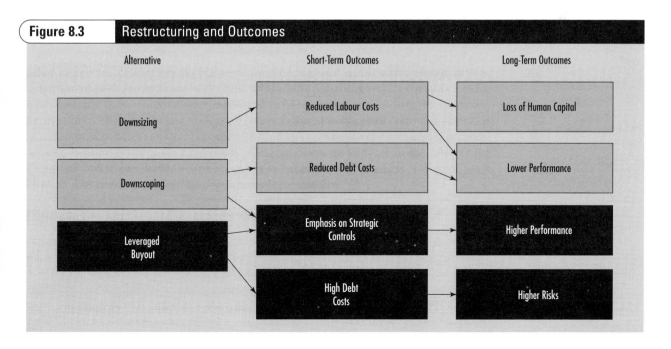

Figure 8.3   Restructuring and Outcomes

As shown in Figure 8.3, downsizing tends to result in a loss of human capital in the long term. Losing employees with many years of experience with the firm represents a major loss of knowledge. As noted in Chapter 4, knowledge is vital to competitive success in the global economy.[124] Thus, in general, research evidence and corporate experience suggest that downsizing may be of more tactical (or short-term) value than strategic (or long-term) value.

As Figure 8.3 indicates, downscoping generally leads to more positive outcomes in both the short and the long term than does downsizing or engaging in a leveraged buyout. Downscoping's desirable long-term outcome of higher performance is a product of reduced debt costs and the emphasis on strategic controls derived from concentrating on the firm's core businesses. In so doing, the refocused firm should be able to increase its ability to compete.

While whole-firm LBOs have been hailed as a significant innovation in the financial restructuring of firms, there can be negative trade-offs. First, the resulting large debt increases the financial risk of the firm, as is evidenced by the number of companies that filed for bankruptcy in the 1990s, after executing a whole-firm LBO. Sometimes, the intent of the owners to increase the efficiency of the bought-out firm and then sell it within five to eight years creates a short-term and risk-averse managerial focus. As a result, these firms may fail to invest adequately in R&D or take other major actions designed to maintain or improve the company's core competence.[125] However, research also suggests that in firms with an entrepreneurial mind-set, buyouts can lead to greater innovation, especially if the debt load is not too excessive.[126]

Summary

- Acquisition strategies are increasingly popular. Because of globalization, deregulation of multiple industries in many different economies, and favourable legislation, the number and size of domestic and cross-border acquisitions continues to increase.

- Firms use acquisition strategies to (1) increase market power, (2) overcome entry barriers to new markets or regions, (3) avoid the costs of developing new products and increase the speed of new market entries, (4) reduce the risk of entering a new business, (5) become more diversified, (6) reshape their competitive scope by developing a different portfolio of businesses, and (7) enhance their learning, thereby adding to their knowledge base.

- Among the problems associated with the use of an acquisition strategy are (1) the difficulty of effectively integrating the firms involved, (2) incorrectly evaluating the target firm's value, (3) creating debt loads that preclude adequate long-term investments (e.g., R&D), (4) overestimating the potential for synergy, (5) creating a firm that is too diversified, (6) creating an internal environment in which managers devote increasing amounts of their time and energy to analyzing and completing the acquisition, and (7) developing a combined firm that is too large, necessitating extensive use of bureaucratic, rather than strategic, controls.

- Effective acquisitions have the following characteristics: (1) both the acquiring and target firms have complementary resources that can be the basis of core competencies in the newly created firm, (2) the acquisition is friendly, thereby facilitating integration of the two firms' resources, (3) the target firm is selected and purchased based on thorough due diligence, (4) the acquiring and target firms have considerable slack in the form of cash or debt capacity, (5) the merged firm maintains a low or moderate level of debt by selling off portions of the acquired firm or some of the acquiring firm's poorly performing units, (6) the acquiring and acquired firms have experience in terms of adapting to change, and (7) R&D and innovation are emphasized in the new firm.

- Restructuring is used to improve a firm's performance by correcting for problems created by ineffective management. Restructuring by downsizing involves reducing a number of employees and hierarchical levels in the firm. Although such actions can lead to short-term cost reductions, these results may be realized at the expense of long-term success, because of the loss of valuable human resources (and knowledge).

- The goal of restructuring through downscoping is to reduce the firm's level of diversification. Often, the firm divests unrelated businesses to achieve this goal. Eliminating unrelated businesses makes it easier for the firm and its top-level managers to refocus on the core businesses.

- Leveraged buyouts (LBOs) represent an additional restructuring strategy. Through an LBO, a firm is purchased so that it can become a private entity. LBOs usually are financed largely through debt. There are three types of LBOs: management buyouts (MBOs), employee buyouts (EBOs), and whole-firm LBOs. Because they provide clear managerial incentives, MBOs have been the most successful of the three. Oftentimes, the intent of a buyout is to improve efficiency and performance to point where the firm can be sold successfully within five to eight years.

- Commonly, restructuring's primary goal is gaining or re-establishing effective strategic control of the firm. Of the three restructuring strategies, downscoping is aligned the most closely with establishing and using strategic controls.

Review Questions

1. Why are acquisition strategies popular in many firms competing in the global economy?

2. What reasons account for firms' decisions to use an acquisition strategy as one means of achieving strategic competitiveness?

3. What are the seven primary problems that affect a firm's efforts to successfully use an acquisition strategy?

4. What are the attributes associated with a successful acquisition strategy?

5. What is the restructuring strategy and what are its common forms?

6. What are the short-term and long-term outcomes associated with the different restructuring strategies?

Experiential Exercise

Mergers and Acquisitions

You are on the executive board of an information technology firm that provides trafficking software to the trucking industry. One of the firm's managers feels the company should grow and has suggested expanding by creating trafficking software for rail shipments or by offering truck-trafficking services online. You know your firm is in a position to expand, but you are not sure what is the best approach.

Part One. Should the firm consider a merger with or an acquisition of a firm that offers the suggested services, or should it develop the suggested services internally? List the advantages and disadvantages of each strategic option.

Part Two. Based on your findings and other information, assume that your firm decides to obtain trafficking software for rail shipments through an acquisition of an existing firm. Predict some general problems your firm might encounter in an acquisition and how they might be resolved.

Notes

1. R. Whittington, 1999, In praise of the evergreen conglomerate, Mastering Strategy (Part Six), *Financial Times*, November 1, 4–6; P. Moran & S. Ghoshal, 1999, Markets, firms, and the process of economic development, *Academy of Management Review*, 24: 390–412; M. A. Hitt, R. E. Hoskisson, R. D. Ireland, & J. S. Harrison, 1991, Effects of acquisitions on R&D inputs and outputs, *Academy of Management Journal*, 34: 693–706.

2. M. A. Hitt, J. S. Harrison, & R. D. Ireland, 2001, *Mergers and Acquisitions: A Guide to Creating Value for Stakeholders*, New York: Oxford University Press.

3. 2000, How M&As will navigate the turn into a new century, *Mergers & Acquisitions*, January, 29–35.

4. J. A. Schmidt, 2002, Business perspective on mergers and acquisitions, in J. A. Schmidt (ed.), *Making Mergers Work*, Alexandria, VA: Society for Human Resource Management, 23–46.

5. M. A. Hitt, R. D. Ireland, & J. S. Harrison, 2001, Mergers and acquisitions: A value creating or a value destroying strategy? In M. A. Hitt, R. E. Freeman, & J. S. Harrison, *Handbook of Strategic Management*, Oxford, UK: Blackwell Publishers, 385–408.

6. J. Stewart, 2004, M&A: 2004 heading for a record year? *Global Finance*, 18(2): 18–21; L. Saigol, 2002, Thin pickings in dismal year for dealmaking, *Financial Times*, http://www.ft.com, January 2; Economist, 2001, Waiting for growth, *Economist*, http://www.economist.com, April 27; Wall Street Journal, 2002, Mergers snapshot:

2001 deal volume, *Wall Street Journal*, January 4, C12; Economist, 2001, The great merger wave breaks, *Economist*, January 27, 59–60

7. P. Chattopadhyay, W. H. Glick, & G. P. Huber, 2001, Organizational actions in response to threats and opportunities, *Academy of Management Journal*, 44: 937–55.

8. H. T. J. Smit, 2001, Acquisition strategies as option games, *Journal of Applied Corporate Finance*, 14(2): 79–89.

9. J. Anand, 1999, How many matches are made in heaven, Mastering Strategy (Part Five), *Financial Times*, October 25: 6–7.

10. M. C. Jensen, 1988, Takeovers: Their causes and consequences, *Journal of Economic Perspectives*, 1(2): 21–48.

11. A. Rappaport & M. L. Sirower, 1999, Stock or cash? *Harvard Business Review*, 77(6): 147–58.

12. R. F. Bruner, 2004, A Merger of Equals? *Wall Street Journal*, January 20, B2.

13. Financial Post, 2004, Cingular in US$27B bid for AT&T Wireless: Offer may spark fight, *National Post (Financial Post)*, January 21, FP4; Weekly Corporate Growth Report, 2004 Cingular Wireless wins auction for AT&T Wireless, *Weekly Corporate Growth Report*, February 23, 3.

14. E. Thorton, F. Keesnan, C. Palmeri, & L. Himelstein, 2002, It sure is getting hostile, *Business Week*, January 14, 28–30.

15. S. McGovern, 2003, Axcan fails in bid for Salix, *Montreal Gazette*, June 20, B3.

16. P. Haspeslagh, 1999, Managing the mating dance in equal mergers, Mastering Strategy (Part Five), *Financial Times*, October 25, 14–15.

17. P. Wright, M. Kroll, & D. Elenkov, 2002, Acquisition returns, increase in firm size and chief executive officer compensation: The moderating role of monitoring, *Academy of Management Journal*, 45(3): 599–621.

18. G. Anders, 2002, Lessons from WaMU's M&A playbook, *Fast Company*, January, 100–7.

19. L. Capron, 1999, Horizontal acquisitions: The benefits and risks to long-term performance, *Strategic Management Journal*, 20: 987–1018.

20. M. Lubatkin, W. S. Schulze, A. Mainkar, & R. W. Cotterill, 2001, Ecological investigation of firm effects in horizontal mergers, *Strategic Management Journal*, 22: 335–57; K. Ramaswamy, 1997, The performance impact of strategic similarity in horizontal mergers: Evidence from the U.S. banking industry, *Academy of Management Journal*, 40: 697–715.

21. D. Eisler, 1998, Pipeline Partnership, *Maclean's*, 111(6): 68.

22. C. Howes, 2001, There's more to a successful merger than making a buck: Making the cultures fit, *National Post (Financial Post)*, February 2, C5.

23. Montreal Gazette, 2004, Aber purchases jeweler Winston, *Montreal Gazette*, April 3, B4.

24. N. Sutton, 2003, OpenText adds content management to tool set, *Computing Canada*, 29(21): 10; Open Text, 2004, The game just got bigger: Open Text acquires 88% of Ixos under final stage of tender offer, *Open Text website*, http://www.opentext.com/ixos, accessed April 15.

25. L. Capron, W. Mitchell, & A. Swaminathan, 2001, Asset divestiture following horizontal acquisitions: A dynamic view, *Strategic Management Journal*, 22: 817–44.

26. M. Lerner, 2001, Israeli antitrust authority's general director David Tadmor on corporate mergers, *Academy of Management Executive*, 15(1): 8–11.

27. S. J. Chang & P. M. Rosenzweig, 2001, The choice of entry mode in sequential foreign direct investment, *Strategic Management Journal*, 22: 747–76.

28. Marketing Magazine, 2002, Best Buy faces its own competition, *Marketing Magazine*, 107(35): 2.

29. J. A. Gingrich, 1999, Five rules for winning emerging market consumers, *Strategy & Business*, 15: 19–33.

30. Hitt, Harrison, & Ireland, *Mergers and Acquisitions*; D. Angwin & B. Savill, 1997, Strategic perspectives on European cross-border acquisitions: A view from the top European executives, *European Management Review*, 15: 423–35.

31. Schmidt, Business perspective on mergers and acquisitions.

32. A. Swift, 2004, Acquisition transforms Coutu into U.S. company; Buys ailing Eckerd stores from J.C. Penney 85% of stores, 90% of sales to be derived from U.S., *Toronto Star*, April, 6, D3.

33. J. K. Shank & V. Govindarajan, 1992, Strategic cost analysis of technological investments, *Sloan Management Review*, 34(3): 39–51.

34. Hitt, Harrison, & Ireland, *Mergers and Acquisitions*.

35. M. A. Hitt, R. E. Hoskisson, R. A. Johnson, & D. D. Moesel, 1996, The market for corporate control and firm innovation, *Academy of Management Journal*, 39: 1084–119.

36. R. Coff, 2003, Bidding wars over R&D intensive firms: Knowledge, opportunism and the market for corporate control, *Academy of Management Journal*, 46(1), 74–97.

37. Chemical Market Reporter, 2002, Biovail strengthens its delivery platform with Pharma Pass buy, *Chemical Market Reporter*, 262(22): 2.

38. K. F. McCardle & S. Viswanathan, 1994, The direct entry versus takeover decision and stock price performance around takeovers, *Journal of Business*, 67: 1–43.

39. J. W. Lu & P. W. Beamish, 2001, The internationalization and performance of SMEs, *Strategic Management Journal*, 22(special issue): 565–86.

40. G. Ahuja & C. Lampert, 2001, Entrepreneurship in the large corporation: A longitudinal study of how established firms create breakthrough inventions, *Strategic Management Journal*, 22(special issue): 521–43.

41. F. Rothaermel, 2001, Incumbent's advantage through exploiting complementary assets via Interfirm cooperation, *Strategic Management Journal*, 22(special issue): 687–99.

42. G. Ahuja & R. Katila, 2001, Technological acquisitions and the innovation performance of acquiring firms: A longitudinal study, *Strategic Management Journal*, 22: 197–220; M. A. Hitt, R. E. Hoskisson, & R. D. Ireland, 1990, Mergers and acquisitions and managerial commitment to innovation in M-form firms, *Strategic Management Journal*, 11(special summer issue): 29–47.

43. R. Langreth, 2002, Betting on the brain, *Forbes*, January 7, 57–59.

44. Hitt, Hoskisson, Johnson, & Moesel, The market for corporate control.

45. Hitt, Hoskisson, Ireland, & Harrison, Effects of acquisitions on R&D inputs and outputs.

46. D. D. Bergh, 1997, Predicting divestiture of unrelated acquisitions: An integrative model of ex ante conditions, *Strategic Management Journal*, 18: 715–31.

47. M. Drapes, 2004, Onex Corporation profile, *Hoover's Online*, http://www.hoovers.com/onex/—ID__52539—/free-co-factsheet.xhtml, accessed April 23, 2004.

48. Onex Corporation 2004, *Onex Corporation website*, http://www.onexcorp.com/cp/cp_entgp/cp_entgp.asp, accessed April 23, 2004.

49. Hitt, Harrison, & Ireland, *Mergers and Acquisitions*.

50. J. Anand & H. Singh, 1997, Asset redeployment, acquisitions and corporate strategy in declining industries, *Strategic Management Journal*, 18(special summer issue): 99–118.

51. M. Raynor, 2001, *Strategic Flexibility in the Financial Services Industry*, report, Toronto, ON: Deloitte Consulting and Deloitte & Touche.

52. W. J. Ferrier, 2001, Navigating the competitive landscape: The drivers and consequences of competitive aggressiveness, *Academy of Management Journal*, 44: 858–77.

53. A. Biesada, 2004, Jim Pattison Group profile, *Hoover's Online*, http://www.hoovers.com/jim-pattison-group/—ID__43507—/free-co-factsheet.xhtml, accessed April 23, 2004; A. Biesada, 2004, Overwaitea Food Group Profile, *Hoover's Online*, http://www.hoovers.com/overwaitea/—ID__107275—/free-co-factsheet.xhtml, accessed April 23, 2004; Jim Pattison Group, 2004, *Jim Pattison Group website*, http://www.jimpattison.com, accessed April 23, 2004.

54. F. Vermeulen & H. Barkema, 2001, Learning through acquisitions, *Academy of Management Journal*, 44: 457–76.

55. J. S. Harrison, M. A. Hitt, R. E. Hoskisson, & R. D. Ireland, 2001, Resource complementarities in business combinations: Extending the logic to organizational alliances, *Journal of Management*, 27: 679–90.

56. Agiotech Pharmaceuticals, 2004, *Angiotech Pharmaceuticals website*, http://www.angiotech.com/?seek=124&searchweb=acquisition, accessed April 22 and April 24, 2004.

57. M. Killick, I. Rawoot, & G. J. Stockport, 2001, *Cisco Systems Inc.—Growth Through Acquisitions*, Crawley, Western Australia: Graduate School of Management, University of Western Australia; A. Muoio, 2000, Cisco's quick study, *Fast Company*, October, 287–95.

58. Schmidt, Business perspective on mergers and acquisitions.

59. D. Olive, 2002, Merger: A strategy of growth by acquisition sent many high-flying companies tumbling into financial turmoil, leaving badly burned investors wary of future, *Toronto Star*, August 27, C1.

60. Hitt, Harrison, & Ireland, *Mergers and Acquisitions*.

61. A. J. Viscio, J. R. Harbison, A. Asin, & R. P. Vitaro, 1999, Post-merger integration: What makes mergers work? *Strategy & Business*, 17: 26–33; D. K. Datta, 1991, Organizational fit and acquisition performance: Effects of post-acquisition integration, *Strategic Management Journal*, 12: 281–97.

62. M. Zollo, 1999, M&A—the challenge of learning to integrate, Mastering Strategy (Part Eleven), *Financial Times*, December 6, 14–15.

63. P. Verberg, T. Watson, & J. Kirby, 2004, You win some, *Canadian Business*, 77(4): 70–71.

64. M. A. Hitt, L. Bierman, K. Shimizu, & R. Kochhar, 2001, Direct and moderating effects of human capital on strategy and performance in professional service firms, *Academy of Management* Journal, 44: 13–28.

65. G. G. Dess & J. D. Shaw, 2001, Voluntary turnover, social capital and organizational performance, *Academy of Management Review*, 26: 446–56.

66. Verberg, Watson, & Kirby, You win some.

67. J. A. Krug & H. Hegarty, 2001, Predicting who stays and leaves after an acquisition: A study of top managers in multinational firms, *Strategic Management Journal*, 22: 185–96.

68. Verberg, Watson, & Kirby, You win some.

69. Rappaport & Sirower, Stock or cash? 149.

70. R. Abelson, 2001, Enron board comes under a storm of criticism, *New York Times Interactive*, http://www.nytimes.com, December 16; D. Ackman, 2001, Enron's mysterious, troubled core, *Forbes*, http://www.forbes.com, December 15; R. A. Oppel Jr. & A. R. Sorkin, 2001, Enron files largest U.S. claim for bankruptcy, *New York Times Interactive*, http://www.nytimes.com, December 3.

71. G. Yago, 1991, *Junk Bonds: How High Yield Securities Restructured Corporate America*, New York: Oxford University Press, 146–48.

72. M. C. Jensen, 1986, Agency costs of free cash flow, corporate finance, and takeovers, *American Economic Review*, 76: 323–29.

73. M. Fraser, 2003, Peladeau is going to need one mighty big slingshot, *National Post (Financial Post)*, January 13, FP3.

74. G. Koch, 2003, Survival of the skittish, *National Post*, December 1, 50.

75. M. A. Hitt & D. L. Smart, 1994, Debt: A disciplining force for managers or a debilitating force for organizations? *Journal of Management Inquiry*, 3: 144–52.

76. Hitt, Harrison, & Ireland, *Mergers and Acquisitions*.

77. T. N. Hubbard, 1999, Integration strategies and the scope of the company, Mastering Strategy (Part Eleven), *Financial Times*, December 6, 8–10.

78. Hitt, Harrison, & Ireland, *Mergers and Acquisitions*.

79. Ibid.

80. Harrison, Hitt, Hoskisson, & Ireland, Resource complementarity; J. B. Barney, 1988, Returns to bidding firms in mergers and acquisitions: Reconsidering the relatedness hypothesis, *Strategic Management Journal*, 9(special summer issue): 71–78.

81. O. E. Williamson, 1999, Strategy research: Governance and competence perspectives, *Strategic Management Journal*, 20: 1087–108.

82. Hitt, Hoskisson, Johnson, & Moesel, The market for corporate control.

83. C. W. L. Hill & R. E. Hoskisson, 1987, Strategy and structure in the multiproduct firm, *Academy of Management Review*, 12: 331–41.

84. R. A. Johnson, R. E. Hoskisson, & M. A. Hitt, 1993, Board of director involvement in restructuring: The effects of board versus managerial controls and characteristics, *Strategic Management Journal*, 14(special issue): 33–50; C. C. Markides, 1992, Consequences of corporate refocusing: Ex ante evidence, *Academy of Management Journal*, 35: 398–412.

85. R. Sobel, 1984, *The Rise and Fall of the Conglomerate Kings*, Briarcliff Manor, NY: Stein and Day.

86. D. Palmer & B. N. Barber, 2001, Challengers, elites and families: A social class theory of corporate acquisitions, *Administrative Science Quarterly*, 46: 87–120.

87. Hitt, Harrison, & Ireland, *Mergers and Acquisitions*.

88. Ibid.

89. Hitt, Johnson, & Moesel, The market for corporate control.

90. J. Brand, 2002, What is an ASP? *Darwin Magazine Online*, October 15, http://www.darwinmag.com/learn/curve/column.html?ArticleID=556, accessed July 29, 2004.

91. M. McClearn, 2002, To Hell and back, *Canadian Business*, 75(2): 59–60.

92. Hitt, Harrison, & Ireland, Mergers and Acquisitions; R. E. Hoskisson, M. A. Hitt, & R. D. Ireland, 1994, The effects of acquisitions and restructuring (strategic refocusing) strategies on innovation, in G. von Krogh, A. Sinatra, & H. Singh (eds.), *Managing Corporate Acquisitions*, London: Macmillan Press, 144–69.

93. Hitt, Hoskisson, & Ireland, The effects of acquisitions.

94. T. Lowry, 2001, How many magazines did we buy today? *Business Week*, January 22, 98–99.

95. Hitt, Harrison, & Ireland, *Mergers and Acquisitions*.

96. Ibid.

97. M. A. Hitt, R. D. Ireland, J. S. Harrison, & A. Best, 1998, Attributes of successful and unsuccessful acquisitions of U.S. firms, *British Journal of Management*, 9: 91–114.

98. Harrison, Hitt, Hoskisson, & Ireland, Resource complementarity.

99. J. Reuer, 2001, From hybrids to hierarchies: Shareholder wealth effects of joint venture partner buyouts, *Strategic Management Journal*, 22: 27–44.

100. D. D. Bergh, 2001, Executive retention and acquisition outcomes: A test of opposing views on the influence of organizational tenure, *Journal of Management*, 27: 603–22;

J. P. Walsh, 1989, Doing a deal: Merger and acquisition negotiations and their impact upon target company top management turnover, *Strategic Management Journal*, 10: 307–22.

101. M. L. Marks & P. H. Mirvis, 2001, Making mergers and acquisitions work: Strategic and psychological preparation, *Academy of Management Executive*, 15(2): 80–92.

102. Hitt, Harrison, & Ireland, *Mergers and Acquisitions*; Q. N. Huy, 2001, Time, temporal capability and planned change, *Academy of Management Review*, 26: 601–23; L. Markoczy, 2001, Consensus formation during strategic change, *Strategic Management Journal*, 22: 1013–31.

103. R. W. Coff, 2002, Human capital, shared expertise, and the likelihood of impasse in corporate acquisitions, *Journal of Management*, 28(1): 107–27.

104. A. Hill, 2001, GE pins expansion plans on acquisitions, *Financial Times*, http://www.ft.com, December 19; D. Jones, 2001, Welch book trips on merger hurdle, *Wall Street Journal*, July 24, D3; Arizona Republic, 2001, European foes stall merger with GE: Focus is misplaced in Honeywell deal, *Arizona Republic*, June 20, V4; L. Zuckerman & A. R. Sorkin, 2001, G.E. calls its $45 billion bid for Honeywell all but dead, *New York Times Interactive*, http://www.nytimes.com, June 17.

105. Anand, How many matches, 6.

106. R. A. Johnson, 1996, Antecedents and outcomes of corporate refocusing, *Journal of Management*, 22: 437–81; J. E. Bethel & J. Liebeskind, 1993, The effects of ownership structure on corporate restructuring, *Strategic Management Journal*, 14(special summer issue): 15–31.

107. R. E. Hoskisson, R. A. Johnson, D. Yiu, & W. P. Wan, 2001, Restructuring strategies of diversified groups: Differences associated with country institutional environments, in M. A. Hitt, R. E. Freeman, & J. S. Harrison (eds.), *Handbook of Strategic Management*, Oxford, UK: Blackwell Publishers, 433–63; S. R. Fisher & M. A. White, 2000, Downsizing in a learning organization: Are there hidden costs? *Academy of Management Review*, 25: 244–51; A. Campbell & D. Sadtler, 1998, Corporate breakups, *Strategy & Business*, 12: 64–73; E. Bowman & H. Singh, 1990, Overview of corporate restructuring: Trends and consequences, in L. Rock & R. H. Rock (eds.), *Corporate Restructuring*, New York: McGraw-Hill.

108. R. Starr, 2003, TransCanada Pipelines, *Canadian Business*, 76(8): 81–82; Hitt, Harrison, & Ireland, *Mergers and Acquisitions*.

109. W. McKinley, J. Zhao, & K. G. Rust, 2000, A sociocognitive interpretation of organizational downsizing, *Academy of Management Review*, 25: 227–43.

110. W. McKinley, C. M. Sanchez, & A. G. Schick, 1995, Organizational downsizing: Constraining, cloning, learning, *Academy of Management Executive*, IX(3): 32–44.

111. P. Patsuris, 2002, Forbes.com layoff tracker surpasses 1M mark, *Forbes*, http://www.forbes.com/2002/01/10/0110layoffs.html, January 10.

112. D. Roth, 2002, How to cut pay, lay off 8,000 people, and still have workers who love you, *Fortune*, 145(3) 62–66; Agilent Technologies, 2004, Agilent Technologies reports first quarter 2004 financial results, *Agilent Technologies website*, http://www.investor.agilent.com/ReleaseDetail.cfm?ReleaseID=128913 (news release), February 17, accessed April 28, 2004; Agilent Technologies, 2003, 2003 annual report to shareholders, *Agilent Technologies website*, http://www.investor.agilent.com/downloads/AR2003.pdf, accessed April 28, 2004.

113. R. E. Hoskisson & M. A. Hitt, 1994, *Downscoping: How to Tame the Diversified Firm*, New York: Oxford University Press.

114. R. Johnson, R. E. Hoskisson, & M. A. Hitt, 1993, Board of director involvement in restructuring: The effects of board versus managerial controls and characteristics, *Strategic Management Journal*, summer: 38–50; R. E. Hoskisson & M. A. Hitt, 1990, Antecedents and performance outcomes of diversification: A review and critique of theoretical perspectives, *Journal of Management*, 16: 461–509.

115. Hoskisson, Johnson, Yiu, & Wan, Restructuring strategies.

116. Fording Canadian Coal Trust, 2001, Canadian Pacific arrangement circular, *Fording Canadian Coal Trust website*, August 3, http://www.fording.ca/data/1/rec_docs/143_Complete_CP_FINAL_CIRCLE.PDF, accessed April 27, 2004; Wall Street Journal, 2001, Canadian Pacific's plan for breakup includes distributions of cash, *Wall Street Journal*, July 14, C8; A. Bary, 1998, From sleepy to sleeper, *Barrons*, 78(20): 30–32; A. Freeman, 1985, Canadian Pacific plans a merger with subsidiary, *Wall Street Journal*, September 9, 1.

117. D. D. Bergh & G. F. Holbein, 1997, Assessment and redirection of longitudinal analysis: Demonstration with a study of the diversification and divestiture relationship, *Strategic Management Journal*, 18: 557–71; C. C. Markides & H. Singh, 1997, Corporate restructuring: A symptom of poor governance or a solution to past managerial mistakes? *European Management Journal*, 15: 213–19.

118. M. F. Wiersema & J. P. Liebeskind, 1995, The effects of leveraged buyouts on corporate growth and diversification in large firms, *Strategic Management Journal*, 16: 447–60.

119. A. Seth & J. Easterwood, 1995, Strategic redirection in large management buyouts: The evidence from post-buyout restructuring activity, *Strategic Management Journal*, 14: 251–74; P. H. Phan & C. W. L. Hill, 1995, Organizational restructuring and economic performance in leveraged buyouts: An ex-post study, *Academy of Management Journal*, 38: 704–39.

120. M. Wright, R. E. Hoskisson, L. W. Busenitz, & J. Dial, 2000, Entrepreneurial growth through privatization: The upside of management buyouts, *Academy of Management Review*, 25: 591–601.

121. M. Wright, R. E. Hoskisson, & L. W. Busenitz, 2001, Firm rebirth: Buyouts as facilitators of strategic growth and entrepreneurship, *Academy of Management Executive*, 15(1): 111–25.

122. P. M. Lee, 1997, A comparative analysis of layoff announcements and stock price reactions in the United States and Japan, *Strategic Management Journal*, 18: 879–94.

123. D. Williamson, 2002, Ford to cut 35,000 jobs, automaker to close up to seven plants in bid to "turn company around," *Vancouver Sun*, January 12, A12.

124. Fisher & White, Downsizing in a learning organization.

125. W. F. Long & D. J. Ravenscraft, 1993, LBOs, debt, and R&D intensity, *Strategic Management Journal*, 14(special summer issue): 119–35.

126. Wright, Hoskisson, Busenitz, & Dial, Entrepreneurial growth through privatization.

Chapter Nine

International Strategy

Knowledge Objectives

Studying this chapter should provide you with the strategic management knowledge needed to:

1. Explain traditional and emerging motives for firms to pursue international diversification.

2. Explore the four factors that lead to a basis for international business-level strategies.

3. Define the three international corporate-level strategies: multidomestic, global, and transnational.

4. Discuss the environmental trends affecting international strategy, especially liability of foreignness and regionalization.

5. Name and describe the five alternative modes for entering international markets.

6. Explain the effects of international diversification on firm returns and innovation.

7. Name and describe two major risks of international diversification.

8. Explain why the positive outcomes from international expansion are limited.

China Enters the World Trade Organization

On September 17, 2001, Beijing and its Chinese leaders formally accepted the requirements to enter the World Trade Organization (WTO). Over the next five years, this agreement promises to create a more open market and lower tariffs for importing and exporting goods into and out of China, as the country increases both its world trade and its number of trading partners. Because of the size of the Chinese market, the agreement's effect on globalization is expected to be significant.

China's orientation toward increased trade actually began in 1979, when the late Chinese leader Deng Xiaoping introduced reforms leading toward more of a market economy. This change was phased in through a decentralization process, during which most enterprises were turned over to local government officials. At the same time, state-owned enterprises were gradually introduced to a market economy. Thus, Chinese leaders have been preparing for entrance into the WTO for more than 20 years. However, because most Chinese firms are still all or partially state-owned, significant changes must occur in these firms as they encounter more efficient and competitive foreign firms in the global marketplace. In fact, Premier Zhu Rongji, the current leader of the reforms, said that to meet the competition, state-owned enterprises would need to reduce their work forces by "two-thirds." This reduction would result in 25 million people being added to China's unemployment rolls over five years.

On the one hand, China seeks to compete strongly in high-tech industries. For instance, the country hopes to supplant India as the number two software producer in the world after the United States. Currently, India holds this position, but like India, China also offers a well-educated, hard-working technology and engineering work force.

To learn more about the Indian approach, the Chinese minister of higher education recently visited India's Bangalore software district, where Chinese software firm Huawei Technologies has a centre. The firm's biggest operation outside of China, Huawei's Bangalore operation employs 536 people—180 Chinese employees work alongside Indian programmers to learn how the Indian employees approach the development of software code. As a professor from China says, "They are learning how Indian programmers work together, how they coordinate."

In 2001, India exported about $8 billion (CDN) worth of software, while China had $1.1 billion (CDN) in software exports. This is a ratio that favours India, seven to one. In 2002, India's software exports increased 35 per cent to about $11 billion (CDN). China's software exports rose 120 percent to $2.4 billion (CDN). If these rates continue, the software export ratio will favour China by seven to one by 2009.

On the other hand, however, China has a number of state-owned firms that are not competitive in world markets. Even though many firms have made significant changes during previous reforms, more change is necessary for them to be competitive. For instance, Angang Iron & Steel was listed in 1997 as a "red chip" firm on the Hong Kong exchange (only the best state-owned firms

Several Chinese companies, such as China Unicom and PetroChina, were involved in IPOs to help them develop better management efficiencies as they prepared for China's entry into the WTO.

中国加入世界贸易组织签字仪式
SIGNING CEREMONY ON CHINA'S ACCESSION TO THE WTO
11 November 2001, Doha

© HUSSEIN MALLA/AFP

(continued)

have qualified to be listed on Hong Kong or Shanghai stock exchanges). Since 1995, to make improvements in productivity, Angang has cut tens of thousands of people from its employment rolls (the company still employs more than 100,000). However, relative to South Korean steel producer Posco, Angang still needs to be more competitive. Posco produces 26 million tons of steel with 20,000 workers, while Angang produces 9.5 million tons with 43,000 workers—Posco is six times as productive as Angang. Even though Chinese wages are lower than those in South Korea, this example indicates that many of China's more productive employers have a long way to go to be competitive in world markets.

Still, China is a magnet for foreign direct investment and has an economy that has grown 8 percent per year in the recent past. In 2002, China's foreign direct investment was up 13 percent to more than $70 billion (CDN), more than the combined investment received by the rest of Asia (not including Japan). Although the country should grow and develop a strong middle class as a result of the direct foreign investment and its economic growth, it will also suffer from market liberalization. Thus, China's entrance into the WTO creates both a challenge and an opportunity for the country.

China will pursue its typical incremental strategy of change as it moves into world markets and is not likely to follow the WTO rules as strictly as preferred for new foreign entrants. In fact, China's decentralization from 1979 to the present will likely make implementation of the WTO rules somewhat difficult. Because local Chinese governments have more control now, the implementation will largely fall to local government officials, making the process of change more incremental than revolutionary. These local barriers are likely to facilitate an increase in foreign direct investment, however, because foreign firms will have to invest to overcome them. Consequently, although change represents an important opportunity with a significant risk of social upheaval, it will lead to more globalization both for China and for those investing in that nation's future.

SOURCES. BizAsia, 2003, Investment: China reports record direct foreign investment, *BizAsia website*, http://www.bizasia.com/investment_/f932c/china_reports_record_direct.htm, January 15, accessed February 17, 2004; Angang Iron & Steel Group, 2004, *Angang Iron & Steel website*, http://www.ansteel.com.cn/egsjj.htm, accessed February 10, 2004; F. Patel & A. Subramanian, 2003, China's software boom manna for Indian pros, *Rediff website*, http://www.rediff.com/money/2003/feb/11china.htm, February 11; S. Rai, 2002, Chinese race to supplant India software, *New York Times*, http://www.nytimes.com, January 5; Economist, 2001, Asia: Ready for the competition? China and the WTO, *Economist*, September 15, 35–36; B. Einhorn, C. Dawson, I. Kunii, D. Roberts, A. Webb, & P. Engardio, 2001, China: Will its entry into the WTO unleash new prosperity or further destabilize the world economy? *Business Week*, October 29, 38; Economist, 2001, Finance and economics: China's economy, celebration, and concern, *Economist*, November 10, 102; D. Murphy, 2001, Riding the tiger of trade, *Far Eastern Economic Review*, November 22, 38–44; B. Powell, 2001, China's great step forward, *Fortune*, September 17, 128–42; A. Tanzer, 2001, Chinese walls, *Forbes*, November 12, 74–75.

As the opening case indicates, China's entry into the World Trade Organization (WTO) has put significant focus on this huge potential market. While more firms will enter China in the coming years, many foreign firms who have entered China have found it difficult to establish legitimacy.[1] This difficulty is most likely due to China's recent history.

"Collective property party" is the Chinese translation of the term *communist party*. Although law has established property rights, many Chinese (still under a Communist regime) do not share this mind-set. Their opposition to property rights is mainly of two types: ideological and practical. First, many local government and communist party officials feel that private enterprise is undermining the socialist ideal. As a result, many of the local policies (e.g., taxes and licence fees) toward private firms are punitive. Second, as pointed out in the opening case, many officials fear that foreign-owned private domestic competitors will undermine state-owned enterprises, which provide social, educational, medical, and retirement benefits to their employees. Although China's reforms include funds for social programs, there may be uncertainty as to how these funds will be distributed locally. Thus, private firms and those that are becoming more market oriented must work hard to establish legitimacy with local government officials, suppliers, and customers.

China and its entrance into the WTO clearly illustrate how entering international markets features both opportunities and threats for firms that choose to compete in global markets. This chapter examines opportunities facing firms as they seek to develop and exploit core competencies by diversifying into global markets. In addition, we discuss different problems, complexities, and threats that might accompany use of the firm's international strategies. Although national boundaries, cultural differences, and geographical distances all pose barriers to entry into many markets, significant opportunities draw businesses into the international arena. A business that plans to operate globally must formulate a successful strategy to take advantage of these global opportunities.[2] Furthermore, to mould their firms into truly global companies, managers must develop global mind-sets. Especially in regard to managing human resources, traditional means of operating with little cultural diversity and without global sourcing are no longer effective.[3]

As firms move into international markets, they develop relationships with suppliers, customers, and partners, and then learn from these relationships. Siemens, for example, sells its products in 190 countries and uses 31 websites in 38 languages to facilitate development and use of relationships as well as opportunities to learn from them. Firms also learn from their competitors in international markets. In essence, they begin to imitate each other's policies in order to compete more effectively.[4] Such activity is evident in the pharmaceuticals industry where firms compete against each other in global markets.[5]

In this chapter, as illustrated in Figure 1.1, on page 8, we discuss the importance of international strategy as a source of strategic competitiveness and above-average returns. The chapter focuses on the incentives to internationalize. Once a firm decides to compete internationally, it must select its strategy and choose a mode of entry into international markets. It may enter international markets by exporting from domestic-based operations, licensing some of its products or services, forming joint ventures with international partners, acquiring a foreign-based firm, or establishing a new subsidiary. Such international diversification can extend product life cycles, provide incentives for more innovation, and produce above-average returns. These benefits are tempered by political and economic risks and the problems of managing a complex international firm with operations in multiple countries.

Figure 9.1 on page 266 provides an overview of the various choices and outcomes. Both the relationships among international opportunities and the exploration of resources and capabilities resulting in strategies and modes of entry that are based on core competencies are explored in this chapter.

Figure 9.1 Opportunities and Outcomes of International Strategy

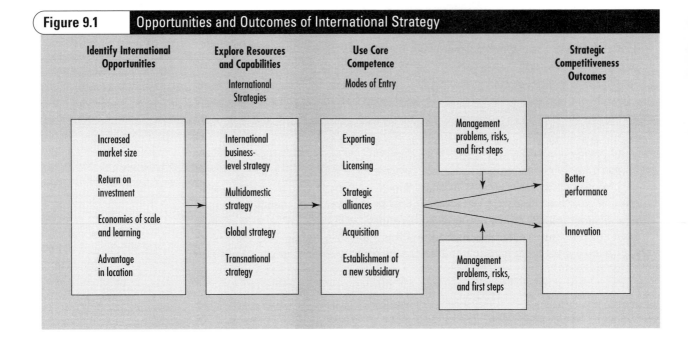

Identify International Opportunities	Explore Resources and Capabilities	Use Core Competence		Strategic Competitiveness Outcomes
	International Strategies	Modes of Entry		
Increased market size	International business-level strategy	Exporting	Management problems, risks, and first steps	Better performance
Return on investment	Multidomestic strategy	Licensing		
Economies of scale and learning	Global strategy	Strategic alliances		Innovation
Advantage in location	Transnational strategy	Acquisition	Management problems, risks, and first steps	
		Establishment of a new subsidiary		

Identifying International Opportunities: Incentives to Use an International Strategy

An **international strategy** is a strategy through which the firm sells its goods or services outside its domestic market.

An **international strategy** is a strategy through which the firm sells its goods or services outside its domestic market.[6] One of the primary reasons for implementing an international strategy (as opposed to a strategy focused on the domestic market) is that international markets yield potential new opportunities.

Raymond Vernon captured the classic rationale for international diversification.[7] He suggested that, typically, a firm discovers an innovation in its home-country market, especially in an advanced economy, such as those found in Canada and the United States. Some demand for the product may then develop in other countries, and exports are provided by domestic operations. Increased demand in foreign countries justifies direct foreign investment in production capacity abroad, especially because foreign competitors also organize to meet increasing demand. As the product becomes standardized, the firm may rationalize its operations by moving production to a region with low manufacturing costs.[8] Vernon, therefore, suggests that firms pursue international diversification to extend a product's life cycle.

Another traditional motive for firms to become multinational is to secure needed resources. Key supplies of raw material—especially minerals and energy—are important in some industries. For instance, aluminium producers need a supply of bauxite, tire firms need rubber, and oil companies scour the world to find new petroleum reserves. Other industries, such as clothing, electronics, and watch making, seek low-cost factors of production, and have moved portions of their operations to foreign locations in pursuit of lower costs.

Research shows that reasons for investing in China differ by the type of firm.[9] Large multinational firms invest primarily to gain access to the large demand potential of China's domestic market. Smaller firms from newly industrializing economies, such as Hong Kong, that use more mundane technologies, are more interested in low-cost sources of inputs, such as labour and land, to maintain their cost advantages.

Although these traditional motives persist, other emerging motivations also drive international expansion (see Chapter 1). For instance, pressure has increased for a global integration of operations, mostly driven by more universal product demand. As nations industrialize, the demand for some products and commodities appears to become more similar. This "nation-less" or borderless, demand for globally branded products may be due to similarities in lifestyle in developed nations. Increases in global communication media also facilitate the ability of people in different countries to visualize and model lifestyles in different cultures. Benetton, an Italian casual-wear apparel company, has used its global brand and well-established worldwide retail presence as the foundation needed to more effectively manage its supply and manufacturing networks with improved communications technology.[10]

The need to go international is particularly important for Canadian companies. Not only is the domestic market a limited one—particularly relative to the U.S.—but also there is a threat posed by potential U.S. competitors entering the Canadian market. Yet, while the first logical market for Canadian firms to enter is the U.S., and while Americans may certainly hear less about Canada than Canadians hear about the U.S., such knowledge may not assure success. The next Strategic Focus box, "The First International Step: To the U.S." on page 268, discusses some of the promise and some the pitfalls of taking that first international step.

In some industries, technology drives globalization because the economies of scale necessary to reduce costs to the lowest level often require an investment greater than that needed to meet domestic market demand, as discovered by major Korean car makers Daewoo and Hyundai.[11] There is also pressure for cost reductions, achieved by purchasing from the lowest cost global suppliers. For instance, research and development expertise for an emerging business start-up may not exist in the domestic market.[12]

New large-scale, emerging markets, such as China and India, provide a strong internationalization incentive because of the potential demand in their countries.[13] Because of currency fluctuations, firms may also choose to distribute their operations across many countries, including emerging ones, in order to reduce the risk of devaluation in one country.[14] However, the uniqueness of emerging markets presents both opportunities and challenges.[15] While China, for example, differs from Western countries in many respects, including culture, politics, and the precepts of its economic system,[16] it also offers a huge potential market. Many international firms perceive Chinese markets as almost untouched markets, without exposure to many modern and sophisticated products. Once China is exposed to these products, international firms believe that demand will develop. However, the differences between China and Western countries pose serious challenges to Western competitive paradigms that emphasize the skills needed to manage financial, economic, and political risks.

While a large majority of Canadian-based companies' international business is in U.S. markets—where 50 percent of Canadian firms' assets that are located outside the domestic market are invested—Europe has been the hot market for investment. Twenty years ago, about 70 percent Canadian direct investment abroad was devoted to the U.S.—today this figure is down to 50 percent. During the same period, Canadian direct investment into Europe rose from 14 percent to 23 percent.[17] While the U.S. has subtle regional differences that should not be ignored, companies seeking to internationalize their operations in Europe face complex pressures to respond to greatly differing local, national, or regional customs. This is especially important where goods or services require either customization because of cultural differences or effective marketing to entice customers to try a different product.[18]

Of course, all firms encounter challenges when using an international strategy. For example, Unilever is a large European-centred global food and consumer products firm that adapts its products to local tastes as it moves into new national markets. Its investors expect Unilever executives to create global megabrands, which have the most growth

The First International Step: To the U.S.

The U.S. should be a good place for Canadians to do business—we share one of the world's longest borders, and we are each other's main trading partners. Yet, developing profitable operations in the U.S. can be challenging. Canadian businesses, such as Second Cup, Canadian Tire, and E.D. Smith, all faired poorly when they tried to replicate their success south of the border. "Whenever you go cross-border," says Donald Chu, a senior analyst at Standard and Poor's Corp., "the biggest difficulty is that people think it's the same marketplace, but it's not. When companies come from the U.S. up to Canada, they often get their heads handed to them on a platter, and the same goes for Canadian companies going down to the U.S." Yet, while there have been some Canadian retreats from the U.S. market, and there are some significant differences between the two countries, there are some noteworthy success stories.

When Quebec's Jean Coutu Group went to the U.S., it started small and close to home—taking over a five-store chain in New England. They were conscious of the need to change basic attributes of their business. "Jean Coutu" was not easy to for Americans to pronounce so they used the MaxiDrug name in the U.S. Now with hundreds of U.S. stores, Jean Coutu has become very quickly involved in the day-to-day details of operations, discovering, hands-on, what works, what doesn't work, what local competitors are doing, and what customers expect. Over the years, this kind of hands-on management has allowed Jean Coutu to develop the fourth largest group of drugstores in North America.

When Keg Restaurants concentrated on locations in Washington and Oregon, near its Vancouver home, the company paid attention to subtle differences. U.S. food portions have to be larger—not because Americans really eat more, but because they want to "be sure they're getting value." Their U.S. customers prefer local wines; Canadian wine tastes are more diverse. Finally, compared to its Canadian locations, the Keg's U.S. restaurants do a bigger Thanksgiving business, and their bars do a bigger Halloween business.

For many firms, successfully penetrating the U.S. market begins with sales. Bob Lavery, president of Winnipeg's Winpak Ltd., stated, "You've got to establish a sales organization in the U.S. first. … If you think it necessary to have a sales rep in Montreal, you should find it just as necessary to have one in Chicago." Within its first year, this manufacturer of food and dairy plastic-packaging products hired sales staff in Atlanta, Chicago, Denver, and Los Angeles. This move was made, despite not setting up a manufacturing facility in the U.S. for a number of years.

The markets view the acquisition of U.S. operations as a plus. Montreal convenience store operator Alimentation Couche-Tard (who operates Mac's, Becker's, and Provi-Soir) found this out in late 2003, when it acquired the U.S. chain Circle-K. The acquisition gave Couche-Tard more than 4500 stores and made it the fourth largest convenience store operator in North America. News of the acquisition immediately moved Couche-Tard's stock up by almost 22 per cent. While the acquisition was a coup, it also had to be viewed as part of an overall strategy to move into the American heartland. In 2001, the company had purchased the 225-store Bigfoot convenience store chain, and in 2002, it acquired about 400 Dairy Mart convenience stores. As was the case with Circle-K—and a handful of smaller chains Couche-Tard picked up along the way—the stores were primarily in the U.S. Midwest, and thus gave the company a strong base of operations south of the border. In an industry known for standardized centrally managed stores, Couche-Tard has demonstrated sensitivity to regional differences by decentralizing and customizing store designs and merchandise offerings to local tastes.

Waterloo, Ontario's Open Text has become a market leader in commercial knowledge-management software. Since its founding, the firm has opened sales offices in the U.S. and acquired about a dozen U.S. software developers. Having a large research centre near Chicago and being listed on the Nasdaq gives the firm a U.S. appearance. Open Text views these U.S. attributes as important tools in gaining U.S. customers. CEO Tom Jenkins insists that companies have to be prepared to pay the price to be close to their customers: "If Canadians make any mistake in the

(continued)

U.S., it would be the same mistake they might make in Vancouver or Calgary ... not locating salespeople close to your customers."

E.D. Smith found that it is not just consumers in the U.S. that differ from Canadians but the workers differ as well. In the early 1990s, the family-run maker of jams, pie fillings, and sauces, made its entry into the U.S. by opening a plant south of the border. Making the plant work correctly was another story. For E.D. Smith, a properly operating facility meant defect-free product with zero shortages. Such goals require a culture with significant employee dedication. Smith found that the Canadians in its Winona, Ontario plant produced a unique corporate culture and dedication to the 110-year-old company that was very different from the devotion to the newcomer in Byhalia, Mississippi. The firm could not meet product standards in the U.S. and, after four years, had to close its U.S. plant.

Then there are moves that include U.S. entry as part of a broader global view. As part of a strategy to remain a viable contender in the consolidating global insurance industry, Manulife Financial pursued a mega merger with Boston's John Hancock Insurance. The Toronto insurance company gained a major presence in the U.S. in individual life insurance and mutual funds. Both companies have operations in Asia, where Manulife wants to expand.

The jury may be out for quite some time on whether the Manulife's colossal cross-border move will work out, as in most mergers, there are the cultural differences to overcome. Hancock has a greater penchant for risk. Speculative-grade securities make up 8 to 10 percent of Hancock's investment portfolio. This percentage is more than double the average for most Canadian insurers. Hancock also carries some riskier and unfamiliar product lines, such as long-term care and fixed annuities. Thus, developing a consistent approach to risk management—critical for any insurance company—will be vital to the combination.

More critically, it will be important how the company's CEOs—both named D'Alessandro—will get along. Former Hancock CEO David D'Alessandro will become Manulife's new chief operating officer and will remain in charge of the U.S. operations. David is a chatty, big-picture kind of businessperson. He is known more for his marketing expertise than his financial skill. Manulife's CEO Dominic D'Alessandro, on the other hand, is a driven, demanding, gruff stickler for detail. Also, he's not one to shy away from making tough decisions if the merger is not working. When Manulife's international acquisition of Daihyaku Insurance appeared to be failing in 2001, hundreds of salespeople were replaced, costs were slashed, and operations centralized. Shakeups are likely if Hancock's financials go south as well.

SOURCE: The Jean Coutu Group, 2004, *Jean Coutu website*, http://www.jeancoutu.com/finance/english/profil/historique, accessed July 31, 2004; K. Kalawsky, 2003, Dominic finally gets his big catch. Now what?..., *Financial Post* (*National Post*), November 10, DM03; S Silcoff & R. Gibbens, 2003, Couche-Tard grows in U.S. on $1.1B deal: "Massive acquisition" of 2,000 U.S. stores to double revenue, stock hits record high, *Financial Post* (*National Post*), October 7, FP01, FP08; Financial Post, 1999, How to succeed in the U.S. market by really really trying, *Financial Post* (*National Post*), June 3, 76; T. Belford and K. Vermond, 1999, Mr. Smith goes to Mississippi and turns back....., *Financial Post* (*National Post*), December 15, E14; R. Steiner, 1999, Year after year...., *National Post Business*, October, 70–77.

potential and margins, despite most of Unilever's growth arising from acquisitions and the selling of the acquired, unique local brands. Establishing megabrands while also dealing with the forces for localization is difficult. As noted in Chapter 12, Unilever is restructuring to meet these challenges.[19]

Local repair and service capabilities are another factor influencing an increased desire for local country responsiveness. This localization may even affect industries that are seen as needing more global economies of scale, for example, white goods (home appliances, such as refrigerators). Alternatively, suppliers often follow their customers, particularly large ones, into international markets, which eliminates the firm's need to find local suppliers.[20] The transportation costs of large products and their parts, such as heavy earthmoving equipment, are significant, which may preclude a firm's suppliers following the firm to an international market.

Chapter 9 / International Strategy

Employment contracts and labour forces differ significantly in international markets. For example, it is more difficult to lay off employees in Europe than in the Canada and United States because of employment contract differences. In many cases, host governments demand joint ownership, which allows the foreign firm to avoid tariffs. Also, host governments frequently require a high percentage of procurements, manufacturing, and R&D to use local sources. These issues increase the need for local investment and responsiveness compared to seeking global economies of scale.[21]

We've discussed incentives influencing firms to use international strategies. When successful, firms can derive four basic benefits from using international strategies: (1) increased market size; (2) greater returns on major capital investments or on investments in new products and processes; (3) greater economies of scale, scope, or learning; and (4) a competitive advantage through location (e.g., access to low-cost labour, critical resources, or customers). We examine these benefits in terms of both their costs (such as higher coordination expenses and limited access to knowledge about host country political influences)[22] and their managerial challenges.

Increased Market Size

Firms can expand the size of their potential market—sometimes dramatically—by moving into international markets. As part of its expansion efforts, Bombardier has learned how to be successful in a wide range of geographic and product markets. By providing local production and maintenance facilities as part of its construction of rapid transit lines, the company has gained experience in working a wide range of governments around the world. While North American demand for rapid transit is expected to increase, the ability to market its product overseas is still important to Bombardier because any one North American customer could represent a sizable order that, if lost to a competitor, would impact the company greatly. Thus, if the company restricted itself to North America alone, the result could be disastrous if the company were unable, for whatever reason, to obtain any contract for providing construction, railcar, and after-sales operating and maintenance services to any one customer.[23]

The size of an international market also affects a firm's willingness to invest in R&D to build competitive advantages in that market. Larger markets usually offer higher potential returns and thus pose less risk for a firm's investments. The strength of the science base in the country in question also can affect a firm's foreign R&D investments. Most firms prefer to invest more heavily in those countries with the scientific knowledge and talent to produce value-creating products and processes from their R&D activities. However, research indicates that simultaneously pursuing R&D and collaborative foreign R&D joint ventures reduces effectiveness.[24]

Return on Investment

Large markets may be crucial for earning a return on significant investments, such as plant and capital equipment or R&D. Therefore, most R&D-intensive industries, such as electronics, are international. For example, significant R&D expenditures by multinational firms in Singapore's electronics industry must meet return on investment requirements. Besides meeting these requirements, the R&D project must also be "consistent with [regional] customer demands, the achievement of time-based competitiveness, the training of R&D manpower, and the development of conducive innovation environments."[25] Thus, most firms investing in the Singapore electronics industry use approaches framed around the need to satisfy multiple project outcome requirements.

In addition to the need for a large market to recoup heavy investment in R&D, the development pace for new technology is increasing. As a result, new products become obsolete more rapidly. Therefore, investments need to be recouped more quickly.

Moreover, firms' abilities to develop new technologies are expanding, and because of different patent laws across country borders, imitation by competitors is more likely. Through reverse engineering, competitors are able to take apart a product, learn the new technology, and develop a similar product that imitates the new technology. Because their competitors can imitate the new technology relatively quickly, firms need to recoup new-product development costs even more rapidly. Consequently, the larger markets provided by international expansion are particularly attractive in many industries such as computer hardware, because these markets expand the opportunity for the firm to recoup a large capital investment and large-scale R&D expenditures.[26]

Regardless of any other reason, however, the primary reason for making investments in international markets is to generate above-average returns on investments. For example, with its domestic growth in the low single digits, Yum! Brands—owner of Kentucky Fried Chicken (KFC), Pizza Hut, Taco Bell, and U.S.-based A&W, among others—has increased its overall growth by expanding globally. Yum! has around 5000 KFC restaurants in the U.S. currently and has opened more than 6000 locations internationally. Overall, the company operates more than 33,000 restaurants in more than 100 countries worldwide—more than any other restaurant company. Even though the firm focused on growth, its global expansion realized an improved return on investment. Yum!'s margin on its investments was up to more than 15 percent in 2002 from 11.6 percent in 1997. This success has come from the company's strategy of adapting to local tastes and preferences.[27]

Expected returns from the investments represent a primary predictor of firms moving into international markets. Still, firms from different countries have different expectations and use different criteria to decide whether to invest in international markets.[28]

Economies of Scale and Learning

By expanding their markets, firms may be able to enjoy economies of scale, particularly in their manufacturing operations. To the extent that a firm can standardize its products across country borders and use the same or similar production facilities, thereby coordinating critical resource functions, it is more likely to achieve optimal economies of scale.[29]

Economies of scale are critical in the global auto industry. China's decision to join the World Trade Organization will allow carmakers from other countries to enter the country, and they will pay lower tariffs (in the past, Chinese carmakers have had an advantage over foreign carmakers due to tariffs). Ford, Honda, General Motors, and Volkswagen are each producing an economy car to compete with the existing cars in China. Because of global economies of scale, all of these companies are likely to obtain market share in China.[30] As a result, Chinese carmakers will have to change the way they do business to compete with foreign carmakers.

Firms may also be able to exploit core competencies in international markets through resource and knowledge sharing between units across country borders.[31] This sharing generates synergy, which helps the firm produce higher quality goods or services at lower cost. In addition, working across international markets provides the firm with new learning opportunities. Multinational firms have substantial occasions to learn from the different practices they encounter in separate international markets. Even firms based in developed markets can learn from operations in emerging markets.[32]

Location Advantages

Firms may locate facilities in other countries to lower the basic costs of the goods or services they provide.[33] These facilities may provide easier access to lower cost labour and other natural resources, such as energy. Other location advantages include access to critical supplies and to customers.

Once they have positioned favourably with an attractive location, firms must manage their facilities effectively to gain the full benefit of a location advantage.[34] In Eastern Europe, Hungary is a prime location for many manufacturers. Flextronics, a large electronics contract manufacturer, is locating critical resources there. Hungary has good safety regulations and rapidly approves new projects. This small country borders seven nations and connects Europe to the emerging economies east of it. In 2001, 57 percent of Hungary's exports were in electronics equipment, providing a strong and growing market for Flextronics. Furthermore, it has lower labour costs than Ireland, another important producer of electronic components in Europe.[35]

In North America, Mexico has well-developed infrastructures and a skilled, although inexpensive, labour force, and it has received significant amounts of foreign direct investment. The costs of locating in Mexico are significantly lower than other countries regionally.[36] Flextronics found the country's reasonably low wage rate and proximity to its customers in North America ideal. As such, it located a 50 hectare industrial park in Guadalajara, Mexico, where everything from handheld computers to routers is manufactured.

International Strategies

Firms choose to use one or both of two basic types of international strategies: business-level international strategy and corporate-level international strategy. At the business level, firms follow generic strategies: cost leadership, differentiation, focused cost leadership, focused differentiation, or integrated cost leadership/differentiation. There are three corporate-level international strategies: multidomestic, global, or transnational (a combination of multidomestic and global). To create competitive advantage, each strategy must realize a core competence based on difficult-to-duplicate resources and capabilities.[37] As discussed in Chapters 5 and 7, firms expect to create value through the implementation of a business-level strategy and a corporate-level strategy.[38]

International Business-Level Strategy

Each business must develop a competitive strategy focused on its own domestic market. We discuss business-level generic strategies in Chapter 5 and competitive rivalry and competitive dynamics in Chapter 6. International business-level strategies have some unique features. In an international business-level strategy, the home country of operation is often the most important source of competitive advantage.[39] The resources and capabilities established in the home country frequently allow the firm to pursue its strategy into markets located in other countries. However, as a firm continues its growth into multiple international locations, research indicates that the country of origin diminishes in importance as the dominant factor.[40]

Michael Porter's model, illustrated in Figure 9.2, describes the factors contributing to the advantage of firms in a dominant global industry and associated with a specific country or regional environment.[41] The first dimension in Porter's model is *factors of production*. This dimension refers to the inputs—labour, land, natural resources, capital, and infrastructure (e.g., transportation, postal, and communication systems)—necessary to compete in any industry. There are basic factors (e.g., natural and labour resources) and advanced factors (e.g., digital communication systems and a highly educated workforce). Other production factors are generalized (highway systems and the supply of debt capital) and specialized (skilled personnel in a specific industry, such as the workers in a port that specialize in handling bulk chemicals). If a country has both advanced and specialized production factors, it is likely to serve an industry well by spawning strong home-country competitors that also can be successful global competitors.

Ironically, countries often develop advanced and specialized factors because they lack critical basic resources. For example, some Asian countries, such as South Korea, lack

Figure 9.2 | Determinants of National Advantage

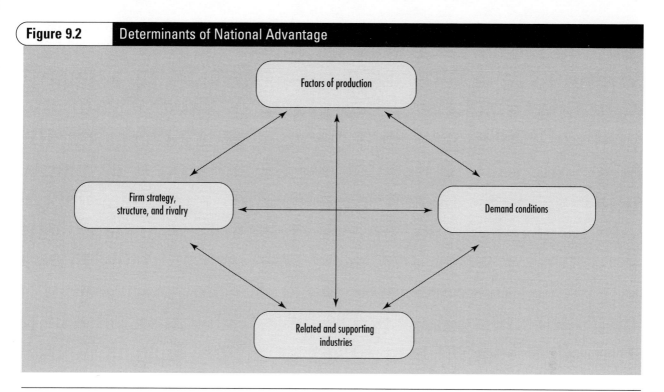

abundant natural resources but offer a strong work ethic, a large number of engineers, and systems of large firms to create an expertise in manufacturing. Similarly, Germany developed a strong chemical industry, partly because Hoechst and BASF spent years creating a synthetic indigo dye to reduce their dependence on imports, unlike Britain, whose colonies provided large supplies of natural indigo.[42]

The second dimension in Porter's model, *demand conditions*, is characterized by the nature and size of buyers' needs in the home market for the industry's goods or services. The sheer size of a market segment can produce the demand necessary to create scale-efficient facilities. This efficiency can also lead to domination of the industry in other countries. Specialized demand may also create opportunities beyond national boundaries. For example, Swiss firms have long led the world in tunnelling equipment because of the need to create rail and highway passage through the mountains in Switzerland. Japanese firms have created a niche market for compact, quiet air conditioners, which are important in Japan because homes are often small and located closely together.[43]

Related and supporting industries are the third dimension in Porter's model. Italy has become the leader in the shoe industry because of related and supporting industries; a well-established leather-processing industry provides the leather needed to construct shoes and related products. Also, many people travel to Italy to purchase leather goods, providing support in distribution. The supporting industries in leather-working machinery and design services also contribute to the success of the shoe industry. In fact, the design services industry supports its own related industries, such as the manufacturing of ski boots, fashion apparel, and furniture. In Japan, cameras and copiers are related industries. Denmark's dairy products industry is related to an industry focused on food enzymes.

Firm strategy, structure, and *rivalry* make up the final country dimension and also foster the growth of certain industries. The dimension of strategy, structure, and rivalry among firms varies greatly from nation to nation. Because of the excellent technical training system in Germany, there is a strong emphasis on methodical product and process improvements. In Japan, unusual cooperative and competitive systems have facilitated the cross-functional management of complex assembly operations. In Italy, the national pride of the country's designers has spawned strong industries in sports cars, fashion apparel, and furniture.

The four basic dimensions of the "diamond" model in Figure 9.2 emphasize the environmental or structural attributes of a national economy that contribute to national advantage. Government policy also clearly contributes to the success and failure of many firms and industries, as exemplified by the Turkish construction industry.[44] Relatively lower wages, the country's geographic and cultural proximity to several promising markets, the existence of a rivalrous home market, and the accompanying pressures to continuously upgrade their capabilities have helped Turkish contractors achieve international success. Turkish government policy, however, has created financing difficulties for foreign projects. Related industries, such as the weak Turkish design, engineering, and consultant service industries, have also weakened Turkey's international position versus other international competitors.

Although each firm must create its own success, not all firms will survive to become global competitors—not even those operating with the same country factors that spawned the successful firms. The actual strategic choices managers make may be the most compelling determinants of success or failure. Accordingly, the factors illustrated in Figure 9.2 are likely to produce competitive advantages only when the firm develops and implements an appropriate strategy that takes advantage of distinct country factors. Thus, these distinct country factors are necessary to consider when analyzing the business-level strategies (i.e., cost leadership, differentiation, focused cost leadership, focused differentiation, and integrated cost leadership/differentiation discussed in Chapter 5) in an international context.

International Corporate-Level Strategy

International business-level strategies are based at least partly on the type of international corporate-level strategy the firm has chosen. Some corporate strategies give individual country units the authority to develop their own business-level strategies; other corporate strategies dictate the business-level strategies to be used in order to standardize the firm's products and sharing of resources across countries.[45]

International corporate-level strategy focuses on the scope of a firm's operations through both product and geographic diversification.[46] International corporate-level strategy is required when the firm operates in multiple industries and multiple countries or regions.[47] The headquarters unit guides the strategy, although business-level or country-level managers can have substantial strategic input, given the type of international corporate level strategy followed. The three international corporate-level strategies are multidomestic, global, and transnational, as shown in Figure 9.3.

Multidomestic Strategy

A **multidomestic strategy** is an international strategy in which strategic and operating decisions are decentralized to the strategic business unit in each country to allow that unit to tailor products to the local market.[48] A multidomestic strategy focuses on competition within each country, based on the assumption that the markets differ and, therefore, are segmented by country boundaries. In other words, consumer needs and desires, industry conditions (e.g., the number and type of competitors), political and legal structures, and social norms vary by country. With multidomestic strategies, the firm can customize its products to meet the specific needs and preferences of local customers.

A **multidomestic strategy** is an international strategy in which strategic and operating decisions are decentralized to the strategic business unit in each country to allow that unit to tailor products to the local market.

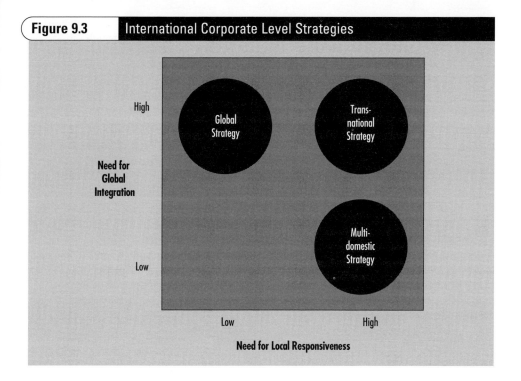

Figure 9.3 | International Corporate Level Strategies

Therefore, these strategies should maximize a firm's competitive response to the idiosyncratic requirements of each market.[49]

The use of multidomestic strategies usually expands the firm's local market share because the firm can pay attention to the needs of the local clientele.[50] However, the use of these strategies results in more uncertainty for the corporation as a whole, because of the differences across markets and thus the different strategies employed by local country units.[51] Moreover, multidomestic strategies do not allow for the achievement of economies of scale and can be more costly. As a result, firms employing a multidomestic strategy decentralize their strategic and operating decisions to the business units operating in each country. The multidomestic strategy has been more commonly used by European multinational firms because of the variety of cultures and markets found in Europe.

As mentioned earlier, Yum! Brands has a strong incentive to compete internationally with its restaurant concepts (KFC, Pizza Hut, Taco Bell, and U.S.-based A&W). Yum! pursues a multidomestic strategy by trying to localize as much as possible. The firm does not open restaurants based solely on the North American model. It consistently adapts to local tastes and negotiates well when cultural and political climates change. Of course, KFC serves poutine in Canada, but the menu adjustments need to be made world over. "In Japan, for instance, KFC sells tempura crispy strips. In northern England, KFC stresses gravy and potatoes, while in Thailand it offers fresh rice with soy or sweet chili sauce. In Holland, the company makes a potato-and-onion croquette. In France, it sells pastries alongside chicken. And in China, the chicken gets spicier the farther inland you travel. More and more, if it's a … brand without a regional appeal, it's going to be difficult to market."[52]

Global Strategy

In contrast to a multidomestic strategy, a global strategy assumes more standardization of products across country markets.[53] As a result, a global strategy is centralized and controlled by the home office. The strategic business units operating in each country are

A **global strategy** is an international strategy through which the firm offers standardized products across country markets, with competitive strategy being dictated by the home office.

assumed to be interdependent, and the home office attempts to achieve integration across these businesses. A **global strategy** is an international strategy through which the firm offers standardized products across country markets, with competitive strategy being dictated by the home office. Thus, a global strategy emphasizes economies of scale and offers greater opportunities to utilize innovations developed at the corporate level or in one country in other markets.

While a global strategy produces lower risk, the firm may forgo growth opportunities in local markets, either because those markets are less likely to identify opportunities or because opportunities require that products be adapted to the local market.[54] The global strategy is not as responsive to local markets and is difficult to manage because of the need to coordinate strategies and operating decisions across country borders. Consequently, achieving efficient operations with a global strategy requires sharing of resources and coordination and cooperation across country boundaries, which in turn require centralization and headquarters control. Many Japanese firms have successfully used the global strategy.[55]

Cemex, a Monterrey, Mexico-based cement maker, is the world's third largest cement manufacturer. Cemex acquired Southdown, the U.S. cement company for $3 billion at the end of 2001 and began to consolidate this operation with its other U.S. assets. Cemex has the leading market position in Spain with around 72 percent of the production capacity in the Spanish cement industry. Besides its significant assets in North and South America and southern Europe, the firm is also making inroads in Asia through acquisitions.

To integrate its businesses globally, Cemex uses the Internet as one way of increasing revenue and lowering its cost structure. The firm takes advantage of its dominant presence in Mexico and other Latin American locations by providing more than 3000 points of distribution through the Internet. Through its e-business subsidiary CxNetworks, Cemex launched the construction materials website Arkio.com; it expects to recoup the cost of implementation within a year.

By using the Internet to improve logistics and manage an extensive supply network, Cemex can significantly reduce costs. With the savings derived from its Internet supply chain management efforts and by consolidating operations such as the Southdown acquisition into its existing U.S. operations, Cemex expects, within three years, to cut $100 million from its operating costs in the U.S. Thus, Cemex is using a global strategy to integrate many aspects of its worldwide operations.[56]

Transnational Strategy

A **transnational strategy** is an international strategy through which the firm seeks to achieve both global efficiency and local responsiveness.

A **transnational strategy** is an international strategy through which the firm seeks to achieve both global efficiency and local responsiveness. Realizing these goals is difficult: one requires close global coordination while the other requires local flexibility. "Flexible coordination"—building a shared vision and individual commitment through an integrated network—is required to implement the transnational strategy.[57] In reality, it is difficult to successfully use the transnational strategy because of its conflicting goals (see Chapter 12 for more on implementation of this and other corporate-level international strategies). On the positive side, effective implementation of a transnational strategy often produces higher performance than does implementation of either the multidomestic or global international corporate-level strategies.[58]

For example, Bombardier's rail operations suggest that the company may be pursuing a transnational strategy to deal with global trends. Passenger rail transportation has significant pressures for local responsiveness, such as the desire of the governments who run the services to employ local manufacturing and maintenance providers. To meet these requests, Bombardier has numerous plants and maintenance facilities around the globe. At the same time, there are global pressures for world-class computerized scheduling, vehicle programming for driverless systems, and innovations in project design and construction engineering. Bombardier pursues these technological initiatives at fewer locations to take advantage of a critical mass of engineering and programming expertise.[59]

Environmental Trends

Although the transnational strategy is difficult to implement, emphasis on global efficiency is increasing as more industries begin to experience global competition. To add to the problem, there is also an increased emphasis on local requirements: global goods and services often require some customization to meet government regulations within particular countries or to fit customer tastes and preferences. In addition, most multinational firms desire coordination and sharing of resources across country markets to hold down costs, as illustrated by the Cemex example above. Furthermore, some products and industries may be better suited than others for standardization across country borders.

As a result, most large multinational firms with diverse products employ a multidomestic strategy with certain product lines and a global strategy with others. Many multinational firms may require this type of flexibility if they are to be strategically competitive, in part due to trends that change over time. Two important trends are the liability of foreignness, which has increased after the terrorist attacks on September 11, 2001, and the trend towards regionalization.

Liability of Foreignness

The dramatic success of Japanese firms such as Toyota and Sony in North American and other international markets in the 1980s was a powerful jolt to managers, awakening them to the importance of international competition in what were rapidly becoming global markets. In the 1990s, Eastern Europe and China represented potential major international market opportunities for firms from many countries, including Canada, the United States, Japan, Korea, and European nations.[60] Research shows that global strategies are not as prevalent as once thought and are very difficult to implement, even when using Internet-based strategies.[61] In the 21st century, firms may focus less on truly global markets and more on regional adaptation. Although parallel developments in the Internet and mobile telecommunication facilitate communications across the globe, the implementation of web-based strategies also requires local adaptation.

The Thomson Corporation demonstrates the globalization of businesses with local strategies. Toronto's Thomson is organized into four market groups: Legal & Regulatory, Learning, Financial, and Scientific & Healthcare. Some of these market groups have products that are global in scope, such as the financial securities databases or, in the case of Legal & Regulatory, its scientific database *Derwent World Patent Index*. Other areas, such as Learning or Legal & Regulatory, are split up so that the company appears to be very much a local resource provider to its customers. For example, Thomson may be better known in the U.S. as the publishing companies South-Western and Gale. In Canada, Thomson Learning is the publisher of this text, under the Nelson imprint; in Latin America, it is known as Thomson Learning Iberoamerica; in Spain, it would be Thomson Paraninfo; and in Europe, it would be Thomson Learning EMEA. The company is more recognizable in the Far East as Thomson Learning Asia and in Australia as Thomson Learning Australia.[62]

Thompson's legal and tax publications seem to have little connection to the company. They are known (among other names) as Sweet & Maxwell Asia in the Far East, Brookers in New Zealand, Forlaget Thomson in Denmark, Westlaw in Sweden, West in North America, and several different names for several different subsidiaries in Australia, the UK, Spain, and Ireland. The legal and publications group also publishes *Bellamy & Child: European Community Law of Competition* in Europe and *Juris Síntese Millennium* in Brazil and owns Argentina's leading provider of legal and regulatory information services,

La Ley. By maintaining the names and subsidiaries as local providers, the company can provide a measure of local responsiveness while, at the same time, tapping into the financial and information resources of the larger parent.

Regionalization

Regionalization is the second trend that has become more common in global markets. Because a firm's location can affect its strategic competitiveness,[63] it must decide whether to compete in all or many global markets, or to focus on a particular region or regions. Competing in all markets provides economies that can be achieved from the combined market size. Research suggests that firms that compete in risky emerging markets can also achieve higher performance.[64]

However, a firm that competes in industries where the international markets differ greatly (in which it must employ a multidomestic strategy) may wish to narrow its focus to a particular region of the world. In so doing, it can better understand the cultures, legal and social norms, and other factors that are important for effective competition in those markets. For example, a firm may focus on Far East markets only, rather than competing simultaneously in the Middle East, Europe, and the Far East. Or, the firm may choose a region of the world where the markets are more similar and some coordination and sharing of resources would be possible. In this way, the firm may be able, not only to better understand the markets in which it competes, but also to achieve some economies, even though it may have to employ a multidomestic strategy. This is the case with Yum! Brands, as we explained earlier.

Countries that develop trade agreements to increase the economic power of their regions may promote regional strategies. The European Union (EU) and South America's Organization of American States (OAS) in South America are country associations that developed trade agreements to promote the flow of trade across country boundaries within their respective regions.[65] Many European firms acquire and integrate their businesses in Europe to better coordinate pan-European brands since the EU creates more unity in European markets.

The North American Free Trade Agreement (NAFTA), signed by Canada, Mexico, and the United States, facilitates free trade across country borders in North America and may be expanded to include other countries in South America, such as Argentina, Brazil, and Chile.[66] NAFTA loosens restrictions on international strategies within a region and provides greater opportunity for international strategies. Between 1988 (the year before the NAFTA went into effect) and 1993, the two-way exchange of goods, services, and income between Canada and the U.S. increased by one-third. After the agreement was expanded in 1994 to include Mexico, trade between Canada and the U.S. grew by 50 percent. Transactions between the U.S. and Canada are now valued at more than $1.5 billion (CDN) per day. One-quarter of all U.S. exports go to Canada. U.S. exports to the province of Ontario alone were worth almost twice as much as those to Japan in 2001.[67]

Most firms enter regional markets sequentially, beginning in markets with which they are more familiar. They also introduce their largest and strongest lines of business into these markets first, followed by their other lines of business once the first lines are successful.[68] After the firm selects its international strategies and decides whether to employ them in regional or world markets, it must choose a market entry mode.[69]

Choice of International Entry Mode

International expansion is accomplished by exporting products, negotiating licensing agreements, forging strategic alliances, securing acquisitions, and establishing new wholly owned subsidiaries. These means of entering international markets and their characteristics are shown in Table 9.1. Each means of market entry has its advantages and disadvantages. Thus, choosing the appropriate mode or path to enter international markets affects the firm's performance in those markets.[70] As shown in next Strategic Focus box, "Beer: Four Ingredients and Five Entry Strategies" on page 280, entry strategies—even within a single industry—can get quite complicated.

Exporting

Many industrial firms begin their international expansion by exporting goods or services to other countries.[71] Exporting does not require the expense of establishing operations in the host countries, but exporters must establish some means of marketing and distributing their products. Usually, exporting firms develop contractual arrangements with host-country firms.

The disadvantages of exporting include the often high costs of transportation and possible tariffs placed on incoming goods. Furthermore, the exporter has less control over the marketing and distribution of its products in the host country and must either pay the distributor or allow the distributor to add to the price to recoup its costs and earn a profit. As a result, it may be difficult to market a competitive product through exporting or to provide a product that is customized to each international market.[72] However, evidence suggests that cost-leadership strategies enhance the performance of exports in developed countries, whereas differentiation strategies are more successful in emerging economies.[73]

Firms export most frequently to countries that are closest to their facilities because of the lower transportation costs and the usually greater similarity between geographic neighbours. As noted earlier, U.S. exports to the province of Ontario alone are worth almost twice as much as U.S. exports to Japan.[74] The Internet has also made exporting easier. Even small firms can access critical information about foreign markets, examine a target market, research the competition, and acquire lists of potential customers. Governments also use the Internet to facilitate applications for export and import licences. Although the terrorist threat is likely to slow its progress, high-speed technology is still the wave of the future.[75]

Small businesses are most likely to use the exporting mode of international entry.[76] Currency exchange rates are one of the most significant problems small businesses face. While larger firms have specialists that manage the exchange rates, small businesses rarely have this expertise. On January 1, 2002, 12 countries began using Euro notes and coins for the first time. This change to a common currency in Europe is helpful to small businesses operating in European markets. Instead of 12 different exchange rates, firms exporting to EU countries only have to obtain information on one exchange rate, which should relieve tension and facilitate exports.[77]

Table 9.1	Global Market Entry: Choice of Entry Mode
Type of Entry	**Characteristics**
Exporting	High cost, low control.
Licensing	Low cost, low risk, little control, low returns.
Strategic alliances	Shared costs, shared resources, shared risks, problems of integration (e.g., two corporate cultures).
Acquisition	Quick access to new market, high cost, complex negotiations, problems of merging with domestic operations.
New wholly owned subsidiary	Complex, often costly, time consuming, high risk, maximum control, potential above-average returns.

Beer: Four Ingredients and Five Entry Strategies

Beer is four simple ingredients: malt, hops, yeast, and water. Yet, for international companies that brew beer, getting the beer to their buyers is anything but simple. The simplest method, exporting, actually has some advantages. The beer can maintain an image of quality because it is still brewed at the original brewery, with the exact same ingredients, by the same brewing company as the original product. Since 1867, the Oland family has brewed Moosehead beer in Saint John, New Brunswick. From this one brewery, Moosehead is exported to 14 countries and is available in 48 of the 50 U.S. states (Arizona and Utah are the exceptions).

The problem with beer is that exporting is not only expensive but also relatively unnecessary. The ingredients that impart flavour to the beer—the malt, hops, and yeast—only make up about 5 percent of the volume of the brew. The rest is water, and any mineral differences in water can, and sometimes do, get corrected by adding or removing minerals from the water used to brew the beer. This is why bringing in the raw materials and brewing the beer in the market in which it is to be sold makes some sense.

In many developed markets, where there are already established breweries, licensing makes sense. While Molson exports its own beers to the U.S., it has licences to brew Heineken and Miller in Canada (Heineken and SAB Miller UK are among the world's five largest breweries). Molson also brews America's Coors, Mexico's Corona, Japan's Asahi, and Australia's Foster's under licence. Belgium's Interbrew—also one of the world's five largest breweries and owner of Labatt—has a licence to produce Budweiser in Canada for U.S. giant Anheuser-Busch. Going to the opposite extreme from brewing the American beer, Labatt also brews Guinness Stout for the Canadian market under licence from Arthur Guinness Son & Company. Guelph, Ontario's Sleeman Brewing has acquired the Canadian rights to sell and distribute the U.S. brand Stroh from its parent, Texas-based Pabst Brewing. Sleeman also brews beer under licence in Canada for Japan's Sapporo Breweries.

Strategic alliances abound in the brewing industry. In 2000, Sleeman entered a partnership with the Boston Beer Company to represent its Samuel Adams brand in Canada. Boston Beer is obligated to conduct market research in the U.S. to identify potential markets for Sleeman and assist with brand development and selling strategies if sufficient market potential is identified. There are other brewers that are involved in strategic alliances, particularly in emerging markets. For example, to operate breweries in China, Anheuser-Busch has partnered with Tsingtao Brewery, SAB Miller with Harbin, and Foster with Shanghai.

Acquisitions are also another way Canadian companies can break into foreign markets. Molson's purchase of Brazil's Bavaria Breweries in December 2000 gave it a foothold into the Brazilian market. To bring the Brazilian investment up to an economically efficient size, Molson acquired Kaiser in March 2002. The acquisition increased Molson's market share in Brazil from about 3 percent to about 18 percent and firmly positioned Molson as the second largest brewer in Brazil. Given the presence in many markets of pre-existing popular local competitors, acquisitions may make sense. However, given the presence of a far larger Brazilian brewer, Molson started expanding its Brazilian brand more in the North American market than in Brazil.

In developing markets, however, opening a new brewery via a wholly owned subsidiary is one possible strategy. Singapore's Asia Pacific Breweries (APB) operates more than a dozen breweries in eight countries, including its most recent new brewery, its 100 percent-owned Hatay Brewery Limited in Vietnam. Baltic Beverages Holding (BBH) has, since the early 1990s, made acquisitions in more than a dozen breweries in Russia, the Baltic States, and the Ukraine. However, its more recent forays into this market include three new greenfield plants—one in the Ukraine and two in Russia. APB, at about $1 billion (CDN) in sales, and BBH, at about $2 billion (CDN) in sales, are significant competitors in their regions. Both companies are the result of another previously mentioned strategy—strategic alliances. Both APB and BBH are joint ventures. Holland's Heineken and Singapore's Fraser and Neave started APB in the 1930s. BBH was

(continued)

1990s 50–50 joint venture between Sweden's Pripps and Finland's Hartwall. Oddly, neither of these original owners still exists independently, victims of still another entry strategy: acquisition. Denmark's Carlsberg acquired Pripps in 2000, and Britain's Scottish & Newcastle acquired Hartwall in 2002.

SOURCES: T. Healy & D. Hsieh, 2001, Drunk on foreign money? China faces a challenge from joint ventures, *Asia Week website*, http://www.asiaweek.com/asiaweek/96/0823/biz3.html; Reuters, 2004, Factbox—World's largest brewer, *Yahoo! Dan-mark Finans website*, http://dk.biz.yahoo.com/ 040107/49/301u3.html, Jan. 7; the following companies' websites were accessed February 12–15, 2004: Anheuser-Busch Companies, http://www.anheuser-busch.com; Asahi Breweries, Ltd., http://www.Asahibeer.co.jp/english; Asia Pacific Breweries Ltd., http://www.apb.com.sg; Carlsberg, http://www.carlsberg.com; Interbrew, http://www.interbrew.com; Heineken, http://www.heineken.com; Labatt Breweries, http://www.labatt.com; Molson, http://www.molson.com; Moosehead Beer, http://www.mooseheadbeer.com; Pabst Brewing Co., http://www.pabst.com; SAB Miller, http://www.sabmiller.com; Sapporo Breweries, http://www.sapporobeer.com; Scottish and Newcastle, http://www.scottish-newcastle.com; Sleeman Brewing, http://www.ale-sleeman.com.

Licensing

Licensing is one of the forms of organizational networks that are becoming common, particularly among smaller firms.[78] A licensing arrangement allows a foreign firm to purchase the right to manufacture and sell the firm's products within a host country or set of countries.[79] The licenser is typically paid a royalty on each unit produced and sold. The licensee takes the risks and makes the monetary investments in facilities for manufacturing, marketing, and distributing the goods or services. As a result, licensing is possibly the least costly form of international expansion.

Licensing is also a way to expand returns based on previous innovations. Even if product life cycles are short, licensing may be a useful tool. For instance, because the toy industry faces relentless change and an unpredictable buying public, licensing is used, and contracts are often completed in foreign markets where labour may be less expensive.[80]

Licensing also has disadvantages. For example, it gives the firm very little control over the manufacture and marketing of its products in other countries. In addition, licensing provides the least potential returns, because returns must be shared between the licenser and the licensee. Worse, the international firm may learn the technology and produce and sell a similar competitive product after the licence expires. Komatsu, for example, first licensed much of its technology from International Harvester, Bucyrus-Erie, and Cummins Engine to compete against Caterpillar in the earthmoving-equipment business. Komatsu then dropped these licences and developed its own products using the technology it had gained from the North American companies.[81]

In addition, if a firm wants to move to a different ownership arrangement, licensing may create some inflexibility. Thus, it is important for a firm to think ahead and consider sequential forms of entry in international markets.[82]

Strategic Alliances

In recent years, strategic alliances have become a popular means of international expansion.[83] Strategic alliances allow firms to share the risks and the resources required to enter international markets.[84] Moreover, strategic alliances can facilitate the development of new core competencies that contribute to the firm's future strategic competitiveness.[85]

Most strategic alliances are formed with a host-country firm that knows and understands the competitive conditions, legal and social norms, and cultural idiosyncrasies of the country, which should help the expanding firm to manufacture and market a competitive product. In return, the host-country firm may find its new access to the expanding firm's technology and innovative products attractive. Each partner in an alliance brings knowledge or resources to the partnership.[86] Indeed, partners often enter an alliance with the purpose of learning new capabilities. Common among those desired capabilities are technological skills.[87] H.J. Heinz Co., for example, sought growth in the Asia–Pacific market as a way to reduce its operating costs there. The company decided to form an alliance with Japanese food company Kagome Co. The partners planned to use Heinz's existing retail network to enhance distribution of products, while Kagome would take the lead in research and production. For Kagome, whose food division had been struggling, the alliance was attractive, since Heinz has many strong food products. Both companies felt that the alliance would help them cut operating costs as well as expand sales.[88]

Attracted by the huge Chinese market, Pearson PLC—the British education and publishing company that publishes the *Financial Times* and the *Economist*, among others—formed an alliance with CCTV, a unit of China State Television. The venture, named CTV Media Ltd., will provide "conversational English in an entertaining setting" to more than 1 billion viewers each day through CCTV. This venture opens up the Chinese television viewing market to Pearson and also to many international advertisers looking to promote their products in China.[89]

Not all alliances are successful; in fact, many fail. The primary reasons for failure include incompatible partners and conflict between the partners.[90] International strategic alliances are especially difficult to manage.[91] Several factors may cause a relationship to sour. Trust between the partners is critical and is affected by at least four fundamental issues: the initial condition of the relationship, the negotiation process to arrive at an agreement, partner interactions, and external events.[92]

Research has shown that equity-based alliances, over which a firm has more control, tend to produce more positive returns[93] (strategic alliances are discussed in greater depth in Chapter 10). However, if conflict in a strategic alliance or joint venture will not be manageable, an acquisition may be a better option. Research suggests that alliances are more favourable in the face of high uncertainty and where cooperation is needed to bring out the knowledge dispersed between partners and where strategic flexibility is important; acquisitions are better in situations with less need for strategic flexibility and when the transaction is used to maintain economies of scale or scope.[94]

Acquisitions

As free trade has continued to expand in global markets, cross-border acquisitions have also been increasing significantly. In recent years, cross-border acquisitions have comprised more than 45 percent of all acquisitions completed worldwide.[95] As explained in Chapter 8, acquisitions can provide quick access to a new market. In fact, acquisitions may provide the fastest, and often the largest, initial international expansion of any of the alternatives.

Although acquisitions have become a popular mode of entering international markets, they are not without costs. International acquisitions carry some of the disadvantages of domestic acquisitions (see Chapter 8). In addition, they can be expensive and often require debt financing, which also carries an extra cost. International negotiations for acquisitions can be exceedingly complex and are generally more complicated than for domestic acquisitions. For example, it is estimated that only 20 percent of cross-border bids lead to a completed acquisition, compared to 40 percent for domestic acquisitions.[96] Dealing with the legal and regulatory requirements in the target firm's country and obtaining appropriate information to negotiate an agreement frequently presents significant problems. Finally, the problems of merging the new firm into the acquiring firm often are more complex than in domestic acquisitions. The acquiring firm must deal, not only with different corporate cultures, but also with potentially different social cultures and practices. Therefore, while international acquisitions have been popular because of the rapid access to new markets they provide, they also carry with them important costs and multiple risks.

While U.S. banks are excluded from making acquisitions in Canada, Canadian banks have bought out a number of regional players south of the border. Royal Bank has been very active in their North American expansion. Since 2000, Royal has completed 10 acquisitions that have boosted its client base by almost 25 percent. TD's acquisition of Waterhouse Investor Services in 1996 made it the second largest discount brokerage in the world. Since buying Chicago's Harris Bank, in 1984, the Bank of Montreal (BOM) has been active in the U.S. BOM merged Harris with Illinois competitor Suburban Bancorp to expand throughout Illinois, Arizona, and Florida. However, Canadian banks may logically be restricted to picking up smaller regional players. Targeting bigger bank chains may call attention to the one-way street Canada has set up—the ability of Canadian banks to buy U.S. financial institutions but the restriction that U.S. banks cannot buy Canadian financial institutions. Taking on bigger U.S. targets may call unwanted attention to this fact.[97]

New Wholly Owned Subsidiary

The establishment of a new wholly owned subsidiary is referred to as a **greenfield venture**. This process is often complex and potentially costly, but it affords maximum control to the firm and has the most potential to provide above-average returns. This potential is especially true in firms with strong intangible capabilities that might be leveraged through a greenfield venture.[98]

The risks are also high, however, because of the costs of establishing a new business operation in a new country. The firm may have to acquire the knowledge and expertise of the existing market by hiring either host-country nationals, possibly from competitors, or consultants, which can be costly. Still, the firm maintains control over the technology, marketing, and distribution of its products. Alternatively, the company must build new manufacturing facilities, establish distribution networks, and learn and implement appropriate marketing strategies to compete in the new market.

When British American Tobacco (BAT) decided to increase its market share in South Korea, a very tough market for imported cigarettes, it resolved to build a new greenfield cigarette factory there. The South Korean cigarette market is very protected, with a state-run monopoly, Korea Tobacco and Ginseng Corporation, controlling most of the market. Also, South Korea has said that it would impose increasingly high tariffs on imported tobacco, and there is a strong antiforeign sentiment of among consumers. John Taylor, president of BAT Korea, hoped that its manoeuvre, which would produce cigarettes "made in Korea, by Koreans and for Koreans," would increase British American Tobacco's market share from 3.7 percent to 10 percent.[99]

Dynamics of Mode of Entry

A firm's choice of mode of entry into international markets is affected by a number of factors.[100] Initially, market entry will often be achieved through export, which requires no foreign manufacturing expertise and investment only in distribution. Licensing can facilitate the product improvements necessary to enter foreign markets, as in the Komatsu example. Strategic alliances have been popular because they allow a firm to connect with an experienced partner already in the targeted market. Strategic alliances also reduce risk through the sharing of costs. All three modes therefore are best for early market development tactics. Also, the strategic alliance is often used in more uncertain situations, such as an emerging economy.[101] However, if intellectual property rights in the emerging economy are not well protected, the number of firms in the industry is growing fast, and the need for global integration is high, the wholly owned entry mode is preferred.[102]

The establishment of a new wholly owned subsidiary is referred to as a **greenfield venture**.

To secure a stronger presence in international markets, acquisitions or greenfield ventures may be required. Many Japanese automobile manufacturers, such as Honda, Toyota, and Suzuki, have gained a presence in the North America through both greenfield ventures and joint ventures.[103] Toyota has particularly strong intangible production capabilities that it has been able to transfer through greenfield ventures.[104] Both acquisitions and greenfield ventures are likely to come at later stages in the development of an international strategy. In addition, both strategies tend to be more successful when the firm making the investment possesses valuable core competencies.[105] Large diversified business groups, often found in emerging economies, not only gain resources through diversification, but also have specialized abilities in managing differences in inward and outward flows of foreign direct investment. In particular, Korean chaebols—conglomerates of many companies clustered around one parent company—have been adept at making acquisitions in emerging economies.[106]

Thus, to enter a global market, a firm selects the entry mode that is best suited to the situation at hand. In some instances, the various options will be followed sequentially, beginning with exporting and ending with greenfield ventures.[107] In other cases, the firm may use several, but not all, of the different entry modes, each in different markets. The decision regarding which entry mode to use is primarily a result of the industry's competitive conditions, the country's situation and government policies, and the firm's unique set of resources, capabilities, and core competencies.

Strategic Competitiveness Outcomes

Once its international strategy and mode of entry have been selected, the firm turns its attention to implementation issues. This focus is important because, as explained next, international expansion is risky and may not result in a competitive advantage (see Figure 9.1). The probability the firm will achieve success by using an international strategy increases when that strategy is effectively implemented.

International Diversification and Returns

International diversification is a strategy through which a firm expands the sales of its goods or services across the borders of global regions and countries into different geographic locations or markets.

As noted earlier, firms have numerous reasons to diversify internationally. **International diversification** is a strategy through which a firm expands the sales of its goods or services across the borders of global regions and countries into different geographic locations or markets. Because of its potential advantages, international diversification should be related positively to firms' returns. Research has shown that, as international diversification increases, firms' returns increase.[108] In fact, the stock market is particularly sensitive to investments in international markets. Firms that are broadly diversified into multiple international markets usually achieve the most positive stock returns.[109] There are also many reasons for the positive effects of international diversification, such as potential economies of scale and experience, location advantages, increased market size, and the opportunity to stabilize returns. The stabilization of returns helps reduce a firm's overall risk.[110] All of these outcomes can be achieved by smaller and newer ventures, as well as by larger and established firms. New ventures can also enjoy higher returns when they learn new technologies from their international diversification.[111]

Firms in the Japanese automobile industry (as indicated in the section "Dynamics of Mode of Entry" on page 283) have found that international diversification may allow them to better exploit their core competencies, because sharing knowledge resources between operations can produce synergy. Also, a firm's returns may affect its decision to diversify internationally. For example, poor returns in a domestic market may encourage a firm to expand internationally in order to enhance its profit potential. In addition, internationally diversified firms may have access to more flexible labour markets (e.g., the experience of Japanese firms in North America) and may thereby benefit from global scanning for competition and market opportunities. Also, through global networks with assets in many countries, firms can develop more flexible structures to adjust to changes that might occur.[112]

Benetton, an Italian casual-wear company, developed a network structure over the years that has allowed it to improve its performance. "Without giving up the strongest aspects of its networked model, it is integrating and centralizing, instituting direct control over key processes throughout the supply chain. The company is also diversifying into sportswear, sports equipment, and communications."[113] To manage the network, the firm has instituted state-of-the-art technology for communication and management of the supply chain. Accordingly, multinational firms with efficient and competitive operations are more likely to produce above-average returns for their investors and better products for their customers than are solely domestic firms. However, as explained later, international diversification can be carried too far.

International Diversification and Innovation

In Chapter 1, we note that the development of new technology is at the heart of strategic competitiveness. As noted in Porter's model (see Figure 9.2, on page 273), a nation's competitiveness depends, in part, on the capacity of its industry to innovate. Eventually and inevitably, competitors outperform firms that fail to innovate and improve their operations and products. Therefore, the only way to sustain a competitive advantage is to upgrade it continually.[114]

International diversification provides the potential for firms to achieve greater returns on their innovations (through larger or more numerous markets) and lowers the often substantial risks of R&D investments. Therefore, international diversification provides incentives for firms to innovate.[115]

In addition, international diversification may be necessary to generate the resources required to sustain a large-scale R&D operation. An environment of rapid technological obsolescence makes it difficult to invest in new technology and the capital-intensive operations required to take advantage of such investment. Firms operating solely in domestic markets may find such investments problematic because of the length of time required to recoup the original investment. If the time is extended, it may not be possible to recover the investment before the technology becomes obsolete.[116] As a result, international diversification improves a firm's ability to appropriate additional and necessary returns from innovation before competitors can overcome the initial competitive advantage created by the innovation. In addition, firms moving into international markets are exposed to new products and processes. If they learn about those products and processes and integrate this knowledge into their operations, further innovation can be developed.[117]

The relationship among international diversification, innovation, and returns is complex. Some level of performance is necessary to provide the resources to generate international diversification, which in turn provides incentives and resources to invest in research and development. The latter, if done appropriately, should enhance the returns of the firm, which then provide more resources for continued international diversification and investment in R&D.[118]

Because of the potential positive effects of international diversification on performance and innovation, such diversification may even enhance returns in product-diversified firms. International diversification would increase market potential in each of these firm's product lines, but the complexity of managing a firm that is both product diversified and internationally diversified is significant. Research suggests that firms in less developed countries gain from being product diversified when partnering with multinational firms from a more developed country that are looking to enter a less developed country in pursuit of increased international diversification.[119]

Switzerland's Asea Brown Boveri (ABB) demonstrates these relationships. This firm's operations involve high levels of both product and international diversification, yet ABB's performance is strong. Some believe that the firm's ability to effectively implement the transnational strategy contributes to its strategic competitiveness. One of ABB's latest moves was in North Korea; it had signed in Pyongyang (the capital of North Korea) "a wide-ranging, long-term cooperation agreement aimed at improving the performance of the country's electricity transmission network and basic industries."[120] To manage itself, ABB assembled culturally diverse corporate and divisional management teams that facilitated the simultaneous achievement of global integration and local responsiveness.

Evidence suggests that more culturally diverse top-management teams often have a greater knowledge of international markets and their idiosyncrasies[121] (top-management teams are discussed further in Chapter 13). Moreover, an in-depth understanding of diverse markets among top-level managers facilitates intrafirm coordination and the use of long-term, strategically relevant criteria to evaluate the performance of managers and their units.[122] In turn, this approach facilitates improved innovation and performance.[123]

Complexity of Managing Multinational Firms

Although firms can realize many benefits by implementing an international strategy, doing so is complex and can produce greater uncertainty.[124] For example, multiple risks are involved when a firm operates in several different countries. Firms can grow only so large and diverse before they either become unmanageable or the costs of managing them exceed their benefits. Other complexities include the highly competitive nature of global markets, multiple cultural environments, potentially rapid shifts in the value of different currencies, and the possible instability of some national governments.

Risks in an International Environment

International diversification carries multiple risks.[125] Because of these risks, international expansion is difficult to implement, and it is difficult to manage after implementation. The chief risks are political and economic. Taking these risks into account, highly internationally diversified firms are accustomed to market conditions yielding competitive situations that differ from the competitive climate that was predicted. Sometimes, these situations contribute to the firm's strategic competitiveness; on other occasions, they have a negative effect on the firm's efforts.[126] Specific examples of political and economic risks are shown in Figure 9.4.

Political Risks

Political risks are risks related to instability in national governments and to war, both civil and international. Instability in a national government creates numerous problems, including economic risks and uncertainty created by government regulation; the existence of many, possibly conflicting, legal authorities; and the potential nationalization of private assets. Foreign firms that invest in another country may have concerns about the stability of the national government and what might happen to their investments or assets because of unrest and government instability. Even among relatively stable and close trading partners, problems can arise—as illustrated in the Strategic Focus box on page 288, "Blame Canada."

Economic Risks

Foremost among the economic risks of international diversification are the differences and fluctuations in the value of different currencies.[127] The value of the dollar relative to

Figure 9.4 Risks in the International Environment

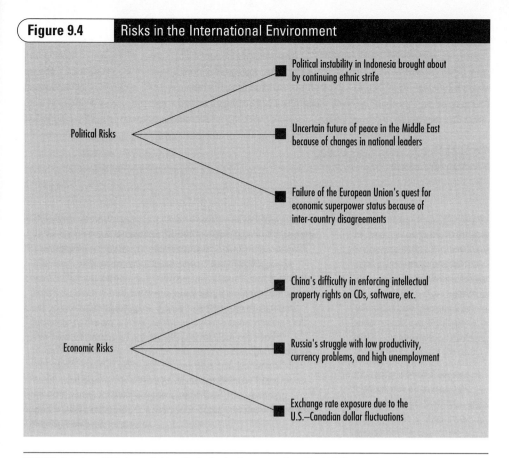

Political Risks
- Political instability in Indonesia brought about by continuing ethnic strife
- Uncertain future of peace in the Middle East because of changes in national leaders
- Failure of the European Union's quest for economic superpower status because of inter-country disagreements

Economic Risks
- China's difficulty in enforcing intellectual property rights on CDs, software, etc.
- Russia's struggle with low productivity, currency problems, and high unemployment
- Exchange rate exposure due to the U.S.–Canadian dollar fluctuations

SOURCES: E. Andrews, 2002, A smooth debut lifts Euro's value in money markets, *New York Times on the web*, http://www.nytimes.com, January 3; M. Kripalani, N. Mangi, F. Balfour, P. Magnusson, & R. Brady, 2002, Now, will India and Pakistan get serious about peace? *Business Week*, January 14, 51; M. Wallin, 2002, Argentina grapples with postdevaluation, *Wall Street Journal*, January 10, A8; B. Einhorn, C. Dawson, I. Kunii, D. Roberts, A. Webb, & P. Engardio, 2001, China: Will its entry into the WTO unleash new prosperity or further destabilize the world economy? *Business Week*, October 29, 38; P. Engardio, R. Miller, G. Smith, D. Brady, M. Kripalani, A. Borrus, & D. Foust, 2001, What's at stake: How terrorism threatens the global economy, *Business Week*, October 22, 33–34; D. Eisenberg, 2001, Arafat's dance of death, *Time*, December 24, 64–65; B. Fulford, 2001, Another enemy, *Forbes*, October 29, 117; K. E. Myer, 2001, Institutions, transaction costs, and entry model choice in Eastern Europe, *Journal of International Business Studies*, 32: 357–67.

other currencies determines the value of the international assets and earnings of U.S. firms; for example, an increase in the value of the U.S. dollar can reduce the value of U.S. multinational firms' international assets and earnings in other countries. Furthermore, because of its effect on the prices of goods manufactured in different countries, the value of different currencies can dramatically affect a firm's competitiveness in global markets. As well, because of the price differential of the products, an increase in the value of the Canadian dollar can harm a firm's exports to international markets. However, such changes also make acquiring U.S. operations less expensive.[128]

Limits to International Expansion: Management Problems

Firms tend to earn positive returns on early international diversification, but the returns often level off and become negative as the diversification increases past some point.[129] There are several reasons for the limits to the positive effects of international diversification. First, greater geographic dispersion across country borders increases the costs of coordination between units and the distribution of products. Second, trade barriers, logistical costs, cultural diversity, and other differences by country (e.g., access to raw

Blame Canada

Canada and the U.S. are as close as any two countries. When the U.S. closed its borders to air traffic on September 11, 2001 (9/11), it was Canada that took in thousands of panicked Americans desperate to get home. Economically, we are each other's number one trading partner. Yet even under such friendly circumstances, problems arise, and there are risks with cross-border trade.

A month before 9/11, the U.S. announced what looked like a different kind of border closing. The U.S. government would be placing a 19.3 percent tariff on Canadian softwood lumber because of the way provinces charged for logging rights. (Despite arguments that Canada's environmental laws on where and how one could log, as well as reforestation requirements, actually made for higher costs, this reasoning fell upon deaf ears with the U.S. regulators.) Even worse, the tariff would be placed on the price of the finished product, not the raw logs—a move that would add another 20 percent to the price. On top of this, tariffs collected might then be paid to subsidize U.S. producers. The U.S. National Association of Homebuilders estimated the tariffs would add $1000 to the cost of building a home and price some 300,000 U.S. homebuyers out of the market. As the Canadian government and the U.S. National Association of Homebuilders geared up to counter the U.S. lumber industry's lobby for tariffs, 9/11 changed the relative importance of the issue.

While 9/11 moved the softwood issue to the government's back burner, the industry sprang into action. The tariff should have raised the cost of Canadian softwood to U.S. buyers and made U.S. softwood relatively cheaper. However, before the tariff came into effect, Canadian producers went all out to ship all the lumber they could across the border. Prices on softwood started dropping. On the U.S. side, an additional 12.6 percent antidumping duty was announced in November 2001. It was a move that, on top of George Bush's failure to thank Canada for its assistance on 9/11, irritated public commentators. Canadian producers, however, realizing what pressure a 30 to 50 percent increase in the price of their product would do to demand, began to cut costs. To reduce per unit costs, inefficient plants were shut down, and production was cranked up in the plants that remained open. This action put further downward pressure on timber prices. The tariffs were actually causing lumber prices to drop, not rise. However, the solution to the trade problem that both sides promised was near, has remained illusive, year after year, and continues to impact the incomes of thousands of Canadian workers and numerous Canadian companies.

If not being able to afford a home because of softwood tariffs is a headache to 300,000 U.S. consumers, maybe those consumers should take a pill. If they want those pills to be affordable, they will probably buy them from a Canadian provider. Thanks to government pricing rules, drugs in Canada can be as much as 80 percent cheaper than they are in the U.S. There are about 100 international pharmacies in Canada that sell primarily to Americans. They have a total annual revenue estimated to be up to, and possibly more than, $1 billion. The Internet pharmacy industry in Manitoba alone pays $150 million in taxes. In fact, governors of several U.S. states have sent delegations to investigate how they too can lower their citizens' drug costs.

The news is not all positive for Canadian pharmacists however. Pharmaceutical companies argue that high U.S. prices are needed to allow for profits that can be plowed back into research into new drugs. Thus, some drug makers, including Pfizer and GlaxoSmithKlein, began limiting supply to Canada to curb exports into the U.S. As well, the industry is threatened by the U.S. Food and Drug Administration warnings to third parties—which could include U.S. insurance companies who provide drug coverage—that they may be violating civil and criminal laws by making it possible for Americans to buy cheaper drugs from Canada. Prosecuting such crimes would certainly put a damper on the growing Canadian Internet pharmacy market.

Some people in the U.S. may be puzzled by Canada's help in providing cheaper lumber for cheaper housing and lower medical prescriptions for Americans. Indeed, it's not the first time Canada has been accused of leaving Americans in the dark. When a power outage left 50 million people in Canada and the U.S. without power in August 2003, New York City Mayor Michael

(continued)

Bloomberg speculated that "It was probably a natural occurrence which disrupted the power system up there [in Canada]." The source turned out to be a problem in Ohio, not Ontario, but the knee-jerk response to blame Canada seemed more out of fiction than reality. In the 1999 film, *South Park: Bigger, Longer & Uncut*, the main characters, the South Park kids, start using the crudest language the town has ever heard, after seeing a movie starring a couple of foul-mouthed Canadian comedians. The parents in the movie urge the U.S. government to wage war on Canada. The film produced an Academy Award–nominated song, "Blame Canada." The Blame Canada effort has certainly found its way into the real world of cross-border business with U.S.—at least in the softwood, pharmaceutical, and electrical power industries.

South Park was not the first time that a movie has suggested a non-trade war between the two countries. In Michael Moore's 1995 comedy, *Canadian Bacon*, the President of the United States—faced with low popularity and a economic decline—planned to win back the support of the American people by creating a new evil empire: Canada. Moore was "amazed at how quickly the American public fell behind the President [in the first Gulf War]." So in 1994, Moore asked himself, "If the President declared any old country to be the enemy, would he receive the support of the entire nation?" Today, Moore, along with some Canadian loggers, could still ask the same question.

SOURCES: S. Bacal, 1995, Un certain regard, U.S., Michael Moore, *Dogeatdogfilms Movie Articles*, http://www.michaelmoore.com/dogeatdogfilms/cbucr.html, May 25, accessed February 16, 2004; R. Simmons, 2001, Don't blame Canada, *Seattle Post Intelligencer*, March 28, 6; J. Greenwood, 2001, US softwood price continues downward drift: trend puzzling in wake of duty on Canadian imports, *Financial Post (National Post)*, August 29, C4; D. Francis, 2001, Softwood duty a tax on success: Lumber law just subsidizes weak US competitors, *Financial Post (National Post)*, September 4, C3; Canadian Press Newswire, 2001, After imposing a 19.3 per cent duty on softwood lumber, the U.S. Commerce Department set an extra preliminary duty at 12.6 per cent average for Canadian lumber products, *Canadian Press Newswire*, November, 1; T. Seskus, 2003, Crackdown shouldn't hurt cross-border drug sales: "Nothing new" in FDA warning, *Financial Post (National Post)*, March 13, FP5; Canadian Press Newswire, 2003, Minnesota governor heads to Manitoba to research its Internet pharmacy industry, *Canadian Press Newswire*, November 11; Canadian Press Newswire, 2003, Some of what was said during the biggest blackout in North American history, *Canadian Press Newswire*, August 15.

materials and different employee skill levels) greatly complicate the implementation of an international diversification strategy.[130]

Institutional and cultural factors can present strong barriers to the transfer of a firm's competitive advantages from one country to another. Marketing programs often have to be redesigned and new distribution networks established when firms expand into new countries. In addition, firms may encounter different labour costs and capital charges. In general, it is difficult to effectively implement, manage, and control a firm's international operations.[131]

Wal-Mart, although a hugely successful company, is not immune to making mistakes in international markets. In fact, Wal-Mart has made some significant mistakes in some Latin American markets. For example, its first Mexican stores carried ice skates, riding lawn mowers, fishing tackle—even clay pigeons for skeet shooting. To get rid of the clay pigeons, they would be radically discounted "only to have automated inventory systems linked to Wal-Mart's U.S. corporate headquarters in Bentonville, Arkansas, order a fresh batch." Once Wal-Mart began to get the right mix of products, the Mexican currency was devalued in 1994. However, over time, Wal-Mart has become very successful in Latin America, especially in Mexico, where it has been able to increase its market share by taking advantage of local sourcing, especially the lower wages in Mexico, as a result of NAFTA.[132]

The amount of international diversification that can be managed will vary from firm to firm and according to the abilities of each firm's managers. The problems of central coordination and integration are mitigated if the firm diversifies into more friendly countries that are geographically close and have cultures similar to its own country's culture. In that case, there are likely to be fewer trade barriers, the laws and customs are better understood, and the product is easier to adapt to local markets.[133] For example, Canadian firms may find it less difficult to expand their operations into the U.S., Mexico, and Western European countries than into Asian countries.

Management must also be concerned with the relationship between the host government and the multinational corporation.[134] Although government policy and regulations are often barriers, many firms, such as Toyota and General Motors, have turned to strategic alliances to overcome those barriers. By forming interorganizational networks, such as strategic alliances, firms can share resources and risks but also build flexibility.[135]

Summary

- The use of international strategies is increasing, not only because of traditional motivations, but also for emerging reasons. Traditional motives include extending the product life cycle, securing key resources, and gaining access to low-cost labour. Emerging motivations focus on the combination of the Internet and mobile telecommunications, which facilitates global transactions. Also, there is increased pressure for global integration as the demand for commodities becomes borderless, and yet pressure is also increasing for local country responsiveness.

- An international strategy usually attempts to capitalize on four benefits: increased market size, the opportunity to earn a return on large investments, economies of scale and learning, and advantages of location.

- International business-level strategies are usually grounded in one or more home-country advantages, as Porter's diamond model suggests. The diamond model emphasizes four determinants: factors of production, demand conditions, related and supporting industries, and patterns of firm strategy, structure, and rivalry.

- There are three types of international corporate-level strategies. A multidomestic strategy focuses on competition within each country in which the firm competes. Firms using a multidomestic strategy decentralize strategic and operating decisions to the business units operating in each country, so that each unit can tailor its goods and services to the local market. A global strategy assumes more standardization of products across country boundaries; therefore, competitive strategy is centralized and controlled by the home office. A transnational strategy seeks to combine aspects of both multidomestic and global strategies in order to emphasize both local responsiveness and global integration and coordination. This strategy is difficult to implement, requiring an integrated network and a culture of individual commitment.

- Although the transnational strategy's implementation is a challenge, environmental trends are causing many multinational firms to consider the need for both global efficiency and local responsiveness. Many large multinational firms—particularly those with many diverse products—use a multidomestic strategy with some product lines and a global strategy with others.

- The threat of terrorist attacks increases the risks and costs of international strategies. Furthermore, research suggests that the liability of foreignness is more difficult to overcome than once thought.

- Some firms decide to compete only in certain regions of the world, as opposed to viewing all markets in the world as potential opportunities. Competing in regional markets allows firms and managers to focus their learning on specific markets, cultures, locations, resources, etc.

- Firms may enter international markets in one of several ways, including exporting, licensing, forming strategic alliances, making acquisitions, and establishing new wholly owned subsidiaries, often referred to as greenfield ventures. Most firms begin with exporting or licensing, because of their lower costs and risks, but later may expand to strategic alliances and acquisitions. The most expensive and risky means of entering a new international market is through the establishment of a new wholly owned subsidiary. On the other hand, such subsidiaries provide the advantages of maximum control by the firm and, if they are successful, the greatest returns.

- International diversification facilitates innovation in a firm, because it provides a larger market to gain more and faster returns from investments in innovation. In addition, international diversification may generate the resources necessary to sustain a large-scale R&D program.

- In general, international diversification is related to above-average returns, but this strategy assumes that the diversification is effectively implemented and that the firm's international operations are well managed. International diversification provides greater economies of scope and learning, which, along with greater innovation, help produce above-average returns.

- Several risks are involved with managing multinational operations. Among these are political risks (e.g., instability of national governments) and economic risks (e.g., fluctuations in the value of a country's currency).

- There are also limits to the ability to manage international expansion effectively. International diversification increases coordination and distribution costs, and management problems are exacerbated by trade barriers, logistical costs, and cultural diversity, among other factors.

Review Questions

1. What are the traditional and emerging motives that cause firms to expand internationally?

2. What four factors provide a basis for international business-level strategies?

3. What are the three international corporate-level strategies? How do they differ from each other? What factors lead to their development?

4. What environmental trends are affecting international strategy?

5. What five modes of international expansion are available, and what is the normal sequence of their use?

6. What is the relationship between international diversification and innovation? How does international diversification affect innovation? What is the effect of international diversification on a firm's returns?

7. What are the risks of international diversification? What are the challenges of managing multinational firms?

8. What factors limit the positive outcomes of international expansion?

Experiential Exercise

International Strategy

Coca-Cola's first international bottling plants opened in 1906, in Canada, Cuba, and Panama. Today the firm produces nearly 300 brands in almost 200 countries, and more than 70 percent of its income comes from outside the United States.

Coca-Cola's German operation began in 1929, and by 1939, was selling 4.5 million cases annually. Germany—Coke's first marketing success outside North America—is the firm's fifth largest market. Nine bottlers, with a total of 24 production plants and 13,000 employees, serve Germany's population of 82 million people. Popular Coca-Cola products in Germany include Fanta (first introduced as a substitute to Coke during World War II) in several flavours, Mezzo Mix (a cola and orange-flavoured beverage), Bonaqa table water, and Lift Apfelsaftschorle (apple juice with carbonated water).

Coca-Cola was introduced in Chile in 1941, with the opening of plants in Santiago and Valparaiso. Brands marketed in Chile include Coca-Cola, Coca-Cola Light, Sprite, Sprite Light, Fanta,

Fanta Sabores, Lift, Vital mineral water, Nordic Mist Ginger Ale, and Nordic Mist Tonic Water. Juice brands are Kapo, Andifrut, and Nectar Andina. The Coca-Cola system in Chile has 11 bottling plants and employs more than 4000 people.

1. Based on the above information, the cultural differences between Germany and Chile (as well as the obvious differences among the other countries in which Coca-Cola operates), and the type of product offered by the firm, compare and contrast the three generic international corporate level strategies (illustrated in Figure 9.3, on page 275) as they apply to Coca-Cola. Which strategy is best for this firm, and why?

2. Describe how Coca-Cola's country operations might be affected by the environmental trends of liability of foreignness and regionalization.

1. D. Ahlstrom & G. D. Bruton, 2001, Learning from successful local private firms in China: Establishing legitimacy, *Academy of Management Executive*, 15(4): 72–83.

2. A. K. Gupta & V. Govindarajan, 2001, Converting global presence into global competitive advantage, *Academy of Management Executive*, 15(2): 45–57.

3. A. McWilliams, D. D. Van Fleet, & P. M. Wright, 2001, Strategic management of human resources for global competitive advantage, *Journal of Business Strategies*, 18(1): 1–24; B. L. Kedia & A. Mukherji, 1999, Global managers: Developing a mindset for global competitiveness, *Journal of World Business*, 34(3): 230–51.

4. B. R. Koka, J. E. Prescott, & R. Madhavan, 1999, Contagion influence on trade and investment policy: A network perspective, *Journal of International Business Studies*, 30: 127–48.

5. G. Bottazzi, G. Dosi, M. Lippi, F. Pammolli, & M. Riccaboni, 2001, Innovation and corporate growth in the evolution of the drug industry, *International Journal of Industrial Organization*, 19: 1161–87.

6. S. Tallman, 2001, Global strategic management, in M. A. Hitt, R. E. Freeman, & J. S. Harrison (eds.), *Handbook of Strategic Management*, Oxford, UK: Blackwell Publishers, 462–90; C. W. L. Hill, 2000, *International Business: Competing in the Global Marketplace*, 3rd ed., Boston: Irwin/McGraw Hill, 378–80.

7. R. Vernon, 1996, International investment and international trade in the product cycle, *Quarterly Journal of Economics*, 80: 190–207.

8. H. F. Lau, C. C. Y. Kwok, & C. F. Chan, 2000, Filling the gap: Extending international product life cycle to emerging economies, *Journal of Global Marketing*, 13(4): 29–51.

9. Y. Shi, 2001, Technological capabilities and international production strategy of firms: The case of foreign direct investment in China, *Journal of World Business*, 18(4): 523–32.

10. A. Camuffo, P. Romano, & A. Vinelli, 2001, Back to the future: Benetton transforms its global network, *Sloan Management Review*, 43(1): 46–52.

11. B. Kim & Y. Lee, 2001, Global capacity expansion strategies: Lessons learned from two Korean carmakers, *Long Range Planning*, 34(3): 309–33.

12. K. Macharzina, 2001, The end of pure global strategies? *Management International Review*, 41(2): 105; W. Kuemmerle, 1999, Foreign direct investment in industrial research in the pharmaceutical and electronics industries—Results from a survey of multinational firms, *Research Policy*, 28(2/3): 179–93.

13. Y. Luo, 2000, Entering China today: What choices do we have? *Journal of Global Marketing*, 14(2): 57–82.

14. C. C. Y. Kwok & D. M. Reeb, 2000, Internationalization and firm risk: An upstream-downstream hypothesis, *Journal of International Business Studies*, 31: 611–29; J. J. Choi & M. Rajan, 1997, A joint test of market segmentation and exchange risk factor in international capital markets, *Journal of International Business Studies*, 28: 29–49.

15. R. E. Hoskisson, L. Eden, C. M. Lau, & M. Wright, 2000, Strategy in emerging economies, *Academy of Management Journal*, 43: 249–67; D. J. Arnold & J. A. Quelch, 1998, New strategies in emerging markets, *Sloan Management Review*, 40: 7–20.

16. M. W. Peng, Y. Lu, O. Shenkar, & D. Y. L. Wang, 2001, Treasures in the China house: A review of management and organizational research on Greater China, *Journal of Business Research*, 52(2): 95–110; S. Lovett, L. C. Simmons, & R. Kali, 1999, Guanxi versus the market: Ethics and efficiency, *Journal of International Business Studies*, 30: 231–48.

17. Statistics Canada, 2003, Foreign direct investment 2002, *The Daily*, http://www.statcan.ca/Daily/English/030326/d030326a.htm, March 26; Industry Canada, 1998, Special report: Canadian foreign direct investment trends in the 1990s, *Industry Canada's Strategis website*, http://strategis.ic.gc.ca/epic/internet/ineas-aes.nsf/vwapj/srmei199807e.PDF/$FILE/srmei199807e.PDF, accessed July 31, 2004.

18. W. Kuemmerle, 2001, Go global—or not? *Harvard Business Review*, 79(6): 37–49; Y. Luo & M. W. Peng, 1999, Learning to compete in a transition economy: Experience, environment and performance, *Journal of International Business Studies*, 30: 269–95.

19. R. Gray, 2001, Local on a global scale, *Marketing*, September 27, 22–23.

20. X. Martin, A. Swaminathan, & W. Mitchell, 1999, Organizational evolution in the interorganizational environment: Incentives and constraints on international expansion strategy, *Administrative Science Quarterly*, 43: 566–601.

21. P. Ghemawat, 2001, Distance still matters: The hard reality of global expansion, *Harvard Business Review*, 79(8): 137–47.

22. S. R. Miller & A. Parkhe, 2002, Is there a liability of foreignness in global banking? An empirical test of banks' x-efficiency, *Strategic Management Journal*, 23: 55–75;

T. Kostova & S. Zaheer, 1999, Organizational legitimacy under conditions of complexity: The case of the multinational enterprise, *Academy of Management Review*, 24: 64–81; S. Zaheer & E. Mosakowski, 1997, The dynamics of the liability of foreignness: A global study of survival in financial services, *Strategic Management Journal*, 18: 439–64.

23. Canadian Commercial Corporation, 2004, Industry sectors: Market opportunities: Rail and guided urban transit vehicles, *Canadian Commercial Corporation website*, http://www.ccc.ca/eng/abo_ind_tra_rail.cfm, accessed February 8, 2004; Bombardier, 2004, *Bombardier website*, http://www.bombardier.com, accessed February 8, 2004.

24. R. C. Shrader, 2001, Collaboration and performance in foreign markets: The case of young high-technology manufacturing firms, *Academy of Management Journal*, 44: 45–60; W. Kuemmerle, 1999, The drivers of foreign direct investment into research and development: An empirical investigation, *Journal of International Business Studies*, 30: 1–24.

25. Z. Liao, 2001, International R&D project evaluation by multinational corporations in the electronics and IT industry of Singapore, *R&D Management*, 31: 299–307.

26. W. Shan & J. Song, 1997, Foreign direct investment and the sourcing of technological advantage: Evidence from the biotechnology industry, *Journal of International Business Studies*, 28: 267–84.

27. Yum! Brands, 2004, *Yum! Brands website*, http://www.yum.com, accessed February 9, 2004; MSN, 2004, Yum! Brands Inc.: Highlights, *MSN Money website*, http://moneycentral.msn.com/investor/invsub/results/hilite.asp?Symbol=YUM, February 9; B. O'Keefe, 2001, Global brands, *Fortune*, November 26, 102–10.

28. W. Chung, 2001, Identifying technology transfer in foreign direct investment: Influence of industry conditions and investing firm motives, *Journal of International Business Studies*, 32: 211–29.

29. A. J. Mauri & A. V. Phatak, 2001, Global integration as inter-area product flows: The internalization of ownership and location factors influencing product flows across MNC units, *Management International Review*, 41(3): 233–49.

30. D. Roberts & A. Webb, 2001, China's carmakers: Flattened by falling tariffs, *Business Week*, December 3, 51.

31. W. Kuemmerle, 2002, Home base and knowledge management in international ventures, *Journal of Business Venturing*, 2: 99–122; H. Bresman, J. Birkinshaw, & R. Nobel, 1999, Knowledge transfer in international acquisitions, *Journal of International Business Studies*, 30: 439–62; J. Birkinshaw, 1997, Entrepreneurship in multinational corporations: The characteristics of subsidiary initiatives, *Strategic Management Journal*, 18: 207–29.

32. Ahlstrom & Bruton, Learning from successful local private firms in China; S. A. Zahra, R. D. Ireland, & M. A. Hitt, 2000, International expansion by new venture firms: International diversity, mode of market entry, technological learning, and performance, *Academy of Management Journal*, 43: 925–50.

33. Mauri & Phatak, Global integration as inter-area product flows.

34. J. Bernstein & D. Weinstein, 2002, Do endowments predict the location of production? Evidence from national and international data, *Journal of International Economics*, 56(1): 55–76.

35. D. Wilson, 2001, Turns to Diamond—Hungary glitters as Central Europe's choice manufacturing site, *EBN*, January 29, 46.

36. R. Robertson & D. H. Dutkowsky, 2002, Labor adjustment costs in a destination country: The case of Mexico, *Journal of Development Economics*, 67: 29–54.

37. D. A. Griffith & M. G. Harvey, 2001, A resource perspective of global dynamic capabilities, *Journal of International Business Studies*, 32: 597–606; D. J. Teece, G. Pisano, & A. Shuen, 1997, Dynamic capabilities and strategic management, *Strategic Management Journal*, 18: 509–33.

38. Y. Luo, 2000, Dynamic capabilities in international expansion, *Journal of World Business*, 35(4): 355–78.

39. L. Nachum, 2001, The impact of home countries on the competitiveness of advertising TNCs, *Management International Review*, 41(1): 77–98.

40. Ibid.

41. M. E. Porter, 1990, *The Competitive Advantage of Nations*, New York: The Free Press.

42. Ibid., 84.

43. Ibid., 89.

44. O. Oz, 2001, Sources of competitive advantage of Turkish construction companies in international markets, *Construction Management and Economics*, 19(2): 135–44.

45. J. Birkinshaw, 2001, Strategies for managing internal competition, *California Management Review*, 44(1): 21–38.

46. W. P. Wan & R. E. Hoskisson, 2002, Home country environments, corporate diversification strategies and firm performance, *Academy of Management Journal*, 46(1): 27–46; J. M. Geringer, S. Tallman, & D. M. Olsen, 2000, Product and international diversification among Japanese multinational firms, *Strategic Management Journal*, 21: 51–80.

47. M. A. Hitt, R. E. Hoskisson, & R. D. Ireland, 1994, A mid-range theory of the interactive effects of international and product diversification on innovation and performance, *Journal of Management*, 20: 297–326.

48. A.-W. Harzing, 2000, An empirical analysis and extension of the Bartlett and Ghoshal typology of multinational companies, *Journal of International Business Studies*, 32: 101–20; S. Ghoshal, 1987, Global strategy: An organizing framework, *Strategic Management Journal*, 8: 425–40.

49. J. Sheth, 2000, From international to integrated marketing, *Journal of Business Research*, 51(1): 5–9; J. Taggart & N. Hood, 1999, Determinants of autonomy in multinational corporation subsidiaries, *European Management Journal*, 17: 226–36.

50. Y. Luo, 2001, Determinants of local responsiveness: Perspectives from foreign subsidiaries in an emerging market, *Journal of Management*, 27: 451–77.

51. M. Carpenter & J. Fredrickson, 2001, Top management teams, global strategic posture, and the moderating role of uncertainty, *Academy of Management Journal*, 44: 533–45; T. T. Herbert, 1999, Multinational strategic planning: Matching central expectations to local realities, *Long Range Planning*, 32: 81–87.

52. O'Keefe, Global brands.

53. Harzing, An empirical analysis and extension of the Bartlett and Ghoshal typology.

54. D. G. McKendrick, 2001, Global strategy and population level learning: The case of hard disk drives, *Strategic Management Journal*, 22: 307–34.

55. M. W. Peng, S. H. Lee, & J. J. Tan, 2001, The keiretsu in Asia: Implications for multilevel theories of competitive advantage, *Journal of International Management*, 7: 253–76; A. Bhappu, 2000, The Japanese family: An institutional logic for Japanese corporate networks and Japanese management. *Academy of Management Review*, 25: 409–15; J. K. Johansson & G. S. Yip, 1994, Exploiting globalization potential: U.S. and Japanese strategies, *Strategic Management Journal*, 15: 579–601.

56. D. Ilott, 2002, Success story—Cemex: The cement giant has managed concrete earnings in a mixed year, *Business Mexico*, January (special ed.), 34; Economist, 2001, Business: The Cemex way, *Economist*, June 16, 75–76.

57. C. A. Bartlett & S. Ghoshal, 1989, *Managing Across Borders: The Transnational Solution*, Boston: Harvard Business School Press.

58. J. Child & Y. Yan, 2001, National and transnational effects in international business: Indications from Sino-foreign joint ventures, *Management International Review*, 41(1): 53–75.

59. Bombardier, 2004, *Bombardier website*, http://www.Bombardier.com, accessed February 11, 2004; Railway Industry Association, 2004, Bombardier Transportation (Rail Control Solutions) UK Ltd., *Railway Industry Association website*, http://www.ria.connect.co.uk/directory/bombrcsolutions.php, accessed February 11, 2004.

60. T. Isobe, S. Makino, & D. B. Montgomery, 2000, Resource commitment, entry timing and market performance of foreign direct investments in emerging economies: The case of Japanese international joint ventures in China, *Academy of Management Journal*, 43: 468–84.

61. S. Zaheer & A. Zaheer, 2001, Market microstructure in a global B2B network, *Strategic Management Journal*, 22: 859–73.

62. Thomson Corporation, 2004, *Thomson website*, http://www.thomson.com, accessed February 11, 2004.

63. F. X. Molina-Morales, 2001, European industrial districts: Influence of geographic concentration on performance of the firm, *Journal of International Management*, 7: 277–94; M. E. Porter & S. Stern, 2001, Innovation: Location matters, *Sloan Management Review*, 42(4): 28–36.

64. C. Pantzalis, 2001, Does location matter? An empirical analysis of geographic scope and MNC market valuation, *Journal of International Business Studies*, 32: 133–55.

65. R. D. Ludema, 2002, Increasing returns, multinationals and geography of preferential trade agreements, *Journal of International Economics*, 56: 329–58; L. Allen & C. Pantzalis, 1996, Valuation of the operating flexibility of multinational corporations, *Journal of International Business Studies*, 27: 633–53.

66. J. I. Martinez, J. A. Quelch, & J. Ganitsky, 1992, Don't forget Latin America, *Sloan Management Review*, 33(winter): 78–92.

67. Government of Canada, 2004, United States–Canada: The world's largest trading relationship: Friends, neighbours—and business partners, *Government of Canada website*, http://www.canadianembassy.org/trade/wltr-en.asp, April, accessed July 31, 2004.

68. J. Chang & P. M. Rosenzweig, 1998, Industry and regional patterns in sequential foreign market entry, *Journal of Management Studies*, 35: 797–822.

69. S. Zahra, J. Hayton, J. Marcel, & H. O'Neill, 2001, Fostering entrepreneurship during international expansion: Managing key challenges, *European Management Journal*, 19: 359–69.

70. Zahra, Ireland, & Hitt, International expansion by new venture firms.

71. M. W. Peng, C. W. L. Hill, & D. Y. L. Wang, 2000, Schumpeterian dynamics versus Williamsonian considerations: A test of export intermediary performance, *Journal of Management Studies*, 37: 167–84.

72. Luo, Determinants of local responsiveness.

73. M. A. Raymond, J. Kim, & A. T. Shao, 2001, Export strategy and performance: A comparison of exporters in a developed market and an emerging market, *Journal of Global Marketing*, 15(2): 5–29; P. S. Aulakh, M. Kotabe, & H. Teegen, 2000, Export strategies and performance of firms from emerging economies: Evidence from Brazil, Chile and Mexico. *Academy of Management Journal*, 43: 342–61.

74. 2004, United States–Canada: The world's largest trading relationship.

75. B. Walker & D. Luft, 2001, Exporting tech from Texas, *Texas Business Review*, August: 1–5.

76. P. Westhead, M. Wright, & D. Ucbasaran, 2001, The internationalization of new and small firms: A resource-based view, *Journal of Business Venturing*, 16: 333–58.

77. D. Fairlamb & R. McNatt, 2002, The Euro: A shopper's best friend, *Business Week*, January 14, 8.

78. M. A. Hitt & R. D. Ireland, 2000, The intersection of entrepreneurship and strategic management research, in D. L. Sexton & H. Landstrom (eds.), *Handbook of Entrepreneurship*, Oxford, UK: Blackwell Publishers, 45–63.

79. A. Arora & A. Fosfuri, 2000, Wholly owned subsidiary versus technology licensing in the worldwide chemical industry, *Journal of International Business Studies*, 31: 555–72.

80. M. Johnson, 2001, Learning from toys: Lessons in managing supply chain risk from the toy industry, *California Management Review*, 43(3): 106–24.

81. C. A. Bartlett & S. Rangan, 1992, Komatsu limited, in C. A. Bartlett & S. Ghoshal (eds.), *Transnational Management: Text, Cases and Readings in Cross-Border Management*, Homewood, IL: Irwin, 311–26.

82. B. Petersen, D. E. Welch, & L. S. Welch, 2000, Creating meaningful switching options in international operations, *Long Range Planning*, 33(5): 688–705.

83. J. W. Lu & P. W. Beamish, 2001, The internationalization and performance of SMEs, *Strategic Management Journal*, 22(special issue): 565–86; M. Koza & A. Lewin, 2000, Managing partnerships and strategic alliances: Raising the odds of success, *European Management Journal*, 18(2): 146–51.

84. J. S. Harrison, M. A. Hitt, R. E. Hoskisson, & R. D. Ireland, 2001, Resource complementarity in business combinations: Extending the logic to organization alliances, *Journal of Management*, 27: 679–90; T. Das & B. Teng, 2000, A resource-based theory of strategic alliances, *Journal of Management*, 26: 31–61.

85. M. Peng, 2001. The resource-based view and international business, *Journal of Management*, 27: 803–29.

86. P. J. Lane, J. E. Salk, & M. A. Lyles, 2002, Absorptive capacity, learning, and performance in international joint ventures, *Strategic Management Journal*, 22: 1139–61; B. L. Simonin, 1999, Transfer of marketing know-how in international strategic alliances: An empirical investigation of the role and antecedents of knowledge ambiguity, *Journal of International Business Studies*, 30: 463–90; M. A. Lyles & J. E. Salk, 1996, Knowledge acquisition from foreign parents in international joint ventures: An empirical examination in the Hungarian context, *Journal of International Business Studies*, 27(special issue): 877–903.

87. Shrader, Collaboration and performance in foreign markets; M. A. Hitt, M. T. Dacin, E. Levitas, J. L. Arregle, & A. Borza, 2000, Partner selection in emerging and developed market contexts: Resource based and organizational learning perspectives, *Academy of Management Journal*, 43: 449–67.

88. J. Eig, 2001, H.J. Heinz and Japan's Kagome are expected to form alliance, *Wall Street Journal Interactive*, http://www.wsj.com, July 26.

89. C. Grande, 2001, Pearson plans to teach English on Chinese TV, *Financial Times*, November 20, 27.

90. Y. Gong, O. Shenkar, Y. Luo, & M.-K. Nyaw, 2001, Role conflict and ambiguity of CEOs in international joint ventures: A transaction cost perspective, *Journal of Applied Psychology*, 86: 764–73.

91. D. C. Hambrick, J. Li, K. Xin, & A. S. Tsui, 2001, Compositional gaps and downward spirals in international joint venture management groups, *Strategic Management Journal*, 22: 1033–53; M. T. Dacin, M. A. Hitt, & E. Levitas, 1997, Selecting partners

for successful international alliances: Examination of U.S. and Korean firms, *Journal of World Business*, 32: 3–16.

92. A. Arino, J. de la Torre, & P. S. Ring, 2001, Relational quality: Managing trust in corporate alliances, *California Management Review*, 44(1): 109–31.

93. Y. Pan & D. K. Tse, 2000, The hierarchical model of market entry modes, *Journal of International Business Studies*, 31: 535–54; Y. Pan, S. Li, & D. K. Tse, 1999, The impact of order and mode of market entry on profitability and market share, *Journal of International Business Studies*, 30: 81–104.

94. W. H. Hoffmann & W. Schaper-Rinkel, 2001, Acquire or ally? A strategy framework for deciding between acquisition and cooperation, *Management International Review*, 41(2): 131–59.

95. M. A. Hitt, J. S. Harrison, & R. D. Ireland, 2001, *Creating Value through Mergers and Acquisitions*, New York: Oxford University Press.

96. Economist, 1999, French dressing, *Economist*, July 10, 53–54.

97. R. Raizel, 2003, Southern exposure: a multibillion-dollar megadeal makes it trickier for Canadian banks stateside. *Canadian Business*, 76(22): 10.

98. A.-W. Harzing, 2002, Acquisitions versus greenfield investments: International strategy and management of entry modes, *Strategic Management Journal*, 23: 211–27; K. D. Brouthers & L. E. Brouthers, 2000, Acquisition or greenfield start-up? Institutional, cultural and transaction cost influences, *Strategic Management Journal*, 21: 89–97.

99. D. Kirk, 2001, British American Tobacco finds opening in South Korea, *New York Times*, http://www.nytimes.com, August 9.

100. S.-J. Chang & P. Rosenzweig, 2001, The choice of entry mode in sequential foreign direct investment, *Strategic Management Journal*, 22: 747–76.

101. K. E. Myer, 2001, Institutions, transaction costs, and entry mode choice in Eastern Europe, *Journal of International Business Studies*, 32: 357–67.

102. Y. Luo, 2001, Determinants of entry in an emerging economy: A multilevel approach, *Journal of Management Studies*, 38: 443–72.

103. A. Takeishi, 2001, Bridging inter- and intra-firm boundaries: Management of supplier involvement in automobile product development, *Strategic Management Journal*, 22: 403–33.

104. D. K Sobek, II, A. C. Ward, & J. K. Liker, 1999, Toyota's principles of set-based concurrent engineering, *Sloan Management Review*, 40(2): 53–83.

105. H. Chen, 1999, International performance of multinationals: A hybrid model, *Journal of World Business*, 34: 157–70.

106. S.-J. Chang & J. Hong, 2002, How much does the business group matter in Korea? *Strategic Management Journal*, 23: 265–74.

107. J. Song, 2002, Firm capabilities and technology ladders: Sequential foreign direct investments of Japanese electronics firms in East Asia, *Strategic Management Journal*, 23: 191–210.

108. M.Ramirez-Aleson & M. A. Espitia-Escuer, 2001, The effect of international diversification strategy on the performance of Spanish-based firms during the period 1991–1995, *Management International Review*, 41(3): 291–315; A. Delios & P. W. Beamish, 1999, Geographic scope, product diversification, and the corporate performance of Japanese firms, *Strategic Management Journal*, 20: 711–27.

109. C. Pantzalis, 2001, Does location matter? An empirical analysis of geographic scope and MNC market valuation, *Journal of International Business Studies*, 32: 133–55; C. Y. Tang & S. Tikoo, 1999, Operational flexibility and market valuation of earnings, *Strategic Management Journal*, 20: 749–61.

110. J. M. Geringer, P. W. Beamish, & R. C. daCosta, 1989, Diversification strategy and internationalization: Implications for MNE performance, *Strategic Management Journal*, 10: 109–19; R. E. Caves, 1982, *Multinational Enterprise and Economic Analysis*, Cambridge, MA: Cambridge University Press.

111. Zahra, Ireland, & Hitt, International expansion by new venture firms.

112. T. W. Malnight, 2002, Emerging structural patterns within multinational corporations: Toward process-based structures, *Academy of Management Journal*, 44: 1187–1210.

113. Camuffo, Romano, & Vinelli, Back to the future: Benetton transforms its global network.

114. G. Hamel, 2000, *Leading the Revolution*, Boston: Harvard Business School Press.

115. L. Tihanyi, R. A. Johnson, R. E. Hoskisson, & M. A. Hitt, 2003. Institutional ownership differences and international diversification: The effects of board of directors and technological opportunity, *Academy of Management Journal*, 46(2): 195–217

116. F. Bradley & M. Gannon, 2000, Does the firm's technology and marketing profile affect foreign market entry? *Journal of International Marketing*, 8(4): 12–36; M. Kotabe,

1990, The relationship between off-shore sourcing and innovativeness of U.S. multi-national firms: An empirical investigation, *Journal of International Business Studies*, 21: 623–38.

117. I. Zander & O. Solvell, 2000, Cross border innovation in the multinational corporation: A research agenda, *International Studies of Management and Organization*, 30(2): 44–67; Y. Luo, 1999, Time-based experience and international expansion: The case of an emerging economy, *Journal of Management Studies*, 36: 505–33.

118. Z. Liao, 2001, International R&D project evaluation by multinational corporations in the electronics and IT industry of Singapore, *R&D Management*, 31: 299–307; M. Subramaniam & N. Venkatraman, 2001, Determinants of transnational new product development capability: Testing the influence of transferring and deploying tacit overseas knowledge, *Strategic Management Journal*, 22: 359–78.

119. Wan & Hoskisson, Home country environments, corporate diversification strategies and firm performance.

120. Business Asia, 2001, Business as usual, or for real? *Business Asia*, January 8, 3–5.

121. M. Carpenter & J. Fredrickson, 2001, Top management teams, global strategic posture, and the moderating role of uncertainty, *Academy of Management Journal*, 44: 533–45; S. Finkelstein & D. C. Hambrick, 1996, *Strategic Leadership: Top Executives and Their Effects on Organizations*, St. Paul, MN: West Publishing Company.

122. A. McWilliams, D. D. Van Fleet, & P. M. Wright, 2001, Strategic management of human resources for global competitive advantage, *Journal of Business Strategies*, 18(1): 1–24.

123. M. A. Hitt, R. E. Hoskisson, & H. Kim, 1997, International diversification: Effects on innovation and firm performance in product-diversified firms, *Academy of Management Journal*, 40: 767–98.

124. D. Rondinelli, B. Rosen, & I. Drori, 2001, The struggle for strategic alignment in multinational corporations: Managing readjustment during global expansion, *European Management Journal*, 19: 404–5; Carpenter & Fredrickson, Top management teams, global strategic posture, and the moderating role of uncertainty.

125. D. M. Reeb, C. C. Y. Kwok, & H. Y. Baek, 1998, Systematic risk of the multinational corporation, *Journal of International Business Studies*, 29: 263–79.

126. C. Pompitakpan, 1999, The effects of cultural adaptation on business relationships: Americans selling to Japanese and Thais, *Journal of International Business Studies*, 30: 317–38.

127. L. L. Jacque & P. M. Vaaler, 2001, The international control conundrum with exchange risk: An EVA framework, *Journal of International Business Studies*, 32: 813–32.

128. J. G. Smith, 2003, The dollar dilemma: a higher Canadian dollar has slashed 2003 profits, and it's only the latest challenge for U.S.-bound exporters, *Canadian Plastics*, 61(11): 3; M. Dacruz, 2003, Exchange rate winners and losers, *Financial Post (National Post)*, December 15, FP12.

129. Wan & Hoskisson, Home country environments, corporate diversification strategies and firm performance; Hitt, Hoskisson, & Kim, International diversification; S. Tallman & J. Li, 1996, Effects of international diversity and product diversity on the performance of multinational firms, *Academy of Management Journal*, 39: 179–96; Hitt, Hoskisson, & Ireland, A mid-range theory of the interactive effects; Geringer, Beamish, & daCosta, Diversification strategy.

130. A. K. Rose & E. van Wincoop, 2001, National money as a barrier to international trade: The real case for currency union, *American Economic Review*, 91: 386–90.

131. I. M. Manev & W. B. Stevenson, 2001, Nationality, cultural distance, and expatriate status: Effects on the managerial network in a multinational enterprise, *Journal of International Business Studies*, 32: 285–303.

132. D. Luhnow, 2001, How NAFTA helped Wal-Mart transform the Mexican market, *Wall Street Journal*, August 31, A1, A2.

133. D. E. Thomas & R. Grosse, 2001, Country-of-origin determinants of foreign direct investment in an emerging market: The case of Mexico, *Journal of International Management*, 7: 59–79.

134. J. Feeney & A. Hillman, 2001, Privatization and the political economy of strategic trade policy, *International Economic Review*, 42: 535–56; R. Vernon, 2001, Big business and national governments: Reshaping the compact in a globalizing economy, *Journal of International Business Studies*, 32: 509–18; B. Shaffer & A. J. Hillman, 2000, The development of business-government strategies by diversified firms, *Strategic Management Journal*, 21: 175–90.

135. B. Barringer & J. Harrison, 2000, Walking the tightrope: Creating value through interorganizational relationships, *Journal of Management*, 26: 367–404.

Chapter Ten

Cooperative Strategy

Knowledge Objectives

Studying this chapter should provide you with the strategic management knowledge needed to:

1. Define cooperative strategies and explain why firms use them.

2. Define and discuss three types of strategic alliances.

3. Name the business-level cooperative strategies and describe their use.

4. Discuss the use of corporate-level cooperative strategies in diversified firms.

5. Understand the importance of cross-border strategic alliances as an international cooperative strategy.

6. Describe cooperative strategies' risks.

7. Describe two approaches used to manage cooperative strategies.

Bigger Than Any of Us: Consortiums Take on the Big Projects

Several factors, including product complexity and research and development costs, make it very difficult for a firm to undertake major projects on its own while competing in the 21st-century competitive landscape. A business analyst speaking about the nature of competition in the aerospace industry said, "If an aerospace company is not good at alliances, it's not in business." Similarly, the chief information officer of international food processor and distributor Cargill believes that successful product innovations require alliances: "To bring something new to the marketplace requires so much cooperation and integration of knowledge that you just can't get it done unless you pick partners."

Cross-border alliances are one type of cooperative strategy used to deal with the realities of the 21st-century competitive landscape and to develop product innovations. As discussed later in the chapter, a cross-border strategic alliance is a partnership formed between firms with headquarters in different nations. Firms use a cross-border alliance to uniquely combine their value-creating resources and capabilities to develop a competitive advantage that neither partner could form on its own.

For example, to address the complex rapid transit needs of the people in York, Ontario, a nine-member consortium was brought in to partner with the government to quickly help bring transit plans to life. The comprehensive $4 billion, 20- to 30-year plan included 95 kilometres of light-rail lines, dedicated bus lanes, and traffic signal priority for transit. The nine companies in the so-called York Consortium 2002, include a U.S. engineering and planning firm, two Canadian engineering companies, a German light-rail vehicle producer, a German financier, an Italian bus maker, Canadian and U.S. construction companies, and a British transit system operator. While this public–private partnership has detractors that may cause sufficient problems to halt execution of the entire plan, it is an example of how companies can get together to deliver a complete solution to a complex customer need.

Transportation is not the only area in which we find such joint ventures. In order to take on a project that was bigger than what any one company was comfortable handling on its own—and involved technology that was unproven on the scale being proposed—a group of companies got together to form Syncrude. Syncrude was formed to take on the development of the Alberta oil sands and turn this resource into usable crude oil. The company is a consortium made up of eight companies, including Petro-Canada, Conoco Phillips, Imperial Oil, Murphy Oil, and Nexen. Syncrude has become one of the largest private sector employers in Alberta.

Syncrude is also one of the top 50 research and development (R&D) investors in Canada. This R&D spending on the part of Syncrude consortium and by others developing the oil sands, has helped create a process for producing crude oil that is reliable enough to allow industry experts to include the oil sands as part of Canada's oil reserves—oil that is commercially recoverable with current technology. By including oil sands in the calculations, Canada

Syncrude is a consortium of eight companies—including Petro-Canada, Conoco, Imperial Oil, and Nexen—formed to develop the Alberta oil sands.

(continued)

increased its oil reserves from 5 billion to 180 billion barrels and made Canada the number two world oil-reserve holder, just behind Saudi Arabia.

Not all joint ventures need to be big projects—just bigger than any one of the partners is willing or able to take on, on its own. Another energy project that was able to get off the ground, albeit smaller than Syncrude, was Edmonton's Windsong Power Inc. When Windsong's 50-metre-high, steel-tube, wind-powered generator went on the Alberta Power Pool grid in 2004, it was the culmination of four years of fundraising and promotion by the 50 environmentally conscious shareholders. Windsong Power Inc.—along with its majority partner, Alberta's Tallon Energy—came together with Holland's Lagerwey Corp. and Windsong Power Cooperative to help build the project. Many of the Windsong coop shareholders have skills (e.g., electrical, engineering, legal) that helped keep costs down. Lagerwey, a Dutch wind-turbine manufacturer, permitted the consortium to make parts (e.g., the 27m turbine blades) in Canada to reduce shipping costs. Finally, Tallon provided the rest of the resources and capabilities needed. Although Tallon's cost certainly could have been great, the entire project only cost $1.1 million—definitely not one of the larger joint ventures.

SOURCES: Syncrude Canada, 2004, *Syncrude website*, http://www.syncrude.ca/who_we_are/index.html, accessed April 30, 2004; K. McGran, 2004, GO staff slam York's transit plan as wasteful: Will duplicate existing routes, report claims York chair says transit authority "missing the point," *Toronto Star*, April 15, B1; D. Finlayson, 2004, Windsong is music to local clean-power investors, *Edmonton Journal*, February 4, G2; K. MacNamara, 2003, Oilsands: Coming to America, *National Post* (*Financial Post*), December 24, FP6; K. McGran, 2003, Light years ahead of its time: York pursues public–private transit plan $4 billion proposal with consortium a first in Canada, *Toronto Star*, January 28, B3.

To this point in the book, we have discussed the two primary means by which firms grow: pursuing internal opportunities (through strategic execution or innovation) and merging with or acquiring other companies. In this chapter, we examine cooperative strategies, the third major alternative that firms use to grow, develop value-creating competitive advantages, and create differences between themselves and their competitors.[1] Defined formally, a **cooperative strategy** is a strategy in which firms work together to achieve a shared objective.[2] Thus, cooperating with other firms is another strategy that is used to create value for a customer that exceeds the value that could be created in other ways[3] and to establish a favourable position, relative to competition (see Chapters 2, 4, 5, and 8).[4] The increasing importance of cooperative strategies as a growth engine shouldn't be underestimated. In fact, some believe that "in a global market tied together by the Internet, corporate partnerships and alliances are proving a more productive way to keep companies growing."[5] In other words, effective competition in the 21st-century landscape results when the firm learns how to cooperate with, as well as compete against, its competitors.[6]

Increasingly, cooperative strategies are formed by firms competing against one another,[7] as shown by the fact that more than half of the strategic alliances (a type of cooperative strategy) established within a recent two-year period were between competitors.[8] For example, when Canada won hockey gold at the 2002 Olympics, Canadian Press (CP) was quick to publish a book. CP had immediately available print and photo material, and there was a market that was hungry for the book. In the future, rather than pursue these kinds of opportunities on its own and compete with other book publishers, CP decided to partner with book publisher John Wiley & Sons on future book publishing efforts. The partnership allows CP access to Wiley's production and distribution, while Wiley gets access to CP's material on current events and in its archives.[9]

Because they are the primary type of cooperative strategy that firms use, strategic alliances (defined in the next section) are this chapter's focus. Although not frequently used, collusive strategies are another type of cooperative strategy discussed in this chapter. In a *collusive strategy*, two or more firms cooperate to raise prices above the fully competitive level.[10]

We examine several topics in this chapter. First, we define and offer examples of different strategic alliances as primary types of cooperative strategies. Next, we discuss the extensive use of cooperative strategies in the global economy and the reasons for their use. In succession, we then describe business-level (including collusive strategies), corporate-level, international, and network cooperative strategies—most in the form of strategic alliances. The chapter closes with discussions of the risks of using cooperative strategies, as well as how the effective management of cooperative strategies can reduce those risks.

> A **cooperative strategy** is a strategy in which firms work together to achieve a shared objective.

Strategic Alliances as a Primary Type of Cooperative Strategy

Strategic alliances are increasingly popular. Researchers describe this popularity by noting that an "unprecedented number of strategic alliances between firms are being formed each year. [These] strategic alliances are a logical and timely response to intense and rapid changes in economic activity, technology, and globalization, all of which have cast many corporations into two competitive races: one for the world and the other for the future."[11]

A **strategic alliance** is a cooperative strategy in which firms combine some of their resources and capabilities to create a competitive advantage.[12] Thus, as linkages between them, strategic alliances involve firms with some degree of exchange and sharing of resources and capabilities to co-develop or distribute goods or services.[13] Strategic alliances let firms leverage their existing resources and capabilities while working with partners to develop additional resources and capabilities as the foundation for new competitive advantages.[14]

Many firms, especially large global competitors, establish multiple strategic alliances. Ballard Power is a Vancouver company working on developing fuel cells that convert

> A **strategic alliance** is a cooperative strategy in which firms combine some of their resources and capabilities to create a competitive advantage.

hydrogen to electricity. The only byproduct is clean water. To tap into this green energy source, Ballard has established strategic alliances with automakers DaimlerChrysler and Ford Motor Company. While Ballard's products can provide power for cars, it can also provide power for stationary generators. Thus, Ballard also has alliances with Japanese industrial equipment maker Ebara, French power-distribution equipment maker ALSTOM, and U.S. utility FirstEnergy.[15] Another example is General Motors, whose alliances cover a wide range of joint activities. These activities "… include collaboration with Honda on internal combustion engines, with Toyota on advanced propulsion, with Renault on medium- and heavy-duty vans for Europe and, in the U.S., with AM General on the brand and distribution rights for the Hummer."[16]

In general, strategic alliance success requires cooperative behaviour from all partners. Actively solving problems, being trustworthy, and consistently pursuing ways to combine partners' resources and capabilities to create value are examples of cooperative behaviour known to contribute to alliance success.[17]

A competitive advantage developed through a cooperative strategy often is called a collaborative or relational advantage.[18] As previously discussed, particularly in Chapter 5, competitive advantages significantly influence the firm's marketplace success.[19] Rapid technological changes and the global economy are examples of factors challenging firms to constantly upgrade current competitive advantages while they develop new ones to maintain strategic competitiveness.[20]

The firms noted in the next Strategic Focus box, "The S-92 Helicopter" on page 302, combined their resources and capabilities to develop competitive advantages while working together as, what the participants called, the Team S-92 alliance. No individual member of the alliance could have developed the *design* and *manufacturing* competitive advantages that were instrumental to the design and production of the Sikorsky's S-92 helicopter—a product with size and cost benefits over competing helicopters.

Three Types of Strategic Alliances

There are three major types of strategic alliances: joint venture, equity strategic alliance, and nonequity strategic alliance.

A **joint venture** is a strategic alliance in which two or more firms create a legally independent company to share some of their resources and capabilities to develop a competitive advantage. Joint ventures are effective in establishing long-term relationships and in transferring tacit knowledge. Because it can't be codified, tacit knowledge is learned through experiences[21] such as the learning that takes place when people from partner firms work together in a joint venture. As discussed in Chapter 4, tacit knowledge is an important source of competitive advantage for many firms.[22]

Typically, partners in a joint venture own equal percentages and contribute equally to its operations. Norampac was created in 1997 as a 50–50 joint venture between two Quebec-based paper companies, Domtar and Cascades. Today, the company is Canada's largest cardboard maker.[23] Overall, evidence suggests that a joint venture may be the optimal alliance when firms need to combine their resources and capabilities to create a competitive advantage that is substantially different from any they possess individually and when the partners intend to enter highly uncertain markets.[24]

An **equity strategic alliance** is an alliance in which two or more firms own different percentages of the company they have formed by combining some of their resources and capabilities to create a competitive advantage. Many foreign direct investments such as those made by Japanese and North American companies in China are completed through equity strategic alliances.[25]

In another example, MTS's Allstream Inc. became one of three companies sharing equal ownership in the venture to provide wireless Internet connections to home and office computers. The other two equal partners were Montreal's Microcell (formally

A **joint venture** is a strategic alliance in which two or more firms create a legally independent company to share some of their resources and capabilities to develop a competitive advantage.

An **equity strategic alliance** is an alliance in which two or more firms own different percentages of the company they have formed by combining some of their resources and capabilities to create a competitive advantage.

operating under the Fido name) and NR Communications, a private U.S. investment firm headed by ex-Rogers executive Nick Kauser. The joint venture is supposed to provide homes and small businesses with a reasonably priced alternative to established products that run through cable or phone lines by allowing customers to bridge what the technical people call "the last mile"—the distance between a user's computer and the closest high-speed wireless connection. Touted as having unheard-of simplicity, customers simply plug in a modem-sized device to their home or office computer, which instantly finds the closest radio tower makes the wireless high-speed connection. The device can also double as a wireless local area network. Finally, the joint venture allows the participants to compete against bigger competitors, such as Bell Canada.[26]

A **nonequity strategic alliance** is an alliance in which two or more firms develop a contractual relationship to share some of their unique resources and capabilities to create a competitive advantage. In this type of strategic alliance, firms do not establish a separate independent company and therefore do not take equity positions. Because of this, nonequity strategic alliances are less formal and demand fewer partner commitments than joint ventures and equity strategic alliances.[27] The relative informality and lower commitment levels characterizing nonequity strategic alliances make them unsuitable for complex projects where success requires effective transfers of tacit knowledge between partners.[28]

> A **nonequity strategic alliance** is an alliance in which two or more firms develop a contractual relationship to share some of their unique resources and capabilities to create a competitive advantage.

However, firms today increasingly use this type of alliance in many different forms, such as licensing agreements, distribution agreements, and supply contracts.[29] For example, Waterloo's Research in Motion (RIM) has a range of alliances that allow various parts of RIM's BlackBerry services to be used on wireless devices worldwide. RIM's products include features that automatically deliver e-mail and other data to and from a range of wireless devices. Included in the list of alliance partners are hardware providers, such as Sony Ericsson, Nokia, Samsung, and Motorola, and service providers, such as Nextel in the U.S., Telus in Canada, and Orange in Europe.[30] A key reason for the growth in types of cooperative strategies, as indicated in the next Strategic Focus box ("The S-92 Helicopter"), is the complexity and uncertainty that characterize most global industries and make it difficult for firms to be successful without some sort of partnerships.[31]

Typically, outsourcing commitments take the form of a nonequity strategic alliance.[32] Discussed in Chapter 4, *outsourcing* is the purchase of a value-creating primary or support activity from another firm. Aurora, Ontario's Magna International Inc., a leading global supplier of technologically advanced automotive systems, components, and modules, has formed many nonequity strategic alliances with automotive manufacturers who have outsourced work to the company. Magna's effectiveness with nonequity strategic alliances is confirmed by the awards honouring the quality of its work received from many of its customers, including General Motors, Ford Motor Company, Honda, DaimlerChrysler, and Toyota.[33]

Reasons Firms Develop Strategic Alliances

As previously noted, the use of cooperative strategies as a path to strategic competitiveness is on the rise[34] in for-profit firms of all sizes, as well as in public organizations.[35] Thus, cooperative strategies are becoming more important to companies.[36] For example, recently surveyed executives of technology companies stated that strategic alliances are central to their firms' success.[37] Speaking directly to the issue of technology acquisition and development for these firms, a manager noted that, "You have to partner today or you will miss the next wave. You cannot possibly acquire the technology fast enough, so partnering is essential."[38]

Some even suggest that strategic alliances "… may be the most powerful trend … in a century."[39] Among other benefits, strategic alliances allow partners to create value that they couldn't develop by acting independently[40] and to enter markets more quickly.[41]

The S-92 Helicopter: A Product of a Cross-Border Alliance

From its facilities in St. John's and Halifax, Cougar Helicopters provides offshore helicopter service to support the oil and gas fields off the coasts of Newfoundland and Nova Scotia. The company, owned by Vancouver Helicopters of B.C., operates a number of different makes and types of helicopters. Given the demands of the jobs it handles and the quality of service it aims to provide, the company is always looking to improve its fleet. In 2000, the company formed a strategic relationship: United Technologies' Sikorsky Aircraft and a group calling itself the "Team S-92" alliance. The relationship—called a launch agreement—gave Cougar the first crack at using Sikorsky's new S-92 helicopter to support its offshore operations. For Sikorsky, the strategic relationship with Cougar facilitated the S-92's successful commercial launch. Cougar gets to give input on possible aircraft modifications that may help the company, and other helicopter users get a better aircraft. Through cooperative interactions with Cougar, Sikorsky is thus discovering possible S-92 modifications that may be needed to ensure the project's long-term success.

Describing the benefits of this strategic relationship, a Sikorsky official stated that, "Cougar is an ideal launch customer. They are extremely professional and innovative. Further, they will put the aircraft to the test with very high utilization, actual icing conditions, and a requirement for the high service levels we have designed in. Sikorsky and our other customers will benefit greatly from the S-92's entry into service with Cougar." The strategic relationship between Cougar and Sikorsky was just the end step of the cross-border alliances set up to produce the S-92.

Five firms from four continents joined with Sikorsky to form this alliance. Using its unique resource and capabilities, each partner assumed different responsibilities for the design and production of the S-92. The combination of the partners' resources and capabilities is thought to have resulted in a competitive advantage for the alliance.

Team S-92 partners and their responsibilities were: (1) Japan's Mitsubishi Heavy Industries (main cabin section), (2) Jingdezhen Helicopter Group/CATIC of China (vertical tail fin and stabilizer), (3) Spain's Gamesa Aeronautica (main rotor pylon, engine nacelles AFT tail, transition section, and cabin interior), (4) Aerospace Industrial Development Corporation of Taiwan (the electrical harness, flight controls, hydraulic lines, and environmental controls forming the cockpit), and (5) Embraer of Brazil (main landing gear and fuel system). As the sixth member of the alliance, Sikorsky was responsible for the main and tail rotor head components and the S-92's transmissions. The "International Wide Area Network" connects alliance members via satellite. This connection enables real-time interactions among partners as they integrate their work.

Sikorsky has alliance responsibilities beyond those described above, including the final assembly of the S-92 and its certification as launch-ready. Following final assembly, the production program to commercially launch the S-92 was initiated in 1999. Commenting about the craft's potential, Sikorsky president Dean Borgman stated that, "The S-92 will be tops in its class in terms of cost and performance. We have numerous opportunities with this aircraft to sell to civil and government operators ..." starting, of course, with Cougar.

SOURCES: VIH Aviation Group, 2004, *VIH Aviation Group website*, http://www.vih.com/index.htm, accessed April 30, 2004; Cougar Helicopters 2004, *Cougar Helicopters website*, http://www.cougar.ca, accessed April 30, 2004; United Technologies Corporation, 2002, The S-92 program, *United Technologies Corporation website*, http://www.utc.com, accessed April 30, 2004; Cougar Helicopters, 2002, Cougar and Sikorsky work accord to launch S-92, *Cougar Helicopters website*, http://www.cougar.com, March 14; D. Donovan, 2001, United Technologies, *Forbes Best of the Web*, May 21, 66; J. Fahey, 2001, Cargill, *Forbes Best of the Web*, May 21, 66.

Moreover, most (if not virtually all) firms lack the full set of resources and capabilities needed to reach their objectives, which indicates that partnering with others will increase the probability of reaching them.[42]

The effects of the greater use of cooperative strategies—particularly in the form of strategic alliances—are noticeable. In large firms, for example, alliances now account for more than 20 percent of revenue.[43] Some experts estimate that alliances may account for about one-third of the revenue for the 1000 largest North American companies.[44] Supporting this expectation is the belief of many senior-level executives that alliances are a prime vehicle for firm growth.[45]

In some industries, alliance versus alliance is becoming more prominent than firm against firm as a point of competition. In the global airline industry, for example, "… competition increasingly is between … alliances rather than between airlines."[46] This increased use of cooperative strategies and their results are not surprising; in the mid-1990s, it was predicted that cooperative strategies would be the wave of the future.[47]

The individually unique competitive conditions of slow-cycle, fast-cycle, and standard-cycle markets[48] find firms using cooperative strategies to achieve slightly different objectives (see Table 10.1). We discuss these three market types in Chapter 6 where we study competitive rivalry and competitive dynamics. *Slow-cycle markets* are markets where the firm's competitive advantages are shielded from imitation for relatively long periods of time and where imitation is costly. These markets are close to monopolistic conditions. Railroads and, historically, telecommunications, utilities, and financial services are examples of industries characterized as slow-cycle markets. In *fast-cycle markets*, the firm's competitive advantages aren't shielded from imitation, preventing their long-term sustainability. Competitive advantages are moderately shielded from imitation in *standard-cycle markets*, typically allowing them to be sustained for a longer period of time compared to fast-cycle market situations, but for a shorter period of time than in slow-cycle markets.

Slow-Cycle Markets

Firms in slow-cycle markets often use strategic alliances to enter restricted markets or to establish franchises in new markets. For example, Dofasco, Canada's second largest steel mill, formed an equity strategic alliance with Paris-based steel maker, Usinor Group, to build a plant to supply car bodies for Honda, Toyota, General Motors, Ford, and DaimlerChrysler. For its 20 percent stake in the new venture, Usinor contributed

Table 10.1	Reasons for Strategic Alliances by Market Type
Market	**Reason**
Slow–Cycle	• Gain access to a restricted market • Establish a franchise in a new market • Maintain market stability (e.g., establish standards)
Fast–Cycle	• Speed up development of new goods or services • Speed up new market entry • Maintain market leadership • Form an industry technology standard • Share risky R&D expenses • Overcome uncertainty
Standard–Cycle	• Gain market power (reduce industry overcapacity) • Gain access to complementary resources • Establish better economies of scale • Overcome trade barriers • Meet competitive challenges from other competitors • Pool resources for very large capital projects • Learn new business techniques

$22 million in cash and technological know-how. Dofasco operates the North American–based plant and distributes its products. Through this alliance, Usinor and Dofasco were able to establish a new franchise "… in the import-averse U.S." steel market.[49]

In another example, the restricted entry to China's insurance market prompted Toronto's Sun Life Financial to form a joint venture—Sun Life Everbright Life Insurance Company—with the China Everbright Group. Because China Everbright is headquartered in Tianjin (near Beijing) the joint venture positioned the company for the opening up of the Beijing market to foreign insurance companies.[50]

Utility companies also use strategic alliances as a means of competing in slow-cycle markets. In the petrochemical industry, for example, Petróleos de Venezuela and Petrobras of Brazil formed a joint venture that calls for cross-investments between the partners. The eventual goal of this cooperative strategy is to form a pan-Latin American energy cooperative with firms in other countries. To reach the goal, the initial partners seek to expand the venture to add other state-owned oil companies in the region, including Petróleos Mexicanos and Colombia's Ecopetrol.[51]

Slow-cycle markets are becoming rare in the 21st-century competitive landscape for several reasons, including the privatization of industries and economies, the rapid expansion of the Internet's capabilities in terms of the quick dissemination of information, and the speed with which advancing technologies make quickly imitating even complex products possible.[52] Firms competing in slow-cycle markets should recognize the future likelihood that they'll encounter situations in which their competitive advantages become partially sustainable (in the instance of a standard-cycle market) or unsustainable (in the case of a fast-cycle market). Cooperative strategies can be helpful to firms making the transition from relatively sheltered markets to more competitive ones.

Fast-Cycle Markets

Fast-cycle markets tend to be unstable, unpredictable, and complex.[53] Combined, these conditions virtually preclude the establishment of long-lasting competitive advantages, forcing firms to constantly seek sources of new competitive advantages while creating value by using current ones. Alliances between firms with current excess resources and capabilities and those with promising capabilities help companies competing in fast-cycle markets to make an effective transition from the present to the future and also to gain rapid entry to new markets.

Sometimes, companies establish venture capital programs to facilitate these efforts.[54] Visa International formed a venture capital program to "… scout technologies and capabilities that will affect the future of financial services and the payments industry and enable (the firm) to deliver value to its more than 21,000 member institutions."[55] Visa International forms strategic alliances with firms that it believes have promising technologies and skills that, when shared with Visa's own resources and capabilities, have the potential to create new competitive advantages, providing the foundation for successfully entering new markets. In particular, Visa seeks partners to help create what it believes is the next generation of commerce—u-commerce, which is the "… merging and integration over time of the physical and the virtual world, where you may not be face-to-face, but still have the levels of trust, convenience, protection and security, in addition to the ease in performing transactions even though you are physically far apart."[56]

Standard-Cycle Markets

In standard-cycle markets, which are often large and oriented toward economies of scale (e.g., commercial aerospace), alliances are more likely to be made by partners with complementary resources and capabilities. For example, Air Canada, Scandinavian Airlines (Sweden), Thai Airways International (Thailand), Lufthansa (Germany), and United

Airlines (United States) formed the Star Alliance in 1997. Since then, eight other airlines have joined this alliance. Star Alliance partners share some of their resources and capabilities to serve almost 900 global airports. The goal of the Star Alliance is to "... combine the best routes worldwide and then offer seamless world travel through shared booking."[57]

Companies also may cooperate in standard-cycle markets to gain market power. As discussed in Chapter 7, market power allows the firm to sell its product above the existing competitive level or to reduce its costs below the competitive level, or both. In 2002, Goodyear Tire spent more than $160 million to expand its tire plant in Dalian, China, created through a 1994 joint venture between Goodyear and Dalian Rubber General Factory. The partners in the already successful venture wanted to expand the manufacturing facility to continue pursuing "... what is clearly destined to be one of the world's biggest long-term business opportunities."[58] Goodyear's investment is expected to increase plant efficiency and to provide even more differentiated and attractive products to those who demand top quality, high-performance tires and are willing to pay an above-average competitive price for them.

Business-Level Cooperative Strategy

A **business-level cooperative strategy** is used to help the firm improve its performance in individual product markets. As discussed in Chapter 5, business-level strategy details what the firm intends to do to gain a competitive advantage in specific product markets. Thus, the firm forms a business-level cooperative strategy when it believes that combining its resources and capabilities with those of one or more partners will create competitive advantages that it can't create by itself and that will lead to success in a specific product market. There are four business-level cooperative strategies (see Figure 10.1).

> A **business-level cooperative strategy** is used to help the firm improve its performance in individual product markets.

Complementary Strategic Alliances

Complementary strategic alliances are business-level alliances in which firms share some of their resources and capabilities in complementary ways to develop competitive advantages.[59] There are two types of complementary strategic alliances: vertical and horizontal (see Figure 10.1).

> **Complementary strategic alliances** are business-level alliances in which firms share some of their resources and capabilities in complementary ways to develop competitive advantages.

Vertical Complementary Strategic Alliance

In a *vertical complementary strategic alliance*, firms share their resources and capabilities from different stages of the value chain to create a competitive advantage (see Figure 10.2 on page 306). For example, Montreal's Van Houtte Coffee formed two vertical complementary alliances: one with Quebec's Couche-Tard and B.C.'s Chevron Convenience Stores for self-serve coffee and a second alliance with Ontario and Western Canada's

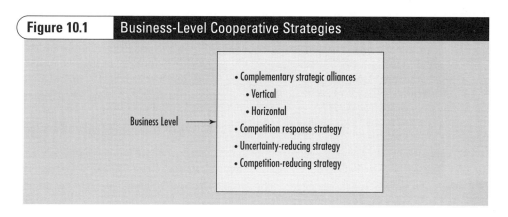

Figure 10.1   **Business-Level Cooperative Strategies**

Business Level →
- Complementary strategic alliances
  - Vertical
  - Horizontal
- Competition response strategy
- Uncertainty-reducing strategy
- Competition-reducing strategy

Safeway supermarkets for ground coffee. Because the units are located in these firms' storefronts, Van Houtte gains access to consumers who can fill up their cars, buy a meal, or pick up items for the home, in just one stop.[60] In another example, Boeing Company formed a vertical complementary alliance that included several partners to design and build the 777 plane—partners who were needed because of the project's scale and size. The partners, including United Airlines and five Japanese companies, each contributed superior resources and capabilities in a different part of the value chain. According to an

Figure 10.2 — Vertical and Horizontal Complementary Strategic Alliances

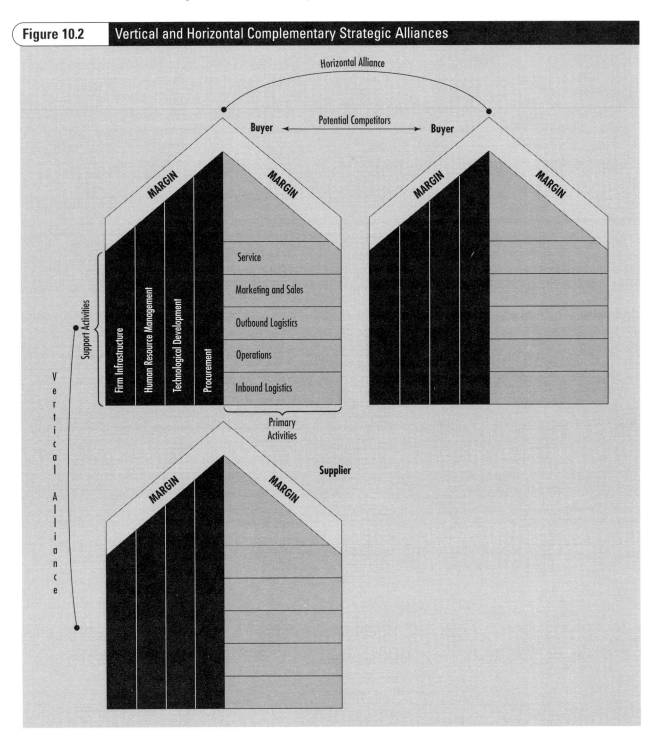

alliance partner, "The development of the 777 was the fastest and most efficient construction of a new commercial aircraft ever."[61]

Horizontal Complementary Strategic Alliance

A *horizontal complementary strategic alliance* is an alliance in which firms share some of their resources and capabilities from the same stage of the value chain to create a competitive advantage (see Figure 10.2). Commonly, firms use this type of alliance to focus on long-term product development and distribution opportunities.[62] Shin Caterpillar Mitsubishi Ltd. (SCM), for example, is a joint venture between Caterpillar Inc. and Mitsubishi Heavy Industries Ltd. that celebrated its 40th anniversary in 2003. These partners continue to share resources and capabilities to produce innovative products that neither firm could design and produce by itself. SCM is a leading supplier of earth-moving and construction equipment in Japan and also sells its products on a global basis to other Caterpillar units.[63]

Two financial and insurance giants—Switzerland's Zurich Financial Services and Holland's ING Group N.V.—are fierce competitors in the Canadian insurance market. ING was looking for a way to expand its personal insurance lines. Zurich wanted to expand its market share of the high-end commercial insurance business (firms with more than $300 million in sales) and get out of its low-return small business and personal insurance lines. The solution was a horizontal complementary alliance between the two companies. Under the provisions of the alliance, ING acquired Zurich's Canadian personal and small business insurance lines, and Zurich Canada is now covering the large commercial policies earlier done by both companies.[64]

Competition Response Strategy

As discussed in Chapter 6, competitors initiate competitive actions to attack rivals and launch competitive responses to their competitors' actions. Strategic alliances can be used at the business level to respond to competitors' attacks. Because they can be difficult to reverse and expensive to operate, strategic alliances are primarily formed to respond to strategic rather than tactical actions.

For example, the toy industry is so competitive that even 75-year-old venerable Toronto toy maker and distributor Irwin Toys (a distributor for Slinky and Etch-a-Sketch, among others) was forced into bankruptcy in 2002. In such an environment, alliances become critical. To improve their chances of success in launching a new product, toy developers have begun establishing licensing agreements with movie studios. Montreal-based Mega Bloks has agreements with Disney to produce construction toys with Disney characters, such as Winnie the Pooh and the Power Rangers. The Mega Bloks action was prompted by a trend in the construction toy industry started by industry leader Lego. In 1999, Lego developed 14 *Star Wars*–themed building kits. To meet the challenge of Lego's themed product, Mega Bloks was pressed into making its agreement with Disney in 2002.[65]

Uncertainty-Reducing Strategy

Particularly in fast-cycle markets, business-level strategic alliances are used to hedge against risk and uncertainty.[66] Global overcapacity and cost competition affected the capabilities of Siemens and Fujitsu to independently reach their objectives in the global PC market. To reduce the risk and uncertainty associated with their PC operations, the two firms formed a joint venture. Called Fujitsu Siemens Computers, this company was formally established on October 1, 1999. Evidence suggests that the formerly independent Fujitsu Computers (Europe) and Siemens Computer Systems are effectively sharing their technological resources and capabilities to create their joint venture. By uniquely combining what Fujitsu Siemens Computers believes is leading-edge

Chapter 10 / Cooperative Strategy

technology from Fujitsu with manufacturing, marketing, and logistics capabilities from Siemens, the joint venture has become Europe's top supplier of PCs for home users and small business firms.[67]

In other instances, firms form business-level strategic alliances to reduce the uncertainty associated with developing new product or technology standards. In this respect, companies are bound by what has been called the ghost of Betamax. When home video cassette recorders (VCRs) were introduced, there were two competing formats. Sony produced VCRs using its proprietary standard, Betamax (Beta). Beta offered smaller tapes and better colour but Sony was unwilling to license the technology to others. Other electronics firms, unwilling to let Sony monopolize a potential multibillion-dollar market, adopted Matsushita's VHS standard. Though VHS was considered technologically inferior, it could be licensed. The sheer number of manufacturers producing VHS VCRs meant that Beta captured an ever-declining percentage of the market. When video rental stores rationalized inventories, it was Betamax tapes they logically eliminated. The triumph of VHS was, however, a loss for the industry because the technologically inferior system became the standard. No manufacturer wants to end up producing another Beta, but no industry wants to end up adopting a technologically inferior standard. Thus, this ghost of Betamax haunts manufacturers who wish to avoid the uncertainties that occurred with the introduction of the home VCR and prompts firms to form standards-setting relationships with others.[68]

Competition-Reducing Strategy

Collusive strategies, an often illegal type of cooperative strategy, separate from strategic alliances, are used to reduce competition. There are two types of collusive strategies: explicit collusion and tacit collusion.

Explicit collusion "… exists when firms directly negotiate production output and pricing agreements in order to reduce competition."[69] Explicit collusion strategies are illegal in Canada, the United States, and most developed economies (except in regulated industries).

Firms that use explicit collusion strategies may face litigation and may be found guilty of noncompetitive actions. In 2002, the Canadian Standard Travel Agent Registry (CSTAR)—a cooperative of 900 travel agencies—began a lawsuit against Air Canada, five U.S. airlines, and the airline's trade group, the International Air Transport Association (IATA). That lawsuit alleged that the airlines and the IATA, "engaged in a conspiracy and collusion as early as 1995 to jointly agree to reduce and eliminate base commissions paid to Canadian travel agencies." The CSTAR claim against Air Canada alone was $1.7 billion.[70] In a 1995 U.S. price-fixing scandal, for example, three Archer Daniels Midland (ADM) executives were convicted and sentenced to jail terms for cooperating with competitors to fix prices on farm commodity products.[71] Similarly, prominent toy retailer Toys "Я" Us was found in violation of U.S. federal trade laws for colluding with toy manufacturers to not sell their popular toy lines to Toys "Я" Us's primary competitors, such as Costco and Sam's Club warehouse clubs.[72]

Tacit collusion exists when several firms in an industry indirectly coordinate their production and pricing decisions by observing each other's competitive actions and responses. Tacit collusion results in production output that is less than fully competitive levels and prices that are higher than fully competitive levels. Unlike explicit collusion, firms engaging in tacit collusion do not directly negotiate output and pricing decisions.

Discussed in Chapter 7, *mutual forbearance* is a form of tacit collusion "… in which firms avoid competitive attacks against those rivals they meet in multiple markets."[73] Rivals learn a great deal about each other when engaging in multimarket competition, including how to deter the effects of their rival's competitive attacks and responses. Given what they know about each other as a competitor, firms choose not to engage in what could be destructive competitions in multiple product markets.

Tacit collusion tends to be used as a business-level competition-reducing strategy in highly concentrated industries, such as breakfast cereals. Firms in these industries recognize that they are interdependent and that their competitive actions and responses significantly affect competitors' behaviour toward them. Understanding this interdependence and carefully observing competitors because of it tend to lead to tacit collusion.

Four brands—Campbell's, Knorr, Maggi, and Progresso—make up about 60 percent of global soup sales. In baby foods, three brands—Enfamil, Gerber, and Similac—account for 70 percent of world sales.[74] In North America, Kellogg, General Mills, Post, and Quaker account for more than 75 percent of sales volume in the ready-to-eat segment of the cereal market. Some believe that this high degree of concentration results in "... prices for branded cereals that are well above (the) costs of production."[75] Prices above the competitive level in these industries suggest the possibility that the dominant firms were using a tacit collusion cooperative strategy.

At a broad level, in free-market economies, governments need to determine how rivals can collaborate to increase their competitiveness without violating established regulations.[76] Reaching this determination is challenging when evaluating collusive strategies, particularly tacit ones. For example, the European Commission recently initiated an investigation of suspicious price fixing by the world's largest music producers and a few large retailers. A Commission spokesperson said, "We're trying to assess whether companies are trying to keep prices higher. It's sufficiently important to consumers to justify an investigation."[77] For individual companies, the issue is to understand the effect of a competition-reducing strategy on their performance and competitiveness.

Assessment of Business-Level Cooperative Strategies

Firms use business-level strategies to develop competitive advantages that can contribute to successful positioning and performance in individual product markets. For a competitive advantage to be developed by using an alliance, the particular set of resources and capabilities that is combined and shared in a particular manner through the alliance must be valuable, rare, imperfectly imitable, and nonsubstitutable (see Chapter 4).

Evidence suggests that complementary business-level strategic alliances, especially those that are vertical, have the greatest probability of creating a sustainable competitive advantage.[78] Strategic alliances designed to respond to competition and to reduce uncertainty can also create competitive advantages. Yet, such advantages tend to be more temporary than those developed through complementary (both vertical and horizontal) strategic alliances. The primary reason is that complementary alliances have a stronger focus on the creation of value, compared to competition-reducing and uncertainty-reducing alliances, which tend to be formed to respond to competitors' actions rather than to attack competitors.

Of the four business-level cooperative strategies, the competition-reducing strategy has the lowest probability of creating a sustainable competitive advantage. In the ready-to-eat breakfast cereal market, for example, annual household purchases of ready-to-eat cereals declined roughly 0.7 kg between 1993 and 1997.[79] Even if the four largest cereal makers did use tacit collusion as a competition-reducing strategy, the results likely failed to meet their performance expectations. The company using competition-reducing, business-level strategic alliances should carefully monitor the degree to which it is facilitating the firm's efforts to develop and successfully use value-creating competitive advantages.

Corporate-Level Cooperative Strategy

A **corporate-level cooperative strategy** is used by the firm to help it diversify, in terms of the products it offers, or the markets it serves, or both. Diversifying alliances, synergistic alliances, and franchising are the most commonly used corporate-level cooperative strategies (see Figure 10.3 on page 310).

A **corporate-level cooperative strategy** is used by the firm to help it diversify, in terms of the products it offers, or the markets it serves, or both.

Figure 10.3   Corporate-Level Cooperative Strategies

Corporate Level →
- Diversifying strategic alliances
- Synergistic strategic alliances
- Franchising

Firms use diversifying alliances and synergistic alliances to grow and diversify their operations through a means other than a merger or acquisition.[80] When a firm seeks to diversify into markets in which the host nation's government prevents mergers and acquisitions, alliances become an especially appropriate option. Corporate-level strategic alliances are also attractive compared to mergers and particularly acquisitions, because they require fewer resource commitments[81] and permit greater flexibility in terms of efforts to diversify partners' operations.[82] An alliance can also be used to determine whether the partners might benefit from a future merger or acquisition between them. This testing process often characterizes alliances that are completed to combine firms' unique technological resources and capabilities.[83]

The collaboration that Wal-Mart, Seiyu Ltd. (a Japanese retail chain), and Sumitomo Corp. (a Japanese trading company) recently formed is partly an attempt to determine if there is a compelling reason for the firms to become more closely aligned in the future. Initially, Wal-Mart took a 6.1 percent interest in Seiyu, with Sumitomo owning 15.6 percent of the company. The firms intend to work together to study and develop retail business opportunities in Japan. If the collaboration is successful, Wal-Mart has the option of increasing its stake in Seiyu across time to as much as 66.7 percent.[84]

Diversifying Strategic Alliance

A **diversifying strategic alliance** is a corporate-level cooperative strategy in which firms share some of their resources and capabilities to diversify into new product or market areas. For example, Winnipeg's Flynn Canada has seen steady growth for more than a decade. While its ascension to a building trade contractor with national reach has been primarily through acquisitions, Flynn has created strategic alliances with U.S. contractors to aid it in diversifying its geographic scope and product range.[85]

Synergistic Strategic Alliance

A **synergistic strategic alliance** is a corporate-level cooperative strategy in which firms share some of their resources and capabilities to create economies of scope. Similar to the business-level horizontal complementary strategic alliance, synergistic strategic alliances create synergy across multiple functions or multiple businesses between partner firms.

Cisco Systems has formed many synergistic strategic alliances to pursue profitable growth. Its synergistic alliance with Hewlett-Packard (HP) is intended to provide an optimized computing environment for Internet players such as telecom service operators and enterprise users. Synergy is expected from this alliance as HP integrates its state-of-the-art telecommunications management solutions with Cisco's industry-leading networking solutions. Working together through this alliance, the two firms anticipate melding "... the worlds of computing and networking, data and voice, and Unix and Windows NT."[86]

In the financial services sector, Rabobank and DG Bank, the Dutch and German cooperative institutions, have formed a joint venture as a synergistic strategic alliance. Called DG-Rabo International, this equally owned venture combines the unique resources and capabilities of each bank in the corporate and investment-banking business areas.

*A **diversifying strategic alliance** is a corporate-level cooperative strategy in which firms share some of their resources and capabilities to diversify into new product or market areas.*

*A **synergistic strategic alliance** is a corporate-level cooperative strategy in which firms share some of their resources and capabilities to create economies of scope.*

Viewed by some as "one of the most important cross-border partnerships yet seen in European banking," the organizations intend to further meld their skills to cooperate in other areas (e.g., asset management transactions) in the future.[87] Thus, this synergistic strategic alliance is different from a complementary business-level alliance in that it diversifies both banks into a new business, but in a synergistic way.

Franchising

Franchising is a corporate-level cooperative strategy in which a firm (the franchiser) uses a franchise as a contractual relationship to describe and control the sharing of its resources and capabilities with partners (the franchisees).[88] A franchise is a "contractual agreement between two legally independent companies whereby the franchiser grants the right to the franchisee to sell the franchiser's product or do business under its trademarks in a given location for a specified period of time."[89]

Franchising is a popular strategy: companies using it account for more than $1 trillion in annual North American sales and compete in more than 75 industries. For example, based on the number of restaurants operating under one banner, B.C.'s Boston Pizza, with almost 200 restaurants in Western Canada, has become the number one casual sit-down dining chain in the country, according to the Toronto market research firm, NPD Canada.[90] However only about 1 percent of the stores are company owned. Boston Pizza franchises are sought after because, as one commentator put it, "Much like Tim Hortons in Atlantic Canada, Boston Pizza's cheap chow and chirpy atmosphere has made the chain a social magnet."[91]

Already frequently used in developed nations, franchising is expected to account for significant portions of growth in emerging economies in the 21st century's first two decades.[92] As with diversifying and synergistic strategic alliances, franchising is an alternative to pursuing growth through mergers and acquisitions.

In the most successful franchising strategy, the partners (the franchiser and the franchisees) closely work together.[93] A primary responsibility of the franchiser is to develop programs to transfer to the franchisees the knowledge and skills that are needed to successfully compete at the local level.[94] In return, franchisees should provide feedback to the franchiser regarding how their units could become more effective and efficient.[95] Working cooperatively, the franchiser and its franchisees find ways to strengthen the core company's brand name, which is often the most important competitive advantage for franchisees operating in their local markets.[96]

Franchising is a particularly attractive strategy to use in fragmented industries, such as retailing. In fragmented industries, a large number of small- and medium-sized firms compete as rivals; however, no firm or small set of firms has a dominant share, making it possible for a company to gain a large market share by consolidating independent companies through contractual relationships.[97] At the retail level, butcher shops exist in a very fragmented industry, and Kitchener, Ontario's M&M Meat Shops has been acting as an industry consolidator. M&M set out to deliver restaurant-quality meat in convenient locations nationally. To do this, M&M ages its meat to the desired degree and then flash-freezes it—quick freezing at very cold temperatures. This process had other implications for the M&M chain that are discussed in the Strategic Focus box "Franchising to Canadian Tastes: A Meaty Topic" on page 312.[98]

Assessment of Corporate-Level Cooperative Strategies

Costs are incurred with each type of cooperative strategy.[99] Compared to those at the business-level, corporate-level cooperative strategies commonly are broader in scope and more complex, making them relatively more costly. Those firms forming and using cooperative strategies, especially corporate-level strategies, should be aware of—and carefully monitor—their alliance costs.

Franchising is a corporate-level cooperative strategy in which a firm (the franchiser) uses a franchise as a contractual relationship to describe and control the sharing of its resources and capabilities with partners (the franchisees).

Franchising to Canadian Tastes: A Meaty Topic

While franchise operations can often be seen as being dominated by the big U.S. chains (such as McDonald's and Subway) Canada has some serious contenders of its own. To survive, they rely on unique market positioning within the country. For example, Harvey's (a division of Toronto's Cara Foods, which also owns Swiss Chalet, Second Cup, Kelsey's, and Montana's), with about 350 outlets across Canada, half of which are franchises, seems like it could be swamped by the U.S. giant McDonald's, with its 1300 Canadian outlets.

The folks at Harvey's would likely claim superiority to McDonald's, at least when it comes to the menu. While McDonald's has the Big Mac, Harvey's has the Big Harv—a 170 gram (six ounce) burger with a uniquely Canadian attitude: Low-carb? Low-fat? Fry my burger? No! No! No! Broil me a burger that is a lot bigger than a Big Mac or Quarter Pounder, put on the toppings I want, and give me onion rings on the side. Live forever? I just want to eat a good slab of meat!

However well the Big Harv sells matters little, compared to the publicity the chain created by bucking any kind of diet trend. This quip from the *Ottawa Citizen* is typical: "Still, it's brave to sell customers what they want these days, with lawyers ready to seek millions in damages on the premise that you made people fat. ... Thanks, Harvey's, for acknowledging we can make up our own minds about what we eat."

Harvey's is not the only franchiser catering to Canadian tastes by offering more. The 600-store Mr. Sub franchise chain stresses its quality product and a broader menu then its rivals. To stand up to Subway's 1800-store chain, Mr. Sub has stated a commitment that it must "sell quality subs, make them fresh, and serve them fast. And above all, give customers value for their money."

Like Harvey's, there is a Canadian uniqueness to Mr. Sub. On the one hand, Mr. Sub has 12 sandwiches containing less than six grams of fat; Subway has only seven sandwiches that can make that claim. Mr. Sub's has almost twice as many low-fat offerings than the U.S.-based firm, yet with characteristic Canadian modesty, Mr. Sub has not claimed the bragging rights to the low-fat sandwiches. Those rights go to Subway, who manages quite nicely in promoting its low-fat sandwiches through weight-loss pitchman Jared Fogel (the Indiana University student who lost 90 kilograms on a diet of low-fat Subway sandwiches). On the other hand, at least one Mr. Sub franchisee is bucking the weight-loss trend. Norman Seyer started serving beer and wine in his Ottawa Mr. Sub franchise in December 2003. Although alcohol sales were modest, the publicity for this act far exceeded any press the chain had received in promoting its low-fat offerings, and it certainly differentiated the chain from the competition.

In another segment of the food market, M&M Meats has made a big beefy name for itself. Actually its name is somewhat deceiving. The M&M Meats objective certainly is the delivery of restaurant quality meat from convenient locations. Yet, because its process involves flash freezing to ensure quality, its stores employ a great deal of freezer space. Thus, the company has expanded its original concept to include frozen meals, other frozen foods, and even ice cream treats.

These moves have made M&M not so much the neighbourhood butcher shop, as a quick meal solutions provider that emphasizes frozen foods for rushed Canadians. With more than 350 stores, the company has also gained some buying power. As well, being a two-time winner of the Canadian Franchise Association's Award of Excellence in Franchise Relations and having been named one of 2001's 50 best run companies in Canada have also helped the company gain franchisees. Except for three company-owned training stores, all M&M Meat Shops are franchises.

SOURCES: Cara Operations Ltd., 2004, Cara announces third quarter results, *Cara Operations website*, http://media.integratir.com/t.cao/PressReleases/3Qpr20041.pdf, press release, February 3, accessed May 10, 2004; McDonald's Canada, 2004, FAQs, *McDonald's Canada website*, http://www.mcdonalds.ca/en/aboutus/faq.aspx, accessed May 10, 2004; Mr. Sub, 2004, *Mr. Sub website*, http://www.mrsub.ca/consumers/about.html, accessed July 29, 2004; Subway, 2004, Welcome to Subway, eh! *Subway website*, http://www.subway.com/subwayroot/AroundTheWorld/Countries/canada/index.aspx, accessed May 10, 2004; M&M Meat Shops, 2004, History of M&M, *M&M Meat Shops website*, http://www.mmmeatshops.com/en/aboutmm/history.asp, accessed May 7, 2004; A. Mayeda, 2004, Mr. Sub banks on beer, *Ottawa Citizen*, January 16, E1; B. Constantineau, 2003, Appetite abounds for flash-frozen M&M Meat Shop offerings, *Edmonton Journal*, July 26, H10; Edmonton Journal, 2003, Harvey's beefs up with monster burger, *Edmonton Journal*, September 18, G3; V. Pilieci, 2002, Mr. Sub takes aim at Subway stronghold: Franchise plans 10 to 12 new stores in Ottawa this year, *Ottawa Citizen*, July 4, D1; H. Shaw, 2002, Revamped Mr. Sub chain hungry for bigger share.... *National Post (Financial Post)*, June 13, FP10.

In spite of these costs, firms can create competitive advantages and value when they effectively form and use corporate-level cooperative strategies.[100] The likelihood of creating competitive advantages increases when successful alliance experiences are internalized. In other words, those firms involved with forming and using corporate-level cooperative strategies can also use the strategies to develop useful knowledge about how to succeed in the future. To gain maximum value, firms should organize this knowledge and verify that it is always properly distributed to those involved with the formation and use of alliances.[101]

We explained in Chapter 7 that firms answer two questions to form a corporate-level strategy—the businesses in which the diversified firm will compete and how those businesses will be managed. These questions are also answered as firms form corporate-level cooperative strategies. Thus, firms able to develop corporate-level cooperative strategies and manage them in ways that are valuable, rare, imperfectly imitable, and are organized to be exploited (see Chapter 4) develop a competitive advantage that is in addition to advantages gained through the activities of individual cooperative strategies. Later in the chapter, we further describe alliance management as a source of competitive advantage.

International Cooperative Strategy

A **cross-border strategic alliance** is an international cooperative strategy in which firms with headquarters in different nations combine some of their resources and capabilities to create a competitive advantage. Taking place in virtually all industries, the number of cross-border alliances being completed continues to increase,[102] in some cases at the expense of mergers and acquisitions.[103] With about $10 billion in assets under supervision, Toronto's Sceptre Investment Counsel Ltd. is one of Canada's largest investment management firms. Under a 2000 alliance agreement, Sceptre became the exclusive Canadian marketing agent for clients of Boston's Putnam Investments. In 2002, the alliance partners launched eight mutual funds. According to Sceptre CEO Richard Knowles "Our strategic alliance with Putnam has proven to be beneficial to our clients and has provided Sceptre with a competitive advantage in the Canadian marketplace."[104]

There are several reasons for the increasing use of cross-border strategic alliances. In general, multinational corporations outperform firms operating on only a domestic basis,[105] so a firm may form cross-border strategic alliances to leverage core competencies that are the foundation of its domestic success, in order to expand into international markets.[106] At Coca-Cola, efforts are underway to cut across the firm's geographic units to identify opportunities to leverage existing brands and competitive advantages. One result from these efforts was the decision to expand the firm's alliance with Nestlé. Called Beverage Partners Worldwide, this cross-border strategic alliance adds herbal beverages to its product line, which already includes Nestea and Nescafé, and will expand into additional global markets.[107]

Limited domestic growth opportunities are another reason firms use cross-border alliances. Diversified and globally oriented Sony Corporation, for example, has long relied on cross-border alliances (more than 100) to pursue growth objectives greater than its home market can support. One of the firm's recent alliances is with Ericsson to make cell phones.[108] Indeed, companies such as Ballard Power (mentioned earlier in this chapter) would not have a sufficient market in Canada alone to make funding their massive R&D spending worthwhile—hence the rationale for their alliances with Ford and DaimlerChrysler.

Cross-border alliances can start out as domestic arrangements with the promise of international expansion. In 2003, Oakville, Ontario's Zenon Industries entered an agreement with U.S. appliance maker Maytag, under which Zenon water filtration systems would be sold under the Maytag brand name in Canada. The hope is that this initial agreement will lead to an expanded relationship for international sales in the future.[109]

A **cross-border strategic alliance** is an international cooperative strategy in which firms with headquarters in different nations combine some of their resources and capabilities to create a competitive advantage.

Another reason for forming cross-border alliances is government economic policies. As discussed in Chapter 9, local ownership is an important national policy objective in some nations. In India, for example, governmental policies reflect a strong preference to license local companies. Only recently, the South Korean government increased the ceiling on foreign investment in South Korean firms.[110] Thus, in some countries, the full range of entry mode choices that we describe in Chapter 9 may not be available to firms wishing to internationally diversify. Indeed, investment by foreign firms in these instances may be allowed only through a partnership with a local firm, such as in a cross-border alliance. A cross-border strategic alliance can also be helpful to foreign partners from an operational perspective, because the local partner has significantly more information about factors contributing to competitive success, such as local markets, sources of capital, legal procedures, and politics.[111]

Firms also use cross-border alliances to help transform themselves or to better use their competitive advantages to take advantage of opportunities surfacing in the rapidly changing global economy. For example, GEC, a U.K.-based company, seeks to move from "a broadly focused group deriving much of its revenues from the defence budget to a full range telecommunications and information systems manufacturer." The uncertainty characterizing many nations' defence budgets is influencing GEC's decision to develop cross-border alliances, such as the one it formed with NEC, the Japanese electronics giant. The alliance has both a commercial and technological focus: NEC distributes GEC products through its extensive marketing channels, and the two companies collaborate in their R&D efforts to develop new technologies.[112]

In general, cross-border alliances are more complex and risky than domestic strategic alliances. However, the fact that firms competing internationally tend to outperform domestic-only competitors suggests the importance of learning how to diversify into international markets. Compared to mergers and acquisitions, cross-border alliances may be a better way to learn this process, especially in the early stages of the firms' geographic diversification efforts. Careful and thorough study of a proposed cross-border alliance contributes to success,[113] as do precise specifications of each partner's alliance role.[114] These points are explored later in our discussion of how to best manage alliances.

Network Cooperative Strategy

Increasingly, firms are involved with more than one cooperative strategy. George Weston, Ltd. is Canada's largest supermarket operator. Weston's outlets include Loblaws, Provigo, and more than a dozen other names. The company is also a giant food producer; it owns Neilson Dairy, is one of North America's largest bakers, and it raises and processes salmon in Chile, B.C., and the U.S. Weston not only produces for its own brands and stores, but has cooperative strategies to produce for others as well. Weston manufactures and markets low-carb bakery products with Atkins Nutritional, and it sells Nestlé-branded shakes and Coffee-Mate liquid coffee whiteners. Weston's Interbake Foods division is a major supplier of Girl Scout cookies in the U.S. For Weston, the cooperative strategies run two ways. Because Weston owns the President's Choice brand, the company requires a wider range of products than it produces. For example, President's Choice pop is made by Toronto food giant Cott Corporation, and CIBC supplies financial services for President's Choice Financial.[115]

A **network cooperative strategy** is a cooperative strategy wherein several firms agree to form multiple partnerships to achieve shared objectives.

In addition to forming their own alliances with individual companies, a growing number of firms are joining forces in multiple cooperative strategies. A **network cooperative strategy** is a cooperative strategy wherein several firms agree to form multiple partnerships to achieve shared objectives.

A network cooperative strategy is particularly effective when it is formed by firms clustered together,[116] as with Silicon Valley in California, Ottawa's Silicon Valley North tech sector, and B.C.'s Silicon Delta.[117] Effective social relationships and interactions among partners, while sharing their resources and capabilities make it more likely that a network cooperative strategy will be successful,[118] as does having a productive strategic centre firm (discussed further in Chapter 12).

For example, because of its previous success with cooperative strategies, Johnson Controls, Inc. (JCI), a leading manufacturer of automotive interior systems, established Peer Partnering. Peer Partnering is a network cooperative strategy between JCI and other U.S. firms Gentex, Jabil Circuit, Microchip Technology, and Yazaki North America, along with Holland's Royal Philips Electronics, France's SAGEM, and Japan's Tokai Rika. The members of this group work with each other to innovatively use advanced electronics to allow automakers to differentiate their products. As the strategic centre firm, JCI manages relationships among partners, holds each accountable for commitments made, and verifies that each firm benefits from participation. JCI supplies innovation and integration capabilities, and partners supply capabilities in advanced, electronic technologies. The network also benefits when members participate in other cooperative strategies. Tokai Rika, for example, has a strategic alliance with Toyoda Gosei to collaborate on automotive safety systems (e.g., air bags and seat belts). Some of the skills Tokai Rika forms via this relationship may enhance the value of its contributions to the Peer Partnering network. [119]

Alliance Network Types

An important advantage of a network cooperative strategy is that firms gain access "to their partners' partners."[120] As discussed above, JCI has access to other relationships with which Gentex, Jabil, Microchip, Philips, and Tokai Rika are involved, and those firms have access to JCI's other collaborative relationships. Having access to multiple collaborations increases the likelihood that additional competitive advantages will be formed, as the set of resources and capabilities being shared expands. In turn, increases in competitive advantages further stimulate the development of product innovations that are critical to strategic competitiveness in the global economy.[121]

The set of partnerships, such as strategic alliances, that result from the use of a network cooperative strategy is commonly called an *alliance network*. The alliance networks that companies develop vary by industry conditions. A *stable alliance network* is formed in mature industries where demand is relatively constant and predictable. Through a stable alliance network, firms try to extend their competitive advantages to other settings while continuing to profit from operations in their core, relatively mature industry. Thus, stable networks are built for *exploitation* of the economies (scale and/or scope) available between firms.[122] *Dynamic alliance networks* are used in industries characterized by frequent product innovations and short product life cycles. Believing that "no single company can hope to anticipate and fulfill all the challenges that are emerging today," Intel is involved with a number of alliances in partnership with several firms, including Nortel, HP, and Microsoft. This dynamic alliance network was created to work together to bring telecommunications and computing closer. The four firms worked on phone systems that use proprietary Nortel hardware and standard Intel-based servers to run, voice, fax, and e-mail messages through a single interface.[123] Dynamic alliance networks are thus used to stimulate rapid, value-creating product innovations and subsequent successful market entries, demonstrating that their purpose is often the exploration of new ideas. [124]

Competitive Risks with Cooperative Strategies

Stated simply, many cooperative strategies fail.[125] In fact, evidence shows that two-thirds of cooperative strategies have serious problems in their first two years and that as many as 70 percent of them fail.[126] This failure rate suggests that even when the partnership has potential complementarities and synergies, alliance success is elusive.[127] Although failure is undesirable, it can be a valuable learning experience. Companies willing to carefully study a cooperative strategy's failure may gain insights that can be used to successfully develop and use future cooperative strategies. Thus, companies should work hard to avoid cooperative strategy failure, but if failure does occur, it should work equally hard to learn from the experience. The firm takes risk when it uses one or more cooperative strategies. Prominent cooperative strategy risks are shown in Figure 10.4.

One cooperative strategy risk is that a partner may act opportunistically. Opportunistic behaviours surface either when formal contracts fail to prevent them or when an alliance is based on a false perception of partner trustworthiness. Not infrequently, the opportunistic firm wants to acquire as much of its partner's tacit knowledge as it can.[128] Full awareness of what a partner wants in a cooperative strategy reduces the likelihood that a firm will suffer from another's opportunistic actions.[129]

Some cooperative strategies fail when it is discovered that a firm has misrepresented the competencies it can bring to the partnership. This risk is more common when the partner's contribution is grounded in some of its intangible assets. Superior knowledge of local conditions is an example of an intangible asset that partners often fail to deliver. Asking the partner to provide evidence that it does possess the resources and capabilities it is to share in the cooperative strategy (even when they are largely intangible) may be an effective way to deal with this risk.

Another risk is that a firm won't actually deliver to its partners the resources and capabilities (e.g., its most sophisticated technologies) that it committed to the cooperative strategy. This risk surfaces most commonly when firms form an international cooperative strategy.[130] In these instances, different cultures can result in different interpretations of contractual terms or trust-based expectations.

A final risk is that the firm may make investments that are specific to the alliance, while its partner does not. For example, the firm might commit resources and capabilities to develop manufacturing equipment that can be used only to produce items arising from the alliance. If the partner isn't also making alliance-specific investments, the firm is at a relative disadvantage in terms of returns earned from the alliance compared to investments made to earn the returns.

Managing Cooperative Strategies

As our discussion has shown, cooperative strategies are an important option for firms competing in the global economy.[131] However, our study of cooperative strategies also shows that they are complex.[132]

Figure 10.4   Managing Competitive Risks in Cooperative Strategies

Competitive Risks
- Inadequate contracts
- Misrepresentation of competencies
- Partners fail to use their complementary resources
- Holding alliance partner's specific investments hostage

Risk and Asset Management Approaches
- Detailed contracts and monitoring
- Developing trusting relationships

Desired Outcome
- Creating value

Firms gain the most benefit from cooperative strategies when they are effectively managed. Managing and flexibly adapting partnerships are crucial aspects of successful cooperative strategies.[133] The firm that learns how to manage cooperative strategies better than its competitors may develop a competitive advantage.[134] This advantage is possible because the ability to effectively manage cooperative strategies is unevenly distributed across organizations.

In general, assigning managerial responsibility for a firm's cooperative strategies to a high-level executive or to a team improves the likelihood that the strategies will be well managed. IBM, Coca-Cola, and Siebel Systems are companies that have made such assignments. (See the Strategic Focus box "Managing Cooperative Strategies to Gain a Competitive Advantage" on page 318 for details on IBM's efforts.) United Airlines has established an alliance division to monitor and create new partnerships and to manage the more than 100 cooperative strategies with which it is currently involved.[135]

Those responsible for managing the firm's set of cooperative strategies coordinate activities, categorize knowledge learned from previous experiences, and ensure that the firm's knowledge about how to effectively form and use cooperative strategies is in the hands of the right people at the right time. Firms, whether or not they have formed a separate cooperative strategy management function, use one of two primary approaches to manage cooperative strategies—cost minimization or opportunity maximization.[136]

In the *cost minimization* management approach, the firm develops formal contracts with its partners. These contracts specify how the cooperative strategy is to be monitored and how partner behaviour is to be controlled. The goal of this approach is to minimize the cooperative strategy's cost and to prevent opportunistic behaviour by a partner. The focus of the second managerial approach, *opportunity maximization*, is on maximizing a partnership's value-creation opportunities. In this case, partners are prepared to take advantage of unexpected opportunities to learn from each other and to explore additional marketplace possibilities.[137] Less formal contracts, with fewer constraints on partners' behaviours, make it possible for partners to explore how their resources and capabilities can be shared in multiple value-creating ways.

Firms can successfully use either approach to manage cooperative strategies. However, the costs to monitor the cooperative strategy are greater with the cost minimization approach, since writing detailed contracts and using extensive monitoring mechanisms are expensive, even though the approach is intended to reduce alliance costs. Although monitoring systems may prevent partners from acting in their own best interests, they also preclude positive responses to those situations where opportunities to use the alliance's competitive advantages surface unexpectedly. Thus, formal contracts and extensive monitoring systems tend to stifle partners' efforts to gain maximum value from their participation in a cooperative strategy and require significant resources to put into place and use.

The relative lack of detail and formality that is a part of the contract developed by firms using the second management approach of opportunity maximization means that firms need to trust each other to act in the partnership's best interests. A psychological state, *trust* is a willingness to be vulnerable because of the expectations of positive behaviour from the firm's alliance partner.[138] When partners trust each other, there is less need to write detailed formal contracts to specify each firm's alliance behaviours,[139] and the cooperative relationship tends to be more stable.[140] On a relative basis, trust tends to be more difficult to establish in international cooperative strategies compared to domestic ones. Differences in trade policies, cultures, laws, and politics that are part of cross-border alliances account for the increased difficulty. When trust exists, partners' monitoring costs are reduced, and opportunities to create value are maximized.

Research showing that trust between partners increases the likelihood of alliance success[141] seems to highlight the benefits of the opportunity maximization approach to

Managing Cooperative Strategies to Gain a Competitive Advantage

To date, effective alliance management skills seem to be in relatively short supply—few firms have developed a competitive advantage through the management of their cooperative strategies. A key reason is the need for the firm to simultaneously learn from its alliance partners while preventing its partners from learning too much from it. In other words, as a partner, a company must develop the skills needed to manage the balance "… between trying to learn and trying to protect" its knowledge and sources of competitive advantages from excessive learning by partners. Finding ways to achieve this balance—a balance that is critical to developing a competitive advantage in terms of the management of cooperative strategies—seems to be difficult for most firms.

Global companies commonly compete against those with whom they are also collaborating. Toyota and General Motors, and Dell and IBM, are examples of companies that are both collaborators and competitors. While sharing some of their resources and capabilities in a partnership, firms exchange knowledge that may be related to a host of issues, including their technological skills, future plans, logistic systems, and hiring and training practices. Part of the successful management of cooperative strategies is to follow procedures preventing partners from being disadvantaged in future competitions, as a result of the resources, capabilities, and knowledge they share to use their cooperative strategy.

In spite of the difficulty, research findings and company experiences yield suggestions about knowledge protection and effective management of cooperative strategies. For example, assigning the responsibility to manage the firm's cooperative strategies to a group of people that reports to a senior-level official is vital. The charge to such a group is broad and should include responsibility to "… coordinate all alliance-related activity within the organization and (to institutionalize) processes and systems to teach, share, and leverage prior alliance-management experience and know-how throughout the company."

To manage its 70-plus cooperative strategies, IBM formed a strategic alliance team. Headed by an upper-level executive, the team handles all of IBM's collaborative ventures to create what it calls an alliance culture within the existing organizational structure. In the desired alliance culture, all parts of the company seek partners who could benefit from using IBM's marketing, sales, and solutions resources while leading with IBM's middleware, server platforms, and services to develop successful new market entries as outputs from each collaboration.

An important part of executing the broad charge given to teams (such as IBM's) that are expected to successfully manage their firm's cooperative strategies is its clear and detailed specification of the benefits of current cooperative strategies, as well as the benefits expected from the integration of new cooperative strategies into the current set. Simultaneously, the team should closely work with all partners to specify the resources and capabilities that will be shared during the partnership and those that will not be shared. Part of this discussion must focus on knowledge that is to remain within the confines of the cooperative strategy, not leaking to other sections of the partner's organization. Collaborations based on trust have a higher probability of being successful in this effort.

SOURCES: R. D. Ireland, M. A. Hitt, & D. Vaidyanath, 2002, Alliance management as a source of competitive advantage, *Journal of Management*, 28(3): 413–30; J. H. Dyer, P. Kale, & H. Singh, 2001, How to make strategic alliances work, *MIT Sloan Management Review*, 42(4): 37–43; A. C. Inkpen, 2001, Strategic alliances, in M. A. Hitt, R. E. Freeman, & J. S. Harrison (eds.), *Handbook of Strategic Management*, Oxford, UK: Blackwell Publishers, 409–32; IBM, 2001, IDC names IBM's strategic alliance program as a best practice in concept and implementation, *IBM website*, http://www-1.ibm.com/press/PressServletForm.wss?MenuChoice=pressreleases&TemplateName=ShowPress ReleaseTemplate&SelectString=t1.docunid=997&TableName=DataheadApplicationClass&SESSIONKEY=any&WindowTitle=Press+Release& STATUS=publish (press release, November 26; D. Ernst & T. Halvey, 2000, When to think alliance, *McKinsey Quarterly*, 4: 46–55; P. Kale, H. Singh, & H. Perlmutter, 2000, Learning and protection of proprietary assets in strategic alliances: Building relational capital, *Strategic Management Journal*, 21: 217–37.

managing cooperative strategies. Trust may also be the most efficient way to influence and control alliance partners' behaviours.[142] Research indicates that trust can be a capability that is valuable, rare, and imperfectly imitable.[143] Thus, firms known to be trustworthy can have a competitive advantage in terms of how they develop and use cooperative strategies. One reason is that it is impossible to specify all operational details of a cooperative strategy in a formal contract. Confidence that its partner can be trusted reduces the firm's concern about the inability to contractually control all alliance details.

Summary

- A cooperative strategy is one in which firms work together to achieve a shared objective. There are two types of cooperative strategies: strategic alliances and collusive strategies. Strategic alliances, which are cooperative strategies in which firms combine some of their resources and capabilities to create a competitive advantage, are the primary form of cooperative strategies. There are three basic types of strategic alliances: joint ventures (where firms create and own equal shares of a new venture that is intended to develop competitive advantages), equity strategic alliances (where firms own different shares of a newly created venture), and nonequity strategic alliances (where firms cooperate through a contractual relationship). Outsourcing, discussed in Chapter 4, commonly occurs as firms form nonequity strategic alliances.

- Collusive strategies are the second type of cooperative strategies. In many economies, and certainly in developed economies, explicit collusive strategies are illegal unless sanctioned by government policies. With increasing globalization, fewer government-sanctioned situations of explicit collusion exist. Tacit collusion, also called mutual forbearance, is a cooperative strategy through which firms tacitly cooperate to reduce industry output below the potential competitive output level, thereby raising prices above the competitive level.

- The reasons firms use cooperative strategies vary by slow-cycle, fast-cycle, and standard-cycle market conditions. To enter restricted markets (slow-cycle), to move quickly from one competitive advantage to another (fast-cycle), and to gain market power (standard-cycle) demonstrate the differences among reasons by market type for use of cooperative strategies.

- Business-level cooperative strategies are used to help firms improve their performance in individual product markets. There are four business-level cooperative strategies: complementary strategic alliances, competition response strategies, uncertainty-reducing strategies, and competition-reducing strategies. Through vertical and horizontal complementary alliances, companies combine their resources and capabilities to create value in different parts (vertical) or the same parts (horizontal) of the value chain. Competition-responding strategies are formed to respond to competitors' actions, especially their strategic actions. Competition-reducing strategies are used to avoid excessive competition while the firm marshals its resources and capabilities to improve its competitiveness. Uncertainty-reducing strategies are used to hedge against the risks created by the conditions of uncertain competitive environments. Complementary alliances have the highest probability of yielding a sustainable competitive advantage; competition-reducing strategies have the lowest probability of doing so.

- Corporate-level cooperative strategies are used when the firm wants to pursue product and/or geographic diversification. Through diversifying strategic alliances, firms agree to share some of their resources and capabilities to enter new markets or produce new products. In a synergistic alliance, firms share resources and capabilities to develop economies of scope. This alliance is similar to the business-level horizontal complementary alliance in which firms try to develop operational synergy; whereas synergistic alliances are used to develop synergy at the corporate level. Franchising is a corporate-level cooperative strategy where the franchiser uses a franchise as a contractual relationship to describe the sharing of its resources and capabilities with franchisees.

- As an international cooperative strategy, cross-border alliances are used for several reasons, including the performance superiority of firms competing in markets outside their domestic market and governmental restrictions on growth through mergers and acquisitions. Cross-border alliances tend to be riskier than their domestic counterparts, particularly when partners aren't fully aware of each other's purpose for participating in the partnership.

- A network cooperative strategy is one wherein several firms agree to form multiple partnerships to achieve shared objectives. One of the primary benefits of a network cooperative strategy is the firm's opportunity to gain access "to its partner's other partnerships." When this happens, the probability greatly increases that partners will find unique ways to share their resources and capabilities to form competitive advantages. Network cooperative strategies are used to form either a stable alliance network or a dynamic alliance network. Used in mature industries, partners use stable networks to extend competitive advantages into new areas. In rapidly changing environments where frequent product innovations occur, dynamic networks are primarily used as a tool of innovation.

- Cooperative strategies aren't risk free. If a contract is not developed appropriately, or if a partner misrepresents its competencies or fails to make them available, failure is likely. Furthermore, a firm may be held hostage through asset-specific investments made in conjunction with a partner, which may be exploited.

- Trust is an increasingly important aspect of successful cooperative strategies. Firms recognize the value of partnering with companies known for their trustworthiness. When trust exists, a cooperative strategy is managed to maximize the pursuit of opportunities between partners. Without trust, formal contracts and extensive monitoring systems are used to manage cooperative strategies. In this case, the interest is to minimize costs rather than to maximize opportunities by participating in a cooperative strategy.

Review Questions

1. What is the definition of cooperative strategy? Why is this strategy important to firms competing in the 21st-century competitive landscape?

2. What is a strategic alliance? What are the three types of strategic alliances firms use to develop a competitive advantage?

3. What are the four business-level cooperative strategies and what are the differences among them?

4. What are the three corporate-level cooperative strategies? How do firms use each one to create a competitive advantage?

5. Why do firms use cross-border strategic alliances?

6. What risks are firms likely to experience as they use cooperative strategies?

7. What are the differences between the cost-minimization approach and the opportunity-maximization approach to managing cooperative strategies?

Experimental Exercise

Cooperative Strategy Risk

Your firm manufactures fasteners for industrial applications. As the senior vice president of sales, you have developed several long-term relationships with your customers. Your main competitor has recently approached you about establishing a strategic alliance with your firm.

1. Because you are not sure if this alliance would be beneficial to your firm, you decide to bring the proposal to your firm's executive committee for a preliminary discussion. You anticipate that the committee will ask several basic questions. What information should you be able to provide?

2. After several weeks of investigating the value of an alliance, your firm decides that it would be financially beneficial, but the executive committee now wants you to present the risks that an alliance might entail and your suggestions for minimizing them. What risks do you foresee? How can they be prevented?

3. Before a contract between your firm and your competitor can be signed, you begin negotiations with one of your competitor's largest customers to provide new products based on a new technology your firm has developed. In your opinion, does the alliance raise legal or ethical issues that your firm should consider before proceeding with your negotiations?

1. K. M. Eisenhardt, 2002, Has strategy changed? *MIT Sloan Management Review*, 43(2): 88–91; T. B. Lawrence, C. Hardy, & N. Phillips, 2002, Institutional effects of interorganizational collaborations: The emergence of proto-institutions, *Academy of Management Journal*, 45: 281–90.

2. J. B. Barney, 2002, *Gaining and Sustaining Competitive Advantage*, 2nd ed., Upper Saddle River, NJ: Prentice-Hall, 339.

3. W. S. Desarbo, K. Jedidi, & I. Sinha, 2001, Customer value in a heterogeneous market, *Strategic Management Journal*, 22: 845–57.

4. C. Young-Ybarra & M. Wiersema, 1999, Strategic flexibility in information technology alliances: The influence of transaction cost economics and social exchange theory, *Organization Science*, 10: 439–59; M. E. Porter & M. B. Fuller, 1986, Coalitions and global strategy, in M. E. Porter (ed.), *Competition in Global Industries*, Boston: Harvard Business School Press, 315–44.

5. M. Schifrin, 2001, Partner or perish, *Forbes Best of the Web*, May 21, 26–28.

6. J. Bowser, 2001, Strategic co-opetition: The value of relationships in the networked economy, *IBM Business Strategy Consulting*, http://www-8.ibm.com/services/pdf/the_value_of_relationships_in_the_networked_economy.pdf, March 12.

7. M. A. Hitt, R. D. Ireland, S. M. Camp, & D. L. Sexton, 2002, Strategic entrepreneurship: Integrating entrepreneurial and strategic management perspectives, in M. A. Hitt, R. D. Ireland, S. M. Camp, & D. L. Sexton (eds.), *Strategic Entrepreneurship: Creating a New Mindset*, Oxford, UK: Blackwell Publishers, 8.

8. J. R. Harbison & P. Pekar, Jr., 1998, Institutionalizing alliance skills: Secrets of repeatable success, *Strategy & Business*, 11: 79–94.

9. Publishers Weekly, 2003, Wiley Canada in deal with Canadian Press, *Publishers Weekly*, 250(41): 13.

10. Barney, *Gaining and Sustaining Competitive Advantage*, 339.

11. Y. L. Doz & G. Hamel, 1998, *Alliance Advantage: The Art of Creating Value through Partnering*, Boston: Harvard Business School Press, xiii.

12. R. D. Ireland, M. A. Hitt, & D. Vaidyanath, 2002, Alliance management as a source of competitive advantage, *Journal of Management*, 28(3): 413–30; J. G. Coombs & D. J. Ketchen, 1999, Exploring interfirm cooperation and performance: Toward a reconciliation of predictions from the resource-based view and organizational economics, *Strategic Management Journal*, 20: 867–88.

13. P. Kale, H. Singh, & H. Perlmutter, 2000, Learning and protection of proprietary assets in strategic alliances: Building relational capital, *Strategic Management Journal*, 21: 217–37.

14. D. F. Kuratko, R. D. Ireland, & J. S. Hornsby, 2001, Improving firm performance through entrepreneurial actions: Acordia's corporate entrepreneurship strategy, *Academy of Management Executive*, 15(4): 60–71; D. Ernst & T. Halevy, 2000, When to think alliance, *The McKinsey Quarterly*, 4: 46–55.

15. Ballard Power Systems, 2004, *Ballard Power Systems website*, http://www.ballard.com, accessed May 2, 2004; Ballard Power Systems, 2002, Coleman Powermate and Ballard Power Systems generate power out of thin air, *Ballard Power Systems website*, http://www.ballard.com/pdfs/29%20Coleman.PDF (press release), December 3, accessed May 2, 2004; Prince George Citizen, 2004, Ballard motors on, *Prince George Citizen*, February 18, 16.

16. Dallas Morning News, 2002, Borrego blurs traditional lines, *Dallas Morning News*, February 24, M4.

17. J. H. Tiessen & J. D. Linton, 2000, The JV dilemma: Cooperating and competing in joint ventures, *Revue Canadienne des Sciences de l'Administration*, 17(3): 203–16.

18. T. K. Das & B.-S. Teng, 2001, A risk perception model of alliance structuring, *Journal of International Management*, 7: 1–29; J. H. Dyer & H. Singh, 1998, The relational view: Cooperative strategy and sources of interorganizational competitive advantage, *Academy of Management Review*, 23: 660–79.

19. A. Afuah, 2002, Mapping technological capabilities into product markets and competitive advantage: The case of cholesterol drugs, *Strategic Management Journal*, 23: 171–79; A. Arino, 2001, To do or not to do? Noncooperative behavior by commission and omission in interfirm ventures, *Group & Organization Management*, 26(1): 4–23; C. Holliday, 2001, Sustainable growth, the DuPont Way, *Harvard Business Review*, 79(8): 129–34.

20. M. A. Geletkanycz & S. S. Black, 2001, Bound by the past? Experienced-based effects on commitment to the strategic status quo, *Journal of Management*, 27: 3–21.

21. S. L. Berman, J. Down, & C. W. L. Hill, 2002, Tacit knowledge as a source of competitive advantage in the National Basketball Association, *Academy of Management Journal*, 45: 13–31.

22. Tiessen & Linton, The JV dilemma, 206; P. E. Bierly III & E. H. Kessler, 1999, The timing of strategic alliances, in M. A. Hitt, P. G. Clifford, R. D. Nixon, & K. P. Coyne (eds.), *Dynamic Strategic Resources: Development, Diffusion and Integration*, Chichester: John Wiley & Sons, 299–345.

23. K. Fortin, 2003, Domtar, Tembec plan $850-million joint venture: Lumber firm will be Canada's second largest, *Ottawa Citizen*, June 20, E1.

24. R. E. Hoskisson & L. W. Busenitz, 2002, Market uncertainty and learning distance in corporate entrepreneurship entry mode choice, in M. A. Hitt, R. D. Ireland, S. M. Camp, & D. L. Sexton (eds.), *Strategic Entrepreneurship: Creating a New Mindset*, Oxford, UK: Blackwell Publishers, 151–72.

25. A.-W. Harzing, 2002, Acquisitions versus greenfield investments: International strategy and management of entry modes, *Strategic Management Journal*, 23: 211–27; S.-J. Chang & P. M. Rosenzweig, 2001, The choice of entry mode in sequential foreign direct investment, *Strategic Management Journal*, 22: 747–76; Y. Pan, 1997, The formation of Japanese and U.S. equity joint ventures in China, *Strategic Management Journal*, 18: 247–54.

26. T. Hamilton, 2003, Joint venture plans wireless network: Expanding choice in broadband communications: "The simplicity of this product is almost unheard of," *Toronto Star*, November 20, C3.

27. S. Das, P. K. Sen, & S. Sengupta, 1998, Impact of strategic alliances on firm valuation, *Academy of Management Journal*, 41: 27–41.

28. Bierly & Kessler, The timing of strategic alliances, 303.

29. Barney, *Gaining and Sustaining Competitive Advantage*, 339; T. B. Folta & K. D. Miller, 2002, Real options in equity partnerships, *Strategic Management Journal*, 23: 77–88.

30. Research in Motion, 2004, *Research in Motion website*, http://www.rim.com/news/press/index.shtml (press releases), accessed May 1, 2004.

31. A. C. Inkpen, 2001, Strategic alliances, in M. A. Hitt, R. E. Freeman, & J. S. Harrison (eds.), *Handbook of Strategic Management*, Oxford, UK: Blackwell Publishers, 409–32.

32. M. Delio, 1999, Strategic outsourcing, *Knowledge Management*, 2(7): 62–68.

33. Magna International, 2004, Company info, *Magna International website*, http://www.magna.com, accessed March 5, 2004.

34. J. J. Reuer, M. Zollo, & H. Singh, 2002, Post-formation dynamics in strategic alliances, *Strategic Management Journal*, 23: 135–51; P. Buxbaum, 2001, Making alliances work, *Computerworld*, 35(30): 30–31; Inkpen, Strategic alliances, 409.

35. D. Campbell, 2001, High-end strategic alliances as fundraising opportunities, *Nonprofit World*, 19(5): 8–12; M. D. Hutt, E. R. Stafford, B. A. Walker, & P. H. Reingen, 2000, Case study: Defining the social network of a strategic alliance, *Sloan Management Review*, 41(2): 51–62.

36. F. M. Lysiak, 2002, M&As create new competencies, *Best's Review*, 102(9): 32–33.

37. M. J. Kelly, J.-L. Schaan, & H. Jonacas, 2002, Managing alliance relationships: Key challenges in the early stages of collaboration, *R&D Management*, 32(1): 11–22.

38. A. C. Inkpen & J. Ross, 2001, Why do some strategic alliances persist beyond their useful life? *California Management Review*, 44(1): 132–48.

39. Schifrin, Partner or perish, 28.

40. Inkpen, Strategic alliances, 411.

41. L. Fuentelsaz, J. Gomez, & Y. Polo, 2002, Followers' entry timing: Evidence from the Spanish banking sector after deregulation, *Strategic Management Journal*, 23: 245–64.

42. K. R. Harrigan, 2001, Strategic flexibility in the old and new economies, in M. A. Hitt, R. E. Freeman, & J. S. Harrison (eds.), *Handbook of Strategic Management*, Oxford, UK: Blackwell Publishers, 97–123.

43. G. W. Dent Jr., 2001, Gap fillers and fiduciary duties in strategic alliances, *Business Lawyer*, 57(1): 55–104.

44. S. Ulfelder, 2001, Partners in profit, http://www.computerworld.com, July/August, 24–28.

45. M. Gonzalez, 2001, Strategic alliances, *Ivey Business Journal*, 66(1): 47–51.

46. M. Johnson, 2001, Airlines rush for comfort alliances, *Global Finance*, 15(11): 119–20.

47. J. Child & D. Faulkner, 1998, *Strategies of Co-operation: Managing Alliances, Networks, and Joint Ventures*, New York: Oxford University Press.

48. J. R. Williams, 1998, *Renewable Advantage: Crafting Strategy through Economic Time*, New York: The Free Press.

49. B. Nelson, 2001, Usinor Group, *Forbes Best of the Web*, May 21, 96.

50. Sun Life Financial, 2004, Sun Life Everbright Life Insurance Company Limited, http://www.sunlife.com/slcorp/genericpage/0,3324,bGFuZy1lbmdsaXNoX3NpdGUtc2xjb3Jw X2Vudi1saXZlX3B6bi1nZW5lcmljX3NlYy0xOF9zdGF0LV9lZC1fbmF2LTMzMzk_,00.html (news release), accessed May 2, 2004; S. D. Gupta, 2002, Chinese market diversification gaining, *National Underwriter*, 106(27): 15; K. Kalawsky, 2001, Sun Life to get OK to sell insurance in China: Joint venture with local insurer...., *National Post (Financial Post)*, December 21, FP7.

51. C. Hoag, 1999, Oil duo plan energy alliance, *Financial Times*, June 30, 17.

52. S. A. Zahra, R. D. Ireland, I. Gutierrez, & M. A. Hitt, 2000, Privatization and entrepreneurial transformation: Emerging issues and a future research agenda, *Academy of Management Review*, 25: 509–24.

53. Eisenhardt, Has strategy changed? 88.

54. H. W. Chesbrough, 2002, Making sense of corporate venture capital, *Harvard Business Review*, 80(3): 90–99.

55. J. Strauss, 2001, Visa International: Creating the next generation of commerce, *Venture Capital Journal*, December 21, 40–41.

56. Ibid., 40.

57. Star Alliance, 2004, Star Alliance website, http://www.star-alliance.com, accessed May 3, 2004; B. Berentson, 2001, United Airlines, *Forbes Best of the Web*, May 21, 68.

58. Goodyear Tire, 2002, *Goodyear Tire website*, http://www.goodyear.com (press releases), March 5, 2002.

59. J. S. Harrison, M. A. Hitt, R. E. Hoskisson, & R. D. Ireland, 2001, Resource complementarity in business combinations: Extending the logic to organizational alliances, *Journal of Management*, 27: 679–99; S. H. Park & G. R. Ungson, 1997, The effect of national culture, organizational complementarity, and economic motivation on joint venture dissolution, *Academy of Management Journal*, 40: 297–307.

60. Van Houtte Coffee, 2004, Van Houtte to install more than 500 single-cup coffee makers in the Couche-Tard network, *Van Houtte website*, http://www.vanhoutte.com/en/Tools/news_item.asp?ID=39 (news release), March 15, accessed May 3, 2004; Van Houtte Coffee, 2003, Van Houtte reports quarterly earnings of $4 million and boosts its presence in Western Canada, *Van Houtte website*, http://www.vanhoutte.com/en/Tools/news_item.asp?ID=37 (news release), November 12, accessed May 3, 2004.

61. C. F. Freidheim, Jr., 1999, The trillion-dollar enterprise, *Strategy & Business*, 14: 60–66.

62. M. Kotabe & K. S. Swan, 1995, The role of strategic alliances in high technology new product development, *Strategic Management Journal*, 16: 621–36.

63. Caterpillar, 2002, Caterpillar announces agreement with Mitsubishi Heavy Industries, Caterpillar website, http://www.caterpillar.com, March 5.

64. P. Zinkewicz, 2002, Zurich Canada alliance with ING brings efficiencies, *Rough Notes*, 145(12): 114–17.

65. C. MacDonald, 2003, Toy story, *Canadian Plastics*, 61(2): 17–18; Mega Bloks Inc., 2002, Mega Bloks Inc. announces licensing agreements with Disney Consumer Products, http://www.megabloks.com/eng/corporate_info/20021112.php?dir=corporate_info, accessed May 5, 2004; C. Fishman, 2001, Why can't Lego click? *Fast Company*, September, 144–60.

66. Hitt, Ireland, Camp, & Sexton, *Strategic Entrepreneurship*, 9; R. G. McGrath, 1999, Falling forward: Real options reasoning and entrepreneurial failure, *Academy of Management Journal*, 22: 13–30.

67. Siemens, 2002, Corporate profile, *Fujitsu Siemens Computers website*, http://www.fujitsu-siemens.com/aboutus/company_information/corporate_profile/index.html, March 7.

68. M. A. Hitt, R. D. Ireland, R. E. Hoskisson, R. G. Rowe, & J. P. Sheppard, 2002, *Strategic Management: Competitiveness & Globalization, Concepts*, 1st Canadian ed., Toronto: Nelson Thompson; D. Coxe, 1999, Visions of techno-sugarplums: owning the best of the best is rarely a losing proposition, *Financial Post (National Post)*, December 24, C8.

69. Barney, *Gaining and Sustaining Competitive Advantage*, 33.

70. P. Vieira, 2003, Travel agents suing Air Canada: Commission cuts, *National Post (Financial Post)*, March 3, FP5; N. Van Praet, 2003, Travel agents file $1.7B claim against Air Canada, *National Post (Financial Post)*, October 31, FP8.

71. M. Freedman, 2000, Planting seeds, *Forbes*, February 7, 62–64.

72. J. M. Broder, 1997, Toys "R" Us led price collusion, judge rules in upholding F.T.C., *New York Times*, http://www.nytimes.com, October 1.

73. S. Jayachandran, J. Gimeno, & P. Rajan, 1999, Theory of multimarket competition: A synthesis and implications for marketing strategy, *Journal of Marketing*, 63(3): 49–66.

74. Mark Gehlhar, 2003, *Regional Concentration in the Global Food Economy*, Paper presented at the First Biennial Conference of the Food System Research Group, June 27, Madison, Wisconsin, http://www.aae.wisc.edu/fsrg/publications/conference/Gehlhar.pdf, accessed May 5, 2004.

75. G. K. Price, 2000, Cereal sales soggy despite price cuts and reduced couponing, *Food Review*, 23(2): 21–28.

76. S. B. Garland & A. Reinhardt, 1999, Making antitrust fit high tech, *Business Week*, March 22, 34–36.

77. B. Mitchener & P. Shishkin, 2001, Price fixing by top five record companies, *Wall Street Journal*, January 29, B1, B4.

78. G. Gari, 1999, Leveraging the rewards of strategic alliances, *Journal of Business Strategy*, 20(2): 40–43.

79. Price, Cereal sales soggy, 21.

80. Harrison, Hitt, Hoskisson, & Ireland, Resource complementarity, 684–85; S. Chaudhuri & B. Tabrizi, 1999, Capturing the real value in high-tech acquisitions, *Harvard Business Review*, 77(5): 123–30; J.-F. Hennart & S. Reddy, 1997, The choice between mergers/acquisitions and joint ventures in the United States, *Strategic Management Journal*, 18: 1–12.

81. Inkpen, Strategic alliances, 413.

82. Young-Ybarra & Wiersema, Strategic flexibility, 439.

83. Folta & Miller, Real options, 77.

84. Wal-Mart, 2002, Wal-Mart Stores, Wal-Mart and Sumitomo agree to acquire strategic stake in Japan's Seiyu, *Wal-Mart website*, general news, March 14.

85. T. Renshaw, 2002, Blue-collar common sense seals steady growth, *National Post*, December 18, SR5.

86. Cisco, 2004, Alliance overview: The HP & Cisco strategic alliance, *Cisco website*, http://www.cisco.com/en/US/partners/pr67/pr29/partners_strategic_summary.html, accessed July 29, 2004.

87. C. Harris & G. Cramb, 1999, Seeking wider co-operation, *Financial Times*, October 19, 20.

88. S. A. Shane, 1996, Hybrid organizational arrangements and their implications for firm growth and survival: A study of new franchisers, *Academy of Management Journal*, 39: 216–34.

89. F. Lafontaine, 1999, Myths and strengths of franchising, Mastering Strategy (Part Nine), *Financial Times*, November 22, 8–10.

90. N. Van Praet, 2004, Boston Pizza set to launch Quebec eateries, *Montreal Gazette*, February 13, B3.

91. N. Van Praet, 2004, Boston Pizza set to launch Quebec eateries, *Montreal Gazette*, February 13, B3.

92. L. Fenwick, 2001, Emerging markets: Defining global opportunities, *Franchising World*, 33(4): 54–55.

93. R. P. Dant & P. J. Kaufmann, 1999, Franchising and the domain of entrepreneurship research, *Journal of Business Venturing*, 14: 5–16.

94. M. Gerstenhaber, 2000, Franchises can teach us about customer care, *Marketing*, March 16, 18.

95. P. J. Kaufmann & S. Eroglu, 1999, Standardization and adaptation in business format franchising, *Journal of Business Venturing*, 14: 69–85.

96. L. Wu, 1999, The pricing of a brand name product: Franchising in the motel services industry, *Journal of Business Venturing*, 14: 87–102.

97. Barney, *Gaining and Sustaining Competitive Advantage*, 110–11.

98. M&M Meat Shops, 2004, History of M&M, *M&M Meat Shops website*, http://www.mmmeatshops.com/en/aboutmm/history.asp, accessed May 7, 2004; B. Constantineau, 2003, Appetite abounds for flash-frozen M&M Meat Shop offerings, *Edmonton Journal*, July 26, H10.

99. P. J. Buckley & M. Casson, 1996, An economic model of international joint venture strategy, *Journal of International Business Studies*, 27: 849–76; M. J. Dowling & W. L. Megginson, 1995, Cooperative strategy and new venture performance: The role of business strategy and management experience, *Strategic Management Journal*, 16: 565–80.

100. Ireland, Hitt, & Vaidyanath, Alliance management.

101. B. L. Simonin, 1997, The importance of collaborative know-how: An empirical test of the learning organization, *Academy of Management Journal*, 40: 1150–74.

102. M. A. Hitt, M. T. Dacin, E. Levitas, J. -L. Arregle, & A. Borza, 2000, Partner selection in emerging and developed market contexts: Resource-based and organizational learning perspectives, *Academy of Management Journal*, 43: 449–67; M. D. Lord &

A. L. Ranft, 2000, Organizational learning about new international markets: Exploring the internal transfer of local market knowledge, *Journal of International Business Studies*, 31: 573–89.

103. A. L. Velocci, Jr., 2001, U.S.–Euro strategic alliances will outpace company mergers, *Aviation Week & Space Technology*, 155(23): 56.

104. Sceptre Investment Counsel, 2004, *Sceptre Investment Counsel website*, http://www.sceptre.ca, accessed May 8, 2004; Toronto Star, 2003, Putnam doubles stake in Sceptre; Cross-border alliance expands Boston firm happy with local partner, *Toronto Star*, September 13, D9.

105. Ireland, Hitt, & Vaidyanath, Alliance management; M. A. Hitt, R. E. Hoskisson, & H. Kim, 1997, International diversification: Effects on innovation and firm performance in product diversified firms, *Academy of Management Journal*, 40: 767–98. R. N. Osborn & J. Hagedoorn, 1997, The institutionalization and evolutionary dynamics of interorganizational alliances and networks, *Academy of Management Journal*, 40: 261–78.

106. J. Hagedoorn, 1995, A note on international market leaders and networks of strategic technology partnering, *Strategic Management Journal*, 16: 241–50.

107. W. Heuslein, 2001, Coca-Cola, *Forbes Best of the Web*, May 21, 72.

108. P. Newcomb, 2001, Sony, *Forbes Best of the Web*, May 21, 84.

109. Appliance Manufacturer, 2003, Purification roundup, *Appliance Manufacturer*, 51(9): 58; National Post, 2003; ZENON in talks with Maytag on home water filter system, *National Post (Financial Post)*, May 15, FP2.

110. M. Schuman, 1996, South Korea raises limit to 18% on foreign investment in firms, *Wall Street Journal*, February 27, A12.

111. S. R. Miller & A. Parkhe, 2002, Is there a liability of foreignness in global banking? An empirical test of banks' x-efficiency, *Strategic Management Journal*, 23: 55–75; Y. Luo, 2001, Determinants of local responsiveness: Perspectives from foreign subsidiaries in an emerging market, *Journal of Management*, 27: 451–77.

112. A. Cane, 1999, GEC and NEC in alliance talks, *Financial Times*, May 11, 20.

113. P. Ghemawat, 2001, Distance matters: The hard reality of global expansion, *Harvard Business Review*, 79(8): 137–47.

114. J. K. Sebenius, 2002, The hidden challenge of cross-border negotiations, *Harvard Business Review*, 80(3): 76–85.

115. George Weston Limited, 2004, About us: corporate profile, *George Weston Limited website*, http://www.weston.ca/en/abt_corprof.html#top, accessed May 9, 2004; Hoover's Online, 2004, George Weston Limited fact sheet, http://www.hoovers.com/george-weston/—ID__41280—/free-co-factsheet.xhtml, accessed May 9, 2004; F. Tomesco, 2004, U.S. sales growth helps boost profit by 42%, *National Post (Financial Post)*, January 30, FP10; T. L. Soblosky, 2003, Brand new, *ABA Bank Marketing*, 35(3): 28–35; George Weston Limited, 2003, George Weston Limited 2003 Annual Information Form, 38, http://www.weston.ca/en/pdf_en/03gwl_aif_en.pdf, accessed July 29, 2004.

116. C. B. Copp & R. L. Ivy, 2001, Networking trends of small tourism businesses in Post-socialist Slovakia, *Journal of Small Business Management*, 39: 345–53.

117. E. Beauchesne, 2004, TD predicts solid growth for Ottawa, *Ottawa Citizen*, January 16, E3; W. Hanley, 1999, Growing up in Silicon Delta …, *National Post*, November 24, D1; S. S. Cohen & G. Fields, 1999, Social capital and capital gains in Silicon Valley, *California Management Review*, 41(2): 108–30; M. E. Porter, 1998, Clusters and the new economics of competition, *Harvard Business Review*, 78(6): 77–90; R. Pouder & C. H. St. John, 1996, Hot spots and blind spots: Geographical clusters of firms and innovation, *Academy of Management Review*, 21: 1192–1225.

118. A. C. Cooper, 2001, Networks, alliances, and entrepreneurship, in M. A. Hitt, R. D. Ireland, S. M. Camp, & D. L. Sexton (eds.), *Strategic Entrepreneurship: Creating a New Mindset*, Oxford, UK: Blackwell Publishers, 203–22.

119. Johnson Controls, 2002, Corporate home: Recognition, *Johnson Controls website*, http://www.johnsoncontrols.com/corp/, March 10; Johnson Controls, 2002, Corporate profile, *Johnson Controls website*, http://www.johnsoncontrols.com, March 10; Johnson Controls, 2002, Johnson Controls partners with MatrixOne, *Johnson Controls Website*, http://www.johnsoncontrols.com, March 10; Johnson Controls, 2002, Peer partners, *Johnson Controls website*, http://www.johnsoncontrols.com, March 10; Fidelity Investments, 2002, Standard & Poor's stock report, *Fidelity Investments website*, http://www.fidelity.com, March 2; B. Berentson, 2001, Johnson Controls, *Forbes Best of the Web*, May 21, 70.

120. R. S. Cline, 2001, Partnering for strategic alliances, *Lodging Hospitality*, 57(9): 42.

121. G. J. Young, M. P. Charns, & S. M. Shortell, 2001, Top manager and network effects on the adoption of innovative management practices: A study of TQM in a public hospital system, *Strategic Management Journal*, 22: 935–51.

122. F. T. Rothaermel, 2001, Complementary assets, strategic alliances, and the incumbent's advantage: An empirical study of industry and firm effects in the biopharmaceutical industry, *Research Policy*, 30: 1235–51.

123. Computing Canada, 1999, HP, Nortel, Microsoft, Intel take aim at convergence, *Computing Canada*, 25(12): 23.

124. H. W. Volberda, C. Baden-Fuller, & F. A. J. van den Bosch, 2001, Mastering strategic renewal: Mobilising renewal journeys in multi-unit firms, *Long Range Planning*, 34(2): 159–78.

125. D. C. Hambrick, J. Li, K. Xin, & A. S. Tsui, 2001, Compositional gaps and downward spirals in international joint venture management groups, *Strategic Management Journal*, 22: 1033–53; T. K. Das & B.-S. Teng, 2000, Instabilities of strategic alliances: An internal tensions perspective, *Organization Science*, 11: 77–101.

126. M. P. Koza & A. Y. Lewin, 1999, Putting the S-word back in alliances, Mastering Strategy (Part Six), *Financial Times*, November 1, 12–13; S. H. Park & M. Russo, 1996, When cooperation eclipses competition: An event history analysis of joint venture failures, *Management Science*, 42: 875–90.

127. A. Madhok & S. B. Tallman, 1998, Resources, transactions and rents: Managing value through interfirm collaborative relationships, *Organization Science*, 9: 326–39.

128. P. M. Norman, 2001, Are your secrets safe? Knowledge protection in strategic alliances, *Business Horizons*, November/December, 51–60.

129. M. A. Hitt, M. T. Dacin, B. B. Tyler, & D. Park, 1997, Understanding the differences in Korean and U.S. executives strategic orientations, *Strategic Management Journal*, 18: 159–68.

130. P. Lane, J. E. Salk, & M. A. Lyles, 2001, Absorptive capacity, learning, and performance in international joint ventures, *Strategic Management Journal*, 22: 1139–61.

131. R. Larsson, L. Bengtsson, K. Henriksson, & J. Sparks, 1998, The interorganizational learning dilemma: Collective knowledge development in strategic alliances, *Organization Science*, 9: 285–305.

132. Ireland, Hitt, & Vaidyanath, Alliance management.

133. Reuer, Zollo, & Singh, Post-formation dynamics, 148.

134. J. H. Dyer, P. Kale, & H. Singh, 2001, How to make strategic alliances work, *MIT Sloan Management Review*, 42(4): 37–43.

135. Berentson, United Airlines, 68.

136. J. H. Dyer, 1997, Effective interfirm collaboration: How firms minimize transaction costs and maximize transaction value, *Strategic Management Journal*, 18: 535–56; M. H. Hansen, R. E. Hoskisson, & J. B. Barney, 1997, Trustworthiness in strategic alliances: Opportunism minimization versus opportunity maximization, working paper, Provo, UT: Brigham Young University.

137. W. Mitchell, 1999, Alliances: Achieving long-term value and short-term goals Mastering Strategy (Part Four), *Financial Times*, October 18, 6–11.

138. Hutt, Stafford, Walker, & Reingen, Defining the social network, 53.

139. D. F. Jennings, K. Artz, L. M. Gillin, & C. Christodouloy, 2000, Determinants of trust in global strategic alliances: Amrad and the Australian biomedical industry, *Competitiveness Review*, 10(1): 25–44.

140. H. K. Steensma, L. Marino, & K. M. Weaver, 2000, Attitudes toward cooperative strategies: A cross-cultural analysis of entrepreneurs, *Journal of International Business Studies*, 31: 591–609.

141. A. Arino & J. de la Torre, 1998, Learning from failure: Towards and evolutionary model of collaborative ventures, *Organization Science*, 9: 306–25; J. B. Barney & M. H. Hansen, 1994, Trustworthiness: Can it be a source of competitive advantage? *Strategic Management Journal*, 15(special winter issue): 175–203.

142. R. Gulati & H. Singh, 1998, The architecture of cooperation: Managing coordination costs and appropriation concerns in strategic alliances, *Administrative Science Quarterly*, 43: 781–814; R. Gulati, 1996, Social structure and alliance formation patterns: A longitudinal analysis, *Administrative Science Quarterly*, 40: 619–52.

143. J. H. Davis, F. D. Schoorman, R. C. Mayer, & H. H. Tan, 2000, The trusted general manager and business unit performance: Empirical evidence of a competitive advantage, *Strategic Management Journal*, 21: 563–76; R. C. Mayer, J. H. Davis, & F. D. Schoorman, 1995, An integrative model of organizational trust, *Academy of Management Review*, 20: 709–34.

Part Three

Strategic Actions: Strategy Implementation

3

Chapter Eleven

Corporate Governance

Knowledge Objectives

Studying this chapter should provide you with the strategic management knowledge needed to:

1. Define corporate governance and explain why it is used to monitor and control managers' strategic decisions.

2. Explain how ownership came to be separated from managerial control in the modern corporation.

3. Define an agency relationship and managerial opportunism and describe their strategic implications.

4. Explain how three internal governance mechanisms—ownership concentration, the board of directors, and executive compensation—are used to monitor and control managerial decisions.

5. Discuss trends among the three types of compensation executives receive and their effects on strategic decisions.

6. Describe how the external corporate governance mechanism—the market for corporate control—acts as a restraint on top-level managers' strategic decisions.

7. Discuss the use of corporate governance in international settings, in particular in Germany and Japan.

8. Describe how corporate governance fosters ethical strategic decisions and the importance of such behaviours on the part of top-level executives.

Corporate Governance and CEO Pay

Corporate governance has become a much debated topic in the last few years. Very high profile corporate scandals involving the senior leaders of companies such as Nortel, Enron, WorldCom, and Tyco have exacerbated this debate. Plunges in stock prices related to these scandals have helped to ensure that increased attention is focused on performance and related governance practices, at an increasing pace among public corporations. The compensation of senior managers, especially CEOs, is being much more critically examined by each firm's stakeholders.

In addition, increased scrutiny is being given to boards and their responsibilities to the firm, in particular the duties of directors to assess the expectations of, and to compensate, senior executives. Directors are more cognizant of the scrutiny that their actions receive and are becoming more alert to the fact that their competence and integrity are being examined as if under a microscope.

The critical board function of aligning management interests with those of shareholders is often accomplished through the skillful structuring of compensation packages that try to compel appropriate management actions to meet firm objectives. Historically, board compensation committees have been known to meet infrequently, often just once per year, to set annual compensation figures. With recent events and increased scrutiny, compensation professionals say that the process of establishing compensation figures now requires significant deliberation on the part of committee members, as time is spent on the consideration of new best practices. This deliberation includes redesigning option plans and instituting more stringent performance measures.

Research shows that compensation of Canadian executives has typically trailed that of their U.S counterparts. Figures reported from the annual CEO compensation survey by Watson Wyatt & Co., released in late 2003, show that the median base salary of a Canadian CEO is up by 6 percent in 2002, down from a rise of 14 percent the previous year. There is also evidence of active change in compensation arrangements; for example, Bank of Montreal (TSX: BMO), a major Canadian company, was one of the first to introduce the use of performance-linked options. In another example, Royal Bank of Canada (TSX: RY) requires executives to hold stock obtained from options for at least one year before selling them.

For some investors, this change is long overdue and is a welcome relief from the excesses of CEO pay in the recent past. J. Richard Finlay, chairman of the Toronto-based Centre for Corporate & Public Governance and a longtime critic of corporate greed, has referred to excessive CEO pay as, "the mad-cow disease of boardrooms. ..." He further suggests that, "We still have a long way to go to bring some sense of sanity back into executive compensation. Especially in light of the trillions of dollars lost in the stock market and what is really the greatest crisis in capitalism since the Great Depression."

One notable display of CEO frugality was that of John Hunkin, chairman and CEO of Canadian Imperial Bank of Commerce (TSX:CM), who, in 2003, refused any pay raises, cash bonuses or options—after the bank

Nortel's board of directors exercised corporate governance when it dismissed Frank Dunn and several senior level managers "for cause."

(continued)

failed to make its yearly performance targets. In a similar move, former TD Bank chairman and CEO Charles Baillie also gave up his bonus in 2003.

Unfortunately, the stories of compensation mismatches still abound, confirming that much work remains to be done. A good example is the experience of Royal Group Technologies (TSX: RYG). Chairman and CEO Vic De Zen received a $5.6 million bonus, despite the facts that the Group's stock fell significantly, beginning in 2002, and the company issued four profit warnings within six months When coupled with his stock option grant, De Zen's total pay package for 2002 was an increase of more than 80 percent over his earnings in 2001. In fact, a review conducted by *Canadian Business*, revealed that more than 50 percent of all companies surveyed saw their CEO's compensation increase, despite the pressure experienced in stock prices and profits.

Investors are becoming savvier and are demanding that their boards be more vigilant in handling issues of executive compensation. Many companies have not yet made public their compensation deals via annual proxy filings. According to Canadian securities regulators, based on a review of compensation disclosures in 2002, 95 percent of the companies reviewed elected to provide general comments about compensation practices, while some 7 percent of the companies had to revise their proxies to correct errors in the data. Compensation consultant Ken Hugessen, of Mercer Human Resources Consulting in Toronto, says, "Even some of the best companies are still reluctant to come out from behind their lawyers and really talk to shareholders about this."

A very controversial example of what might be deemed executive excess is the lucrative compensation deal at Air Canada. If the airline's CEO and its chief restructuring officer remain on board for the next four years of operations, they each receive 1 percent of Air Canada's equity. This bonus offer is estimated at approximately $20 million each and could in fact be substantially higher if it rises with the value of Air Canada's stock. This compensation package comes at a time when Air Canada staff very recently agreed to more than $1 billion in wage cuts per year and layoffs over the next six years. The significant bonus package threatens to further depress the already low employee morale. Douglas Reid, professor of strategy at Queen's University, suggests that this deal could well be one of the turning points in the collapse of Air Canada.

SOURCES: J. Gray, 2003, High on the hog: While stocks tank, some execs are still gorging themselves on plump pay cheques, *Canadian Business*, May 12, 41–44; J. Kirby, 2003, Frank's follies: Let's put the $58-million pay package Magna's Frank Stronach received under the magnifying glass, *Canadian Business*, April 28, 20; J. Gray, 2003, The best and worst boards of directors in Canada: Our survey reveals good news for governance advocates: boards are improving, *Canadian Business*, August 19, 28; J. Gray, 2004, Having their cake. … : More and more companies are explicitly linking superior CEO pay to superior performance, *Canadian Business*, March 15, 69–70; J. Gray, 2004, A tale of two CEOs: Applying the notion that executive pay is the acid test for corporate reform, *Canadian Business*, April 26–May 9, 35–36; J. Gray, 2003, Up in the air: Anger over lavish bonuses for top executives could clip Air Canada's wings, *Canadian Business*, November 24–December 7, 39; P. Kontes, 2003, Rethinking today's CEO pay practices: Executive compensation, *Directors & Boards*, spring, 27; P. Brieger, 2004, Directors fear scandal will rock their firms, *Financial Post*, February 11, FP1.

As the opening case illustrates, corporate governance is an increasingly important part of the strategic management process.[1] If the board makes the wrong decision in compensating the firm's strategic leader—the CEO—then the whole firm suffers, as do its shareholders. Compensation is used to motivate CEOs to act in the best interests of the firm—in particular, the shareholders. When they do, the firm's value should increase.

What are a CEO's actions worth? The opening case suggests that they are worth a significant amount in Canada, as they are in the U.S. and other countries. While some critics argue that CEOs are paid too much, the hefty increases in their compensation in recent years ostensibly have come from linking their pay to their firms' performance, and Canadian and U.S. firms have performed better than many firms in other countries. However, research suggests that firms with a smaller pay gap between the CEO and other top executives perform better, especially when collaboration among top management team members is more important. The performance improvement is attributed to better cooperation among the top management team members. Other research suggests that CEOs receive excessive compensation when corporate governance is the weakest.[2] Also, the benchmark-basing of CEO compensation, by offering salaries comparable to those paid to peers at other companies, appears to be a prevalent cause of excessive compensation.

Corporate governance represents the relationship among stakeholders that is used to determine and control the strategic direction and performance of organizations. At its core, corporate governance is concerned with identifying ways to ensure that strategic decisions are made effectively. Governance can also be thought of as a means used by corporations to establish order among parties (the firm's owners and its top-level managers) whose interests may be in conflict. Thus, corporate governance reflects and enforces the company's values. In modern corporations—especially those in Canada, the United States, and the United Kingdom—a primary objective of corporate governance is to ensure that the interests of top-level managers are aligned with the interests of the shareholders. Corporate governance involves oversight in areas where owners, managers, and members of boards of directors may have conflicts of interest. These areas include the election of directors, the general supervision of CEO pay and more focused supervision of director pay, and the corporation's overall structure and strategic direction.[3]

Corporate governance has been emphasized in recent years because corporate governance mechanisms occasionally fail to adequately monitor and control top-level managers' decisions. This situation has resulted in changes in governance mechanisms at corporations throughout the world, especially with respect to efforts intended to improve the performance of boards of directors. A second and more positive reason for this interest is that evidence suggests that a well-functioning corporate governance and control system can create a competitive advantage for an individual firm. For example, one governance mechanism—the board of directors—has been suggested to be rapidly evolving into a major strategic force in U.S. business firms.[4] It is considered that this trend is also developing in Canadian firms. Thus, in this chapter, we describe actions designed to implement strategies that focus on monitoring and controlling mechanisms, which can help to ensure that top-level managerial actions contribute to the firm's strategic competitiveness and its ability to earn above-average returns.

Effective corporate governance is also of interest to nations. As stated by one scholar, "Every country wants the firms that operate within its borders to flourish and grow in such ways as to provide employment, wealth, and satisfaction, not only to improve standards of living materially but also to enhance social cohesion. These aspirations cannot be met unless those firms are competitive internationally in a sustained way, and it is this medium- and long-term perspective that makes good corporate governance so vital."[5]

Corporate governance, then, reflects company standards, which in turn collectively reflect societal standards. In many individual corporations, shareholders hold top-level

> **Corporate governance** represents the relationship among stakeholders that is used to determine and control the strategic direction and performance of organizations.

managers accountable for both their decisions and the results generated by making these decisions. As with these individual firms and their boards, nations that effectively govern their corporations may gain a competitive advantage over rival countries. For example, during the 1997 currency crisis in Asia, weak governance in the emerging economies resulted in asset prices falling lower than would have been the case had there been strong governance.[6]

In a range of countries, but especially in Canada, the United States, and the United Kingdom, the fundamental goal of business organizations is to maximize shareholder value. Traditionally, shareholders are treated as the firm's key stakeholders, because they are the company's legal owners. The firm's owners expect top-level managers and others influencing the corporation's actions (e.g., the board of directors) to make decisions that will result in the maximization of the company's value and, hence, of the owners' wealth.[7]

As mentioned in Chapter 2, Ipsos-Reid publishes the list of Canada's Most Respected Corporations each year. As part of this release, it also publishes the top 10 most admired and respected corporations with respect to corporate governance. The results are tabulated from a poll of Canadian CEOs. The poll is sponsored by KPMG and conducted by Ipsos-Reid. Table 11.1 reports the results for 2003 and 2002. One interesting result is that four of the "Big Five" banks remained in 2003 from the 2002 rankings, with only TD Canada Trust dropping out of the top 10 in this one category.

In the first section of this chapter, we describe the relationship providing the foundation on which the modern corporation is built: the relationship between owners and managers. The rest of this chapter is then used to explain various mechanisms owners use to govern managers and to ensure that they comply with their responsibility to maximize shareholder value.

Three internal governance mechanisms and a single external one are used in the modern corporation (see Table 11.2). The three internal governance mechanisms we describe in this chapter are (1) ownership concentration, as represented by types of

Table 11.1	Top Ten Most Admired and Respected Corporations in Canada, Based on How CEOs Perceive Corporate Governance		
Firm		**2003**	**2002**
RBC Financial Group		1	1
BCE Inc.		2	3
Canadian Imperial Bank of Commerce		3	6*
TransCanada Pipelines Ltd.		4*	7
BMO Financial Group		4*	5
EnCana Corporation		5	10
Bombardier Inc.		6	6*
Bank of Nova Scotia		7	8
TransAlta Corporation		8	12
Suncor Energy Inc.		9*	10
Canadian National Railway Co.		9*	9
Manulife Financial Corporation		10	4

*ties

SOURCES: 2003, RBC Financial Group (Royal Bank) selected by CEOs as Canada's most respected corporation for 2002, *Ipsos-Reid Press Release*, January 20, 2003; 2004, RBC Financial Group again selected by CEOs as Canada's most respected corporation for 2003, *Ipsos-Reid Press Release*, January 19, 2004.

Table 11.2	Internal Governance Mechanisms

Ownership Concentration
- Relative amounts of stock owned by individual shareholders and institutional investors

Board of Directors
- Individuals responsible for representing the firm's owners by monitoring top-level managers' strategic decisions

Executive Compensation
- Use of salary, bonuses, and long-term incentives to align managers' interests with shareholders' interests

External Governance Mechanism
Market for Corporate Control
- The purchase of a company that is underperforming relative to industry rivals in order to improve the firm's strategic competitiveness

shareholders and their different incentives to monitor managers, (2) the board of directors, and (3) executive compensation. We then consider the market for corporate control, an external corporate governance mechanism. Essentially, this market is a set of potential owners seeking to acquire undervalued firms and earn above-average returns on their investments by replacing ineffective top-level management teams.[8] Closing our analysis of corporate governance is a consideration of the need for these control mechanisms to encourage and support ethical behaviour in organizations.

Importantly, the mechanisms discussed in this chapter can positively influence the governance of the modern corporation, which has placed significant responsibility and authority in the hands of top-level managers. The most effective managers understand their accountability for the firm's performance and respond positively to corporate governance mechanisms. In addition, the firm's owners should not expect any single mechanism to remain effective over time. Rather, the use of several mechanisms allows owners to govern the corporation in ways that maximize strategic competitiveness and increase the financial value of their firm. With multiple governance mechanisms operating simultaneously, however, it is also possible for some of the governance mechanisms to conflict.[9] Later, we review how these conflicts can occur.

Separation of Ownership and Managerial Control

Historically, the founders–the owners and their descendants—managed Canadian and U.S. firms. In these cases, corporate ownership and control resided in the same persons. As firms grew larger, "the managerial revolution led to a separation of ownership and control in most large corporations, where control of the firm shifted from entrepreneurs to professional managers while ownership became dispersed among thousands of unorganized stockholders who were removed from the day-to-day management of the firm."[10] These changes created the modern public corporation, which is based on the efficient separation of ownership and managerial control. Supporting the separation is a basic legal premise suggesting that the primary objective of a firm's activities is to increase the corporation's profit and, thereby, the financial gains of the owners (the shareholders).[11]

The separation of ownership and managerial control allows shareholders to purchase stock, which entitles them to income (residual returns) from the firm's operations after paying expenses. This right, however, requires that they also take a risk that the firm's

Chapter 11 / Corporate Governance

expenses may exceed its revenues. To manage this investment risk, shareholders maintain a diversified portfolio by investing in several companies to reduce their overall risk.[12] As shareholders diversify their investments over a number of corporations, their risk declines. The poor performance or failure of any one firm in which they invest has less overall effect. Thus, successful shareholders specialize in managing their investment risk.

In small firms, managers often are high-percentage owners, so there is less separation between ownership and managerial control, but as these firms grow and become more complex, their owners–managers may contract with managerial specialists. These managers oversee decision making in the owner's firm and are compensated on the basis of their decision-making skills. As decision-making specialists, managers are agents of the firm's owners and are expected to use their decision-making skills to operate the owners' firm, in ways that will maximize the return on the owners' investment.[13]

Without the owner (shareholder) specialization in risk bearing and the management specialization in decision making that we have described, a firm probably would be limited by the abilities of its owners to manage and make effective strategic decisions. Thus, the separation and specialization of ownership (risk bearing) and managerial control (decision making) should produce the highest returns for the firm's owners.

Shareholder value is reflected by the price of the firm's stock. As stated earlier, corporate governance mechanisms, such as the board of directors or compensation based on the performance of a firm, provide reasons for CEOs to show general concern about the firm's stock price. For example, Cisco earned the dubious honour, in 2001, of being the firm to lose the most in shareholder value: $156 billion for the year. Furthermore, it lost $456 billion between March 2000 and December 2001. Although Cisco CEO John Chambers had been considered an excellent CEO, by the mid-2002, the firm's losses since early 2000, as well as its possible future prospects, caused some to begin questioning their view of Chambers's leadership. On a more positive note, it is fair to report that over its lifetime, Cisco has created significant wealth for its investors and managers; it ranks 11th overall in regard to wealth creation. Moreover, a study of 2001's business landscape shows that Cisco's performance in that year was not unlike that of many other U.S. companies, which lost a combined total of $2.5 trillion in shareholder wealth.[14]

In 2002, more than half of the top Canadian CEOs saw their pay jump an average of 17 percent. These increases occurred during a period when the S&P/TSX Composite Index fell 11 percent. As mentioned in the opening case, Vic De Zen (chair and CEO, Royal Group Technologies Ltd., Woodbridge, Ontario) received a pay increase of more than 80 percent while his company's stock fell to nearly half its former value and the company issued four profit warnings in a six-month timeframe. On the other hand, there were some high-profile Canadian CEOs who took a pay cut. Gerry Schwartz, chair, CEO and president of Onex, took home a total of $49.2 million in salary, bonuses, and stock option gains in 2001. In 2002, he took home $1 million in salary with no bonus and no option grants or any exercised options.[15]

Agency Relationships

An **agency relationship** exists when one or more persons (the principal or principals) hire another person or persons (the agent or agents) as decision-making specialists to perform a service.

The separation between owners and managers creates an agency relationship. An **agency relationship** exists when one or more persons (the principal or principals) hire another person or persons (the agent or agents) as decision-making specialists to perform a service. Thus, an agency relationship exists when one party delegates decision-making responsibility to a second party for compensation (see Figure 11.1). In addition to shareholders and top executives, other examples of agency relationships are consultants and clients, and insured and insurer. Moreover, within organizations, an agency relationship exists between managers and their employees, as well as between the firm's owners and its top executives. In the modern corporation, managers must understand the links between these relationships and the firm's effectiveness. Although the agency relation-

Figure 11.1 | An Agency Relationship

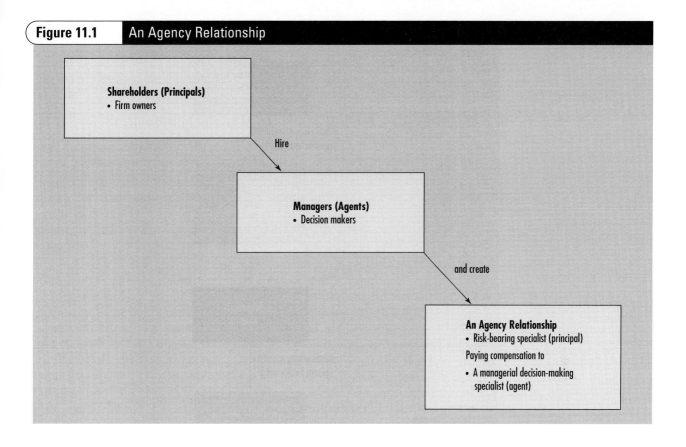

ship between managers and their employees is important, in this chapter we focus on the agency relationship between the firm's owners (the principals) and top-level managers (the principals' agents), because this relationship is related directly to how the firm's strategies are implemented.[16]

The separation between ownership and managerial control can be problematic. Research evidence indicates a variety of agency problems in the modern corporation.[17] Problems can surface because the principal and the agent have different interests and goals, or because shareholders lack direct control of large publicly traded corporations. Problems also arise when an agent makes decisions that result in the pursuit of goals that conflict with those of the principals. Firms that were previously owned by a single person but have since gone through an initial public offering (IPO) may see this problem exacerbated in the following manner. Sole owners, (i.e., CEOs/owners) are accustomed to making decisions that benefit themselves. However, after an IPO, these same CEOs have to make decisions that enhance the wealth of the many shareholders who now own the firm, not just themselves. Thus, the separation of ownership and control potentially allows divergent interests (between principals and agents) to surface, which can lead to managerial opportunism.

Managerial opportunism is the seeking of self-interest with guile (i.e., cunning or deceit). Opportunism is both an attitude (e.g., an inclination) and a set of behaviours (i.e., specific acts of self-interest). It is not possible for principals to know beforehand which agents will or will not act opportunistically. The reputations of top executives are an imperfect predictor, and opportunistic behaviour cannot be observed until it has occurred. Thus, principals establish governance and control mechanisms to prevent agents from acting opportunistically, even though theory suggests that only a few are

Managerial opportunism is the seeking of self-interest with guile (i.e., cunning or deceit).

likely to do so. Any time that principals delegate decision-making responsibilities to agents, the opportunity for conflicts of interest exists. Top executives, for example, may make strategic decisions that maximize their personal welfare and minimize their personal risk. Decisions such as these prevent the maximization of shareholder wealth. Decisions regarding product diversification demonstrate these possibilities.[18]

Product Diversification as an Example of an Agency Problem

As explained in Chapter 7, a corporate-level strategy to diversify the firm's product lines can enhance a firm's strategic competitiveness and increase its returns, both of which serve the interests of shareholders and the top executives. However, product diversification can result in two benefits to managers that shareholders do not enjoy, so top executives may prefer product diversification to a greater degree than do shareholders.[19]

First, diversification usually increases the size of a firm, and size is positively related to executive compensation. Also, diversification increases the complexity of managing both a firm and its network of businesses and may thus require greater compensation because of this complexity. Thus, increased product diversification provides an opportunity for top executives to increase their compensation.[20]

Second, product diversification and the resulting diversification of the firm's portfolio of businesses can reduce top executives' employment risk. Managerial employment risk includes the possibilities of job loss, loss of compensation, and loss of managerial reputation.[21] These risks are reduced with increased diversification, because a firm and its upper-level managers are less vulnerable to the reduction in demand associated with a limited number of product lines or businesses. For example, France-based Gemplus International named Antonio Perez as its CEO in 2000. With his 25-year career at Hewlett-Packard, Perez had a good reputation in the business world, and his Hewlett-Packard experience seemed to be perfect preparation for his new position. Gemplus is the world's top producer of smart cards, "microchip-embedded cards used for everything from phone calls to credit-card transactions," and is very focused on a narrow product market. Perez's appointment was met with outrage by the French media, because of the $97 million worth of stock and options he received when he was hired. When demand for the Gemplus smart cards dropped sharply with slowing sales of mobile phones that used Gemplus chips, the company, worth approximately $3 billion in December 2000, lost more than 65 percent of its worth in the ensuing 15 months. Perez cut his own pay by 20 percent, but his decision to cut some of the company's 7800-person workforce and the ensuing battle with Marc Lassus, company founder and chairman, led to both being forced to resign by the firm's major shareholders. Perez's employment risk was higher because the firm lacked significant product diversification, which is probably why he received significant compensation in the form of stock and options when he began his tenure with Gemplus.[22]

Another concern that may represent an agency problem is the control that top executives have over a firm's free cash flows. Free cash flows are resources remaining after the firm has invested in all projects that have positive net present values within its current businesses. In anticipation of positive returns, managers may decide to invest these funds in products that are not associated with the firm's current lines of business to increase the firm's level of diversification. The managerial decision to use free cash flows to overdiversify the firm is an example of self-serving and opportunistic managerial behaviour. In contrast to managers, shareholders may prefer that free cash flows be distributed as dividends, so they can control how the cash is invested.[23]

Curve S in Figure 11.2 on page 336 depicts the shareholders' optimal level of diversification. Owners seek the level of diversification that reduces the risk of the firm's total failure while simultaneously increasing the company's value through the development of economies of scale and scope (see Chapter 7). Of the four corporate-level diversification strategies shown in Figure 11.2, shareholders likely prefer the diversified position noted by point A on curve S—a position that is located between the dominant business and related-constrained diversification strategies. Of course, the optimum level of diversification owners seek varies from firm to firm.[24] Factors that affect shareholders' preferences include the firm's primary industry, the intensity of rivalry among competitors in that industry, and the top management team's experience with implementing diversification strategies.

As do principals, upper-level executives—as agents—also seek an optimal level of diversification. Declining performance resulting from too much product diversification increases the probability that corporate control of the firm will be acquired in the market. Once a firm is acquired, the employment risk for the firm's top executives increases substantially. Furthermore, a manager's employment opportunities in the external managerial labour market are affected negatively by a firm's poor performance. Therefore, top executives prefer diversification, but not to a point that it increases their employment risk and reduces their employment opportunities.[25] Curve M in Figure 11.2 shows that executives prefer higher levels of product diversification than shareholders. Top executives might prefer the level of diversification shown by point B on curve M.

In general, shareholders prefer riskier strategies and more focused diversification. They reduce their risk by holding a diversified portfolio of equity investments. Alternatively, managers obviously cannot balance their employment risk by working for a diverse portfolio of firms. Therefore, top executives may prefer a level of diversification that maximizes firm size and their compensation and reduces their employment risk. Product diversification, therefore, is a potential agency problem that could result in principals incurring costs to control their agents' behaviours.

Agency Costs and Governance Mechanisms

The potential conflict illustrated by Figure 11.2, coupled with the fact that principals do not know which managers might act opportunistically, demonstrates why principals establish governance mechanisms. However, the firm incurs costs when it uses one or more governance mechanisms. **Agency costs** are the sum of incentive costs, monitoring costs, enforcement costs, and individual financial losses incurred by principals, because governance mechanisms cannot guarantee total compliance by the agent. If a firm is diversified, governance costs increase because it is more difficult to monitor what is going on inside the firm.[26]

In general, managerial interests may prevail when governance mechanisms are weak, as is exemplified by allowing managers a significant amount of autonomy to make strategic decisions. If, however, the board of directors controls managerial autonomy, or if other strong governance mechanisms are used, the firm's strategies should better reflect the interests of the shareholders.

Recent research suggests that even using more governance mechanisms may produce major changes in strategies. In the 1980s, firms acquired unrelated businesses at approximately the same rate as they did in the 1960s, even though more governance mechanisms were employed in the 1980s. Thus, governance mechanisms are an imperfect means of controlling managerial opportunism. Alternatively, other current evidence suggests that active shareholders, especially institutional investors, are more willing to try to remove the CEO leading a firm that is performing poorly. The actions taken at Gemplus International, as explained above, demonstrate this willingness.[27]

A recent issue in Canada is the belief that good governance may be too costly. One business writer reported that while top Canadian executives are willing to accept new corporate governance rules, many also believe that the gains will be minimal. The majority of these executives expected the cost of higher governance standards to increase. Many believe that balancing the costs versus the perceived benefits to be gained is a grave concern for corporations.[28] The co-CEO of Power Corp. of Canada, Paul DesMarais, considers that

Agency costs are the sum of incentive costs, monitoring costs, enforcement costs, and individual financial losses incurred by principals, because governance mechanisms cannot guarantee total compliance by the agent.

Figure 11.2 | Manager and Shareholder Risk and Diversification

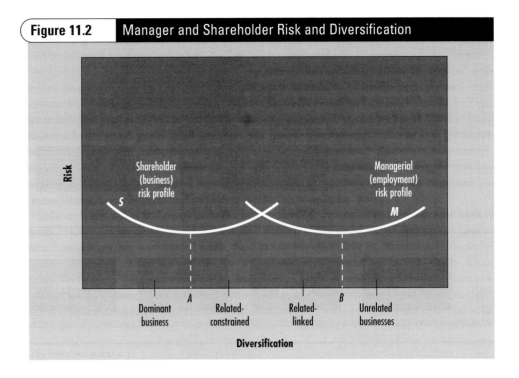

corporate governance concerns have reached hysterical proportions, and he is concerned many directors will not be willing to take the risks necessary to make their firms grow and prosper.[29] Next, we explain the effects of different governance mechanisms on the decisions managers make about the choice and the use of the firm's strategies.

Ownership Concentration

Ownership concentration is defined by both the number of large-block shareholders and the total percentage of shares they own.

Large-block shareholders typically own at least 10 percent of a corporation's issued shares.

Both the number of large-block shareholders and the total percentage of shares they own define **ownership concentration**. **Large-block shareholders** typically own at least 10 percent of a corporation's issued shares. (In the U.S., it is 5 percent.) Ownership concentration as a governance mechanism has received considerable interest because large-block shareholders are increasingly active in their demands that corporations adopt effective governance mechanisms to control managerial decisions.[30]

In general, diffuse ownership (a large number of shareholders with small holdings and few, if any, large-block shareholders) produces weak monitoring of managers' decisions. Among other problems, diffuse ownership makes it difficult for owners to effectively coordinate their actions. Diversification of the firm's product lines beyond the shareholders' optimum level might result from weak monitoring of managers' decisions. Higher levels of monitoring could encourage managers to avoid strategic decisions that do not create greater shareholder value. In fact, research evidence shows that ownership concentration is associated with lower levels of firm diversification.[31] Thus, with high degrees of ownership concentration, the probability is greater that managers' strategic decisions will be intended to maximize shareholder value.

Ownership concentration is a natural consequence of deregulated industries. For example, after the airline industry was deregulated, the ownership of the airlines became more concentrated. A similar pattern has occurred in the banking industry in the U.S., where there has been substantial consolidation through acquisitions. Much of this concentration has come from increasing equity ownership by institutional investors.[32]

The Growing Influence of Institutional Owners

A classic work published in the 1930s argued that the "modern" corporation had become characterized by a separation of ownership and control. This change occurred primarily because growth prevented founders–owners from maintaining their dual positions in their increasingly complex companies. More recently, another shift has occurred: ownership of many modern corporations is now concentrated in the hands of institutional investors rather than individual shareholders.[33]

Institutional owners are financial institutions such as stock mutual funds and pension funds that control large-block shareholder positions. Because of their prominent ownership positions, institutional owners, as large-block shareholders, are a powerful governance mechanism. Institutions of these types now own more than 50 percent of the stock in large U.S. corporations, and of the top 1000 corporations, they own, on average, 59 percent of the stock. Pension funds alone control at least one-half of corporate equity.[34] The Vancouver Fraser Institute estimates that from 65 percent to 70 percent of publicly traded stocks in Canada are owned by institutional investors.

> **Institutional owners** are financial institutions such as stock mutual funds and pension funds that control large-block shareholder positions.

These ownership percentages suggest that, as investors, institutional owners have both the size and the incentive to discipline ineffective top-level managers and can significantly influence a firm's choice of strategies and overall strategic decisions. Research evidence indicates that institutional and other large-block shareholders are becoming more active in their efforts to influence a corporation's strategic decisions. Initially, these shareholder activists and institutional investors concentrated on the performance and accountability of CEOs and contributed to the ouster of a number of them. They are now targeting what they believe are ineffective boards of directors.[35]

For example, at the 2004 annual general meeting of Magna International, it was expected that several institutional investors would withhold their votes as a protest against the 12-person board of directors. Three of these institutions were the Ontario Teachers' Pension Plan Board, the Royal Bank of Canada's investment arm, and Meritas Mutual Funds. They had earlier criticized chairman Frank Stronach's salary, the company's board of directors, and other governance issues. However, in the end, no shareholders discussed or opposed the appointees to the board. One long-time shareholder Denise Altman did indicate that she was unhappy with Stronach's $54 million salary in 2003, but only after she was asked about it by Stronach himself.[36]

In the U.S., the California Public Employees' Retirement System (CalPERS) provides retirement and health coverage to more than 1.3 million current and retired public employees. One of the largest public employee pension funds in the United States, CalPERS is generally thought to act aggressively to promote decisions and actions that it believes will enhance shareholder value in companies in which it invests. To pressure boards of directors to make what it believes are needed changes, CalPERS has advocated for board reform. In 1990, 66 percent of all directors on U.S. company boards were outsiders; by 2000, the level had risen to 78 percent. CalPERS believes that all but the CEO should be outsiders, "which translates into 92 percent of all company directors should be independent non-executives." The largest institutional investor, TIAA-CREF, has taken actions similar to those of CalPERS, but with a less publicly aggressive stance. To date, research suggests that these institutions' activism may not have a direct effect on firm performance, but that its influence may be indirect through its effects on important strategic decisions, such as those concerned with innovation.[37]

Shareholder Activism: How Much Is Possible?

As the earlier example regarding Magna International illustrates, sometimes shareholders find it hard to be activists in the area of corporate governance. In the U.S., the Securities and Exchange Commission (SEC) has issued several rulings that support shareholder involvement and control of managerial decisions. For example, the SEC eased its rule regarding communications among shareholders. Historically, shareholders could communicate among themselves only through a cumbersome and expensive filing process. Now, with a simple notification to the SEC of an upcoming meeting, shareholders can convene to discuss a corporation's strategic direction. If consensus exists on an issue, shareholders can vote as a block. The Internet has facilitated proxy battles because "the web makes it easier and cheaper to contact and organize other investors."[38]

Some argue that greater latitude should be extended to those managing the funds of large institutional investor groups; if fund managers were allowed to hold positions on boards of firms in which their organizations have significant investments, they might be able to better represent the interests of those they serve. However, the actions of traditionally activist institutional investor CalPERS were potentially compromised by its investments in Enron. Institutional activism should create a premium for companies with good corporate governance. However, trustees for these funds sometimes have other relationships that compromise their effectiveness. It is more often the case that large *private* pension funds, which have other business relationships with companies in their fund's portfolio, reduce effective monitoring.[39]

Also, the degree to which institutional investors can effectively monitor the decisions being made in all of the companies in which they have investments is questionable. Given limited resources, even large-block shareholders tend to concentrate on corporations in which they have significant investments. Thus, although shareholder activism has increased, institutional investors face barriers to the amount of active governance they can realistically employ. One major barrier may be the amount of stock owned in a firm. If the amount is substantial, selling the stock to punish the board and senior managers may reduce the proceeds because selling the stock could depress the stock's price. Furthermore, at times, activist institutional shareholders may have conflicting goals. Other means of corporate governance are needed.[40]

Besides institutional owners, other owners are able to influence the decisions that managers make as agents. Although other investors have significant influence, institutional investors are currently such significant shareholders that battles are not likely to be won or lost unless they are involved.

Corporate governance may also by affected by the recent phenomenon of increased managerial ownership of the firm's stock. There are many positive reasons for managerial ownership, including the use of stock options to link managerial pay to the performance of a firm. However, an unexpected outcome of managerial ownership has been reduced support for shareholder-sponsored proposals to repeal anti-takeover provisions. Institutional owners generally support the repeal of these provisions because shareholder wealth is typically increased if a takeover is offered, while managerial owners, whose jobs are at risk if a takeover is executed, generally oppose their repeal. Thus, managerial ownership provides managers with power to protect their own interests.[41]

Board of Directors

Typically, shareholders monitor the managerial decisions and actions of a firm through the board of directors. Shareholders elect members to their firm's board. Those who are elected are expected to oversee managers and to ensure that the corporation is operated in ways that will maximize its shareholders' wealth. As we have described, the practices of large institutional investors have resulted in an increase in ownership concentration in Canadian and U.S. firms. Nonetheless, diffuse ownership still describes the status of most Canadian and U.S. firms, which means that monitoring and control of managers by individual shareholders is limited in large corporations. Furthermore, large financial institutions, such as banks, are prevented from directly owning stock in firms and from having representatives on companies' boards of directors, although this is not the case in Europe and elsewhere. These conditions highlight the importance of the board of directors for corporate governance. Unfortunately, over time, boards of directors have not always been highly effective in monitoring and controlling top management's actions. However, while boards of directors are imperfect, they can positively influence both managers and the companies they serve.[42]

The **board of directors** is a group of elected individuals whose primary responsibility is to act in the owners' interests by formally monitoring and controlling the corporation's top-level executives. Boards have power to direct the affairs of the organization, punish and reward managers, and protect shareholders' rights and interests. Thus, an appropriately structured and effective board of directors protects owners from managerial opportunism. Board members are seen as stewards of their company's resources, and the way they carry out these responsibilities affects the society in which their firm operates.[43]

A fair division of responsibility is for the senior management team, led by the CEO, to recommend strategic actions to the board, for the board to approve these strategic actions, for the CEO and the senior management team to implement the strategic actions, and for the board to monitor this implementation. Some consider this a problem when the chair of the board and the CEO are the same person, as such CEOs are placed in a position of having to monitor and assess themselves. Others agree with the CEO and chair being the same person, as it means that there is unity of command and no doubt in anyone's mind as to who is responsible for the firm's performance. The preponderance of opinion seems to be for having two different people in these positions to avoid even the appearance of a conflict. When the same person fills the positions of CEO and board chair, some boards appoint a lead director who chairs meetings when the CEO/chair is absent.

Generally, board members (often called directors) are classified into one of three groups (see Table 11.3 on page 340). *Insiders* are active top-level managers in the corporation who are elected to the board because they are a source of information about the firm's day-to-day operations. Examples are the CEO, the chief operating officer, and the chief financial officer. *Related outsiders* have some relationship with the firm, contractual or otherwise, that may create questions about their independence, but these individuals are not involved with the corporation's day-to-day activities. Examples are lawyers from the firm's external legal counsel or CEOs of firms that are large customers. *Outsiders* provide independent counsel to the firm and may hold top-level managerial positions in other companies or may have been elected to the board prior to the beginning of the current CEO's tenure. Members who were elected before the current CEO's tenure are considered to be more independent than those appointed during the CEO's tenure.[44]

Some argue that many boards are not fulfilling their primary fiduciary duty to protect shareholders. Among other possibilities, it may be that boards are a managerial tool: they do not question managers' actions, and they readily approve managers' self-serving initiatives. In general, those critical of boards as a governance mechanism believe that inside managers dominate boards and exploit their personal ties with them. A widely accepted view is that a board with a significant percentage of its membership from the firm's top executives tends to provide relatively weak monitoring and control of managerial decisions.[45] Critics advocate reforms to ensure that independent outside directors represent a significant majority of the total membership of a board.

Because successful high-tech start-up firms usually operate in a dynamic environment, they often have strong entrepreneurial leaders or founders who guide them through rapid changes. However, such entrepreneurs often put together weak boards of directors. By creating strong boards with independent outsiders who can help foster the entrepreneurial spirit, such high-flying firms can maintain their momentum and

The **board of directors** is a group of elected individuals whose primary responsibility is to act in the owners' interests by formally monitoring and controlling the corporation's top-level executives.

Table 11.3	Classifications of Boards of Directors' Members

Insiders
- The firm's CEO and other top-level managers

Related outsiders
- Individuals not involved with the firm's day-to-day operations, but who have a relationship with the company

Outsiders
- Individuals who are independent of the firm in terms of day-to-day operations and other relationships

profitability if and when their founders leave. Some examples of these strong leaders are Jeff Bezos at Amazon, Stephen Case at AOL Time Warner, and Bill Gates at Microsoft.[46]

One criticism of boards has been that some have not been vigilant enough in hiring and then monitoring the behaviour of CEOs. For example, Albert Dunlap, the former CEO at Sunbeam, agreed to settle, out of his own pocket, a $15 million shareholder lawsuit brought against him (and other former executives). A number of questionable acquisitions had been made by the Dunlap team, ultimately spreading the company too thin and causing Sunbeam to file for Chapter 11 bankruptcy. Although Dunlap and his colleagues claimed that they did nothing wrong, there were significant performance problems, and the accounting at the company lacked transparency. The Sunbeam board must share the blame in the failure for two reasons. First, it selected the CEO. Second, the board should have been actively involved in the development of the firm's strategy—if the strategy fails, the board has failed.[47]

Other issues, in addition to criticisms of their work, affect today's corporate boards. For example, there is some disagreement about the most appropriate role of outside directors in a firm's strategic decision-making process. Because of external pressures, board reforms have been initiated. To date, these reforms have generally called for an increase in the number of outside directors, relative to insiders, serving on a corporation's board. For example, the New York Stock Exchange requires that listed firms have board audit committees composed solely of outside directors. In Canada, the Dey Report on Corporate Governance suggested establishing a separate audit committee composed only of outsiders.[48] As a result of external pressures, boards of large corporations have more outside members. Research shows that outside board members can influence the strategic direction of companies. Therefore, there are potential strategic implications associated with the movement toward having corporate boards dominated by outsiders.[49]

Alternatively, a large number of outside board members can create some issues. Outsiders do not have contact with the firm's day-to-day operations and typically do not have easy access to the level of information about managers and their skills that is required to effectively evaluate managerial decisions and initiatives. Outsiders can, however, obtain valuable information through frequent interactions with inside board members, during board meetings and otherwise. Insiders possess such information by virtue of their organizational positions. Thus, boards with a critical mass of insiders typically are better informed about intended strategic initiatives, the reasons for the initiatives, and the outcomes expected from them. Without this type of information, outsider-dominated boards may emphasize the use of financial, as opposed to strategic, controls to gather performance information to evaluate managers' and business units' performances. A virtually exclusive reliance on financial evaluations shifts risk to top-level managers, who, in turn, may make decisions to maximize their own interests and reduce their own employment risk. Reductions in R&D investments, additional diversification of the firm, and the pursuit of greater levels of compensation are some of the results of managers' actions to achieve financial goals set by outsider dominated boards.[50]

Enhancing the Effectiveness of the Board of Directors

Because of the importance of boards of directors in corporate governance and the increased scrutiny from shareholders—in particular, large institutional investors—the performances of both individual board members and entire boards are being evaluated more formally and with greater intensity. Given the demand for greater accountability and improved performance, many boards have initiated voluntary changes. Among these changes are (1) increased diversity in the backgrounds of board members (e.g., a greater number of directors from public service, academic, and scientific settings; a greater percentage of boards with ethnic minorities and women; and members from different countries on boards of Canadian and U.S. firms that operate internationally), (2) the strengthening of internal management and accounting control systems, and (3) the establishment and consistent use of formal processes to evaluate the board's performance.[51]

Because boards have become more involved in the strategic decision-making process, they must work collaboratively. Research shows that boards working collaboratively make higher quality strategic decisions, and they make them faster. Sometimes, there is conflict among board members regarding the appropriate strategic direction for a company. In addition, because of the increased pressure from owners and the potential conflict, procedures are necessary to help boards function effectively in facilitating the strategic decision-making process.[52]

Besides being increasingly involved in important strategic decisions, boards also are becoming more active in expressing their views about CEO succession, as opposed to readily supporting the incumbent's choice. In general, however, boards have relied on precedence (past decisions) for guidance in the selection process. Also, they are most likely to consider inside candidates before looking for outside candidates. Outside directors have the power to facilitate the firm's transition to a new CEO. When an internal, heir apparent CEO-candidate is associated with a high-performing firm, outside directors are likely to help the heir apparent make the transition. However, if firm performance is problematic, outside directors are less likely to support the chosen successor and are often skeptical of someone chosen to follow in the footsteps of the former CEO.[53]

Increasingly, outside directors are being required to own significant equity stakes as a prerequisite to holding a board seat. In fact, some research suggests that firms perform better if outside directors have such a stake. Another study suggests that the performance of inside directors also improves if they hold an equity position. Therefore, an inside director's knowledge of the firm can be used appropriately. Finally, an inside director's relationship to the CEO does not necessarily lead to entrenchment of that CEO if the inside director has a strong ownership position. One activist concludes that boards need three foundational characteristics to be effective: director stock ownership, executive meetings to discuss important strategic issues, and a serious nominating committee that truly controls the nomination process to strongly influence the selection of new board members.[54]

An issue surfacing in Canada in recent years is whether high-quality candidates are going to continue to be willing to serve on boards. One business writer reported that Jay Taylor, CEO of Placer Dome Ltd., was not keen on being a director after he retired as CEO. Apparently, Taylor saw the role as 90 percent governance and stated that he did not have the traffic cop mentality needed to do the job. He said that, "Watching people and looking for infractions and fraud and embezzlement is not what it's all about for me."[55]

Executive Compensation

As the opening case illustrates, the compensation of top-level managers, especially CEOs, generates a great deal of interest and strongly held opinions. (See also the Strategic Focus box "CEO Compensation: A Big Deal" on page 346.) One reason for this widespread interest can be traced to a natural curiosity about extremes and excesses. Another stems from the more substantive view that CEO pay is tied in an indirect but very tangible way to the fundamental governance processes in large corporations: Who has power? What are the bases of power? How and when do owners and managers exert their relative preferences? How vigilant are boards? Who is taking advantage of whom?[56]

Executive compensation is a governance mechanism that seeks to align the interests of managers and owners through salaries, bonuses, and long-term incentive compensation, such as stock options. Stock options are a mechanism used to link executives' performance to the performance of their company's stock. Increasingly, long-term incentive plans are becoming a critical part of compensation packages in Canadian and U.S. firms. The use of longer term pay helps firms cope with or avoid potential agency problems. Because of this approach, the stock market generally reacts positively to the introduction of a long-range incentive plan for top executives.[57]

Sometimes the use of a long-term incentive plan prevents major stockholders (e.g., institutional investors) from pressing for changes in the composition of the board of directors, because they assume that the long-term incentives will ensure that top executives will act in shareholders' best interests. Alternatively, stockholders largely assume that top-executive pay and the performance of a firm are more closely aligned when firms have boards that are dominated by outside members.[58]

Effectively using executive compensation as a governance mechanism is particularly challenging to firms implementing international strategies. For example, the interests of owners of multinational corporations may be best served when there is less uniformity among the firm's foreign subsidiaries' compensation plans. Developing an array of unique compensation plans requires additional monitoring and increases the firm's agency costs. Importantly, levels of pay vary by regions of the world. For example, managers in the United States receive the highest compensation, while it is somewhat lower in Canada and much lower in Asia. Compensation is lower in India partly because many of the largest firms have strong family ownership and control. As corporations acquire firms in other countries, the managerial compensation puzzle becomes more complex and may cause additional executive turnover. For instance, when Daimler-Benz acquired Chrysler, the top executives of Chrysler made substantially more than the executives at Daimler-Benz—but the Chrysler executives ended up reporting to the Daimler executives.[59]

A Complicated Governance Mechanism

For several reasons, executive compensation—especially long-term incentive compensation—is complicated. First, the strategic decisions made by top-level managers are typically complex and nonroutine, so direct supervision of executives is inappropriate for judging the quality of their decisions. The result is a tendency to link the compensation of top-level managers to measurable outcomes, such as the firm's financial performance. Second, an executive's decision often affects a firm's financial outcomes over an extended period, making it difficult to assess the effect of current decisions on the corporation's performance. In fact, strategic decisions are more likely to have long-term, rather than short-term, effects on a company's strategic outcomes. Third, a number of other factors affect a firm's performance besides top-level managerial decisions and behaviour. Unpredictable economic, social, or legal changes (see Chapter 3) make it difficult to discern the effects of strategic decisions. Thus, although performance-based

Executive compensation is a governance mechanism that seeks to align the interests of managers and owners through salaries, bonuses, and long-term incentive compensation, such as stock options.

compensation may provide incentives to top management teams to make decisions that best serve shareholders' interests, such compensation plans, alone, are imperfect in their ability to monitor and control managers. Still, annual bonuses, as incentive compensation, represent a significant portion of many executives' total pay. For example, in a 1999 study, annual bonuses composed an average of about 60 percent of the CEO's total compensation in the United States, about 45 percent in the United Kingdom, approximately 30 percent in Canada, while only 19 percent in France.[60] A more recent look at a specific year (2002) in Canada saw annual bonuses at 14.3 percent of total compensation for the 25 highest paid CEOs.[61]

Although incentive compensation plans may increase the value of a firm in line with shareholder expectations, such plans are subject to managerial manipulation. For instance, annual bonuses may provide incentives to pursue short-run objectives at the expense of the firm's long-term interests. Supporting this conclusion, some research has found that bonuses based on annual performance were negatively related to investments in R&D when the firm was highly diversified, which may affect the firm's long-term strategic competitiveness. In high-tech firms, where uncertainty is higher, short-term (salary and bonus) compensation was related to innovation, but no such relationship was found in low-tech firms. However, no relationship between innovation and long-term compensation was found among either high-tech or low-tech firms.[62]

Although long-term, performance-based incentives may reduce the temptation to underinvest in the short run, they increase executive exposure to risks associated with uncontrollable events, such as market fluctuations and industry decline. The longer the focus of incentive compensation, the greater the long-term risks borne by top-level managers. Also, because long-term incentives tie a manager's overall wealth to the firm in a way that is inflexible, such incentives and ownership may not be valued as highly by a manager as by outside investors who have the opportunity to diversify their wealth in a number of other financial investments.[63] Thus, firms may have to overcompensate managers using long-term incentives, especially stock options, as the next section suggests.

The Effectiveness of Executive Compensation

The compensation recently received by some top-level managers, especially CEOs, has angered many stakeholders, including shareholders. Table 11.4 lists the compensation received by the highest paid Canadian CEOs in 2002, and Table 11.5 shows the largest value of stock options for Canadian CEOs for the year (see page 344 for both). As the tables show, Frank Stronach had both the highest valued stock options and the highest total compensation.[64]

As Tables 11.4 and 11.5 indicate, stock and stock options are a primary component of large compensation packages. This trend is likely to continue in the 21st century, partly because of the long-term incentive plans that compensate executives in stock options and stock.[65]

The primary reason for compensating executives in stock is that the practice affords them with an incentive to keep the stock price high and hence aligns managers' interests with shareholders' interests. However, there may be some unintended consequences. Managers who own greater than 1 percent of their firm's stock may be less likely to be forced out of their jobs, even when the firm is performing poorly. Furthermore, a review of the research suggests "that firm size accounts for more than 40 percent of the variance in total CEO pay, while firm performance accounts for less than 5 percent of the variance."[66] Thus, the effectiveness of pay plans as a governance mechanism is suspect.

Another way that boards may choose to compensate executives is through loans with either a favourable interest rate or no interest rate, for the purpose of buying company stock. If appropriately used, this practice can be a governance tool, since it aligns executives'

Table 11.4   Highest Paid Canadian CEOs, 2002

Name	Company	Total Compensation
Frank Stronach, chair	Magna International Inc.	$52,124,000
Robert Burton, chair/CEO/pres	Moore Corp. Ltd.	$20,926,946
Richard George, CEO/pres	Suncor Energy Inc.	$16,273,375
Conrad Black, chair/CEO	Hollinger International	$15,836,628
Pierre Lessard, CEO/pres	Metro Inc.	$15,275,200
Gwyn Morgan, CEO/pres	EnCana Corp.	$13,133,116
Travis Engen, CEO/pres	Alcan Inc.	$11,356,775
Peter Godsoe, chair/CEO	Bank of Nova Scotia	$10,446,908
Gordon Nixon, CEO/pres	Royal Bank of Canada	$9,706,233
Joe Houssian, chair/CEO/pres	Intrawest Corp.	$9,371,629
Paul Tellier, CEO/pres	Canadian National Railway	$9,333,588
Jean Monty, chair/CEO	BCE Inc.	$8,832,730
Vic De Zen, chair/CEO	Royal Group Technologies	$8,541,548
Tony Comper, chair/CEO	Bank of Montreal	$8,423,530
Dominic D'Alessandro, CEO/pres	Manulife Financial Corp.	$8,321,400

Note: Compensation includes salary, bonuses, "other" compensation, and an estimate of the present value of options grants.
SOURCE: From "High on the hog" by J. Gray in *Canadian Business*, May 12, 2003, 41–44. Reprinted with permission.

Table 11.5   Largest Options Grants, 2002

Name	Company	Option Value (millions)
Frank Stronach, chair	Magna International Inc.	$0
Robert Burton, chair/CEO/pres	Moore Corp. Ltd.	$0
Richard George, CEO/pres	Suncor Energy Inc.	$3,614,820
Conrad Black, chair/CEO	Hollinger International	$1,956,836
Pierre Lessard, CEO/pres	Metro Inc.	$14,025,000
Gwyn Morgan, CEO/pres	EnCana Corp.	$4,351,500
Travis Engen, CEO/pres	Alcan Inc.	$6,804,075
Peter Godsoe, chair/CEO	Bank of Nova Scotia	$4,589,550
Gordon Nixon, CEO/pres	Royal Bank of Canada	$3,904,245
Joe Houssian, chair/CEO/pres	Intrawest Corp.	$2,407,500
Paul Tellier, CEO/pres	Canadian National Railway	$6,910,200
Jean Monty, chair/CEO	BCE Inc.	$6,513,000
Vic De Zen, chair/CEO	Royal Group Technologies	$2,400,000
Tony Comper, chair/CEO	Bank of Montreal	$5,116,749
Dominic D'Alessandro, CEO/pres	Manulife Financial Corp.	$4.679,992

SOURCE: From "High on the hog" by J. Gray in *Canadian Business*, May 12, 2003, 41–44. Reprinted with permission.

priorities with the shareholders: executives hold stock, not just options on the stock, gaining or losing money along with the shareholders. "When people exercise most stock options, they pay the regular income-tax rate—close to 45 to 50 percent for executives—on the difference between the option's exercise price and the share price at that time. But if executives buy shares with borrowed money instead of receiving options, the government considers their profit to be an investment gain, not a part of their salary, and they pay only the capital-gains tax of 20 percent or less."[67] Despite the positive benefits of providing loans for buying stock, the practice can be devastating if the value of the stock falls.

To foster improved performances from their companies during the recessionary year 2001, many boards in the U.S. granted more stock options to executives than they had in the past. This trend of increasing stock options to compensate managers after a bad year seems to run counter to the concept of pay for performance. For example, Larry Ellison, CEO of Oracle, cashed in options for 23 million shares of stock worth $700 million in January 2001. To make good on these options and provide Ellison with 23 million shares, Oracle must issue that many new shares of stock, repurchase that amount from investors, or do a combination of the two. No matter which approach Oracle takes, shareholder value or available cash decreases (this phenomenon is often called shareholder dilution).

While some stock option–based compensation plans are well designed with option strike prices substantially higher than current stock prices, too many plans have been designed simply to give executives more wealth that will not immediately show up on the balance sheet. Research of stock option repricing, where the strike price value of the option has been changed to lower than it was originally set, suggests that such a step is taken more frequently in high-risk situations. However, it is also used to restore the incentive effect for the option when firm performance has been poor. But evidence also suggests that politics are often involved. Again, this evidence shows that no internal governance mechanism is perfect.[68]

Market for Corporate Control

The **market for corporate control** is an external governance mechanism that becomes active when a firm's internal controls fail.[69] The market for corporate control is composed of individuals and firms that buy ownership positions in, or take over, potentially undervalued corporations so they can form new divisions in established diversified companies or merge two previously separate firms. Because the undervalued firm's executives are assumed to be the party responsible for formulating and implementing the strategy that led to poor performance, that team is usually replaced. For instance, HP has performed better than Compaq recently, and the merger between the two firms may turn out to be controlled by HP. Thus, when the market for corporate control operates effectively, it ensures that managers who are ineffective or act opportunistically are disciplined.[70]

The market for corporate control governance mechanism should be triggered by a firm's poor performance, relative to industry competitors. A firm's poor performance, often demonstrated by the firm earning below-average returns, is an indicator that internal governance mechanisms have failed; that is, their use did not result in managerial decisions that maximized shareholder value.

In North America, the market for corporate control has been active for some time. The 1980s were known as a time of merger mania in the U.S., with almost 55,000 acquisitions valued at approximately $1.3 trillion. However, there were many more acquisitions in the 1990s, and the value of mergers and acquisitions in that decade was more than $10 trillion.[71] During an economic downturn, unsolicited takeover bids increase because poorly managed firms are more easily identified.[72]

Managerial Defence Tactics

Hostile takeovers are the major activity in the market for corporate control governance mechanism. Not all hostile takeovers are prompted by poorly performing targets, and firms targeted for hostile takeovers may use multiple defense tactics to fend off the

The **market for corporate control** is an external governance mechanism that becomes active when a firm's internal controls fail.

CEO Compensation: A Big Deal

With the increased scrutiny on corporate leadership, CEO roles, responsibility, and compensation have received their fair share of commentary by many business writers. Many argue that CEO compensation does not necessarily reflect company performance during the year.

In an apparent attempt to turn things around and change the perceived excesses in executive compensation, the 2003 proxy period proceeded with a significant number of shareholder proposals aimed specifically at executive compensation. Proposals appeared to target compensation in its totality, including pay, bonuses, stock option packages, and the composition of CEO pay among these three areas. Several writers commented on the negative publicity received by executive compensation—in particular, CEO compensation—which became the subject of several calls for reform.

The rationale behind the calls for reform varied, depending on the issuing group, and included the social engineer perspective (pay is too high in relation to that of the ordinary employee), the financial engineer perspective (pay is not linked effectively to economic performance), and the legal engineer perspective (the process of setting CEO pay is not sufficiently objective nor independent).

What exactly do compensation packages look like, and why all the attention? A quick look shows Manulife CEO Dominic D'Alessandro, received approximately $7.5 million in 2003, a figure more than double his prior package. A spokesperson for Manulife Financial Corporation explained that D'Alessandro gets paid for performance, and the company performed extremely well that year. However, increases in excess of 100 percent are likely to draw attention.

Frank Weise, the outgoing CEO of the Canadian soft-drink maker Cott Corp., made nearly $22 million in 2003, including about 2 million in base salary and bonus payments; Dan O'Neill, CEO of Molson Inc., took home $18.8 million in the same year; and, in an extreme and history-making example, the CEO of Power Financial Corp., Robert Gratton, exercised stock options for a gain of about $170 million in early 2004. In each of the given examples, compensation packages included significant stock option components.

Despite the noise in the trenches, or perhaps because of it, there are several companies that sought to control or better align executive compensation with firm performance. Among these was Magna International Inc. Magna's board compensation committee, in response to criticisms (regarding what was perceived as insufficient justification for the pay of founder and chairman Frank Stronach) arising from the stockholders' review of the annual management proxy circular, went to great lengths to justify the executive raises. The committee's response included detailed explanations of revised pay policies and indications that expectations had been instituted that Stronach was expected to meet for the 2004 fiscal period.

In another example, Gwyn Morgan, the president and chief executive officer of EnCana Corporation (an oil and gas company), took a 14 percent pay cut in fiscal 2003. His pay packet dropped from $10.1 million in 2002 to $8.65 million in 2003 (both including option gains and long-term pay units). In contrast, at other Calgary-based oil and gas companies, pay packets increased. For examples, at Enbridge Inc., president and CEO Patrick Daniel's pay packet more than doubled, while at Talisman Energy Inc., president and CEO James Buckee's compensation increased by 41 percent. Encana's stock price on the TSX rose 5 percent during the year, while Enbridge shares rose 26 percent, and Talisman jumped 29 percent.

SOURCES: J. G. Kaiser, 2001, Compensation literacy and other fires to be lit under boards, *Directors & Boards*, fall, 26; R. H. Rock, 2003, Comping the CEO, *Directors & Boards*, spring, 27; Korn/Ferry International, 2003, Fortune 1000 board members are turning down directorships at twice the rate of last year due to personal liability risk, *Canadian Corporate News*, October 28; G. Keenan, 2004, Magna Entertainment CEO got $200,000 bonus last year, *Globe and Mail Report on Business*, April 7, B5; S. Stewart, 2004, Manulife CEO's pay doubled last year, *Globe and Mail Report on Business*, April 2; R. Bloom, 2004, Cott CEO among top earners in Canada, *Globe and Mail Report on Business*, April 1; G. Keenan, 2004, Stronach's pay rose last year: Board went to great lengths to justify raise, *Globe and Mail Report on Business*, April 1; B. Jang, 2004, EnCana CEO's pay cut 14% in '03: Morgan's total package reduced to $8.65-million, *Globe and Mail Report on Business*, March 30.

takeover attempt. Historically, the increased use of the market for corporate control has enhanced the sophistication and variety of managerial defence tactics that are used to reduce the influence of this governance mechanism. The market for corporate control tends to increase risk for managers. As a result, managerial pay is often augmented indirectly through golden parachutes (a practice by which CEOs can receive up to three years' salary if their firm is taken over).

Among other outcomes, takeover defences increase the costs of mounting a takeover, causing the incumbent management to become entrenched, while reducing the chances of introducing a new management team. Some defence tactics require asset restructuring created by divesting one or more divisions in the diversified firm's portfolio. Others necessitate only changes in the financial structure of the firm, such as repurchasing shares of the firm's outstanding stock.[73] Some tactics (e.g., reincorporation of the firm in another state) require shareholder approval, but the greenmail tactic, wherein money is used to repurchase stock from a corporate raider to avoid the takeover of the firm, does not. These defence tactics are controversial, and research on their effects is inconclusive, despite opposition of their use by most institutional investors.

A potential problem with the market for corporate control is that it may not be totally efficient. A study of several of the most active corporate raiders in the U.S. in the 1980s showed that approximately 50 percent of their takeover attempts targeted firms with above-average performance in their industry—corporations that were neither undervalued nor poorly managed. The targeting of high-performance businesses may lead to both acquisitions at premium prices and decisions by managers of the targeted firm to establish what may prove to be costly takeover defence tactics to protect their corporate positions.[74]

Although the market for corporate control lacks the precision of internal governance mechanisms, the fear of acquisition and influence by corporate raiders is an effective constraint on the managerial-growth motive. The market for corporate control has been responsible for significant changes in many firms' strategies and, when used appropriately, has served shareholders' interests.[75] But this market and other means of corporate governance vary by world region and by country. Accordingly, we next address the topic of international corporate governance.

Global Corporate Governance

Understanding the corporate governance structure of Canada and the United States is inadequate for a multinational firm in today's global economy.[76] The 21st-century competitive landscape is fostering the creation of a relatively uniform governance structure that will be used by firms throughout the world.[77] As markets become more global and customer demands become more similar, shareholders are becoming the focus of managers' efforts in an increasing number of companies. Investors are growing more and more active throughout the world.

Changes in governance are evident in many countries and are moving the governance models closer to that of Canada and the United States. For example, in France, very little information about top executives' compensation has traditionally been provided. However, this practice has come under pressure with increasing foreign investment in French companies. One report recommended that the positions of CEO and chairman of the board be held by different individuals; it also recommended reducing the tenure of board members and disclosing their pay. In South Korea, changes went much further. Principles of corporate governance were adopted that "provide proper incentives for the board and management to pursue objectives that are in the interests of the company and the shareholders and facilitate effective monitoring, thereby encouraging firms to use resources more efficiently."[78]

Even in transitional economies, such as those of China and Russia, changes in corporate governance are occurring. In 1999 and 2000, several state-owned enterprises, such as China National Petroleum Corporation and the Unicom Group, restructured to allow a subsidiary (PetroChina and China Unicom, respectively) to be publicly listed on the New York Stock Exchange and the Hong Kong Stock Exchange. In addition to raising much needed capital, these initiatives were instituted to bring corporate governance in line with the corporate governance practices in more developed economies. Also, Chinese firms have found it helpful to use stock-based compensation plans, thereby providing an incentive for foreign companies to invest in China. Because Russia has reduced controls on the economy and on business activity much faster than China has, the country needs more effective governance systems to control its managerial activities. In fact, research suggests that ownership concentration leads to lower performance in Russia, primarily because minority shareholder rights are not well protected through adequate governance controls.[79]

Governance Mechanism and Ethical Behaviour

The governance mechanisms described in this chapter are designed to ensure that the agents of the firm's owners—the corporation's top executives—make strategic decisions that best serve the interests of the entire group of stakeholders, as described in Chapter 1. In Canada and the United States, shareholders are recognized as a company's most significant stakeholder. Thus, governance mechanisms focus on the control of managerial decisions to ensure that shareholders' interests will be served, but product market stakeholders (e.g., customers, suppliers, and host communities) and organizational stakeholders (e.g., managerial and nonmanagerial employees) are important as well.[80] Therefore, at least the minimal interests or needs of all stakeholders must be satisfied through the firm's actions. Otherwise, dissatisfied stakeholders will withdraw their support from one firm and provide it to another (e.g., customers will purchase products from a supplier offering an acceptable substitute).

A firm's strategic competitiveness is enhanced when its governance mechanisms take into consideration the interests of all stakeholders. Although the idea is subject to debate, some believe that ethically responsible companies design and use governance mechanisms that serve all stakeholders' interests. There is, however, a more critical relationship between ethical behaviour and corporate governance mechanisms. The Strategic Focus box "Nortel: The Importance of Ethics in Governance" illustrates the devastating effect of poor ethical behaviour on a firm's stakeholders, including the Canadian economy, given Nortel's size relative to the Canadian economy.

In addition, as the Strategic Focus box demonstrates, all corporate owners are vulnerable to unethical behaviours by their employees, including top-level managers—the agents who have been hired to make decisions that are in the shareholders' best interests. The decisions and actions of a corporation's board of directors can be an effective deterrent to these behaviours. In fact, some believe that the most effective boards participate actively to set boundaries for their firms' business ethics and values.[81] Once formulated, the board's expectations related to ethical decisions and actions of all of the firm's stakeholders must be clearly communicated to its top-level managers. Moreover, as shareholders' agents, these managers must understand that the board will hold them fully accountable for the development and support of an organizational culture that results in ethical decisions and behaviours. As explained in Chapter 13, CEOs can be positive role models for ethical behaviour.

Only when the proper corporate governance is exercised can strategies be formulated and implemented that will help the firm achieve strategic competitiveness and earn above-average returns. As the discussion in this chapter suggests, corporate governance mechanisms are a vital, yet imperfect, part of firms' efforts to select and successfully use strategies.

Nortel: The Importance of Ethics in Governance

In late April 2004, Nortel Networks fired three of its top executives "for cause." Fired were CEO Frank Dunn, CFO Douglas Beatty and controller Michael Gollogly. Around the same time, Nortel suspended with pay four divisional finance officials, after Nortel was plunged into an accounting scandal. These officials were Doug Hamilton of Optical Networks, Craig Johnson of Wireline Networks, James Kinney of Wireless Networks, and Ken Taylor of Enterprise Networks. Nortel announced that it would have to restate its financial results for the past several years and that its profit for 2003 would be cut in half, to $366 million (U.S.) from the $732 million (U.S.) it had reported in January 2004. This would be the second time in less than a year that Nortel would have to restate several years of results. Nortel hired William Owen, former vice-chief of the Joint Chiefs of Staff in the U.S. military to replace former CEO Frank Dunn.

The accounting scandal had several ramifications that illustrate the importance of ethics in governance. A drop in the Canadian dollar was linked to the accounting scandal. The dollar dropped $0.31 against the U.S. dollar—the greatest single-day drop in 20 years. The TSX Index, which was heavily influenced by changes in Nortel's stock, dropped 3.5 percent. Nortel's stock dropped $2.32 from $5.26, seriously affecting the wealth of Nortel's shareholders. Nortel's bond-holders had the right to issue a notice of default, since, as of May 2004, Nortel had not filed official 2003 results. Bondholders of a small $150 million (U.S.) bond due in 2026 had seen their bond trading at about $0.92 on the dollar.

Nortel needed to obtain a waiver from Export Development Canada (EDC) to not have to pay back $326 million by May 29, 2004, because of the late filing of 2003 results. One analyst suggested that EDC would pull its support, leaving Nortel to put up its own cash. Nortel had about $3.6 billion in cash with $3.9 billion in long-term debt at that time. The analyst argued that Nortel would have to look for a new line of credit even though the threat of having to pay back the debt was very low. He suggested that Nortel would have to reassure debtholders and investors that the company had the ability to repay debt even in a worst case scenario. A Nortel spokesperson said that Nortel had requested a new waiver from EDC and had not received any notices from debtholders.

The three senior executives mentioned above had all of their outstanding stock options cancelled. Frank Dunn, CEO, had 2.25 million stock options revoked because of his termination for cause; CFO Doug Beatty lost 435,000 stock options, while controller Michael Gollogly lost 78,000 stock options.

In related news, Nortel was subpoenaed to produce documents, which included accounting records going back more than four years, as part of a criminal investigation in Dallas, Texas. In 2003 and 2004, Nortel was recovering from seeing its stock fall from a high of $124.50 in 2000, at the height of the tech boom.

SOURCES: M. Evans and W. Dabrowski, 2004, Nortel clears decks for Admiral, *National Post*, April 29, A1, A8; S. Maich, 2004, How greed took down Nortel, *National Post, Financial Post*, April 29, FP1; M. Morrison, 2004, Stocks flatten on inflation data: Nortel falls as financial info subpoenaed, *Canada.com website*, http://www.canada.com, accessed May 14, 2004; M. Morrison, 2004, Stocks face on interest rates: Nortel subpoenaed in criminal probe, *Canada.com website*, http://www.canada.com, May 14, accessed May 14, 2004; Globe and Mail, 2004, Nortel revokes options of 3 former executives, *Globe and Mail website*, http://www.theglobeandmail.com, May 12, accessed May 14, 2004; D. Ebner, 2004, Bondholders could force Nortel to seek new financing, *Globe and Mail website*, http://www.theglobeandmail.com, May 11, accessed May 14, 2004; G. Pitts, 2004, Nortel enlists a uniform to rally the suits, *Globe and Mail website*, http://www.theglobeandmail.com, May 10, accessed May 14, 2004; S. Stewart, 2004, Nortel releases names of suspended officials, *Globe and Mail website*, http://www.theglobeandmail.com, May 8, accessed May 14, 2004.

Summary

- Corporate governance is a relationship among stakeholders that is used to determine a firm's direction and control its performance. How firms monitor and control top-level managers' decisions and actions affects the implementation of strategies. Effective governance that aligns managers' decisions with shareholders' interests can be a competitive advantage.

- There are three internal governance mechanisms in the modern corporation: ownership concentration, the board of directors, and executive compensation. The market for corporate control is the single external governance mechanism influencing both managers' decisions and the outcomes that result from their decisions.

- Ownership is separated from control in the modern corporation. Owners (principals) hire managers (agents) to make decisions that maximize the firm's value. As risk-bearing specialists, owners diversify their risk by investing in multiple corporations with different risk profiles. As decision-making specialists, owners expect their agents (the firm's top-level managers) to make decisions that will lead to maximization of the value of their firm. Thus, modern corporations are characterized by an agency relationship that is created when one party (the firm's owners) hires and pays another party (top-level managers) to use its decision-making skills.

- Separation of ownership and control creates an agency problem when an agent pursues goals that conflict with the principals' goals. Principals establish and use governance mechanisms to control this problem.

- Ownership concentration is based on the number of large-block shareholders and the percentage of shares they own. With significant ownership percentages, such as those held by large mutual funds and pension funds, institutional investors often are able to influence top executives' strategic decisions and actions. Thus, unlike diffuse ownership, which tends to result in relatively weak monitoring and control of managerial decisions, concentrated ownership produces more active and effective monitoring. As an increasingly powerful force in corporate Canada, institutional investors actively use their positions of concentrated ownership to force managers and boards of directors to make decisions that maximize a firm's value.

- In Canada, the United States, and the United Kingdom, a firm's board of directors, composed of insiders, related outsiders, and outsiders, is a governance mechanism that shareholders expect to represent their collective interests. On many boards, the percentage of outside directors now exceeds the percentage of inside directors. Outsiders are expected to be more independent of a firm's top-level managers, compared to those selected from inside the firm.

- Executive compensation is a highly visible and often criticized governance mechanism. Salary, bonuses, and long-term incentives are used to strengthen the alignment between managers' and shareholders' interests. A firm's board of directors is responsible for determining the effectiveness of the firm's executive compensation system. An effective system elicits managerial decisions that are in shareholders' best interests.

- In general, evidence suggests that shareholders and boards of directors have become more vigilant in their control of managerial decisions. Nonetheless, these mechanisms are insufficient to govern managerial behaviour in many large companies. Therefore, the market for corporate control is an important governance mechanism. Although it, too, is imperfect, the market for corporate control has been effective in causing corporations to combat inefficient diversification and to implement more effective strategic decisions.

- Corporate governance structures that are used internationally differ from each other and from the structure that is used in Canada. Historically, the Canadian governance structure has focused on maximizing shareholder value.

- Effective governance mechanisms ensure that the interests of all stakeholders are served. Thus, long-term strategic success results when firms are governed in ways that permit at least minimal satisfaction of capital market stakeholders (e.g., shareholders), product market stakeholders (e.g., customers and suppliers), and organizational stakeholders (managerial and nonmanagerial employees, see Chapter 3). Moreover, effective governance produces ethical behaviour in the formulation and implementation of strategies.

1. What is corporate governance? What factors account for the considerable amount of attention corporate governance receives from several parties, including shareholder activists, business press writers, and academic scholars? Why is governance necessary to control managers' decisions?

2. What does it mean to say that ownership is separated from control in the modern corporation? Why does this separation exist?

3. What is an agency relationship? What is managerial opportunism? What assumptions do owners of modern corporations make about managers as agents?

4. How is each of the three internal governance mechanisms—ownership concentration, boards of directors, and executive compensation—used to align the interests of managerial agents with those of the firm's owners?

5. What trends exist regarding executive compensation? What is the effect of the increased use of long-term incentives on executives' strategic decisions?

6. What is the market for corporate control? What conditions generally cause this external governance mechanism to become active? How does the mechanism constrain top executives' decisions and actions?

7. How can corporate governance foster ethical strategic decisions and behaviours on the part of managers as agents?

Corporate Governance and the Board of Directors

The composition and actions of the firm's board of directors have a profound effect on the firm. "The most important thing a board can ask itself today is whether it is professionally managed in the same way that the company itself is professionally managed," says Carolyn Brancato, director of the Global Corporate Governance Research Center at The Conference Board, which creates and disseminates knowledge about management and the marketplace. "The collegial nature of boards must give way to a new emphasis on professionalism, and directors must ask management the hard questions."

Break into small groups and use the content of this chapter to discuss the following questions about boards of directors and corporate governance. Be prepared to defend your answers.

1. How can corporate governance keep a company viable and maintain its shareholders' confidence?

2. How should boards evaluate CEOs? How can the board learn of problems in the CEO's performance? How does a board decide when a CEO needs to be replaced? How should succession plans be put in place?

3. Who should serve on a board? What human factors affect board members' interactions with each other, and how can those factors be used to best advantage?

4. Should independent directors meet on a regular basis without management present? Does the board have a role in setting corporate strategy?

5. What should a CEO expect of directors? How can a CEO move unproductive participants off a board?

6. What processes can be put in place to help make the board more aware of problems in company operations? How can the board be assured of receiving appropriate information? How can the board fulfill its monitoring role while relying on information provided by management and external accountants?

1. M. Carpenter & J. Westphal, 2001, Strategic context of external network ties: Examining the impact of director appointments on board involvement in strategic decision making, *Academy of Management Journal*, 44: 639–60.

2. A. Henderson & J. Fredrickson, 2001, Top management team coordination needs and the CEO pay gap: A competitive test of economic and behavioral views, *Academy of Management Journal*, 44: 96–117; F. Elloumi & J.-P. Gueyie, 2001, CEO compensation, IOS and the role of corporate governance, *Corporate Governance*, 1(2): 23–33; J. E. Core, R. W. Holthausen, & D. F. Larcker, 1999, Corporate governance, chief executive officer compensation, and firm performance, *Journal of Financial Economics*, 51: 371–406.

3. A. J. Hillman, G. D. Keim, & R. A. Luce, 2001, Board composition and stakeholder performance: Do stakeholder directors make a difference? *Business and Society*, 40: 295–314; R. K. Mitchell, B. R. Agle, & D. J. Wood, 1997, Toward a theory of stake-

holder identification and salience: Defining the principle of who and what really counts, *Academy of Management Review*, 22: 853–86; P. Stiles, 2001, The impact of the board on strategy: An empirical examination, *Journal of Management Studies*, 38: 627–50; J. H. Davis, F. D. Schoorman, & L. Donaldson, 1997, Toward a stewardship theory of management, *Academy of Management Review*, 22: 20–47; D. Finegold, E. E. Lawler III, & J. Conger, 2001, Building a better board, *Journal of Business Strategy*, 22(6): 33–37; E. F. Fama & M. C. Jensen, 1983, Separation of ownership and control, *Journal of Law and Economics*, 26: 301–25.

4. R. Charan, 1998, *How Corporate Boards Create Competitive Advantage*, San Francisco: Jossey-Bass; A. Cannella Jr., A. Pettigrew, & D. Hambrick, 2001, Upper echelons: Donald Hambrick on executives and strategy, *Academy of Management Executive*, 15(3): 36–52; J. D. Westphal & E. J. Zajac, 1997, Defections from the inner circle: Social exchange, reciprocity and diffusion of board independence in U.S. corporations, *Administrative Science Quarterly*, 42: 161–212.

5. J. McGuire & S. Dow, 2002, The Japanese keiretsu system: An empirical analysis, *Journal of Business Research*, 55: 33–40; J. Charkham, 1994, *Keeping Good Company: A Study of Corporate Governance in Five Countries*, New York: Oxford University Press, 1.

6. A. Cadbury, 1999, The future of governance: The rules of the game, *Journal of General Management*, 24: 1–14; S. Johnson, P. Boone, A. Breach, & E. Friedman, 2000, Corporate governance in the Asian financial crisis, *Journal of Financial Economics*, 58: 141–86.

7. Cadbury Committee, 1992, *Report of the Cadbury Committee on the Financial Aspects of Corporate Governance*, London: Gee; C. K. Prahalad & J. P. Oosterveld, 1999, Transforming internal governance: The challenge for multinationals, *Sloan Management Review*, 40(3): 31–39.

8. M. A. Hitt, R. A. Harrison, & R. D. Ireland, 2001, *Creating Value through Mergers and Acquisitions: A Complete Guide to Successful M&As*, New York: Oxford University Press; M. A. Hitt, R. E. Hoskisson, R. A. Johnson, & D. D. Moesel, 1996, The market for corporate control and firm innovation, *Academy of Management Journal*, 39: 1084–1119; J. P. Walsh & R. Kosnik, 1993, Corporate raiders and their disciplinary role in the market for corporate control, *Academy of Management Journal*, 36: 671–700.

9. Davis, Schoorman & Donaldson, Toward a stewardship theory of management; R. C. Anderson, T. W. Bates, J. M. Bizjak, & M. L. Lemmon, 2000, Corporate governance and firm diversification, *Financial Management*, 29(1): 5–22; C. Sundaramurthy, J. M. Mahoney, & J. T. Mahoney, 1997, Board structure, antitakeover provisions, and stockholder wealth, *Strategic Management Journal*, 18: 231–46; K. J. Rediker & A. Seth, 1995, Boards of directors and substitution effects of alternative governance mechanisms, *Strategic Management Journal*, 16: 85–99; R. E. Hoskisson, M. A. Hitt, R. A. Johnson, & W. Grossman, 2002, Conflicting voices: The effects of ownership heterogeneity and internal governance on corporate strategy, *Academy of Management Journal*, 45(4): 697–716.

10. G. E. Davis & T. A. Thompson, 1994, A social movement perspective on corporate control, *Administrative Science Quarterly*, 39: 141–73

11. R. Bricker & N. Chandar, 2000, Where Berle and Means went wrong: A reassessment of capital market agency and financial reporting, *Accounting, Organizations and Society*, 25: 529–54; M. A. Eisenberg, 1989, The structure of corporation law, *Columbia Law Review*, 89(7): 1461 as cited in R. A. G. Monks & N. Minow, 1995, *Corporate Governance*, Cambridge, MA: Blackwell Business, 7.

12. R. M. Wiseman & L. R. Gomez-Mejia, 1999, A behavioral agency model of managerial risk taking, *Academy of Management Review*, 23: 133–53.

13. E. E. Fama, 1980, Agency problems and the theory of the firm, *Journal of Political Economy*, 88: 288–307.

14. J. A. Byrne & B. Elgin, 2002, Cisco: Behind the hype, *Business Week*, January 21, 56–61; D. Stires, 2001, America's best & worst wealth creators, *Fortune*, December 10, 137–42.

15. J. Gray, 2003, High on the hog, *Canadian Business*, May 12, 41–44.

16. M. Jensen & W. Meckling, 1976, Theory of the firm: Managerial behavior, agency costs, and ownership structure, *Journal of Financial Economics*, 11: 305–60; L. R. Gomez-Mejia, M. Nunez-Nickel, & I. Gutierrez, 2001, The role of family ties in agency contracts, *Academy of Management Journal*, 44: 81–95; H. C. Tosi, J. Katz, & L. R. Gomez-Mejia, 1997, Disaggregating the agency contract: The effects of monitoring, incentive alignment, and term in office on agent decision making, *Academy of Management Journal*, 40: 584–602; M. G. Jacobides & D. C. Croson, 2001, Information policy: Shaping the value of agency relationships, *Academy of Management Review*, 26: 202–23; R. Mangel & M. Useem, 2001, The strategic role of gainsharing, *Journal of Labor Research*, 2: 327–43; T. M. Welbourne & L. R. Gomez-

Mejia, 1995, Gainsharing: A critical review and a future research agenda, *Journal of Management*, 21: 577.

17. Jacobides & Croson, Information policy: Shaping the value of agency relationships.

18. O. E. Williamson, 1996, *The Mechanisms of Governance*, New York: Oxford University Press, 6; O. E. Williamson, 1993, Opportunism and its critics, *Managerial and Decision Economics*, 14: 97–107; C. C. Chen, M. W. Peng, & P. A. Saparito, 2002, Individualism, collectivism, and opportunism: A cultural perspective on transaction cost economics, *Journal of Management*, 28(4):567–83; S. Ghoshal & P. Moran, 1996, Bad for practice: A critique of the transaction cost theory, *Academy of Management Review*, 21: 13–47; K. H. Wathne & J. B. Heide, 2000, Opportunism in interfirm relationships: Forms, outcomes, and solutions, *Journal of Marketing*, 64(4): 36–51; Y. Amihud & B. Lev, 1981, Risk reduction as a managerial motive for conglomerate mergers, *Bell Journal of Economics*, 12: 605–17.

19. Anderson, Bates, Bizjak & Lemmon, Corporate governance and firm diversification; R. E. Hoskisson & T. A. Turk, 1990, Corporate restructuring: Governance and control limits of the internal market, *Academy of Management Review*, 15: 459–77.

20. M. A. Geletkanycz, B. K. Boyd, & S. Finkelstein, 2001, The strategic value of CEO external directorate networks: Implications for CEO compensation, *Strategic Management Journal*, 22: 889–98; P. Wright, M. Kroll, & D. Elenkov, 2002, Acquisition returns, increase in firm size and chief executive officer compensation: The moderating role of monitoring, *Academy of Management Journal*, 45(3): 599–608; S. Finkelstein & D. C. Hambrick, 1989, Chief executive compensation: A study of the intersection of markets and political processes, *Strategic Management Journal*, 10: 121–34; H. C. Tosi & L. R. Gomez-Mejia, 1989, The decoupling of CEO pay and performance: An agency theory perspective, *Administrative Science Quarterly*, 34: 169–89.

21. Hoskisson & Turk, Corporate restructuring; Gomez-Mejia, Nunez-Nickel, & Gutierrez, The role of family ties in agency contracts.

22. C. Matlack, 2001, Gemplus: No picnic in Provence, *Business Week Online*, http://www.businessweek.com, August 6; C. Matlack, 2001, A global clash at France's Gemplus, *Business Week Online*, http://www.businessweek.com, December 21.

23. M. S. Jensen, 1986, Agency costs of free cash flow, corporate finance, and takeovers, *American Economic Review*, 76: 323–29; T. H. Brush, P. Bromiley, & M. Hendrickx, 2000, The free cash flow hypothesis for sales growth and firm performance, *Strategic Management Journal*, 21: 455–72; H. DeAngelo & L. DeAngelo, 2000, Controlling stockholders and the disciplinary role of corporate payout policy: A study of the Times Mirror Company, *Journal of Financial Economics*, 56: 153–207.

24. K. Ramaswamy, M. Li, & R. Veliyath, 2002, Variations in ownership behavior and propensity to diversify: A study of the Indian corporate context, *Strategic Management Journal*, 23: 345–58.

25. P. Wright, M. Kroll, A. Lado, & B. Van Ness, 2002, The structure of ownership and corporate acquisition strategies, *Strategic Management Journal*, 23: 41–53.

26. R. Rajan, H. Servaes, & L. Zingales, 2001, The cost of diversity: The diversification discount and inefficient investment, *Journal of Finance*, 55: 35–79; A. Sharma, 1997, Professional as agent: Knowledge asymmetry in agency exchange, *Academy of Management Review*, 22: 758–98.

27. P. Lane, A. A. Cannella, Jr., & M. H. Lubatkin, 1999, Agency problems as antecedents to unrelated mergers and diversification: Amihud and Lev reconsidered, *Strategic Management Journal*, 19: 555–78; D. Champion, 2001, Off with his head? *Harvard Business Review*, 79(9): 35–46.

28. P. Fitzpatrick, 2003, Is good governance too costly? Many CEOs say yes, *National Post, Financial Post*, December 3, FP1.

29. S. Silcoff, 2004, Governance run amok: DesMarais, *National Post, Financial Post*, May 13, FP1.

30. J. Coles, N. Sen, & V. McWilliams, 2001, An examination of the relationship of governance mechanisms to performance, *Journal of Management*, 27: 23–50.

31. S.-S. Chen & K. W. Ho, 2000, Corporate diversification, ownership structure, and firm value: The Singapore evidence, *International Review of Financial Analysis*, 9: 315–26; R. E. Hoskisson, R. A. Johnson, & D. D. Moesel, 1994, Corporate divestiture intensity in restructuring firms: Effects of governance, strategy, and performance, *Academy of Management Journal*, 37: 1207–51.

32. S. R. Kole & K. M. Lehn, 1999, Deregulation and the adaptation of governance structure: The case of the U.S. airline industry, *Journal of Financial Economics*, 52: 79–117; K. C. Banning, 1999, Ownership concentration and bank acquisition strategy: An empirical examination, *International Journal of Organizational Analysis*, 7(2): 135–52.

33. A. Berle & G. Means, 1932, *The Modern Corporation and Private Property*, New York: Macmillan; P. A. Gompers & A. Metrick, 2001, Institutional investors and equity prices,

Quarterly Journal of Economics, 116: 229–59; M. P. Smith, 1996, Shareholder activism by institutional investors: Evidence from CalPERS, *Journal of Finance*, 51: 227–52.

34. M. Useem, 1998, Corporate leadership in a globalizing equity market, *Academy of Management Executive*, 12(3): 43–59; Hoskisson, Hitt, Johnson, & Grossman, Conflicting Voices; C. M. Daily, 1996, Governance patterns in bankruptcy reorganizations, *Strategic Management Journal*, 17: 355–75.

35. Hoskisson, Hitt, Johnson, & Grossman, Conflicting voices; Useem, Corporate leadership in a globalizing equity market; R. E. Hoskisson & M. A. Hitt, 1994, *Downscoping: How to Tame the Diversified Firm*, New York: Oxford University Press; K. Rebeiz, 2001, Corporate governance effectiveness in American corporations: A survey, *International Management Journal*, 18(1): 74–80.

36. G. Keenan, 2004, Stronach critics hold their tongues at meeting, *Globe and Mail website*, http://www.globeandmail.com/servlet/ArticleNews/TPPrint/LAC/20040507/RMAGNA07/TPBusiness/, May 7, accessed May 13, 2004.

37. CalPERS, 2002, CalPERS at a glance, *CalPERS website*, http://www.calpers.com, April 24; Economist, 2001, The fading appeal of the boardroom series, *Economist*, February 10(business special): 67–69; Hoskisson, Hitt, Johnson, & Grossman, Conflicting voices; P. David, M. A. Hitt, & J. Gimeno, 2001, The role of institutional investors in influencing R&D, *Academy of Management Journal*, 44: 144–57; B. J. Bushee, 2001, Do institutional investors prefer near-term earnings over long-run value? *Contemporary Accounting Research*, 18: 207–46.

38. Investor Relations Bureau, 2001, Shareholder activism is rising, *Investor Relations Business*, August 6, 8; Business Week, 2000, Now, a gadfly can bite 24 hours a day, *Business Week*, January 24, 150.

39. M. J. Roe, 1993, Mutual funds in the boardroom, *Journal of Applied Corporate Finance*, 5(4): 56–61; R. A. G. Monks, 1999, What will be the impact of active shareholders? A practical recipe for constructive change, *Long Range Planning*, 32(1): 20–27.

40. B. S. Black, 1992, Agents watching agents: The promise of institutional investor's voice, *UCLA Law Review*, 39: 871–93; Hoskisson, Hitt, Johnson, & Grossman, Conflicting voices; T. Woidtke, 2002, Agents watching agents? Evidence from pension fund ownership and firm value, *Journal of Financial Economics*, 63, 99–131.

41. C. Sandaramurthy & D. W. Lyon, 1998, Shareholder governance proposals and conflict of interests between inside and outside shareholders, *Journal of Managerial Issues*, 10: 30–44.

42. Wright, Kroll, Lado, & Van Ness, The structure of ownership and corporate acquisition strategies; S. Thomsen & T. Pedersen, 2000, Ownership structure and economic performance in the largest European companies, *Strategic Management Journal*, 21: 689–705; D. R. Dalton, C. M. Daily, A. E. Ellstrand, & J. L. Johnson, 1998, Meta-analytic reviews of board composition, leadership structure, and financial performance, *Strategic Management Journal*, 19: 269–90; M. Huse, 1998, Researching the dynamics of board-stakeholder relations, *Long Range Planning*, 31: 218–26; A. Dehaene, V. De Vuyst, & H. Ooghe, 2001, Corporate performance and board structure in Belgian companies, *Long Range Planning*, 34(3): 383–98;

43. Rebeiz, Corporate governance effectiveness in American corporations; J. K. Seward & J. P Walsh, 1996, The governance and control of voluntary corporate spinoffs, *Strategic Management Journal*, 17: 25–39; S. Young, 2000, The increasing use of non-executive directors: Its impact on UK board structure and governance arrangements, *Journal of Business Finance & Accounting*, 27(9/10): 1311–42; P. Mallete & R. L. Hogler, 1995, Board composition, stock ownership, and the exemption of directors from liability, *Journal of Management*, 21: 861–78; J. Chidley, 2001, Why boards matter, *Canadian Business*, October 29, 6; D. P. Forbes & F. J. Milliken, 1999, Cognition and corporate governance: Understanding boards of directors as strategic decision-making groups, *Academy of Management Review*, 24: 489–505.

44. Hoskisson, Hitt, Johnson, & Grossman, Conflicting voices; B. D. Baysinger & R. E. Hoskisson, 1990, The composition of boards of directors and strategic control: Effects on corporate strategy, *Academy of Management Review*, 15: 72–87; Carpenter & Westphal, Strategic context of external network ties; E. J. Zajac & J. D. Westphal, 1996, Director reputation, CEO-board power, and the dynamics of board interlocks, *Administrative Science Quarterly*, 41: 507–29.

45. A. Hillman, A. Cannella Jr., & R. Paetzold, 2000, The resource dependence role of corporate directors: Strategic adaptation of board composition in response to environmental change, *Journal of Management Studies*, 37: 235–55; J. D. Westphal & E. J. Zajac, 1995, Who shall govern? CEO/board power, demographic similarity, and new director selection, *Administrative Science Quarterly*, 40: 60–83; J. Westphal & L. Milton, 2000, How experience and network ties affect the influence of demographic minorities on corporate boards, *Administrative Science Quarterly*, June, 45(2): 366–98; R. P. Beatty & E. J. Zajac, 1994, Managerial incentives, monitoring, and risk

bearing: A study of executive compensation, ownership, and board structure in initial public offerings, *Administrative Science Quarterly*, 39: 313–35.

46. A. L. Ranft & H. M. O'Neill, 2001, Board composition and high-flying founders: Hints of trouble to come? *Academy of Management Executive*, 15(1): 126–38.

47. K. Greene, 2002, Dunlap agrees to settle suit over Sunbeam, *Wall Street Journal*, January 15, A3, A8; Stiles, The impact of the board on strategy; J. A. Byrne, 1999, Commentary: Boards share the blame when the boss fails, *Business Week Online*, http://www.businessweek.com, December 27.

48. R. M. Corbin, 1999, *Report on Corporate Governance, Five Years to the Dey*, Toronto: Toronto Stock Exchange, 35.

49. E. Perotti & S. Gelfer, 2001, Red barons or robber barons? Governance and investment in Russian financial-industrial groups, *European Economic Review*, 45(9): 1601–17; I. M. Millstein, 1997, Red herring over independent boards, *New York Times*, April 6, F10; W. Q. Judge Jr. & G. H. Dobbins, 1995, Antecedents and effects of outside directors' awareness of CEO decision style, *Journal of Management*, 21: 43–64; I. E. Kesner, 1988, Director characteristics in committee membership: An investigation of type, occupation, tenure and gender, *Academy of Management Journal*, 31: 66–84; T. McNulty & A Pettigrew, 1999, Strategists on the board, *Organization Studies*, 20: 47–74.

50. J. Coles & W. Hesterly, 2000, Independence of the chairman and board composition: Firm choices and shareholder value, *Journal of Management*, 26: 195–214; S. Zahra, 1996, Governance, ownership and corporate entrepreneurship among the Fortune 500: The moderating impact of industry technological opportunity, *Academy of Management Journal*, 39: 1713–35; Hoskisson, Hitt, Johnson, & Grossman, Conflicting Voices.

51. A. Conger, E.E. Lawler, & D.L. Finegold, 2001, *Corporate Boards: New Strategies for Adding Value at the Top*, San Francisco: Jossey-Bass; J. A. Conger, D. Finegold, & E. E. Lawler III, 1998, Appraising boardroom performance, *Harvard Business Review*, 76(1): 136–48; J. Marshall, 2001, As boards shrink, responsibilities grow, *Financial Executive*, 17(4): 36–39.

52. C. A. Simmers, 2000, Executive/board politics in strategic decision making, *Journal of Business and Economic Studies*, 4: 37–56; Hoskisson, Hitt, Johnson, & Grossman, Conflicting voices.

53. W. Ocasio, 1999, Institutionalized action and corporate governance, *Administrative Science Quarterly*, 44: 384–416; A. A. Cannella Jr. & W. Shen, 2001, So close and yet so far: Promotion versus exit for CEO heirs apparent, *Academy of Management Journal*, 44: 252–70.

54. M. Gerety, C. Hoi, & A. Robin, 2001, Do shareholders benefit from the adoption of incentive pay for directors? *Financial Management*, 30: 45–61; D. C. Hambrick & E. M. Jackson, 2000, Outside directors with a stake: The linchpin in improving governance, *California Management Review*, 42(4): 108–27; S. Rosenstein & J. G. Wyatt, 1997, Inside directors, board effectiveness, and shareholder wealth, *Journal of Financial Economics*, 44: 229–50; J. Kristie, 2001, The shareholder activist: Nell Minow, *Directors and Boards*, 26(1): 16–17.

55. D. Hasselback, 2004, Placer's Taylor snubs governance "cop" job—refuses directorships, *National Post, Financial Post*, May 6, FP1.

56. D. C. Hambrick & S. Finkelstein, 1995, The effects of ownership structure on conditions at the top: The case of CEO pay raises, *Strategic Management Journal*, 16: 175–93.

57. J. S. Miller, R. M. Wiseman, & L. R. Gomez-Mejia, 2002, The fit between CEO compensation design and firm risk, *Academy of Management Journal*, 45(4): 745–56; L. Gomez-Mejia & R. M. Wiseman, 1997, Reframing executive compensation: An assessment and outlook, *Journal of Management*, 23: 291–374; S. Finkelstein & B. K. Boyd, 1998, How much does the CEO matter? The role of managerial discretion in the setting of CEO compensation, *Academy of Management Journal*, 41: 179–99; W. G. Sanders & M. A. Carpenter, 1998, Internationalization and firm governance: The roles of CEO compensation, top team composition and board structure, *Academy of Management Journal*, 41: 158 78; N. T. Hill & K. T. Stevens, 2001, Structuring compensation to achieve better financial results, *Strategic Finance*, 9: 48–51; J. D. Westphal & E. J. Zajac, 1999, The symbolic management of stockholders: Corporate governance reform and shareholder reactions, *Administrative Science Quarterly*, 43: 127–53.

58. Elloumi & Gueyie, CEO compensation, IOS and the role of corporate governance; M. J. Conyon & S. I. Peck, 1998, Board control, remuneration committees, and top management compensation, *Academy of Management Journal*, 41: 146–57; Westphal & Zajac, The symbolic management of stockholders.

59. S. O'Donnell, 2000, Managing foreign subsidiaries: Agents of headquarters, or an interdependent network? *Strategic Management Journal*, 21: 521–48; K. Roth & S. O'Donnell, 1996, Foreign subsidiary compensation: An agency theory perspective,

Academy of Management Journal, 39: 678–703; K. Ramaswamy, R. Veliyath, & L. Gomes, 2000, A study of the determinants of CEO compensation in India, *Management International Review*, 40(2): 167–91; J. Krug & W. Hegarty, 2001, Predicting who stays and leaves after an acquisition: A study of top managers in multinational firms, *Strategic Management Journal*, 22: 185–96; S. Fung, 1999, How should we pay them? *Across the Board*, June, 37–41.

60. M. A. Carpenter & M. G. Sanders, 2002, Top management team compensation: The missing link between CEO pay and firm performance, *Strategic Management Journal*, 23(4): 367–75; S. Bryan, L. Hwang, & S. Lilien, 2000, CEO stock-based compensation: An empirical analysis of incentive-intensity, relative mix, and economic determinants, *Journal of Business*, 73: 661–93; C. Peck, H. M. Silvert, & K. Worrell, 1999, Top executive compensation: Canada, France, the United Kingdom, and the United States, *Chief Executive Digest*, 3: 27–29.

61. Gray, High on the hog.

62. R. E. Hoskisson, M. A. Hitt, & C. W. L. Hill, 1993, Managerial incentives and investment in R&D in large multiproduct firms, *Organization Science*, 4: 325–41; D. B. Balkin, G. D. Markman, & L. Gomez-Mejia, 2000, Is CEO pay in high-technology firms related to innovation? *Academy of Management Journal*, 43: 1118–29.

63. L. K. Meulbroek, 2001, The efficiency of equity-linked compensation: Understanding the full cost of awarding executive stock options, *Financial Management*, 30(2), 5–44.

64. Gray, High on the hog.

65. S. Strom, 2002, Even last year, option spigot was wide open, *New York Times*, http://www.nytimes.com, February 3; C. G. Holderness, R. S. Kroszner, & D. P. Sheehan, 1999, Were the good old days that good? Changes in managerial stock ownership since the Great Depression, *Journal of Finance*, 54: 435–69.

66. J. Dahya, A. A. Lonie, & D. A. Power, 1998, Ownership structure, firm performance and top executive change: An analysis of UK firms, *Journal of Business Finance & Accounting*, 25: 1089–1118; H. Tosi, S. Werner, J. Katz, & L. Gomez-Mejia, 2000, How much does performance matter? A meta-analysis of CEO pay studies, *Journal of Management*, 26: 301–39.

67. D. Leonhardt, 2002, It's called a "loan," but it's far sweeter, *New York Times*, http://www.nytimes.com, February 3.

68. Strom, Even last year, option spigot was wide open; T. G. Pollock, H. M. Fischer, & J. B. Wade, 2002, The role of politics in repricing executive options, *Academy of Management Journal*, 45(6): 1172–82; M. E. Carter & L. J. Lynch, 2001, An examination of executive stock option repricing, *Journal of Financial Economics*, 2: 207–25; D. Chance, R. Kumar, & R. Todd, 2001, The "repricing" of executive stock options, *Journal of Financial Economics*, 57: 129–54.

69. R. Coff, 2003, Bidding wars over R&D intensive firms: Knowledge, opportunism and the market for corporate control, *Academy of Management Journal*, 46(1): 74–85; Hitt, Hoskisson, Johnson, & Moesel, The market for corporate control and firm innovation; Walsh & Kosnik, Corporate raiders.

70. D. Goldstein, 2000, Hostile takeovers as corporate governance? Evidence from 1980s, *Review of Political Economy*, 12: 381–402.

71. Hitt, Harrison, & Ireland, *Creating Value through Mergers and Acquisitions*.

72. E. Thorton, F. Keesnan, C. Palmeri, & L. Himelstein, 2002, It sure is getting hostile, *Business Week*, January 14, 28–30.

73. Sundaramurthy, Mahoney, & Mahoney, Board structure, antitakeover provisions, and stockholder wealth; J. Westphal & E. Zajac, 2001, Decoupling policy from practice: The case of stock repurchase programs, *Administrative Science Quarterly*, 46: 202–28.

74. Walsh & Kosnik, Corporate raiders; A. Chakraborty & R. Arnott, 2001, Takeover defenses and dilution: A welfare analysis, *Journal of Financial and Quantitative Analysis*, 36: 311–34.

75. A. Portlono, 2000, The decision to adopt defensive tactics in Italy, *International Review of Law and Economics*, 20: 425–52; C. Sundaramurthy, 2000, Antitakeover provisions and shareholder value implications: A review and a contingency framework, *Journal of Management*, 26: 1005–30.

76. B. Kogut, G. Walker, & J. Anand, 2002, Agency and institutions: National divergence in diversification behavior, *Organization Science*, 13: 162–78; D. Norburn, B. K. Boyd, M. Fox, & M. Muth, 2000, International corporate governance reform, *European Business Journal*, 12(3): 116–33; Useem, Corporate leadership in a globalizing equity market.

77. J. B. White, 2000, The company we'll keep, *Wall Street Journal interactive*, http://www.wsj.com, January 17.

78. A. Alcouffe & C. Alcouffe, 2000, Executive compensation-setting practices in France, *Long Range Planning*, 33(4): 527–43; J. Groenewegen, 2001, European integration and changing corporate governance structures: The case of France, *Journal of Economic Issues*, 34: 471–79; C. P. Erlich & D.-S. Kang, 1999, South Korea: Corporate governance reform in Korea: The remaining issues—Part I: Governance structure of the large Korean firm, *East Asian Executive Reports*, 21: 11–14.

79. P. Mar & M. Young, 2001, Corporate governance in transition economies: A case study of two Chinese airlines, *Journal of World Business*, 36(3): 280–302; M. W. Peng, 2000, *Business Strategies in Transition Economies*, Thousand Oaks, CA: Sage; L. Chang, 1999, Chinese firms find incentive to use stock-compensation plans, *Wall Street Journal*, November 1, A2; T. Clarke & Y. Du, 1998, Corporate governance in China: Explosive growth and new patterns of ownership, *Long Range Planning*, 31(2): 239–51; I. Filatotchev, R. Kapelyushnikov, N. Dyomina, & S. Aukutsionek, 2001, The effects of ownership concentration on investment and performance in privatized firms in Russia, *Managerial and Decision Economics*, 22(6): 299–313; E. Perotti & S. Gelfer, 2001, Red barons or robber barons? Governance and investment in Russian financial-industrial groups, *European Economic Review*, 45(9): 1601–17; T Buck, I. Filatotchev, & M. Wright, 1998, Agents, stakeholders and corporate governance in Russian firms, *Journal of Management Studies*, 35: 81–104.

80. Hillman, Keim, & Luce, Board composition and stakeholder performance; R. Oliver, 2000, The board's role: Driver's seat or rubber stamp? *Journal of Business Strategy*, 21: 7–9.

81. A. Felo, 2001, Ethics programs, board involvement, and potential conflicts of interest in corporate governance, *Journal of Business Ethics*, 32: 205–18.

Chapter Twelve

Organizational Structure and Controls

Knowledge Objectives

Studying this chapter should provide you with the strategic management knowledge needed to:

1. Define organizational structure and controls and discuss the difference between strategic and financial controls.

2. Describe the relationship between strategy and structure.

3. Discuss the functional structures used to implement business-level strategies.

4. Explain the use of three versions of the multidivisional (M-form) structure to implement different diversification strategies.

5. Discuss the organizational structures used to implement three international strategies.

6. Define strategic networks and strategic centre firms.

Aligning Strategy and Structure at Zurich Financial Services

Zurich Financial Services was founded in Switzerland in 1872, primarily as a property and casualty insurer and reinsurer. Part of the reason for Zurich's historical success was the firm's rapid movement into markets outside its home nation. International expansion intensified during the early 1990s when Rolf Hüppi, Zurich CEO, concluded that the dynamic global economy created significant opportunities for firms to profitably sell financial products and services to customers in different regions of the world.

Convinced that acquisition was the route for Zurich to become a diversified, global financial powerhouse, Hüppi acted quickly and boldly. In 1996, Zurich gained a strong presence in the asset management business by spending $2 billion to acquire Kemper, a U.S. life insurer and asset manager. One year later, Scudder, Stevens & Clark, a U.S. fund manager, was purchased for an additional $2 billion, significantly expanding Zurich's asset management position. The two acquisitions were then combined to form Zurich Scudder Investments, which became Zurich's global fund management arm. Zurich's size doubled in 1998, when it merged with the financial service arm of British American Tobacco.

Study of Zurich's transactions shows that by 2000, the firm had become a diversified, global financial corporation with more than 70,000 employees and operations in more than 60 countries, serving more than 35 million customers. By this time, a new organizational structure had been formed. This structure grouped the firm's diversified businesses into five segments: non–life insurance (e.g., property, accident, and car and liability), life insurance, reinsurance, farmers management services, and asset management. Investors responded favourably to Zurich's diversification, as shown by the company's quick growth to a market capitalization of more than $50 billion.

Hüppi touted the merits of what Zurich had become and confidently claimed that the company should be worth $100 billion because of its large, lucrative customer base. However, all was not well at Zurich. In fact, in 2001, the company surprised investors when it issued a series of profit warnings and hints of unexpected and significant losses in its fund management business unit. Zurich's market value quickly tumbled by half, to $25 billion. In response, Zurich announced plans to divest several large holdings to raise $4 billion to reduce the firm's debt and the burden of servicing that debt.

What caused Zurich's problems? How could the value of a firm that appeared to have effectively diversified its operations tumble so quickly? In the words of a business analyst, "It was not Zurich's expansion (diversification strategy) that got it into trouble. It was its failure to adapt its structure to its new incarnation (strategy)."

Throughout the time Zurich was quickly diversifying its operations, Hüppi focused on driving top-line sales revenue growth, but little attention was paid to the company's organizational structure. In fact, the structure in place prior to diversification—a hybrid of centralization and decentralization designed to coordinate and control roughly a dozen business units—remained relatively unchanged as Zurich became more

Rolf Hüppi led Zurich Financial Services through an intense period of international expansion in the early 1990s that eventually caused its structure to collapse.

© STEFFEN SCHMIDT/AFP

(continued)

diversified. This structure could not accommodate the complexity of the 350 or so business units that resulted from rapid growth and diversification. Without an organizational structure that could support the firm's new and more diversified corporate-level strategy, decisions about how to best integrate Zurich's recently acquired businesses with existing units were slow in the making.

The lack of integration was particularly pronounced in the Scudder Investments division. Kemper and Scudder, Stevens & Clark were combined to form Zurich's asset management business, but the two firms had very different cultures. Well-known in the Midwestern United States, Kemper sold funds through brokers and financial advisors. Scudder, on the other hand, was an old-line, Boston-based money manager selling mutual funds directly to investors. The decision to have Scudder executives run the asset management unit complicated things, as these executives had little experience in convincing brokerage firms and banks to sell mutual funds. The decisions made by inexperienced decision makers appear to have contributed to former Kemper investors withdrawing $7 billion in assets in 1999, and another $5.3 billion in 2000.

Convinced that a lack of fit between its diversification strategy and organizational structure was contributing to its financial difficulties, in late 2001, Zurich's top-level managers changed their firm's structure while simultaneously reshaping its portfolio of businesses (e.g., Zurich left the reinsurance business by spinning off Converium, its reinsurance operation formerly known as Zurich Re). In the new organizational structure, 11 global and regional businesses were grouped into 5 business units, each headed by an executive reporting directly to Hüppi. As shown in the chart, four of the units are organized across geographic lines with the fifth framed around global asset and investment businesses. An eight-member Group Executive Committee, consisting of Hüppi, the five unit heads, the chief financial officer, and the chief operating officer, considers strategic and financial issues for all of Zurich. The 25-person Group Management Board is an information and networking body working to ensure horizontal collaboration across the segments.

By creating these larger, regional geographic business units, Zurich intends to capitalize on economies of scale in purchasing and back office functions, and it also plans to

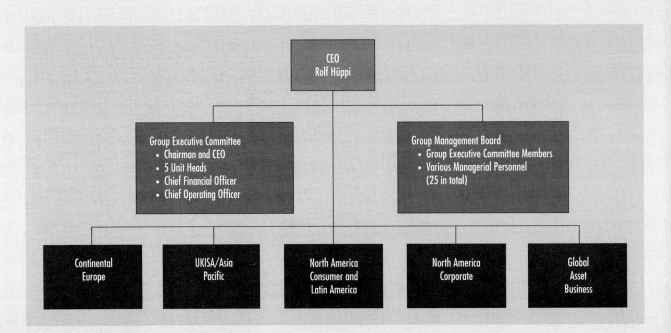

customize its product offerings to satisfy the needs of local clientele. Scale economies should help Zurich reduce its costs, while local product customization should increase revenue. Hüppi believes in the new structure's value, suggesting that it "... is an important step in creating the platform for an efficient and focused development of our Group (business firm)." In mid-2002, new CEO James J. Schiro remained committed to using the structure shown here.

SOURCES: B. Rigby & T. Johnson, 2002, Zurich scraps plan to sell U.S. unit, *Reuters Business News*, http://www.fidelity.com, January 9; Zurich Financial Services, 2001, Zurich Financial Services and Deutsche Bank have signed definitive agreements, *Zurich Financial Services website*, http://www.zurich.com/main/mediarelations/mediareleases/2001/english/ARTICLE171.htm, December 4; Zurich Financial Services, 2001, Zurich Financial Services: Refining the management structure and streamlining the organization, *Zurich Financial Services website*, http://www.zurich.com/main/mediarelations/mediareleases/2001/english/ARTICLE141.htm, July 9; Economist, 2001, Re structure: The Swiss group badly needs a structure to fit its strategy, *The Economist*, September 8, 80–82; H. Deogun & T. Lauricella, 2001, Zurich Financial seeks a merger to reinvigorate its Scudder unit, *Wall Street Journal*, April 23; W. Hall, 2001, Zurich financial profits fall amid fund management fears, *Financial Times*, September 6; S. Tuckey, 2001, Zurich CEO sees consolidation, *Insurance Accounting*, December 3; Zurich Financial Services, 2000, Analyst's day presentation, *Zurich Financial Services website*, http://www.zurich.com/presentations, November; Zurich Financial Services Group, 2000, Zurich Financial Services Group: New organizational structure, *Zurich Financial Services Group website*, http://www.zurich.com/main/mediarelations/mediareleases/2000/english/ARTICLE110.htm, October 31.

As described in Chapter 5, all firms use one or more business-level strategies. In Chapters 7–10, we discuss the other strategies that might be used (corporate-level, restructuring, international, and cooperative strategies). Once selected, strategies can't be implemented in a vacuum. Organizational structure and controls, this chapter's topic, provide the framework within which strategies are used. However, as we explain, separate structures and controls are required to successfully implement different strategies. Top-level managers have the final responsibility for ensuring that the firm has matched each of its strategies with the appropriate organizational structure and that changes to both take place when needed. The match or degree of fit between strategy and structure influences the firm's attempts to earn above-average returns. Thus, the ability to select an appropriate strategy and match it with the appropriate structure is an important characteristic of effective strategic leadership.[1]

This chapter opens with an introduction to organizational structure and controls. We then provide more details about the need for the firm's strategy and structure to be properly matched. Critical to this match is the fact that strategy and structure influence each other. As we discuss, strategy has a more important influence on structure, although once in place, structure influences strategy.[2]

The chapter then describes the relationship between growth and structural change that successful firms experience, which is followed by discussions of the different organizational structures that firms use to implement the separate business-level, corporate-level, international, and cooperative strategies. A series of figures highlights the different structures firms match with strategies. Across time and based on their experiences, organizations, especially large and complex ones, customize these general structures to meet their unique needs. Typically, the firm tries to form a structure that is complex enough to facilitate use of its strategies but simple enough for all to effectively implement.[3] The chapter closes with brief discussions of alternative organizational structures and controls.

Organizational Structure and Controls

Research shows that organizational structure and the controls that are a part of it affect firm performance. In particular, when the firm's strategy isn't matched with the most appropriate structure and controls, performance declines. This relationship is shown in the opening case: the mismatch between strategy and structure contributed to Zurich Financial Services' declining performance. Recognizing this mismatch, the firm is changing its structure and controls to be a better match with its strategy. Even though mismatches between strategy and structure do occur, the evidence suggests that managers try to act rationally when forming or changing their firm's structure.[4]

Organizational Structure

Organizational structure
specifies the firm's formal reporting relationships, procedures, controls, and authority and decision-making processes.

Organizational structure specifies the firm's formal reporting relationships, procedures, controls, and authority and decision-making processes. Developing an organizational structure that will effectively support the firm's strategy is difficult, especially because of the uncertainty about cause–effect relationships in the global economy's rapidly changing and dynamic competitive environments. When a structure's elements (e.g., reporting relationships, procedures, and so forth) are properly aligned with one another, that structure facilitates effective implementation of the firm's strategies.[5]

Organizational structure influences how managers work and the decisions resulting from that work.[6] As explained in the opening case, in Zurich's structure prior to diversification, former CEO Hüppi's decisions were oriented to driving the firm's growth through sales volume increases. However, greater diversification created a need for Hüppi and the top management team to choose a structure that facilitated coordination and integration among the firm's rapidly growing number of business units.

A firm's structure specifies the work to be done and how to do it, given the firm's strategy or strategies. Supporting the implementation of strategies, structure is concerned with processes used to complete organizational tasks. Effective structures provide the stability a firm needs to successfully implement its strategies and maintain its current competitive advantages, while simultaneously providing the flexibility to develop competitive advantages that will be needed for its future strategies. Thus, *structural stability* provides the capacity the firm requires to consistently and predictably manage its daily work routines, while *structural flexibility* provides the opportunity to explore competitive possibilities and then allocate resources to activities that will shape the competitive advantages the firm will need to be successful in the future. An effective organizational structure allows the firm to *exploit* current competitive advantages while *developing* new ones.[7]

Modifications to the firm's current strategy or selection of a new strategy call for changes to its organizational structure. As explained in the opening case, Zurich's existing structure—developed when Zurich had far fewer business units and when it was much less diversified—became incapable of supporting implementation of the firm's new corporate-level diversification strategy. However, Zurich's structure wasn't changed until the firm's performance had dramatically declined.

Research shows that Zurich's experience with strategy and structure isn't unusual. Once in place, organizational inertia often inhibits efforts to change structure, even when the firm's performance suggests that it is time to do so. In his pioneering work, Alfred Chandler found that organizations change their structures only when inefficiencies force them to do so. Firms seem to prefer the structural status quo and its familiar working relationships until the firm's performance declines to the point where change is absolutely necessary. In addition, top-level managers hesitate to conclude that there are problems with the firm's structure (or its strategy, for that matter), in that doing so suggests that their previous choices weren't the best ones.[8]

Because of these inertial tendencies, structural change is often induced instead by the actions of stakeholders who are no longer willing to tolerate the firm's performance. For example, continuing losses of customers who have become dissatisfied with the value created by the firm's products could force change, as could reactions from capital market stakeholders (see Chapter 3). In Zurich's case, changes were made to form a match between strategy and structure when the firm's shareholders and debtholders became quite dissatisfied with the firm's financial performance.

In spite of the timing of structural change described above, many companies make changes prior to substantial performance declines. Appropriate timing of structural change happens when top-level managers quickly recognize that a current organizational structure no longer provides the coordination and direction needed for the firm to successfully implement its strategies.[9] Effective organizational controls help managers recognize when it is time to change the firm's structure.

Organizational Controls

Organizational controls are an important aspect of structure. **Organizational controls** guide the use of strategy, indicate how to compare actual results with expected results, and suggest corrective actions to take when the difference between actual and expected results is unacceptable. The fewer the differences between actual and expected outcomes, the more effective are the organization's controls. It is hard for the company to successfully exploit its competitive advantages without effective organizational controls. Properly designed organizational controls provide clear insights regarding behaviours that enhance firm performance. Firms rely on strategic controls and financial controls as part of their structures to support use of their strategies.[10]

Strategic controls are largely subjective criteria intended to verify that the firm is using appropriate strategies for the conditions in the external environment and the

Organizational controls guide the use of strategy, indicate how to compare actual results with expected results, and suggest corrective actions to take when the difference between actual and expected results is unacceptable.

Strategic controls are largely subjective criteria intended to verify that the firm is using appropriate strategies for the conditions in the external environment and the company's competitive advantages.

company's competitive advantages. Thus, strategic controls are concerned with examining the fit between what the firm *might do* (as suggested by opportunities in its external environment) and what it *can do* (as indicated by its competitive advantages) (see Figure 4.1, on page 104). Effective strategic controls help the firm understand what it takes to be successful. Strategic controls demand that the managers who use them (to judge the firm's performance) share rich communications with those managers (e.g., middle- and first-level managers) with the primary responsibility for implementing the firm's strategies. These frequent exchanges are both formal and informal in nature.[11]

Strategic controls are also used to evaluate the degree to which the firm focuses on the requirements to implement its strategies. For a business-level strategy, for example, the strategic controls are used to study primary and support activities (see Table 4.8, on page 124) to verify that those critical to successful execution of the business-level strategy are being properly emphasized and executed. With related corporate-level strategies, strategic controls are used to verify the sharing of appropriate strategic factors, such as knowledge, markets, and technologies across businesses. To effectively use strategic controls when evaluating related diversification strategies, executives must have a deep understanding of each unit's business-level strategy.[12]

Financial controls are largely objective criteria used to measure the firm's performance against previously established quantitative standards.

Partly because strategic controls are difficult to use with extensive diversification, financial controls are emphasized to evaluate the performance of the firm following the unrelated diversification strategy. The unrelated diversification strategy's focus on financial outcomes (see Chapter 7) requires the use of standardized financial controls to compare performances between units and managers.[13] **Financial controls** are largely objective criteria used to measure the firm's performance against previously established quantitative standards. Accounting-based measures (e.g., return on investment and return on assets) and market-based measures (e.g., economic value added) are examples of financial controls. (In the next chapter, Table 13.1, on page 419, shows examples of strategic and financial controls.)

When using financial controls, firms evaluate their current performance against previous outcomes as well as their performance compared to both competitors and industry averages. In the global economy, technological advances are being used to develop more sophisticated financial controls, making it possible for firms to more thoroughly analyze their performance results. Pfizer Inc.'s expectations of sophisticated financial controls are that they will: "(1) safeguard the firm's assets, (2) ensure that transactions are properly authorized, and (3) provide reasonable assurance, at reasonable cost, of the integrity, objectivity, and reliability of the financial information."[14]

Both strategic and financial controls are important aspects of each organizational structure, and any structure's effectiveness is determined by using a combination of strategic and financial controls. However, the relative use of controls varies by type of strategy. For example, companies and business units of large diversified firms using the cost leadership strategy emphasize financial controls (e.g., quantitative cost goals), while companies and business units using the differentiation strategy emphasize strategic controls (e.g., subjective measures of the effectiveness of product development teams).[15] As explained above, a corporate-wide emphasis on sharing among business units (as called for by related diversification strategies) results in an emphasis on strategic controls, while financial controls are emphasized for strategies in which activities or capabilities aren't shared (e.g., in an unrelated diversification).

Relationships between Strategy and Structure

Strategy and structure have a reciprocal relationship. This relationship highlights the interconnectedness between strategy formulation (Chapter 5 and Chapters 7–10) and strategy implementation (Chapters 11–14). In general, this reciprocal relationship finds structure flowing from or following the selection of the firm's strategy. Once in place, structure can influence current strategic actions as well as choices about future strategies. The general nature of the strategy–structure relationship means that changes to the firm's strategy create the need to change how the organization completes its work. In the "structure influences strategy" direction, firms must be vigilant in their efforts to verify that the way in which their structure prescribes that work is to be completed remains consistent with the implementation requirements of chosen strategies. Research shows, however, that "… strategy has a much more important influence on structure than the reverse."[16]

Regardless of the strength of the reciprocal relationships between strategy and structure, those choosing the firm's strategy and structure should be committed to matching each strategy with a structure that provides both the stability needed to use current competitive advantages as well as the flexibility required to develop future advantages. This means, for example, that when changing strategies, the firm should simultaneously consider the structure that will be needed to support use of the new strategy. Moreover, a proper strategy–structure match can be a competitive advantage. Based on the four criteria of sustainability discussed in Chapter 4, the firm's strategy–structure match is a sustained competitive advantage when that match is valuable, rare, imperfectly imitable, and part of the organized to be exploited condition. When the firm's strategy–structure combination is a sustained competitive advantage, it contributes to the earning of above-average returns.[17]

Actions at Charles Schwab & Co. demonstrate these issues. A premier discount broker, Schwab, was challenged by declines in its online trading volume and its overall financial performance. At least partly as a result of uncertainty created by the events of September 11, 2001, Schwab's average daily trades in the third-quarter of 2001 fell 26 percent, compared to the same period a year earlier. In turn, revenue declines were instrumental in the 50.6 percent fall in year-to-year (2000–01) net income. Following analysis of these data, as well as current and possible future conditions in the global financial industry, Schwab concluded that its website and discount trades could no longer be the foundation for the firm's strategy in what were rapidly changing financial markets. Supporting this conclusion was feedback indicating that an increasing number of investors, when making their investment choices, want a relationship in the form of financial advice, in addition to low trading costs. This feedback is not surprising—recent evidence suggests that customers prefer to receive all types of financial services through relationships rather than through encounters. Commenting about the importance of the trend of customers wanting personal relationships, one analyst noted, "If Schwab doesn't offer advice, it risks losing the customer relationship altogether."[18] As a result of Schwab's evaluation of its current situation and future possibilities, the firm decided to change its cost leadership strategy as a discount broker to an integrated cost leadership–differentiation strategy. This change was made so Schwab could offer relatively low-cost financial advice while simultaneously becoming more of a full-service brokerage house.

Schwab's decision makers recognized that the firm's structure would have to change to support the new strategy. Historically, the firm's strategy called for Schwab brokers to take orders rather than sell them. In that structure, the brokers served as intermediaries between customers who had decided what they wanted to buy with the sellers of those products. The firm's new structure must now support brokers' efforts to find customers and sell advice and a broad array of products. Work in the previous structure was largely centralized and dictated by rules and procedures. To support a marketing, advice-driven strategy, Schwab's structure needs to be more decentralized with greater decision responsibility at the individual broker level.

Efforts are underway at Schwab to match structure with the new strategy. If that match proves to be valuable, rare, and imperfectly imitable, the firm will have a competitive advantage based on its integration between strategy and structure.

Evolutionary Patterns of Strategy and Organizational Structure

Research suggests that most firms experience a certain pattern of relationships between strategy and structure. Chandler found that firms tended to grow in somewhat predictable patterns: "… first by volume, then by geography, then integration (vertical, horizontal) and finally through product/business diversification."[19] (See Figure 12.1.) Chandler interpreted his findings to indicate that the firm's growth patterns determine its structural form.

As shown in Figure 12.1, sales growth creates problems of coordination and control that the existing organizational structure can't efficiently handle. Organizational growth creates the opportunity for the firm to change its strategy to try to become even more successful. However, the existing structure's formal reporting relationships, procedures, controls, and authority and decision-making processes lack the sophistication required to support use of the new strategy. A new structure is needed that can help decision makers gain access to the knowledge and understanding required to effectively coordinate and integrate the actions to implement the new strategy.[20]

Three major types of organizational structures are used to implement strategies: simple structure, functional structure, and multidivisional structure.

Simple Structure

The **simple structure** is a structure in which the owner–manager makes all major decisions and monitors all activities, while the staff serves as an extension of the manager's supervisory authority.

The **simple structure** is a structure in which the owner–manager makes all major decisions and monitors all activities, while the staff serves as an extension of the manager's supervisory authority.[21] Typically, the owner–manager actively works in the business on a daily basis. Informal relationships, few rules, limited task specialization, and unsophisticated information systems describe the simple structure. Frequent and informal communications between the owner–manager and employees make it relatively easy to coordinate the work that is to be done. The simple structure is matched with focus strategies and business-level strategies as firms commonly compete by offering a single product line in a single geographic market. Local restaurants, repair businesses, and other specialized enterprises are examples of firms relying on the simple structure to implement their strategy.

As the small firm grows larger and becomes more complex, managerial and structural challenges emerge. For example, the amount of competitively relevant information requiring analysis substantially increases, placing significant pressure on the owner–manager. Still additional growth and success may cause the firm to change its strategy. Even if the strategy remains the same, the firm's larger size dictates the need for more sophisticated workflows and integrating mechanisms. At this evolutionary point, firms tend to move from the simple structure to a functional organizational structure.[22]

Functional Structure

The **functional structure** is a structure consisting of a chief executive officer and a limited corporate staff, with functional line managers in dominant organizational areas, such as production, accounting, marketing, R&D, engineering, and human resources.

The **functional structure** is a structure consisting of a chief executive officer and a limited corporate staff, with functional line managers in dominant organizational areas, such as production, accounting, marketing, R&D, engineering, and human resources. This structure allows for functional specialization, thereby facilitating active sharing of knowledge within each functional area. Knowledge sharing facilitates career paths as well as the professional development of functional specialists. However, a functional orientation can have a negative effect on communication and coordination among those representing different organizational functions. Because of this effect, the CEO must work hard to verify that the decisions and actions of individual business functions promote the entire firm rather than a single function. The functional structure supports implementation of business-level strategies and some corporate-level strategies (e.g., single or dominant business) with low levels of diversification.[23]

Figure 12.1 | Strategy and Structure Growth Pattern

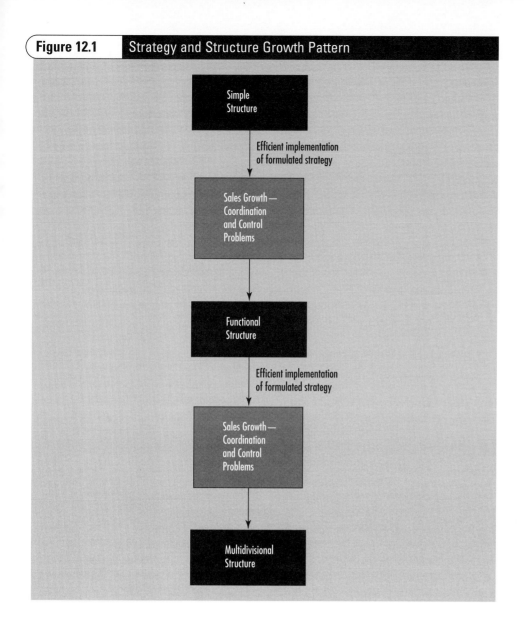

Multidivisional Structure

With continuing growth and success, firms often consider greater levels of diversification. However, successful diversification requires analysis of substantially greater amounts of data and information when the firm offers the same products in different markets (market or geographic diversification) or offers different products in several markets (product diversification). In addition, trying to manage high levels of diversification through functional structures creates serious problems of coordination and control. Thus, greater diversification leads to a new structural form.[24]

The **multidivisional (M-form) structure** consists of operating divisions, each representing a separate business or profit centre in which the top corporate officer delegates responsibilities for day-to-day operations and business-unit strategy to division managers. Each division represents a distinct, self-contained business with its own functional hierarchy. As initially designed, the M-form was thought to have three major benefits:

The **multidivisional (M-form) structure** consists of operating divisions, each representing a separate business or profit centre in which the top corporate officer delegates responsibilities for day-to-day operations and business-unit strategy to division managers.

"(1) it enabled corporate officers to more accurately monitor the performance of each business, which simplified the problem of control; (2) it facilitated comparisons between divisions, which improved the resource allocation process; and (3) it stimulated managers of poorly performing divisions to look for ways of improving performance." Active monitoring of performance through the M-form increases the likelihood that decisions made by managers heading individual units will be in shareholders' best interests. Diversification is a dominant corporate-level strategy in the global economy, resulting in extensive use of the M-form.[25]

Used to support implementation of related and unrelated diversification strategies, the M-form helps firms successfully manage the many demands (including those related to processing vast amounts of information) of diversification. Chandler viewed the M-form as an innovative response to problems of coordination and control that surfaced during the 1920s in the functional structures then used by large firms such as DuPont and General Motors. Research shows that the M-form is appropriate when the firm grows through diversification. Partly because of its value to diversified corporations, some consider the multidivisional structure to be one of the 20th century's most significant organizational innovations.[26]

No organizational structure (simple, functional, or multidivisional) is inherently superior to the other structures.[27] As a result, managers concentrate on developing proper matches between strategies and organizational structures rather than searching for an optimal structure. We now describe the strategy–structure matches that evidence shows positively contribute to firm performance.

Matches between Business-Level Strategies and the Functional Structure

Different forms of the functional organizational structure are used to support implementation of the cost leadership, differentiation, and integrated cost leadership–differentiation strategies. The differences in these forms are accounted for primarily by different uses of three important structural characteristics or dimensions—*specialization* (concerned with the type and number of jobs required to complete work), *centralization* (the degree to which decision-making authority is retained at higher managerial levels), and *formalization* (the degree to which formal rules and procedures govern work).[28]

Using the Functional Structure to Implement the Cost Leadership Strategy

Firms using the cost leadership strategy want to sell large quantities of standardized products to an industry's or a segment's typical customer. Simple reporting relationships, few layers in the decision-making and authority structure, a centralized corporate staff, and a strong focus on process improvements through the manufacturing function (rather than the development of new products through an emphasis on product R&D) characterize the cost leadership form of the functional structure[29] (see Figure 12.2). This structure contributes to the emergence of a low-cost culture—a culture in which all employees constantly try to find ways to reduce the costs incurred to complete their work.

In terms of centralization, decision-making authority is centralized in a staff function to maintain a cost-reducing emphasis within each organizational function (e.g., engineering and marketing). While encouraging continuous cost reductions, the centralized staff also verifies that further cuts in costs in one function won't adversely affect the productivity levels in other functions.

Jobs are highly specialized in the cost leadership functional structure. Job specialization is accomplished by dividing work into homogeneous subgroups. Organizational functions are the most common subgroup, although work is sometimes batched on the

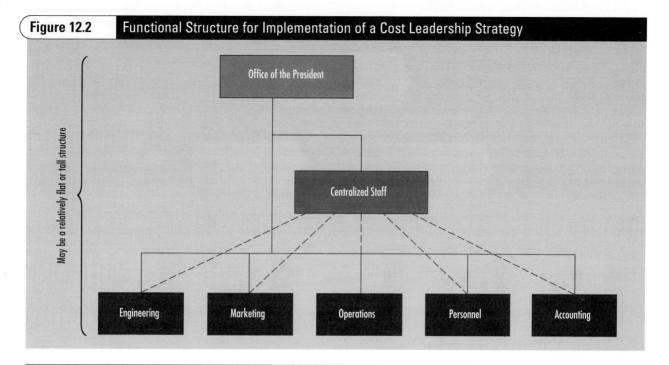

Figure 12.2   Functional Structure for Implementation of a Cost Leadership Strategy

Notes: • Operations is the main function
- Process engineering is emphasized rather than new product R&D
- Relatively large centralized staff coordinates functions
- Formalized procedures allow for emergence of a low-cost culture
- Overall structure is mechanical; job roles are highly structured

basis of products produced or clients served. Specializing in their work allows employees to increase their efficiency, reducing the firm's costs as a result. Highly formalized rules and procedures, often emanating from the centralized staff, guide the work completed in the cost leadership form of the functional structure. Predictably following formal rules and procedures creates cost-reducing efficiencies. Known for its commitment to EDLP (everyday low price), Wal-Mart's functional organizational structures in both its retail (e.g., Wal-Mart Stores, Supercenters, and Sam's Club) and specialty (e.g., Wal-Mart Vacations and Wal-Mart Used Fixture Auctions) divisions are formed to continuously drive costs lower.[30] Competitors' efforts to duplicate the success of Wal-Mart's cost leadership strategies have failed, partly because of Wal-Mart's effective strategy–structure configurations in its business units.

Using the Functional Structure to Implement the Differentiation Strategy

Firms using the differentiation strategy produce products that customers perceive as being different in ways that create value for them. With this strategy, the firm wants to sell nonstandardized products to customers with unique needs. Relatively complex and flexible reporting relationships, frequent use of cross-functional product development teams, and a strong focus on marketing and product R&D rather than manufacturing and process R&D (as with the cost leadership form of the functional structure) characterize the differentiation form of the functional structure (see Figure 12.3 on page 368). This structure contributes to the emergence of a development-oriented culture—a culture in which employees try to find ways to further differentiate current products and to develop new, highly differentiated products.

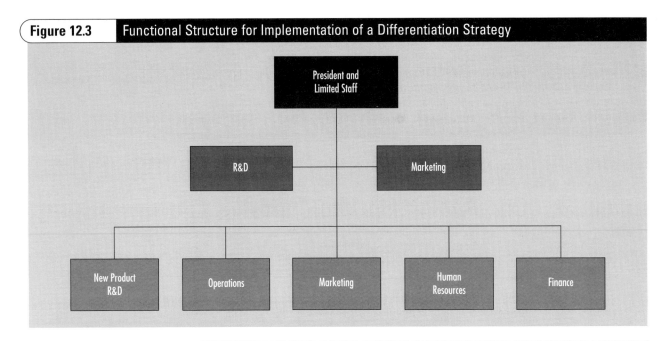

| Figure 12.3 | Functional Structure for Implementation of a Differentiation Strategy |

Notes:
- Marketing is the main function for keeping track of new product ideas
- New product R&D is emphasized
- Most functions are decentralized, but R&D and marketing may have centralized staffs that work closely with each other
- Formalization is limited so that new product ideas can emerge easily and change is more readily accomplished
- Overall structure is organic; job roles are less structured

Continuous product innovation demands that people throughout the firm be able to interpret and take action, based on information that is often ambiguous, incomplete, and uncertain. With a strong focus on the external environment to identify new opportunities, employees often gather this information from people outside the firm, such as customers and suppliers. Commonly, rapid responses to the possibilities indicated by the collected information are necessary, suggesting the need for decision-making responsibility and authority to be decentralized. To support creativity and the continuous pursuit of new sources of differentiation and new products, jobs in this structure are not highly specialized. This lack of specialization means that workers have a relatively large number of tasks in their job descriptions. Few formal rules and procedures also characterize this structure. Low formalization, decentralization of decision-making authority and responsibility, and low specialization of work tasks combine to create a structure in which people interact frequently to exchange ideas about how to further differentiate current products while developing ideas for new products that can be differentiated to create value for customers.

Using the Functional Structure to Implement the Integrated Cost Leadership–Differentiation Strategy

Firms using the integrated cost leadership–differentiation strategy want to sell products that create value because of their "relatively" low cost and "reasonable" sources of differentiation: the cost of these products is low, *relative* to the cost leader's prices, while their differentiation is *reasonable* compared to the clearly unique features of the differentiator's products.

The integrated cost leadership–differentiation strategy is used frequently in the global economy, although it is difficult to successfully implement. This difficulty is due largely to the fact that different primary and support activities (see Chapter 4) must be emphasized when using the cost leadership and differentiation strategies. To achieve the low-cost position, emphasis is placed on production and process engineering, with infrequent product changes. To achieve a differentiated position, marketing and new-product R&D are emphasized while production and process engineering are not. Thus, use of the integrated strategy results when the firm successfully combines activities intended to reduce costs with activities intended to create additional differentiation features. As a result, the integrated form of the functional structure must have decision-making patterns that are partially centralized and partially decentralized. Additionally, jobs are semi-specialized, and rules and procedures call for some formal and some informal job behaviour.

Matches between Corporate-Level Strategies and the Multidivisional Structure

As explained earlier, Chandler's research showed that the firm's continuing success leads to product or market diversification or both.[31] The firm's level of diversification is a function of decisions about the number and type of businesses in which it will compete as well as how it will manage the businesses (see Chapter 7). Geared to managing individual organizational functions, increasing diversification eventually creates problems in information processing, coordination, and control that the functional structure can't handle. Thus, use of a diversification strategy requires the firm to change from the functional structure to the multidivisional structure to develop an appropriate strategy–structure match.

As defined in Figure 7.1, on page 209, in Chapter 7, corporate-level strategies have different degrees of product and market diversification. The demands created by different levels of diversification highlight the need for each strategy to be implemented through a unique organizational structure (see Figure 12.4 on page 370).

Using the Cooperative Form of the Multidivisional Structure to Implement the Related-Constrained Strategy

The **cooperative form** is a structure in which horizontal integration is used to bring about interdivisional cooperation. The divisions in the firm using the related-constrained diversification strategy commonly are formed around products, markets or both. The objective of related-constrained firm Procter & Gamble (P&G), to "think globally, act locally," for example, is supported by a cooperative structure of five global business product units (baby, feminine and family care, fabric and home care, food and beverage, and health and beauty care) and seven market development organizations (MDOs), each formed around a region of the world, such as Northeast Asia. Using the five global product units to create strong brand equities through ongoing innovation is how P&G thinks globally; interfacing with customers to ensure that a division's marketing plans fully capitalize on local opportunities is how P&G acts locally. Information is shared between the product-oriented and the marketing-oriented efforts to enhance the corporation's performance. Indeed, some corporate staff members are responsible for focusing on making certain that knowledge is meaningfully categorized and then rapidly transferred throughout P&G's businesses.[32]

In Figure 12.5 on page 370, we use product divisions as part of the representation of the cooperative form of the multidivisional structure, although as the P&G example suggests, market divisions could be used instead of or in addition to product divisions to develop the figure. Thus, P&G has slightly modified the core cooperative form of the multidivisional structure to satisfy its unique strategy–structure match requirements.

All of the related-constrained firm's divisions share one or more corporate strengths. Production competencies, marketing competencies, or channel dominance are examples

The **cooperative form** is a structure in which horizontal integration is used to bring about interdivisional cooperation.

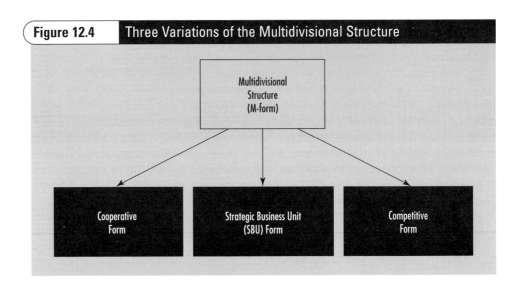

Figure 12.4 Three Variations of the Multidivisional Structure

Figure 12.5 Cooperative Form of the Multidivisional Structure for Implementation of a Related-Constrained Strategy

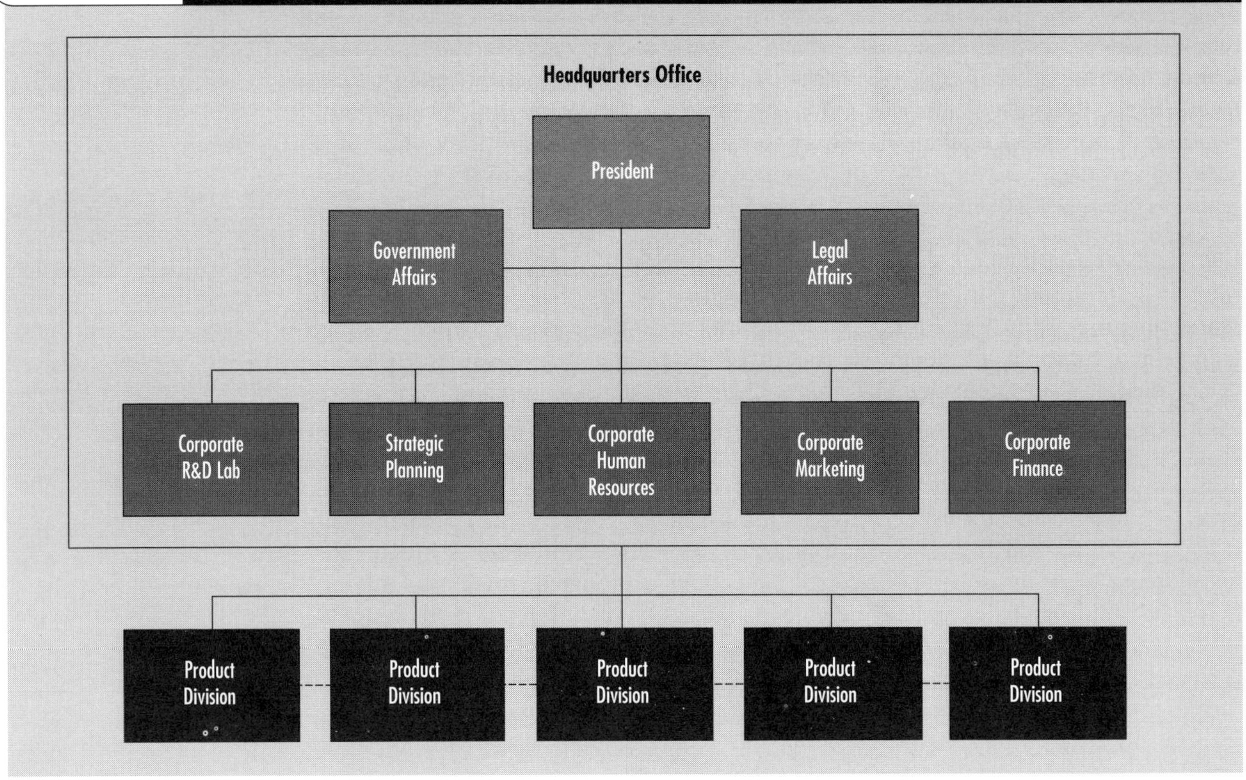

Headquarters Office

President

Government Affairs

Legal Affairs

Corporate R&D Lab

Strategic Planning

Corporate Human Resources

Corporate Marketing

Corporate Finance

Product Division

Product Division

Product Division

Product Division

Product Division

Notes: • Structural integration devices create tight links among all divisions
• Corporate office emphasizes centralized strategic planning, human resources, and marketing to foster cooperation between divisions
• R&D is likely to be centralized
• Rewards are subjective and tend to emphasize overall corporate performance in addition to divisional performance
• Culture emphasizes cooperative sharing

of strengths that the firm's divisions might share. Production expertise is one of the strengths shared across P&G's divisions.

The sharing of divisional competencies facilitates the corporation's efforts to develop economies of scope. As explained in Chapter 7, economies of scope (cost savings resulting from the sharing of competencies developed in one division with another division) are linked with successful use of the related-constrained strategy. Interdivisional sharing of competencies depends on cooperation, suggesting the use of the cooperative form of the multidivisional structure. Increasingly, it is important that the links resulting from effective use of integration mechanisms support the cooperative sharing of both intangible resources (e.g., knowledge) as well as tangible resources (e.g., facilities and equipment).[33]

Different characteristics of structure are used as integrating mechanisms by the cooperative structure to facilitate interdivisional cooperation. Defined earlier in the discussion of functional organizational structures, centralization is one of these mechanisms. Centralizing some organizational functions (human resource management, R&D, marketing, and finance) at the corporate level allows the linking of activities among divisions. Work completed in these centralized functions is managed by the firm's central office with the purpose of exploiting common strengths among divisions by sharing competencies. The intent is to develop a competitive advantage in the divisions as they implement their cost leadership, differentiation, or integrated cost leadership–differentiation, business-unit strategies that exceed the value created by the advantages used by undiversified rivals' implementation of these strategies.[34]

Frequent, direct contact between division managers, another integrating mechanism, encourages and supports cooperation and the sharing of either competencies or resources that have the possibility of being used to create new advantages. Sometimes, liaison roles are established in each division to reduce the amount of time division managers spend integrating and coordinating their unit's work with the work taking place in other divisions. Temporary teams or task forces may be formed around projects whose success depends on sharing competencies that are embedded within several divisions. Formal integration departments might be established in firms frequently using temporary teams or task forces. Ultimately, a matrix organization may evolve in firms implementing the related-constrained strategy. A *matrix organization* is an organizational structure in which there is a dual structure combining both functional specialization and business product or project specialization. Although complicated, an effective matrix structure can lead to improved coordination among a firm's divisions.[35] Figure 12.6 on page 372 gives an example of a matrix structure.

The success of the cooperative multidivisional structure is significantly affected by how well information is processed among divisions. But because cooperation among divisions implies a loss of managerial autonomy, division managers may not readily commit themselves to the type of integrative information-processing activities that this structure demands. Moreover, coordination among divisions sometimes results in an unequal flow of positive outcomes to divisional managers. In other words, when managerial rewards are based at least in part on the performance of individual divisions, the manager of the division that is able to benefit the most by the sharing of corporate competencies might be viewed as receiving relative gains at others' expense. Strategic controls are important in these instances, as divisional managers' performance can be evaluated at least partly on the basis of how well they have facilitated interdivisional cooperative efforts. Furthermore, using reward systems that emphasize overall company performance, besides outcomes achieved by individual divisions, helps overcome problems associated with the cooperative form.

Figure 12.6 | A Typical Product and Matrix Structure

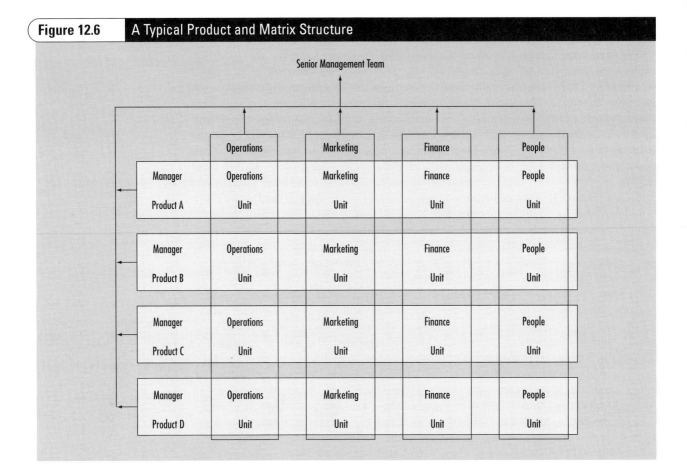

Using the Strategic Business Unit Form of the Multidivisional Structure to Implement the Related-Linked Strategy

When the firm has fewer links or less constrained links among its divisions, the related-linked diversification strategy is used. The strategic business unit form of the multidivisional structure supports implementation of this strategy. The **strategic business unit (SBU) form** is a structure consisting of three levels: corporate headquarters, strategic business units (SBUs), and SBU divisions (see Figure 12.7).

The divisions within each SBU are related in terms of shared products or markets or both, but the divisions of one SBU have little in common with the divisions of the other SBUs. Divisions within each SBU share product or market competencies to develop economies of scope and possibly economies of scale. The integration mechanisms used by the divisions in a cooperative structure can be equally well used by the divisions within the individual strategic business units that are part of the SBU form of the multi-divisional structure. In the SBU structure, each SBU is a profit centre that is controlled and evaluated by the headquarters office. Although both financial and strategic controls are important, on a relative basis, financial controls are vital to headquarters' evaluation of each SBU; strategic controls are critical when the heads of SBUs evaluate their divisions' performance. Strategic controls are also critical to the headquarters' efforts to determine if the company has chosen an effective portfolio of businesses and if those businesses are being effectively managed.

Used by large firms, the SBU structure can be complex, with the complexity reflected by the organization's size and product and market diversity. Related-linked firm GE, for

> The **strategic business unit (SBU) form** is a structure consisting of three levels: corporate headquarters, strategic business units (SBUs), and SBU divisions.

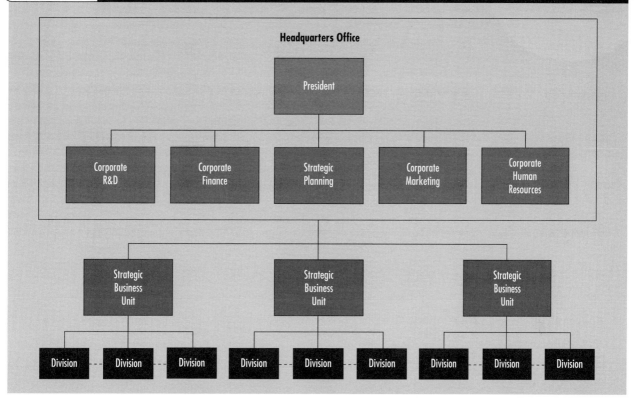

Notes: • Structural integration is emphasized among divisions within SBUs, but independence exists across SBUs
• Strategic planning may be the most prominent function in headquarters for managing the strategic planning approval process of SBUs for the president
• Each SBU may have its own budget for staff to foster integration
• Corporate headquarters staff serve as consultants to SBUs and divisions, rather than having direct input to product strategy, as in the cooperative form

example, has 28 strategic business units, each with multiple divisions. GE Aircraft Engines, GE Appliances, GE Power Systems, NBC, and GE Capital are a few of the firm's SBUs. As is frequently the case with large diversified corporations, the scale of GE's business units is striking. GE Aircraft Engines, for example, is the world's leading manufacturer of jet engines for civil and military aircraft. With almost 30 divisions, GE Capital is a diversified financial services company creating comprehensive solutions to increase client productivity and efficiency. The GE Power Systems business unit has 21 divisions, including GE Energy Rentals, GE Distributed Power, and GE Water Technologies.[36]

In many of GE's SBUs, efforts are undertaken to form competencies in services and technology as a source of competitive advantage. Recently, technology was identified as an advantage for the GE Medical Systems SBU, as that unit's divisions share technological competencies to produce an array of sophisticated equipment, including computed tomography (CT) scanners, magnetic resonance imaging (MRI) systems, nuclear medicine cameras, and ultrasound systems. Once a competence is developed in one of GE Medical Systems' divisions, it is quickly transferred to the other divisions in that SBU so that the competence can be leveraged to increase the unit's overall performance.[37]

Eastman Kodak also uses the SBU structure. In the next Strategic Focus box, "Kodak Implements the Strategic Business Unit Form to Regain Growth" on page 374, we describe this firm's evolution to the SBU structure. To date, it is not clear whether the

Kodak Implements the Strategic Business Unit Form to Regain Growth

The world's largest manufacturer of photographic film, Kodak has struggled recently with intense competitive pressures from several sources. Kodak is engaged in a fierce price war with Fuji Photo Film, its biggest competitor, to maintain its market share in film sales both in the United States and in international markets. Posing an even greater potential competitive threat are the revolutionary changes taking place in photography with the advent of digital technology. In growing numbers, consumers are abandoning traditional film, in favour of digital cameras.

Shareholder concerns about future performance pushed Kodak's stock price down from near $70 in late 2000 to the $30–$35 range in mid-2002. Contributing to shareholders' actions were recent earnings per share figures. Kodak's third-quarter 2001 earnings were $0.15 per share, significantly below the expected $0.46 per share. Although the firm's fourth-quarter 2001 earnings of $0.12 per share beat analysts' expectation of $0.09, shareholders remained unimpressed. The events of September 11 may have influenced these results, when consumers cancelled or curtailed their travel plans (less travel leads to fewer film purchases). In addition, Hollywood studios cancelled film projects and commercials, negatively affecting Kodak's entertainment business. Even Kodak's traditionally dependable medical imaging business suffered, as hospitals banded together to demand lower prices from their suppliers.

For years, Kodak used the cooperative form of the multidivisional structure to implement the related-constrained diversification strategy. In this structure, primary organizational functions, such as manufacturing, customer care, and strategic planning, were centralized, which allowed their expertise to be shared among its seven product divisions. Consistent with the cooperative structure's mandates, headquarters personnel encouraged interdivisional cooperation. In addition to the product divisions, Kodak also maintained separate divisions organized according to geographic region.

The cooperative structure worked well for Kodak, as it used the related-constrained strategy to compete in what for many years had been relatively stable markets. However, innovative technologies and increased competition disrupted these markets, making the sharing of the firm's technologies and related skills across product divisions less competitively valuable. Moreover, sharing key resources and their corresponding costs across many business units with increased competition in unstable markets made it difficult for Kodak to assess the profitability of its product divisions. The inability to pinpoint the firm's revenue and profitability sources was an issue, as Kodak had decided that it wanted to develop "anything that helps people capture, use, or store images, including digital technology." However, the firm also concluded that being able to pinpoint the revenue and profitability outcomes of all new product offerings would influence these attempts to improve its overall financial performance.

Study of its external environment and its competitive advantages found Kodak concluding that it should reduce the number of links between its business units and their products and services. In October 2000, Kodak moved to the SBU structure. As shown in the figure, this structure combined seven previous product divisions into two broad customer-oriented SBUs: the Consumer Business Group and the Commercial Business Group. Global Operations, the third SBU included in the structure, continued to handle Kodak's supply chain and operational needs.

Although this SBU structure halved the number of direct reports to the CEO, the structure did not yield the robust feedback needed to assess products on a stand-alone profitability basis, as competencies were shared within individual SBU product divisions. Furthermore, the customer groupings were too broad to generate scope and scale economies among the product divisions. Executives concluded that another form of the SBU structure was necessary.

Kodak completed a new version of its SBU structure in November 2001, as shown below. The firm believes that this version is a proper match with its newly selected related-linked diversification strategy and that it offers the benefits it had been seeking. Each product division is now

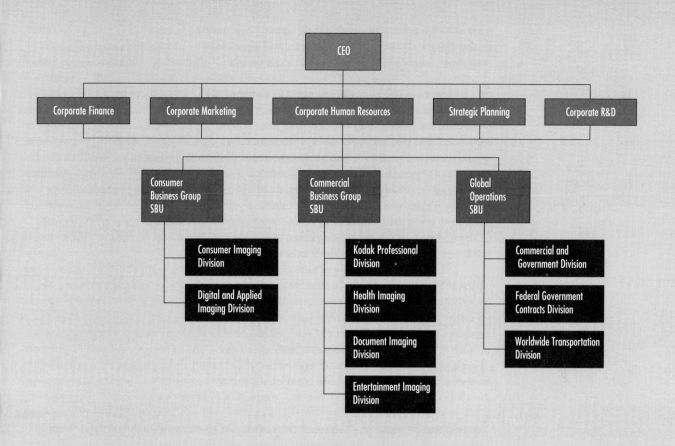

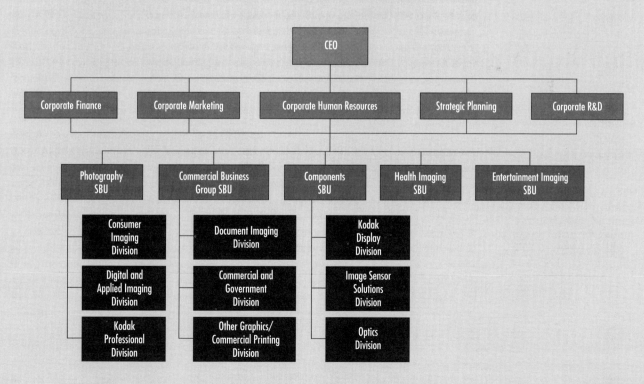

(continued)

responsible for managing all activities that affect earnings, including supply chain management, inventory, marketing, and customer service. Each product division also generates its own independent financial statements. Financial controls can be used to measure performance within divisions, creating the data required to identify the profitability of individual products and product lines. The additional autonomy this form of the SBU structure provides to division heads should allow product-related decisions to be made more quickly. The rapidly changing nature of Kodak's competitive arena affords a premium to the firm able to quickly satisfy consumers' emerging needs with new products. Finally, Kodak's product divisions should be able to realize scope and possible scale economies because they have been grouped based on a similar customer orientation, technology platform, and channel structure. Strategic controls can be used to determine the degree to which divisions are effectively sharing common competencies in terms of customers, technologies, and distribution channels.

SOURCES: Eastman Kodak Co., 2002, Kodak press center, *Eastman Kodak website*, http://www.kodak.com/US/en/corp/pressCenter/pressCenter.shtml, January 15; S. Rosenbush, 2002, A lengthy honeymoon at Lucent? *Business Week*, January 31, 34; Business Wire, 2001, Kodak's Eric Steenburgh announces retirement, *Business Wire*, November 14; C. Deutsch, 2001, Kodak realigns operations as slump in demand persists, *New York Times*, http://www.nyt.com, November 15; Reuters, 2001, Eastman Kodak restructures business units, *Reuters*, November 14; A. Hill & P. Russo, 2001, Kodak puts its faith in group reorganization, *Financial Times*, http://www.ft.com, November 15; Hoovers Online, 2001, Eastman Kodak Company, *Hoovers Online*, http://www.hoovers.com, December 12; A. Tsao, 2001, Kodak: Not enough positive developments? Its shares are off their lows, but long-term question marks over its transition to a digital world linger, *Business Week Online*, http://www.businessweek.com, November 26; Eastman Kodak Co., 2001, Kodak announces new operating model, business alignment to build profitable growth, businesses given more direct responsibility for sales and profits, *Eastman Kodak website*, http://www.kodak.com/US/en/corp/pressReleases/pr20011114-01.shtml (press release), November 14; Eastman Kodak Co., 2001, Kodak reports third-quarter 2001 sales and earnings; Operating results within expectations, economic downturn deepens, *Eastman Kodak website*, http://www.kodak.com/US/en/corp/pressReleases/pr20011024-01.shtml (press release), October 24; D. Shook, 2000, Why Kodak is worth focusing on again: The company's plausible digital strategy could slowly start to improve its image on the Street, *Business Week Online*, http://www.businessweek.com, June 27.

diversification strategy and structure are now properly matched at Kodak. This latest structural change occurred under Patricia Russo's leadership as CEO. However, Russo departed after only eight months at Kodak to accept the CEO position at Lucent Technologies.[38] In spite of this disruption to the firm's operations, Kodak's current leadership is confident that it has the strategy and structure in place that will lead to competitive success.

Using the Competitive Form of the Multidivisional Structure to Implement the Unrelated Diversification Strategy

Firms using the unrelated diversification strategy want to create value through efficient internal capital allocations or by restructuring, buying, and selling businesses.[39] The competitive form of the multidivisional structure supports implementation of this strategy.

The **competitive form** is a structure in which there is complete independence among the firm's divisions.

The **competitive form** is a structure in which there is complete independence among the firm's divisions (see Figure 12.8). Unlike the divisions included in the cooperative structure, the divisions that are part of the competitive structure do not share common corporate strengths (e.g., marketing competencies or channel dominance). Because strengths aren't shared, integrating devices aren't developed for use by the divisions included in the competitive structure.

The efficient internal capital market that is the foundation for use of the unrelated diversification strategy requires organizational arrangements that emphasize divisional competition rather than cooperation. Three benefits are expected from the internal competition that the competitive form of the multidivisional structure facilitates. First, internal competition creates flexibility—corporate headquarters can have divisions working on different technologies to identify those with the greatest future potential. Resources can then be allocated to the division that is working with the most promising technology to fuel the entire firm's success. Second, internal competition challenges the

Figure 12.8 Competitive Form of the Multidivisional Structure for Implementation of an Unrelated Strategy

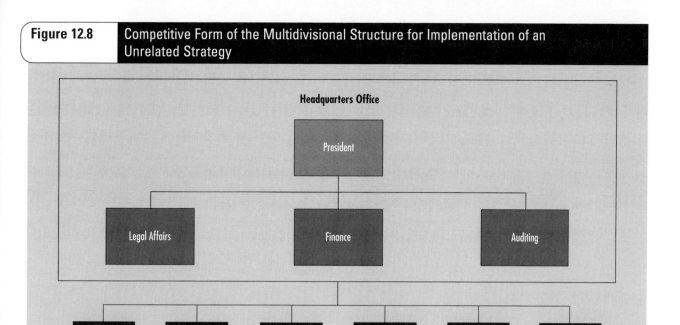

Notes: • Corporate headquarters has a small staff
   • In the headquarters office, finance and auditing are the most prominent functions, managing cash flow and ensuring the accuracy of performance data coming from divisions
   • The legal affairs function becomes important when the firm acquires or divests assets
   • Divisions are independent and separate for financial evaluation purposes
   • Divisions retain strategic control, but cash is managed by the corporate office
   • Divisions compete for corporate resources

status quo and inertia, because division heads know that future resource allocations are a product of excellent current performance as well as superior positioning of their division in terms of future performance. Lastly, internal competition motivates effort. The challenge of competing against internal peers can be as great as the challenge of competing against external marketplace competitors.[40]

Independence among divisions, as shown by a lack of sharing of corporate strengths and the absence of integrating devices, allows the firm using the unrelated diversification strategy to form specific profit performance expectations for each division to stimulate internal competition for future resources. The benefits of internal capital allocations or restructuring cannot be fully realized unless divisions are held accountable for their own independent performance. In the competitive structure, organizational controls (primarily financial controls) are used to emphasize and support internal competition among separate divisions and as the basis for allocating corporate capital based on divisions' performances.

To emphasize competitiveness among divisions, the headquarters office maintains an arms-length relationship with them and does not intervene in divisional affairs, except to audit operations and discipline managers whose divisions perform poorly. In this situation, the headquarters office relies on strategic controls to set rate-of-return targets and financial controls to monitor divisional performance relative to those targets. The headquarters office then allocates cash flow on a competitive basis, rather than automatically returning cash to the division that produced it. Thus, the focus of the headquarters' work is on performance appraisal, resource allocation, and long-range planning to verify that the firm's portfolio of businesses will lead to financial success.[41]

Toronto-based Onex Corporation is an example of a Canadian firm that pursues a corporate-level strategy of unrelated diversification along with the associated competitive form of the M-Form structure. Onex achieves financial economies through both risk reduction and the buying and selling of other firms to restructure their assets. Onex has been successful in growing shareholder value (29 percent) when compared to indexes such as the TSX (12 percent), the S&P 500 (15 percent) and the S&P/TSX Composite (10 percent). Among Onex's operating principles are risk reduction through the deliberate development of a portfolio of businesses that earns appropriate returns for appropriate risks and helping the existing management of acquired businesses increase value over the long term. Onex owns businesses as diverse as computer components, electronic components, movie theatres, financial services, and health care services.

The three major forms of the multidivisional structure should each be paired with a particular corporate-level strategy. Table 12.1 shows these structures' characteristics. Differences are seen in the degree of centralization, the focus of the performance appraisal, the horizontal structures (integrating mechanisms), and the incentive compensation schemes. The most centralized and most costly structural form is the cooperative structure. The least centralized, with the lowest bureaucratic costs, is the competitive structure. The SBU structure requires partial centralization and involves some of the mechanisms necessary to implement the relatedness among divisions. Also, the divisional incentive compensation awards are allocated according to both SBUs and corporate performance.

Matches between International Strategies and Worldwide Structures

As explained in Chapter 8, international strategies are becoming increasingly important for long-term competitive success. Along with other benefits, international strategies allow the firm to search for new markets, resources, core competencies, and technologies as part of its efforts to outperform competitors.[42]

| Table 12.1 | Characteristics of the Structures Necessary to Implement the Related-Constrained, Related-Linked, and Unrelated Diversification Strategies |

	Overall Structural Form		
Structural Characteristics	Cooperative M-Form (Related-Constrained Strategy)[a]	SBU M-Form (Related-Linked Strategy)[a]	Competitive M-Form (Unrelated Diversification Strategy)[a]
Centralization of operations	Centralized at corporate office	Partially centralized (in SBUs)	Decentralized to divisions
Use of integration mechanisms	Extensive	Moderate	Nonexistent
Divisional performance appraisals	Emphasize subjective (strategic) criteria	Use a mixture of subjective (strategic) and objective (financial) criteria	Emphasize objective (financial) criteria
Divisional incentive compensation	Linked to overall corporate performance	Mixed linkage to corporate, SBU, and divisional performance	Linked to divisional performance

[a]Strategy implemented with structural form.

As with business-level and corporate-level strategies, unique organizational structures are necessary to successfully implement the different international strategies. Forming proper matches between international strategies and organizational structures facilitates the firm's efforts to effectively coordinate and control its global operations. More importantly, recent research findings confirm the validity of the international strategy–structure matches we discuss here.[43]

Using the Worldwide Geographic Area Structure to Implement the Multidomestic Strategy

The *multidomestic strategy* decentralizes the firm's strategic and operating decisions to business units in each country so that product characteristics can be tailored to local preferences. Firms using this strategy try to isolate themselves from global competitive forces by establishing protected market positions or by competing in industry segments that are most affected by differences among local countries. The worldwide geographic area structure is used to implement this strategy. The **worldwide geographic area structure** is a structure emphasizing national interests and facilitating the firm's efforts to satisfy local or cultural differences (see Figure 12.9).

The **worldwide geographic area structure** is a structure emphasizing national interests and facilitating the firm's efforts to satisfy local or cultural differences.

Because using the multidomestic strategy requires little coordination between different country markets, integrating mechanisms among divisions in the worldwide geographic area structure aren't needed. Hence, formalization is low, and coordination among units in a firm's worldwide geographic area structure is often informal.

| Figure 12.9 | Worldwide Geographic Area Structure for Implementation of a Multidomestic Strategy |

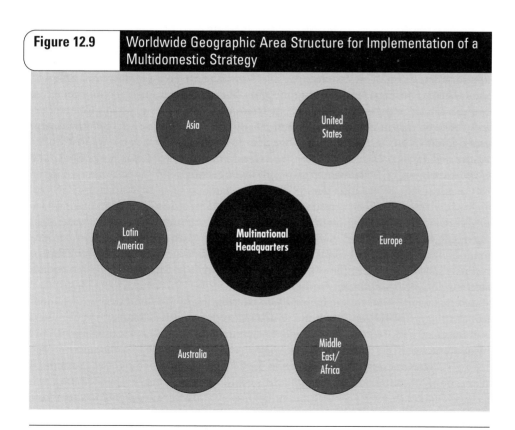

Notes: • The perimeter circles indicate decentralization of operations
   • Emphasis is on differentiation by local demand to fit an area or country culture
   • Corporate headquarters coordinates financial resources among independent subsidiaries
   • The organization functions like a decentralized federation

The multidomestic strategy–worldwide geographic area structure evolved as a natural outgrowth of the multicultural European marketplace. Friends and family members of the main business who were sent as expatriates into foreign countries to develop the independent country subsidiary often implemented this type of structure for the main business. The relationship to corporate headquarters by divisions took place through informal communication among family members.[44]

Unilever, the giant Dutch consumer products firm, has refocused its business operations. As a result, the firm grouped its worldwide operations into two global divisions—foods and home and personal care. The firm uses the worldwide geographic area structure. For the foods division (known as Unilever Bestfoods), regional presidents are responsible for results from operations in the region to which they have been assigned. Asia, Europe, North America, Africa, Middle East and Turkey, and Latin America are the regions of the foods division. The firm describes the match between the multidomestic strategy and Unilever's worldwide geographic structure (in terms of the firm's foods division): "Unilever Bestfoods' strength lies in our ability to tailor products to different markets as well as to anticipate consumer trends and demands. This comes from our deep understanding of the countries in which we operate and our policy of listening to our customers."[45]

A key disadvantage of the multidomestic strategy–worldwide geographic area structure is the inability to create global efficiency. With an increasing emphasis on lower cost products in international markets, the need to pursue worldwide economies of scale has also increased. These changes have fostered the use of the global strategy and its structural match, the worldwide product divisional structure.

Using the Worldwide Product Divisional Structure to Implement the Global Strategy

With the corporation's home office dictating competitive strategy, the *global strategy* is one through which the firm offers standardized products across country markets. The firm's success depends on its ability to develop and take advantage of economies of scope and scale on a global level. Decisions to outsource some primary or support activities to the world's best providers are particularly helpful when the firm tries to develop economies of scale.

The **worldwide product divisional structure** is a structure in which decision-making authority is centralized in the worldwide division headquarters to coordinate and integrate decisions and actions among divisional business units.

The worldwide product divisional structure supports use of the global strategy. In the **worldwide product divisional structure**, decision-making authority is centralized in the worldwide division headquarters to coordinate and integrate decisions and actions among divisional business units (see Figure 12.10). This structure is often used in rapidly growing firms seeking to manage their diversified product lines effectively, as in Japan's Kyowa Hakko. With businesses in pharmaceuticals, chemicals, biochemicals, and liquor and food, this company uses the worldwide product divisional structure to facilitate its decisions about how to successfully compete in what it believes are rapidly shifting global competitive environments.[46]

Integrating mechanisms are important to effective use of the worldwide product divisional structure. Direct contact between managers, liaison roles between departments, and temporary task forces, as well as permanent teams are examples of these mechanisms. One researcher describes the use of these mechanisms in the worldwide structure, "There is extensive and formal use of task forces and operating committees to supplement communication and coordination of worldwide operations."[47] The evolution of a shared vision of the firm's strategy and how structure supports its implementation is one of the important outcomes resulting from these mechanisms' effective use. The disadvantages of the global strategy–worldwide structure combination are the difficulty involved with coordinating decisions and actions across country borders and the inability to quickly respond to local needs and preferences.

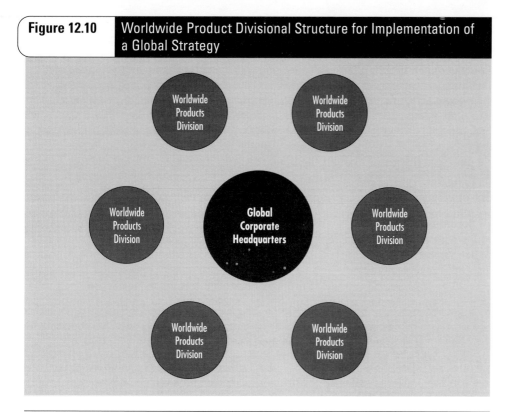

Notes: • The headquarters circle indicates centralization to coordinate information flow among worldwide products
• Corporate headquarters uses many intercoordination devices to facilitate global economies of scale and scope
• Corporate headquarters also allocates financial resources in a cooperative way
• The organization functions like a centralized federation

Using the Combination Structure to Implement the Transnational Strategy

The *transnational strategy* calls for the firm to combine the multidomestic strategy's local responsiveness with the global strategy's efficiency. Thus, firms using this strategy are trying to gain the advantages of both local responsiveness and global efficiency.[48] The combination structure is used to implement the transnational strategy. The **combination structure** is a structure drawing characteristics and mechanisms from both the worldwide geographic area structure and the worldwide product divisional structure.

The fits between the multidomestic strategy and the worldwide geographic area structure and between the global strategy and the worldwide product divisional structure are apparent. However, when a firm wants to implement both the multidomestic and the global strategy simultaneously through a combination structure, the appropriate integrating mechanisms for the two structures are less obvious. The structure used to implement the transnational strategy must be simultaneously centralized and decentralized, integrated and nonintegrated, formalized and nonformalized. These seemingly opposite characteristics must be managed by an overall structure that is capable of encouraging all employees to understand the effects of cultural diversity on a firm's operations.

This requirement highlights the need for a strong educational component to change the whole culture of the organization. If the cultural change is effective, the combination structure should allow the firm to learn how to gain competitive benefits in local economies by adapting its core competencies, which often have been developed and

The **combination structure** is a structure drawing characteristics and mechanisms from both the worldwide geographic area structure and the worldwide product divisional structure.

nurtured in less culturally diverse competitive environments. As firms globalize and move toward the transnational strategy, the idea of a corporate headquarters has become increasingly important in fostering leadership and a shared vision to create a stronger company identity.[49]

Matches between Cooperative Strategies and Network Structures

As discussed in Chapter 10, a network strategy exists when partners form several alliances together in order to improve the performance of the alliance network itself through cooperative endeavours. The greater levels of environmental complexity and uncertainty that companies face in today's competitive environment are causing increasing numbers of firms to use cooperative strategies, such as strategic alliances and joint ventures.[50]

The breadth and scope of firms' operations in the global economy create many opportunities for firms to cooperate. In fact, the firm can develop cooperative relationships with many of its stakeholders, including customers, suppliers, and competitors. When the firm becomes involved with combinations of cooperative relationships, it is part of a strategic network.[51]

A *strategic network* is a group of firms that has been formed to create value by participating in multiple cooperative arrangements, such as alliances and joint ventures. An effective strategic network facilitates the discovery of opportunities beyond those identified by individual network participants. A strategic network can be a source of competitive advantage for its members when its operations create value that is difficult for competitors to duplicate and that network members can't create by themselves. Strategic networks are used to implement business-level, corporate-level, and international cooperative strategies.[52]

Commonly, a strategic network is a loose federation of partners who participate in the network's operations on a flexible basis. At the core or centre of the strategic network, the *strategic centre firm* is the one around which the network's cooperative relationships revolve (see Figure 12.11).

Because of its central position, the strategic centre firm is the foundation for the strategic network's structure. Concerned with various aspects of organizational structure, such as formal reporting relationships and procedures, the strategic centre firm manages what are often complex, cooperative interactions among network partners. The strategic centre firm is engaged in four primary tasks as it manages the strategic network and controls its operations:[53]

Strategic Outsourcing

The strategic centre firm outsources and partners with more firms than do other network members. At the same time, the strategic centre firm requires network partners to be more than contractors. Members are expected to find opportunities for the network to create value through its cooperative work.

Competencies

To increase network effectiveness, the strategic centre firm seeks ways to support each member's efforts to develop core competencies that can benefit the network.

Technology

The strategic centre firm is responsible for managing the development and sharing of technology-based ideas among network members. The structural requirement that members submit formal reports detailing the technology-oriented outcomes of their efforts to the strategic centre firm facilitates this activity.

Figure 12.11 | A Strategic Network

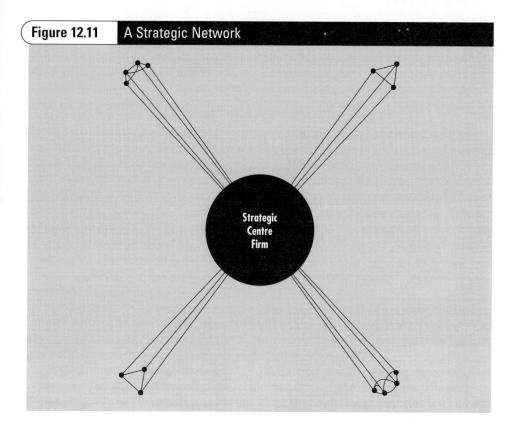

Race to Learn

The strategic centre firm emphasizes that the principal dimensions of competition are among value chains and among networks of value chains. Because of this structure, the strategic network is only as strong as its weakest value-chain link. With its centralized decision-making authority and responsibility, the strategic centre firm guides participants in efforts to form network-specific competitive advantages. The need for each participant to have capabilities that can be the foundation for the network's competitive advantages encourages friendly rivalry among participants seeking to develop the skills needed to quickly form new capabilities that create value for the network.[54]

Implementing Business-Level Cooperative Strategies

As noted in Chapter 10, there are two types of business-level complementary alliances: vertical and horizontal. Firms with competencies in different stages of the value chain form a vertical alliance to cooperatively integrate their different, but complementary, skills. Firms who agree to combine their competencies to create value in the same stage of the value chain form a horizontal alliance. Vertical complementary strategic alliances, such as those developed by Toyota Motor Corporation, are formed more frequently than horizontal alliances. Acting as the strategic centre firm, Toyota fashioned its lean production system around a network of supplier firms.[55]

A strategic network of vertical relationships, such as the network in Japan between Toyota and its suppliers, often involves a number of implementation issues. First, the strategic centre firm encourages subcontractors to modernize their facilities and provides them with technical and financial assistance, if necessary. Second, the strategic centre firm reduces its transaction costs by promoting longer term contracts with subcontractors, so that supplier-partners increase their long-term productivity. This approach is diametrically opposed to that of continually negotiating short-term contracts based on unit pricing. Third, the strategic centre firm enables engineers in upstream companies (suppliers) to have better communication with those companies with whom it has contracts for services. As a result, suppliers and the strategic centre firm become more interdependent and less independent.[56]

The lean production system pioneered by Toyota has been diffused throughout the Japanese and Canadian–U.S. automobile industries. However, no automobile company has learned how to duplicate the manufacturing effectiveness and efficiency Toyota derives from the cooperative arrangements in its strategic network.[57] A key factor accounting for Toyota's manufacturing-based competitive advantage is the cost other firms would incur to imitate the structural form used to support Toyota's application. Thus, in part, the structure of Toyota's strategic network that it created as the strategic centre firm facilitates cooperative actions among network participants that competitors can't fully understand or duplicate.

In vertical complementary strategic alliances, such as the one between Toyota and its suppliers, the strategic centre firm is obvious, as is the structure that that firm establishes. However, this is not always the case with horizontal complementary strategic alliances where firms try to create value in the same part of the value chain, as with airline alliances that are commonly formed to create value in the primary activity segment of the value chain, marketing and sales (see Table 4.8, on page 124).

As strategic networks, airline alliances have not been very stable. An airline may decide to change alliances, as when Delta left a network with Swiss Air and Sabena, its primary partners, to join Air France, Korean Air, and Aero Mexico to form the Sky Team alliance (Alitalia has since joined this network). Alternatively, an airline may simultaneously participate in several strategic networks. American Airlines (AA) and British Airways (BA) are members of the Oneworld alliance of eight airlines. However, BA formed another network (and serves as the strategic centre firm) to provide region-specific service to customers and to extend its reach by offering a broader set of destination choices to its customers. Called franchise carriers, its partners (including British Mediterranean Airways, Brymon Airlines, Loganair, and Maersk Air) fly aircraft featuring the BA cabin interior and in-flight service is provided by personnel wearing BA uniforms. In addition, BA has a separate partnership with AA and Iberia Airlines, all of whom are also members of Oneworld. Participating in multiple networks makes it difficult to select the strategic centre firm and may cause firms to question partners' true loyalties and intentions. For these reasons, horizontal complementary alliances are used less frequently than their vertical counterpart.[58]

Strategic networks have been important to Cisco Systems, Inc. The worldwide leader in networking for the Internet, Cisco provides a broad line of solutions for transporting data, voice, and video in multiple settings and has been involved with a number of strategic networks in its pursuit of competitive success. Historically, the firm's structure featured three primary business units—enterprise, service provider, and commercial. In late 2001, Cisco changed its structure to create 11 technology areas.[59] Will cooperative strategies be as critical to the firm as it completes its work through the dictates of a new organizational structure? In all likelihood, this will be the case, although the evolution of strategy and structure at Cisco will ultimately decide this issue.

Implementing Corporate-Level Cooperative Strategies

Corporate-level cooperative strategies (e.g., franchising) are used to facilitate product and market diversification. As a cooperative strategy, franchising allows the firm to use its competencies to extend or diversify its product or market reach, but without completing a merger or acquisition. For example, McDonald's, the largest fast-food company in the world, has more than 50 percent of its almost 30,000 restaurants outside the United States (with 1300 in Canada) and serves more than 46 million customers daily.[60]

The McDonald's franchising system is a strategic network. McDonald's headquarters office serves as the strategic centre firm for the network's franchisees. The headquarters office uses strategic controls and financial controls to verify that the franchisees' operations create the greatest value for the entire network. One strategic control issue is the location of franchisee units. McDonald's believes that its greatest expansion opportunities are outside the United States. Density percentages seem to support this conclusion. In the United States and Canada, there are 22,000 to 23,000 people per McDonald's, in the rest of the world there is only one McDonald's for every 605,000 people.[61] As a result, as the strategic centre firm, McDonald's is devoting its capital expenditures (more than 70 percent in the last three years) primarily to develop units in non–U.S. and Canadian markets. Financial controls are framed around requirements an interested party must satisfy to become a McDonald's franchisee as well as performance standards that are to be met when operating a unit.[62]

McDonald's Canada is an example of a firm that uses vertical and horizontal complementary alliances. It has a vertical network of more than 120 Canadian suppliers from whom it purchased $680 million worth of paper and food goods in 2002, representing in excess of 90 percent of McDonald's Canada's total purchases for that year. In addition, 65 percent of McDonald's Canada's restaurants are owned and operated by Canadian entrepreneurs. Finally, an example of its horizontal alliances is the placement of approximately 200 nontraditional restaurants in Wal-Mart stores across Canada.[63]

As the strategic centre of its cooperative network of franchisees, McDonald's concentrates on finding ways for all network units to improve their performance. Currently, the headquarters office is developing an evaluation system to improve customer service, especially in the U.S. and Canadian units. Increased training for personnel and simplification of processes used to take and deliver orders are actions that the strategic centre firm is requiring of all network members. In addition, the financial controls used to determine the bonuses for regional teams are being changed. The intent is to increase managers' accountability for the performance of units for which they are responsible.

Improving service throughout a strategic network as large as the McDonald's franchise system is challenging.[64] However, being able to do this is necessary for the strategic centre firm to increase the value created by its corporate-level cooperative franchising strategy.

Implementing International Cooperative Strategies

Strategic networks formed to implement international cooperative strategies result in firms competing in several countries. Differences among countries' regulatory environments increase the challenge of managing international networks and verifying that, at a minimum, the network's operations comply with all legal requirements.[65]

Distributed strategic networks are the organizational structure used to manage international cooperative strategies. As shown in Figure 12.12 on page 386, several regional strategic centre firms are included in the distributed network to manage partner firms' multiple cooperative arrangements. Strategic centres for Ericsson (a supplier of telecommunications exchange equipment) and Electrolux (a producer of white goods, such as washing machines) are located in countries throughout the world, instead of only in Sweden where the firms are headquartered. Ericsson, for example, is active in more than 140 countries and employs more than 90,000 people. Using the SBU structure, Ericsson has five strategic business units and has formed cooperative agreements with companies throughout the world in each unit. As a founding member of an Ethernet alliance (Intel

Figure 12.12 A Distributed Strategic Network

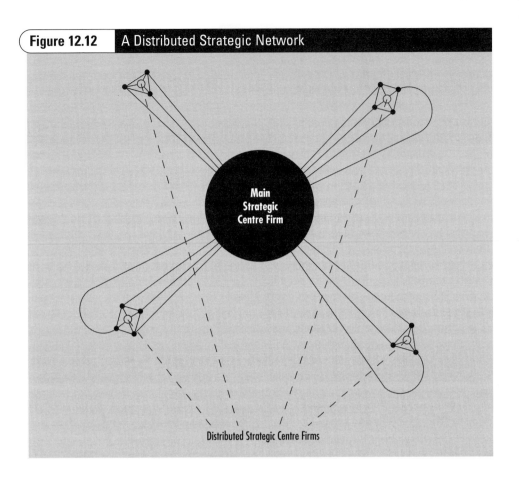

Distributed Strategic Centre Firms

and Cisco are also members), Ericsson acts as the strategic centre firm for this cooperative arrangement, which seeks to solve the wireline access bottleneck by promoting open industry standards.[66]

Organizational Structure and Controls: An Additional Perspective

As noted in Chapter 5, no business-level strategy is inherently superior to the others. In this chapter, we note that the same is true for organizational structures. The objective when dealing with strategy and structure is to design a way for the firm's work to be completed, as called for by a strategy's focus and details. Peter Drucker's words address this matter: "There is no one right organization anymore. Rather, the task … is to select the organization for the particular task and mission at hand."[67] In our context, Drucker is suggesting that the firm must select a structure that is right for the particular strategy that has been chosen to pursue the firm's strategic intent and strategic mission.

The increasingly competitive global economy finds firms continuously modifying the use of their strategies to improve performance. An important theme of this chapter is that once a strategy has been modified, the firm should also change how its work is to be done through changing its structure, control, and reward systems. Thus, 21st-century companies, especially global competitors, are in a stream of strategy and structure changes. In all cases, the outcome sought is to develop an effective match between what the firm intends to do (as indicated by strategy) with how it intends to do it (as indicated by structure, controls, and reward systems).

Semco's Unique Organizational Structure

Semco is a diversified Brazilian manufacturing company specializing in marine and food service equipment. The firm's strategy is to grow by sharing ideas, people, technologies, and distribution channels. Thus, Semco essentially follows a dominant-business diversification strategy (one in which there is some, but not extensive product and market diversification). Supporting the use of this strategy is a unique organizational structure that appears to be effectively matched with the firm's strategy.

Semco was teetering on the brink of bankruptcy in the early 1980s when Ricardo Semler, the founder's son, became president at the age of 22. Semler thought that management control in the form of pyramidal hierarchy stifled creativity and flexibility. He believed that employees should be treated as adults and managed by common sense rather than by rules, procedures, and formal decision-making processes. To implement his unconventional ideas, Semler streamlined Semco's organizational structure into an organizational circle. Pictured here, this structure consists of three concentric circles, each representing a management level. One level is corporate and the other two are operating levels.

The smaller circle depicts the corporate level, containing the six individuals (called counsellors) who are jointly responsible for coordinating Semco's operations. Rather than having a permanent CEO, Semco rotates each counsellor into the CEO position for a six-month period. This structural characteristic allows responsibility for the firm's performance to be shared rather than isolated to one key executive. In Semler's view, "When financial performance is one person's problem, then everyone else can relax. In our system, no one can relax. You get to pass on the baton, but it comes back again two-and-a-half years later." The middle circle depicts the operating level of Semco's divisions and includes the division heads (called partners). The outer, largest circle also depicts an operating level and holds Semco's remaining employees, the

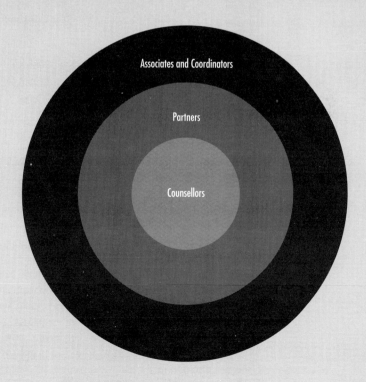

(continued)

majority of whom are classified as associates. Without direct reports, associates perform the research, design, sales, and manufacturing work at Semco. They select their own permanent and temporary task leaders, called coordinators, who are openly evaluated every six months. Depending on the uniqueness of their skill sets, associates often earn greater compensation than coordinators and partners. Moreover, associates can increase their corporate status and compensation through continuing excellence in their work, unlike employees at other firms, who more commonly must move into managerial positions to increase their status and total compensation.

The amount of authority and responsibility given to individual employees also differentiates Semco's structure from more traditional ones. Examples of empowerment by the firm's structure are the absence of a dress code, set work hours, assigned offices, and employee manuals. Indeed, employees determine their own hours, decide when to take holidays, and choose how they will be compensated. Staff functions such as human resources and marketing also are not part of Semco's structure. The firm feels that its turnover rate of roughly 1 percent precludes the need to allocate resources to examine personnel issues, and marketing is the responsibility of every employee. To support individuals' marketing efforts, all employees are provided cost and pricing information for the firm's products.

Semco does not hire individuals for specific jobs. Instead, it allows employees to choose their work and the location in which they perform it. All entry-level new hires participate in a program called "Lost in Space," in which they spend six months to a year rotating through at least 12 different business units and job functions until a preferred position is found. Employees are also encouraged to rotate positions at least every five years to prevent boredom and develop new skills.

Finally, Semco does not have a corporate mission and refuses to define its business. "Once you say what business you are in," explains Semler, "you put your employees in a mental straitjacket. You place boundaries around their thinking and, worst of all, you hand them a ready-made excuse for ignoring new opportunities."

Despite Semco's success, critics aren't convinced that the firm's unique structure is transferable. At present, Semco operates with approximately 1000 employees and generates about $40 million in annual sales. This relatively small size, some argue, requires a less formal structure and fewer organizational controls compared to those needed by large organizations. In addition, its smaller size facilitates communication within the firm, as well as between the firm and its stakeholders. As a privately held company with Semler holding the majority ownership position, Semco encounters minimal pressure for growth from investors. Although the applicability of Semco's ideas to mainstream businesses is debatable, Semco is an interesting example of an efficient and successful organization built and operated without conventional rules and controls.

SOURCES: G. Colvin, 2001, The anti-control freak, *Fortune*, November 26, 60; R. Semler, 2000, How we went digital without a strategy, *Harvard Business Review*, 78(5): 51–58; J. F. Wolff, 1999, In the organization of the future, competitive advantage will lie with inspired employees, *Research Technology Management*, 42(4): 2–4; R. Semler, 1994, Why my former employees still work for me, *Harvard Business Review*, 72(1): 64–74; R. Semler, 1989, Managing without managers, *Harvard Business Review*, 89(5): 76–84.

There is no inherently superior strategy or structure, and there is no inherently superior strategy–structure match. In the next Strategic Focus box, "Semco's Unique Organizational Structure" above, we describe an informal structure that seems to be effectively matched with a firm's strategy.

How appropriate are Semco's organizational structure and controls for other companies? For similar firms (i.e., relatively small companies committed to resource sharing across somewhat diversified product lines and markets) there are lessons to be learned. However, the primary message remains the same—firms must match strategy and structure to increase the probability of competitive success. Not set in concrete, strategy–structure matches evolve with changes in the firm's external and internal environments and should be grounded in the core matches discussed in this chapter.

Summary

- Organizational structure specifies the firm's formal reporting relationships, procedures, controls, and authority and decision-making processes. Influencing managerial work, structure essentially details the work to be done and how that work is to be accomplished. Organizational controls guide the use of strategy, indicate how to compare actual and expected results, and suggest actions to take to improve performance when it falls below expectations. When properly matched with the strategy for which they were intended, structure and controls can be a competitive advantage.

- Strategic controls (largely subjective criteria) and financial controls (largely objective criteria) are the two types of organizational controls used to successfully implement the firm's chosen strategy. Both types of controls are critical, although their degree of emphasis varies, based on individual matches between strategy and structure.

- Strategy and structure influence each other, although strategy has an overall stronger influence on structure. Research indicates that firms tend to change structure when declining performance forces them to do so. Effective managers anticipate the need for structural change, quickly modifying structure to better accommodate the firm's strategy implementation needs when evidence calls for that action.

- Business-level strategies are implemented through the functional structure. The cost leadership strategy requires a centralized functional structure—one in which manufacturing efficiency and process engineering are emphasized. The differentiation strategy's functional structure decentralizes implementation-related decisions, especially those concerned with marketing, to those involved with individual organizational functions. Focus strategies, often used in small firms, require a simple structure until such time that the firm diversifies in terms of products and/or markets.

- Unique combinations of different forms of the multidivisional structure are matched with different corporate-level diversi-

fication strategies to properly implement these strategies. The cooperative M-form, used to implement the related-constrained, corporate-level strategy, has a centralized corporate office and extensive integrating mechanisms. Divisional incentives are linked to overall corporate performance. The related-linked SBU M-form structure establishes separate profit centres within the diversified firm. Each profit centre may have divisions offering similar products, but the centres are unrelated to each other. The competitive M-form structure, used to implement the unrelated diversification strategy, is highly decentralized, lacks integrating mechanisms, and utilizes objective financial criteria to evaluate each unit's performance.

- The multidomestic strategy, implemented through the worldwide geographic area structure, emphasizes decentralization and locates all functional activities in the host country or geographic area. The worldwide product divisional structure is used to implement the global strategy. This structure is centralized in order to coordinate and integrate different functions' activities so as to gain global economies of scope and scale. Decision-making authority is centralized in the firm's worldwide division headquarters.

- The transnational strategy—a strategy through which the firm seeks the local responsiveness of the multidomestic strategy and the global efficiency of the global strategy—is implemented through the combination structure. Because it must be simultaneously centralized and decentralized, integrated and nonintegrated, and formalized and nonformalized, the combination structure is difficult to organize and manage successfully.

- Increasingly important to competitive success, cooperative strategies are implemented through organizational structures framed around strategic networks. Strategic centre firms are critical to the management of strategic networks.

Review Questions

1. What is organizational structure and what are organizational controls? What are the differences between strategic controls and financial controls?

2. What does it mean to say that strategy and structure have a reciprocal relationship?

3. What are the characteristics of the functional structures that are used to implement the cost leadership, differentiation, integrated cost leadership–differentiation, and focused business-level strategies?

4. What are the differences among the three versions of the multidivisional (M-form) organizational structures that are used to implement the related-constrained, related-linked, and unrelated corporate-level diversification strategies?

5. What organizational structures are used to implement the multidomestic, global, and transnational international strategies?

6. What is a strategic network? What is a strategic centre firm?

Organizational Structure and Controls

As an executive board member for a successful 50-partner firm that provides accounting services to corporate clients, you are interested in expanding to offer management consulting services to these clients. Another possibility for your firm is offering both types of services to smaller clients.

Part One. You are concerned about how your organizational structure may need to change to support these services. Based on the material in the chapter, use the chart to rank each type of organizational structure against the activities—information processing, coordination, and control—that you anticipate will need to be strengthened.

Part Two. You are also very concerned that there may be a potential conflict of interest if your firm provides both accounting and management consulting services to the same client. In small groups, discuss whether it is possible for a firm to use organizational structure and controls to achieve its strategic objectives but also to prevent conflicts of interest among its divisions.

	Information Processing	Coordination	Control
Simple structure			
Functional structure			
Multidivisional structure			

Notes

1. R. J. Herbold, 2002, Inside Microsoft: Balancing creativity and discipline, *Harvard Business Review*, 80(1): 73–79; R. E. Miles & C. C. Snow, 1978, *Organizational Strategy, Structure and Process*, New York: McGraw-Hill; M. van Clieaf, 2001, Leading & creating value in the knowledge economy, *Ivey Business Journal*, 65(5): 54–59.

2. T. Amburgey & T. Dacin, 1994, As the left foot follows the right? The dynamics of strategic and structural change, *Academy of Management Journal*, 37: 1427–52; B. Keats & H. O'Neill, 2001, Organizational structure: Looking through a strategy lens, in M. A. Hitt, R. E. Freeman, & J. S. Harrison (eds.), *Handbook of Strategic Management*, Oxford, UK: Blackwell Publishers, 520–42.

3. R. E. Hoskisson, C. W. L. Hill, & H. Kim, 1993, The multidivisional structure: Organizational fossil or source of value? *Journal of Management*, 19: 269–98; F. Warner, 2002, Think lean, *Fast Company*, February, 40–42.

4. T. Burns & G. M. Stalker, 1961, *The Management of Innovation*, London: Tavistock; P. R. Lawrence & J. W. Lorsch, 1967, *Organization and Environment*, Homewood, IL: Richard D. Irwin; J. Woodward, 1965, *Industrial Organization: Theory and Practice*, London: Oxford University Press; P. Jenster & D. Hussey, 2001, *Company Analysis: Determining Strategic Capability*, Chichester: John Wiley & Sons, 135–71; D. J. Teece, G. Pisano, & A. Shuen, 1997, Dynamic capabilities and strategic management, *Strategic Management Journal*, 18: 509–33; B. Keats & H. O'Neill, 2001, Organizational structure: Looking through a strategy lens, in M. A. Hitt, R. E. Freeman & J. S. Harrison (eds.), *Handbook of Strategic Management*, Oxford, UK: Blackwell Publishers, 520–42; J. R. Galbraith, 1995, *Designing Organizations*, San Francisco: Jossey-Bass, 6.

5. Keats & O'Neill, Organizational structure, 533; Galbraith, *Designing Organizations*, 6; V. P. Rindova & S. Kotha, 2001, Continuous "morphing": Competing through dynamic capabilities, form, and function, *Academy of Management Journal*, 44: 1263–80; J. G. Covin, D. P. Slevin, & M. B. Heeley, 2001, Strategic decision making in an intuitive vs. technocratic mode: Structural and environmental consideration, *Journal of Business Research*, 52: 51–67.

6. M. A. Schilling & H. K. Steensma, 2001, The use of modular organizational forms: An industry-level analysis, *Academy of Management Journal*, 44: 1149–68.

7. Jenster & Hussey, Company Analysis, 169; L. Donaldson, 1997, A positivist alternative to the structure-action approach, *Organization Studies*, 18: 77–92; D. C. Hambrick & J. W. Fredrickson, 2001, Are you sure you have a strategy? *Academy of Management Executive*, 15(4): 48–59; G. G. Dess & G. T. Lumpkin, 2001, Emerging issues in strategy process research, in M. A. Hitt, R. E. Freeman, & J. S. Harrison (eds.), *Handbook of Strategic Management*, Oxford, UK: Blackwell Publishers, 3–34; C. A. De Kluyver, 2000, *Strategic Thinking: An Executive Perspective*, Upper Saddle River: Prentice Hall, 52;

G. A. Bigley & K. H. Roberts, 2001, The incident command system: High-reliability organizing for complex and volatile task environments, *Academy of Management Journal*, 44: 1281–99; J. Child & R. M. McGrath, 2001, Organizations unfettered: Organizational form in an information-intensive economy, *Academy of Management Journal*, 44: 1135–48; T. W. Malnight, 2001, Emerging structural patterns within multinational corporations: Toward process-based structures, *Academy of Management Journal*, 44: 1187–1210; A. Sharma, 1999, Central dilemmas of managing innovation in firms, *California Management Review*, 41(3): 146–64; H. A. Simon, 1991, Bounded rationality and organizational learning, *Organization Science*, 2: 125–34.

8. B. W. Keats & M. A. Hitt, 1988, A causal model of linkages among environmental dimensions, macroorganizational characteristics, and performance, *Academy of Management Journal*, 31: 570–98; A. Chandler, 1962, *Strategy and Structure*, Cambridge, MA.: MIT Press; Keats & O'Neill, *Organizational structure*, 535.

9. C. H. Noble, 1999, The eclectic roots of strategy implementation research, *Journal of Business Research*, 45: 119–34.

10. S. Venkataraman & S. D. Sarasvathy, 2001, Strategy and entrepreneurship: Outlines of an untold story, in M. A. Hitt, R. E. Freeman, & J. S. Harrison (eds.), *Handbook of Strategic Management*, Oxford, UK: Blackwell Publishers, 650–68; J. Matthews, 1999, Strategic moves, *Supply Management*, 4(4): 36–37; D. F. Kuratko, R. D. Ireland, & J. S. Hornsby, 2001, Improving firm performance through entrepreneurial actions: Acordia's corporate entrepreneurship strategy, *Academy of Management Executive*, 15(4): 60–71; J. S. Harrison & C. H. St. John, 2002, *Foundations in Strategic Management*, 2nd ed., Cincinnati: South-Western College Publishing, 118–29.

11. D. Incandela, K. L. McLaughlin, & C. S. Shi, 1999, Retailers to the world, *The McKinsey Quarterly*, 3: 84–97; R. E. Hoskisson, M. A. Hitt, & R. D. Ireland, 1994, The effects of acquisitions and restructuring strategies (strategic refocusing) on innovation, in G. von Krogh, A. Sinatra, & H. Singh (eds.), *Managing Corporate Acquisition*, London: MacMillan Press, 144–69.

12. M. A. Hitt, R. E. Hoskisson, R. A. Johnson, & D. D. Moesel, 1996, The market for corporate control and firm innovation, *Academy of Management Journal*, 39: 1084–1119.

13. R. E. Hoskisson & M. A. Hitt, 1988, Strategic control and relative R&D investment in multiproduct firms, *Strategic Management Journal*, 9: 605–21; D. J. Collis, 1996, Corporate strategy in multibusiness firms, *Long Range Planning*, 29: 416–18.

14. K. Massaro, 2000, FTI and PeopleSoft ally to offer financial control solution, *Wall Street & Technology*, 18(11): 84; Pfizer Inc., 2004, Pfizer., Management's report, http://www.pfizer.com/are/investors_reports/annual_2003/financial/p2003fr21.htm (annual report), February 26.

15. J. B. Barney, 2002, *Gaining and Sustaining Competitive Advantage*, 2nd ed., Upper Saddle River: Prentice Hall.

16. M. Sengul, 2001, Divisionalization: Strategic effects of organizational structure, Paper presented during the 21st Annual Strategic Management Society Conference, San Francisco, CA, October 21–24.; Keats & O'Neill, Organizational structure, 531.

17. K. J. Euske & A. Riccaboni, 1999, Stability to profitability: Managing interdependencies to meet a new environment, *Accounting, Organizations & Society*, 24: 463–81; D. Miller & J. O. Whitney, 1999, Beyond strategy: Configuration as a pillar of competitive advantage, *Business Horizons*, 42(3): 5–17; S. Tallman, 2001, Global strategic management, in M. A. Hitt, R. E. Freeman, & J. S. Harrison (eds.), *Handbook of Strategic Management*, Oxford, UK: Blackwell Publishers, 464–90.

18. B. A. Gutek & T. Welsh, 2000, *The Brave New Service World*, New York: AMACOM; L. Lee, 2002, Will investors pay for Schwab's advice? *Business Week*, January 21, 36.

19. Chandler, *Strategy and Structure*; Keats & O'Neill, Organizational structure, 524.

20. G. M. McNamara, R. A. Luce, & G. H. Thompson, 2002, Examining the effect of complexity in strategic group knowledge structures on firm performance, *Strategic Management Journal*, 23: 153–70; J. P. Walsh, 1995, Managerial and organizational cognition: Notes from a trip down memory lane, *Organization Science*, 6: 280–321.

21. C. Levicki, 1999, *The Interactive Strategy Workout*, 2nd ed., London: Prentice-Hall.

22. J. J. Chrisman, A. Bauerschmidt, & C. W. Hofer, 1998, The determinants of new venture performance: An extended model, *Entrepreneurship Theory & Practice*, 23(3): 5–29; H. M. O'Neill, R. W. Pouder, & A. K. Buchholtz, 1998, Patterns in the diffusion of strategies across organizations: Insights from the innovation diffusion literature, *Academy of Management Review*, 23: 98–114.

23. Galbraith, *Designing Organizations*, 25; Keats & O'Neill, Organizational structure, 539; Lawrence & Lorsch, *Organization and Environment*.

24. O. E. Williamson, 1975, *Markets and Hierarchies: Analysis and Anti-trust Implications*, New York: The Free Press; Chandler, Strategy and Structure.

25. J. Greco, 1999, Alfred P. Sloan, Jr. (1875–1966): The original organizational man, *Journal of Business Strategy*, 20(5): 30–31; Hoskisson, Hill, & Kim, The multidivisional structure, 269–98; W. G. Rowe & P. M. Wright, 1997, Related and unrelated diversification and their effect on human resource management controls, *Strategic Management Journal*, 18: 329–38; D. C. Galunic & K. M. Eisenhardt, 1996, The evolution of intracorporate domains: Divisional charter losses in high-technology, multidivisional corporations, *Organization Science*, 7: 255–82.

26. A. D. Chandler, 1994, The functions of the HQ unit in the multibusiness firm, in R. P. Rumelt, D. E. Schendel, & D. J. Teece (eds.), *Fundamental Issues in Strategy*, Cambridge, MA: Harvard Business School Press, 327; O. E. Williamson, 1994, Strategizing, economizing, and economic organization, in R. P. Rumelt, D. E. Schendel, & D. J. Teece (eds.), *Fundamental Issues in Strategy*, Cambridge, MA: Harvard Business School Press, 361–401; R. M. Burton & B. Obel, 1980, A computer simulation test of the M-form hypothesis, *Administrative Science Quarterly*, 25: 457–76; O. E. Williamson, 1985, *The Economic Institutions of Capitalism: Firms, Markets, and Relational Contracting*, New York: MacMillan.

27. Keats & O'Neill, Organizational structure, 532.

28. R. H. Hall, 1996, *Organizations: Structures, Processes, and Outcomes*, 6th ed., Englewood Cliffs: Prentice-Hall, 13; S. Baiman, D. F. Larcker, & M. V. Rajan, 1995, Organizational design for business units, *Journal of Accounting Research*, 33: 205–29.

29. Barney, *Gaining and Sustaining Competitive Advantage*, 257.

30. Wal-Mart Stores, 2002, Wal-Mart stores pricing policy, http://www.walmart.com, February 2.

31. Ibid.

32. Procter & Gamble, 2004, Corporate structure: How the structure works, *Procter & Gamble website*, http://www.pg.com/jobs/corporate_structure/how_the_structure.jhtml, accessed July 21, 2004.

33. C. C. Markides & P. J. Williamson, 1996, Corporate diversification and organizational structure: A resource based view, *Academy of Management Journal*, 39: 340–67; C. W. L. Hill, M. A. Hitt, & R. E. Hoskisson, 1992, Cooperative versus competitive structures in related and unrelated diversified firms, *Organization Science*, 3: 501–21; P. F. Drucker, 2002, They're not employees, they're people, *Harvard Business Review*, 80(2): 70–77; J. Robins & M. E. Wiersema, 1995, A resource-based approach to the multibusiness firm: Empirical analysis of portfolio interrelationships and corporate financial performance, *Strategic Management Journal*, 16: 277–99.

34. C. C. Markides, 1997, To diversify or not to diversify, *Harvard Business Review*, 75(6): 93–99.

35. J. G. March, 1994, *A Primer on Decision Making: How Decisions Happen*, New York: The Free Press, 117–18.

36. General Electric Co., 2004, Business directory, *General Electric website*, http://www.ge.com/en/company/businesses/index.htm, accessed July 21, 2004.

37. Argus Research, 2002, General Electric Co., *Argus Research website*, http://argusresearch.com, February 4; J. Welch with J. A. Byrne, 2001, *Jack: Straight from the Gut*, New York: Warner Business Books.

38. S. Rosenbush, 2002, A lengthy honeymoon at Lucent? *Business Week*, January 21, 34.

39. R. E. Hoskisson & M. A. Hitt, 1990, Antecedents and performance outcomes of diversification: A review and critique of theoretical perspectives, *Journal of Management*, 16: 461–509.

40. Hill, Hitt, & Hoskisson, Cooperative versus competitive structures, 512; J. Birkinshaw, 2001, Strategies for managing internal competition, *California Management Review*, 44(1): 21–38.

41. T. R. Eisenmann & J. L. Bower, 2000, The entrepreneurial M-form: Strategic integration in global media firms, *Organization Science*, 11: 348–55.

42. Y. Luo, 2002, Product diversification in international joint ventures: Performance implications in an emerging market, *Strategic Management Journal*, 23: 1–20; Tallman, Global strategic management, 467.

43. Malnight, Emerging structural patterns, 1188; J. Wolf & W. G. Egelhoff, 2002, A reexamination and extension of international strategy-structure theory, *Strategic Management Journal*, 23: 181–89.

44. C. A. Bartlett & S. Ghoshal, 1989, *Managing across Borders: The Transnational Solution*, Boston: Harvard Business School Press.

45. Unilever, 2002, Unilever today, http://www.unilever.com/company/unilevertoday/, February 5.

46. Kyowa Hakko, 2001, Kyowa Hakko consolidated financial summary for the interim period ended September 20, 2001, http://www.kyowa.co.jp/eng/intext/pdf2001_11/tkr_e2001_01.pdf (semiannual report), September 30.

47. Malnight, Emerging structural patterns, 1197.

48. Barney, *Gaining and Sustaining Competitive Advantage*, 533.

49. R. J. Kramer, 1999, Organizing for global competitiveness: The corporate headquarters design, *Chief Executive Digest*, 3(2): 23–28.

50. Y. L. Doz & G. Hamel, 1998, *Alliance Advantage: The Art of Creating Value through Partnering*, Boston: Harvard Business School Press, 222; A. C. Inkpen, 2001, Strategic alliances, in M. A. Hitt, R. E. Freeman, & J. S. Harrison (eds.), *Handbook of Strategic Management*, Oxford, UK: Blackwell Publishers, 409–32.

51. Luo, Product diversification in international joint ventures, 2; R. Gulati, N. Nohira, & A. Zaheer, 2000, Strategic networks, *Strategic Management Journal*, 21(special issue): 203–15; B. Gomes-Casseres, 1994, Group versus group: How alliance networks compete, *Harvard Business Review*, 72(4): 62–74.

52. C. Lee, K. Lee, & J. M. Pennings, 2001, Internal capabilities, external networks, and performance: A study on technology-based ventures, *Strategic Management Journal*, 22(summer special issue): 615–40; M. B. Sarkar, R. Echambadi, & J. S. Harrison, 2001, Alliance entrepreneurship and firm market performance, *Strategic Management Journal*, 22(summer special issue): 701–11.

53. S. Harrison, 1998, *Japanese Technology and Innovation Management*, Northampton, MA: Edward Elgar.

54. P. Dussauge, B. Garrette, & W. Mitchell, 2000, Learning from competing partners: Outcomes and duration of scale and link alliances in Europe, North America and Asia, *Strategic Management Journal*, 21: 99–126; G. Lorenzoni & C. Baden-Fuller, 1995, Creating a strategic center to manage a web of partners, *California Management Review*, 37(3): 146–63.

55. J. H. Dyer & K. Nobeoka, 2000, Creating and managing a high-performance knowledge-sharing network: The Toyota case, *Strategic Management Journal*, 21(special issue): 345–67; J. H. Dyer, 1997, Effective interfirm collaboration: How firms minimize transaction costs and maximize transaction value, *Strategic Management Journal*, 18: 535–56.

56. T. Nishiguchi, 1994, *Strategic Industrial Sourcing: The Japanese Advantage*, New York: Oxford University Press.

57. W. M. Fruin, 1992, *The Japanese Enterprise System*, New York: Oxford University Press.

58. Delta Air Lines, 2002, About Delta, http://www.delta.com, February 10; British Airways, 2004, Our global network, http://www.britishairways.com/travel/routeintro/public/en_ca, accessed July 21, 2004; 2002, Iberia's History, http://www.iberia.com, February 10.

59. Cisco Systems, 2002, News@Cisco, http://newsroom.cisco.com/dlls/index.html, February 10; 2002, Q&A with John Chambers, http://www.cisco.com, February 10.

60. McDonald's Canada, 2004, FAQs, http://www.mcdonalds.ca/en/aboutus/faq.aspx, accessed May 23; Fidelity Investments, 2002, McDonald's Corp., Standard & Poor's stock report, *Fidelity Investments website*, http://www.fidelity.com, January 26.

61. McDonald's Canada, 2004, Facts about McDonald's Canada, http://www.mcdonalds.ca, accessed May 23, 2004; Fidelity Investments, 2002, McDonald's Corp., Standard & Poor's stock report, *Fidelity Investments website*, http://www.fidelity.com, January 26.

62. McDonald's Corporation, 2004, Frequently asked questions about acquiring a McFranchise inside the USA, http://www.media.mcdonalds.com/secured/company/franchising/usfaq/, accessed July 21, 2004.

63. McDonald's Canada, 2004, FAQs, *McDonald's Canada website*, http://www.mcdonalds.ca/en/aboutus/faq.aspx, accessed May 23; 2004, McDonald's Canada: Canadian milestones, http://www.mcdonalds.ca/en/aboutus/mcdcanada_milestones.aspx, accessed May 23.

64. Argus Research Company, 2002, Argus company report: McDonald's Corp., *Argus Research Company website*, http://argusresearch.com, February 10.

65. C. Jones, W. S. Hesterly, & S. P. Borgatti, 1997, A general theory of network governance: Exchange conditions and social mechanisms, *Academy of Management Review*, 22: 911–45; J. M. Mezias, 2002, Identifying liabilities of foreignness and strategies to minimize their effects: The case of labor lawsuit judgments in the United States, *Strategic Management Journal*, 23: 229–44.

66. R. E. Miles, C. C. Snow, J. A. Mathews, G. Miles, & J. J. Coleman, Jr., 1997, Organizing in the knowledge age: Anticipating the cellular form, *Academy of Management Executive*, 11(4): 7–20; Ericsson, 2002, Ericsson NewsCenter, *Ericsson website*, http://www.ericsson.com, February 10.

67. M. F. Wolff, 1999, In the organization of the future, competitive advantage will be inspired, *Research Technology Management*, 42(4): 2–4.

Chapter Thirteen

Strategic Leadership

Knowledge Objectives

Studying this chapter should provide you with the strategic management knowledge needed to:

1. Define strategic leadership and describe top-level managers' importance as a resource.

2. Differentiate among the concepts of strategic, visionary, and managerial leadership.

3. Define top management teams and explain their effects on firm performance and their ability to innovate and make appropriate strategic changes.

4. Discuss the value of strategic leadership in determining the firm's strategic direction.

5. Explain strategic leaders' role in exploiting and maintaining core competencies.

6. Describe the importance of strategic leaders in developing human capital.

7. Define organizational culture and explain what must be done to sustain an effective culture.

8. Explain what strategic leaders can do to establish and emphasize ethical practices.

9. Discuss the importance and use of organizational controls.

Women in Leadership Roles: The Canadian Experience

Catalyst, a North American nonprofit research and advisory association focuses on the advancement of women in business over time and issues related to women in business. Since 1998, Catalyst researchers, sponsored by Canadian corporations, have conducted a number of studies and censuses that survey high-level women in major Canadian corporations and professional firms, as well as male and female CEOs from hundreds of leading Canadian corporations. The intent is to establish a database on the advancement of women in corporate and professional Canada. Some of that research indicated that 6 in 10 CEOs consider women's advancement to be critical or very important for their organizations. In that same research, views expressed by at least three-quarters of Canadian CEOs suggested that opportunities for advancement by women had improved greatly.

However, Catalyst Canada's vice president, Susan Black, said in a 2003 report, "... there is still not parity in the executive suite.... We have to keep awareness on this issue in order to move it forward." Much of the impetus for the studies conducted by Catalyst arises from the fact that while women are a significant and growing percentage of entry- and mid-level managers in Canada, only a few firms have been successful in removing the structural and attitudinal barriers to women's advancement into senior management positions.

A census of Women Board Directors of Canada, taken in March 1998, showed that women held 6.2 percent of the board positions (257 out of a total of 4,154) on the companies of the 1998 Financial Post 500 (FP500). In addition, in that same year, Catalyst found that of Canada's 560 most influential companies, only 234 (41.7 percent) of those companies had any women board members at all.

By 2003, the new Catalyst Census of Women Board Directors of Canada showed that the number of women board members in FP500 companies had increased to 11.2 percent, while the number of companies with no women board directors had risen to 51.4 percent (a figure unchanged since 2001).

A similar census conducted of "Women Corporate Officers and Top Earners of Canada" in 2002 indicated that women represented 14 percent of corporate officer positions in the FP500. At the same time, women held approximately 6.7 percent of corporate titles out of a total of 1423 persons holding corporate titles such as Chairman, CEO, Vice-Chairman, President, COO, SEVP and EVP. Research also indicated that women lead 14 FP500 companies while 3.9 percent (44 of 1128) of top earners are women.

In a report published by *The Globe and Mail* in March 2003, reporters indicated that there was some progress, albeit slow, for women moving into the top ranks of Canadian companies. Of note, it was reported that the financial services industry was ahead of others in promoting women to top ranks. Specifically, of the 88 women in Canada with corporate titles, 30 of them work for banks. Indeed, research presented indicates that women make up 22.6 percent of corporate officers at Canada's banks.

Belinda Stronach's leadership at Magna International was parlayed into an almost-successful run for the leadership of the Conservative Party of Canada—she came in second.

CP PHOTO/AARON HARRIS

(continued)

In comparing progress in Canada to that in the U.S., statistics show that in Canada, women are behind in achieving the top ranks. For example, in the U.S. 15.7 percent of officers at Fortune 500 companies are women, compared to 14 percent in Canada, while 85.6 percent of these same companies have at least one female corporate officer compared to 62.5 percent in Canada.

Conversely, in Canada, 13 women are CEOs in the 500 largest companies, compared to 6 women CEOs in the U.S. Fortune 500. In a more recent report (February 2004), it was suggested that the biggest opportunities for advancement of women to senior positions exist at crown corporations, where women represented 23.7 percent of board positions. Unfortunately, research shows that the percentage of companies that do not have women on their boards has not changed since 2001.

On an individual level, in a special edition of *Time* magazine issued in April 2004, the editors included Belinda Stronach (along with 3 other Canadians) in the list of the 100 most influential people in the world who affected, for good or bad, countless lives around the globe in 2004. In 2000, Stronach, former president and CEO of Magna International, was among 13 women in Canada named to lead one of the 500 largest Canadian businesses. In 2001, she was named "... the most powerful business woman in Canada," by the *National Post*, while in 2002, Stronach was number two on *Fortune* magazine's list of the world's most powerful women in business. In 2003, Stronach resigned her position at Magna International in order to run for the leadership of the new Conservative Party of Canada—she came second. This success suggests she is one woman leader to continue to watch in the future.

SOURCES: J. McFarland, 2004, Women still find slow rise to power positions: Hold only 14% of corporate officer jobs in Canada, *Globe and Mail, Report on Business*, March 13; Catalyst, 2004, Catalyst census of women board directors of Canada, *Catalyst website*, www.catalyst-women.org/research/censuses.htm, accessed May 11, 2004; J. Frew, 2004, It's still a man's world: Glass ceiling continues to block women from top echelon of business report shows, *Toronto Observer*, February 20; The Belinda Stronach Team, 2004, *The Belinda Stronach Team website*, www.belinda.ca/page.asp, accessed May 18, 2004.

As the opening case illustrates, CEOs and their senior management teams need to know and understand the human resources available to them and their organizations. A major resource that has gone largely untapped are women and minorities. Strategic leaders discover and utilize untapped resources to the benefit of their organizations. We are expecting that greater numbers of women and minorities will be in the ranks of senior management and on boards of directors in the 21st century, as more CEOs and boards of directors understand the benefits of a more diverse senior management team and board. Of course, developing an organization's human capital is just one of several dimensions of effective strategic leadership.

As this chapter makes clear, it is through effective strategic leadership that firms are able to successfully use the strategic management process. As strategic leaders, top-level managers must guide the firm in ways that result in the formation of strategic intent and strategic mission. This guidance may lead to goals that stretch everyone in the organization to improve their performance.[1] Moreover, strategic leaders must facilitate the development of appropriate strategic actions and determine how to implement them. These actions on the part of strategic leaders culminate in strategic competitiveness and above-average returns,[2] as shown in Figure 13.1 on page 398.

This chapter begins with a definition of strategic leadership and its importance as a potential source of competitive advantage. Then, we discuss the differences among managerial, visionary, and strategic leadership. Next, we examine top management teams and their effects on innovation, strategic change, and firm performance. Closing the chapter are descriptions of the six key components of effective strategic leadership: determining a strategic direction, exploiting and maintaining core competencies, developing human capital, sustaining an effective organizational culture, emphasizing ethical practices, and establishing balanced organizational control systems.

The impermanence of success is well documented by the frequent changes in leadership at Xerox. Xerox's board of directors promoted Anne Mulcahy to president in May 2000, after it ousted CEO G. Richard Thoman, who lasted 13 months. Thoman had followed Paul A. Allaire as CEO, who remained chairman of the board. Even though Xerox invented the idea of the personal computer and was the innovator of the copier machine, it was not able to capitalize on the computer and has stumbled in copiers. For example, Hewlett-Packard's division that manufactures and sells laser printers (based on the same technology as the copier) has more total revenue than all of Xerox. Even with these strategic blunders, Xerox has enjoyed significant success in its digital copiers.[3] However, because of significant weakness in its many businesses, "the company was close to floundering after years of weak sales and high costs; employees were as disgruntled as customers." Mulcahy, who was named CEO and chairman in July 2001, after several unsuccessful leaders, is trying to turn the situation at Xerox around by divesting businesses, such as financial services, and not only selling copiers and printers, but also by strengthening its services and solutions business, as IBM did.

Strategic Leadership

The word *strategy* originated with the Greeks. Originally, *strategos* alluded to a role such as a general in command of an army. Subsequently, it referred to the psychological and behavioural skills with which the general occupied the role and came to mean the "art of the general." By 450 B.C., it had come to mean managerial skills such as administration, leadership, oration, and power. And by 330 B.C., it meant the ability to employ forces to defeat opposing forces and to develop a unified system of global governance.[4] **Strategic leadership** is defined as the ability to influence those with whom you work in your organization to *voluntarily* make decisions on a day-to-day basis that enhance the long-term viability of the organization, while at the same time maintaining the short-

Strategic leadership is defined as the ability to influence those with whom you work in your organization to *voluntarily* make decisions on a day-to-day basis that enhance the long-term viability of the organization, while at the same time maintaining the short-term financial stability of the organization.

Figure 13.1 Strategic Leadership and the Strategic Management Process

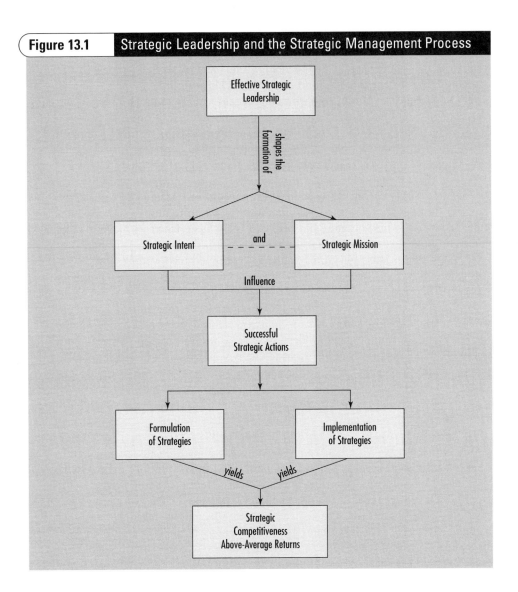

term financial stability of the organization.[5] This definition of strategic leadership makes several presumptions:

- It presumes an ability to influence those with whom one works—subordinates, peers, and superiors.
- It presumes that the leader understands the emergent strategy process, which, according to Henry Mintzberg,[6] is more important than the intended strategic process.
- It presumes a shared vision of what the organization is to be, so that the day-to-day decision making, or the emergent strategy process, is consistent with this vision.
- It presumes agreement among the senior managers and board members on the opportunities that can be taken advantage of and the threats that can be neutralized, given the resources and capabilities of the organization.[7]
- It presumes visionary leadership that entails many characteristics, such as a willingness to take risks.
- It presumes managerial leadership that entails many characteristics, such as an intended rational way of looking at the world.

- It presumes that visionary leadership and managerial leadership can exist together.
- It presumes that strategic leadership synergistically combines visionary leadership and managerial leadership.
- Finally, it presumes leaders' beliefs in their ability to change their organizations in such a way that the environment in which the organization operates will also change versus believing that the actions they take are constrained by the environment and organization in which they work.

In the next two sections, the concepts of managerial and visionary leadership are discussed. A major portion of this discussion is based on the classic *Harvard Business Review* (HBR) article by Abraham Zaleznik.[8]

A Comparison of Managerial, Visionary, and Strategic Leadership

In the 21st century, many managers who work in nations around the world will be challenged to change their frames of reference to cope with the rapid and complex changes occurring in the global economy. A **managerial frame of reference** is the set of assumptions, premises, and accepted wisdom that bounds—or *frames*—a manager's understanding of the firm, the industry or industries in which it competes, and the core competencies it uses in the pursuit of strategic competitiveness. A frame of reference is the foundation on which a manager's mind-set is built (see Chapter 4).

A firm's ability to achieve strategic competitiveness and earn above-average returns is compromised when leaders fail to respond appropriately and quickly to mind-set–related changes that an increasingly complex and global competitive environment demands. Research suggests that a firm's "long-term competitiveness depends on managers' willingness to challenge continually their managerial frames" and that global competition is more than product versus product or company versus company—it is also a case of "mind-set versus mind-set, managerial frame versus managerial frame."[9] Competing on the basis of mind-set requires that strategic leaders learn how to deal with diverse and cognitively complex competitive situations. One of the most challenging mind-set changes is overcoming one's own success when change is required. Managers who are able to successfully complete challenging assignments that are linked to achieving strategic competitiveness, early and frequently in their career, appear to improve their ability to make appropriate changes to their mind-set.[10]

A **managerial frame of reference** is the set of assumptions, premises, and accepted wisdom that bounds—or *frames*—a manager's understanding of the firm, the industry or industries in which it competes, and the core competencies it uses in the pursuit of strategic competitiveness.

Managerial Leadership

Organizations implicitly and explicitly train their people to be managerial leaders. For example, in governments, managerial leaders are required to address public accountability for every penny spent, to provide unrelated diversification as an organization, to work within the political context, and, for most governments, managerial leaders are needed to deal with an enormous debt load. These factors lead to the imposition of a financial control system that enhances the use of managerial leadership and curtails the use of strategic and visionary leadership. Managerial leaders adopt impersonal, passive attitudes toward goals, leading to goals that arise from necessity rather than from desires or dreams. These goals are based on the organization's history and are deeply embedded in the history and culture of the organization as it currently stands.[11] Managerial leaders view work as an enabling process that involves some combination of ideas and people interacting to establish strategies and make decisions. In this process, they negotiate and bargain and/or use rewards, punishments, or other forms of coercion.[12]

In their relations with others, managerial leaders relate to people according to their role in the decision-making process. Although managerial leaders may seek out involvement with others, they will maintain a low level of emotional involvement in these relationships. They may lack empathy; managerial leaders need order, not the potential chaos inherent in human relations.[13] Managerial leaders see themselves as conservators and regulators of the existing order of affairs with which they personally identify. Strengthening and perpetuating the existing institution enhances these managers' self-worth. For example, if people feel that they are members of an institution and contributing to that institution's well-being, then they will consider that a mission in life has been fulfilled and will feel rewarded for having measured up to an ideal. This reward transcends material gains and answers the more fundamental desire for personal integrity that is achieved by identifying with existing institutions.[14] However, when managerial leaders have devoted their career to perpetuating and strengthening an institution, which then gets ripped apart and put back together again, as happens in restructuring, these leaders feel as if they are being torn apart, too.

Managerial leaders influence only the actions and decisions of those with whom they work.[15] They are involved in situations and contexts characteristic of day-to-day activities,[16] and they are concerned with, and more comfortable in, functional areas of responsibilities.[17] They possess more expertise about their functional areas than visionary leaders.[18] In some instances, managerial leaders make decisions that are not subject to value-based constraints,[19] which does not mean that these leaders are not moral, ethical people on a personal level; as managers, values might not be included in their decision making because of certain pressures, such as being financially controlled. These leaders engage in, and support, short-term, least cost behaviour activities, to enhance financial performance figures in the short term.[20] They focus on managing the exchange and combination of explicit knowledge and ensuring compliance to standard operating procedures.[21] They use a linear thought process. Finally, managerial leaders believe in determinism—that is, they believe that their organization's internal and external environments determine what they do.[22]

To summarize, **managerial leaders** want stability and order, and they strive to preserve the existing order. They are more comfortable handling day-to-day activities, and are short-term–oriented. They guide without a strategic vision constrained by values and by using explicit knowledge. We need to emphasize that this is not a bad way to be—it is more a recognition of some of the defining characteristics of managerial leadership. Organizations need managerial leadership; however, it is possible that managerial leaders lead too many organizations. In the longer term, managerial leadership causes organizational performance to decline.

Visionary Leadership

Visionary leadership is touted as the cure for many of the ills that affect organizations in today's fast changing environment. Unfortunately, visionary leaders are not readily embraced by organizations, and without the support of managerial leaders, they may not be appropriate for most organizations. Being visionary and having an organizational tendency to use visionary leaders is risky. Ultimately, visionary leadership requires power to influence the thoughts and actions of people. This means putting power in the hands of one person, which entails risk on several dimensions. First, there is the risk of equating power with the ability to achieve immediate results; second, there is the risk of losing self-control in the desire for power; and third, the presence of visionary leaders may undermine the development of managers who become anxious in the relative disorder that visionary leaders tend to generate.

Because they are relatively more proactive, visionary leaders have attitudes towards goals that are different from those of managerial leaders. Visionary leaders shape ideas, as opposed to reacting to them. They exert influence in a way that determines the direction an organization will take, by altering moods, evoking images and expectations, and

Managerial leaders want stability and order, and they want to preserve the existing order. They are more comfortable handling day-to-day activities, and are short-term oriented. They guide without a strategic vision constrained by values and by using explicit knowledge.

establishing specific desires and objectives. Their influence changes the way people think about what is desirable, possible, and necessary.[23] Visionary leaders strive to develop choices and fresh approaches to long-standing problems. They create excitement in work. Visionary leaders work from high-risk positions; in fact, they seek out risky ventures, especially when the rewards are high.[24]

Visionary leaders are concerned with ideas and relate to people in intuitive and empathetic ways, focusing on what events and decisions mean to people. With visionaries in charge, human relations are more turbulent, intense, and, sometimes, even disorganized. This atmosphere may intensify individual motivation and produce unanticipated, positive outcomes.[25] With respect to their sense of self, visionary leaders feel separate from their environment, and, sometimes, from other people. The key point is that they work in—but do not belong to—organizations. Their sense of identity does not depend on their work, roles, or memberships, but on their created sense of identity, which may result from major events in their lives.[26]

Visionary leaders influence the opinions and attitudes of others within their organizations.[27] They are concerned with insuring the future of an organization through the development and management of people.[28] Visionaries immerse themselves in complexity, ambiguity, and information overload. Their task is multifunctional, and because they have a much more complex integrative task,[29] they come to know less than their functional area experts about each of the functional areas for which they are responsible.[30]

Visionaries are more likely to make decisions that are based on values,[31] and they are more willing to invest in innovation, human capital, and creating and maintaining an effective culture to ensure long-term viability.[32] Visionary leaders focus on tacit knowledge and develop strategies as communal forms of tacit knowledge that promote the enactment of a vision.[33] They utilize nonlinear thinking, and they believe in strategic choice—that is, they believe that their choices make a difference in what their organizations do and these differences affect their organizations' environments.[34]

In summary, visionary leadership is future-oriented and concerned with risk taking, and visionary leaders are not dependent on their organizations for their sense of identity. Under these leaders, organizational control is maintained through socialization and the sharing of, and compliance to, a commonly held set of norms, values, and shared beliefs. Organizations need visionary leadership to ensure their long-term viability; however, organizations that are led by visionaries without the constraining influence of managerial leaders are probably more in danger of failing in the short-term than those led by managers. One solution is a combination of managers and visionaries to lead organizations with visionaries having more influence than managers.[35] This was the solution used by The Body Shop, with Anita Roddick as the visionary leader and Gordon Roddick (her husband) as the managerial leader. A better solution is to have an individual who can exercise both visionary and managerial leadership. Herein is the problem; Zaleznik argues that leaders and managers are different and that no one person can exercise both types of leadership simultaneously.[36] His perspective suggests that visionary leaders and managerial leaders are at opposite ends of a continuum and that trying to be both causes the individual to end up in the centre and unable to exercise either style of leadership.

This is not an unreasonable perspective when we consider the following: managerial leaders want stability and order, and they strive to preserve the existing order; whereas, **visionary leaders** want creativity, innovation, and chaos, and they strive to change the existing order. For an organization in a transition phase, being driven by a visionary is very hard on those who are managerial leaders. The organization they have worked so hard to build, and that is part of their identity, is being ripped apart and put together as something else. Under visionary leaders, this climate of transition will be more the norm than the stability and order experienced under managerial leadership. In fact, the environment being created by today's technological and global forces is one of change and complexity. John

Visionary leaders want creativity, innovation, and chaos, and they strive to change the existing order.

Kotter, one of the foremost experts on organizational leadership, suggests that organizations need leaders to cope with change and managers to cope with complexity.[37]

Having said this, it is necessary to reiterate and emphasize that both visionary and managerial leadership are vital for long-term viability and short-term financial stability. As we said earlier, visionary leadership without managerial leadership may be more detrimental to organizational performance in the short term.[38] Having visionary and managerial leadership can be accomplished by having the two different organizational mind-sets that co-exist—but with the visionary approach being more influential than the managerial approach. However, an organization will be more viable in the long term and better able to maintain its financial stability in the short term, if strategic leadership is prevalent. To conceptualize strategic leadership, it is necessary to think of visionary leadership and managerial leadership as existing on separate continuums that are perpendicular to each other. This conceptualization of strategic leadership provides a synergistic combination of visionary and managerial leadership that was not possible under previous thinking.

Strategic Leadership

Earlier, *strategic leadership* was defined as the ability to influence those with whom you work in your organization to *voluntarily* make decisions on a day-to-day basis that enhance the long-term viability of the organization, while at the same time maintaining the short-term financial stability of the organization. Strategic leaders are different from managerial and visionary leaders. They are a synergistic combination of managerial and visionary leadership. This means that a strategic leader creates more wealth[39] than a combination of two individuals—one of whom is a visionary leader and one of whom is a managerial leader.[40] Strategic leaders emphasize ethical behaviour.[41] Strategic leaders are probably very rare in most organizations.[42] They oversee operating (day-to-day) and strategic (long-term) responsibilities.[43] They formulate and implement strategies for immediate impact and the preservation of long-term goals to enhance organizational growth, survival, and long-term viability.[44] Strategic leaders have strong, positive expectations of the performance they expect from their superiors, peers, subordinates—and from themselves. They use strategic controls and financial controls—with the emphasis on strategic controls.[45] They utilize and interchange tacit and explicit knowledge both on the individual and organizational levels.[46] And they use both linear and nonlinear thinking patterns. Finally, they believe in strategic choice—that is, they believe that their choices make a difference in what their organizations do and that their choices will affect their organizations' environments,[47] while at the same time they understand that managerial leaders are deterministic.

Strategic leaders manage the paradox created by the use of managerial and visionary leadership models. They use metaphors, analogies, and models to allow the juxtaposition of apparently contradictory concepts by defining boundaries of mutual co-existence. They guide the organizational knowledge creation process by encouraging contradictory combinative capabilities.

In summary, **strategic leaders** manage the paradox created by the use of managerial and visionary leadership models. They use metaphors, analogies, and models to allow the juxtaposition of apparently contradictory concepts by defining boundaries of mutual co-existence. They guide the organizational knowledge creation process by encouraging contradictory combinative capabilities—that is, the organization's ability to combine individual, group, and organizational tacit and explicit knowledge to generate organizational and technological innovations.[48] Organizations need to let a critical mass of their managers develop the skills and abilities required to exercise strategic leadership.[49] This means that managerial leaders need to bear with and actively support the strategic leaders, who create chaos, destroy order, take risks, and maybe destroy a part of the organization that is near and dear to them. This does not mean throwing out managerial leadership—it means including visionary and managerial leadership to enhance long-term viability and short-term financial stability. In fact, strategic leaders need to understand what managerial and visionary leaders bring to the organization and utilize the skills, knowledge and abilities that of both.

Multifunctional in nature, strategic leadership involves managing through others, managing an entire enterprise (rather than a functional subunit), and coping with change that seems to be increasing exponentially in today's new competitive landscape. Because of the complexity and global nature of this new landscape, strategic leaders must learn how to influence human behaviour effectively in an uncertain environment. By word and/or personal example and through their ability to dream pragmatically, strategic leaders meaningfully influence the behaviours, thoughts, and feelings of those with whom they work.[50] The ability to manage human capital may be the most critical of the strategic leader's skills.[51] In the opinion of one well-known leadership observer, the key to competitive advantage "... will be the capacity of top leadership to create the social architecture capable of generating intellectual capital.... By intellectual capital, I mean know-how, expertise, brainpower, innovation (and) ideas."[52] Strategic leaders also establish the context through which stakeholders (e.g., employees, customers, and suppliers) are able to perform at peak efficiency.[53]

Strategic leaders are willing to make candid, courageous, yet pragmatic, decisions—decisions that may be difficult, yet necessary, in light of internal and external conditions facing the firm.[54] Strategic leaders solicit corrective feedback from their peers, superiors, and employees about the value of their difficult decisions. Often, this feedback is sought through face-to-face communications. The unwillingness to accept feedback may be a key reason other talented executives fail, highlighting the need for strategic leaders to consistently solicit feedback from those affected by their decisions.[55]

The primary responsibility for strategic leadership rests at the top—in particular, with the CEO, but other commonly recognized strategic leaders include members of the board of directors, the top management team, and division general managers. Regardless of title and organizational function, strategic leaders have substantial decision-making responsibilities that cannot be delegated.[56]

Strategic leadership is an extremely complex but critical form of leadership. Strategies cannot be formulated and implemented to achieve above-average returns without strategic leadership. Because it is a requirement of strategic success, and because organizations may be poorly led and over-managed, firms competing in the new competitive landscape are challenged to develop strategic leaders.[57] Wayne Calloway, PepsiCo's former CEO, has suggested that "... most of the companies that are in life-or-death battles got into that kind of trouble because they didn't pay enough attention to developing their leaders."[58]

Constraints on Strategic Leadership

Unfortunately, there are many organizations that may constrain the exercise of strategic leadership. Some of these constraints are examined using government as an example because some of the principles that affect large businesses also affect governments. Governments are sometimes thought of as a monopoly with the power to impose its will on the people. However, governments compete with other organizations for human resources and with other governments for tax dollars and for new businesses to set up in their constituency (country, state, or province).[59] Unfortunately, they also grow large and unrelatedly diversified. This high level of diversification *plus* the massive debt loads of many state, provincial, and national governments *plus* public accountability for every cent spent *plus* the political context of an election every four years forces governments to use financial controls only and to push the use of strategic controls aside. This forces leaders with the potential to be strategic leaders to do one of three things: (1) to be managerial leaders, (2) to leave the organization, or (3) to fight within the system that uses the strategic energy they should be expending on leading and managing their part of the organization.[60]

Is strategic leadership possible in this type of organization? The answer is "probably not," except under two very hard to impose conditions: autonomy and protection.[61] Giving a subunit some autonomy could enhance the exercise of strategic leadership in the subunit if the autonomy is coupled with protection from those to whom the strategic leaders report. In this way, the subunit can exercise strategic controls as well as financial controls. Unfortunately, as the subunit becomes more successful and achieves visibility (because it is taking risks and "bruising" the bureaucracy), it is much more difficult to maintain this autonomy and to be protected from the managerial leadership of the organization—especially when that leadership controls financially and bureaucratically because the organization is unrelatedly diversified, has a massive debt load, operates in a political context, and must be publicly accountable for every dollar it spends. Doug House, a professor of sociology who was seconded to the Provincial Government of Newfoundland and Labrador from Memorial University of Newfoundland, considers it difficult to exercise strategic leadership in government:

> The organization of the Newfoundland and Labrador public service is very bureaucratic and hierarchical. There is a place for everyone and everyone should know his or her place. Communications go up the hierarchy from officer to manager to director to assistant deputy minister to deputy minister, and possibly to the minister, and down the hierarchy in a reverse chain. Much gets lost or reinterpreted along the way, and it is often a slow process. Not surprisingly, the public and the business community who deal with government as "clients," often complain about "red tape" and "bureaucracy."

> Such a system is not well suited to dealing with change. To the extent that change has to occur—and able senior officials recognize that it does—they prefer that it takes place at a modest pace under their control and direction. They are naturally skeptical about and resistant to premiers, ministers, and other agencies that want to initiate a lot of change on a number of fronts within a short period of time.

> This system also tends to select out or mould certain personality types for career success. The premium is on reliability, steadfastness, and loyalty to the service rather than on creativity, innovation, and critical thinking. People who do not fit the mould either stagnate, leave, or are forced out of the service. Creative individuals are usually damned with faint praise in epithets such as "He's a smart guy but he can't manage people" or "She's got some good ideas but she's a bit of a loose cannon."[62]

Managers as an Organizational Resource

As we have suggested, top-level managers are an important resource for firms seeking to formulate and implement strategies effectively. The strategic decisions made by top-level managers influence how the firm is designed and whether goals will be achieved. Thus, a critical element of organizational success is having a top-management team with superior managerial skills.[63]

A recent poll of Canadian CEOs suggest that an increasingly important part of the CEO's skill set is to build respect for their firm among the general public. Two-thirds (67 percent) of CEOs engaged in this activity in 2003, up slightly from 2002, when 64 percent indicated that this was a greater part of their job. The reason that a firm's reputation is becoming more important is that 90 percent of the CEOs surveyed believe that firms that are more respected by the public enjoy a premium in their share price.[64]

Managers often use their discretion (or latitude for action) when making strategic decisions, including those concerned with the effective implementation of strategies.[65]

Managerial discretion differs significantly across industries. The primary factors that determine the amount of decision-making discretion a manager (especially a top-level manager) has include (1) external environmental sources (e.g., the industry structure, the rate of market growth in the firm's primary industry, and the degree to which products can be differentiated), (2) characteristics of the organization (e.g., its size, age, resources, and culture), and (3) characteristics of the manager (e.g., commitment to the firm and its strategic outcomes, tolerance for ambiguity, skills in working with different people, and aspiration levels) (see Figure 13.2). Because strategic leaders' decisions are intended to help the firm gain a competitive advantage, how managers exercise discretion when determining appropriate strategic actions is critical to the firm's success.[66] Top executives must be action-oriented; thus, the decisions that they make should spur the company to action. In addition to determining new strategic initiatives, top-level managers also develop the appropriate organizational structure and reward systems of a firm. (In Chapter 12, we described how organizational structure and reward systems affect strategic actions taken to implement different types of strategies.) Furthermore, top-level managers have a major effect on a firm's culture. Evidence suggests that managers' values

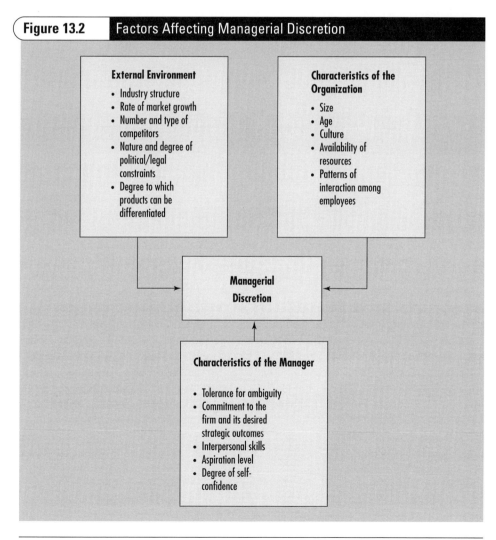

| Figure 13.2 | Factors Affecting Managerial Discretion |

External Environment
- Industry structure
- Rate of market growth
- Number and type of competitors
- Nature and degree of political/legal constraints
- Degree to which products can be differentiated

Characteristics of the Organization
- Size
- Age
- Culture
- Availability of resources
- Patterns of interaction among employees

Managerial Discretion

Characteristics of the Manager
- Tolerance for ambiguity
- Commitment to the firm and its desired strategic outcomes
- Interpersonal skills
- Aspiration level
- Degree of self-confidence

SOURCE: Adapted from S. Finkelstein & D. C. Hambrick, 1996, *Strategic Leadership: Top Executives and Their Effects on Organizations*, St. Paul, MN: West Publishing Company.

are critical in shaping a firm's cultural values.[67] As this discussion shows, top-level managers have an important effect on organizational activities and performance.[68] The significance of this effect should not be underestimated.

The potential effect of strategic leadership is illustrated by Mitt Romney's successful turnaround of the 2002 Winter Olympic Games. When Romney took over as CEO of the Salt Lake Organizing Committee in 1999, it had a $379 million deficit, resulting from the loss of sponsors following the Olympic bid scandal and allegations of bribery. Romney's ability, not only to cut costs, but also to attract new sponsors, saved the games financially. Moreover, his approach and integrity won over many and helped heal the wounds from the bid controversy. "If we do our job well, people will go away feeling like they have had a fire lit within them or they've been inspired by the athletes and by the people they've met here and by their fellow citizens from around the world."[69] Romney's leadership was very effective in accomplishing these aspirations.

The decisions and actions of strategic leaders can make them a source of competitive advantage for the firm. In accordance with the criteria of sustainability discussed in Chapter 4, strategic leaders can be a source of sustained competitive advantage only when their work is valuable, rare, costly to imitate, and nonsubstitutable. Effective strategic leaders become a source of sustained competitive advantage when they focus their work on the key issues that ultimately shape the firm's ability to earn above-average returns. Accordingly, managerial beliefs affect strategic decisions, which in turn, affect the firm's performance.[70] For example, Mitt Romney certainly believed that the 2002 Winter Olympic Games could be turned into a success. However, Romney's vision was achieved through a team of leaders.

Top Management Teams

The complexity of the challenges faced by the firm and the need for substantial amounts of information and knowledge require teams of executives to provide the strategic leadership of most firms. The **top management team** is composed of the key managers who are responsible for selecting and implementing the firm's strategies. Typically, the top management team includes the officers of the corporation, defined by the title of vice president and above or by service as a member of the board of directors. The quality of the strategic decisions made by a top management team affects the firm's ability to innovate and engage in effective strategic change.[71]

Top Management Team, Firm Performance, and Strategic Change

The job of top-level executives is complex and requires a broad knowledge of the firm's operations and the three key parts of the firm's external environment—the general environment, the industry environment, and the competitor environment—as discussed in Chapter 3. Therefore, firms try to form a top management team that has the appropriate knowledge and expertise to operate the internal organization, yet also can deal with all the firm's stakeholders, as well as its competitors.[72] This approach typically requires a **heterogeneous top management team**. A heterogeneous top management team is composed of individuals with different functional backgrounds, experience, and education. The more heterogeneous a top management team is, with varied expertise and knowledge, the more capacity it has to provide effective strategic leadership in *formulating* strategy.

Members of a heterogeneous top management team benefit from discussing the different perspectives advanced by team members. In many cases, these discussions increase the quality of the top management team's decisions, especially when the diverse perspectives result in a synthesis that is generally superior to any one individual perspective. The net benefit of actions taken by heterogeneous teams has been positive, in

The **top management team** is composed of the key managers who are responsible for selecting and implementing the firm's strategies.

A **heterogeneous top management team** is composed of individuals with different functional backgrounds, experience, and education.

terms of market share and above-average returns. Research shows that greater heterogeneity among top management team members promotes debate, which often leads to better strategic decisions. In turn, better strategic decisions produce higher firm performance.[73]

It is also important that the top management team members function cohesively. In general, the more heterogeneous and the larger the top management team, the more difficult it is for the team to effectively implement strategies. Comprehensive and long-term strategic plans can be inhibited by communication difficulties among top executives who have different backgrounds and different cognitive skills. As a result, a group of top executives with diverse backgrounds may inhibit the process of decision making if it is not effectively managed. In these cases, top management teams may fail to comprehensively examine threats and opportunities, leading to a suboptimal strategic decision.[74]

Having members with substantive expertise in the firm's core functions and businesses is also important to the effectiveness of a top management team. In a high-technology industry, it may be critical for a firm's top management team to have R&D expertise, particularly when growth strategies are being implemented.[75]

The characteristics of top management teams are related to innovation and strategic change. For example, more heterogeneous top management teams are associated positively with innovation and strategic change. The heterogeneity may force the team or some of the members to "think outside of the box" and thus be more creative in making decisions. Therefore, firms that need to change their strategies are more likely to do so if they have top management teams with diverse backgrounds and expertise. A top management team with various areas of expertise is more likely to identify environmental changes (opportunities and threats) or changes within the firms that require a different strategic direction.[76]

CEO Daniel Vasella, chairman of Novartis, runs the world's seventh largest pharmaceutical company, which was formed through the merger of Swiss drug makers Sandoz and Ciba-Geigy in 1996. Vasella, formerly a physician, has transformed the once stodgy Swiss conglomerate into an aggressive innovator, partly by putting together an energetic but diverse top management team. One analyst noted, "Although the top executives at Novartis contain a diversity of strong personalities, their oft-used term 'alignment' rings true in their teamwork.... Yet, each team member carries a different charge and perspective."[77]

The CEO and Top Management Team Power

As noted in Chapter 11, the board of directors is an important governance mechanism for monitoring a firm's strategic direction and for representing stakeholders' interests, especially those of shareholders. In fact, higher performance typically is achieved when the board of directors is more directly involved in shaping a firm's strategic direction.[78]

Boards of directors, however, may find it difficult to direct the strategic actions of powerful CEOs and top management teams. It is not uncommon for a powerful CEO to appoint a number of sympathetic outside board members or have inside board members who are on the top management team and report to the CEO. In either case, the CEO may have significant control over the board's actions. "A central question is whether boards are an effective management control mechanism ... or whether they are a 'management tool,' ... a rubber stamp for management initiatives ... and often surrender to management their major domain of decision-making authority, which includes the right to hire, fire, and compensate top management."[79]

Xerox has stumbled, partly due to its board. *Fortune* named it one of the "dirty half dozen" in 2001: "Xerox is a textbook example of a high-profile board asleep at the wheel ... the once proud document giant has been plagued by everything short of locusts: missed earnings estimates, plummeting stock, mounting debt, and an SEC investigation of dodgy accounting practices in Xerox's Mexican operations. What have the venerable directors done? Very little—perhaps because they were busy at other meetings (most of Xerox's directors serve on at least four other boards)."[80]

Alternatively, recent research shows that social ties between the CEO and board members may actually increase board members' involvement in strategic decisions. Thus, strong relationships between the CEO and the board of directors may have positive or negative outcomes.[81]

CEOs and top management team members can achieve power in other ways. A CEO who also holds the position of board chair usually has more power than the CEO who is not simultaneously serving as chair of the firm's board. Although this practice of CEO duality (when the CEO and the chair of the board are the same) has become more common in Canadian and U.S. businesses, it has come under heavy criticism. Duality has been blamed for poor performance and slow response to change in a number of firms.[82]

DaimlerChrysler CEO Jürgen Schrempp, who holds the dual positions of chairman of the board and CEO, has substantial power in the firm. In fact, insiders suggest that he was purging those individuals who were outspoken and who represented potential threats to his dominance. In particular, former Chrysler executives are leaving the firm, although research suggests that retaining key employees after an acquisition contributes to improved post-acquisition performance. Thus, it has been particularly difficult to turn around the North American operations.[83] Dieter Zetsche, a German, who is likely next in line to be CEO at DaimlerChrysler, is leading the team that is seeking to reverse Chrysler's fortunes. Schrempp's future may depend on how Zetsche's team does. It is ironic that six of the turnaround team members are former Chrysler executives. The loss of some of these key executives, such as Thomas Stallkamp, has been blamed in part for the poor performance.

Although it varies across industries, duality occurs most commonly in the largest firms. Increased shareholder activism, however, has brought CEO duality under scrutiny and attack in Canadian, U.S., and European firms. Historically, an independent board leadership structure, in which the same person does not hold the positions of CEO and chair, was believed to enhance a board's ability to monitor top-level managers' decisions and actions, particularly in terms of the firm's financial performance. Stewardship theory, on the other hand, suggests that CEO duality facilitates effective decisions and actions. In these instances, the increased effectiveness gained through CEO duality accrues from the individual who wants to perform effectively and desires to be the best possible steward of the firm's assets. Because of this person's positive orientation and actions, extra governance and the coordination costs resulting from an independent board leadership structure would be unnecessary.[84]

Top-management team members and CEOs who have long tenure—on the team and in the organization—have a greater influence on board decisions. Long tenure is known to restrict the breadth of an executive's knowledge base. With the limited perspectives associated with a restricted knowledge base, long-tenured top executives typically develop fewer alternatives to evaluate in making strategic decisions. However, long-tenured managers also may be able to exercise more effective strategic control, thereby obviating the need for board members' involvement because effective strategic control generally produces higher performance.[85]

To strengthen the firm, boards of directors should develop an effective relationship with the firm's top management team. The relative degrees of power held by the board and top management team members should be examined in light of an individual firm's situation. For example, the abundance of resources in a firm's external environment and the volatility of that environment may affect the ideal balance of power between boards and top-management teams. Moreover, a volatile and uncertain environment may create a situation where a powerful CEO is needed to move quickly, but a diverse top management team may create less cohesion among team members and prevent or stall a necessary strategic move. By developing effective working relationships, boards, CEOs, and other top management team members are able to serve the best interests of the firm's stakeholders.[86]

Key Strategic Leadership Actions

Several identifiable actions characterize strategic leadership that positively contributes to effective use of the firm's strategies.[87] We present the most critical of these actions in Figure 13.3. Many of the actions interact with each other. For example, developing human capital through executive training contributes to establishing a strategic direction, fostering an effective culture, exploiting core competencies, using effective organizational control systems, and establishing ethical practices. The next Strategic Focus box, "Changing the Guard" on page 410, highlights a change in leadership at Scotiabank and examines the impact this change will have on the strategic direction of Scotiabank.

Determining Strategic Direction

Determining the strategic direction of a firm involves developing a long-term vision of the firm's strategic intent. A long-term vision typically looks at least 5 to 10 years into the future. A philosophy with goals, this vision consists of the image and character the firm seeks.[88]

The ideal long-term vision has two parts: a core ideology and an envisioned future. While the core ideology motivates employees through the company's heritage, the envisioned future encourages employees to stretch beyond their expectations of accomplishment and requires significant change and progress in order to be realized.[89] The envisioned future serves as a guide to many aspects of a firm's strategy implementation process, including motivation, leadership, employee empowerment, and organizational design.

Determining the strategic direction of a firm involves developing a long-term vision of the firm's strategic intent.

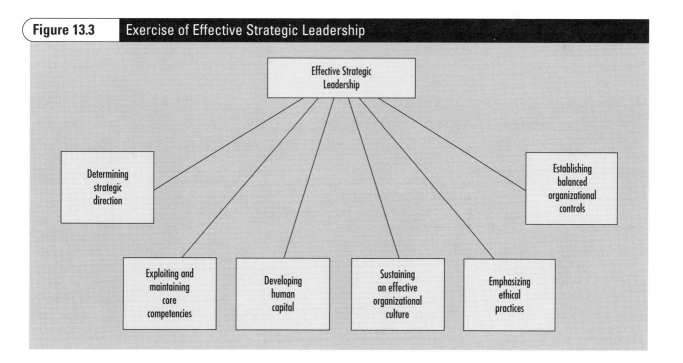

Figure 13.3 Exercise of Effective Strategic Leadership

Changing the Guard: Scotiabank Transitions from Godsoe to Waugh

Scotiabank promoted Richard (Rick) Waugh to the CEO position in December 2003. The search for a successor to outgoing CEO Peter C. Godsoe lasted approximately five years and saw Waugh prevail over colleagues Robert Chisholm (head of domestic banking) and David Wilson (CEO of Scotia Capital).

Waugh joined the bank at its Winnipeg branch as a trainee in 1970. It is expected that he will be challenged to maintain, if not surpass, the heights attained by the bank over the last 30 years. The challenge lies not only externally, as the bank continues to compete in an increasingly competitive market, but also internally, as Waugh brings his own style of leadership, which he calls "evolutionary change." Analysts are divided on whether Waugh's leadership style will be as effective as that of his predecessors, Cedric Ritchie and Peter Godsoe. On the one hand, some suggest that Waugh's gentler more relaxed approach is what the bank needs for growth, while other analysts think that his style may not fit well with the culture that developed under his predecessors—a culture where a strong personality made the decisions and was a forceful presence.

Perhaps the key to Waugh's success will reside in his ability to bring his demonstrated experience in the international market to bear on the bank's operations. The international banking operation that Waugh headed up generates almost one-third of Scotiabank's earnings and employs approximately 40 percent of its 48,000 staff. With intense domestic competition, exploiting the potential for international growth may be the only formula for success.

Recognized as the most international bank in Canada, Scotiabank has more than 1800 branches and offices in 50 countries on 6 continents. The international network has well-established operations (e.g., a branch in Jamaica was established in 1889, before operations were in place in Toronto), as well as relatively new operations (e.g., a Mexican branch was established in the 1960s). Scotiabank enjoys the position of being one of only six banks to operate in Mexico and was recently ranked as number one in customer service by *La Reforma*, Mexico's leading newspaper.

Scotiabank, with Rick Waugh at the helm, is positioned for growth in Mexico. For example, in his analysis of growth potential, Waugh stated that trade between Canada and Mexico had increased by 300 percent in the last 10 years, making Canada the second most important export market behind the U.S. He sees the growing market in Mexico, with a population of close to 100 million people, along with rapid growth in the retail banking sector, as a tremendous opportunity for Scotiabank. In his address to the Economic Club of Toronto in January 2004, Waugh made it clear that growth was expected in nontraditional markets, such as the Caribbean, Central America, and Mexico, and Scotabank was prepared for the opportunities and challenges this growth would bring.

Scotiabank, which was founded in 1832, in Halifax, Nova Scotia, has been nurtured and challenged by a number of leaders over its 172-year history to achieve its goal—to be the best and most successful Canadian-based international financial services group. Thirty years under the leadership of Cedric Ritchie and Peter Godsoe saw the bank move from the bottom of the "Big Five" banks to its current ranking in 2004, as Canada's number two bank, as ranked by assets and market capitalization.

The tremendous achievements and growth over the period are attributed to the strategic leadership and personal management styles of Ritchie and Godsoe. Some analysts have suggested their styles were "autocratic" and "undemocratic." Their attitudes differed from the more relaxed and inclusive approach attributed to Waugh, and it remains to be seen what impact his leadership style will have on the bank's performance. If he sets the right strategic direction, develops and aligns the bank's human capital with the strategic direction, exploits and maintains core competencies, sustains an effective corporate culture, emphasizes ethical practices, and establishes an appropriate combination of strategic and financial controls, Waugh will prove to be an effective strategic leader who will have a positive impact on Scotiabank's performance.

SOURCES: J. Kirby, 2004, In the vault, *Canadian Business*, March 1–14, 68–74; Scotiabank, 2004, Info centre: Corporate profile, corporate governance, speeches and presentations, *Scotiabank website*, http://www.scotiabank.com/cda/eventindex/0,1004,LIDen_SID35,00.html, accessed May 19, 2004.

Matthew D. Heyman came out of Harvard Business School in 1993, with a vision of building lavish movie theatres in Mexico City, a metropolis with 20 million inhabitants. The Mexican theatre industry was in shambles because of government price controls, and so a vacuum existed for quality movie theatres. For six months, Heyman and his partners, Miguel Angel Dávila and Adolfo Fastlicht, were told by investors that their idea was too risky. After finding financial backing for their company, Cinemex, they began constructing movie theatres, but then the Mexican economy crashed. Heyman decided to push through anyway, as much of his competition disappeared as a result of the crash. He decided early on to target the largest market in Mexico City, the working poor. His theatres charged about half as much for tickets in poor areas of the city compared to the price charged by theatres in wealthy areas, even though these theatres were just as extravagant. In 2001, Cinemex was expected to generate a profit of approximately $40 million. This accomplishment is largely due to Heyman's vision and the employees of Cinemex who were inspired by Heyman's leadership to implement his vision.[90]

A charismatic CEO may foster employees' commitment to a new vision and strategic direction. Nonetheless, it is important not to lose sight of the strengths of the organization in making changes required by a new strategic direction. Most top executives obtain inputs regarding their vision from many people with a range of skills to help them analyze various aspects of the firm's operations. In addition, executives must structure the firm effectively to help achieve their vision.[91] The goal is to balance the firm's short-term need to adjust to a new vision while maintaining its long-term survivability by emphasizing its current and valuable core competencies. One CEO who has garnered the respect of his peers partially because of his ability to set a direction is Paul Tellier, who leads Bombardier Inc. (See the Strategic Focus box "Paul Tellier" on page 412.)

Exploiting and Maintaining Core Competencies

Examined in Chapters 1 and 4, *core competencies* are resources and capabilities that serve as a source of sustained competitive advantage for a firm over its rivals. Typically, core competencies relate to an organization's functional skills, such as manufacturing, finance, marketing, and research and development. As shown by the descriptions that follow, firms develop and exploit core competencies in many different functional areas. Strategic leaders must verify that the firm's competencies are emphasized in strategy implementation efforts. Intel, for example, has core competencies of *competitive agility* (an ability to act in a variety of competitively relevant ways) and *competitive speed* (an ability to act quickly when facing environmental and competitive pressures).[92]

In many large firms, and certainly in related diversified ones, core competencies are effectively exploited when they are developed and applied across different organizational units (see Chapter 7). For example, PepsiCo purchased Quaker Oats, which makes the sports drink Gatorade. Pepsi plans to use its competence in distribution systems to build market share outside the United States. Accordingly, Pepsi soft drinks (e.g., Pepsi Cola and Mountain Dew) and Gatorade will share the logistics activity. Similarly, Quaker Oats's healthy snacks and Frito Lay's salty snacks (already owned by Pepsi) can use this competence and be distributed through the same channels.[93] PepsiCo's human capital will play a critical role in the firm's attempt to develop the core competencies that are required to successfully compete in the markets PepsiCo is now targeting.

Developing Human Capital

Human capital refers to the knowledge and skills of a firm's entire workforce. From the perspective of human capital, employees are viewed as a capital resource that requires investment. These investments are productive, in that much of the development of industry in Canada and the U.S. can be attributed to the effectiveness of its human

Human capital refers to the knowledge and skills of a firm's entire workforce.

Paul Tellier: Most Respected Canadian CEO in 2003

In 2003, Paul Tellier, CEO of Bombardier Inc., was selected by his peers as the most respected CEO in Canada. Interestingly, he had also been selected for this honour in 2002, while serving as the CEO of Canadian National Railway, prior to moving to Bombardier in late 2002. The number of CEOs selecting Tellier increased from 6 percent in 2002 to 15 percent in 2003.

Most Admired and Respected Canadian CEOs in 2003

Name	Company	Percent
Paul Tellier	Bombardier Inc.	15
Dominic D'Alessandro	Manulife Financial Corp.	6
Rick George	Suncor Energy	3
Clive Beddoe	WestJet Airlines	3
Ray Royer	Domtar Inc.	3
Peter Godsoe	The Bank of Nova Scotia	3
Gwyn Morgan	EnCana Corporation	3
Remi Marcoux	Transcontinental Inc.	2
Frank Stronach	Magna International Inc.	2
Gordon Nixon	RBC Financial Group	2
Isadore (Izzy) Sharp	Four Seasons Hotels and Resorts	2

The survey is sponsored by KPMG and conducted by Ipsos-Reid each year. CEOs are asked to write in the name of the CEO they most admire and respect. The table above lists the top CEOs and the percentage of CEOs who selected them.

In addition, each respondent was asked to identify what they most admired and respected about the CEO they had selected. Ipsos-Reid compiled a list of the 11 attributes and the percentage of times they were identified: vision, focus, discipline, or good strategy (42 percent); track record (39 percent); financial performance (38 percent); corporate governance or leadership (34 percent); shareholder or investment value (21 percent); honest, trustworthy, or ethical (15 percent); global presence/international expansion (15 percent); innovative or creative (15 percent); driven or aggressive (14 percent); good staff, management, or employee relations (12 percent); and social responsibility, community involvement, or corporate citizenship (11 percent).

SOURCE: 2004, Press Release, For second year running, Paul Tellier named most respected CEO by peers, Ipsos News Center, January 20, http://www.ipsos-na.com/news, retrieved May 10, 2004.

capital, leading to the conviction, in many business firms today, that "as the dynamics of competition accelerate, people are perhaps the only truly sustainable source of competitive advantage." Human capital's increasing importance suggests a significant role for the firm's human resource management activities. As a support activity (see Chapter 4), human resource management practices facilitate people's efforts to successfully select and especially to use the firm's strategies.[94]

Finding the human capital necessary to run an organization effectively is a challenge that many firms attempt to solve by using temporary employees. Other firms try to improve their recruiting and selection techniques. Solving the problem, however, requires more than hiring temporary employees; it requires building effective commitment to organizational goals, as well. Hiring star players is also insufficient; rather, a strategic leader needs to build an effective organizational team committed to achieving the company's vision and goals.[95]

Increasingly, international experience has become essential to the development necessary for strategic leaders. Because nearly every industry is targeting fast-growing foreign markets, more companies are requiring "global competency" among their top managers. Thus, companies trying to learn how to compete successfully in the global economy should find opportunities for their future strategic leaders to work in locations outside of their home nation. When multinational corporations invest in emerging economies, they are also wise to invest in human capital in foreign subsidiaries. Also, because international management capabilities are becoming important, managing "inpatriation" (the process of transferring host-country or third-country national managers into the domestic market of multinational firms) has become an important means of building global core competencies.[96]

Effective training and development programs increase the probability that a manager will be a successful strategic leader. These programs have grown progressively important as knowledge has become more integral to gaining and sustaining a competitive advantage. Additionally, such programs build knowledge and skills, inculcate a common set of core values, and offer a systematic view of the organization, thus promoting the firm's strategic vision and organizational cohesion. The programs also contribute to the development of core competencies. Furthermore, they help strategic leaders improve skills that are critical to completing other tasks associated with effective strategic leadership, such as determining the firm's strategic direction, exploiting and maintaining the firm's core competencies, and developing an organizational culture that supports ethical practices. Thus, building human capital is vital to the effective execution of strategic leadership.[97]

Strategic leaders must acquire the skills necessary to help develop human capital in their areas of responsibility. This challenge is significant, given that most strategic leaders need to enhance their human resource management abilities. For example, firms that place value on human resources and have effective reward plans for employees obtained higher returns on their initial public offerings. When human capital investments are successful, the result is a workforce capable of learning continuously. Continuous learning and leveraging the firm's expanding knowledge base are linked with strategic success.[98]

Although Barclays Group lost its position among the world's largest banks in the 1980s (it was ranked fifth in the world in assets in the early 1980s), its prestige was rising again in 2000. Its return on equity was 23 percent in fiscal year 2000, up from 15 percent in 1997, thanks, in part, to the leadership of Matthew Barrett, named CEO of Barclays in October 1999. Barrett was CEO of the Bank of Montreal prior to moving to England in 1999. Much of Barrett's accomplishments can be attributed to hiring significant leadership talent away from other firms to form formidable top management teams for various business groups at Barclays. For instance, he hired Robert Diamond from Morgan Stanley to lead the capital unit. Barrett has developed a new long-term vision of the firm's strategic intent by taking the position that: "I want us to be the premier European investment bank for debt finance." While competitors are downsizing, Barclays is adding key people, partly by raiding its German rival Deutsche Bank for additional talent. The firm has also hired 25 senior investment bankers for its New York unit and hired Michael O'Neill from Bank of America to be the chief executive of its long-term capital management group. In summary, as he did at the Bank of Montreal, Barrett is relying on the human capital at Barclays to pursue the firm's newly determined strategic direction.[99]

Programs that achieve outstanding results in the training of future strategic leaders become a competitive advantage for a firm. General Electric's system of training and development of future strategic leaders is comprehensive and thought to be among the best.[100] Accordingly, it may be a source of competitive advantage for the firm.

Because of the economic downturn in 2001 and early 2002, many firms laid off key people. Layoffs can result in a significant loss of the knowledge possessed by a firm's human capital. Although it is also not uncommon for restructuring firms to reduce their expenditures on, or investments in, training and development programs, restructuring may actually be an important time to increase investments in these programs. Restructuring firms have less slack and cannot absorb as many errors; moreover, the employees who remain after layoffs may find themselves in positions without all of the skills or knowledge they need to perform the required tasks effectively. Improvements in information technology can facilitate better use of human resources when a downsizing event occurs.[101]

Viewing employees as a resource to be maximized, rather than a cost to be minimized, facilitates the successful implementation of a firm's strategies. The implementation of such strategies also is more effective when strategic leaders approach layoffs in a manner that employees believe is fair and equitable.[102]

Sustaining an Effective Organizational Culture

An **organizational culture** consists of a complex set of ideologies, symbols, and core values that is shared throughout the firm and influences the way business is conducted.

An **organizational culture** consists of a complex set of ideologies, symbols, and core values that is shared throughout the firm and influences the way business is conducted. Evidence suggests that a firm can develop core competencies in terms of both the capabilities it possesses and the way the capabilities are used to produce strategic actions. In other words, because the organizational culture influences how the firm conducts its business and helps regulate and control employees' behaviour, it can be a source of competitive advantage. Thus, shaping the context within which the firm formulates and implements its strategies—that is, shaping the organizational culture—is a central task of strategic leaders.[103]

Entrepreneurial Orientation

An organizational culture often encourages (or discourages) the pursuit of entrepreneurial opportunities, especially in large firms. Entrepreneurial opportunities are an important source of growth and innovation.[104] In Chapter 14, we describe how large firms use strategic entrepreneurship to pursue entrepreneurial opportunities and to gain first-mover advantages. Medium and small firms also rely on strategic entrepreneurship when trying to develop innovations as the foundation for profitable growth. In firms of all sizes, strategic entrepreneurship is more likely to be successful when employees have an entrepreneurial orientation. Five dimensions characterize a firm's entrepreneurial orientation: autonomy, innovativeness, risk taking, proactiveness, and competitive aggressiveness.[105] In combination, these dimensions influence the activities of a firm to be innovative and launch new ventures.

The first of an entrepreneurial orientation's five dimensions, *autonomy*, allows employees to take actions that are free of organizational constraints and permits individuals and groups to be self-directed. The second dimension, *innovativeness*, "reflects a firm's tendency to engage in and support new ideas, novelty, experimentation, and creative processes that may result in new products, services, or technological processes." Cultures with a tendency toward innovativeness encourage employees to think beyond existing knowledge, technologies, and parameters, in efforts to find creative ways to add value. *Risk taking* reflects a willingness by employees and their firm to accept risks when pursuing entrepreneurial opportunities. These risks can include assuming significant levels of debt and allocating large amounts of other resources (e.g., people) to projects that may not be completed. The fourth dimension of an entrepreneurial orientation, *proactiveness*, describes a firm's ability to be a market leader rather than a follower.

Proactive organizational cultures constantly use processes to anticipate future market needs and to satisfy them before competitors learn how to do so. Finally, *competitive aggressiveness* is a firm's propensity to take actions that allow it to consistently and substantially outperform its rivals.[106]

Changing the Organizational Culture and Business Re-engineering

Changing a firm's organizational culture is more difficult than maintaining it, but effective strategic leaders recognize when change is needed. Incremental changes to the firm's culture typically are used to implement strategies. More significant changes—and, sometimes, even radical changes—to organizational culture are used to support the selection of strategies that differ from those the firm has implemented historically. Regardless of the reasons for change, shaping and reinforcing a new culture require effective communication and problem solving, along with the selection of the right people (those who have the values desired for the organization), effective performance appraisals (establishing goals and measuring individual performance toward goals that fit in with the new core values), and appropriate reward systems (rewarding the desired behaviours that reflect the new core values).[107]

Evidence suggests that cultural changes succeed only when the firm's CEO, other key top management team members, and middle-level managers actively support them. To effect change, middle-level managers, in particular, need to be highly disciplined to energize the culture and foster alignment with the strategic vision.[108]

Selecting new top management team members from the external managerial labour market is a catalyst for changes to organizational culture. This concept is illustrated in the Strategic Focus box about Carlos Ghosn. A Brazilian-born manager working for Renault, Ghosn was charged with turning around Nissan, partially owned by Renault, which was suffering from lost market share. As the Strategic Focus box "An Outsider from Brazil Facilitates Change at Nissan" on page 416 illustrates, transforming an organization and its culture is challenging.

Emphasizing Ethical Practices

The effectiveness of processes used to implement the firm's strategies increases when they are based on ethical practices. Ethical companies encourage and enable people at all organizational levels to act ethically when doing what is necessary to implement the firm's strategies. In turn, ethical practices and the judgment on which they are based create social capital in the organization by increasing the goodwill available to individuals and groups. Thus, while "money motivates, it does not inspire" as social capital can. Alternately, when unethical practices evolve in an organization, they become like a contagious disease.[109]

To properly influence employees' judgment and behaviour, ethical practices must shape the firm's decision-making process and be an integral part of an organization's culture. In fact, research has found that a value-based culture is the most effective means of ensuring that employees comply with the firm's ethical requirements. As discussed in Chapter 11, in the absence of ethical requirements, managers may act opportunistically, making decisions that are in their own best interests, but not in the firm's best interests. In other words, managers acting opportunistically take advantage of their positions, making decisions that benefit them to the detriment of the firm's owners (shareholders).[110]

Managerial opportunism may explain the behaviour and decisions of a few key executives at Enron, where stockholders lost almost all the value in their Enron stock in the firm's bankruptcy proceeding. Accounting firm Arthur Andersen, Enron's auditor, was also severely damaged by the disaster. Due to the unethical practices of both the company and the auditor, many accounting firms—and other firms unrelated to Enron but

An Outsider from Brazil Facilitates Change at Nissan

In 1999, Renault assumed $5.4 billion of Nissan's debt in return for 36.6 percent of Nissan's equity, giving it a controlling stake in the Japanese automaker. The combined assets of Renault and Nissan made it the fourth largest carmaker in the world. However, Nissan was struggling with shrinking market share, both domestically in Japan and worldwide. Renault turned to Carlos Ghosn to lead a turnaround for the Japanese carmaker.

Ghosn came to Renault from Michelin's Brazilian subsidiary. He was given a complex challenge—not only did he face the difficulty of overcoming conservatism among Nissan car designers, which had allowed engineers to dominate for the past decade of slow market share loss, but he also had to face the cultural challenge of being an outsider in the homogeneous Japanese culture. Although the challenge was daunting, Ghosn was able to win over key Japanese inside managers necessary to implement his plan, as well as suppliers and labour leaders who might have been expected to resist more intensely. Furthermore, the car designs created under Ghosn's leadership had much more flare than in the recent past. As a result, in 2001, Nissan posted a profit of $2.7 billion; the largest in its 68-year history and its first annual profit in 4 years. How was Ghosn, a manager who was selected from the external managerial labour market, able to accomplish this significant strategic turnaround? Although he continues to indicate that his strategic change agenda is not complete because facilitating a change in the organization culture takes time, several actions can be identified. For example, he charged Itaru Koeda with the task of drastic cost reduction with specific targets and tactics. To accomplish this reduction, Ghosn brought together a younger set of Nissan managers, "35- and 45-year-old managers," to participate in identifying issues to focus on in the cost reduction. Although this action may not sound that unusual outside of Japan, it was revolutionary to have "young people in the company to debate things and propose what we should do."

Next, he changed the way the supply chain was managed by reducing the number of suppliers and, at the same time, sought to create deeper partnerships with them. To fund this new way of managing the supply chain, Ghosn dismantled the cross shareholding associated with Nissan's keiretsu investments (investments with companies with shared common interests and organized for their mutual benefit). Ghosn found that $4 billion was tied up in cross shareholdings with keiretsu partner companies, which often had no relationship with Nissan.

Another difficult action Ghosn took was to close a number of plants, although in Japan lifetime employment is still seen as an important labour movement objective. To facilitate closure of a plant in a Tokyo suburb, Ghosn worked with Nissan's unions to show that no matter how painful, in the long run, such actions would be good for workers as well. He negotiated a generous one-time bonus of 5.2 months' pay for those workers who were laid off. Because other companies were challenging the practice of lifetime employment, Ghosn' efforts had some legitimacy.

Although Nissan knew such actions were needed before it put Ghosn in charge, it needed someone like him to "push the button." Kenichi Ohmae, a Japanese management expert, has indicated that a large majority of Japanese companies face problems similar to Nissan's. However, few have the "power to heal themselves from within." In Ghosn's words, "a good corporate culture taps into the productive aspects of a country's culture, and in Nissan's case we have been able to exploit the uniquely Japanese combination of keen competitiveness and sense of community that has driven the likes of Sony and Toyota—and Nissan itself in earlier times." A Japanese manager will likely take over Nissan after Ghosn leaves. However, he will have left a legacy of significant cultural change that will likely foster success in the future.

SOURCES: C. Dawson, 2002, Nissan bets big on small, *Business Week Online*, http://www.businessweek.com, March 4; C. Ghosn, 2002, Saving the business without losing the company, *Harvard Business Review*, 80(1): 37–45; M. S. Mayershon, 2002, Nissan's U-turn to profits, *Chief Executive*, January, 12–16; A. Raskin, 2002, Voulez-vous completely overhaul this big, slow company and start making some cars people actually want avec moi? *Business 2.0*, January, 61–67; G. S. Vasilash, 2002, Managing design; Design management, *Automotive Design and Production*, February, 34–35; C. Ahmadjian & P. Robinson, 2001, Safety in numbers: Downsizing and the deinstitutionalization of permanent employment in Japan, *Administrative Science Quarterly*, 46: 622–54; C. Dawson & S. Prasso, 2001, Pow! Bam! Zap! Meet Nissan's super hero, *Business Week*, April 30, 12; L. P. Norton, 2001, Meet Mr. Nissan, *Barron's*, November 19, 17–19.

with aggressive accounting methods—have not only been criticized, but have lost customers or been devalued by investors. Firms that have been reported to have poor ethical behaviour, such as acts of fraud or having to restate financial results, see their overall corporate value in the stock market drop precipitously.[111]

These incidents suggest that firms need to employ ethical strategic leaders—leaders who include ethical practices as part of their long-term vision for the firm, who desire to do the right thing, and for whom honesty, trust, and integrity are important. Strategic leaders who consistently display these qualities inspire employees as they work with others to develop and support an organizational culture in which ethical practices are the expected behavioural norms.[112]

Strategic leaders are challenged to take actions that increase the probability that an ethical culture will prevail in their organizations. One action that has gained favour is to institute a formal program to manage ethics. Operating much like control systems, these programs help inculcate values throughout the organization.[113] Therefore, when these efforts are successful, the practices associated with an ethical culture become institutionalized in the firm; that is, they become the set of behavioural commitments and actions accepted by most of the firm's employees and other stakeholders with whom employees interact.

Additional actions that strategic leaders can take to develop an ethical organizational culture include (1) establishing and communicating specific goals to describe the firm's ethical standards (e.g., developing and disseminating a code of conduct); (2) continuously revising and updating the code of conduct, based on inputs from people throughout the firm and from other stakeholders (e.g., customers and suppliers); (3) disseminating the code of conduct to all stakeholders to inform them of the firm's ethical standards and practices; (4) developing and implementing methods and procedures to use in achieving the firm's ethical standards (e.g., using internal auditing practices that are consistent with the standards); (5) creating and using explicit reward systems that recognize acts of courage (e.g., rewarding those who use proper channels and procedures to report observed wrongdoings); and (6) creating a work environment in which all people are treated with dignity.[114] The effectiveness of these actions increases when they are taken simultaneously, thereby making them mutually supportive. When managers and employees do not engage in such actions—perhaps because an ethical culture has not been created—problems are likely to occur. As we discuss next, formal organizational controls can help prevent further problems and reinforce better ethical practices.

Establishing Balanced Organizational Controls

Organizational controls have long been viewed as an important part of strategy implementation processes. Controls are necessary to help ensure that firms achieve their desired outcomes. Defined as the "formal, information-based ... procedures used by managers to maintain or alter patterns in organizational activities," controls help strategic leaders build credibility, demonstrate the value of strategies to the firm's stakeholders, and promote and support strategic change.[115] Most critically, controls provide the parameters within which strategies are to be implemented, as well as corrective actions to be taken when implementation-related adjustments are required. In this chapter, we focus on two organizational controls—strategic and financial—that are introduced in Chapter 12. Our discussion of organizational controls here emphasizes strategic and financial controls because strategic leaders are responsible for their development and effective use.

Evidence suggests that, although critical to the firm's success, organizational controls are imperfect. *Control failures* have a negative effect on the firm's reputation and divert managerial attention from actions that are necessary to effectively use the strategic management process.

As explained in Chapter 12, financial control focuses on short-term financial outcomes. In contrast, strategic control focuses on the *content* of strategic actions, rather than their *outcomes*. Some strategic actions can be correct, but poor financial outcomes may still result because of external conditions, such as a recession in the economy, unexpected domestic or foreign government actions, or natural disasters.[116] Therefore, an emphasis on financial control often produces more short-term and risk-averse managerial decisions, because financial outcomes may be caused by events beyond managers' direct control. Alternatively, strategic control encourages lower-level managers to make decisions that incorporate moderate and acceptable levels of risk because outcomes are shared between the business-level executives making strategic proposals and the corporate-level executives evaluating them.

The Balanced Scorecard

The **balanced scorecard** is a framework that firms can use to verify that they have established both strategic and financial controls to assess their performance.

The **balanced scorecard** is a framework that firms can use to verify that they have established both strategic and financial controls to assess their performance.[117] This technique is most appropriate for use when dealing with business-level strategies, but can also apply to corporate-level strategies.

As discussed in Chapter 2, the underlying premise of the balanced scorecard is that firms jeopardize their future performance possibilities when financial controls are emphasized at the expense of strategic controls, since financial controls provide feedback about outcomes achieved from past actions, but do not communicate the drivers of the firm's future performance. Thus, an overemphasis on financial controls could promote organizational behaviour that has a net effect of sacrificing the firm's long-term value-creating potential for short-term performance gains. An appropriate balance of strategic controls and financial controls, rather than an overemphasis on either, allows firms to effectively monitor their performance.[118]

Four perspectives are integrated to form the balanced scorecard framework: *financial* (concerned with growth, profitability, and risk from shareholders' perspective), *customer* (concerned with the amount of value customers perceive was created by the firm's products), *internal business processes* (with a focus on the priorities for various business processes that create customer and shareholder satisfaction), and *learning and growth* (concerned with the firm's effort to create a climate that supports change, innovation, and growth). Thus, using the balanced scorecard's framework allows the firm to understand how it looks to shareholders (financial perspective), how customers view it (customer perspective), the processes it must emphasize to successfully use its competitive advantage (internal perspective), and what it can do to improve its performance in order to grow (learning and growth perspective).[119] Generally speaking, strategic controls tend to be emphasized when the firm assesses its performance relative to the learning and growth perspective, while financial controls are emphasized when assessing performance in terms of the financial perspective. Study of the customer and internal business processes perspectives often is completed through an equal emphasis on strategic controls and financial controls.

Strategic leaders play an important role in determining a proper balance between strategic controls and financial controls for their firm. This is true in single business firms as well as in diversified firms. A proper balance between controls is important, in that, "Wealth creation for organizations where strategic leadership is exercised is possible because these leaders make appropriate investments for future viability [through strategic control], while maintaining an appropriate level of financial stability in the present [through financial control]." In fact, most corporate restructuring is designed to refocus the firm on its core businesses, thereby allowing top executives to reestablish strategic control of their separate business units.[120] Thus, as emphasized in Chapter 12, both strategic controls and financial controls support effective use of the firm's corporate-level strategy. Table 13.1 lists several characteristics of a strategically controlled organization and a financially controlled organization.

Successful use of strategic control by top executives frequently is integrated with appropriate autonomy for the various subunits so that they can gain a competitive advantage in their respective markets. Strategic control can be used to promote the sharing of both tangible and intangible resources among interdependent businesses within a firm's portfolio. In addition, the autonomy provided allows the flexibility necessary to take advantage of specific marketplace opportunities. As a result, strategic leadership promotes the simultaneous use of strategic control and autonomy.[121]

Balancing strategic and financial controls in diversified firms can be difficult. Failure to maintain an effective balance between strategic controls and financial controls in these firms often contributes to a decision to restructure the company. For example, following

Table 13.1	Characteristics of Strategic and Financial Control Systems

Strategic Controls
- High level of interaction among divisions
- High level of interaction between corporate HQ and divisions
- Ability to share resources and capabilities among divisions
- Ability to transfer core competencies among divisions
- Information sharing among divisions
- Corporate managers with an in-depth knowledge of the work being done in divisions
- A long-term perspective and a willingness to accept risky ventures
- Relatively more is spent on:
  - Research and development
  - Managerial/employee training and development
  - Capital and equipment
  - Market research
- A good system to monitor product market/operational/financial data
- Open communication between corporate and divisional managers
- Employees evaluated on the basis of an open, subjective appraisal of what was done to achieve financial results

Financial Controls
- A least cost behaviour approach
- Capital funds are channelled to divisions that yield higher financial returns—and financial returns are the only criteria used
- A short-term perspective and risk avoidance
- Corporate managers have a superficial knowledge of divisional operations
- Competition among divisions
- Managers and employees evaluated on the basis of short-term financial criteria
- Relatively less is spent on:
  - Research and development
  - Managerial/employee training and development
  - Capital and equipment
  - Market research
- Focus is on:
  - Short-term ROI (return on investment)
  - Cash flow
  - Revenue growth
  - Market share

Chapter 13 / Strategic Leadership

the 1997 Southeast Asian currency crisis, Samsung Electronics, a large Korean firm, was heading into a significant crisis in its Chinese operations. It was a large diversified firm, which had businesses throughout the world. Its Chinese operations were selling everything from washing machines to VCRs. Each product division had established Chinese factories and a nationwide sales organization by the mid-1990s. However, in China, these divisions encountered significant losses, losing $37 million in 1998.

When Yun Jong Yong took over as Samsung's CEO in 1997, he shut down all 23 sales offices and declared that each of the 7 mainland factories would have to become profitable on their own to survive. Thus, he instituted strong financial controls that were to be followed to verify that each division was operating profitably. Additionally, based on market survey results, Samsung executives decided that the firm would focus on 10 major cities in China. Furthermore, the firm carefully selected products and supported them with intense marketing. Thus, the firm improved strategic controls using a top-down marketing strategy. As a result, in 2001, Samsung sold products worth $1.81 billion in China, a fivefold increase since 1998, and profits increased more than 70 percent to $228 million. A more effective balance between strategic and financial controls has helped Samsung to improve its performance and to make progress towards its goal of establishing marquee brands in China, comparable to Sony and Motorola.[122]

Summary

- Effective strategic leadership is a prerequisite to successfully using the strategic management process. Strategic leadership is defined as the ability to influence those with whom you work in your organization to voluntarily make decisions on a day-to-day basis that enhance the long-term viability of the organization, while at the same time maintaining the short-term financial stability of the organization.

- Top-level managers are an important resource for firms to develop and exploit temporary and sustained competitive advantages. In addition, when they and their work are valuable, rare, imperfectly imitable, and organized to be exploited, strategic leaders can themselves be a source of competitive advantage.

- The top management team is composed of key managers who play a critical role in the selection and implementation of the firm's strategies. Generally, they are officers of the corporation or members of the board of directors.

- There is a relationship among the top management team's characteristics, a firm's strategies, and its performance. For example, a top management team that has significant marketing and R&D knowledge positively contributes to the firm's use of growth strategies. Overall, most top management teams are more effective when they have diverse skills.

- When the board of directors is involved in shaping a firm's strategic direction, that firm generally improves its performance. However, the board may be less involved in decisions about strategy formulation and implementation when CEOs have more power. CEOs increase their power when they appoint people to the board and when they simultaneously serve as the CEO and board chair.

- Effective strategic leadership has six major components: determining the firm's strategic direction, exploiting and maintaining core competencies, developing human capital, sustaining an effective organizational culture, emphasizing ethical practices, and establishing balanced organizational controls.

- A firm must develop a long-term vision of its strategic intent. A long-term vision is the driver of strategic leaders' behaviour in terms of the remaining five components of effective strategic leadership.

- Strategic leaders must ensure that their firm exploits its core competencies, which are used to produce and deliver products that create value for customers, through the implementation of strategies. In related-diversified and large firms in particular, core competencies are exploited by sharing them across units and products.

- A critical element of strategic leadership and the effective implementation of strategy is the ability to develop a firm's human capital. Effective strategic leaders and firms view human capital as a resource to be maximized, rather than as a cost to be minimized. Resulting from this perspective is the development and use of programs intended to train current and future strategic leaders to build the skills needed to nurture the rest of the firm's human capital.

- Shaping the firm's culture is a central task of effective strategic leadership. An appropriate organizational culture encourages the development of an entrepreneurial orientation among employees and an ability to change the culture as necessary.

- In ethical organizations, employees are encouraged to exercise ethical judgment and to behave ethically at all times. Improved ethical practices foster social capital. Setting specific goals to describe the firm's ethical standards, using a code of conduct, rewarding ethical behaviours, and creating a work environment in which all people are treated with dig-

nity are examples of actions that facilitate and support ethical behaviour within the firm.

- Developing and using balanced organizational controls is the final component of effective strategic leadership. An effective balance between strategic and financial controls allows for the flexible use of core competencies, but within the parameters indicated by the firm's financial position. The balanced scorecard is a tool used by the firm and its strategic leaders to develop an appropriate balance between its strategic and financial controls.

Review Questions

1. What is strategic leadership? In what ways are top executives considered important resources for an organization?

2. What is a top-management team, and how does it affect a firm's performance and its abilities to innovate and make appropriate strategic changes?

3. How does strategic leadership affect the determination of the firm's strategic direction?

4. Why is it important for strategic leaders to make certain that their firms exploit their core competencies in the pursuit of strategic competitiveness and above-average returns?

5. What is the importance of human capital and its development for strategic competitiveness?

6. What is organizational culture? What actions must strategic leaders take to develop and sustain an effective organizational culture?

7. As a strategic leader, what actions could you take to establish and emphasize ethical practices in your firm?

8. What are organizational controls? Why are strategic controls and financial controls important parts of the strategic management process?

Experiential Exercise

Strategic, Visionary, and Managerial Leaders

This chapter contains descriptions of strategic, visionary, and managerial leaders. Using these descriptions and characteristics, assess three well-known CEOs to determine whether they are strategic, visionary, or managerial leaders. Choose one leader for each type of leadership and use published material (e.g., the Internet, books, annual reports, interviews, etc.) to help you in your assessment.

Part 1 (individual). Use the information provided within this chapter and your own perceptions to complete the following chart. Be prepared to discuss in class.

Part 2 (in small groups). Find other students who selected the same CEOs as you did and discuss with them the leadership styles of the CEOs you selected.

CEOs	Strategic	Visionary	Managerial

Notes

1. D. Ireland, M. A. Hitt, S. M. Camp, & D. L. Sexton, 2001, Integrating entrepreneurship and strategic management actions to create firm wealth, *Academy of Management Executive*, 15(1): 49–63; K. R. Thompson, W. A. Hochwarter, & N. J. Mathys, 1997, Stretch targets: What makes them effective? *Academy of Management Executive*, 11(3): 48–59.

2. A. A. Cannella Jr., A. Pettigrew, & D. Hambrick, 2001, Upper echelons: Donald Hambrick on executives and strategy, *Academy of Management Executive*, 15(3): 36–52; R. D. Ireland & M. A. Hitt, 1999, Achieving and maintaining strategic competitiveness in the 21st century: The role of strategic leadership, *Academy of Management Executive*, 12(1): 43–57; D. Lei, M. A. Hitt, & R. Bettis, 1996, Dynamic core competencies through meta-learning and strategic context, *Journal of Management*, 22: 547–67.

3. A. Bianco & P. L. Moore, 2001, Downfall: The inside story of the management fiasco at Xerox, *Business Week*, March 5, 82–92.

4. R. Evered, 1980, So what is strategy? working paper, Monterey, CA: Naval Postgraduate School; J. B. Quinn, 1980, *Strategies for Change: Logical Incrementalism*, Homewood, IL: Richard D. Irwin; H. Mintzberg & J. B. Quinn, 1996, *The Strategy Process: Concepts, Contexts, Cases*, 3rd ed., Upper Saddle River, NJ: Prentice Hall.

5. W. G. Rowe, 2001, Creating wealth in organizations: The role of strategic leadership, *Academy of Management Executive*, 15(2), 81–94.

6. H. Mintzberg, 1987, Five Ps for Strategy, *California Management Review*, fall, in H. Mintzberg & J. B. Quinn, 1996, *The Strategy Process: Concepts, Contexts, Cases*, 3rd ed., Upper Saddle River, NJ: Prentice Hall, 10–17; H. Mintzberg, 1987, Crafting Strategy, *Harvard Business Review*, July–August, in H. Mintzberg & J. B. Quinn, 1996, *The Strategy Process: Concepts, Contexts, Cases*, 3rd ed., Upper Saddle River, NJ: Prentice Hall, 101–9.

7. J. B. Barney, 1997, *Gaining and Sustaining Competitive Advantage*, New York: Addison-Wesley Publishing Company, 65–133.

8. A. Zaleznik, 1977, Managers and leaders: Are they different? *Harvard Business Review*, May–June, 67–78.

9. G. Hamel & C. K. Prahalad, 1993, Strategy as stretch and leverage, *Harvard Business Review*, 71(2): 75–84.

10. S. Sherman, 1995, How tomorrow's best leader's are learning their stuff, *Fortune*, November, 27, 99; R. Calori, G. Johnson, & P. Sarnin, 1994, CEOs' cognitive maps and the scope of the organization, *Strategic Management Journal*, 15: 437–57.

11. Zaleznik, Managers and leaders: Are they different? 70–71.

12. Ibid., 71–72.

13. Ibid., 72–74.

14. Ibid., 74–75.

15. L. T. Hosmer, 1982, The importance of strategic leadership, *Journal of Business Strategy*, 3(2), fall, 47–57.

16. D. Schendel, 1989, Introduction to the special issue on "strategic leadership," *Strategic Management Journal*, special issue, 10, 1–3.

17. D. Hambrick, 1989, Guest's editor's introduction: Putting top managers back in the strategy picture, *Strategic Management Journal*, special issue, 10, 5–15.

18. Ibid., 5–15.

19. Hosmer, 1982, The importance of strategic leadership; R. Evans, 1997, Hollow the leader, *Report on Business*, November, 56–63; I. Sooklal, 1989, The leader as a broker of dreams, *Human Relations*, 44(8): 833–56; A. Zaleznik, 1990, The leadership gap, *Academy of Management Executive*, 4(1): 7–22.

20. C. W. L. Hill & R. E. Hoskisson, 1987, Strategy and structure in the multiproduct firm, *Academy of Management Review*, 12(2): 1987, 331–41; R. E. Hoskisson & M. A. Hitt, 1994, *Downscoping: How to Tame the Diversified Firm*, New York: Oxford University Press; A. Zaleznik, The leadership gap, 7–22.

21. G. Hedlund, 1994, A model of knowledge management and the N-Form corporation, *Strategic Management Journal*, 15(special issue), summer, 73–90; B. Kogut & U. Zander, 1992, Knowledge of the firm, combinative abilities, and the replication of technology, *Organization Science*, 3, 383–97

22. R. Trigg, 1996, *Ideas of Human Nature: An Historical Introduction*, Cambridge, MA: Blackwell Publishers; J. Child, 1972, Organizational structure, environment and performance: The role of strategic choice, *Sociology*, 6: 1–22.

23. Zaleznik, Managers and leaders: Are they different? 70–71.

24. Ibid., 71–72.

25. Ibid., 72–74.

26. Zaleznik, Managers and leaders: Are they different? 74–75; A. Zaleznik, 1990, The leadership gap, *Academy of Management Executive*, 4(1): 7–22.

27. Hosmer, The importance of strategic leadership, 47–57.

28. Schendel, Introduction to the special issue on "strategic leadership," 1–3.

29. Hambrick, Guest editor's introduction: Putting top managers back into the strategy picture, 5–15; H. Mintzberg, 1973, *The Nature of Managerial Work*, chapters 15–17, New York: Harper and Row.

30. Hambrick, Guest editor's introduction: Putting top managers back into the strategy picture, 5–15.

31. Evans, Hollow the leader, 56–63; Hosmer, The importance of strategic leadership, 47–57; Sooklal, The leader as a broker of dreams, 833–56; Zaleznik, The leadership gap, 7–22.

32. Hoskisson & Hitt, *Downscoping: How to Tame the Diversified Firm*.

33. M. Polanyi, 1966, *The Tacit Dimension*, Garden City, NY: Anchor; R. Reed & R. J. DeFillippi, 1990, Causal ambiguity, barriers to imitation, and sustainable competitive advantage, *Academy of Management Review*, 15: 88–102; R. Nelson & S. Winter, 1982, *An Evolutionary Theory of Economic Change*, Cambridge, MA: Belknap Press; H. Itami, 1987, *Mobilizing Invisible Assets*, Cambridge, MA: Harvard University Press; J. Kotter & J. Heskett, 1992, *Corporate Culture and Performance*, New York: The Free Press; W. G. Ouchi & M. Maguire, 1975, Organizational control: Two functions, *Administrative Sciences Quarterly*, 20: 559–69; E. H. Schein, 1993, On dialogue, culture, and organizational learning, *Organizational Dynamics*, 22(2): 40–51.

34. Trigg, *Ideas of Human Nature: An Historical Introduction*; Child, Organizational structure, environment and performance, 1–22; H. Mintzberg, B. Ahlstrand, & J. Lampel, 1998, *Strategy Safari*, chapter 5, New York: The Free Press.

35. J. P. Kotter, 1990, What leaders really do, *Harvard Business Review*, May–June, reprinted in *Harvard Business Review on Leadership*, Boston: Harvard Business School Press, 37–60.

36. Zaleznik, Managers and leaders: Are they different? 74–75; Zaleznik, The leadership gap, 7–22.

37. Kotter, What leaders really do.

38. Ibid.

39. Rowe, Creating wealth in organizations: The role of strategic leadership, 81–94.

40. Ibid., 81–94

41. Ireland & Hitt, Achieving and maintaining strategic competitiveness in the 21st century, 43–57.

42. J. Conger, 1991, Inspiring others: The language of leadership, *Academy of Management Executive*, 5(1): 31–45; M. Nathan, 1996, What is organizational vision? Ask chief executives, *Academy of Management Executive*, 10(1): 82–83.

43. Hambrick, Guest editor's introduction: Putting top managers back in the strategy picture, 5–15; Schendel, Introduction to the special issue on "strategic leadership," 1–3.

44. Hoskisson & Hitt, *Downscoping: How to Tame the Diversified Firm*.

45. Ibid.

46. I. Nonaka, 1994, A dynamic theory of organizational knowledge creation, *Organization Science*, 5(1): 14–37; I. Nonaka & H. Takeuchi, 1995, *The Knowledge Creating Company*, New York: Oxford University Press.

47. Trigg, *Ideas of Human Nature: An Historical Introduction*; Child, Organizational structure, environment and performance: The role of strategic choice, 1–22.

48. I. Nonaka & H. Takeuchi, 1995, *The Knowledge Creating Company*; Kogut & Zander, Knowledge of the firm, combinative abilities, and the replication of technology, 383–97; S. Sherman & W. G. Rowe, 1996, Leadership and strategic value: A resource-based typology, Proceedings of the Texas Conference on Organizations, March 1.

49. H. Mintzberg, 1975, The manager's job: Folklore and fact, *Harvard Business Review*, July–August, reprinted in 1998, *Harvard Business Review on Leadership*, Boston: Harvard Business School Press, 1–36.

50. H. Gardner, 1995, *Leading Minds: An Anatomy of Leadership*, New York: Basic Books; S. Sherman, 1995, How tomorrow's best leaders are learning their stuff, *Fortune*, November 27, 90–102.

51. J. B. Quinn, P. Anderson, & S. Finkelstein, 1996, Managing professional intellect: Making the most of the best, *Harvard Business Review*, 74(2): 71–80.

52. M. Loeb, 1994, Where leaders come from, *Fortune*, September 19, 241–42.

53. M. F. R. Kets de Vries, 1995, *Life and Death in the Executive Fast Lane*, San Francisco: Jossey-Bass.

54. Loeb, Where leaders come from, 241; N. Nohria & J. D. Berkley, 1994, Whatever happened to the take-charge manager? *Harvard Business Review*, 72(1): 128–37.

55. M. Hammer & S. A. Stanton, 1997, The power of reflection, *Fortune*, November 24, 291–96.

56. S. Finkelstein & D. C. Hambrick, 1996, *Strategic Leadership: Top Executives and Their Effects on Organizations*, St. Paul, MN: West Publishing Company, 2.

57. J. A. Byrne & J. Reingold, 1997, Wanted: A few good CEOs, *Business Week*, August 11, 64–70; Kotter, What leaders really do?

58. Sherman, How tomorrow's best, 102.

59. Rowe, Creating wealth in organizations: The role of strategic leadership, 81–94.

60. Ibid., 81–94.

61. Ibid., 81–94.

62. J. D. House, 1999, *Against the Tide: Battling for Economic Renewal in Newfoundland and Labrador*, Toronto: University of Toronto Press.

63. R. Castanias & C. Helfat, 2001, The managerial rents model: Theory and empirical analysis, *Journal of Management*, 27: 661–78; H. P. Gunz & R. M. Jalland, 1996, Managerial careers and business strategy, *Academy of Management Review*, 21: 718–56; M. Beer & R. Eisenstat, 2000, The silent killers of strategy implementation and learning, *Sloan Management Review*, 41(4): 29–40; C. M. Christensen, 1997, Making strategy: Learning by doing, *Harvard Business Review*, 75(6): 141–56; M. A. Hitt, B. W. Keats, H. E. Harback, & R. D. Nixon, 1994, Rightsizing: Building and maintaining strategic leadership and long-term competitiveness, *Organizational Dynamics*, 23: 18–32.

64. Ipsos-Reid, 2004, For second year running, Paul Tellier named most respected CEO by peers, *Ipsos-Reid website*, http://www.ipsos-na.com/news/pressrelease.cfm?id=2021 (press release), January 20, accessed May 10, 2004.

65. M. Wright, R. E. Hoskisson, L. W. Busenitz, & J. Dial, 2000, Entrepreneurial growth through privatization: The upside of management buyouts, *Academy of Management Review*, 25: 591–601; M. J. Waller, G. P. Huber, & W. H. Glick, 1995, Functional background as a determinant of executives' selective perception, *Academy of Management Journal*, 38: 943–74; N. Rajagopalan, A. M. Rasheed, & D. K. Datta, 1993, Strategic decision processes: Critical review and future directions, *Journal of Management*, 19: 349–84.

66. Rowe, Creating wealth in organizations: The role of strategic leadership, 81–94; Finkelstein & Hambrick, *Strategic Leadership*, 26–34; D. C. Hambrick & E. Abrahamson, 1995, Assessing managerial discretion across industries: A multimethod approach, *Academy of Management Journal*, 38: 1427–41; D. C. Hambrick & S. Finkelstein, 1987, Managerial discretion: A bridge between polar views of organizational outcomes, in B. Staw & L. L. Cummings (eds.), *Research in Organizational Behavior*, Greenwich, CT: JAI Press, 369–406.

67. R. C. Mayer, J. H. Davis, & F. D. Schoorman, 1995, An integrative model of organizational trust, *Academy of Management Review*, 20: 709–34.

68. N. Rajagopalan & D. K. Datta, 1996, CEO characteristics: Does industry matter? *Academy of Management Journal*, 39: 197–215.

69. J. Call, 2002, The fire within, *BYU Magazine*, winter, 34–39.

70. J. E. Dutton, S. J. Ashford, R. M. O'Neill, & K. A. Lawrence, 2001, Moves that matter: Issue selling and organizational change. *Academy of Management Journal*, 44: 716–36; W. Ferrier, 2001, Navigating the competitive landscape: The drivers and consequences of competitive aggressiveness, *Academy of Management Journal*, 44: 858–77; P. Chattopadhyay, W. H. Glick, C. C. Miller, & G. P. Huber, 1999, Determinants of executive beliefs: Comparing functional conditioning and social influence, *Strategic Management Journal*, 20: 763–89.

71. I. Goll, R. Sambharya, & L. Tucci, 2001, Top management team composition, corporate ideology, and firm performance, *Management International Review*, 41(2): 109–29; L. Markoczy, 2001, Consensus formation during strategic change, *Strategic Management Journal*, 22: 1013–31; A. L. Iaquito & J. W. Fredrickson, 1997, Top management team agreement about the strategic decision process: A test of some of its determinants and consequences, *Strategic Management Journal*, 18: 63–75.

72. C. Pegels, Y. Song, & B. Yang, 2000, Management heterogeneity, competitive interaction groups, and firm performance, *Strategic Management Journal*, 21: 911–23; N. Athanassiou & D. Nigh, 1999, The impact of U.S. company internationalization on top management team advice networks: A tacit knowledge perspective, *Strategic Management Journal*, 20: 83–92.

73. Markoczy, Consensus formation during strategic change; D. Knight, C. L. Pearce, K. G. Smith, J. D. Olian, H. P. Sims, K. A. Smith, & P. Flood, 1999, Top management team diversity, group process, and strategic consensus, *Strategic Management Journal*, 20: 446–65; J. J. Distefano & M. L. Maznevski, 2000, Creating value with diverse teams in global management, *Organizational Dynamics*, 29(1): 45–63; T. Simons, L. H. Pelled, & K. A. Smith, 1999, Making use of difference, diversity, debate, and decision comprehensiveness in top management teams, *Academy of Management Journal*, 42: 662–73.

74. Finkelstein & Hambrick, *Strategic Leadership*, 148; S. Barsade, A. Ward, J. Turner, & J. Sonnenfeld, 2000, To your heart's content: A model of affective diversity in top management teams, *Administrative Science Quarterly*, 45: 802–36; C. C. Miller, L. M. Burke, & W. H. Glick, 1998, Cognitive diversity among upper-echelon executives: Implications for strategic decision processes, *Strategic Management Journal*, 19: 39–58.

75. U. Daellenbach, A. McCarthy, & T. Schoenecker, 1999, Commitment to innovation: The impact of top management team characteristics, *R&D Management*, 29(3): 199–208; D. K. Datta & J. P. Guthrie, 1994, Executive succession: Organizational antecedents of CEO characteristics, *Strategic Management Journal*, 15: 569–77.

76. S. Wally & M. Becerra, 2001, Top management team characteristics and strategic changes in international diversification: The case of U.S. multinationals in the European community, *Group & Organization Management*, 26: 165–88; W. Boeker, 1997, Strategic change: The influence of managerial characteristics and organizational growth, *Academy of Management Journal*, 40: 152–70; A. Tomine, 2000, Fast Pack 2000, *Fast Company Online*, http://www.fastcompany.com/online/32/fast-pack.html, March 1; L. Tihanyi, C. Daily, D. Dalton, & A. Ellstrand, 2000, Composition of the top management team and firm international diversification, *Journal of Management*, 26: 1157–78; M. E. Wiersema & K. Bantel, 1992, Top management team demography and corporate strategic change, *Academy of Management Journal*, 35: 91–121; K. Bantel & S. Jackson, 1989, Top management and innovations in banking: Does the composition of the top team make a difference? *Strategic Management Journal*, 10: 107–24.

77. 2002, The top 25 managers: Daniel Vasella, *Business Week*, January 14, 58; W. Koberstein, 2001, Executive profile: Novartis inside out, *Pharmaceutical Executive*, November, 36–50.

78. B. Taylor, 2001, From corporate governance to corporate entrepreneurship, *Journal of Change Management*, 2(2): 128–47; W. Q. Judge Jr. & C. P. Zeithaml, 1992, Institutional and strategic choice perspectives on board involvement in the strategic decision process, *Academy of Management Journal*, 35: 766–94; J. A. Pearce II & S. A. Zahra, 1991, The relative power of CEOs and boards of directors: Associations with corporate performance, *Strategic Management Journal*, 12: 135–54.

79. B. R. Golden & E. J. Zajac, 2001, When will boards influence strategy? Inclination times power equals strategic change, *Strategic Management Journal*, 22: 1087–1111; M. Carpenter & J. Westphal, 2001, Strategic context of external network ties: Examining the impact of director appointments on board involvement in strategic decision making, *Academy of Management Journal*, 44: 639–60; J. D. Westphal & E. J. Zajac, 1995, Who shall govern? CEO/board power, demographic similarity, and new director selection, *Administrative Science Quarterly*, 40: 60.

80. M. Boyle, 2001, The dirty half-dozen: America's worst boards, *Fortune*, May 14, 249–52.

81. J. D. Westphal, 1999, Collaboration in the boardroom: Behavioral and performance consequences of CEO-board social ties, *Academy of Management Journal*, 42: 7–24.

82. Ibid., 16; J. Roberts & P. Stiles, 1999, The relationship between chairmen and chief executives: Competitive or complementary roles? *Long Range Planning*, 32(1): 36–48; J. Coles, N. Sen, & V. McWilliams, 2001, An examination of the relationship of governance mechanisms to performance, *Journal of Management*, 27: 23–50; J. Coles & W. Hesterly, 2000, Independence of the chairman and board composition: Firm choices and shareholder value, *Journal of Management*, 26: 195–214; B. K. Boyd, 1995, CEO duality and firm performance: A contingency model, *Strategic Management Journal*, 16: 301.

83. D. Bergh, 2001, Executive retention and acquisition outcomes: A test of opposing views on the influence of organizational tenure, *Journal of Management*, 27: 603–22; J. Muller, J. Green, & C. Tierney, 2001, Chrysler's Rescue Team, *Business Week*, January 15, 48–50.

84. C. M. Daily & D. R. Dalton, 1995, CEO and director turnover in failing firms: An illusion of change? *Strategic Management Journal*, 16: 393–400; R. Albanese, M. T. Dacin, & I. C. Harris, 1997, Agents as stewards, *Academy of Management Review*, 22: 609–11; J. H. Davis, F. D. Schoorman, & L. Donaldson, 1997, Toward a stewardship theory of management, *Academy of Management Review*, 22: 20–47.

85. M. A. Carpenter, 2002, The implications of strategy and social context for the relationship between top management team heterogeneity and firm performance, *Strategic Management Journal*, 23: 275–84; J. D. Westphal & E. J. Zajac, 1997,

Defections from the inner circle: Social exchange, reciprocity and diffusion of board independence in U.S. corporations, *Administrative Science Quarterly*, 161–83; Rajagopalan & Datta, CEO characteristics, 201; R. A. Johnson, R. E. Hoskisson, & M. A. Hitt, 1993, Board involvement in restructuring: The effect of board versus managerial controls and characteristics, *Strategic Management Journal*, 14(summer special issue): 33–50.

86. Boyd, CEO duality and firm performance: A contingency model; M. Carpenter & J. Fredrickson, 2001, Top management teams, global strategic posture, and the moderating role of uncertainty, *Academy of Management Journal*, 44: 533–45; M. Schneider, 2002, A stakeholder model of organizational leadership, *Organization Science*, 13: 209–20.

87. B. Dyck, M. Mauws, F. Starke, & G. Mischke, 2002, Passing the baton: The importance of sequence, timing, technique and communication in executive succession, *Journal of Business Venturing*, 17: 143–62.

88. J. J. Rotemberg & G. Saloner, 2000, Visionaries, managers, and strategic direction, *RAND Journal of Economics*, 31: 693–716.

89. I. M. Levin, 2000, Vision revisited, *Journal of Applied Behavioral Science*, 36: 91–107; J. C. Collins & J. I. Porras, 1996, Building your company's vision, *Harvard Business Review*, 74(5): 65–77.

90. G. Gori, 2001, An American directs Mexico City's cinema revival, *New York Times*, http://www.nytimes.com, July 15.

91. P. W. Beamish, 1999, Sony's Yoshihide Nakamura on structure and decision making, *Academy of Management Executive*, 13(4): 12–16; R. M. Hodgetts, 1999, Dow Chemical's CEO William Stavropoulos on structure and decision making, *Academy of Management Executive*, 13(4): 29–35.

92. R. A. Burgelman, 2001, *Strategy Is Destiny: How Strategy-Making Shapes a Company's Future*, New York: The Free Press.

93. S. Jaffe, 2001, Do Pepsi and Gatorade mix? *Business Week Online*, http://www.businessweek.com, August 14.

94. C. A. Lengnick-Hall & J. A. Wolff, 1999, Similarities and contradictions in the core logic of three strategy research streams, *Strategic Management Journal*, 20: 1109–32; M. A. Hitt, L. Bierman, K. Shimizu, & R. Kochhar, 2001, Direct and moderating effects of human capital on strategy and performance in professional service firms: A resource-based perspective, *Academy of Management Journal*, 44: 13–28; S. A. Snell & M. A. Youndt, 1995, Human resource management and firm performance: Testing a contingency model of executive controls, *Journal of Management*, 21: 711–37; P. Caligiuri & V. Di Santo, 2001, Global competence: What is it, and can it be developed through global assignments? *Human Resource Planning*, 24(3): 27–35; A. McWilliams, D. D. Van Fleet, & P. M. Wright, 2001, Strategic management of human resources for global competitive advantage, *Journal of Business Strategies*, 18(1): 1–24; J. Pfeffer, 1994, *Competitive Advantage through People*, Cambridge, MA: Harvard Business School Press, 4.

95. L. Gratton, 2001, *Living Strategy: Putting People at the Heart of Corporate Purpose*, London: Financial Times/Prentice Hall, London.

96. Caligiuri & Di Santo, Global competence; M. W. McCall & G. P. Hollenbeck, 2001, *Developing Global Executives: The Lessons of International Experience*, Boston, MA: Harvard Business School Press; C. F. Fey & I. Bjorkman, 2001, The effect of human resource management practices on MNC subsidiary performance in Russia, *Journal of International Business Studies*, 32: 59–75; M. G. Harvey & M. M. Novicevic, 2000, The influences of inpatriation practices on the strategic orientation of a global organization, *International Journal of Management*, 17: 362–71; M. G. Harvey & M. R. Buckley, 1997, Managing inpatriates: Building a global core competency, *Journal of World Business*, 32(1): 35–52.

97. C. A. Bartlett & S. Ghoshal, 2002, Building competitive advantage through people, *MIT Sloan Management Review*, 43(2): 34–41; D. M. DeCarolis & D. L. Deeds, 1999, The impact of stocks and flows of organizational knowledge on firm performance: An empirical investigation of the biotechnology industry, *Strategic Management Journal*, 20: 953–68; J. Sandberg, 2000, Understanding human competence at work: An interpretative approach, *Academy of Management Journal*, 43: 9–25; J. Lee & D. Miller, 1999, People matter: Commitment to employees, strategy and performance in Korean firms, *Strategic Management Journal*, 20: 579–93.

98. T. M. Welbourne & L. A. Cyr, 1999, The human resource executive effect in initial public offering firms, *Academy of Management Journal*, 42: 616–29; J. Pfeffer & J. F. Veiga, 1999, Putting people first for organizational success, *Academy of Management Executive*, 13(2): 37–48; Bartlett & Ghoshal, Building competitive advantage through people.

99. J. H. Christy, 2001, Eagle aloft, *Forbes*, August 6, 60.

100. H. Collingwood & D. L. Coutu, 2002, Jack on Jack, *Harvard Business Review*, 80(2): 88–94.

101. J. Di Frances, 2002, 10 reasons why you shouldn't downsize, *Journal of Property Management*, 67(1): 72–73; M. A. Hitt, R. E. Hoskisson, J. S. Harrison, & B. Summers, 1994, Human capital and strategic competitiveness in the 1990s, *Journal of Management Development*, 13(1): 35–46; A. Pinsonneault & K. Kraemer, 2002, The role of information technology in organizational downsizing: A tale of two American cities, *Organization Science*, 13: 191–208.

102. M. David, 2001, Leadership during an economic slowdown, *Journal for Quality and Participation*, 24(3): 40–43; C. L. Martin, C. K. Parsons, & N. Bennett, 1995, The influence of employee involvement program membership during downsizing: Attitudes toward the employer and the union, *Journal of Management*, 21: 879–90.

103. A. K. Gupta & V. Govindarajan, 2000, Knowledge management's social dimension: Lessons from Nucor Steel, *Sloan Management Review*, 42(1): 71–80; C. M. Fiol, 1991, Managing culture as a competitive resource: An identity-based view of sustainable competitive advantage, *Journal of Management*, 17: 191–211; J. B. Barney, 1986, Organizational culture: Can it be a source of sustained competitive advantage? *Academy of Management Review*, 11: 656–65; V. Govindarajan & A. K. Gupta, 2001, Building an effective global business team, *Sloan Management Review*, 42(4): 63–71; S. Ghoshal & C. A. Bartlett, 1994, Linking organizational context and managerial action: The dimensions of quality of management, *Strategic Management Journal*, 15: 91–112.

104. D. F. Kuratko, R. D. Ireland, & J. S. Hornsby, 2001, Improving firm performance through entrepreneurial actions: Acordia's corporate entrepreneurship strategy, *Academy of Management Executive*, 15(4): 60–71; T. E. Brown, P. Davidsson, & J. Wiklund, 2001, An operationalization of Stevenson's conceptualization of entrepreneurship as opportunity-based firm behavior, *Strategic Management Journal*, 22: 953–68.

105. G. T. Lumpkin & G. G. Dess, 1996, Clarifying the entrepreneurial orientation construct and linking it to performance, *Academy of Management Review*, 21: 135–72.

106. Ibid., 137, 142.

107. R. R. Sims, 2000, Changing an organization's culture under new leadership, *Journal of Business Ethics*, 25: 65–78; R. A. Burgelman & Y. L. Doz, 2001, The power of strategic integration, *Sloan Management Review*, 42(3): 28–38; P. H. Fuchs, K. E. Mifflin, D. Miller, & J. O. Whitney, 2000, Strategic integration: Competing in the age of capabilities, *California Management Review*, 42(3): 118–47.

108. J. S. Hornsby, D. F. Kuratko, & S. A. Zahra, 2002, Middle managers' perception of the internal environment for corporate entrepreneurship: Assessing a measurement scale, *Journal of Business Venturing*, 17: 253–73; J. E. Dutton, S. J. Ashford, R. M. O'Neill, E. Hayes, & E. E. Wierba, 1997, Reading the wind: How middle managers assess the context for selling issues to top managers, *Strategic Management Journal*, 18: 407–25; B. Axelrod, H. Handfield-Jones, & E. Michaels, 2002, A new game plan for C players, *Harvard Business Review*, 80(1): 80–88.

109. P. S. Adler & S.-W. Kwon, 2002, Social capital: Prospects for a new concept, *Academy of Management Review*, 27: 17–40; T. A. Stewart, 2001, Right now the only capital that matters is social capital, *Business 2.0*, December, 128–30; D. J. Brass, K. D. Butterfield, & B. C. Skaggs, 1998, Relationships and unethical behavior: A social network perspective, *Academy of Management Review*, 23: 14–31.

110. L. K. Trevino, G. R. Weaver, D. G. Toffler, & B. Ley, 1999, Managing ethics and legal compliance: What works and what hurts, *California Management Review*, 41(2): 131–51; C. W. L. Hill, 1990, Cooperation, opportunism, and the invisible hand: Implications for transaction cost theory, *Academy of Management Review*, 15: 500–13.

111. K. Brown, G. Hitt, S. Liesman, & J. Weil, 2002, Andersen fires partner it says led shredding of Enron documents, *Wall Street Journal*, January 16, A1, A18; W. Wallace, 2000, The value relevance of accounting: The rest of the story, *European Management Journal*, 18(6): 675–82.

112. E. Soule, 2002, Managerial moral strategies: In search of a few good principles, *Academy of Management Review*, 27: 114–24; J. Milton-Smith, 1995, Ethics as excellence: A strategic management perspective, *Journal of Business Ethics*, 14: 683–93; L. M. Leinicke, J. A. Ostrosky, & W. M. Rexroad, 2000, Quality financial reporting: Back to the basics, *CPA Journal*, August, 69–71.

113. J. R. Cohen, L. W. Pant, & D. J. Sharp, 2001, An examination of differences in ethical decision-making between Canadian business students and accounting professionals, *Journal of Business Ethics*, 30: 319–36; G. R. Weaver, L. K. Trevino, & P. L. Cochran, 1999, Corporate ethics programs as control systems: Influences of executive commitment and environmental factors, *Academy of Management Journal*, 42: 41–57.

114. P. E. Murphy, 1995, Corporate ethics statements: Current status and future prospects, *Journal of Business Ethics*, 14: 727–40.

115. J. H. Gittell, 2000, Paradox of coordination and control, *California Management Review*, 42(3): 101–17; L. J. Kirsch, 1996, The management of complex tasks in organizations: Controlling the systems development process, *Organization Science*, 7: 1–21; M. D. Shields, F. J. Deng, & Y. Kato, 2000, The design and effects of control systems: Tests of direct- and indirect-effects models, *Accounting, Organizations and Society*, 25: 185–202; R. Simons, 1994, How new top managers use control systems as levers of strategic renewal, *Strategic Management Journal*, 15: 170–71.

116. K. J. Laverty, 1996, Economic "short-termism": The debate, the unresolved issues, and the implications for management practice and research, *Academy of Management Review*, 21: 825–60.

117. R. S. Kaplan & D. P. Norton, 2001, The strategy-focused organization, *Strategy & Leadership*, 29(3): 41–42; R. S. Kaplan & D. P. Norton, 2000, *The Strategy-Focused Organization: How Balanced Scorecard Companies Thrive in the New Business Environment*, Boston, MA: Harvard Business School Press.

118. B. E. Becker, M. A. Huselid, & D. Ulrich, 2001, *The HR Scorecard: Linking People, Strategy, and Performance*, Boston: Harvard Business School Press, 21; Kaplan & Norton, *The Strategy-Focused Organization*; R. S. Kaplan & D. P. Norton, 2001, Transforming the balanced scorecard from performance measurement to strategic management: Part I, *Accounting Horizons*, 15(1): 87–104.

119. R. S. Kaplan & D. P. Norton, 1992, The balanced scorecard—measures that drive performance, *Harvard Business Review*, 70(1): 71–79.

120. Rowe, Creating wealth in organizations: The role of strategic leadership; R. E. Hoskisson, R. A. Johnson, D. Yiu, & W. P. Wan, 2001, Restructuring strategies of diversified business groups: Differences associated with country institutional environments, in M. A. Hitt, R. E. Freeman, J. S. Harrison (eds.), *Handbook of Strategic Management*, Oxford, UK: Blackwell Publishers, 433–63; R. A. Johnson, 1996, Antecedents and outcomes of corporate refocusing, *Journal of Management*, 22: 437–81; Hoskisson & Hitt, *Downscoping: How to Tame the Diversified Firm*.

121. J. Birkinshaw & N. Hood, 2001, Unleash innovation in foreign subsidiaries, *Harvard Business Review*, 79(3): 131–37; Ireland & Hitt, Achieving and maintaining strategic competitiveness.

122. M. Ihlwan & D. Roberts, 2002, How Samsung plugged into China, *Business Week Online*, http://www.businessweek.com, March 4.

14

Chapter Fourteen

Strategic Entrepreneurship

Knowledge Objectives

Studying this chapter should provide you with the strategic management knowledge needed to:

1. Define and explain strategic entrepreneurship.

2. Describe the importance of entrepreneurial opportunities, innovation, and entrepreneurial capabilities.

3. Discuss the importance of international entrepreneurship and describe why its practice is increasing.

4. Describe the two forms of internal corporate venturing: autonomous and induced strategic behaviours.

5. Discuss how cooperative strategies, such as strategic alliances, are used to develop innovation.

6. Explain how firms use acquisitions to increase their innovations and enrich their innovative capabilities.

7. Describe the importance of venture capital and initial public offerings to entrepreneurial activity.

8. Explain how the practice of strategic entrepreneurship creates value for customers and shareholders of all types of firms, large and small, new and established.

What Makes Entrepreneurs Successful?

There is a wide variety of types of entrepreneurs, but no one formula for success. However, there are many successful entrepreneurs. For example, Lino Saputo co-founded Montreal's Saputo Inc. in 1954, with his parents, $500 in equipment, and a bicycle that he used to deliver his cheese. By the 1970s, Saputo was Canada's leading producer of mozzarella.

In 1997, Saputo shares went public, and the company put the proceeds of its initial public offering (IPO) to good use by making a number of acquisitions. The company moved into fluid milk and frozen novelties, by buying Quebec's Three Rivers Creamery. It bought Stella Cheese to triple the company's size and establish it as one of the leading natural cheese producers in the U.S. Several other purchases of cheese makers on both sides of the border followed. In addition, Saputo purchased Montreal's Culinar Inc. to give the company a presence in snack cakes, fine breads, soup, and cookies.

In the new millennium, Saputo acquired Dairyworld Foods to move into yogurt, cheese, butter, skim milk powder, juices, and related food ingredients. As well, Saputo acquired Molfino Hermanos S.A., the third largest dairy processor in Argentina. Today, the company has annual revenues of more than $3 billion and more than 7500 employees working in 45 plants across North America and Argentina.

The Saputo family had been making cheese for generations and their knowledge of the product certainly helped start the company. Yet, when Lino Saputo Sr. turned the reigns of the company over to his son, Lino Jr., in 2004, its growth into a multibillion-dollar empire can also be attributed to good governance and good management. For example, the elder Saputo's annual salary never reached seven figures. In fact, the company president and chief operating officer were paid more, over the last three years, than the elder Saputo made when he headed the company (however, the president received stock options, while Lino Sr. did not). Since the company is still about 60 percent owned by the Saputo family, there is an excellent alignment between the interests of management and shareholders. David Newman, an analyst at National Bank Financial in Toronto, notes that, "Saputo is very cautious and disciplined in everything.... They make good acquisitions, integrate them well into the operations and never overpay."

Anatoly Karachinsky originally had no thoughts of starting his own business. However, in 1992, he was invited to attend a conference in Arizona, where he met the CEO of EDS, Mort Myerson. After a several-hour conversation with Myerson, Karachinsky returned to Russia and took over a friend's computer consulting firm. In 1994, Karachinsky met Michael Dell and became the exclusive distributor of Dell computers in Russia. Several U.S. investors were impressed with his company, Informatsionniye Biznes Sistemy (IBS), and how he managed it. So impressed were the investors that two of them—Citigroup and AIG Brunswick Millennium Fund—invested $30 million of capital in his firm. IBS has continued to grow and now controls much of the IT market in Russia. In 2001, IBS earned more than $5 million of pre-tax income on total revenues of $200 million. Karachinsky was successful because he had a good idea and

Lino Saputo's success as an entrepreneur led his company to $3 billion in annual sales of cheese products.

(continued)

implemented it without help from the Russian government or the black market. He was able to obtain the critical venture capital for these reasons.

A visionary leader, Jonathan Coon, started his business in 1995. By 2001, his mail-order contact lens business—the name of the business is also its phone number: 1-800 CONTACTS—had become the largest direct-to-consumer contact lens business in the world. The company stocks 9 million lenses, selling more than 100,000 per day. Before he started the business, Coon developed an effective business plan that has produced a strong cash flow. He also has an effective distribution system and built-in repeat business because the product is disposable. Coon's employees are empowered to do whatever is necessary to satisfy customers. He also encourages them to participate in developing company policies and provides stock options to all employees.

Each of these three successful entrepreneurs took some unique actions and had some special traits, but they all had a passion for the businesses they developed. According to Michael Dell, passion must be the driving force for starting a company. Dell also emphasizes the importance of identifying and exploiting opportunities. All of the entrepreneurs described identified opportunities and obviously were passionate about exploiting them.

SOURCES: J. Gray, 2004, A tale of two CEOs, *Canadian Business*, 77(9): 35–36; T. Singer, 2002, What business would you start? *Inc.*, March, 68–76; Chain Store Age, 2000, Retail entrepreneurs of the year: Jonathan Coon, *Chain Store Age*, 76(12): 115; T. Kellner, 2001, Entrepreneurs, *Forbes*, April 30, 116–17.

The opening case provides examples of three successful entrepreneurs. While the descriptions are brief, several factors can be identified as important for each person's success. They all have a passion for their business. Furthermore, they had strong business knowledge and planned well (for example, they each developed a business plan). Each identified opportunities and exploited them. Other factors, such as knowledge and determination (Lino Saputo), strong values and independence (Anatoly Karachinsky), and creativity and empowering employees (Jonathan Coon) also contributed to their success.

Understanding why some entrepreneurs succeed while others fail is important to help future entrepreneurs in their efforts to be successful. Entrepreneurship is the economic engine driving many nations' economies in the global competitive landscape. Entrepreneurship and innovation have become important for young and old firms and for large and small firms in all types of industries. Research conducted by Statistics Canada and the Center for Entrepreneurial Leadership at the Kauffman Foundation has shown that small entrepreneurial firms are creating the vast majority of new jobs in North America.[1] As a result, this chapter focuses on strategic entrepreneurship. **Strategic entrepreneurship** is the use of entrepreneurial actions based on a strategic perspective. More specifically, it involves engaging in simultaneous opportunity seeking and competitive advantage seeking behaviours to design and implement entrepreneurial strategies to create wealth.[2] These actions can be taken by individuals or by corporations. Such activity is particularly important in the evolving 21st-century landscape.

Strategic entrepreneurship is the use of entrepreneurial actions based on a strategic perspective.

The competitive landscape that has evolved in the 21st century presents firms with substantial change, a global marketplace, and significant complexity and uncertainty.[3] Because of this uncertain environment, firms cannot easily predict the future. As a result, they must develop strategic flexibility to have a range of strategic alternatives that they can implement as needed. To do so, they must acquire resources and build the capabilities that allow them to take necessary actions to adapt to a dynamic environment in, or proactive toward, that environment.[4] In this environment, entrepreneurs and entrepreneurial managers design and implement actions that capture more of existing markets from less aggressive and less innovative competitors while simultaneously creating new markets.[5] In effect, they are trying to create tomorrow's businesses.[6]

Creating tomorrow's businesses requires identifying opportunities, as argued by Michael Dell in the opening case, and developing innovation. In other words, firms must be entrepreneurial and innovative. Innovations are critical to companies' efforts to differentiate their goods or services from competitors in ways that create additional or new value for customers.[7] Thus, entrepreneurial competencies are important for firms to achieve and sustain competitive advantages for a period of time.[8]

To describe how firms produce and manage innovation, we examine several topics in this chapter. To set the stage, we first examine entrepreneurship and innovation in a strategic context. Next, we discuss international entrepreneurship, a phenomenon reflecting the increased use of entrepreneurship in countries throughout the world. Internally, firms innovate through either autonomous or induced strategic behaviour. After our descriptions of these internal corporate venturing activities, we discuss actions taken by firms to implement the innovations resulting from those two types of strategic behaviour. In addition to innovating through internal activities, firms can gain access to other companies' innovations or innovative capabilities through strategic alliances and acquisitions. Following our discussion of these topics is a description of entrepreneurship in start-up ventures and smaller firms. This section closes both the chapter and our analysis of actions that firms take to successfully implement strategies.

Strategic Entrepreneurship and Innovation

Joseph Schumpeter viewed entrepreneurship as a process of "creative destruction," through which existing products or methods of production are destroyed and replaced with new ones.[9] Thus, entrepreneurship is "concerned with the discovery and exploitation of profitable opportunities."[10] Entrepreneurial activity is an important mechanism for creating changes, as well as for helping firms adapt to changes created by others. Firms that encourage entrepreneurship are risk takers, who are committed to innovation and act proactively in that they try to create opportunities rather than waiting to respond to opportunities created by others.[11]

Entrepreneurial opportunities represent conditions in which new products or services can satisfy a need in the market. The essence of entrepreneurship is to identify and exploit these opportunities.[12] Importantly, entrepreneurs or entrepreneurial managers must be able to identify opportunities not perceived by others. Identifying these opportunities in a dynamic and uncertain environment requires an entrepreneurial mind-set that entails the passionate pursuit of opportunities.[13] As we noted in Chapter 13, Matthew Heyman and two Harvard classmates found opportunity in the chaos of Mexico City's movie theatre industry to create profit out of what many considered a largely unprofitable market that many of the competitors had given up on. However, Heyman and his colleagues had the vision to start Cinemex in 1994. They obtained venture capital from J. P. Morgan and used it to attract other investors. They built attractive theatres and were able to dominate the market (by 2001, Cinemex reported revenues of almost $200 million).[14] The effort paid off well for investors after Toronto's Onex and partners acquired the chain for $440 million in 2002.[15] As in the previous chapter, we described the long-term vision (one of the actions associated with effective strategic leadership) that supported Heyman and his partners as they started their entrepreneurial venture. As we now see, these strategic leaders were successful in their pursuit of what they recognized to be an entrepreneurial opportunity.

After identifying the opportunities, entrepreneurs take actions to exploit them and establish a competitive advantage. The process of identifying and pursuing opportunities is entrepreneurial, but this activity alone is rarely enough to create maximum wealth or even to survive over time. Actions must be valuable, rare, difficult to imitate, and non-substitutable to create and sustain a competitive advantage (as described in Chapter 4). Without the competitive advantage, success will be only temporary (as explained in Chapter 1). An innovation may be valuable and rare early in its life, if a market perspective is used in its development. However, strategic actions must be taken to introduce the new product to the market and protect its position in the market against competitors (difficult to imitate) to gain a competitive advantage. These actions combined represent strategic entrepreneurship.

Peter Drucker argues that "innovation is the specific function of entrepreneurship, whether in an existing business, a public service institution, or a new venture started by a lone individual." Moreover, Drucker suggests that innovation is "the means by which the entrepreneur either creates new wealth-producing resources or endows existing resources with enhanced potential for creating wealth."[16] Thus, entrepreneurship and the innovation resulting from it are important for large and small firms, as well as for start-up ventures, as they compete in the 21st-century competitive landscape. Therefore, we can conclude that, "Entrepreneurship and innovation are central to the creative process in the economy and to promoting growth, increasing productivity and creating jobs."[17]

Innovation

Innovation is a key outcome firms seek through entrepreneurship and is often the source of competitive success. In Rosabeth Moss Kanter's words, "Winning in business today

---

Entrepreneurial opportunities represent conditions in which new products or services can satisfy a need in the market.

demands innovation. Companies that innovate reap all the advantages of a first mover."[18] For example, research results show that firms competing in global industries that invest more in innovation also achieve the highest returns.[19] In fact, investors often react positively to the introduction of a new product, thereby increasing the price of a firm's stock. Innovation, then, is an essential feature of high-performance firms.[20] Furthermore, "innovation may be required to maintain or achieve competitive parity, much less a competitive advantage in many global markets."[21]

In his classic work, Schumpeter argued that firms engage in three types of innovative activity.[22] **Invention** is the act of creating or developing a new product or process. **Innovation** is the process of creating a commercial product from an invention. Thus, an invention brings something new into being, while an innovation brings something new into use. Accordingly, technical criteria are used to determine the success of an invention, whereas commercial criteria are used to determine the success of an innovation.[23] Finally, **imitation** is the adoption of an innovation by similar firms. Imitation usually leads to product or process standardization, and products based on imitation often are offered at lower prices, but without as many features. As noted in the next Strategic Focus box, "Imitation Is More Than the Sincerest Form of Flattery" on page 432, protecting the innovation, although difficult, can be accomplished in a number of ways.

Innovation is perhaps the most critical of the three types of innovative activity that occur in firms. Many companies are able to create ideas that lead to inventions, but commercializing those inventions through innovation has, at times, proved difficult. Approximately 80 percent of R&D occurs in large firms, but these same firms produce fewer than 50 percent of the patents.[24]

Innovations produced in large established firms are often referred to as corporate entrepreneurship. **Corporate entrepreneurship** is a process whereby an individual or a group in an existing organization creates a new venture or develops an innovation. Overall, corporate entrepreneurship is the sum of a firm's innovation, renewal, and venturing efforts. Evidence suggests that corporate entrepreneurship practices are facilitated through the effective use of both a firm's strategic management process and its human capital.[25] Determining how to harness the ingenuity of a firm's employees and how to appropriately reward them, while retaining some of the rewards of the entrepreneurial efforts for the shareholders' benefit facilitates the emergence of value-creating corporate entrepreneurship.[26]

Entrepreneurs and Entrepreneurial Capabilities

Entrepreneurs are individuals, acting independently or as part of an organization, who create a new venture or develop an innovation and take risks entering it into the marketplace. Entrepreneurs can be independent individuals, or they can surface in an organization at any level. Thus, top-level managers, middle- and first-level managers, staff personnel, and those producing the company's good or service can all be entrepreneurs.

Firms need employees who think entrepreneurially. Top-level managers should try to establish an entrepreneurial culture that inspires individuals and groups to engage in corporate entrepreneurship.[27] Apple Computer's Steve Jobs is committed to this effort, believing one of his key responsibilities is to help Apple become more entrepreneurial. Apple has introduced some innovatively designed products, such as its iMac with its 15-inch liquid crystal display attached to the base computer with a chrome swivel bar.[28] Some believe that it looks more like a desk lamp. Apple is using the new design to capture a larger share of the PC market.

Of course, to create and commercialize products such as the iMac requires not only intellectual capital, but an entrepreneurial mind-set as well. It also requires entrepreneurial competence. Returning to the opening case, entrepreneurial competence involves effective knowledge of the business and technology, a passion for the business, and a risk

---

Invention is the act of creating or developing a new product or process.

Innovation is the process of creating a commercial product from an invention.

Imitation is the adoption of an innovation by similar firms.

Corporate entrepreneurship is a process whereby an individual or a group in an existing organization creates a new venture or develops an innovation.

Entrepreneurs are individuals, acting independently or as part of an organization, who create a new venture or develop an innovation and take risks entering it into the marketplace.

Imitation Is More Than the Sincerest Form of Flattery

Sooner or later, someone will try to copy the innovator's product. How does the innovator protect against this? The most obvious way is through legal intellectual property protection: patents, trademarks, and copyrights. However, patents can be expensive and time-consuming to register and defend. Instead, one can avoid the patent route and doggedly pursue the first-mover advantage. Daniel Muzyka, dean and professor of entrepreneurship at the University of British Columbia's Sauder School of Business, advises, "Go to market early. ... Staking out territory will force others to back off. ..." In order to sustain such a first-mover advantage, it helps to have a branded differentiated product and some way to lock in customers. Thus, even before potential competitors appear, innovators should figure out how to differentiate their product and continue that differentiation as competitors arrive. Muzyka also notes the need to make the brand one that creates customer "expectations of quality and value ... that can't be beat."

For example, in 1992, Toronto's Shery Leeder developed the first nursing bra that stressed comfort over fashion. Her product used stretchy fabrics, wide bands—and no underwire. To add some fun to the design, the fabric choices included polka dot and leopard-skin prints. Leeder's Bravado Designs started producing the bra, and, by 1994, the product was selling well throughout North America and through its distributor in the U.K. The grassroots distribution via childbirth educators and midwives was working well.

However, Leeder had no patent on her product—Bravado did not have the $5000 to $20,000 to secure a patent. Thus, when Bravado's distributor in London, England, developed its own bra and stopped selling Bravado's, Leeder could not pursue a legal route. She did respond by writing letters to British customers that there was a problem with the firm's wholesaler, and the company would be glad to serve them directly from Toronto. Customers rallied to Leeder's side, and, eventually, one childbirth educator and her husband took over U.K. distribution.

Brand loyalty can go a long way in protecting companies against copycats—particularly for products in which quality is important. Thus, Bravado's focus on forming an emotional connection with customers was critical in protecting the firm from copycat products. "It's brand quality that is our protection," Leeder noted. While other copycats followed, none have had much impact on Bravado's sales. Bravado used its first-mover advantage to establish strong relationships with people who could reach expectant mothers: midwives and childbirth educators. They then supported the effort through moves that enhanced the firm's stature in customers' minds (e.g., support of local and international breastfeeding initiatives). "We're more than just the product," explains Bravado CEO Kathryn From. "We're the whole experience. And that separates us from our competition."

In 1993, Linda Butler created Kidzpace Interactive. Collingwood, Ontario's Kidzpace produces game consoles and other electronic games for children that, among other things, allow kids to try out video games. Kidzpace started out by targeting places where kids faced stressful situations, like dentists' offices, hospitals, and funeral homes. Orders poured in—so did a copycat. In response, Butler increased the range of products—making a wider range of models, sizes, and prices and developed service standards that included immediate phone response, same-day parts shipping, and a 100 percent customer satisfaction guarantee. The first copycat and several others have come and gone.

Not only was Kidzpace branded and differentiated, but Butler found ways to lock in customers. The best lock-in is Butler's exclusive contract to supply product to interested McDonald's outlets. In 1996, a McDonald's franchisee saw a Kidzpace kiosk at a hospital and decided to put one in his restaurant. After three months, sales increased by 15 percent, and Butler won McDonald's Canadian distribution rights. She then went to the U.S. and, after giving the product a three-month test run, was able to sell to 17 McDonald's locations. The product passed durability tests, increased restaurant sales, and within three years, McDonald's approved Kidzpace products for

(continued)

its 27,000 restaurants worldwide. Butler's agreement with the fast-food giant allows her access to McDonald's biannual conferences, where franchisees view the latest ideas for their stores.

This access to McDonald's also brings to her door the gaming companies who are looking for a way into McDonald's. Thus, the company has been able to form strong connections with games manufacturers, such as Nintendo, Microsoft, and Sony. This relationship gives Kidzpace access to the latest games and allows it to further differentiate its product. For example, some Kidzpace units housed Sony PlayStation's EyeToy (a video game that allows the user to become part of the game) months before it was available to the public in North America.

SOURCES: H. Schachter, 2004, Double danger, *Profit*, 23(1): 62–65; K. Balpataky, 2002, Canada's top 100 women business owners: Katheryn From & Shery Leeder, smart, sexy—and lots of fun, *Profit*, 21(6): 32; S. Baillie & S. Nerberg, 2001, In leaps and bounds: Is doing business all that difficult? As four of Canada's top women entrepreneurs show, it takes simple strategies to spur go-go growth, *Profit*, 20(6): 38–40.

orientation.[29] In most cases, knowledge must be transferred to others in the organization, even in smaller ventures, to enhance the entrepreneurial competence of the firm. The transfer is likely to be more difficult in larger firms. Research has shown, however, that units within firms are more innovative if they have access to new knowledge.[30]

Transferring knowledge can be difficult, because the receiving party must have adequate absorptive capacity to learn the knowledge.[31] This capability requires that the new knowledge be linked to the existing knowledge. Thus, managers will need to develop the capabilities of their human capital to build on their current knowledge base, while incrementally expanding that knowledge.[32] Developing innovations and achieving success in the marketplace requires effective human capital. In particular, firms must have strong intellectual capital in their R&D organization.[33] However, a firm must have strong human capital throughout its workforce if employees are to be innovative. Having the intellectual talent is only part of the challenge. The appropriate management of the talent in order to realize its potential is critical for a firm to be entrepreneurial.[34] Managers must develop the culture and infuse it with the values espoused by successful entrepreneurs, such as those discussed in the opening case. Additionally, managers should empower employees at all levels to act independently, as Jonathan Coon of 1-800 CONTACTS did, as described in the opening case.[35]

International Entrepreneurship

Entrepreneurship is a global phenomenon.[36] It is at the top of public policy agendas in many of the world's countries, including Finland, Germany, Israel, Ireland, and France, among others. In Northern Ireland, for example, the minister for enterprise, trade, and investment told businesspeople that their current and future commercial success would be affected by the degree to which they decided to emphasize R&D and innovation (critical components of entrepreneurship).[37]

According to some researchers who are studying economies throughout the world, virtually all industrial nations "are experiencing some form of transformation in their economies, from the dramatic move from centrally planned to market economies in East-Central Europe … to the efforts by Asian countries to return to their recent high growth levels."[38] Entrepreneurship can play central roles in those transformations, in that it has a strong potential to fuel economic growth, create employment, and generate prosperity for citizens.[39]

While entrepreneurship is a global phenomenon, there are differences in the rates of entrepreneurship across countries. A recent study of 41 countries found that the percentage of adults involved in entrepreneurial activity ranged from a high of about 28 percent in Venezuela and Uganda to a low of approximately 3 percent in France; Canada's rate is about 8 percent. Importantly, this study also found a strong positive relationship between the national level of entrepreneurship and national economic growth in the country.[40]

Culture is one of the reasons for the varying rates of entrepreneurship among different countries. For example, the tension between individualism and collectivism is important for entrepreneurship; research shows that entrepreneurship declines as collectivism is emphasized. Simultaneously, however, research results suggest that exceptionally high levels of individualism might be dysfunctional for entrepreneurship. Viewed collectively, these results appear to call for a balance between individual initiative and a spirit of cooperation and group ownership of innovation. For firms to be entrepreneurial, they must provide appropriate autonomy and incentives for individual initiative to surface, but they must also promote cooperation and group ownership of an innovation if it is to be implemented successfully. Thus, entrepreneurship often requires teams of people with unique skills and resources, especially in cultures where collectivism is a valued historical norm.[41]

Another important dimension of international entrepreneurship is the level of investment made by young ventures outside of the home country. In fact, with increasing globalization, a greater number of new ventures have been "born global."[42] Research has shown that new ventures that enter international markets increase their learning of new technological knowledge and thereby enhance their performance.[43] Because of these outcomes, the amount of international entrepreneurship has been increasing in recent years.[44]

The probability of entering international markets increases when the firm has top executives with international experience. Furthermore, the firm has a higher likelihood of successfully competing in international markets when its top executives have international experience.[45] Because of the learning and economies of scale and scope afforded by operating in international markets, both young and established internationally diversified firms often are stronger competitors in their domestic market as well. As well, internationally diversified firms are generally more innovative, as research has shown.[46]

International entrepreneurship has been an important factor in the economic development of Asia. In fact, private companies owned by Chinese families outside of China compose the fourth largest economic power in the world. Significant learning from their international ventures occurs in these businesses, and this learning enhances their success with future ventures.[47] The learning that occurs contributes to a firm's knowledge of operating in international markets.[48] It also contributes knowledge that can enhance a firm's new product development, on which we focus in the next section.

New Product Development and Internal Corporate Ventures

Most corporate innovation is developed through research and development (R&D). In many industries, the competitive battle for the market begins in the R&D labs. In fact, R&D may be the most critical factor in gaining and sustaining a competitive advantage in some industries, such as pharmaceuticals. Larger established firms use R&D labs to create the competence-destroying new technology and products envisioned by Schumpeter. Such radical innovation has become an important component of competition in many industries.[49]

Incremental and Radical Innovation

Firms can create incremental or more radical innovations. Most innovations are *incremental*—that is, they build on existing knowledge bases and provide small improvements in the current product lines. Alternatively, *radical innovations* usually provide

Where Did All This Come From?

The Canadian innovators discussed here hate slow kayaks and dead batteries, but really have a thing for tent rot and lightweight engines. All of these things are behind some diverse new Canadian innovations that help get people moving. They come from individuals acting alone, from small companies, and from federally sponsored research groups—anywhere, in fact, where people are driven to create something better.

After cruising up and down Canada's West Coast for years, Bob Blad, "got tired of listening to motors and tired of running up and down the middle of channels." Bob and his wife, Karen, found their salvation in kayaking. Blad remembers, "We saw things that we used to blow by. … We found rock caves in the wall along the shore—things like that. We didn't even know they existed and we were able to take our kayaks right inside. Kayaking opened up a whole new world for us."

Kayaking for days at a time, however, is no quick or easy task. Why not put a sail on a kayak to speed the trip and lessen the burden of paddling? The simple answer is because kayak sails had ropes and an awkward system of rigging. A lightweight kayak and canoe sail that could be put up in seconds was what Blad wanted. So after extensive experimentation and modification, Blad found a way to attach a standard rod-holder to his kayak. Then he used a V-shaped sail for propulsion. Blad's incremental innovation was employing a special Y-shaped yoke that allowed the sail to be raised or lowered in seconds. After a couple of grants, positive product evaluations, a patent, finding sources for product materials and a $100,000 investment, he began manufacturing his Spirit Sails in 2001. Blad says, "I built this business to employ myself and at times I can barely keep up." It took only 18 months for Blad to recoup his investment and he now manufactures about 400 sails a year.

David Green had a different nautical problem. Green woke up many mornings with a drained boat battery. The culprit was an energy-wasting incandescent bulb on his sailboat. An engineer by trade, Green set out to design something better: a solar-powered, light-emitting diode (LED). LEDs use about one-tenth the power of a normal bulb, so even with small amounts of solar power, a battery can be charged to power the LED. By 1998, he had founded Victoria's Carmanah Technologies to produce his product.

Carmanah lights now sit on navigation buoys worldwide, they light bus stops and transit schedules in London, England, and in several U.S. cities, and they mark airstrips and helipads at U.S. air-force bases in Iraq and Afghanistan. The self-contained light systems can run as long as five years without maintenance and do not have to be wired into an electrical grid, making them ideal for remote sites. The company's profit goes back into R&D to reduce cost and improve the brightness of the lights. The goal is to get the brightness and purchase price to an acceptable level for mass-market consumers.

While Carmanah's solution to the world's energy problems involves using less energy through the use of LEDs, Ottawa's Iogen Corp. wants to make clean power. Forget the hi-tech hydrogen fuel-cell stuff though, Iogen—a biotech company—has found the answer to the world's greenhouse-gas problems in a fungus. Currently, most ethanol is made from fermented and distilled grain. The problem is that making ethanol in this way means consuming oil to plant corn, make fertilizer, harvest, and transport the crop. Starting with organic waste—such as wheat straw—Iogen's system employs an enzyme derived from fungus that ate army tents during World War II. The enzyme breaks the sugars out of the straw so that they can be fermented and distilled into ethanol. The company claims the reduction in greenhouse-gas emissions with its ethanol is about 90 percent, compared to 30 percent for the conventional method. As well, the company has some big backers for its innovation. Shell Chemicals Canada has already invested about $40 million in the company.

Of course putting Iogen's ethanol into a lighter weight vehicle would also help the environment. This is where Auto21—a federally sponsored alliance of automotive researchers, based in 34 different Canadian universities comes in. The 250 professors and 350 graduate students who

(continued)

make up Auto21 now comprise the largest research group in Canada. One of its accomplishments comes from a research team headed by University of Windsor professor Jerry Sokolowski. Sokolowski's team figured out a way to make aluminum harder—hard enough, in fact, so that the aluminum can be used in any part of an engine block. Currently, iron piston sleeves are required to line the cylinders of virtually all aluminum block engines because aluminum is generally too soft to be durable on its own. Iron sleeves are typically shrink-fitted into the blocks—a time-consuming and expensive extra step in engine manufacture—and one that adds extra weight to the engine as well.

Sokolowski's treatment pumps low-frequency sound waves into molten aluminum, pulverizing and rearranging silicon crystals in the alloy. This somewhat radical innovation reduces brittleness, makes the final casting stronger, and produces a major increase in alloy strength. Aluminum sleeves made with the process match the strength of steel versions and will allow cars in the future to be lighter and thus more fuel-efficient.

SOURCES: C. Vander Doelen, 2004, Casting off sleeves: U of W professor hardens aluminium, *Windsor Star*, May 11, C3; K. MacQueen, 2003, A brighter future, *Maclean's*, 116(48): 50; I. Austen, 2003, Magic mushroom, *Canadian Business*, 76(23): 14; G. Niosi, 2003, Kayak sails are going up, *Times-Colonist*, October 4, C1.

significant technological breakthroughs and create new knowledge.[50] In the Strategic Focus box "Where Did All This Come From?" above, we discuss where some surprising new inventions come from: some are radical innovations, some are incremental, and some … you can decide for yourself.

Radical innovations are rare because of the difficulty and risk involved in developing them. There is substantial uncertainty regarding the technology and the market opportunities for radical innovations.[51] Because radical innovation creates new knowledge and uses only some or little of a firm's current product or technological knowledge, creativity is required. However, creativity does not create something from nothing. Rather, creativity discovers, combines, or synthesizes current knowledge, often from diverse areas.[52] This knowledge is then used to develop new products or services that can be used in an entrepreneurial manner to move into new markets, capture new customers, and gain access to new resources.[53] Such innovations are often developed in separate units that start internal ventures.[54]

Internal corporate venturing is the set of activities used to create inventions and innovations through internal means.[55] Spending on R&D is linked to success in internal corporate venturing. Put simply, firms are unable to invent or innovate without significant R&D investments. Because of the importance of innovation to the competitiveness of multinational firms, the effectiveness of their internal venturing process is critical.

As shown in Figure 14.1, there are two forms of internal corporate venturing: autonomous strategic behaviour and induced strategic behaviour.

Autonomous Strategic Behaviour

Autonomous strategic behaviour is a bottom-up process in which product champions pursue new ideas, often through a political process, to develop and coordinate the commercialization of a new good or service until it achieves success in the marketplace. A *product champion* is an organizational member with an entrepreneurial vision of a new good or service who seeks to create support for its commercialization. Evidence suggests that product champions play critical roles in moving innovations forward.[56] Autonomous strategic behaviour is based on a firm's wellsprings of knowledge and

---

Internal corporate venturing is the set of activities used to create inventions and innovations through internal means.

Autonomous strategic behaviour is a bottom-up process in which product champions pursue new ideas, often through a political process, to develop and coordinate the commercialization of a new good or service until it achieves success in the marketplace.

Figure 14.1

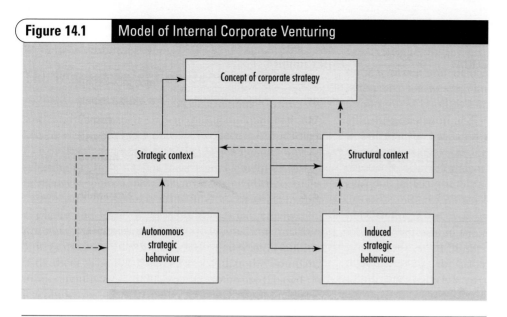

SOURCE: Adapted from R. A. Burgelman, 1983, A model of the interactions of strategic behavior, corporate context, and the concept of strategy, *Academy of Management Review*, 8: 65.

resources that are the sources of the firm's innovation. Thus, a firm's technological capabilities and competencies are the basis for new products and processes.[57]

GE depends on autonomous strategic behaviour on a regular basis to produce innovations. Essentially, "the search for marketable services can start in any of GE's myriad businesses. [For example], an operating unit seeks out appropriate technology to better do what it already does. Having mastered the technology, it then incorporates it into a service it can sell to others." In response to frequent crisis calls and requests from customers, GE's Industrial Systems division took six months to develop a program that uses artificial intelligence to help assign field engineers to customer sites. Quite sophisticated, the program handles thousands of constraints while making assignments. The division's customer relationship manager was a champion for this product. The manager observed that the program "reduced the average time to dispatch an engineer from 18 hours to 4 hours."[58] In addition to facilitating the operations of one of GE's units, the program is being sold as a marketable item that developed through autonomous strategic behaviour.

Changing the concept of corporate-level strategy through autonomous strategic behaviour results when a product is championed within strategic and structural contexts (see Figure 14.1). The strategic context is the process used to arrive at strategic decisions (often requiring political processes to gain acceptance). The best firms keep changing their strategic context and strategies because of the continuous changes in the current competitive landscape. Thus, some believe that the most competitively successful firms reinvent their industry or develop a completely new one across time as they engage in competition with current and future rivals.[59]

To be effective, an autonomous process for developing new products requires that new knowledge be continuously diffused throughout the firm. In particular, the diffusion of tacit knowledge is important for development of more effective new products.[60] Interestingly, some of the processes important for the promotion of autonomous new product development behaviour vary by the environment and country in which a firm operates. For example, the Japanese culture is high on uncertainty avoidance. As such, research has found that Japanese firms are more likely to engage in autonomous behaviours under conditions of low uncertainty.[61]

Induced Strategic Behaviour

Induced strategic behaviour is a top-down process whereby the firm's current strategy and structure foster product innovations that are closely associated with that strategy and structure.

The second of the two forms of internal corporate venturing, **induced strategic behaviour**, is a top-down process whereby the firm's current strategy and structure foster product innovations that are closely associated with that strategy and structure. In this form of venturing, the strategy in place is filtered through a matching structural hierarchy.

Implementing New Product Development and Internal Ventures

To be innovative and develop internal ventures requires *an entrepreneurial mind-set*. In Chapter 13, we discuss an entrepreneurial orientation that includes several dimensions, such as risk propensity. Clearly, firms and individuals must be willing to take risks in order to commercialize new products. While they must continuously attempt to identify opportunities, they must also select and pursue the best opportunities and do so with discipline. Thus, employing an entrepreneurial mind-set entails not only developing new products and markets but also an emphasis on execution. According to Rita McGrath and Ian MacMillan, those with an entrepreneurial mind-set "engage the energies of everyone in their domain," both inside and outside the organization.[62]

Having processes and structures in place through which a firm can successfully implement the outcomes of internal corporate ventures and commercialize the innovations is critical. The successful introduction of innovations into the marketplace reflects implementation effectiveness.[63] In the context of internal corporate ventures, processes are the "patterns of interaction, coordination, communication, and decision making employees use" to convert the innovations resulting from either autonomous or induced strategic behaviours into successful market entries.[64] As we described in Chapter 12, organizational structures are the sets of formal relationships supporting organizational processes.

Effective integration of the various functions involved in innovation processes—from engineering to manufacturing and, ultimately, market distribution—is required to implement (that is, to effectively use) the innovations that result from internal corporate ventures.[65] Increasingly, product development teams are being used to integrate the activities associated with different organizational functions. Product development teams are commonly used to produce cross-functional integration. Such coordination involves coordinating and applying the knowledge and skills of different functional areas in order to maximize innovation.[66]

Cross-Functional Product Development Teams

Cross-functional teams facilitate efforts to integrate activities associated with different organizational functions, such as design, manufacturing, and marketing. In addition, new product development processes can be completed more quickly and the products more easily commercialized when cross-functional teams work effectively.[67] Using cross-functional teams, product development stages are grouped into parallel or overlapping processes to allow the firm to tailor its product development efforts to its unique core competencies and to the needs of the market.

Horizontal organizational structures support the use of cross-functional teams in their efforts to integrate innovation-based activities across organizational functions.[68] Therefore, instead of being built around vertical hierarchical functions or departments, the organization is built around core horizontal processes that are used to produce and manage innovations. Some of the core horizontal processes that are critical to innovation efforts are formal; they may be defined and documented as procedures and practices. More commonly, however, these processes are informal: "They are routines or ways of working that evolve over time."[69] Often invisible, informal processes are critical to successful product innovations and are supported properly through horizontal organizational structures more so than through vertical organizational structures.

Two primary barriers that may prevent the successful use of cross-functional teams as a means of integrating organizational functions are independent frames of reference of team members and organizational politics.[70]

Team members working within a distinct specialization (i.e., a particular organizational function) may have an independent frame of reference typically based on common backgrounds and experiences. They are likely to use the same decision criteria to evaluate issues such as product development efforts as they do within their functional units. Research suggests that functional departments vary along four dimensions: time orientation, interpersonal orientation, goal orientation, and formality of structure.[71] Thus, individuals from different functional departments having different orientations on these dimensions can be expected to perceive product development activities in different ways. For example, a design engineer may consider the characteristics that make a product functional and workable to be the most important of the product's characteristics. Alternatively, a person from the marketing function may hold characteristics that satisfy customer needs most important. These different orientations can create barriers to effective communication across functions.[72]

Organizational politics is the second potential barrier to effective integration in cross-functional teams. In some organizations, considerable political activity may centre on allocating resources to different functions. Interunit conflict may result from aggressive competition for resources among those representing different organizational functions. This dysfunctional conflict between functions creates a barrier to their integration.[73] Methods must be found to achieve cross-functional integration without excessive political conflict and without changing the basic structural characteristics necessary for task specialization and efficiency.

Facilitating Integration and Innovation

Shared values and effective leadership are important to achieve cross-functional integration and implement innovation.[74] Highly effective shared values are framed around the firm's strategic intent and mission and become the glue that promotes integration between functional units. Thus, the firm's culture promotes unity and internal innovation.[75]

Strategic leadership is also highly important for achieving cross-functional integration and promoting innovation. Leaders set the goals and allocate resources. The goals include integrated development and commercialization of new goods and services. Effective strategic leaders remind organizational members continuously of the value of product innovations. In the most desirable situations, this value-creating potential becomes the basis for the integration and management of functional department activities.

Effective strategic leaders also ensure a high quality communication system to facilitate cross-functional integration. A critical benefit of effective communication is the sharing of knowledge among team members.[76] Effective communication thus helps create synergy and gains team members' commitment to an innovation throughout the organization. Shared values and leadership practices shape the communication systems that are formed to support the development and commercialization of new products.[77]

Creating Value from Innovation

The model in Figure 14.2 on page 440 shows how the firm can create value from the internal processes it uses to develop and commercialize new goods and services. An entrepreneurial mind-set is necessary so that managers and employees will consistently try to identify entrepreneurial opportunities that the firm can pursue by developing new goods and services and new markets. Cross-functional teams are important to promote

Figure 14.2 Creating Value through Internal Innovation Processes

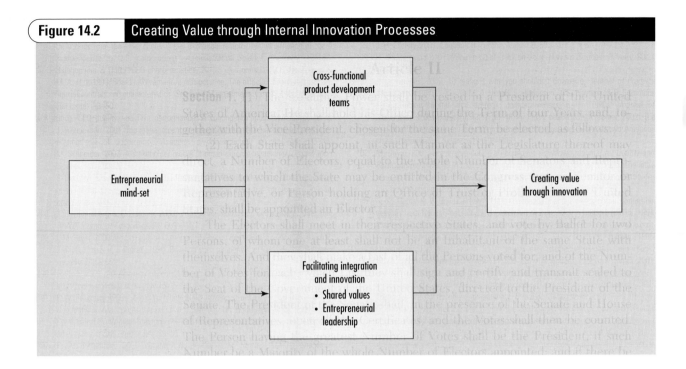

integrated new product design ideas and commitment to their implementation thereafter. Effective leadership and shared values promote integration, vision, and commitment to innovation. The end result for the firm is the creation of value for the customers and shareholders through development and commercialization of new products.[78]

Cooperative Strategies for Entrepreneurship and Innovation

It is unlikely that a firm possesses all the knowledge and resources required for it to be entrepreneurial and innovative in dynamic competitive markets. Knowledge and resources are needed to develop new products and serve new markets.[79] To successfully commercialize inventions, firms may therefore choose to cooperate with other organizations and integrate their knowledge and resources. Entrepreneurial new ventures, for example, may seek investment capital as well as the distribution capabilities of more established firms to implement a new product idea and introduce it to the market.[80] Alternatively, more established companies may need new technological knowledge and can gain access to it through alliances with newer entrepreneurial firms.[81] Alliances between large pharmaceutical firms and biotechnology companies have increasingly been formed to integrate the knowledge and resources of both firms to develop new products and bring them to market.[82] With increasing frequency, alliances are used to produce or manage innovations. To innovate through a cooperative relationship, firms must share their knowledge and skills.[83]

For example, almost 40 percent of the firms that innovated in Canada's pulp and paper sector entered into cooperative arrangements. Paper manufacturers preferred to enter into such arrangements with customers and clients rather than competitors. Thus, within the industry, one can find short-term contracts between equipment suppliers and manufacturers, manufacturers and independent research organizations, and university–industry research consortia. Since a great deal of innovation in the industry involves incremental improvements in process technology, competitors quickly copy such moves. Thus, most competitive advantages to be realized from innovation are quite temporary. Therefore, we find some degree of industry-wide cooperation through a national, independent R&D consortium called Paprican. This consortium accounts for about 30 percent of industry R&D spending and is involved in helping firms in the industry in achieving common goals (e.g., reducing emissions and costs) and enhancing product properties and quality. Paprican is 80 percent funded by fees from its members, who represent more than 80 percent of the pulp and paper production in Canada.[84]

Because of the importance of alliances, particularly in the development of new technology and in commercializing innovations, firms are beginning to build networks of alliances that represent a form of social capital. This social capital in the form of relationships with other firms helps firms to obtain the knowledge and other resources necessary to develop innovations.[85] In turn, knowledge from these alliances helps firms develop new capabilities.[86] Some firms now even allow external firms to participate in their internal new product development processes. It is not uncommon for firms to have supplier representatives on their cross-functional innovation teams because of the importance of the suppliers' input to ensure quality materials for any new product developed.[87]

However, alliances formed for the purpose of innovation are not without risks. A significant risk is that a partner will appropriate a firm's technology or knowledge and use it to enhance its own competitive abilities.[88] To prevent or at least minimize this risk, firms, particularly new ventures, need to select their partners carefully. The ideal partnership is one in which the firms have complementary skills, as well as compatible strategic goals.[89] However, because firms are operating in a network of firms and thus may be participating in multiple alliances simultaneously, they encounter challenges in managing the alliances.[90] An R&D consortium, such as Paprican, can be useful in managing a group of alliance partners. Research has shown that when firms become involved in too many alliances, the complexity of the arrangements can harm, rather than facilitate, their innovation capabilities.[91] Thus, effectively managing the cooperative relationships to produce innovation is critical.

Acquisitions to Buy Innovation

One of the reasons that firms turn to acquisitions is the capital market values' growth; acquisitions provide a means to rapidly extend the product line and increase the firm's revenues. For example, to deepen its knowledge and market share in acrylic bathroom fixtures MAAX Inc., of Saint-Marie de Beauce, Quebec, purchased the third largest maker of fibreglass bathroom equipment in the U.S.—Aker Plastics—in 2002. Similarly, cereal giant Kellogg's product mix changed quickly when it acquired Keebler Foods. Before the acquisition, 75 percent of Kellogg's sales revenues came from cereal products; after the acquisition, 60 percent of its sales came from non-cereal products. Firms can acquire firms with new products or new product development capability. Usually, investing in R&D does not produce new products rapidly.[92]

Similar to internal corporate venturing and strategic alliances, acquisitions are not a risk-free approach to producing and managing innovations. A key risk of acquisitions is that a firm may substitute an ability to buy innovations for an ability to produce innovations internally. In support of this contention, research shows that firms engaging in acquisitions introduce fewer new products into the market.[93] This substitution may take place because firms lose strategic control and focus instead on financial control of their original—and especially of their acquired—business units.

We noted in Chapter 8 that firms can also learn new capabilities from acquired firms. As such, firms can gain capabilities to produce innovation from an acquired firm. Additionally, firms that emphasize innovation and carefully select companies for acquisition and also emphasize innovation are likely to remain innovative.[94]

Capital for Entrepreneurial Ventures

Venture capital is a resource that is typically allocated to entrepreneurs who are involved in projects with high growth potential. The intent of venture capitalists is to achieve a high rate of return on the funds they invest.[95] In the late 1990s, the number of venture capital firms and the amount of capital invested in new ventures reached unprecedented levels. In 1999, the amount of venture capital invested in new ventures reached a high of about $60 billion.[96] Venture capitalists desire to receive large returns on their investments and take major risks by investing in new ventures. Research has shown that venture capitalists may earn large returns or experience significant losses. For example, one study found that 34 percent of venture capitalists experienced a loss, while 23 percent gained a rate of return on their investments of 50 percent or greater.[97]

For the decade of the 1990s, the top quintile of performers in the U.S. Standard & Poor's 500 had average annual growth in revenues and earnings of 20.6 percent and 29.3 percent, respectively. Furthermore, these firms provided average annual returns to their shareholders of 34 percent.[98] Additional research showed that 90 percent of these high-performing firms had created and successfully commercialized a radical innovation or developed a fundamental new business model in an existing industry, both indicative of an entrepreneurial firm.[99]

Venture capitalists place weight on the competence of the entrepreneur or the human capital in the firms in which they consider investing. They also weigh the expected scope of competitive rivalry the firm is likely to experience and the degree of instability in the market addressed.[100] However, the characteristics of the entrepreneur or firm in which venture capitalists invest, as well as the rate of return expected, will vary with the type of venture in which investments are made.[101]

Increasingly, venture capital is being used to support the acquisition of innovations. To provide such support, some firms establish their own venture-capital divisions. These divisions carefully evaluate other companies to identify those with innovations or innovative capabilities that might yield a competitive advantage. In other instances, a firm might decide to serve as an internal source of capital for innovative product ideas that can be spun off as independent or affiliated firms. New enterprises that are backed by venture capital provide an important source of innovation and new technology. The amount of corporate venture capital invested grew exponentially at the end of the 1990s and in 2000. For example, in the U.S., venture capital invested grew from about $2 billion (U.S.) in 1998 to slightly more than $18 billion (U.S.) in 2000.[102]

Some ventures are able to obtain capital through initial public offerings (IPOs). Firms that offer new stock in this way must have high potential in order to sell their stock and obtain adequate capital to finance the growth and development of the firm. This form of capital can be substantial and is often much larger than the amounts obtained from venture capitalists. Investment bankers frequently play major roles in the development and offering of IPOs. Research has shown that founder-managed firms generally receive lower returns from IPOs than professionally managed firms.[103] The IPO market values experienced managers more than founders, who frequently do not have substantial managerial experience. Firms such as WestJet in Canada or JetBlue in the U.S. created a lot of interest from investors because of their low costs, strong customer demand, and highly experienced CEOs (who, in both cases, happened to be each firm's founder).[104] Investors believe that the firm with an experienced CEO is more likely to succeed. Also, firms that have received venture capital backing usually receive greater returns from IPOs.[105]

The next Strategic Focus box, "Show Me the Money," explains how new ventures obtain capital—an often hard to come by commodity necessary to develop a business. While the 2001–02 downturn in the stock market temporarily dried up funding in the IPO market, it meant little to companies so small that even venture capitalists were

Show Me the Money: Capital for Entrepreneurs

To get started, all you need is love. Or, in the case of entrepreneurs, what some have called "love money." Love money is the initial funding from family or friends. They provide funds because of their close relationship to the entrepreneur, rather than for any solid investment purpose. This funding does not go very far in developing the enterprise, and there is a big gap between the love money and the venture capitalist. If a business is to grow, this gap needs to be filled—this is where angel investors come in.

Angel investors are wealthy individuals who fund developing enterprises in need of funding in the range of $125,000 to $1,000,000. In backing entrepreneurs—sometimes with little more than an idea or a prototype—angels are willing to accept large amounts of risk in return for the potential of high rewards. This does not mean that any company will be funded, however. Angel investors are experienced company builders and seek solid business potential and talented founder teams.

Angels are, however, becoming easier to find. They have been gathering in organizations such as the Vancouver Angel Network, Ottawa's Band of Scoundrels and Purple Angels, and the Calgary Angel Network. In 2002, the National Angel Organization (NAO) was formed in Toronto, to bring best practice and other information to angels across the country.

When a business becomes large enough, venture capitalists (VCs) provide the next round of financing. However, there is an increasing gap between the funding angels will supply and that which VCs will supply because both angels and VCs have become more conservative since the stock market downturn in 2001–02. Also, venture capital funds are growing in size. As a result, there are closer relationships on early stage deals between angels and boutique VC funds. For example, Vancouver's Yaletown Venture Partners attracted $30 million for investment in information and energy technology companies in Western Canada from a combination of major institutional investors, as well as respected technology angels. Steve Hnatiuk, co-founder of Yaletown, notes that "We bridge the gap between where angels leave off, and larger, later stage venture funds begin to get interested. … In our market, there is a funding gap for promising angel-backed companies seeking between $1 million and $3 million in a first professional investment round. This is precisely the stage where we get very interested. …"

Thus, an investment chain is forming. The best angel-backed deals feed early stage venture capitalists; the best venture capital deals feed future bank financing, IPOs, or sale of the company to a larger competitor that can afford to continue to invest in the organization. Ideally that would be the progression.

The links to the investment chain do not always mesh all that smoothly. Although it is accepted that angels play a vital role in early stage development, angels have seen their equity greatly diluted when a VC deal is struck for the next round of financing. While VCs concede that in this investment environment, new deals are done at lower valuations, they also note that the rules apply to VCs who have to accept lower valuations when doing another private equity round. David Ferguson, managing director with Toronto's VenGrowth Capital Management, said the low valuations are "… not unique to angel investors. … It is really anyone coming in at an early stage of a company's development. Generally, anyone who does … or did early stage investing is faced with this kind of environment." Despite the economic uncertainty and low appetite for risk, companies are still attracting investment because low initial valuations will allow angels and VCs to collect big should the venture become successful.

SOURCES: 2003, Improving the success of angel investors, *National Angel Organization website* http://www.angelinvestor.ca/library/docs/TheAngelPrimerJuly17v2.pdf, accessed May 26, 2004; T. Wanless, 2003, Angel investors step in where others fear to tread, *Ottawa Citizen*, October 20, C1; M. Evans, 2003, Bear market has clipped the wings of angels: Funding retrenched, *National Post (Financial Post)*, June 30, FP1.

unlikely to look at the firm. Still, attracting the funding is critical for firms to move from idea to reality, and the route by which companies source needed capital can be complex.

Creating Value through Strategic Entrepreneurship

Newer entrepreneurial firms often are more effective than larger firms in identifying opportunities. Some believe that these firms tend to be more innovative as well because of their flexibility and willingness to take risks. Alternatively, larger and well-established firms often have more resources and capabilities to exploit opportunities that are identified.[106] So, younger, entrepreneurial firms are generally opportunity seeking, and more established firms are advantage seeking. However, to compete effectively in the landscape of the 21st century, firms must identify and exploit opportunities, while achieving and sustaining a competitive advantage.[107] Thus, newer entrepreneurial firms must learn how to gain a competitive advantage, and older more established firms must relearn how to identify entrepreneurial opportunities. The concept of strategic entrepreneurship suggests that firms can be simultaneously entrepreneurial and strategic, regardless of their size and age.

To be entrepreneurial, firms must develop an entrepreneurial mind-set among their managers and employees. Managers must emphasize the development of their resources, particularly human capital and social capital. The importance of knowledge to identify and exploit opportunities as well as to gain and sustain a competitive advantage suggests that firms must have strong human capital.[108] Social capital is critical for access to complementary resources from partners in order to compete effectively in domestic and international markets.[109]

There remain many entrepreneurial opportunities in international markets. Thus, firms should seek to enter and compete in international markets. Firms can learn new technologies and management practices from international markets and diffuse this knowledge throughout the firm. Furthermore, the knowledge firms gain can contribute to their innovations. Research has shown that firms operating in international markets tend to be more innovative.[110] Small and large firms are now regularly moving into international markets. Both types of firms must also be innovative to compete effectively. Thus, by developing resources (human and social capital), taking advantage of opportunities in domestic and international markets, and using the resources and knowledge gained in these markets to be innovative, firms are able to achieve competitive advantages. In so doing, they create value for their customers and shareholders.

Firms that practice strategic entrepreneurship contribute to a country's economic development. In fact, some countries, such as Ireland, have made dramatic economic progress by changing the institutional rules for businesses operating in the country, which could be construed as a form of institutional entrepreneurship. Likewise, firms that seek to establish their technology as a standard, also representing institutional entrepreneurship, are engaging in strategic entrepreneurship because creating a standard produces a sustainable competitive advantage for the firm.[111]

Research shows that because of its economic importance and individual motives, entrepreneurial activity is increasing across the globe. Furthermore, more women are becoming entrepreneurs because of the economic opportunity that entrepreneurship provides and the individual independence it affords.[112] In future years, entrepreneurial activity may increase the wealth of less affluent countries and continue to contribute to the economic development of more affluent countries. Regardless, the companies that practice strategic entrepreneurship are likely to be the winners in the 21st century.[113]

Summary

- Strategic entrepreneurship is the use of entrepreneurial actions based on a strategic perspective. More specifically, it involves engaging in simultaneous opportunity seeking and competitive advantage seeking behaviours to design and implement entrepreneurial strategies to create wealth.

- The concepts of entrepreneurial opportunity, innovation, and capabilities are important to firms. Entrepreneurial opportunities represent conditions in which new products or services can satisfy a need in the market. The essence of entrepreneurship is to identify and exploit these opportunities. Innovation is the process of commercializing the products or processes that surfaced through invention. Entrepreneurial capabilities include building an entrepreneurial culture, having a passion for the business, and having a desire for measured risk.

- Increasingly, entrepreneurship is being practiced in many countries. As used by entrepreneurs, entrepreneurship and corporate entrepreneurship are strongly related to a nation's economic growth. This relationship is a primary reason for the increasing use of entrepreneurship and corporate entrepreneurship in countries throughout the global economy.

- Three basic approaches are used to produce and manage innovation: internal corporate venturing, strategic alliances, and acquisitions. Autonomous strategic behaviour and induced strategic behaviour are the two processes of internal corporate venturing. Autonomous strategic behaviour is a bottom-up process through which a product champion facilitates the commercialization of an innovative good or service. Induced strategic behaviour is a top-down process in which a firm's current strategy and structure facilitate product or process innovations that are associated with them. Thus, induced strategic behaviour is driven by the organization's current corporate strategy, structure, and reward and control systems.

- To create incremental and radical innovation requires effective innovation processes and practices. Increasingly, cross-functional integration is vital to a firm's efforts to develop and implement internal corporate venturing activities and to commercialize the resulting innovation. Additionally, integration and innovation can be facilitated by the development of shared values and the practice of entrepreneurial leadership.

- In the complex global economy, it is difficult for an individual firm to possess all the knowledge needed to innovate consistently and effectively. To gain access to the kind of specialized knowledge that often is required to innovate, firms may form a cooperative relationship, such as a strategic alliance with other firms, sometimes even with competitors.

- Acquisitions provide another means for firms to produce and manage innovation. Innovation can be acquired through direct acquisition, or firms can learn new capabilities from an acquisition, thereby enriching their internal innovation processes.

- Entrepreneurial activity requires capital for development. Venture capitalists are a prime source for this capital. The amount of venture capital available increased dramatically in the decade of the 1990s. While it decreased recently due to economic problems, it remains much higher than in earlier years. Initial public offerings (IPOs) also have become a common means of obtaining capital for new ventures.

- The practice of strategic entrepreneurship by all types of firms, large and small, new and more established, creates value for all stakeholders, especially for shareholders and customers. Strategic entrepreneurship also contributes to the economic development of entire nations. Thus, entrepreneurial activity is increasing throughout the world.

Review Questions

1. What is strategic entrepreneurship? Why is it important for firms competing in the global economy?

2. What are entrepreneurial opportunities, innovation, and entrepreneurial capabilities? Explain their significance for entrepreneurial firms.

3. Why is international entrepreneurship important and why is it increasing across the globe?

4. What is autonomous strategic behaviour? What is induced strategic behaviour?

5. How do firms use strategic alliances to help them produce innovations?

6. How can a firm use acquisitions to increase the number of innovations it produces and improve its capability to produce innovations?

7. What is the importance of venture capital and initial public offerings to entrepreneurial activity?

8. How does strategic entrepreneurship create value for customers and shareholders and contribute to economic development?

Strategic Entrepreneurship

Assume that you are a partner in a new venture energy company called Currence. You have approached an investor group for capital to fund the first three years of your operation. Following the preliminary presentation, you find that the group is very impressed by Currence and by its six start-up partners, each of whom brings unique, yet critical skills, experience, contacts, and other knowledge to the venture. Before the investor group decides to fund your company, however, it has asked for a brief presentation about how the Currence partners will be rewarded.

Part 1 (complete individually). Indicate how Currence will determine the approximate salary, fringe benefits, and shares of stock (as a percentage) each partner will be allocated upon closing the financing of your new venture. Also indicate your rationale for these amounts.

Part 2 (in small groups). Compare your responses to Part 1 with others in your small group. Reach a consensus on the criteria your group would use to determine how to reward each partner. Appoint one group member to present your consensus to the class and describe how the consensus was reached.

Part 3 (in small groups). Following the presentations in Part 2, discuss the following issues and indicate any important lessons and implications:

1. Why would an entrepreneurial venture, such as Currence, be asked to provide this type of information to an investor group?

2. What criteria did the groups use concerning salaries and stock? Why?

3. What patterns did you perceive in the approaches taken by each team?

4. Did the groups make salaries or stock equal for all Currence partners? Why or why not? What reasons would there be for providing different rewards for different partners?

5. How difficult was it for the small groups to reach a consensus?

Notes

1. P. D. Reynolds, W. D. Bygrave, E. Autio, P. Arenius, P. Fitzsimons, M. Minniti, S. Murray, C. O'Goran, & F. Roche, 2004, *Global Entrepreneurship Monitor: 2003 Executive Report*, Babson Park, MA: Babson College, http://www.kauffman.org/pdf/gem_2003_global_report_3.pdf, accessed May 27, 2004; G. Picot, J. Baldwin, & R. Dupuy, 1994, *Have Small Firms Created a Disproportionate Share of New Jobs in Canada? A Reassessment of the Facts*, Ottawa: Statistics Canada Micro-Economic Studies and Analysis Division, and Canadian Institute for Advanced Research, http://www.statcan.ca/english/research/11F0019MIE/11F0019MIE1994071.pdf, accessed May 27, 2004, 2004; S. M. Camp, L. W. Cox, & B. Kotalik, 2001, *The Hallmarks of Entrepreneurial Excellence: 2001 Survey of Innovative Practices*, Kansas City, MO: Kauffman Center for Entrepreneurial Leadership, Ewing Marion Kauffman Foundation.

2. M. A. Hitt, R. D. Ireland, S. M. Camp, & D. L. Sexton, 2002, Strategic entrepreneurship: Integrating entrepreneurial and strategic management perspectives, in M. A. Hitt, R. D. Ireland, S. M. Camp, & D. L. Sexton (eds.), *Strategic Entrepreneurship: Creating a New Mindset*, Oxford, UK: Blackwell Publishers, 1–16; M. A. Hitt, R. D. Ireland, S. M. Camp, & D. L. Sexton, 2001, Strategic entrepreneurship: Entrepreneurial strategies for wealth creation, *Strategic Management Journal*, 22(special issue): 479–91; R. D. Ireland, M. A. Hitt, S. M. Camp, & D.L. Sexton, 2001, Integrating entrepreneurship and strategic management actions to create firm wealth, *Academy of Management Executive*, 15(1): 49–63.

3. R. D. Ireland & M. A. Hitt, 1999, Achieving and maintaining strategic competitiveness in the 21st century: The role of strategic leadership, *Academy of Management Executive*, 13(1): 43–57.

4. H. Lee, M. A. Hitt, & E. K. Jeong, 2002, The impact of CEO and TMT characteristics on strategic flexibility and firm performance, working paper, Storrs, CT: University of Connecticut; M. E. Raynor, 2001, *Strategic Flexibility in the Financial Services Industry: Creating Competitive Advantage Out of Competitive Turbulence*, New York: Deloitte Research.

5. G. Hamel, 2000, *Leading the Revolution*, Boston, MA: Harvard Business School Press.

6. S. Michael, D. Storey, & H. Thomas, 2002, Discovery and coordination in strategic management and entrepreneurship, in M. A. Hitt, R. D. Ireland, S. M. Camp, & D. L. Sexton (eds.), *Strategic Entrepreneurship: Creating a New Mindset*, Oxford, UK: Blackwell Publishers, 45–65.

7. M. A. Hitt, R. D. Nixon, P. G. Clifford, & K. P. Coyne, 1999, The development and use of strategic resources, in M. A. Hitt, P. G. Clifford, R. D. Nixon, & K. P. Coyne (eds.), 1999, *Dynamic Strategic Resources: Development, Diffusion and Integration*, Chichester, UK: John Wiley & Sons, Ltd., 1–14.

8. T. W. Y. Man, T. Lau, & K. F. Chan, 2002, The competitiveness of small and medium enterprises: A conceptualization with focus on entrepreneurial competencies, *Journal of Business Venturing*, 17: 123–42.

9. J. Schumpeter, 1934, *The Theory of Economic Development*, Cambridge, MA: Harvard University Press.

10. S. Shane & S. Venkataraman, 2000, The promise of entrepreneurship as a field of research, *Academy of Management Review*, 25: 217–26.

11. B. R. Barringer & A. C. Bluedorn, 1999, The relationship between corporate entrepreneurship and strategic management, *Strategic Management Journal*, 20: 421–44.

12. G. D. Meyer, H. M. Neck, & M. D. Meeks, 2002, The entrepreneurship-strategic management interface, in M. A. Hitt, R. D. Ireland, S. M. Camp, & D. L. Sexton (eds.), *Strategic Entrepreneurship: Creating a New Mindset*, Oxford, UK: Blackwell Publishers, 19–44; I. Kirzner, 1997, Entrepreneurial discovery and the competitive market process: An Austrian approach, *Journal of Economic Literature*, 35(1): 60–85.

13. R. G. McGrath & I. MacMillan, 2000, *The Entrepreneurial Mindset*, Boston, MA: Harvard Business School Press.

14. G. Gori, 2001, An American directs Mexico City's cinema revival, *New York Times*, http://www.nytimes.com, July 15.

15. S. Rubin, 2002, Onex adds Mexican theatre chain: Groupo Cinemex to be folded into Loews, *National Post (Financial Post)*, June 20, FP1.

16. P. F. Drucker, 1998, The discipline of innovation, *Harvard Business Review*, 76(6): 149–57.

17. P. D. Reynolds, M. Hay, & S. M. Camp, 1999, *Global Entrepreneurship Monitor: 1999 Executive Report*, Babson Park, MA: Babson College.

18. R. M. Kanter, 1999, From spare change to real change: The social sector as beta site for business innovation, *Harvard Business Review*, 77(3): 122–32.

19. Hamel, *Leading the Revolution*; R. Price, 1996, Technology and strategic advantage, *California Management Review*, 38(3): 38–56; L. G. Franko, 1989, Global corporate competition: Who's winning, who's losing and the R&D factor as one reason why, *Strategic Management Journal*, 10: 449–74; G. T. Lumpkin & G. G. Dess, 1996, Clarifying the entrepreneurial orientation construct and linking it to performance, *Academy of Management Review*, 21: 135–72; K. M. Kelm, V. K. Narayanan, & G. E. Pinches, 1995, Shareholder value creation during R&D innovation and commercialization stages, *Academy of Management Journal*, 38: 770–86.

20. G. T. Lumpkin & G. G. Dess, 1996, Clarifying the entrepreneurial orientation construct and linking it to performance, *Academy of Management Review*, 21: 135–72; K. M. Kelm, V. K. Narayanan, & G. E. Pinches, 1995, Shareholder value creation during R&D innovation and commercialization stages, *Academy of Management Journal*, 38: 770–86.

21. M. A. Hitt, R. D. Nixon, R. E. Hoskisson, & R. Kochhar, 1999, Corporate entrepreneurship and cross-functional fertilization: Activation, process and disintegration of a new product design team, *Entrepreneurship: Theory and Practice*, 23(3): 145–67.

22. Schumpeter, *The Theory of Economic Development*.

23. P. Sharma & J. L. Chrisman, 1999, Toward a reconciliation of the definitional issues in the field of corporate entrepreneurship, *Entrepreneurship: Theory and Practice*, 23(3): 11–27; R. A. Burgelman & L. R. Sayles, 1986, *Inside Corporate Innovation: Strategy, Structure, and Managerial Skills*, New York: Free Press.

24. R. E. Hoskisson & L. W. Busenitz, 2002, Market uncertainty and learning distance in corporate entrepreneurship entry mode choice, in M. A. Hitt, R. D. Ireland, S. M. Camp, & D. L. Sexton (eds.), *Strategic Entrepreneurship: Creating a New Mindset*, Oxford, UK: Blackwell Publishers, 151–72.

25. J. S. Hornsby, D. F. Kuratko, & S. A. Zahra, 2002, Middle managers' perception of the internal environment for corporate entrepreneurship: Assessing a measurement scale, *Journal of Business Venturing*, 17: 253–73.

26. S. D. Sarasvathy, 2000, Seminar on research perspectives in entrepreneurship (1997), *Journal of Business Venturing*, 15: 1–57.

27. D. F. Kuratko, R. D. Ireland, & J. S. Hornsby, 2001, Improving firm performance through entrepreneurial actions: Acordia's corporate entrepreneurship strategy, *Academy of Management Executive*, 15(4): 60–71; J. Birkinshaw, 1999, The determinants and consequences of subsidiary initiative in multinational corporations, *Entrepreneurship: Theory and Practice*, 24(1): 9–36.

28. Arizona Republic, 2002, Apple unveils its latest iMac, *Arizona Republic*, January 8, D8; P-W. Tam, 2002, Apple unveils sleek new iMac design, hoping to revive struggling business, *Wall Street Journal Interactive*, http://www.wsj.com, January 8.

29. T. Erickson, 2002, Entrepreneurial capital: The emerging venture's most important asset and competitive advantage, *Journal of Business Venturing*, 17: 275–90.

30. W. Tsai, 2001, Knowledge transfer in intraorganizational networks: Effects of network position and absorptive capacity on business unit innovation and performance, *Academy of Management Journal*, 44: 996–1004.

31. S. A. Zahra & G. George, 2002, Absorptive capacity: A review, reconceptualization, and extension, *Academy of Management Review*, 27: 185–203.

32. M. A. Hitt, L. Bierman, K. Shimizu, & R. Kochhar, 2001, Direct and moderating effects of human capital on strategy and performance in professional service firms: A resource-based perspective, *Academy of Management Journal*, 44: 13–28.

33. I. Bouty, 2000, Interpersonal and interaction influences on informal resource exchanges between R&D researchers across organizational boundaries, *Academy of Management Journal*, 43: 5–65.

34. T. W. Brailsford, 2001, Building a knowledge community at Hallmark Cards, *Research Technology Management*, 44(5): 18–25.

35. R. G. McGrath, 2001, Exploratory learning, innovative capacity, and managerial oversight, *Academy of Management Journal*, 44: 118–31.

36. J. W. Lu & P. W. Beamish, 2001, The internationalization and performance of SMEs, *Strategic Management Journal*, 22(special issue): 565–85.

37. Staff reporter, 2000, Business innovation urged, *Irish Times*, February 9, 23.

38. J. E. Jackson, J. Klich, & V. Kontorovich, 1999, Firm creation and economic transitions, *Journal of Business Venturing*, 14: 427–50.

39. M. Kwak, 2002, What's the best commercialization strategy for startups? *MIT Sloan Management Review*, 43(3): 10.

40. P. D. Reynolds, S. M. Camp, W. D. Bygrave, E. Autio, & F. M. Hay, 2002, *Global Entrepreneurship Monitor*, Kaufman Center for Entrepreneurial Leadership, Babson Park, MA: Marion Kaufman Foundation / Babson College.

41. M. H. Morris, 1998, *Entrepreneurial Intensity: Sustainable Advantages for Individuals, Organizations, and Societies*, Westport, CT: Quorum Books, 85–86. M. H. Morris, D. L. Davis, & J. W. Allen, 1994, Fostering corporate entrepreneurship: Cross-cultural comparisons of the importance of individualism versus collectivism, *Journal of International Business Studies*, 25: 65–89.

42. S. A. Zahra & G. George, 2002, International entrepreneurship: The state of the field and future research agenda, in M. A. Hitt, R. D. Ireland, S. M. Camp, & D. L. Sexton (eds.), *Strategic Entrepreneurship: Creating a New Mindset*, Oxford, UK: Blackwell Publishers, 255–88.

43. S. A. Zahra, R. D. Ireland, & M. A. Hitt, 2000, International expansion by new venture firms: International diversity, mode of market entry, technological learning and performance, *Academy of Management Journal*, 43: 925–50.

44. P. P. McDougall & B. M. Oviatt, 2000, International entrepreneurship: The intersection of two paths, *Academy of Management Journal*, 43: 902–8.

45. H. Barkema & O. Chvyrkov, 2002, What sort of top management team is needed at the helm of internationally diversified firms? in M. A. Hitt, R. D. Ireland, S. M. Camp, & D. L. Sexton (eds.), *Strategic Entrepreneurship: Creating a New Mindset*, Oxford, UK: Blackwell Publishers, 290–305.

46. T. S. Frost, 2001, The geographic sources of foreign subsidiaries' innovations, *Strategic Management Journal*, 22: 101–22.

47. E. W. K. Tsang, 2002, Learning from overseas venturing experience: The case of Chinese family businesses, *Journal of Business Venturing*, 17: 21–40.

48. W. Kuemmerle, 2002, Home base and knowledge management in international ventures, *Journal of Business Venturing*, 17: 99–112.

49. R. Leifer, G. Colarelli, & M. Rice, 2001, Implementing radical innovation in mature firms: The role of hubs, *Academy of Management Executive*, 15(3): 102–13.

50. G. Ahuja & M. Lampert, 2001, Entrepreneurship in the large corporation: A longitudinal study of how established firms create breakthrough inventions, *Strategic Management Journal*, 22 (special issue): 521–43.

51. Leifer, Collarelli, & Rice, Implementing radical innovation.

52. R. I. Sutton, 2002, Weird ideas that spark innovation, *MIT Sloan Management Review*, 43(2): 83–87.

53. K. G. Smith & D. Di Gregorio, 2002, Bisociation, discovery, and the role of entrepreneurial action, in M. A. Hitt, R. D. Ireland, S. M. Camp, & D. L. Sexton (eds.), *Strategic Entrepreneurship: Creating a New Mindset*, Oxford, UK: Blackwell Publishers, 129–50.

54. Hoskisson & Busenitz, Market uncertainty and learning distance.

55. R. A. Burgelman, 1995, *Strategic Management of Technology and Innovation*, Boston, MA: Irwin.

56. R. Leifer & M. Rice, 1999, Unnatural acts: Building the mature firm's capability for breakthrough innovation, in M. A. Hitt, P. G. Clifford, R. D. Nixon, & K. P. Coyne (eds.), *Dynamic Strategic Resources: Development, Diffusion and Integration*, Chichester, UK: John Wiley & Sons, 433–53.

57. M. A. Hitt, R. D. Ireland, & H. Lee, 2000, Technological learning, knowledge management, firm growth and performance, *Journal of Engineering and Technology Management*, 17: 231–46; D. Leonard-Barton, 1995, *Wellsprings of Knowledge: Building and Sustaining the Sources of Innovation*, Cambridge, MA: Harvard Business School Press.

58. S. S. Rao, 2000, General Electric, software vendor, *Forbes*, January 24, 144–46.

59. H. W. Chesbrough, 2002, Making sense of corporate venture capital, *Harvard Business Review*, 80(3): 90–99; G. Hamel, 1997, Killer strategies that make shareholders rich, *Fortune*, June 23, 70–88.

60. M. Subramaniam & N. Venkatraman, 2001, Determinants of transnational new product development capability: Testing the influence of transferring and deploying tacit overseas knowledge, *Strategic Management Journal*, 22: 359–78.

61. M. Song & M. M. Montoya-Weiss, 2001, The effect of perceived technological uncertainty on Japanese new product development, *Academy of Management Journal*, 44: 61–80.

62. McGrath and MacMillan, *Entrepreneurial Mindset*.

63. F. Murray, 2002, Innovation as co-evolution of scientific and technological networks … , *Research Policy*, 31(8,9): 1389-1404.

64. C. M. Christensen & M. Overdorf, 2000, Meeting the challenge of disruptive change, *Harvard Business Review*, 78(2): 66–77.

65. L. Yu, 2002, Marketers and engineers: Why can't we just get along? *MIT Sloan Management Review*, 43(1): 13.

66. P. S. Adler, 1995, Interdepartmental interdependence and coordination: The case of the design/manufacturing interface, *Organization Science*, 6: 147–67.

67. B. L. Kirkman & B. Rosen, 1999, Beyond self-management: Antecedents and consequences of team empowerment, *Academy of Management Journal*, 42: 58–74;

A. R. Jassawalla & H. C. Sashittal, 1999, Building collaborative cross-functional new product teams, *Academy of Management Executive*, 13(3): 50–63.

68. Hitt, Nixon, Hoskisson, & Kochhar, Corporate entrepreneurship.

69. Christensen & Overdorf, Meeting the challenge of disruptive change.

70. Hitt, Nixon, Hoskisson, & Kochhar, Corporate entrepreneurship.

71. A. C. Amason, 1996, Distinguishing the effects of functional and dysfunctional conflict on strategic decision making: Resolving a paradox for top management teams, I, 39: 123–48; P. R. Lawrence & J. W. Lorsch, 1969, *Organization and Environment*, Homewood, IL: Richard D. Irwin.

72. D. Dougherty, L. Borrelli, K. Muncir, & A. O'Sullivan, 2000, Systems of organizational sensemaking for sustained product innovation, *Journal of Engineering and Technology Management*, 17: 321–55; D. Dougherty, 1992, Interpretive barriers to successful product innovation in large firms, *Organization Science*, 3: 179–202.

73. Hitt, Nixon, Hoskisson, & Kochhar, Corporate entrepreneurship.

74. E. C. Wenger & W. M. Snyder, 2000, Communities of practice: The organizational frontier, *Harvard Business Review*, 78(1): 139–44.

75. Hamel, *Leading the Revolution*.

76. McGrath & MacMillan, *Entrepreneurial Mindset*.

77. Hamel, *Leading the Revolution*.

78. Hitt, Ireland, Camp, & Sexton, Strategic entrepreneurship; S. W. Fowler, A. W. King, S. J. Marsh, & B. Victor, 2000, Beyond products: New strategic imperatives for developing competencies in dynamic environments, *Journal of Engineering and Technology Management*, 17: 357–77.

79. R. K. Kazanjian, R. Drazin, & M. A. Glynn, 2002, Implementing strategies for corporate entrepreneurship: A knowledge-based perspective, in M. A. Hitt, R. D. Ireland, S. M. Camp, & D. L. Sexton (eds.), *Strategic Entrepreneurship: Creating a New Mindset*, Oxford, UK: Blackwell Publishers, 173–99.

80. A. C. Cooper, 2002, Networks, alliances and entrepreneurship, in M. A. Hitt, R. D. Ireland, S. M. Camp, & D. L. Sexton (eds.), *Strategic Entrepreneurship: Creating a New Mindset*, Oxford, UK: Blackwell Publishers, 204–22.

81. S. A. Alvarez & J. B. Barney, 2001, How entrepreneurial firms can benefit from alliances with large partners, *Academy of Management Executive*, 15(1): 139–48; F. T. Rothaermel, 2001, Incumbent's advantage through exploiting complementary assets via interfirm cooperation, *Strategic Management Journal*, 22 (special issue): 687–99.

82. J. Hagedoorn & N. Roijjakkers, 2002, Small entrepreneurial firms and large companies in inter-firm R&D networks—the international biotechnology industry, in M. A. Hitt, R. D. Ireland, S. M. Camp, & D. L. Sexton (eds.), *Strategic Entrepreneurship: Creating a New Mindset*, Oxford, UK: Blackwell Publishers, 223–52.

83. P. Kale, H. Singh, & H. Perlmutter, 2000, Learning and protection of proprietary assets in strategic alliances: Building relational capital, *Strategic Management Journal*, 21: 217–37.

84. M. Nakamura, H. Nelson, & I. Vertinsky, 2003, Cooperative R&D and the Canadian forest products industry, *Managerial and Decision Economics*, 24: 147–69.

85. H. Yli-Renko, E. Autio, & H. J. Sapienza, 2001, Social capital, knowledge acquisition and knowledge exploitation in young technology-based firms, *Strategic Management Journal*, 22(special issue): 587–613.

86. C. Lee, K. Lee, & J. M. Pennings, 2001, Internal capabilities, external networks and performance: A study of technology-based ventures, *Strategic Management Journal*, 22(special issue): 615–40.

87. A. Takeishi, 2001, Bridging inter- and intra-firm boundaries: Management of supplier involvement in automobile product development, *Strategic Management Journal*, 22: 403–33.

88. R. D. Ireland, M. A. Hitt, & D. Vaidyanath, 2002, Strategic alliances as a pathway to competitive success, *Journal of Management*, 28(3): 413–30.

89. M. A. Hitt, M. T. Dacin, E. Levitas, J.-L. Arregle, & A. Borza, 2000, Partner selection in emerging and developed market contexts: Resource-based and organizational learning perspectives, *Academy of Management Journal*, 43: 449–67.

90. J. J. Reuer, M. Zollo, & H. Singh, 2002, Post-formation dynamics in strategic alliances, *Strategic Management Journal*, 23: 135–51.

91. F. Rothaermel & D. Deeds, 2002, More good things are not always necessarily better: An empirical study of strategic alliances, experience effects, and new product development in high-technology start-ups, in M. A. Hitt, R. Amit, C. Lucier, & R. Nixon (eds.), *Creating Value: Winners in the New Business Environment*, Oxford, UK: Blackwell Publishers, 85–103.

92. A. Swift, 2003, Maax Inc. shares soar on plans for sale; Founder of fixture firm is retiring Analysts expect favourable offers, *Toronto Star*, September, 10, C1; J. Muller, 2001, Thinking outside of the cereal box, *Business Week*, January 15, 54–55.

93. M. A. Hitt, R. E. Hoskisson, R. A. Johnson, & D. D. Moesel, 1996, The market for corporate control and firm innovation, *Academy of Management Journal*, 39: 1084–1119.

94. M. A. Hitt, J. S. Harrison, & R. D. Ireland, 2001, *Mergers and Acquisitions: A Guide to Creating Value for Stakeholders*, New York: Oxford University Press.

95. J. A. Timmons, 1999, *New Venture Creation: Entrepreneurship for the 21st Century*, 5th ed., New York: Irwin/McGraw-Hill.

96. R. Amit, C. Lucier, M. A. Hitt, & R. D. Nixon, 2002, Strategies for the entrepreneurial millennium, in M. A. Hitt, R. Amit, C. Lucier, & R. Nixon (eds.), *Creating Value: Winners in the New Business Environment*, Oxford, UK: Blackwell Publishers, 1–12.

97. C. M. Mason & R. T. Harrison, 2002, Is it worth it? The rates of return from informal venture capital investments, *Journal of Business Venturing*, 17: 211–36.

98. Amit, Lucier, Hitt, & Nixon, Strategies for the entrepreneurial millennium.

99. C. E. Lucier, L. H. Moeller, & R. Held, 1997, 10X value: The engine powering long-term shareholder returns, *Strategy & Business*, 8: 21–28.

100. D. A. Shepherd & A. Zacharakis, 2002, Venture capitalists' expertise: A call for research into decision aids and cognitive feedback, *Journal of Business Venturing*, 17: 1–20.

101. S. Manigart, K. de Waele, M. Wright, K. Robbie, P. Desbrieres, H. J. Sapienza, & A. Beekman, 2002, Determinants of required return in venture capital investments: A five-country study, *Journal of Business Venturing*, 17: 291–312.

102. M. Maula & G. Murray, 2002, Corporate venture capital and the creation of U.S. public companies: The impact of sources of capital on the performance of portfolio companies, in M. A. Hitt, R. Amit, C. Lucier, & R. Nixon (eds.), *Creating Value: Winners in the New Business Environment*, Oxford, UK: Blackwell Publishers, 164–87.

103. S. T. Certo, J. G. Covin, C. M. Daily, & D. R. Dalton, 2001, Wealth and the effects of founder management among IPO-stage new ventures, *Strategic Management Journal*, 22(special issue): 641–58.

104. L. DeCarlo, 2002, JetBlue IPO will fly right for investors, *Forbes*, http://www.forbes.com, February, 13.

105. Maula & Murray, Corporate venture capital.

106. Amit, Lucier, Hitt, & Nixon, Strategies for the entrepreneurial millennium.

107. Hitt, Ireland, Camp, & Sexton, Strategic entrepreneurship.

108. Hitt, Bierman, Shimizu, & Kochhar, Direct and moderating effects of human capital.

109. M. A. Hitt, H. Lee, & E. Yucel, 2002, The importance of social capital to the management of multinational enterprises: Relational networks among Asian and Western firms, *Asia Pacific Journal of Management*, 19(3): 353–73.

110. M. A. Hitt, R. E. Hoskisson, & H. Kim, 1997, International diversification: Effects on innovation and firm performance in product diversified firms, *Academy of Management Journal*, 40: 767–98.

111. R. Garud, S. Jain, & A. Kumaraswamy, 2002, Institutional entrepreneurship in the sponsorship of common technological standards: The case of Sun Microsystems and JAVA, *Academy of Management Journal*, 45: 196–214.

112. Reynolds, Camp, Bygrave, Autio, & Hay, *Global Entrepreneurship Monitor*.

113. Hitt, Ireland, Camp, & Sexton, Strategic entrepreneurship; Amit, Lucier, Hitt, & Nixon, Strategies for the entrepreneurial millennium.

Name Index

A

Aaker, D.A., 132, 169
Abell, D.F., 32, 33, 131
Abelson, R., 259
Abrahamson, E., 202, 423
Ackman, D., 259
Adler, P.S., 230, 424, 447
Afuah, A., 97, 169, 321
Aggarwal, R., 96
Agle, B.R., 34, 351
Ahlstrand, B., 422
Ahlstrom, D., 292
Ahuja, G., 33, 131, 258, 447
Albanese, R., 423
Alchian, A., 60
Alcouffe, A., 354
Alcouffe, C., 354
Alexander, D., 170
Alexander, G.J., 60
Alexander, M., 132, 229
Aley, J., 203
Allaire, Paul A., 397
Allen, J.W., 447
Allen, L., 293
Almeida, J.G., 131
Altman, Denise, 337
Altman, Edward I., 42–43, 60
Alvarez, S.A., 448
Amason, A.C., 448
Ambrosini, V., 133
Amburgey, T., 390
Ames, C., 133
Amihud, Y., 231, 352
Amit, R., 33, 131, 132, 133, 230, 448
Anand, J., 258, 259, 354
Anders, G., 258
Anderson, P., 132, 422
Anderson, R.C., 231, 352
Angwin, D., 258
Anhalt, K.N., 170
Anthanassiou, N., 423
Arenius, P., 446
Argote, L., 132
Arino, A., 294, 321, 323
Armstrong, L., 202, 203
Arnold, D., 33
Arnold, D.J., 292
Arnott, R., 354
Arora, A., 131, 293
Arregle, J.L., 293, 322, 448
Artz, K.W., 97, 131, 132, 323
Ashford, S.J., 423, 424
Asin, A., 258
Audia, P.G., 132

B

Aukutsionek, S., 354
Aulakh, P.S., 293
Autio, E., 96, 131, 446, 447, 448
Axelrod, B., 424
Azamhuzjaev, M., 61

Baden-Fuller, C., 323, 391
Baek, H.Y., 294
Baglole, J., 170
Bagnell, P., 33
Bagozzi, R., 33
Bailey, J.V., 60
Baillie, Charles, 328
Baiman, S., 391
Balakrishnan, U., 61
Baldwin, J., 446
Baldwin, T.T., 132
Balkin, D.B., 354
Bamford, C.E., 169
Banning, K.C., 352
Bansal, P., 96
Bantel, K., 423
Barber, B.N., 259
Barber, C.E., 229
Barefield, R.M., 231
Barenaked Ladies, 163
Barker, V.L., III, 34
Barnes, J.E., 34
Barnes, J.G., 60
Barney, Jay B., 9, 32, 33, 39–40, 47, 60, 131, 132, 133, 169, 170, 229, 259, 321, 322, 323, 391, 422, 424, 448
Barnholt, Ned, 253
Barrett, Matthew, 413
Barringer, B.R., 294, 446
Barsade, S., 423
Bartlett, C.A., 97, 131, 293, 391, 424
Bary, A., 259
Bates, K.A., 132
Bates, T.W., 231, 352
Bauerschmidt, A., 391
Baum, A.C., 202
Baum, I.R., 34
Baumgartner, P., 97
Baysinger, B.D., 353
Beamish, P.W., 97, 258, 293, 294, 424, 447
Beatty, Douglas, 55, 349
Beatty, R.P., 353

Beauchesne, E., 323
Becerra, M., 423
Becker, B.E., 425
Beddoe, Clive, 148, 149, 412
Beekman, A., 448
Beer, M., 423
Beinhocker, E.D., 34
Bell, A., 60
Bell, Don, 148
Belson, K., 202
Bengtsson, L., 323
Bennett, N., 424
Bentson, G., 60
Berenson, A., 96
Berentson, B., 323
Bergh, D.D., 229, 230, 231, 258, 259, 423
Berkley, J.D., 423
Berle, A., 352
Berman, S., 132, 321
Bernstein, J., 292
Berry, L.L., 169
Best, A., 259
Bethel, J.E., 259
Bettis, R.A., 33, 422
Betts, M., 133
Bezos, Jeff, 340
Bhappu, A., 293
Bianco, A., 422
Bierly, P.E., III, 321
Bierman, L., 32, 34, 131, 132, 258, 424, 447, 448
Biesada, A., 258
Bigley, G.A., 390
Billet, M.T., 230
Birkinshaw, J., 33, 292, 293, 391, 425, 447
Bizjak, J.M., 231, 352
Bjorkman, I., 424
Black, B.S., 353
Black, Conrad, 344
Black, J.S., 33
Black, S.S., 169, 321
Black, Susan, 395
Blad, Bob, 435
Blad, Karen, 435
Bliss, R., 231
Bloomberg, Michael, 288–89
Bluedorn, A.C., 446
Bodie, Z., 60
Boeker, W., 34, 423
Bogner, W.C., 95, 96, 132
Bonabeau, E., 32
Boone, P., 352
Borgatti, S.P., 392
Borgman, Dean, 302

Borrelli, L., 448
Borza, A., 293, 322, 448
Bottazzi, G., 292
Boulding, W., 202
Bourgeois, L.J., 202
Bouty, I., 447
Bower, J.L., 391
Bowman, C., 133
Bowman, E.H., 32, 96, 169, 229, 231, 259
Bowser, J., 321
Boyd, B.K., 231, 352, 353, 354, 423, 424
Boyle, Debra, 168
Boyle, M., 423
Bradley, F., 294
Brailsford, T.W., 447
Brancato, Carolyn, 351
Brand, J., 259
Brannen, M.Y., 230
Brass, D.J., 424
Breach, A., 352
Bresman, H., 292
Bricker, R., 352
Brinkerhoff, D., 60
Broder, J.M., 322
Bromiley, P., 34, 229, 352
Brooker, K., 203
Brooks, G.R., 97
Brouthers, K.D., 294
Brouthers, L.E., 294
Brown, K., 169
Brown, R.L., 169
Brown, S.L., 32
Brown, T.E., 424
Bruce, M., 133
Bruner, R.F., 258
Brush, C.G., 131, 132, 133
Brush, T.H., 131, 132, 229, 230, 352
Bruton, G.D., 292
Bryan, A., 170
Bryan, S., 354
Buchholtz, A.K., 391
Buck, T., 354
Buckee, James, 346
Buckley, M.R., 424
Buckley, P.J., 132, 322
Buffet, Warren, 13
Bulkeley, W.M., 231
Burgelman, R.A., 229, 424, 447
Burke, L.M., 423
Burns, T., 390
Burritt, C., 169
Burrows, P., 132

Company Index

Coca-Cola Co., 52, 53, 84, 99, 112, 120, 177, 291, 313, 317
Cognicase, 239
Coldwell Banker, 220
Coles, 142
Compaq Computer Corporation, 178, 194, 208, 214, 242, 345
Computer Networks, 249
Conis Entertainment, 196
Conoco Phillips, 297
Converium, 358
Coors, 280
Corel, 251
Corning, 114
Corona, 280
Corporate Knights, 37, 38, 54, 56
Cosma, 205
Costco, 308
Cott Corporation, 314, 346
Couche-Tard, 305
Cougar Helicopters, 302
Covisint, LLC, 206
CP Hotels, 254
CP Rail, 6, 254
CP Ships, 254
Crest, 208, 224
CTV Inc., 13
CTV Media Ltd., 282
Culinar Inc., 427
Cummins Engine, 281
CxNetworks, 276
Cyborg Worldwide, 127

D
Daewoo, 267
Daihyaku Insurance, 269
Daimler-Benz, 236, 342
DaimlerChrysler, 73, 76, 81, 206, 300, 301, 303, 313, 408
Dairy Mart, 268
Dairyworld Foods, 427
Dalian Rubber General Factory, 305
Datatrak, 125
Days Inn, 28
Dean Witter Reynolds, Inc., 220
Decoma International, 205
Dell Computer Corporation, 52, 79, 103, 119, 126, 128, 178, 179, 194, 216, 318
Delta Air Lines, Inc., 83, 100, 384
Deutsche Bank, 413
DG Bank, 310–11
DG-Rabo International, 310–11
Disney Channel, 215
Dofasco Inc., 55, 58, 103, 303–4
Dominion Securities, 223

Domtar Inc., 38, 58, 300, 412
Donatos Pizza, 213
Duke Energy, 238
DuPont, 100, 366
Dupont Canada, 57
Duracell, 158
Dynatech Action, 189, 190
Dynegy, 245

E
Eastman Kodak, 87, 88, 89, 92, 99, 114, 373, 374–76
easyJet, 148
Eaton's, 13, 14, 40, 146, 193
Ebara, 300
eBay, 186–87
Eckerd Drug Stores, 240
Ecopetrol, 304
EcoTrans Technologies, 57
E.D. Smith, 268, 269
Eden restaurant, 154
EDS, 127, 239, 427
Edward Jones, 113
Edward Jones (Canada), 112, 113
Electrolux, 385
Elektrim, 217
Elektrim Telekomunikacja, 217
Eli Lilly and Company, 123, 125
Embraer, 302
Enbridge Inc., 56, 58, 346
EnCana Corporation, 6, 7, 12, 32, 55, 58, 103, 238, 244–45, 254, 330, 344, 346, 412
Enfamil, 309
Enron, 71, 99, 245, 327, 415–16
Enterprise Networks, 349
Ericsson, 313, 385–86
ESPN, 215
Ethical Funds Company, 57
EthicScan Canada Ltd., 37, 38
Export Development Canada, 349
Exult, Inc., 127
Exxon Mobil Corp., 52, 100

F
Factiva, 93
Fair Labor Association, 155–56
Fairmont Hotels & Resorts Inc., 58
Falconbridge Limited, 58
Fannie Mae, 52
Fast Company, 249
Federal Aviation Administration, 222
Federal Express, 122
Fido, 301

Firestone, 100
FirstEnergy, 300
Fishery Products International, 50, 90, 208
FlexPort, 142
Flextronics, 272
Flynn Canada, 310
Ford Motor Company, 17, 73, 100, 106, 141, 166, 177, 191–92, 206, 216, 255, 271, 300, 301, 303, 313
Fording Coal, 254
Forlaget Thomson, 277
Forster's, 280
Four Seasons Hotels and Resorts, 55, 412
Fox Family Worldwide, 215
Fraser and Neave, 280
Frito Lay's, 212, 411
Fruit of the Loom, 13
Fueling Technologies Inc., 57
Fuji Photo Film, 87, 88, 89, 92, 374
Fujitsu, 307
Fujitsu Computers, 307–8
Fujitsu Siemens Computers, 307–8
Future Shop, 240
FutureLink, 248–49

G
Gale, 277
Game Cube, 152
Gamesa Aeronautica, 302
Gap, Inc., 114
Gateway, 194
Gatorade, 212, 222, 224, 411
GE Aircraft Engines, 373
GE Appliances, 373
GEC, 314
GE Canada Inc., 55
GE Capital, 373
GE Distributed Power, 373
GE Energy Rentals, 373
GE Industrial Systems, 437
GE Medical Systems, 373
Gemplus International, 334, 335
Genentech, 125
General Electric Co., 52, 53, 71, 83, 85, 99, 100, 112, 177, 209, 220, 250–51, 372–73, 413–14, 437. *See also specific GE business units*
General Electric of Canada, 102
General Hydrogen, 20
General Mills, 309
General Motors Corporation (GM), 20, 29, 51, 52, 73, 109, 192, 206, 216, 219, 271, 290, 300, 301, 303, 318, 366
Gentex, 315
George Weston, Ltd., 314

GE Power Systems, 373
Gerber, 309
Get Well Network, 160
GE Water Technologies, 373
Gildan Activewear, 13, 155–56
Gillette, 99, 114
GlaxoSmithKline, 74, 241, 288
Global Crossing, 81
Globe and Mail, 38, 54, 247
GLOBE Foundation, 38, 54
GNG Networks, 138
go.com, 215
Goodyear Tire, 164, 305
GPS Gas Projection System Inc., 57
Grand & Toy, 28
Great-West Lifeco Inc., 58
Greenlight Power Technologies, 20
Groupe Vidéotron ltée, 245
Gruner+Jahr, 249
Guardian, 180
Guinness Stout, 280
Gulf Canada Resources, 238

H
Handspring, 118
Hansen Trust, 220
Harbin, 280
Harley-Davidson, 86, 112, 162
Harley-Davidson Motor Clothes, 112
Harris Bank, 283
Harry Winston Inc., 238
Hartwall, 281
Harvey's, 28, 143, 312
Hasbro, 190
Hatay Brewery Limited, 280
HBO, 13, 217
Heineken, 280
Helena Rubinstein, 156
Hennes & Mauritz, 199
Hewitt Associates, 127
Hewlett-Packard, 178, 208, 214, 242, 252, 310, 315, 334, 345, 397
Hitachi, 90
H.J. Heinz Co., 282
Hoechst, 273
Hollinger International, 344
Holt Renfrew, 154
Home Capital Group, 159
Home Depot, 183, 193
Home Hardware, 193
Honda, 73, 85–86, 192, 213, 271, 284, 300, 301, 303
Honeywell, 85, 250–51
Houghton Mifflin Co., 217, 247
Huawei Technologies, 263
Hudson's Bay Company, 42, 173–75, 176

Subject Index

reasons firms develop, 301–5
synergistic, 310–11
vertical complementary, 305–7
Strategic assets, 115
Strategic behaviour
autonomous, 436–38
induced, 438
Strategic business unit (SBU) form, 372
implementing related-linked strategy using, 372–76
at Kodak, 374–76
Strategic center firm, 382
Strategic competitiveness, 7
of Canadian companies, 5–6
outcomes of, 284–86
Strategic controls, 361–62
Strategic direction, determining, 409–11
Strategic flexibility, 19
Strategic focus: corporate
AIC's competitive advantage, 113
CEO compensation, 346
CEO Paul Tellier, 412
cooperative strategies for competitive advantage, 318
diamond industry's focused differentiation strategy, 161–62
diversification incentives, 222–23
downsizing, 253–54
economic recessions, 83
ethics of strategic leaders, 415–17
franchising, 312
human resource capability at Edward Jones, 113
Hydrogenics Corp. and strategic flexibility, 20
impermanence of success, 14
leadership changes at Scotiabank, 410
limitations of MVA and EVA, 53
MTS acquisition of Allstream, 233–34
multipoint competition among media firms, 215–16
Nissan's new leadership facilitates change, 416
Nortel and ethics in governance, 349
obtaining venture capital, 443

outsourcing of human resources function, 127–28
reputation as performance measure, 55–56
rivalry between major competitors, 88
Root's use of differentiation strategy, 155–56
Semco's unique organizational structure, 387–88
simultaneous operational relatedness and corporate relatedness at Vivendi, 217–18
stakeholders, 25–26
strategic business unit (SBU) form at Kodak, 374–76
synergy failures, 247
value chain, changes in pharmaceutical industry's, 122–23, 125–26
Westjet's cost leadership strategy, 148–49
Strategic focus: international
airplane wars, 185–86
Canada–U.S. software lumber dispute, 78
CGI's related acquisitions, 239
cooperative strategies and consortiums, 297–98
cross-border alliance, 302
entry strategies, 280–81
innovation, 432–33
political risks, 288–89
promises and pitfalls of entering international markets, 268–69
small competitors outperform larger rivals, 190
telco wars, 181
Strategic groups, 91
value of analysis of, 91
Strategic inputs, 7
Strategic intent, 21, 28
Strategic leaders, 395–97, 402
ethics of, 415–17
women, 395–96
Strategic leadership, 397–99
constraints on, 403–4
effective, 409
strategic management process, 398
Strategic management, challenge of, 12–13

Strategic management
process, 7, 29–30
strategic leadership and, 398
Strategic mission, 21–22
Strategic network, 382
distributed, 385–86
Strategic outcomes, 7
Strategic outsourcing, 382
Strategic stakes, high, 90
Strategists, organizational, 26–29
Strategy, 139
defined, 9–12
emergent, 10
intended, 9
realized, 10
Structure. See Organizational structure
Subsidiary, new wholly owned, 283
Substitute products, 153, 158
threat of, 87
Success, impermanence of, 14
Suppliers, bargaining power of, 86, 152, 157
Support activities, 120–24
Sustained (sustainable) competitive advantage, 7
criteria for determining, 115–20
in fast-cycle markets, 197
Switching costs, 84–85
low, 89
Synergistic strategic alliances, 310–11
Synergy, 224
inability to achieve, 246, 247

T

Tacit collusion, 308
Tactical action, 184
Takeovers, 236
differences among mergers, acquisitions and, 236
hostile, 345, 347
Tangible resources, 110, 111
Tax laws, incentive to diversify, as, 221–23
Technological segment, 77–80
Technology
managing in strategic network, 382
rate of change and diffusion in, 18
Threat, 71
new entrants, of, 82–86, 152–53, 157
substitute products, of, 87
Times interest earned, 44
Top management teams, 406–9

CEO and power of, 407–9
firm performance, strategic change, and, 406–7
heterogeneous, 406
Total assets turnover, 45
Total quality management, 191–92
Total quality management systems, 165–66
Trade barriers, 289
Transaction costs, 246
Transnational strategy, 276–77
using combination structure to implement, 381–82
Treynor's measure, 49
Trust, strategic asset, as a, 317

U

Uncertainty reduction strategies, 307–8
Unique competitive position, 106
Unrelated diversification, 211, 218–20
using competitive form to implement, 376–78

V

Valuable capabilities, 116–17
Value, 40, 107, 439–40
Value chain analysis, 120–24, 125–26
Value innovation, 439–40
Venture capital
innovation and, 442–44
obtaining, 443
Vertical acquisitions, 238
Vertical complementary strategic alliances, 305–7
Vertical integration, 214, 216
Virtual integration, 216
Visionary leaders, 401
Visionary leadership, 400–2

W

Wholly owned subsidiary, new, 283
World Trade Organization (WTO), 80, 263–64
Worldwide geographic area structure, implementing multidomestic strategy using, 379–80
Worldwide product divisional structure, implementing global strategy using, 380–81
WTO. See World Trade Organization